HARNESSING GREEN IT

HARNESSING GREEN IT
PRINCIPLES AND PRACTICES

Editors

San Murugesan
BRITE Professional Services and University of Western Sydney, Australia

G.R. Gangadharan
Institute for Development and Research in Banking Technology, India

IEEE computer society

IEEE

WILEY

A John Wiley & Sons, Ltd., Publication

This edition first published 2012

Registered office
John Wiley & Sons Ltd, The Atrium, Southern Gate, Chichester, West Sussex, PO19 8SQ, United Kingdom

For details of our global editorial offices, for customer services and for information about how to apply for permission to reuse the copyright material in this book please see our website at www.wiley.com.

Library of Congress Cataloging-in-Publication Data

Harnessing green IT : principles and practices / San Murugesan, G. R. Gangadharan, editors. – 1st ed.
p. cm.
Includes bibliographical references and index.
ISBN 978-1-119-97005-7 (cloth)
1. Information technology – Environmental aspects. 2. Computer science – Environmental aspects. 3. Information technology – Energy consumption. 4. Green technology. I. Murugesan, San. II. Gangadharan, G. R.
QA76.9.E58H37 2012
004.028′6 – dc23
2012010715

A catalogue record for this book is available from the British Library.

ISBN (H/B): 9781119970057

Typeset in 10/12pt Times by Laserwords Private Limited, Chennai, India

Dedicated to all who are interested in learning and harnessing green IT to create a sustainable environment for the benefit of current and future generations.

Contents

About the Editors

San Murugesan is Director of BRITE Professional Services and Adjunct Professor in the School of Computing and Mathematics at the University of Western Sydney, Australia. He is a Senior Consultant with the Data Insight & Social BI practice of Cutter Consortium, United States. He is also a corporate trainer and an independent IT and education consultant. He held various senior positions at the University of Western Sydney and Southern Cross University, both in Australia, and at Multimedia University in Malaysia. He also worked at the Indian Space Research Organisation, Bangalore, India. He has served as Senior Research Fellow of the US National Research Council at the NASA Ames Research Center, United States. In a career spanning over three decades in academia and industry, Dr Murugesan has led several innovative IT projects, provided leadership in teaching and research, and consulted to business, industry and educational institutions.

His work has focussed on the development, application and management of IT with expertise and interests spanning a range of areas, including green computing, cloud computing, Web 2.0 and 3.0, mobile computing applications, Web engineering, e-business and IT for emerging markets. He has over 150 publications which include journal and conference papers, executive reports, edited books, IEEE CS *EssentialSets* and e-mail advisories. He has developed and delivered professional certificate training programs on green IT and cloud computing. He serves as Associate Editor-in-Chief of IEEE's *IT Professional* magazine and on the editorial boards of other international journals. He also edits and contributes to the IT in Emerging Markets Department of *IT Professional*. He is a Fellow of the Australian Computer Society, a Fellow of IETE, a Senior Member of IEEE and a distinguished visitor and tutorial speaker of the IEEE Computer Society. You can follow him on Twitter @santweets and at LinkedIn and contact him at san.greenit@gmail.com.

G.R. Gangadharan currently serves as an Assistant Professor at the Institute for Development and Research in Banking Technology (IDRBT), Hyderabad, India. He has rich experience of working on several European Framework projects including COMPAS, GAMES, COCKPIT and WATTALYST. His areas of research interests include Internet technologies (service-oriented computing and cloud computing), green information systems and energy-efficient computing, information and communication technology (ICT) for emerging markets, free and open source systems (FOSS) and enterprise information systems. He has over 40 publications in international conference proceedings and journals. He is a member of IEEE. He holds a PhD in Information and Communication Technology from the University of Trento, Trento, Italy and the European University Association; an MS in Information Technology from Scuola Superiore Sant'Anna, Pisa, Italy; and an MSc in Computer Science from Manonmaniam Sundaranar University, Tirunelveli, India. Contact him at geeyaar@gmail.com.

About the Authors

Abhishek Agrawal (abhishek.r.agrawal@intel.com) has over 10 years of industry experience and is currently a Senior Technical Lead in Intel's Software Services Group who drives Intel's initiatives on power efficiency for client and Atom-based platforms. He has significant research experience in energy efficiency and has authored and co-authored several industry white papers and technical papers in refereed international conferences and journals. Abhishek is Intel's representative for Climate Savers Computing Initiative, has participated in numerous industry panels on green computing, has delivered multiple tutorial sessions at industry and academic events and is member of multiple industry power working groups such as the *Extended Battery Life Working Group* (EBLWG) and *Universal Power Adapter for Mobile Devices* (UPAMD).

Felipe Albertao (felipe.albertao@gmail.com) is a Researcher at IBM Research – China who focusses on software solutions for improving urban water systems as part of IBM's Smarter Planet effort. His previous research and activism are related to the use of technology for environmental and social development in Brazil (his native country) and the USA. Felipe has a master's degree in software engineering from Carnegie Mellon University, and two decades of experience in information technology.

Tom Butler (tbutler@afis.ucc.ie) is a Senior Lecturer in Business Information Systems, University College Cork, Ireland. Since joining academia from the Telecommunications Industry in 1998, he has authored over 95 publications. Tom held a Government of Ireland Research Fellowship in green IT from 2009 to 2010. Subsequently he became Champion of the Irish Business and Employers Confederation (IBEC)/Irish Software Innovation Network (ISIN) green information and communication technology (ICT) cluster. Since 2005 he has been conducting research into environmental compliance management systems (ECMSs), which are a type of green IS that enables organizations to, for example, design green IT and remain in compliance with regulations globally. He is currently conducting research on green ICT in the public sector and on the role of green IS for the Smart Grid.

Rajkumar Buyya (raj@csse.unimelb.edu.au) is Director of the Cloud Computing and Distributed Systems (CLOUDS) Laboratory at the University of Melbourne, Australia. He has authored 350 publications and four text books. He also edited several books including

Cloud Computing: Principles and Paradigms (2011). He is a highly cited author in computer science and software engineering worldwide. Software technologies for grid and cloud computing developed under Dr Buyya's leadership are in use at several academic institutions and commercial enterprises in 40 countries around the world.

Enrique G. Castro-Leon (enrique.g.castro-leon@intel.com) is an Enterprise Architect and Technology Strategist with Intel Corporation working on technology integration for highly efficient virtualized cloud data centres for emerging usage models for cloud computing. He is the lead author of two books, *The Business Value of Virtual Service Grids: Strategic Insights for Enterprise Decision Makers* (2008) and *Creating the Infrastructure for Cloud Computing: An Essential Handbook for IT Professionals* (2011).

Vanessa Cooper (vanessa.cooper@rmit.edu.au) is a Senior Lecturer in the School of Business Information Technology and Logistics, RMIT University, Melbourne, Australia. Her research interests include green IT, IT services, knowledge management and organizational learning.

Edward Curry (ed.curry@deri.org) leads the green and sustainable IT research domain at the Digital Enterprise Research Institute. His areas of research include green IT and IS, energy informatics, enterprise-linked data, integrated reporting and cloud computing. Edward has worked extensively with industry and government advising on the adoption patterns, practicalities and benefits of new technologies. He has published in leading journals and books, and has spoken at international conferences including the MIT CIO Symposium. He is an adjunct lecturer at the National University of Ireland, Galway.

Chris Davis (c.b.davis@tudelft.nl) is currently a PhD Candidate at the Energy and Industry group, Faculty of Technology, Policy and Management, at Delft University of Technology. In 2001, he graduated with a bachelor of engineering degree in electrical engineering and computer science from Vanderbilt University. In 2007, he received an MSc in industrial ecology from Leiden University with a thesis combining life cycle assessment within agent-based modelling. His current work involves tackling issues of sustainability through a combination of tools such as the Semantic Web, agent-based models and collaborative software such as wikis.

Haluk Demirkan (haluk.demirkan@asu.edu) is Clinical Full Professor of Information Systems and a Research Faculty member of the Center for Services Leadership at Arizona State University. His main research interests are service science and innovation, cloud-based IT services, analytics and business process engineering for sustainable innovation. He is the recent recipient of the IBM Faculty Award for the research project 'Design Science for Self Service Systems'. In 2011, he was ranked 50th in the 'Top 100 Rankings of World-wide Researchers' according to the Association for Information Systems' sanctioned worldwide research rankings (based the 2008–2010 publication records of premier IS journals *MIS Quarterly*, *Information Systems Research* and *Journal of Management Information Systems*). His research has been supported by American Express, Intel, IBM, Teradata and MicroStrategy. He has a PhD in information systems and operations management from the University of Florida.

Gerard Dijkema (G.P.J.Dijkema@tudelft.nl) is an Associate Professor at the Energy and Industry group, Faculty of Technology, Policy and Management, Delft University of Technology. Gerard graduated as a Chemical Engineer (honours) from Twente University of Technology (Enschede, the Netherlands) in 1986 and holds a PhD from Delft University of Technology (PhD thesis: 'Process System Innovation by Design – Towards a Sustainable Petrochemical Industry', 2004). His expertise spans energy technology, large-scale process industry, transition, networked process system innovation, the modelling of large-scale systems for decision support and the relation between industrial infra-systems and applicable policy, law and economics.

Brian Donnellan (brian.donnellan@nuim.ie) is Professor of Information Systems Innovation at the National University of Ireland Maynooth and Co-director of the Innovation Value Institute. Prior to joining NUI Maynooth, Professor Donnellan was a faculty member in the National University of Ireland, Galway. He has spent 20 years working in the ICT industry where he was responsible for the provision of IS to support product development. He is an expert evaluator for the European Commission and has been guest and associate editor of several leading IS journals, including *Journal of IT, Journal of Strategic Information Systems* and *MIS Quarterly*.

Keith A. Ellis (keith.a.ellis@intel.com) is an Applied Researcher within Intel Labs, the R&D arm of Intel Corporation, where he primarily focusses on sustainable ICT and ICT enablement in the context of energy efficiency. Keith has worked on both internal sustainability projects in the data centre arena and also on European FP7-funded sustainability research. His prime interest areas are energy data analytics and impact assessment technology and practices. Keith holds an MSc in innovation and technology management, a BSc (honours) in technology and diplomas in information technology and systems thinking, and he is Lean Six Sigma certified. He has 13 years of industrial experience, primarily in manufacturing. Roles have included operational management, hardware, maintenance and process engineering, business process improvement (BPI) engineering primarily in lean, Lean Six Sigma, systems analyses and people systems.

Christopher P. Fowler (chrisx.fowler@intel.com) has worked in computing science research since 2001. He has held research fellowships with leading research groups focussed on system architectures for distributed e-science, intelligent transport systems and sensor networks. He has an MSc and PhD from Newcastle University, United Kingdom. He is currently focussed on the design, integration and demonstration of applied ICT for sustainable energy management.

G.R. Gangadharan (geeyaar@gmail.com) see his biography under 'About the Editors' on page xx.

Saurabh Kumar Garg (sgarg@csse.unimelb.edu.au) is currently working as a research fellow in the Cloud Computing and Distributed Systems (CLOUDS) Laboratory, University of Melbourne, Australia. He completed his PhD in the area of meta-scheduling in market-oriented grids and utility computing from the University of Melbourne in 2010. In Melbourne University, he received various special scholarships for his PhD candidature. He has also worked with IBM India Research Laboratory, where he designed and optimized the FFT and Random Access benchmarks for Blue Gene/L. His research interests include resource management, scheduling, utility and grid computing, cloud computing, green computing, wireless networks and ad hoc networks.

Aditya Ghose (aditya@uow.edu.au) is Professor of Computer Science at the University of Wollongong (UoW) and Director of its Decision Systems Lab. He holds a PhD and MSc in computing science from the University of Alberta, Canada. He is Research Leader of the Cooperative Research Centre for Smart Services, Co-Director of the Centre for Oncology Informatics at the UoW Health and Medical Research Institute, Co-leader of the UoW Carbon-Centric Computing Initiative, Co-convenor of the Australian Computer Society's New South Wales Branch Special Interest Group (NSW SIG) on Green ICT and Vice President of the Computing Research and Education Association of Australasia (CORE) (Australia's apex body for computing academics).

Robert R. Harmon (harmonr@pdx.edu) is Professor of Marketing and Technology Management and Cameron Research Fellow in the School of Business at Portland State University. His research interests are service innovation, cloud-based sustainable IT services, ecological design factors for technology products and the strategic migration of manufacturing companies to service enterprise business models. His research has been supported by the National Science Foundation, Intel Corporation, IBM and Tata Consultancy Services, among others. He has a PhD in marketing and information systems from Arizona State University.

Konstantin Hoesch-Klohe (konstantin.hoesch@gmail.com) holds a BSc in Business Information Systems from the Hochschule Furtwangen, Germany. Since 2010 he has been a PhD student at the School of Computer Science and Software Engineering at the University of Wollongong (UoW). Konstantin's research interests include business process management, enterprise architectures, service science, formal methods and conceptual modelling.

Sateesh S. Kannegala (sateeshks@hp.com) received his PhD from the University of Massachusetts in Physics after receiving his MSc from IIT Kanpur. Since 1994 he has been in the IT Industry and has worked in security and IT service management. He worked as a Solution Architect with HP until 2005. Sateesh currently works as a Senior IT Specialist in IBM, primarily focussing on analytics and optimization of systems and software development. Sateesh is the IBM India Standards Leader and runs the standards programme in India. In addition, Sateesh chairs TEC (Technology Experts Council) India, an affiliate of the IBM Academy of Technology. He is also an elected member of the IBM Academy of Technology. Since April 2012, Sateesh is working as a Senior Technical Manager in Hewlett Packard.

Ashok Pon Kumar (ashokponkumar@in.ibm.com) is a Technical Staff Member at IBM India Research Lab. His research interests include Smarter Energy, Social Networking and Ubiquitous Computing. Before joining IBM Research, he worked with IBM Rational where he was part of the core team that developed Rational Insight, a cognos based reporting solution for software development. He speaks regularly on Android at conferences. He currently is working on smarter energy related research where he is working on optimizing energy usage in laptops and in optimizing electricity distribution networks.

Nagapramod Mandagere (pramod@us.ibm.com) is a Researcher in the Service Innovation Lab at IBM Almaden Research Center and is concurrently pursuing his PhD. He received his bachelor's degree from Vishveshwaraiah Technological University, Bangalore, India in 2003, after which he received a master's degree at the University of Wyoming in 2005. He worked as a Storage Area Networking (SAN) Consultant for EMC^2, following which he started pursuing a PhD at University of Minnesota working on storage systems. In 2008, he started working at IBM focussing on systems resiliency management. His research interests range from resiliency management, replication management and data centre power management to data de-duplication.

Sally McClean (si.mcclean@ulster.ac.uk) is Professor of Mathematics at the University of Ulster, Northern Ireland. Her main research interests are in statistical modelling and optimization, particularly for health care planning, and computer science, particularly databases, sensor technology and telecommunications. She is currently a grant holder on over £7M worth of funding, mainly from the UK *Engineering and Physical Sciences Research Council* (EPSRC) and other government sources. Sally is a Fellow of the Royal Statistical Society, and a past President of the Irish Statistical Association. She is a recipient of Ulster's Senior Distinguished Research Fellowship.

Alemayehu Molla (alemayehu.molla@rmit.edu.au) is currently an Associate Professor of Information Systems, and Convener of the Green IT Research Cluster at the School of Business Information Technology and Logistics, RMIT University. He has previously been a Lecturer at the University of Manchester, United Kingdom and at Addis Ababa University, Ethiopia. His main research areas are green information technology, e-business, enterprise systems and development informatics. His publications appeared in top-tier information systems, e-business and development informatics journals.

Philip Morrow (pj.morrow@ulster.ac.uk) is a Senior Lecturer at the University of Ulster, Northern Ireland. He has a BSc in applied mathematics and computer science (1981), an MSc in electronics (1982) and a PhD in computing (1993). His research interests lie in image processing and telecommunications. Specific areas of interest include energy efficiency in network management, resource modelling for multimedia distribution and wireless sensor networks. He is co-investigator on the India–UK Centre of Excellence in Next Generation Networks, funded by the UK Engineering and Physical Sciences Research Council (EPSRC) and India's Department of Science and Technology (DST). He has over 100 peer-reviewed publications and has been an investigator in a number of other externally funded research projects.

San Murugesan (san.greenit@gmail.com) see his biography under 'About the Editors' on page xix.

Igor Nikolic (I.Nikolic@tudelft.nl) is an Assistant Professor at the Energy and Industry group, Faculty of Technology, Policy and Management, Delft University of Technology. In his research he specializes in applying complex adaptive systems theory, agent-based modelling and evolutionary theory to model industry and infrastructure network evolution. He takes a heavy hint from evolutionary biology and ecosystem behaviour in his understanding of industrial ecology and sociotechnical system evolution. He is an active networker and promoter of open source and social software that enables collaborative, multidisciplinary research work.

Gerard Parr (gp.parr@ulster.ac.uk) holds the Full Chair in Telecommunications Engineering at the University of Ulster, Northern Ireland. Research areas within the group include intelligent mobile agents in xDSL, real-time data analytics for network management systems (NMS), energy-aware infrastructure, resource management protocols, application performance management, bandwidth provision over synchronous optical networking (SONET) and synchronous digital hierarchy (SDH) in the presence of chaotic impulses and fuzzy inference systems for multicriteria hand-off in tactical communications. He is the UK principal investigator of the EPSRC–DST-funded India–UK Centre of Excellence in Next Generation Networks of which BT Group is the lead industrial partner, and he is also principal investigator in the EPSRC-funded project Sensing Unmanned Autonomous Aerial Vehicles (SUAAVE).

Cathryn Peoples (c.peoples@ulster.ac.uk) is a Post-Doctoral Research Associate in the Faculty of Computing and Engineering at the University of Ulster, Northern Ireland and works on the EPSRC–DST-funded project 'Cross-Layer Energy-Aware Network Management: A Green ICT Solution' with the India–UK Centre of Excellence in Next Generation Networks. She holds a BA (honours) in business and computing (2004), MSc in telecommunications and Internet systems (2005) and PhD in telecommunications (2009) from the University of Ulster. Research interests include cross-layer energy-aware protocol stack optimization and autonomic network operation driven by context awareness and policy-based management, with domains of interest including data centres and delay-tolerant networks.

Joseph Sarkis (jsarkis@clarku.edu) is Professor of Operations and Environmental Management at Clark University. He has a PhD in management science from the State University of New York at Buffalo. He was Assistant and Associate Professor at the University of Texas at Arlington School of Business for about five years. His teaching interests cover a wide range of topics including operations management, logistics, supply chain management, corporate environmental management, management of technology, international management, information systems and technology and also some entrepreneurship. He has published over 250 publications.

Charles G. Sheridan (charles.g.sheridan@intel.com) leads Intel Labs Europe's Sustainability and Energy research programme which is focussed on the application of ICTs to drive and enable the shift to a more sustainable economy and society. He is currently involved in research projects related to Smart Buildings and Grids in addition to electromobility, at both the national and European levels. Charlie has worked with Intel for 17 years with important roles in both TMG Automation and IT Innovation before joining Intel Labs Europe. He has published a number of white papers and journal publications and is co-author of the book *Creating the Infrastructure for Cloud Computing: An Essential Handbook for IT Professionals* (2011).

Bob Steigerwald (Bob.steigerwald@intel.com) is an engineering manager at Intel Corporation. He has over 30 years of industry experience as a software engineer, Associate Professor of Computer Science, program manager and engineering manager. He has spent the past four years leading an Intel team researching methods to improve software performance and energy efficiency. Bob earned a BS in computer science from the US Air Force Academy, a master's degree from the University of Illinois, an MBA from Rensselaer Polytechnic Institute and a PhD from the Naval Postgraduate School.

Bhuvan Unhelkar (bhuvan@methodscience.com) (BE, MDBA, MSc, PhD, FACS) has more than two decades of strategic as well as hands-on professional experience in the ICT industry. As a Founder of MethodScience.com, he has demonstrated consulting and training expertise in business analysis, software engineering, collaborative web services, green IT and mobile business. His domain experience includes banking, financial, insurance, government as well as telecommunication organizations. Dr Unhelkar earned his doctorate in the area of object orientation from the University of Technology, Sydney in 1997. Since then, he has authored or edited 17 books in the areas of collaborative business, globalization, mobile business, software quality, business analysis an processes, Unified Modeling Language (UML) and green ICT, and has extensively presented and published papers and case studies. He is an adjunct Associate Professor at the University of Western Sydney. Dr Unhelkar is a sought-after orator, Fellow of the Australian Computer Society (elected to this prestigious membership grade in 2002 for distinguished contribution to the field of ICT), life member of the Computer Society of India, Rotarian at St Ives (President and Paul Harris Fellow), discovery volunteer at New South Wales Parks and Wildlife and a previous TiE (The Indus Entrepreneurs) Mentor.

Linda R. Wilbanks (Linda.wilbanks@navy.mil) serves as Command Information Officer at the US Naval Criminal Investigative Service, where she is responsible for all aspects of information technology at 144 locations worldwide, supporting law enforcement and the US Department of the Navy. Prior to this position she served as Chief Information Officer for the National Nuclear Security Administration within the US Department of Energy and for NASA Goddard Space Flight Center. With over 35 years of experience in information technology, she continues to serve on educational committees at several universities, and contributes as an Associate Editor and Author for the IEEE journal *IT Professional*. Dr Wilbanks earned her PhD from the University of Maryland Baltimore with research in software engineering.

Pin Zhou (pinzhou@us.ibm.com) is a Research Staff Member at the Storage Systems Research Group in the IBM Almaden Research Center. She joined IBM Research in 2006 after obtaining her PhD from the Computer Science Department of University of

Illinois at Urbana-Champaign. At IBM, she has been involved with a wide variety of projects on storage systems, such as archive and backup storage, data de-duplication, storage resiliency and management, thermal and power management for data centers and so on. Her research interests are storage and operating systems, and software and system reliability. Her work has been published at various international journals and conferences. She has more than 15 patent applications on various topics in computer science, mostly in storage systems.

Foreword

I am delighted to see *Harnessing Green IT* by Murugesan and Gangadharan. Sustainability is growing in significance on a global scale. It attracts political attention, public notice, marketing interest, investment, innovation, technology development and more. The IT industry is facing increased scrutiny due to IT products' and services' impact on sustainability throughout their life cycle. Mitigating the risks and exploiting the opportunities that green IT offers require a holistic and strategic approach with sound principles and best practices. Business leaders, policy makers, IT professionals, researchers, students and the general public need practical and useful guidance on how to harness green IT.

Unfortunately, there have been relatively few practical and useful books on green IT. Murugesan and Gangadharan bring to this book accomplished experts from industry and academia who have hands-on experience and in-depth knowledge in specific areas of green IT. Their connections and involvement with business leaders, researchers, IT professionals and IT consumers add a tremendous amount of real-world insight and relevance. Their personal experiences as both practitioners and researchers are also clear throughout the book.

One of the most impressive aspects of this book is its holistic perspective towards greening IT. Modern IT systems rely upon a complicated mix of people, processes and products. Holistically, this book outlines how green-conscious people adopt green processes to produce or consume green products and services. Specifically, the first part of this book details how green IT can be achieved in and by hardware, software, network communication and data centre operations. The second part of this book discusses the strategies, frameworks, processes and management of greening IT initiatives. The third part of this book highlights innovation to enable greater efficiency of IT products and services.

This book is dedicated to all who are interested in learning and harnessing green IT to create a sustainable environment for the benefit of current and future generations. The information here is presented in such a way that one need not be a professional to understand and use it. Some of this information cannot be found in other books as it captures years of practice and lessons learned by industrial practitioners and academic experts who have real-world expertise and keen knowledge in specific areas of green IT.

I had to learn many of the topics covered in this book in real time, and sometimes by making a mistake on the first attempt. Those of us who work in the IT industry play a key role in harnessing green IT. With this book, many IT leaders and professionals will get to learn the extensive and keen insights of Murugesan, Gangadharan and other experts on sound principles and best practices that make tomorrow's IT greener and sustainable.

Whether you are a provider or consumer of IT products and services, arm yourself with the principles and practices required to make the right green IT decisions to create a sustainable society embracing IT power that benefits our current and future generations. This book is an excellent resource for the necessary knowledge and tools to achieve that goal.

Ultimately, this is a remarkable book, a practical testimonial and a comprehensive bibliography rolled into one. It is a single, bright sword that cuts across the various murky green IT topics. And if the mistakes and lessons that I learned through my green IT journey are any indication, this book will be used every day by folks interested in greening IT. I congratulate Murugesan and Gangadharan on this excellent book that provides an invaluable resource. I enjoyed reading the book and found it exceptionally practical and extremely useful. I think you will, too. Enjoy!

Simon Y. Liu, PhD, EdD
Editor-in-Chief, *IT Professional* Magazine, IEEE Computer Society
Director, US National Agricultural Library

Preface

Though some disagreement still surrounds the scientific, political and social aspects of global warming, there is growing acceptance regarding the dangerous consequences of not taking action now to address this and other environmental problems. Climate change is a reality, and its main cause is manmade greenhouse gas (GHG) emissions, most notably carbon dioxide (CO_2). Tackling environmental issues and adopting environmentally responsible practices comprise a new important agenda for enterprises, governments and society at large. And, several other factors including the soaring cost of energy, environmental legislations and regulations, the rising cost of waste disposal, an electric energy shortage and corporate image and public perception concerns are pushing enterprises and individuals to go green.

As part of this global agenda of growing significance, we are called upon to make our information technology (IT) systems and work practices greener and to harness the power of IT to address environmental problems facing us. So chief information officers (CIOs), IT managers, IT professionals and businesses and individuals that use IT as well as government agencies seek answers to questions such as: What are the key environmental impacts arising from IT? What are the major environmental IT issues that we must address? How can we make our IT infrastructure, products, services, operations, applications and practices environmentally responsible? How do we measure and compare the effectiveness of our green efforts? What are the regulations or standards with which we need to comply? What benefits can an organization gain by adopting greener IT practices? How can IT assist businesses and society at large in their efforts to improve our environmental sustainability?

Green IT refers to environmentally sound information technologies and systems, applications and practices and encompasses three complementary IT-enabled approaches to improving environmental sustainability: (i) minimize the energy consumption and environmental impacts of computing resources – hardware, software and communication systems – over their life cycle; (ii) harness the power of IT and information systems (IS) to empower – that is, to support, assist and leverage – other environmental initiatives by businesses and (iii) leverage IT to help create awareness among stakeholders and promote a green agenda and green initiatives. Green IT is an economic as well as environmental imperative. And, as many green advocates will attest, it is our social responsibility.

The green movement is creating new career opportunities for IT professionals, auditors and others with special skills in areas such as green IT, energy efficiency, ethical IT asset disposal, carbon footprint estimation and the reporting and development of green products, applications and services. A few universities and training institutes have taken the lead and offer courses on green IT, and others are expected to follow suit. To help create a more sustainable environment, stakeholders need informed understanding of green IT and its promises. But a disparity exists among companies, as well as IT professionals, students and users, in their level of green IT understanding. Many of them do not know how or where to begin when it comes to implementing green IT.

Harnessing Green IT: Principles and Practices is aimed at helping those in the IT field gain an informed and holistic understanding of green IT, its potential and its adoption.

About the Book

In this book, we comprehensively discuss what green IT is, how IT can be made greener and how IT can help improve environmental sustainability. The book covers a wide range of topics: green technologies, design, standards, maturity models, strategies and adoption methodologies. To help readers explore this new discipline further and keep abreast of ongoing developments, we also provide, for each chapter, a list of additional information resources. The topics and coverage are well aligned with current technology and market trends and with the green movement which is gaining greater awareness and significance.

This book is intended for anyone interested in understanding the principles and practices of green IT and in adopting or deploying green IT in their areas of interest. The book assumes no prior knowledge in this area, and presents in-depth comprehensive coverage. It will be of interest and value to IT professionals, students, academics, researchers, executives and policy makers. It will help them to get better informed about the promise of green IT and create a sustainable environment embracing the power of IT that benefits our current and future generations.

The book features 18 chapters written by green IT experts drawn from academia and industry. The chapters can be read in sequence or the reader, after getting an overview of green IT in Chapter 1, can jump to a selected chapter or chapters of interest. Each chapter also presents a set of review and discussion questions that helps the readers to further examine and explore the green IT domain. The book also features a glossary and a companion Web site at wiley.com. For instructors adopting this book for courses, supplementary PowerPoint presentation material is available (contact the publisher's representative in your area).

Chapter Preview

Chapter 1 introduces the concept of green IT, illustrating the principles and practices of IT *by* greening and IT *for* greening. It examines the environmental impacts of IT, outlines a definition of green IT and delineates the notion of green IT 1.0 and 2.0. It presents a holistic approach to greening IT and briefly outlines how data centres, cloud computing, storage systems, software and networks can be made greener. It also highlights how IT could help businesses' environmental initiatives and reduce their carbon emissions, and thus sets the backdrop for the remaining chapters.

The next three chapters illustrate green IT's hardware and software aspects, detailing how sustainability could be achieved in (and by) hardware and software. Chapter 2 provides comprehensive coverage of green hardware including PC power management, energy-efficient power converters, the use of multicore processors, newer types of displays and the use of less toxic materials. Chapter 3 discusses how you can make software greener and energy efficient, and focuses on ways, methods and options by which software can be made greener. As a continuation, Chapter 4 discusses how software characteristics impact the sustainability or greenness of computing applications, and outlines the notion of sustainable software engineering.

Key sustainability challenges associated with data centres and strategies to minimize data centres' energy consumption and carbon footprint are discussed in Chapter 5, which describes a holistic approach to IT and facilities energy management in a data centre. Chapter 6 presents comprehensive coverage of energy-efficient storage technologies and data storage systems. Computer networks and communications can also be made greener. Chapter 7 examines the need for making computer networks and communications energy efficient, and describes emerging greener network protocols and related ongoing developments.

To realize fuller benefits, business goals and green strategies for carbon reduction need to be aligned more closely. Chapter 8 emphasizes the need for this alignment and describes the crucial steps and considerations in developing green IT strategies. Chapter 9 examines the information requirements at multiple levels including the organization, business function, product and service and individual levels, and discusses sustainability frameworks, principles and tools. It also presents a model for assessing an organization's sustainability capability. Chapter 10 proposes a green IT readiness (G-readiness) framework to display the input, transformational and output capabilities of greening IT, offers a series of propositions linking the G-readiness dimensions and shows the framework's utility by drawing on data collected in Australia, the United States and New Zealand.

IT is a key enabler, and can be a primary driver, of an overall corporate sustainability strategy. Chapter 11 discusses sustainable IT services, applications that provide innovative solutions for corporate ecological and societal issues. It also examines the dimensions of sustainable IT services and their value from different stakeholder perspectives, and outlines the criteria for improving the alignment between these services and a sustainability strategy. Chapter 12 highlights the need for the entire enterprise (or as many of its units as possible) to go greener and presents an overview of various green initiatives within and between organizations. It also discusses the role of IT and IS in greening enterprises.

The needs to address and reengineer business processes from an environmental perspective and to make business and physical processes greener are outlined in Chapter 13. Chapter 14 elicits management's role as well as managerial and implementation issues in greening IT and one's enterprise. It also discusses the life cycle of green IT initiatives and illustrates it with a case study. Chapter 15 delineates the mix of regulatory, nonregulatory and other influences affecting business and the IT industry to make them more environmentally sustainable. It describes the global regulations governing green IT and discusses the scope of emerging green IT regulations and public policy.

The next two chapters outline the roles of Semantic Web and cloud computing in the green IT context. Chapter 16 discusses cloud computing in the context of environmental sustainability and various elements of clouds which contribute to total energy consumption, and outlines key concepts in building greener clouds. Chapter 17 deals with information management for sustainability. It discusses how semantic Web technologies and concepts could be applied for collecting and sharing information, and describes an ecosystem of tools, based on Semantic MediaWiki, that enable greater efficiency of data use.

Chapter 18, the concluding chapter, examines how some emerging technologies support green IT initiatives, explores opportunities and challenges in green IT and emerging trends and identifies research directions.

We believe this book, covering a range of key topics and solutions in green IT, would be helpful to a spectrum of readers who wish to gain an informed understanding of the promise and potential of green IT and create a sustainable environment that harnesses the power of IT to benefit current and future generations. You can start making a difference by taking the steps and measures outlined in the book. As Mahatma Gandhi once said, 'Be the change you want to see in the world'. Now, we're delighted to pass on the book to you. We welcome your comments on the book and suggestions at greenITbook@gmail.com.

For more information, please visit the companion website –
www.wiley.com/go/murugesan_green

San Murugesan
G.R. Gangadharan
greenITbook@gmail.com
June 2012

Acknowledgements

Publication of this book wouldn't have been possible without the contribution, support and cooperation of several people. We would like to acknowledge them.

We would like to thank each one of the chapter authors for enthusiastically contributing to the book, and thereby sharing their expertise, experiences and insights with the readers. We gratefully acknowledge their support and cooperation. We also extend our gratitude to the reviewers who have provided valuable comments on the book chapters.

We profusely thank Simon Liu, Editor-in-Chief of the IEEE Computer Society's *IT Professional* magazine, for writing a foreword to this book.

The editorial team at Wiley deserves our commendation for their key roles in publishing this volume and in ensuring its quality. In particular, we would like to thank Anna Smart, Susan Barclay and Mariam Cheok for their excellent enthusiasm, support and cooperation. We would like to thank Cheryl Adam, our copy editor, and Lavanya and her team at Laserwords in India, our typesetter, for their excellent work on this book.

Finally, we would like to thank our family members for their encouragement, support and cooperation which enabled us to make this venture a reality.

San Murugesan
G.R. Gangadharan

1

Green IT: An Overview

San Murugesan[1] and G.R. Gangadharan[2]
[1]*BRITE Professional Services and University of Western Sydney, Sydney, Australia*
[2]*Institute for Development and Research in Banking Technology, Hyderabad, India*

Key Points

- Explains what green IT is and examines the significance of green IT.
- Discusses environmental concerns, global warming and the principles of sustainable development.
- Examines the environmental impacts of IT.
- Describes the three key dimensions of green IT and explains green IT 1.0 and 2.0.
- Presents a holistic approach to greening IT.
- Discusses how data centres, cloud computing, storage systems, software and networks can be made greener.
- Highlights how IT could help businesses in their environmental initiatives and reduce their carbon emissions.
- Outlines enterprise green IT strategy.

1.1 Introduction

Enterprises, governments and societies at large have a new important agenda: tackling environmental issues and adopting environmentally sound practices. Over the years, information technology (IT) has fundamentally altered our work and life and improved our productivity, economy and social well-being. IT now has a new role to play – helping to create a greener, more sustainable environment whilst offering economic benefits. But IT has been contributing to environmental problems which most people do not realize. Computers and other IT infrastructure consume significant amounts of electricity, which is increasing day by day, placing a heavy burden on our electric grids and contributing to greenhouse gas (GHG) emissions. Additionally, IT hardware poses environmental problems during both its production and its disposal.

Harnessing Green IT: Principles and Practices, First Edition. Edited by San Murugesan and G.R. Gangadharan.

Whilst many people consider IT to be part of the problem to environmental pollution, it can be its saviour too. In other words, IT is both a solution and a problem for environmental sustainability. We can exploit the power of IT in innovative ways to address mounting environmental issues (Aronson, 2008; Ruth, 2009) and make our IT systems – and their use – greener. Green IT, also known as green computing, is the study and practice of designing, manufacturing and using computers, servers, monitors, printers, storage devices and networking and communications systems efficiently and effectively, with zero or minimal impact on the environment (Murugesan, 2007, 2008). Green IT is also about using IT to support, assist and leverage other environmental initiatives and to help create green awareness (Murugesan, 2008). Thus, green IT encompasses hardware, software, tools, strategies and practices that improve and foster environmental sustainability.

Green IT benefits the environment by improving energy efficiency, lowering GHG emissions, using less harmful materials and encouraging reuse and recycling. Thus green IT includes the dimensions of environmental sustainability, the economics of energy efficiency and the total cost of ownership, which includes the cost of disposal and recycling. Increased awareness of the harmful effects of GHG emissions, new stringent environmental legislation, concerns about electronic waste disposal practices and corporate image concerns are driving businesses and individuals to go green.

Green IT is an economic as well as environmental imperative. And, as many green advocates will attest, it is our social responsibility as well (Murugesan, 2007). The imminent introduction of more green taxes and regulations will trigger a major increase in demand for green IT products, solutions and services. Hence a growing number of IT vendors and users have begun to develop and offer green IT products and services. As business and governments try to balance growth with environmental risks, we will be legally, ethically and/or socially required to 'green' our IT products, applications, services and practices.

To foster green IT, we should understand the following issues: What are the key environmental impacts arising from IT? What are the major environmental IT issues that we must address? How can we make our IT infrastructure, products, services, operations, applications and practices environmentally sound? What are the regulations or standards with which we need to comply? How can IT assist businesses and society at large in their efforts to improve our environmental sustainability?

Beginning with a brief account of IT's environmental impact, this chapter outlines what green IT means and presents a holistic approach to greening IT. It also highlights how IT can help in different ways to improve our environmental sustainability, and outlines a green IT strategy for enterprises.

1.2 Environmental Concerns and Sustainable Development

Numerous scientific studies and reports offer evidence of climate change and its potential harmful effects. Specifically, the growing accumulation of GHGs is changing the world's climate and weather patterns, creating droughts in some countries and floods in others and pushing global temperatures slowly higher, posing serious worldwide problems. Global data show that storms, droughts and other weather-related disasters are growing more severe and frequent.

Global warming is an average increase in the temperature of the atmosphere near the Earth's surface which can contribute to changes in global climate patterns (EPA, 2009,

2012). Global warming can occur from a variety of causes, both natural and human induced. In common usage, however, *global warming* often refers to warming that can occur due to increased GHG emissions from human activities which trap heat that would otherwise escape from Earth. This phenomenon is called the greenhouse effect. GHGs comprise a range of different elements, and the common characteristics of them are that they can absorb thermal infrared radiation (heat) which is emitted from the Earth, and then re-emit it, increasing the Earth's temperature. The most significant constituents of GHG are carbon dioxide (CO_2), methane, nitrous oxide and chlorofluorocarbon (CFC) gases. Electricity is a major source of GHGs as it is generated by burning coal or oil, which releases CO_2 into the atmosphere. Reducing electric power consumption is a key to reducing CO_2 emissions and their impacts on our environment and global warming. The 1997 Kyoto Protocol mandates reducing carbon emissions. The Protocol requires computer manufacturers to undertake energy audits to calculate the electricity used by devices over their lifetime and determine the quantum of CO_2 emissions to take remedial action. In order to stop the accumulation of GHGs in the atmosphere, global emissions would have to stop growing and be reduced by an astonishing 60% from today's levels by 2050 (Lash and Wellington, 2007).

1.2.1 The Inconvenient Truth

Climate change presents a new kind of risk; its impact is global and long term, and the damage it causes is essentially irreversible. The imminent dangers of climate change and the state of global warming are highlighted by former US Vice President and environment activist Al Gore in the Oscar®-winning documentary film *An Inconvenient Truth* and the book *An Inconvenient Truth* (Gore, 2006). Sir Nicholas Stern, in his landmark report, discussed the economics of global warming and warned, 'It was not action, but inaction, on climate change that would devastate global economies' (Stern, 2007).

Not everyone agrees, however, with these predictions regarding global warming and its impacts. For instance, controversies exist concerning the causes of global warming, whether this warming trend is unprecedented or within normal climatic variations, predictions of additional warming, what the consequences are and what actions should be taken. These controversies are scientific, political and/or social in nature (for a good overview of these, see Wikipedia's article on 'Global Warming Controversy'). Environmental groups, numerous governmental reports and many in the media are, however, in agreement with the scientific community in support of human-caused warming. Several scientific societies and academies of science, including all major countries' national academies of science, endorse that global warming is mainly caused by human activity and will continue if GHG emissions are not reduced.

Driven by the disastrous impact of recent storms, floods, droughts and excessive heat that many people have experienced around the world, various studies on global warming and its impact and major global campaigns, many people have begun to think seriously about global warming and its impacts and to do whatever they can to address this problem. Governments, enterprises and people all have roles in combating global warming and building a sustainable environment. There is now greater awareness and a growing commitment to address environmental problems. Inaction to arrest environmental degradation would significantly affect not only current but also future generations and our further progress, and there is need for multipronged action. The highlighted awareness drives us to ask: What can, and should, IT do in creating a greener, sustainable environment? What can each of us – those in business and industry or in IT departments, CEOs, CIOs, CTOs, IT professionals and employees – do individually and collectively to stop global warming and create a sustainable environment?

1.2.2 Sustainable Development

Sustainability is all about meeting needs and seeking a balance between people, the environment and the economy. According to the United Nations Global Commission on the Environment and Development's 1987 *Brundtland Report*, sustainable development is the 'development that meets the needs of the present without compromising the ability of future generations to meet their own needs'. Sustainable development comprises economic, environmental and social dimensions.

1.2.3 Why Should You Go Green?

Enterprises are now increasingly interested in creating strategies that will help them to handle environmental issues and pursue new opportunities. The reasons for going green are manifold: increasing energy consumption and energy prices, growing consumer interest in environmentally friendly goods and services, higher expectations by the public on enterprises' environmental responsibilities and emerging stricter regulatory and compliance requirements. Enterprise will increasingly feel the effects of environmental issues that impact their competitive landscape in ways not envisaged earlier. For instance, investors have started discounting the share prices of companies that poorly address the environmental problems they create. When making purchasing, leasing or outsourcing decisions, many customers now take into consideration the company's environmental records and initiatives. Investors are increasingly placing their money on initiatives that are green or that develop and promote green products and services. Government agencies, investors and the public are demanding more disclosures from companies regarding their carbon footprint and their environmental initiatives and achievements. Companies with the technology and vision to provide products and services that address environmental issues will enjoy a competitive edge (Lash and Wellington, 2007).

1.3 Environmental Impacts of IT

As mentioned in this chapter, IT affects our environment in several different ways. Each stage of a computer's life, from its production, through its use and to its disposal, presents environmental problems. Manufacturing computers and their various electronic and non-electronic components consume electricity, raw materials, chemicals and water, and generate hazardous waste. All these directly or indirectly increase carbon dioxide emissions and impact the environment.

Total electrical energy consumption by servers, computers, monitors, data communications equipment and data centre cooling systems is steadily increasing. This increase results in greater GHG emissions, as most electricity is generated by burning fossil fuel like coal, oil and gas. For instance, each PC in use generates about a ton of carbon dioxide every year. Computer components contain toxic materials. Increasingly, consumers discard a large number of old computers, monitors and other electronic equipment 2–3 years after purchase, and most of this ends up in landfills, polluting the Earth and contaminating water.

The increased number of computers and their use, along with their frequent replacements, make IT's environmental impact a major concern. Consequently, there is increasing pressure on the IT industry, businesses and individuals to make IT environmentally friendly throughout its life cycle, from birth to death to rebirth. As many believe, it's our social and corporate responsibility to safeguard our environment.

1.4 Green IT

IT now has a new role to play in creating a greener, more sustainable environment, whilst offering economic benefits by becoming greener.

Green IT is an umbrella term referring to environmentally sound information technologies and systems, applications and practices. It encompasses three complementary IT-enabled approaches to improving environmental sustainability (Murugesan, 2008) (see Figure 1.1):

1. the efficient and effective design, manufacture, use and disposal of computer hardware, software and communication systems with no or minimal impact on the environment;
2. the use of IT and information systems to empower – that is, support, assist and leverage – other enterprise-wide environmental initiatives and
3. the harnessing of IT to help create awareness among stakeholders and promote the green agenda and green initiatives.

Green IT is not just about creating energy-efficient IT systems (hardware, software and applications), though this is an important component, especially as the use of IT proliferates. Green IT is also about the application of IT to create energy-efficient, environmentally sustainable business processes and practices, transportation and buildings. IT can support, assist and leverage environmental initiatives in several areas and also help create green awareness. IT contributes to only about 2–3% of GHG emissions. The vast majority of emissions come from non-IT sources. So, broader applications of IT in

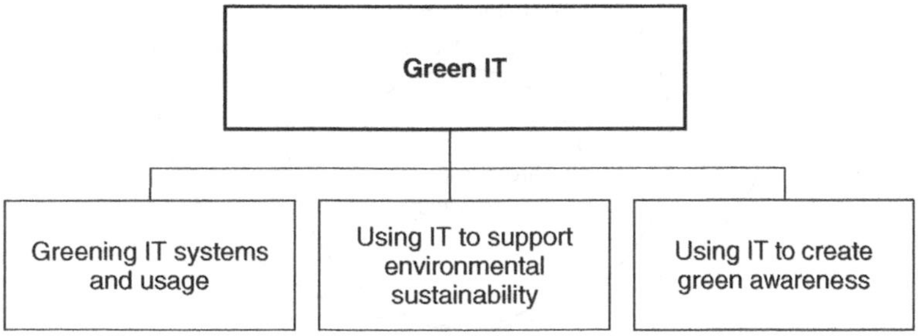

Figure 1.1 Green IT dimensions.

other areas of the economy could bring significant energy savings and improve overall environmental sustainability. According to the SMART 2020 report, IT's largest influence will be by enabling energy efficiencies in other sectors, an opportunity that could deliver carbon savings five times larger than the total emissions from the entire information and computer technology (ICT) sector in 2020. IT can help organizations to minimize their environmental impacts in areas such as GHG emissions, toxic contamination and energy and water consumption.

1.4.1 OCED Green IT Framework

The Organisation for Economic Co-operation and Development (OECD) has proposed a green IT framework consisting of three analytical levels (OCED, 2010) (Figure 1.2). Its objectives are similar to the 'Green IT Dimensions' described in this chapter:

1. **Direct impacts of IT:** These are IT's first-order effects on the environment and include both positive and negative impacts due to the physical existence of IT goods and services and related processes. The sources of IT's direct environmental impacts are IT manufacturing and services firms, including intermediaries and goods producers and final consumers and users of ICTs.
2. **Enabling impacts of IT:** These are the second-order effects that arise from IT applications that reduce environmental impacts across several economic and social activities. For instance, IT can be harnessed to streamline and modify how other products are designed, produced, consumed, used and disposed of, making production and consumption more resource efficient and environmentally sound. This may include consolidations, integration, optimization, dematerialization and substitution.
3. **Systemic impacts of IT:** These impacts and their application on the environment, also called third-order effects, involve behavioural change, process change and other nontechnological factors.

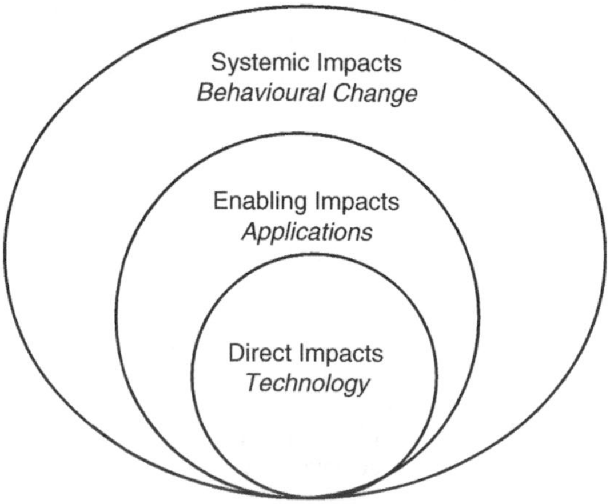

Figure 1.2 OCED green IT framework.

1.4.2 Green IT 1.0 and 2.0

The first wave of green IT – the greening of IT, or Green IT 1.0 – was internally focussed on reengineering IT products and processes to improve IT's energy efficiency, maximize its use and meet compliance requirements. However, as mentioned the vast majority of GHG emissions that deteriorate our environment come from non-IT sources. So, to create significant energy savings and improve overall environmental sustainability, we need to focus our attention and efforts on other areas.

The second wave of green IT, Green IT 2.0, is externally focussed and empowers a range of other green initiatives aimed at reducing environmental degradation and reducing GHG emissions. It is focussed on environmentally sound business transformation, IT-based sustainability innovation, sustainability-based IT innovations and enterprise-wide sustainability. For instance, in addition to being green itself, IT can help create a more sustainable environment by

- coordinating, reengineering and optimizing the supply chain, manufacturing activities and organizational workflows to minimize their environmental impact;
- making business operations, buildings and other systems energy efficient;
- helping decision making by analysing, modelling and simulating environmental impacts;
- providing platforms for eco-management and emissions trading;
- auditing and reporting energy consumption and savings; and
- offering environmental knowledge management systems and decision support systems.

1.5 Holistic Approach to Greening IT

To comprehensively and effectively address the environmental impacts of IT, we must adopt a holistic approach that addresses the problems along these six complementary directions (Murugesan, 2008) (see Figure 1.3):

1. **Green design.** Design energy-efficient and environmentally sound components, computers, servers and cooling equipment.
2. **Green manufacturing.** Manufacture electronic components, computers and other associated subsystems with minimal or no impact on the environment.
3. **Green use.** Reduce the energy consumption of computers and other information systems, and use them in an environmentally sound manner.
4. **Green disposal.** Refurbish and reuse old computers, and properly recycle unwanted computers and other electronic equipment.
5. **Green standards and metrics.** These are required for promoting, comparing and benchmarking sustainability initiatives, products, services and practices.
6. **Green IT strategies and policies.** These effective and actionable strategies and policies add value and focus on both short- and long-term benefits. These are aligned with business strategies and practices, and are key components of greening IT.

By focussing our efforts on these six fronts, we can achieve total environmental sustainability for IT and make IT greener throughout its entire life cycle.

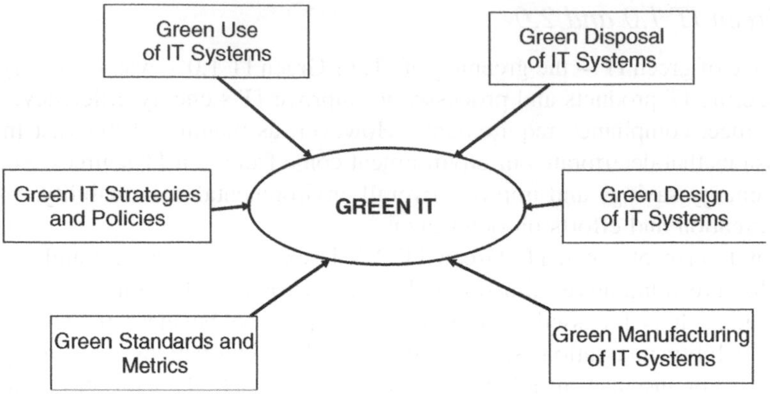

Figure 1.3 Holistic, multipronged approach to greening IT.

1.5.1 Greening Computer's Entire Life Cycle

As shown in Figure 1.4, the entire life cycle of a computer, server and storage system could be made greener, reducing their GHG emissions and carbon footprint and minimizing or eliminating toxic materials used and/or released to the environment. Chapter 2 discusses environmental issues arising from electronic devices, offers a range of solutions to address this problem and highlights best practices in each of the life cycle phases.

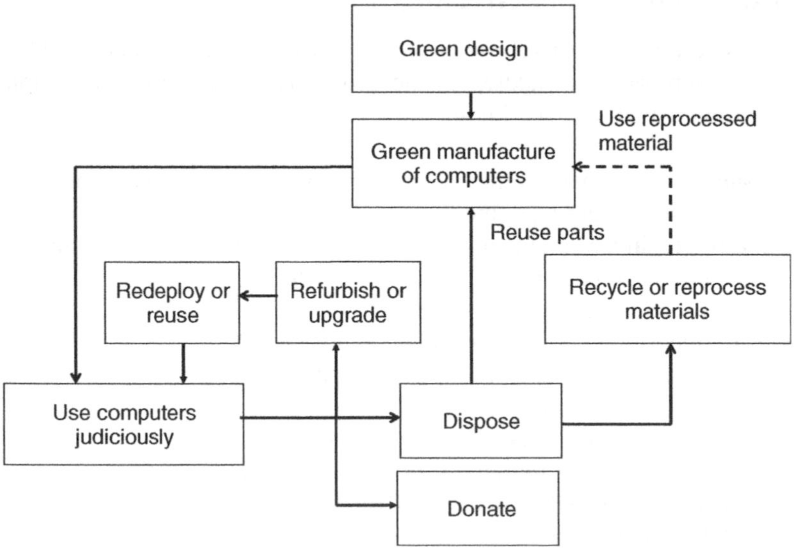

Figure 1.4 Greening computer's entire life cycle.

1.5.2 The Three Rs of Green IT

Unwanted computers, monitors and other hardware should not be thrown away as rubbish, as they will then end up in landfills and cause serious environmental problems. Instead, we should refurbish and reuse them, or dispose them in environmentally sound ways. *Reuse*, *refurbish* and *recycle* are the three 'Rs' of greening unwanted hardware.

- **Reuse.** Many organizations and individuals buy new computers for each project or once every 2–3 years. Instead, we should make use of an older computer if it meets our requirements. Otherwise, we should give it to someone who could use it in another project or unit. By using hardware for a longer period of time, we can reduce the total environmental footprint caused by computer manufacturing and disposal.
- **Refurbish.** We can refurbish and upgrade old computers and servers to meet our new requirements. We can make an old computer and other IT hardware almost new again by reconditioning and replacing some parts. Rather than buying a new computer to our specifications, we can also buy refurbished IT hardware in the market. More enterprises are now open to purchasing refurbished IT hardware, and the market for refurbished equipment is growing. If these options are unsuitable, we can donate the equipment to charities, schools or someone in need, or we can trade in our computers.
- **Recycle.** When we cannot refurbish or otherwise reuse computers, we must dispose of them in environmentally friendly ways by depositing them with recognized electronic recyclers or electronic waste (e-waste) collectors. E-waste – discarded computers and electronic goods – is one of the fastest-growing waste types and poses serious environmental problems. The United Nations Environment Program estimates that 20–50 million tons of e-waste are generated worldwide each year, and this is increasing. IT hardware contains toxic materials like lead, chromium, cadmium and mercury. If we bury IT hardware in landfills, toxic materials can leach harmful chemicals into waterways and the environment. If burned, they release toxic gases into the air we breathe. So if e-waste is not discarded properly, it can harm the environment and us. Waste electrical and electronic equipment (WEEE) regulations aim to reduce the amount of e-waste going to landfills and increase recovery and recycling rates.

Disposal of e-waste, if not properly done, causes serious environmental damage and health problems particularly to those directly involved in the disposal or recycling. Despite bans on the export and import of e-waste, e-waste gets into developing countries (such as India, China and Philippines) for 'recycling' as the cost of recycling is lower there. Unfortunately, as environmental regulations and proper means of e-waste disposal and recycling are not enforced in practice in these countries, e-waste is handled 'informally' in unofficial recycling markets by manual, crude, hazardous means to extract metals and other valuables.

Computer manufacturers should take their share of responsibility and take action to reduce pollution caused by their products' end of life. For instance, they should widely adopt a take-back option, whereby they take from consumers the computers that they no longer need, and arrange for their disposal in an environmentally friendly manner through an e-waste recycling plant. They should educate customers on what they should with do their old computers. They should also gradually eliminate or minimize the use of toxic materials in computers, which some computer manufacturers are doing.

1.6 Greening IT

One might wonder how we should go about greening IT, and what subsystems of IT can be greened. In fact, every subsystem and peripheral of IT can be greened. The key among them are PCs, notebooks and servers, data centres and cloud computing, software (system and application software, along with the processes of software design and development), storage systems and networking and communication systems and protocols. Peripherals such as printers can be made energy efficient and environmentally friendly.

1.6.1 Green PCs, Notebooks and Servers

We can significantly reduce energy consumption by making small changes to the ways we use computers. Most desktop computers run even when they aren't being used, because users needlessly leave them on, wasting electricity (Nordman and Christensen, 2009). Furthermore, computers generate heat and require additional cooling, which add to the total power consumption and cost. Whilst the savings in energy costs per PC may not seem like much, the combined savings for hundreds of computers in an enterprise is considerable. We can reduce PC energy consumption by adopting several measures.

- **Enabling power management features.** Without sacrificing performance, we can program computers to automatically power down to an energy-saving state when we are not using them.
- **Turning off the system when not in use.** This is the most basic energy conservation strategy for most systems.
- **Using screensavers.** A blank screensaver conserves more power than a screensaver that displays moving images, which continually interacts with the CPU. But even that reduces the monitor's energy consumption by only a small percentage.
- **Using thin-client computers.** Users can choose to employ thin-client computers, which draw about a fifth of the power of a desktop PC.

These measures, though easily adoptable, will not become a practical reality without users' wholehearted willingness and active participation. Even simple steps by one individual or organization can make a huge difference when leveraged across the vast number of individuals and organizations across the world. Smart companies will adopt innovative environmental strategies to innovate, create value and build a competitive advantage. Chapter 2 describes the concept of green hardware including PC power management, energy-efficient power converters, the use of multicore processors, newer types of displays, the use of less toxic materials and related topics.

1.6.2 Green Data Centres

Enterprise data centres, the modern engine rooms that power the Internet and corporate computing, are growing in their number, capacity and power consumption. For instance, according to an IBM estimate, the power demanded worldwide by data centres currently stands at 100 billion kWh a year, and data centres are one of the fastest-growing users of power (Pritchard, 2007). The carbon footprint of data centres has been increasing dramatically as they consume much energy to power their IT systems and data centre cooling systems.

A study by Jonathan Koomey reveals that the total power used by servers represented 0.6% of total US electricity consumption in 2005 (Pritchard, 2007). With the power needed for cooling and other auxiliary services, electricity use rises to 1.2%, equivalent to the power used by all the country's colour televisions. Aggregate electricity use for servers doubled between 2000 and 2005, and most of this came from businesses installing large numbers of new servers (Pritchard, 2007).

The continued rise of Internet and Web applications is driving the rapid growth of data centres and an increase in energy use. To handle more transactions in less time, to process and store more data and to automate more business processes, enterprises are installing more servers or expanding their capacity, all of which demands more computing power. As energy prices increase worldwide, data centres' operational costs also increases. Energy costs now account for nearly 30% of a data centre's operating costs. As a result, IT is increasingly coming under scrutiny, and data centre efficiency is a major issue facing IT departments.

The number of server computers in data centres has increased sixfold, to 30 million, in the last decade, and each server draws far more electricity than earlier models. Besides the cost, the availability of electrical power is becoming a critical issue for many companies whose data centres have expanded steadily. Energy suppliers need time to design, build and supply the huge amounts of additional electrical power (a few megawatts) demanded by data centres. These social, financial and practical constraints force businesses and IT departments to consider how to reduce, or at least limit, energy consumption by data centres.

So data centres must become greener as well. A green data centre is one in which IT system, air-conditioning systems, electrical and mechanical systems and the buildings that house the data centre are designed and operated for maximum energy efficiency, low carbon footprint and minimum environmental impacts. The data centre uses advanced cooling, heating and IT systems to tailor power consumption to processing and operational needs. Ways to save data centre energy consumption include server, storage and network virtualization, the use of blade servers, server clustering and consolidation and the use of energy-efficient power supplies. Chapter 5 details key sustainability challenges facing data centres and discusses strategies to minimize energy consumption and reduce the carbon footprint of IT systems and data centre facilities.

The EU Code of Conduct on Data Centres' Energy Efficiency is a voluntary initiative aimed at reducing the environmental, economic and energy supply security impact of data centres. The scope of the Code of Conduct encompasses both the equipment and system levels, focussing on two primary areas: the IT load (i.e. the IT capacity available for the power consumed) and facilities load (equipment and systems that support the IT load, such as cooling systems, power distribution units (PDUs) and uninterruptable power supply (UPS)). The flexible and adaptable Code of Conduct encourages data centre operators and owners to undertake a cost-effective adoption of energy-efficient practices without hampering their data centres' mission-critical functions.

1.6.3 Green Cloud Computing

Cloud computing represents a paradigm shift. It is a transition from computing-as-a-product to computing-as-a-service, which is shared and scalable on demand. Driven by the benefits that cloud computing offers, businesses, educational institutions, governments and individuals in both developed and emerging markets have begun to use it for several applications. Cloud offerings and use are growing, and hence these created huge demands on data centres that house the clouds. To cater to the growing demands of cloud-computing services, vendors use large-scale data centres which consolidate thousands of servers with other infrastructure such as cooling, storage and communication networks. With the growth of the cloud, therefore, comes increasing energy consumption by data centres. Then how can clouds be greener? Cloud computing is a green solution as cloud infrastructure embraces two critical elements of a green IT: resource efficiency and energy efficiency. Chapter 16 gives further details on on-going developments to make cloud computing greener.

1.6.4 Green Data Storage

Data and information storage requirements keep growing drastically. Storage systems in data centres consume significant amounts of power and cooling. For instance, in a data centre, storage systems consume anywhere between 24% and 40% of total IT power usage and are the centre's biggest power hogs. So, besides making servers energy efficient, the focus is on greening data storage. Several approaches including MAID (Massive Array of Idle Disks), disk spin down, tiered storage and solid-state drives (SSDs) are used for improving energy efficiency and cutting the overall costs of storing persistent data. System-level approaches such as storage virtualization, thin provisioning (TP) and data de-duplication helps reduce required storage space and make effective utilization of available space. For in-depth coverage of green data storage, refer to Chapter 6. Green storage has to be part of a bigger 'greener ICT' strategy.

Data de-duplication is the elimination of coarse-grained redundant data, typically to improve storage utilization. De-duplication may occur *in line*, as data are flowing, or *post process* after data have been written. It reduces the required storage capacity since only the unique data are stored. Depending on the type of information stored, de-duplication of data can yield a compression ratio from 3:1 to 10:1. Data de-duplication also reduces the data that must be sent across a network for remote backups, replication and disaster recovery.

TP is a method of storage resource management and virtualization that lets IT administrators limit the allocation of actual physical storage to what applications immediately need. TP operates by allocating disk storage space in a flexible manner among multiple users, based on the minimum space required by each user at any given time. NetApp, EMC, Compellent, Xiotech, Dell, 3PAR and several others offer tiering and TP systems.

Tiering, in addition to filtering out unnecessary data and files, allocates business data and files to the most efficient layer of storage available: for example, Tier 1 (on-demand data), Tier 2 (data not critical but still timely) and Tier 3 (archival data). Tiering also provides immediate access to timely business data so they can be used for internal corporate analytics if needed. Chapter 6 discusses the power consumption characteristics of different storage solutions and media, and highlights different energy management techniques for hard disks and system-level green measures.

1.6.5 Green Software

Does software impact the environment? Yes. Software plays an important role in determining overall energy consumption and computational efficiency. For instance, a single ill-behaving, computationally inefficient or power-unfriendly software component on a system can thwart all of the power management benefits built into the hardware.

Software is a key element in improving environmental sustainability. Green software is environmentally friendly software that helps improve the environment. Green software can be classified into four broad categories:

- Software that is greener – consumes less energy to run;
- Embedded software that assists other things in going green (smart operations);
- Sustainability reporting software, or carbon management software (CMS);
- Software for understanding climate change, assessing its implications and forming suitable policy responses.

The manner in which software is developed and the quality attributes of software impact the environment. *Sustainable software development* refers to creating software addressing environmental requirements and perspectives. Development-related attributes such as modifiability, reusability and portability and performance attributes such as computational time and efficiency, usability and dependability influence software's environmental impact. For further discussion on green software and on software design considerations and software methodologies to improve software energy efficiency, refer to Chapters 3 and 4.

Using open source methodologies for application development is expected to result in energy savings as collaborative development processes tend to be more efficient than traditional processes.

Organizations are now required to account and manage their carbon footprint, the amount of GHGs (in CO_2 equivalent) that they produce. This requires IT systems that can measure, analyse and manage carbon emissions in a cost-effective and efficient manner, called a carbon management system. A number of carbon management systems such as Carbonview (www.carbon-view.com), Carbon Planet (www.carbonplanet.com), Greenstone (www.greenstonecarbon.com/software.php) and EmissionsLogic (www.cemsus.com/cems/emissions-logic) are available in the market (see also the CMS Directory at www.carbonmanagementsoftware.com). CMS is also integrated with ERP software from vendors like SAP, Oracle and Microsoft.

1.6.6 Green Networking and Communications

Networks and communications play more significant roles than ever before, and facilitate data transfer and sharing. They enable us to communicate and share information, shop, learn and socialize online, make our work environment smarter and do many other things. The demands on communication networks, wired and wireless, have been constantly increasing, and as a result the energy consumption of communication systems has increased considerably. Traditional networking systems and communication protocols are not particularly designed for energy efficiency. Thus they have some negative impact on the environment.

Green networking refers to ways of minimizing networks' impact on the environment using energy-efficient networking technologies, protocols and products and minimizing resource use whenever possible. Green networking practices include the following:

- Using newer, more energy-efficient techniques, technologies and products;
- Upgrading older equipment with newer, greener networking gears;
- Employing smart systems, user management and energy conservation across IT networks to increase energy efficiency;
- Substituting telecommuting, remote administration and video conferencing for travel.

Chapter 7 describes energy-efficient networking solutions and network protocols, and outlines energy-efficient networking objectives, solutions and management strategies.

1.7 Applying IT for Enhancing Environmental Sustainability

IT can be a key driver in greening several industries and activities, and a positive force towards environmental sustainability initiatives. We should make IT a positive force in environmental change. As mentioned in this chapter, several studies reveal that IT contributes only about 3% of GHG emissions; thus the vast majority of emissions come from non-IT sources, almost all of which can realize enhanced energy efficiency and minimize their environmental pollution through the smarter use of IT (Aronson, 2008; Ruth, 2009).

Besides IT becoming green, it can also be a very helpful enabler and aid to create a better environment. Some of the opportunities for this are as follows:

- Software tools for analysing, modelling and simulating environmental impacts and for environmental risk management;
- Platforms for eco-management, emission trading and ethical investing;
- Tools for auditing and reporting energy consumption and savings and for monitoring GHG emissions;
- Environmental knowledge management systems, meaning the acquisition and transfer of environmental knowledge, decision support systems and collaborative environments; environmental ontologies;
- Environmental information systems engineering, including geographic information systems and environmental (meta-)data standards;
- Urban environment planning tools and systems;
- Technologies and standards for interoperable environmental monitoring networks; smart *in situ* sensor networks;
- Integration and optimization of existing environmental monitoring networks, easy plug-in new sensors, sensor cooperation and networks;
- Tools and systems for optimizing organizational workflows.

To reduce their carbon footprint, organisations can dematerialise some of their products and activities embracing IT. Dematerialization refers to the transformation of physical goods to information goods represented in digital form – "turning atoms to bits." Organisations can adopt electronic billing (e-billing) instead of paper-based billing, offer music and videos for online download rather than on CDs, use e-books and electronic documents rather than printed documents and do video conferencing rather holding face-to-face meetings.

Chapters 11–13 explore further how the power of IT could be harnessed in several different ways to reduce carbon emissions and improve environmental sustainability. Chapter 17 discusses how Semantic Web technologies can be harnessed for the environmental sustainability of production systems.

1.8 Green IT Standards and Eco-Labelling of IT

To promote and adopt standardization, a number of green IT standards and directives have emerged. Key among them are EPEAT (Electronic Product Environmental Assessment Tool), RoHS (Restriction of Hazardous Substances Directive), WEEE, Energy Star, LEED (Leadership in Energy and Environmental Design), the ISO14001 core set of standards for designing and implementing an effective environmental management system and the EN 16001 Energy Management System. EPEAT is a popular, easy-to-use assessment tool to help organizations compare computer desktops, laptops and monitors based on their environmental attributes. EPEAT-registered products are classified as bronze, silver or gold (www.epeat.net) and they have reduced levels of cadmium, lead and mercury to better protect human health. They are more energy efficient and easier to upgrade and recycle. In fact, manufacturers of EPEAT products must offer safe recycling options for their products when they are no longer usable. For further information on green IT standards and regulation, see Chapter 15.

1.9 Enterprise Green IT Strategy

Green IT and green initiatives are becoming a key agenda for enterprises and governments. They are driven by the benefits they offer and by several on-going developments such as concerns about climate change, government regulations and peer pressure and influence, as shown in Figure 1.5.

Each enterprise must develop a holistic, comprehensive green IT strategy, which should be a component of, and aligned with, an enterprise-wide green strategy. It should then develop a green IT policy outlining aims, objectives, goals, plans of action and schedules. Large enterprises should also appoint an environmental sustainability officer to implement their green policy and to monitor their progress and achievements. To green their IT, enterprises can take any one or a combination of the following three approaches:

1. **Tactical incremental approach.** In this approach, an enterprise preserves the existing IT infrastructure and policies and incorporates simple measures to achieve moderate green goals such as reducing energy consumption. These measures include adopting policies and practices such as power management, switching off computers when not in use, using compact energy-efficient light bulbs and maintaining an optimal room temperature. These measures are generally easy to implement without much cost. However, enterprises should work towards these measures only as short-term, ad hoc solutions.

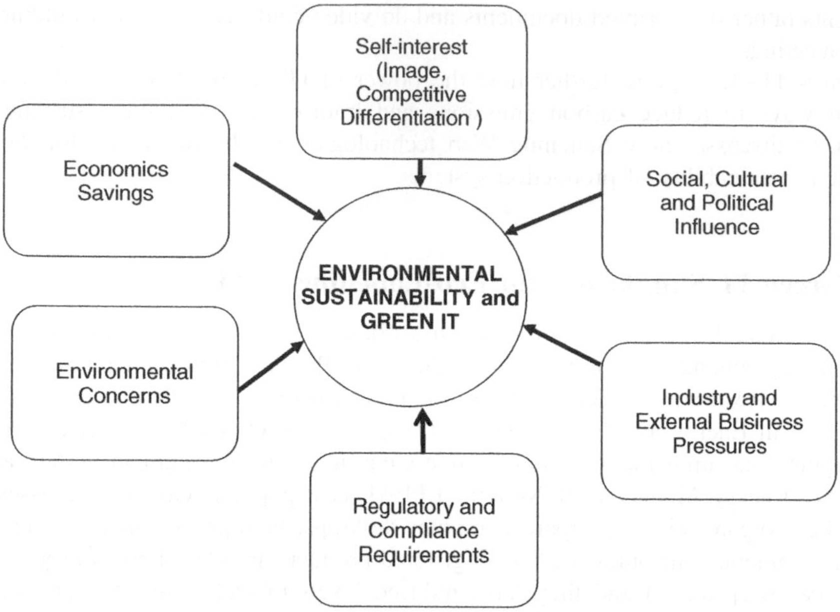

Figure 1.5 Drivers of environmental sustainability and green IT.

2. **Strategic approach.** In this approach, an enterprise conducts an audit of its IT infrastructure and its use from an environmental perspective, develops a comprehensive plan addressing broader aspects of greening its IT and implements distinctive new initiatives. For example, an enterprise may deploy new energy-efficient, environmentally friendly computing systems, or it may develop and implement new policies on procuring, operating and/or disposing of computing resources. Whilst the primary rationale is still cost efficiency and a reduced carbon footprint, this approach also considers other factors such as branding, image creation and marketing.
3. **Deep green approach.** This approach expands upon the measures highlighted in the strategic approach, wherein an enterprise adopts additional measures such as implementing a carbon offset policy to neutralize GHG emissions – including planting trees, buying carbon credits from one of many carbon exchanges or using green power generated from solar or wind energy.

An Accenture Report suggests that about 96% of CEOs are in favour of integrating sustainability issues with organizational strategies (Lacy *et al.*, 2010). Chapter 8 discusses crucial steps and considerations in developing green IT strategies, and challenges in implementing green strategies and policies. Chapters 9 and 10 deal with 'Sustainable Information Systems and Green Metrics' and 'Enterprise Green IT Readiness', respectively. Chapter 14 outlines how to manage IT with a focus on environmental sustainability.

1.9.1 Green Washing

Green washing refers to the practice of organizations exaggerating their green credentials and environmental sustainability attributes, and making false claims. Green washing is an amalgam of the terms green and whitewash. It is an unjustified appropriation of environmental virtue. This socially irresponsible and unethical practice misleads customers and the public regarding the company's environmental practices or the environmental benefits of its product or services. It is a marketing ploy to establish an eco-friendly image to consumers, investors, businesses and regulators. It also uses vague claims regarding products' or services' environmental impact. In several developed countries including Australia, the United States, Canada and Norway, companies that provide misleading environmental claims are liable for punishment. For further information, refer to Greenpeace's Green Washing web site at www.stopgreenwash.org and Wikipedia's article on green washing (http://en.wikipedia.org/wiki/Greenwashing).

1.10 Green IT: Burden or Opportunity?

The green philosophy in general, and the 'go green' movement and green demands on corporate IT in particular, do not excessively or unduly burden IT systems, corporate IT departments or functional units. In fact, these initiatives provide an opportunity to revisit and examine our IT systems and their operations in terms of energy efficiency and resource utilization, and thereby enable us to go lean on IT, minimize IT's energy consumption and save on energy bills. Until recently, IT functions and activities primarily focussed on meeting their functional and performance requirements. Very little attention was paid to aspects such as energy consumption, effective utilization of IT resources, IT's operational costs or IT's negative impact on environments at the stages of design, manufacturing, use, reuse and disposal. There is a pressing need to address these neglected or overlooked aspects as they are now important for safeguarding our environment. IT is required to go green. It is good for IT, businesses and the entire planet. Though initially some might view going green as a burden, a closer examination of green philosophy reveals that it includes improving energy efficiency, improving resource utilization, reducing waste, promoting reuse and recycling and more such benefits. This will give the necessary impetus and motivation to turn IT green and use IT in innovative new ways to green all other corporate functions.

We also need to look at green requirements from another viewpoint. The implications of not going green might cost a lot in the context of emerging stricter environmental regulations, stakeholder demands, competitiveness, brand or corporate image and social responsibility. A holistic and objective view would reveal green IT – greening *of* IT and greening *by* IT – to soon become a necessity, not an option. Even if one feels overburdened with 'go green' initiatives and demands, it is better to adopt them in the interest of self and our planet.

Green IT will be a top priority for several years to come, as it is both an economic and environmental imperative. Several case studies on greening efforts reveal that businesses that reduce their environmental (carbon) footprint can also reduce costs and improve their public image. IT professionals, CIOs and IT support staff are thus being called upon to deliver environmentally sustainable IT solutions (Wilbanks, 2008). Even simple steps that one individual or organization takes can make a huge difference when leveraged across the vast number of individuals and organizations across the world.

However, there is a disparity in the level of green IT understanding across companies, IT professionals, students and IT users. Many do not know how or where to begin or are unwilling to implement green IT. Although green initiatives are catching the attention of the corporate world, some IT professionals, executives and IT departments feel excessively burdened by the green philosophy. However, upon closer examination, they will find that going green is a sound strategy.

Green initiatives let us revisit and examine our IT systems and their operations in terms of energy efficiency and resource utilization, and thus can reduce energy bills. Until recently, very little attention was given to IT's energy consumption, effective use of resources, operational costs and negative environmental impacts during manufacturing, use and disposal. Now, however, a spotlight has been turned on IT, and there is a pressing need to address these overlooked aspects, which are important in safeguarding the environment for future generations.

Businesses also need to look at green requirements from another viewpoint – that is the implications of not going green in the context of stricter environmental regulations, stakeholder demands, competitiveness, branding and corporate image and social responsibility. Smart companies will adopt an environmental strategy to innovate, create value and build a competitive advantage. They will benefit by viewing these challenges as strategic opportunities.

Again, the greening of and by IT will soon be necessities – not options. To help create a more sustainable environment, IT professionals must understand green IT and its potential. Publications that describe new advances, outline current trends and present solid case studies demonstrating green IT's benefits will help provide this understanding and the motivation to 'green' IT.

1.11 Conclusion

As the climate debate heats up, IT finds itself part of the problem – and part of the solution. Environmentalism and economic growth can go hand in hand in the battle against global warming.

A vigorous green IT plan is an economic – as well as an environmental – imperative. Companies can outcompete their peers by tackling sustainability head on, engaging stakeholders, developing partnerships and adding environmental stewardship to their corporate culture. Every business, big or small, faces environmental risks and opportunities. Companies have benefited from taking these challenges as strategic opportunities (Esty and Winston, 2006).

Businesses must develop a positive attitude towards addressing environmental concerns and adopt forward-looking, green-friendly policies and practices. The challenges are immense; however, recent developments indicate that the IT industry has the will and conviction to tackle these environmental issues head on.

As Albert Einstein once said, 'The significant problems we have cannot be solved at the same level of thinking with which we created them'. The green IT agenda represents a major shift in priorities for the IT industry, and IT professionals, educators, researchers and users must be prepared to adjust their 'level of thinking' to realize IT's potential.

Review Questions

1. Briefly describe climate change, global warming, greenhouse gases and the greenhouse effect.
2. What is meant by green IT? Why is it gaining greater relevance and importance now?
3. What are the different dimensions or directions of green IT?
4. How can software impact the environment and the energy consumption of computing systems?
5. What are key subsystems of IT that could be made greener? Briefly explain.
6. Describe the 3Rs of green IT.
7. Why there is growing demand, and need, for greening data centres?
8. What is meant by 'green washing'? Explain with examples.

Discussion Questions

1. Is IT is more of a problem or a solution to environmental sustainability and sustainable development? Discuss.
2. For enterprises, do green initiatives and green IT present a burden or an opportunity to leverage their benefits?
3. Would you advocate effective use of power management features in enterprise computers?
4. What is meant by dematerialization in the context of environmental sustainability? Discuss with examples of how IT and the Internet can help in dematerialization.
5. Discuss how one can use social media, IT and the Internet to create awareness of environmental problems and promote green initiatives among individuals and businesses.
6. Discuss any two smart mobile phone or tablet computer applications (apps) that help individuals or enterprises become greener and environmentally more responsible.
7. Choose three types of carbon management software (CMS) and discuss their features and limitations.
8. Discuss the philosophy, pros and cons of carbon trading.
9. In your view, what are the barriers to individual and enterprise adoption of green IT? Discuss.

References

Aronson, S.J. (2008) Making IT a positive force in environmental change. *IT Professional*, **10** (1), 43–45.

EPA (2009) *Global Warming and Climate Change: Back to Basics*, Environmental Protection Agency, http://www.epa.gov/climatechange/downloads/Climate_Basics.pdf (accessed April 2012).

EPA (2012) *Climate Change: Basic Information, Video and Factsheets*, Environmental Protection Agency, http://www.epa.gov/climatechange/basicinfo.html (accessed April 2012).

Esty, D.C. and Winston, A.S. (2006) *Green to Gold: How Smart Companies Use Environmental Strategy to Innovate, Create Value, and Build Competitive Advantage*, Yale University Press, New Haven, CT.

Gore, A.L. (2006) *An Inconvenient Truth: The Planetary Emergency of Global Warming and What We Can Do about It*, Rodale Books, Emmaus, PA.

Lacy, P., Cooper, T., Hayward, R. *et al.* (2010) *A New Era of Sustainability: UN Global Compact – Accenture CEO Study 2010*, United Nations Global Compact, Chicago.

Lash, J. and Wellington, F. (2007) Competitive advantage on a warming planet. *Harvard Business Review*, **85**, 95–102.

Murugesan, S. (2007) Going green with IT: Your responsibility toward environmental sustainability. *Cutter Consortium Business – IT Strategies Executive Report*, **10** (8), 1–24.

Murugesan, S. (2008) Harnessing green IT: Principles and practices. *IEEE IT Professional*, **10** (1), 24–33.

Nordman, B. and Christensen, K. (2009) Greener PCs for the enterprise. *IT Professional*, **11** (4), 28–37.

OCED (2010) Greener and Smarter: ICTs, the Environment and Climate Change, OCED, September, http://www.oecd.org/dataoecd/27/12/45983022.pdf (accessed April 2012).

Pritchard, S. (2007) IT going green: Forces pulling in different directions. *Financial Times* (May 30).

Ruth, S. (2009) Green IT: More than a three percent solution. *IEEE Internet Computing*, **13** (4), 74–78.

Stern, N. (2007) Stern Review on the Economics of Climate Change, Cambridge University Press, www.hm-treasury.gov.uk/independent_reviews/stern_review_economics_climate_change/stern_review_report.cfm (accessed April 2012).

Wilbanks, L. (2008) Green: My favorite color. *IT Professional*, **10** (6), 64, 63.

Further Reading and Useful Web Sites

These additional resources will help you to explore green IT further and to keep abreast of on-going developments (all sites accessed April 2012).

Special Issues

- *IT Professional*, special issue on green IT, January–February 2011: http://www.computer.org/portal/web/csdl/abs/mags/it/2011/01/mit201101toc.htm. Download it for free from: http://bitly.com/HOu1bR.
- *IT Professional*, special issue on green computing, January–February 2008: http://www.computer.org/portal/web/csdl/abs/mags/it/2008/01/mit200801toc.htm.
- *SETLab Briefings*, special issue on green IT, 2011: http://www.infosys.com/infosys-labs/publications/setlabs-briefings/Pages/green-IT.aspx.
- Green High Performance Computing', *IEEE Computing in Science & Engineering*, no. 6, 2010: http://www.computer.org/portal/web/csdl/abs/mags/cs/2010/06/mcs201006toc.htm
- *Microsoft Architectural Journal*, special issue on green computing, no. 18, 2010: http://research.microsoft.com/pubs/78813/AJ18_EN.pdf.

Reports

- S. Murugesan, ed., 'Understanding and implementing green IT', Essential Set, IEEE CS Press, 2010: http://www.computer.org/portal/web/store?product_id=TS0000030&category_id=TechSets.
- Smart 2020: Enabling the low carbon economy in the information age,' Global eSustainability Institute, 2010: http://www.gesi.org/LinkClick.aspx?fileticket=tbp5WRTHUoY%3d&tabid=60.
- *Using ICT to Tackle Climate Change*, Global eSustainability Institute, 2010: http://www.gesi.org/LinkClick.aspx?fileticket=fzmFL3kXfOU%3d&tabid=60.
- Tom Worthington, *ICT Sustainability: Assessment and Strategies for a Low Carbon Future, 2011:* http://www.tomw.net.au/ict_sustainability/.
- Evaluating the Carbon-Reducing Impacts of ICT: An Assessment Methodology', Global eSustainability Institute, 2010: http://www.gesi.org/ReportsPublications/AssessmentMethodology/tabid/193/Default.aspx.

- Best Practices for the EU Code of Conduct on Data Centres', 2011: http://re.jrc.ec.europa.eu/energyefficiency/pdf/CoC/Best%20Practices%20v3.0.1.pdf.
- EU Code of Conduct for Data Centres, 2008: http://re.jrc.ec.europa.eu/energyefficiency/pdf/CoC%20data%20centres%20nov2008/CoC%20DC%20v%201.0%20FINAL.pdf.

Government Legislations

The Carbon Reduction Commitment (CRC) Scheme: http://www.decc.gov.uk/en/content/cms/emissions/crc_efficiency/crc_efficiency.aspx.

Web Sites

- Green Computing, IEEE Technical Committee on Scalable Computing (TCSC) – Technical Area of Green Computing: http://sites.google.com/site/greencomputingproject/ (requires log-in).
- Green Communications and Computing, Technical Subcommittee of IEEE Communications Society: http://sites.google.com/site/gcccomsoc/home.
- The Green Grid (www.thegreengrid.org) – industry-supported research and commentary site aimed at data centre activity with reports about design, energy measurement and so on.
- The Uptime Institute: http://uptimeinstitute.org/.
- Sustainable IT: http://weblog.infoworld.com/sustainableit.
- GreenBiz: www.greenbiz.com.

2

Green Devices and Hardware

Ashok Pon Kumar[1] and Sateesh S. Kannegala[2]
[1]*IBM Research India, Bangalore, India*
[2]*Hewlett-Packard Globalsoft Pvt Limited, Bangalore, India*

Key Points

- Introduces the concept of green devices and hardware.
- Sensitizes the reader to environmental issues arising from electronic devices.
- Describes the life cycle of electronic devices.
- Examines electronic devices' impact on the environment during each phase of their life cycle, and possible causes for this impact.
- Discusses a range of solutions to address this problem and highlights best practices in each life cycle phase.

2.1 Introduction

Electronic devices have become ubiquitous and are an intrinsic part of our lives. Whilst these devices provide the convenience of faster and better access to people, information and services, the downside is their negative impact on available resources and our environment. With the threat of global warming looming large, prudent use of these devices becomes urgent. Awareness of our usage patterns' impact and ways to minimize the impact comprises the first step towards a more sustainable practice.

The number of computers and other electronic devices in use has been increasing exponentially, and newer more powerful devices continue to replace older versions. This has led to a very short useful lifetime of devices, leaving behind a trail of obsolete devices.

During the early stages of the electronic revolution, also called the digital revolution, the manufacture, distribution, use and disposal of devices had only a small impact on our environment. For instance, power consumed by these devices during use was not a major constraint. Development efforts were focussed primarily on improving processing speed, increasing device density (number of transistors per integrated circuit) and

Harnessing Green IT: Principles and Practices, First Edition. Edited by San Murugesan and G.R. Gangadharan.

reducing the cost of production. Until recently, little attention was paid to minimizing or optimizing devices' power consumption. With the advent of battery-powered devices such as notebook computers and mobile phones, power consumption in these devices started to become an important consideration. However, environmental impact, especially in the disposal stage of the devices, was largely ignored.

It has become increasingly clear that there are opportunities for improving the energy use characteristics of devices we use every day. Most CPUs today provide options to optimize power consumption. Newer operating systems (e.g. Windows XP, Mac OS X 10.3 and Linux kernel 2.6 and later) that drive these devices are increasingly taking advantage of these options (as discussed in Chapter 3). These features coupled with users' behavioural changes can go a long way in optimizing devices' energy consumption.

The process of manufacturing the devices also has a significant environmental impact. It is important to examine manufacturing processes to ensure minimal negative impact.

Yet another dimension to the phenomenon of unprecedented growth in the number of devices is the accumulation of electronic waste (e-waste) as these devices become obsolete. Given that many devices, especially ones built during the early phase of the electronic revolution, contain toxic materials that are potentially harmful, disposing them safely poses a major problem. This makes it imperative to closely examine the materials used in manufacturing to ensure minimal impact on the environment even during the disposal stage. The problem of e-waste disposal is further aggravated by the proliferation of newer, better devices.

With these backdrop, we explore 'green IT' from different perspectives – that of the producer and the user. Following the green IT definition of Murugesan (2008), we use the term green devices and hardware to explore the aspects of 'greenness' in hardware. In this chapter, we explore the environmental impact of electronic devices, primarily hardware devices, at every stage of their life cycle. We examine the manufacturing process in an attempt to identify best practices. We also explore resource usage patterns in bringing products to market. Further, we look at usage patterns and the adoption of environmentally friendly practices, and make the reader sensitive to these issues.

2.2 Life Cycle of a Device or Hardware

A green device cannot be built by just having an additional step in the life cycle of the device. There needs to be a concerted effort at every stage of the device life cycle – from the moment the device is conceived, to its development, to the time when it is used and recycled or disposed (i.e. from cradle to grave). Each stage of the cycle has varying levels of impact on the environment. In this section, we will look into each stage that a computer device goes through and discuss green considerations for each stage. The typical life cycle of a device, shown in Figure 2.1, consists of five stages:

1. Design.
2. Manufacture and facilities.
3. Packaging and transportation.
4. Usage.
5. Reuse or disposal.

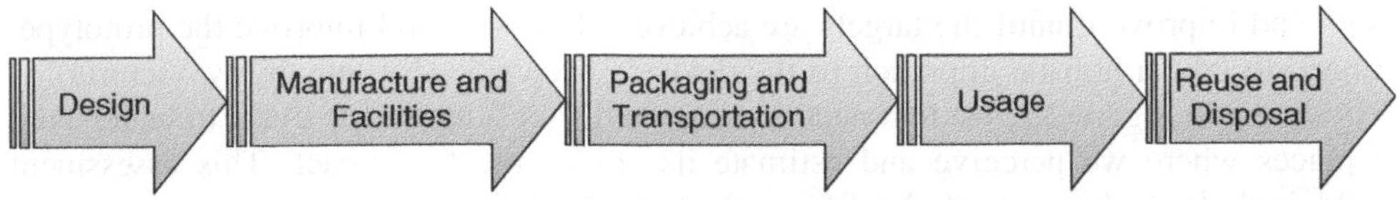

Figure 2.1 Life cycle of a device.

2.2.1 Design

In the design stage, the idea is conceptualized and the device is designed, prototyped and tested. Though this stage does not have direct impact on the environment, design stage decisions such as those regarding architecture, constituent components or materials and layout have a huge effect on the environmental impact of other stages. Hence, it is important to design devices so as to keep their environmental impact as low as possible during subsequent stages whilst meeting performance and other requirements. We will look at a possible process improvement that will help design a green device.

Figure 2.2 shows the typical steps in the design process. When a device gets into the design stage, the first step should be to set environment targets for it (Samsung, 2011). As indicated in Figure 2.2, setting environmental targets should be done in parallel to conceptualization. These targets can be derived from the device's environmental objectives, and also based on environmental impact assessment reports of similar devices that are in the market. These form a minimum set of targets that the device has to meet when released to the market. These targets should act as a benchmark and should help with decision making whilst designing the device.

As the device is being prototyped, one of the goals should be to meet all environment targets that have been set. To achieve this, we need to continuously assess the prototype's

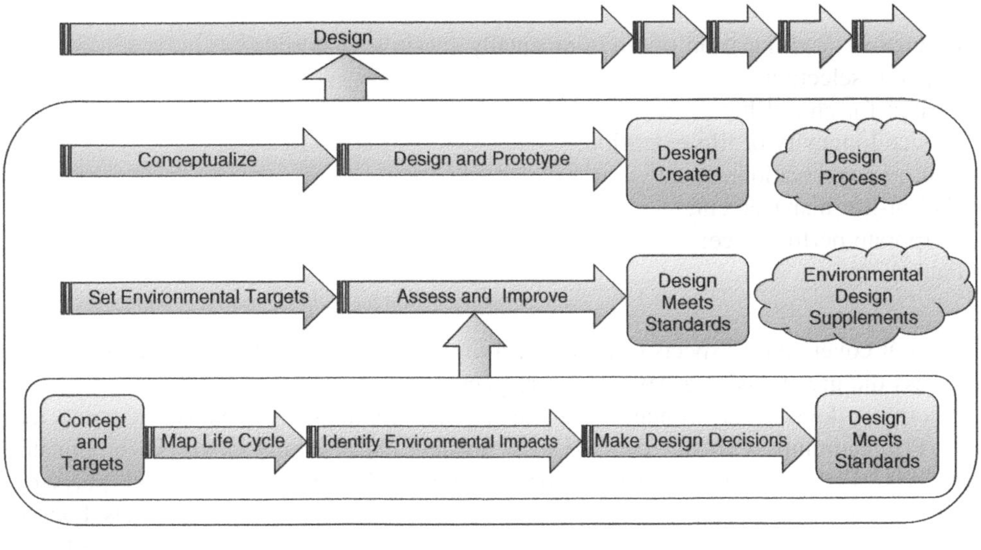

Figure 2.2 Typical steps in design of a device.

design and improve it until the targets are achieved. To assess and improve the prototype, we need to take a holistic approach to the device's life cycle (Sustainability Victoria).

As shown in Figure 2.2, we first need to map the device's entire life cycle to understand the places where we perceive and estimate its environmental impact. This assessment should include each stage of the life cycle from manufacturing and transportation to usage and disposal. Effort should be made to quantify the impact at every stage of the life cycle. This will help us identify main sources of environmental impact. Design alternatives to reduce the environmental impact need to be considered. Design changes have to be implemented and the prototype has to be assessed again for environmental impact. This process should go on until the device meets the environmental targets set for the device.

2.2.2 *Manufacturing*

The manufacturing process is one of the main sources of environmental impact in the life cycle of a device. Manufacturing processes are resource intensive and consume a lot of raw materials, water and energy; they create many different categories of waste, some which are toxic. For instance, according to a UN report, production of a desktop personal computer (PC) consumes 240 kg of fossil fuels, 22 kg of chemicals (which includes hazardous chemicals) and 1.5 tonnes of water (United Nations Environment Programme, 2004). It is very important to minimize the use of environmentally sensitive substances and reduce the amount of harmful waste.

The EPEAT (Electronic Product Environmental Assessment Tool, n.d.) ratings system serves as a good guideline for understanding how green a device is. EPEAT grades electronic devices and computer systems into three grades (bronze, silver and gold), helps customers identify how green a device is and helps them to make informed choices.

The rating system takes into account the following aspects:

- Reduction or elimination of environmentally sensitive materials;
- Material selection;
- Design for end of life;
- Device longevity or life extension;
- Energy conservation;
- End-of-life management;
- Corporate performance;
- Packaging.

Since it covers most aspects of a manufacturing process, EPEAT serves as a good way to assess the greenness of a device with respect to its manufacturing.

Electronic devices may contain hazardous and environmentally sensitive materials like lead (Pb), cadmium (Cd), mercury (Hg), hexavalent chromium ($Cr6+$), polybrominated biphenyls (PBBs), polybrominated diphenyl ethers (PBDEs), arsenic and polyvinyl chloride (PVC). It is important to reduce, if not eliminate, these materials both in the device and in its manufacturing process. The Restriction of Hazardous Substances (RoHS, n.d.) directive restricts the hazardous substances commonly used in electronics and electronic equipment.

Table 2.1 Summary of hazardous chemicals used in the manufacturing of electronic devices

Chemical	Used in	Effect on humans
Lead	Circuits, motherboards and glass monitors	Affects nervous system, hematopoietic system and kidneys
Cadmium	Low-temperature soldering, plating for corrosion protection, colorants in plastics and contact buttons in relays	Affects the liver and kidneys
Mercury	Monitors and batteries	Affects immune system, alters genetic and enzyme systems and damages the nervous system
Polybrominated diphenyl ethers (PBDEs) and polybrominated biphenyls (PBBs)	Flame retardants	Extremely toxic
Arsenic	Manufacture of semiconductors	Affects cellular longevity
Polyvinyl chloride	Manufacture of computer parts	Carcinogen and also has effect on the human reproductive system

Table 2.1 presents a brief summary of the hazardous chemicals used in manufacturing various electronic devices and their effects on humans. The impact of some of those key materials is as follows:

- **Lead** is generally used in printed circuit boards and in glass monitors. The pathological effects of lead are most prominent in the nervous system, hematopoietic system and kidneys. Excessive exposure to lead (Pb) results in clinical toxicity. There has been extensive research to find a replacement for lead (Norwegian University of Science and Technology, 2010). There are also on-going efforts to recover lead from the e-waste (Duffy, 2008).
- **Cadmium** is generally used in low-temperature soldering, plating for corrosion protection, colorants in plastics and contact buttons in relays (Penica and Hilty, 2004). Cadmium when ingested affects the liver and kidneys. Research is on-going to produce alternatives for its various uses.
- **Mercury** is mainly used in monitors and batteries. Mercury is a well-known pollutant (US Geological Survey, 2000), and it affects the immune system, alters genetic and enzyme systems and damages the nervous system. New light-emitting diode (LED) backlit technologies have been developed which make monitors mercury free. Mercury use in batteries has also been reduced considerably over the past few years.
- **PBDEs and PBBs** are used as flame retardants (Wisconsin Department of Natural Resources, 2011). These materials are ubiquitous environmental pollutants; they are

extremely toxic and are banned in many countries. Efforts are on-going to remove these materials from the manufacture of computers.

- **Arsenic** is used in glasses and in manufacturing semiconductors. Arsenic interferes with cellular longevity by allosteric inhibition of an essential metabolic enzyme. Many arsenic prevention and recovery methodologies have been devised, and these need to be actively deployed to reduce arsenic usage in the manufacturing process.
- **PVC** is one of the most commonly used plastics worldwide. It has been used extensively in the manufacture of computer parts. Vinyl chloride, one of the main ingredients of PVC, is a carcinogen and also affects the human reproductive system (US Environmental Protection Agency (EPA), 2011). Of late, many companies have eliminated the use of PVC in their devices.

The EPA Web site gives further information on these and other toxic materials and how each of these chemicals affects the environment.

It is important that electronic device manufacturers avoid using these chemicals in their devices and use environmentally friendly alternatives. Further, their facilities' carbon footprint can be reduced by employing energy conservation techniques and by using energy from renewable sources. Energy conservation techniques like sensors for switching off lights automatically, and shutting down servers during weekends (where possible), not only help reduce the carbon footprint but also result in lower energy bills. In addition, environmentally sensitive materials like chlorofluorocarbons (CFCs) should be avoided in air conditioning and cooling facilities. Such measures also help companies in projecting a good public image.

2.2.3 Packaging and Transportation

Packaging and transportation also contribute to the carbon footprint in a device's life cycle. The two main contributors in this segment are the materials used for packaging and the carbon footprint of the vehicles used in transportation.

Since the materials used in packaging a device have an effect on the device's carbon footprint, the amount of material used for packaging needs to be kept at a minimum. The packaging should be done in such a way that it minimizes the amount of material used whilst ensuring the integrity and security of the device.

The size of the device has an effect on the amount of packaging required, so even during the design stage, effort must be made to make the device as compact as possible. Eco-friendly materials like recycled paper, potato starch and recycled board can be used as packaging materials, and soy ink can be used for printing. The following are general recommendations for designing suitable packaging (US Environmental Protection Agency, 2011):

1. Packaging materials should be recyclable.
2. The amount of packaging materials should be kept at a minimum.
3. Various materials used in packaging should be easily separable to ease the recycling process.
4. Adhesive use should be reduced by using folds and tabs instead.

5. All the additives, coatings and inks that get added to the package should be eco-friendly.
6. Printed documentation can be avoided wherever possible. Instead, documentation could be provided through the device's Web page.

In addition, freight transportation leads to a lot of carbon emission. Along with making the transport system efficient, the design of the device should facilitate smarter transportation. For example, the smaller the device, the more of them can be transported in a given space, thus reducing the number of vehicles required to transport them from manufacturing facilities to distribution centres.

2.2.4 *Use*

Quite a significant amount of energy is consumed by devices when they are being used (powered). This increases a device's carbon footprint, thus resulting in a profound impact on the environment. The Energy Star rating system helps customers chose the most energy-efficient devices and, thereby, reduce their energy consumption and cost.

Often people tend to apply a usage pattern without being aware of a device's characteristic. For example, the commonly held belief that, to ensure longer life of a battery, the battery needs to be drained completely before recharging is not necessarily true for all battery types. In case of lithium-ion batteries, commonly known as Li-ion batteries, the maximum number of charge cycles decreases with increase in depth of discharge (Buchmann, 2011). Since the best usage patterns are tightly tied with a device's characteristics, it is important that manufacturers provide guidelines on its best usage practices from environmental and energy perspectives.

Devices like 'Kill a Watt' (P3 International, 2011) help measure the amount of energy consumed by a device over time. When 'Kill a Watt' is plugged between the device and the power socket, it measures the amount of energy that the device consumes. This can be used to measure the amount of energy consumed over time and with different configurations of the device, and thus helps one find an optimum configuration that consumes the least energy. It also helps one figure out whether older devices are still energy efficient.

The amount of energy consumed by different kinds of electronic devices varies widely, and ways to reduce their energy use vary widely too, hence we will look into different device categories separately, and look at ways to reduce energy usage in notebook computers, desktop computers, servers, mobile devices and other special devices.

2.2.4.1 Notebook Computers

Though notebook computers are designed to be energy economical compared to desktops, the energy consumption of a laptop depends on the usage pattern. To reduce energy consumption, it is necessary to have a usage pattern that results in optimal energy consumption. Let's examine the power consumption of a laptop's different components and discuss how each component's power consumption could be reduced or optimized.

Notebook computers are generally powered by a rechargeable battery, which when in good condition powers the device for about 3–5 hours. The battery is recharged with the help of a charger, which can charge the battery irrespective of whether the device is running or is in a powered-down state. The lifetime of a battery is generally short: They last for only about 300–600 charge cycles. This results in the need to replace the battery a few times during the life of a laptop, thereby contributing to e-waste. A few companies are also coming out with notebook computers which run on solar power.

Notebook computers are also characterized by their liquid crystal display (LCD) or LED monitors, which are integrated into the device. The monitors and CPU consume the largest share of power that is utilized by the laptop (Mahesri and Vardhan, 2005; Roberson *et al.*, 2012). The larger the monitors, the greater the laptop's power consumption (Albert, 2009); and the more intensive the operations performed by the processor, the higher its power consumption.

Energy can be conserved in a laptop in several ways. According to various studies, quite a lot of the energy wasted in a laptop happens when the laptop is being charged (Snyder, 2009). The chargers convert the AC to DC and steps down the voltage. This happens as long as the charger is connected to the power socket, irrespective of whether the laptop is connected to the charger or not, thus resulting in wasted energy. Hence it is important to switch off the power supply and unplug the charger from the power socket when it is not in use. This will reduce power wastage. Of late there have also been green chargers (such as the iGo Green Charger) available which can detect whether a charger is connected to a notebook computer or any other device, and reduce the power consumption when a charger is not connected to a device.

Monitors consume about 20–30% (Mahesri and Vardhan, 2005) of the total energy used by a laptop; hence it is important to reduce their power consumption. Strategies that help in reducing their power consumption include the following:

1. Reduce the brightness of the monitor to an appropriate level. A brighter screen consumes more energy.
2. When some background task is running on the computer and there is no need to use the monitor during this time, switch off the monitor instead of using screen savers as screen savers also consume some energy.
3. Most computer operating systems provide power-saving profiles which, when enabled, reduce the amount of energy consumed by the computer. For example, when the laptop is starting up or shutting down, these applications reduce screen brightness to a minimum.

Laptop processors also consume a lot of power particularly when carrying out computationally intensive tasks such as encryption, analytics, computer games and image and video processing. Many aspects of applications that run on a system impact power consumption. The following guidelines will help in optimizing energy consumption:

1. The background processes and other applications which are not being used are kept running to keep the processor active, thus resulting in energy wastage. So when an application is not in use, close the application and also stop the background processes that are not being used.
2. Multitasking is a trade-off between CPU time spent executing tasks and inefficiencies brought in by context switching. When a task starts running slower than it would normally run, one of the likely causes is due to inefficiencies due to context switching. It is advisable to reduce the number of tasks when such slowing down is noticed.

3. The more processes that are set to start at start-up, the longer amount of time the laptop needs to boot up, thus resulting in more unproductive time for the processor and the monitor. So keep the number of processes at start-up to a minimum. The required applications can be started when needed.
4. When playing games or other multimedia applications, the greater the level of detail, the greater the processing power consumed. So it is better to keep the level of detail to the required level; most games support this feature.

The higher the speed at which a processor runs, the more energy is consumed, so advanced users could run the processor at a lower frequency (i.e. 'under-clocking' it) to save power. This can be done by going to the basic input–output system (BIOS) of the laptop and setting the appropriate processor speed. In most computers going to the BIOS is easy, though it depends on the computer configuration. In contrast, if a computer is perceived to be slow and you are contemplating replacing the processor, a better option would be to try over-clocking the processor to see whether the increased speed meets the need. Over-clocking a processor can harm the computer, so practice caution and have a computer expert do it. In addition multicore processors consume relatively less energy for the same amount of processing done by multiple single-core processors. This is primarily because of the decreased power required to drive signals external to the chip.

The other major component of the laptop that consumes a lot of power is the hard disk. Since hard disks are physical devices, they consume relatively more energy than many other components. Hence it is important to keep hard disk access to a minimum and use it only when necessary. The spinning of the hard disk is one of the important parts that results in higher energy usage. Lessening the spin of the hard disk results in lower energy consumption. The spin of the disk is greater when the files are fragmented and scattered all over the hard disk. Defragmenting the hard disk reduces the spin of the hard disk and will result in less energy usage. Solid-state drives (SSDs) are known to consume less energy than comparable hard disk drives (HDDs). In addition, many power-saving options are available on computers that switch off the hard disk when it is not in use. For detailed coverage of energy-efficient, environmentally friendly computer storage, refer to Chapter 6.

Peripheral devices connected to a computer also consume energy, even though they might not be in active use. For example, devices connected to USB ports in a computer draw power even when the device is not in use. So when these external devices are not in use, it is better to unplug them.

Most notebook computers can operate in at least two idle power modes – standby and hibernate. These modes help keep the laptop's energy consumption to a minimum whilst still retaining the state of the computer. In standby mode, the laptop's internal devices and optical drives are powered off, but the power is still maintained to the RAM, where the state of the device is preserved to facilitate instant resumption. Though this state requires considerably less power compared to when the computer is running, it still requires some power, which needs to be supplied by the battery or an external power source, or else the system will shut down immediately, thus losing the state. Retaining the state is very helpful when we are away from the computer for a short period of time.

The hibernate mode makes the laptop completely shut down whilst still retaining the powered-on state, thus reducing the start-up time. When a laptop goes to hibernate mode, the current state of the machine is stored in the hard disk, and all the devices including the RAM are powered off. When the computer is resumed from this state, the state information from the hard disk is reloaded into RAM. It takes more time to resume from hibernate mode than from standby mode, but it is more energy efficient. This mode can be used when the state of the computer needs to be retained for a longer period of time.

Most laptops today are provided with power management features and software. Power management software can help in regulating the use of the battery and electric power. It monitors the load on the hard disk, the activities on the laptop and the ambient brightness, and changes various computer settings to make optimal use of power. This software also allows users to set timings when the computers can automatically go to standby or hibernate mode. For example, notebook computers can be set to go to standby mode after 20 minutes of inactivity or when the laptop lid is closed. This helps in automatically managing the power consumption of the laptops.

2.2.4.2 Desktop Computer

Desktops are personal computers that are meant for use from a single location and are not portable. Though these devices are being replaced by laptops, there are certain applications where these devices are still used, such as intensive processing applications (but not in a scale where servers are required) like image processing.

The architecture and physical configuration of desktops support upgrading and replacing individual defective subunits and parts. Since desktops are quite rapidly being discarded in favour of laptops, the biggest problem facing the industry is disposing of or recycling these devices. In addition, quite a few desktop users are home users who are not fully aware of disposal mechanisms unlike the enterprises that are obliged to safely dispose of their assets.

A typical desktop uses about 115 W of power. By US rates if a 115 W desktop is used continuously for one full year, it costs about US$100 (8760 hours/year × 115 W × US$0.10/kW h). Cathode ray tube (CRT) monitors were the primary output device used in desktop PCs until a few years ago. CRT monitors consume a lot of energy and are inefficient. A typical 17" CRT monitor consumes about 80 W compared to 28 W consumed by a 19" LCD (Display Link, 2008). It also contains a lot of environmentally sensitive materials. LCD and LED monitors are energy efficient (Roberson *et al.*, 2012) and small in size. The power management systems and techniques for monitors that were described in Section 2.2.4.1 on laptops also apply to desktops. The processors used in desktops consume a lot more power than their laptop counterparts. The processor and hard disk power optimization techniques that were used in laptops also apply here.

One of the areas where a desktop varies from laptops is in its mode of usage. Desktops are powered from external power, so, in many cases, they are kept always on so that they can be remotely accessed from a laptop or some other desktop. In most cases desktops are left on 24/7 even during holidays. Hence most of the time desktops remain idle and waste a lot of energy. To avoid having desktops switched on all the time, remote wake-up methodologies have been devised. In the 1990s, Advanced Micro Devices (AMD) and several other companies came together to develop the magic packet technology to accomplish this. It is commonly referred to as Wake On LAN (WOL). This relies on a special kind of packet called the magic packet to wake up the computer. When the computer is in sleep state, the Ethernet Network Interface Controller (NIC) is left powered on. This network interface controller can detect the magic packet and trigger an interrupt which wakes up the desktop. Using this technology, desktops can be awakened at any time from remote locations, thus removing the need to have the desktops switched on all the time.

In enterprises, where there are many desktops in use, it is important to globally monitor the usage of all desktops to get a holistic picture on their usage efficiency. Tools like Night Watchman (www.1e.com), The Energy Detective (TED) (www.theenergydetective.com), eMonitor (www.powerhousedynamics.com) and Conserve Insight (http://www.belkin.com/conserve/insight/) help managers in assessing the power usage trends of many of their desktops over time by monitoring these trends and presenting the data in the form of a dashboard. The dashboard helps managers understand the desktops' power usage patterns and set power conservation targets, which will make the company greener. Several online energy calculators are available (e.g. 1e, n.d.), which help in calculating the amount of energy that can be saved.

In addition to monitoring tools, enterprises also need management tools which allow remote control of desktops. Though most operating systems have group policies which allow certain configurations to be enforced on desktops, they are not as effective as management tools which allow granular control over the desktops. Tools like Night Watchman help enterprises have more control over the desktops. These tools allow enterprises to securely, remotely and centrally power down desktops. They also allow enterprises to apply power schemes at different times in multiple locations, globally from a single console, maximizing power savings without impacting users. Though there might be resistance from employees to the implementation of such systems, it is important to make employees understand the benefits and advantages of the system and then implement solutions.

2.2.4.3 Servers

Servers are computers designed to serve the needs of other computers. In general, server computers run one or more services that will be used by other computers in the network. They have powerful CPUs and a large amount of memory (RAM). They are generally placed in racks. Examples of servers are mail servers, database servers, file servers and others. They are on most of the time, and in most cases to provide increased reliability redundant servers are used. These servers are generally placed in data centres. Even though the growth of energy usage of data centres was less than predicted (Koomey, 2011), it still accounts for between 1.1% and 1.5% of total electricity use.

Servers in general generate a large amount of heat due to their large power consumption, and hence they require better cooling mechanisms. The energy efficiency aspects of servers are discussed in detail in Chapter 5.

2.2.4.4 Mobile Devices

Mobile devices comprise mobile phones, personal digital assistants (PDAs) and other smart devices that people carry around. These devices are small in size and are powered by a small rechargeable battery. These devices are produced in large numbers and are designed for operation with low power consumption. These are used by people all over the world from both developed countries and developing countries. The International Telecommunication Union (ITU) estimates that by October 2010, over 5 billion mobile phones were in use (International Telecommunication Union, 2010).

Mobile devices use external chargers for their batteries. The power efficiency of these chargers is low, and most people keep the charger powered even whilst mobile devices are disconnected after being charged. Chargers consume power even whilst not changing a battery and hence waste power. So, chargers should be switched off or unplugged when they are not charging, or disconnected from mobile devices. Awareness needs to be created among users to switch off chargers when they are not needed.

2.2.4.5 Specialized Devices

Specialized devices are designed for a specific purpose, such as set-top boxes, play stations and medical equipment like X-ray machines and computerized tomography (CT) scanners. Since these devices are designed to accomplish a specific purpose, the designer can optimize the device for the particular use and for low power consumption.

Devices like set-top boxes and play stations consume power even when they are not in use (idle), and idle power could be as much as about two-thirds of the power the device consumes when it is used. For such devices, it is important to switch off the devices so that they do not consume (waste) power when not in use. Play stations in general have powerful graphics processors which consume a lot of power. It is a common practice among users of play stations to leave them in pause mode for long periods of time, which results in power wastage. It is important to create awareness among users of special devices to switch them off when they are not in use.

2.3 Reuse, Recycle and Dispose

Mobile phones and computers, as well as some other electronic gadgets, become obsolete quickly, typically about every two years, due to continued advancements in technology and the introduction of new gadgets with enhanced features. This leads to an accumulation of much e-waste. Most of these devices end up in landfills or get exported to developing countries for recycling. In many developing countries, however, due to lack of sufficient knowledge about the toxicity of the chemicals involved and lack of regulations enforcement relating to e-waste recycling, unhealthy recycle methodologies are used, leading to health hazards and pollution.

One way to reduce waste is to increase the lifespan of the devices. Increasing the lifespan of devices saves life cycle energy[1] and resources and reduces the amount of hazardous materials ending up in landfills. Reusing an old computer is a great way to increase its lifespan. Reusing a computer is environmentally friendlier than recycling. It has been shown that reusing a computer is 20 times more effective at saving life cycle energy than recycling (Computer Aid International, 2010). As there is a lot of environmental cost involved in a device's production, it becomes important to use a computer to its fullest life before discarding it.

[1] Life cycle energy is a term used to refer to all energy inputs to a product, not only direct energy inputs during its manufacture, but also all energy inputs needed to produce components, materials and services needed for the manufacturing process.

Once we have decided to replace a device, the first option to consider is to send the computer for reuse to some other place like an educational institution. Both the EPA in the United States and WEEE in the European Union provide guidelines on enabling computer reuse. Before sending the device for reuse, adhere to the following guidelines (U.S. Environmental Protection Agency, 2011):

1. Make sure that the receiving organization does need the device being sent and can reuse it. A better alternative would be to send the device to a local refurbisher who will make sure the device is in a working state and can send it to an appropriate organization that is in need of it.
2. Copy the information that has been stored in the device to a backup device or another device.
3. Wipe off personal or sensitive information in the device using tools specific for this purpose like Symantec's WipeInfo.

Another way to increase the lifespan of a device is by enabling easy upgrade of its various parts. This will encourage people and organizations to use their device longer by upgrading certain parts of their device that have become obsolete. Some design considerations that enable the easy upgrade of a computer are as follows:

1. The device should be modular.
2. Each part of the device should be easy to replace.
3. The device should be easy to disassemble and reassemble. Techniques like screw-less casing make it easy.

Wherever reuse is not a viable option, the next best option is to recycle. In the process of recycling, most of the original device's materials are reused as raw materials for a new device, thus resulting in less waste. To enable recycling, it is important to collect back the old devices from customers. Many manufacturers have their own recycling programs. Take-back, mail-in and trade-in programs are some of the popular programs that encourage customers to return devices to the manufacturers. In addition, companies also support local organizations to collect the devices. In order to increase awareness, collection events and local recycling events are conducted. These programs help individual users easily recycle their computers. In 2009, the United States generated 3.19 million tons of e-waste. Of this amount, according to the EPA (2011), only 600 000 tons or 17.7% was recycled. The rest was trashed – in landfills or incinerators.

An electronic device consists of various materials which take quite a lot of energy to extract from ores. During recycling these materials can be recovered and some of the recovered materials can be used in making new devices, thus reducing the amount of environmental emissions compared to making these devices from virgin materials. Materials like gold, silver, copper and plastic can be recovered and reused. Some companies use a measurement called recycling rate, which is the weight of the materials the company recycles each year as compared to the total weight of the devices the company sold a few years earlier.

As discussed in this chapter, one of the problems regarding recycling of e-waste is the export of e-waste to developing countries for recycling. Developed countries export their e-waste to developing countries since the cost of recycling is cheaper there. For example, recycling a computer in the United States costs about US$20.00, whereas recycling a computer in developing countries like India or China costs only about US$2.00. But e-waste is not properly recycled in developing countries. In many cases, the labourers involved in recycling simply burn off the e-waste, follow crude unhealthy practices to remove components and metals from e-waste or dump the waste into rivers, resulting in huge environmental impact. They are unaware of the environmental and health hazards posed by the chemicals and poisonous gases released in the crude recycling process they follow. They are not required to wear protective clothing, and thus face severe health problems. Efforts have been made by organizations such as Greenpeace to regulate the export of e-waste to developing countries and to adopt healthy e-waste recycling processes.

Whereas refurbishing and recycling are effective techniques for the end-of-life management of electronic devices, often they are not practical. The only option left at this stage would be disposal. There are a few known techniques of waste disposal that are commonly used in e-waste disposal as well. These are incineration, chemical decomposition and landfill. There is no single silver bullet that works in all cases for all materials or all kinds of e-waste. Incineration may result in the release of toxic gases and can pose a hazard. On the positive side, the heat generated may be used in generating electricity. Due to the nonbiodegradability of materials used in electronic devices, landfill may not be a viable option either. Chemical decomposition may be an option in some cases and will have to be executed in a managed manner. In short, safe disposal is a major problem and the solution depends on the specific material used in manufacturing the device.

2.4 Conclusions

The last couple of decades have seen an explosion in the use of electronic devices. We now face the problem of e-waste emerging as a significant challenge. This, coupled with increasing concerns on global warming, has made the need to manage and contain the environmental problems caused by electronic devices and IT significant and very urgent.

In this chapter, we explored 'green' aspects of electronic devices and computers. We examined the environmental problems created by electronic devices and hardware and explored how the industry is addressing these issues. We outlined best 'green' practices from the perspective of manufacturers, and discussed practical green measures that users should adopt. We also outlined the importance of designing a device with environmental considerations in mind so that the entire life cycle of the device could be better managed. We highlighted some of the major problems we encounter in recycling e-waste.

Many governments and other agencies have realized that the cost of inaction is enormous and the consequences of inaction – that is, the resulting environmental damage – may be irreversible. This has led governments, the United Nations and other agencies to come up with guidelines and regulations to address the environmental impacts of electronic devices throughout their life cycle – from design and manufacturing to their use and disposal followed by recycling.

Review Questions

1. Briefly outline different stages in the life cycle of an electronic device. Order these stages in decreasing order based on their environmental impact from your perspective, and give your rationale.
2. How would you design the manufacturing process of a product (say, a mobile phone) while also considering its environmental impact during manufacturing?
3. What environmentally sensitive materials are typically used in the manufacturing of a product (e.g. a notebook computer or a smart mobile phone), and what are their impacts? Suggest safer alternatives for each of those materials.
4. What are the tools that can be used to monitor and manage the power consumption, or usage patterns, of an organization's computers? Briefly describe the features of three of those tools, and compare them.
5. What are the various e-waste disposal techniques, and which is the most effective among them and why?

Discussion Questions

1. Discuss the various chemicals used in manufacturing a typical electronic device, identify the safest disposal mechanism for each of the chemicals and discuss the economics of your proposal. What would be an optimal solution for this problem?
2. Discuss, with supporting analysis, the problems and impact of accumulating e-waste and what measures you would recommend to effectively address this issue. Include an analysis of impact on human health (of current and future generations), the cost of disposal and the benefits of planned disposal.
3. Identify an electronic device that you use most, and outline the application for which you use the device and your usage pattern. Discuss the measures you would take to minimize its energy consumption. Where applicable, identify the configuration and features that you would enable to minimize the device's energy consumption, meeting your application requirements.

References

1e (n.d.) Energy Campaign Calculator, http://www.1e.com/energycampaign/calculation.aspx (accessed April 2012).

Albert, M. (2009) Power Consumption: 30 LCDs Tested, March 19, http://www.pcgameshardware.com and http://www.pcgameshardware.com/aid,679385/Power-consumption-30-LCDs-tested/Reviews/ (both accessed April 2012).

Buchmann, I. (2011) How to Prolong Lithium-Based Batteries, http://batteryuniversity.com and http://batteryuniversity.com/learn/article/how_to_prolong_lithium_based_batteries (both accessed April 2012).

Computer Aid International (2010) ICT and the Environment, August, http://www.computeraid.org/uploads/ICTs-and-the-Environment – Special-Report-1 – Reuse-(Aug10).pdf (accessed April 2012).

Display Link (2008) Multiple Monitor Energy Use, http://www.displaylink.com and http://www.displaylink.com/pdf/dl_wp_energy_use.pdf (both accessed April 2012).

Duffy, J. (2008) Researchers Getting the Lead Out of Electronics, Network World (November 18), http://www.networkworld.com/news/2008/111808-researchers-electronics.html (accessed April 2012).

Electronic Product Environmental Assessment Tool (n.d.) http://www.epeat.net (accessed April 2012).

Energy Star (n.d.) http://www.energystar.gov (accessed April 2012).

International Telecommunication Union (2010) Key Global Telecom Indicators for the World Telecommunication Service Sector, October, http://www.itu.int; http://www.itu.int/ITU-D/ict/statistics/at_glance/KeyTelecom.html (accessed April 2012).

Koomey, J.G. (2011) *Growth in Data Center Electricity Use 2005 to 2010*, Analytics Press, Burlingame, CA.

Mahesri, A. and Vardhan, V. (2005) Power consumption breakdown on a modern laptop. *Power-Aware Computer Systems*, **10** (1), 165–180.

Murugesan, S. (2008) Harnessing green IT: Principles and practices. *IT Professional Technology Solutions for the Enterprise*, **347**, 24–33.

Norwegian University of Science and Technology (2010) An alchemist's dream: Lead-free electronics. ScienceDaily (July 10), http://www.sciencedaily.com/releases/2010/06/100610095047.htm (accessed April 2012).

P3 International (2011) Kill a Watt, http://www.p3international.com/products/special/P4400/P4400-CE.html (accessed April 2012).

Penica, J.R. and Hilty, R.D. (2004) Chromate and Cadmium: Use and Alternatives. Texas Electronics, http://www.te.com/customersupport/rohssupportcenter/pdf/tyco_hex_chrome_and_cad_overview.pdf (accessed April 2012).

Restriction of Hazardous Substances (RoHS) (n.d.) http://www.rohs.gov.uk (accessed April 2012).

Roberson, J.A., Homan, G.K., Mahajan, A., *et al.* (2002) Energy Use and Power Levels in New Monitors and Personal Computer. Lawrence Berkeley Lab, http://enduse.lbl.gov/Info/Pubs.html (accessed April 2012).

Samsung (2011) Eco Design, http://www.samsung.com/us/aboutsamsung/sustainability/environment/eco_products/eco_design.html (accessed April 2012).

Snyder, G.F. (2009) Power Supply/Charger Energy Waste Explained, April 21 2009, http://www.gordostuff.com and http://www.gordostuff.com/2009/04/power-supplycharger-energy-waste.html (both accessed April 2012).

Sustainability Victoria (n.d.) Design for Environment, Resource Smart, http://www.resourcesmart.vic.gov.au/documents/DfE_brochure.pdf (accessed April 2012).

United Nations Environment Programme (2004) United Nations Environment Programme: The Environment in the News, March 9, http://www.unep.org; http://www.unep.org/cpi/briefs/Brief09March04.doc (accessed April 2012).

US Environmental Protection Agency (2011) EPA: US Environmental Protection Agency, http://www.epa.gov (accessed April 2012).

US Geological Survey (2000) Mercury in the Environment, October, http://www.usgs.gov and http://www.usgs.gov/themes/factsheet/146-00/ (both accessed April 2012).

Wisconsin Department of Natural Resources (2011) PBDE/PBB (Brominated Flame Retardants), June 6, http://dnr.wi.gov/environmentprotect/pbt/chemicals/pbde.htm (accessed April 2012).

3

Green Software

Bob Steigerwald and Abhishek Agrawal
Software & Services Group, Intel Corporation, Folsom, CA, USA

Key Points

- Describes software methodologies, designs and software development tools that help to improve the energy efficiency of application software.
- Discusses methods to reduce energy consumption during software development.
- Recommends a set of tools for evaluating and measuring the energy consumption of software.

3.1 Introduction

A green IT infrastructure is incomplete without green software. Software plays an important role in overall platform energy efficiency. Whilst platform hardware designers work diligently to reduce components' power consumption, a single ill-behaving or power-unfriendly software component on the system can thwart all of the power management benefits built into the hardware. This chapter describes the characteristics of green software and the software design considerations and methodologies to improve software energy efficiency.

A computing 'platform' is a combination of hardware, software and other technologies that allow software to run. The techniques we describe in this chapter apply to all types of platforms including embedded platforms, smartphones, tablets, netbooks, notebooks, desktops, data centre servers and supercomputers. Every one of these devices runs software, and every one of them requires energy to do it. Most agree that a platform's energy efficiency is extremely important. Nowadays less than a full day's use of one's smartphone is intolerable to most. Notebook computer manufacturers are still striving for the elusive all-day PC, though some of the thin and light models are getting close. A big concern for data centres is the cost of electricity to run the servers and air-conditioning

Harnessing Green IT: Principles and Practices, First Edition. Edited by San Murugesan and G.R. Gangadharan.

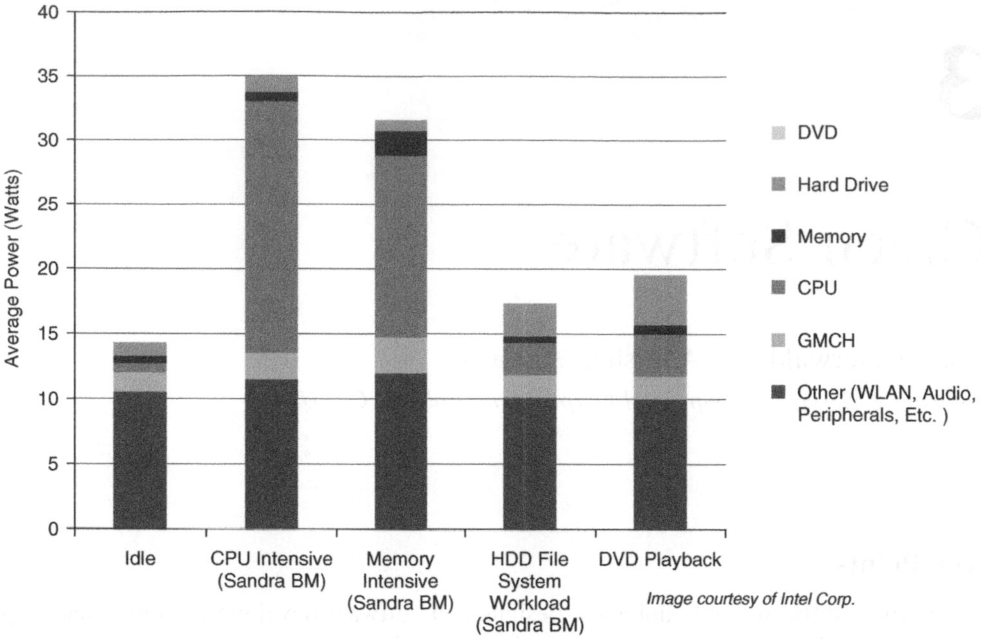

Figure 3.1 Breakdown of power usage on a notebook PC.

units to keep the room and servers cool. To make progress in improving energy efficiency, it is important to understand how energy is consumed. Figure 3.1 shows a typical power breakdown for a notebook PC during various operating conditions (provided by Si Software's Sandra benchmark suite). There are many components to target for improvement, and we believe that a focus on software will lead to significant impact.

3.1.1 Processor Power States

For software developers, the component of primary interest is the central processing unit (CPU). CPUs have defined energy states as well. It makes sense that if the CPU is not actively processing information or performing computations, it should be consuming minimal energy. The CPU has what are called C-states and P-states (Intel, 2011). *C-states* are core power states that define the degree to which the processor is 'sleeping'. In state C0, the processor is active and executing instructions. Whilst in C0, the processor can operate at various frequency levels, designated as *P-states* (performance states).

3.1.1.1 C-States

In the C0 state the CPU is active – it is busy carrying out some task, and it is performing that task at a frequency (P-state) that is appropriate. Between periods of activity the CPU can take the opportunity to rest or 'sleep'. In fact, C-states are often referred to as sleep states. Intel processors support several levels of core and package (resources shared by all the cores) C-states that provide a flexible selection between power consumption and responsiveness. With each successively deeper sleep state, some new part of the CPU is turned off and more energy is saved. Deeper sleep leads to greater energy savings. Even if the sleep period is only 100 μs, a considerable amount of energy can be saved over time.

3.1.1.2 P-States

P-states define the frequency at which the processor is running. Different processor brands showcase their P-states as features, such as SpeedStep in Intel processors, PowerNow! or Cool'n'Quiet in Advanced Micro Devices (AMD) processors and PowerSaver in VIA processors. Typical P-states are as follows:

- P0; maximum power and frequency.
- P1; less than P0; voltage or frequency scaled down.
- Pn; lowest rated voltage and/or frequency.

P-states were developed to save energy overall and deliver the performance you need when you need it. We can see how P-states save energy by studying the following equation:

$$P = CV^2f$$

This means that the power (P) required to run a CPU is the product of the capacitance (C), the frequency (f) and the voltage V. Assuming constant capacitance and voltage, reducing the frequency leads to a corresponding reduction in power. In practice, P-states are realized by adjustments to both voltage and frequency. In general, we consider a lower P-state to be a lower frequency state. An end user can actually control (to a moderate extent) the P-state of the processor by setting the platform power policy.

3.2 Energy-Saving Software Techniques

Many might wonder why a software developer needs to know about the component energy efficiency and states of the CPU. Whilst most of the energy-saving features in the platform are transparent to the software developer and applications have very little direct control, the behaviour of the software has significant influence on whether the energy-saving features built into the platform are effective. Well-behaved software allows the energy-saving features to work. Poorly behaved software inhibits the energy-saving features and leads to lower battery life and higher energy costs. Consider, for example, DVD playback applications; some are more energy efficient than others. A number of techniques are available to the developer to implement a more energy-efficient player. For instance, you could implement a read-ahead buffering methodology and allow the optical drive to take breaks rather than continuously spinning the disk. The application could be developed to use a hardware accelerator for video decode instead of using the CPU. That also saves energy. A third mechanism might be to use an alternate audio decoder when the system is running on battery power, one that may sacrifice a small bit of quality for longer battery life. Software developers have choices and design decisions to make that can influence the energy efficiency of applications.

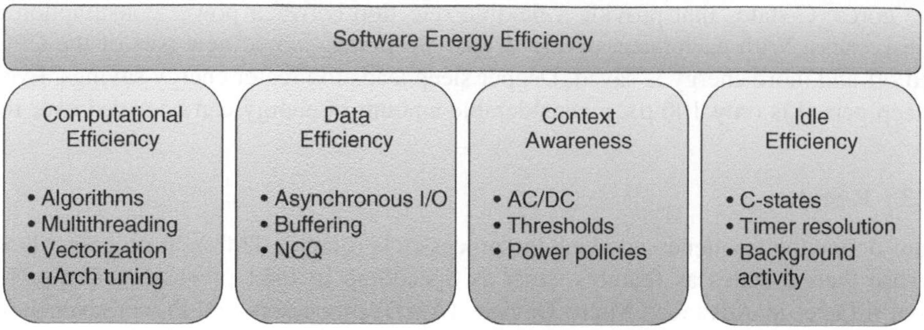

Figure 3.2 Software energy efficiency techniques.

Before examining software energy-saving techniques, it is important to understand the distinction between *active* and *idle* software. Active software is software that is fulfilling its intended purpose such as by computing a spreadsheet, playing music or a movie, uploading photos to a Web site or browsing the Internet. In all of these cases, there is a *workload* that the CPU or graphics processing unit (GPU) is busy working on. Idle software is software that is essentially running but waiting for an event to make it active. Examples of idle software are a browser that is started but has not been pointed to a Web site, an open word processor programme in the background or whose window is minimized, or an instant messaging programme that is running but not sending or receiving a message. The DVD playback scenario provides a good example for both states. It is idle when it is started and not playing a movie, and it is under a workload when it is playing a movie.

Software energy efficiency can be improved by improving computational efficiency, data efficiency and idle efficiency and by enhancing context awareness. Figure 3.2 provides a snapshot of the techniques that can be applied in each of these areas.

3.2.1 Computational Efficiency

Simply put, computational efficiency means getting the workload done quickly, with minimal energy consumption. The amount of effort that computer scientists have put into software performance saves not only time but also energy. We call this the *race to idle*. The faster we can complete the workload and get the computer back to idle, the more energy we can save. For faster processing, approaches such as efficient algorithms, multithreading, vectorization and uArch tuning are used.

3.2.1.1 Efficient Algorithms

Considerable effort has gone into research to find more efficient means to solve problems and to investigate and document the corresponding time and space trade-offs. It is clear from computer science theory that the choice of algorithms and data structures can make a vast difference in an application's performance. All other things being equal, an algorithm that computes a solution in $O(n \log n)$ time is going to perform better than one that does

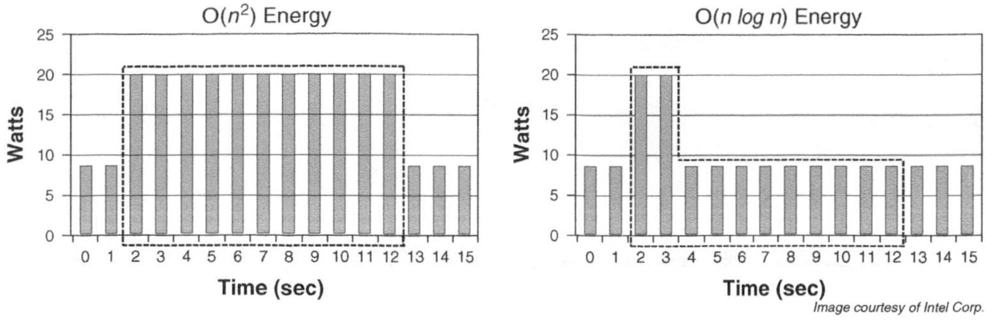

Figure 3.3 Impact of algorithm performance on energy.

the job in $O(n^2)$ time. For a particular problem, a stack may be better than a queue and a B-tree may be better than a binary tree or a hash function. The best algorithm or data structure to use depends on many factors, which indicates that a study of the problem and a careful consideration of the architecture, design, algorithms and data structures can lead to an application that delivers better performance.

Figure 3.3 illustrates how better algorithm performance leads to energy savings. The two diagrams in Figure 3.3 show the simplified, hypothetical power usage over time of two algorithms operating on the same workload. The power at idle for this computer is about 8 W. The areas within the dotted lines represent the total energy consumed over 12 sec. In the first case the total energy was 220 J, and in the second case the total energy was 112 J. The better algorithm saves time and energy.

Of course, the big hole in our logic here is the assumption that both algorithms push the system to consume an identical 20 W. But what if the more time-efficient algorithm has a complexity that drives the system to consume more power than the slower algorithm? Could the total energy for the more time-efficient algorithm be worse? The answer is probably yes, but we believe that in the vast majority of cases, the *race to idle* yields favourable results, and in the rest of this chapter, we'll show a number of case studies that demonstrate why we believe that.

3.2.1.2 Multithreading

Multithreading the software delivers better performance and as well as better energy efficiency. To help you take advantage of the multiple cores available in modern compute platforms, many threading methodologies and libraries such as OpenMP, OpenCL and Thread Building Blocks are available. To illustrate how well-developed, balanced multithreading saves energy, consider a favourite performance benchmarking application – Cinebench 11.5 from Maxon Computer GmbH (Maxon GmbH, 2010) – and the measured energy consumed on a four-core, eight-thread Intel processor. The hypothesis: Completing the Cinebench workload with the full four cores and eight threads available will save energy versus completing the workload with a single thread. Figure 3.4 shows the CPU energy use over time using one, two, four and eight threads. As you can see, completing the workload with a single thread takes considerably longer and uses more energy than any of the multithreaded runs. In fact, the eight-thread case (normalized) uses about 25%

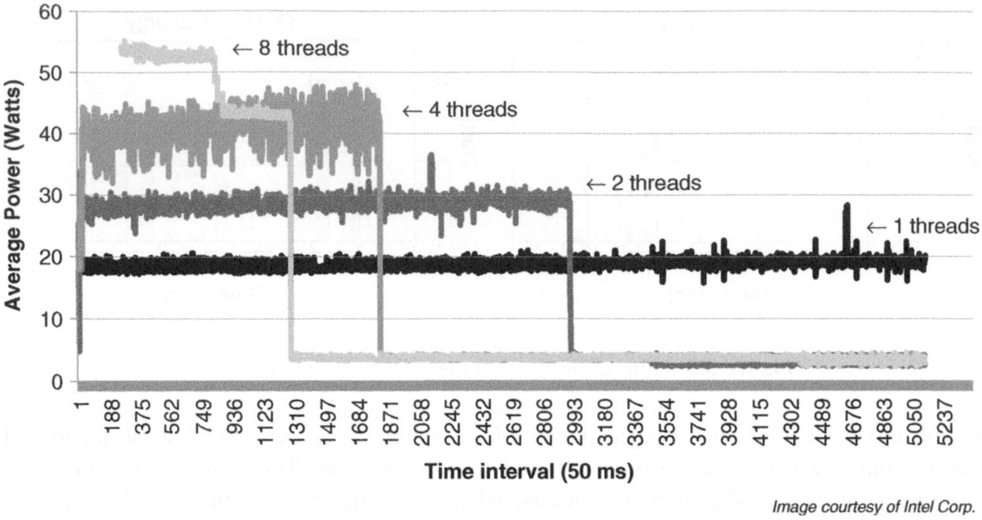

Figure 3.4 CPU energy measurements from various runs of the CINEBENCH 11.5 on an Intel Core i7 system.

less energy than the single-threaded case. A well-balanced multithreaded workload is more energy efficient than running the same workload with a single thread. The added advantage is that the eight-thread run was completed in about one-fourth the time and the processor is available for other computation.

3.2.1.3 Vectorization

Another method used to achieve better computational efficiency is by vectorizing the code instead of using scalar C-code by using advanced instructions such as single-instruction multiple data (SIMD) for instruction-level data parallelism. If you can *vectorize* your solution, you will get better performance and a corresponding power benefit. To test this, we took two different audio decode algorithms and optimized them using Intel's Advanced Vector Extensions (AVX) instruction set. Using a method we have to turn the AVX feature on and off, we measured both the performance and the average power of an audio decode workload. When AVX is enabled, the workloads run considerably faster – by 1.65X and 1.34X – with a huge savings in power. Table 3.1 summarizes the performance and power impact of using AVX.

Table 3.1 Performance and power impact of AVX instructions

Audio decode	Time (s) AVX off	Time (s) AVX on	Speed up	Average power (W) AVX off	Average power (W) (W) AVX on	Savings on average power (W)
#1	144	87	1.65X	12.7	8.4	4.3
#2	203	151	1.34X	13.7	11.1	2.6

3.2.2 *Data Efficiency*

Data efficiency reduces energy costs by minimizing data movement and delivers performance benefits. Data efficiency can be achieved (Arnout, 2005) by designing:

- Software algorithms that minimize data movement;
- Memory hierarchies that keep data close to processing elements;
- Application software that efficiently uses cache memories.

Methods for achieving data efficiency include managing disk input–output (I/O), using block reads, native command queuing, file fragmentation, disk I/O with multithreaded code as well as pre-fetching and caching.

3.2.2.1 Managing Disk I/O

This section summarizes the analysis of a disk's power characteristics during sequential and random reads and native command queuing, and provides an analysis on file fragmentation and disk thrashing. This section also provides guidelines on optimizing the power during disk I/O in various usage models, along with the power impact. For additional details as well as sample code, see Krishnan and De Vega (2009).

The analyses are based on the typical performance characteristics of hard disk drives (HDDs) which are affected by rotational speed, seek time, rotational latency and the sustainable transfer rate. Furthermore, the actual throughput of the system will also depend on the physical location of the data on the drive. Since the angular velocity of the disk is constant, more data can be read from the outermost perimeter of the disk than the inner perimeter in a single rotation. When a read request is placed by an application, the disk may have to be spun up first, the read-write head must be positioned at the appropriate sector, data are then read and optionally placed in an operating system (OS) file system cache and then they are copied to the application buffer. Table 3.2 shows the relative time (in milliseconds) involved in these operations based on the theoretical specification of the serial advanced technology attachment (SATA) drive used. Whilst the actual numbers will vary between different drives, this gives a relative idea of the times taken. Figure 3.5 shows the average power consumed during idle, read-write and spin-up.

It is clear from the data that disk spin-up takes the most time and consumes the most power. Applications performing disk I/O should take this power profile into consideration and optimize for the power and performance of the hard disk. To help better understand the energy usage of HDDs using various I/O methodologies, we present below the setup, results and recommendations of five separate experiments:

- Impact of block size on sequential reads;
- Effect of buffering during multimedia playback;
- Impact of file fragmentation;
- Impact of native command queuing on random reads;
- Disk I/O in multithreaded code.

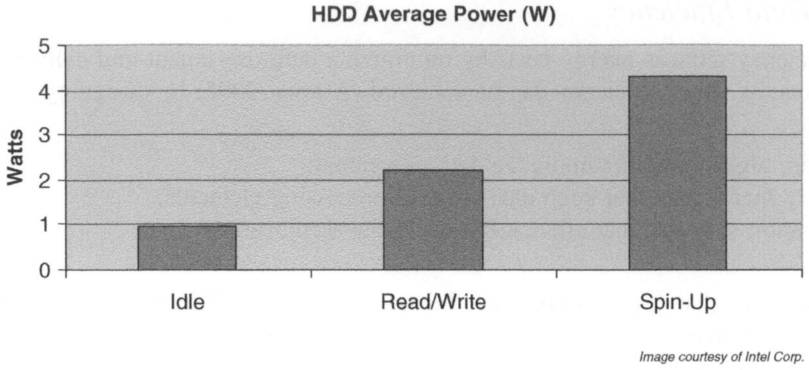

Figure 3.5 HDD average power consumed.

Table 3.2 HDD performance data

Average seek time (ms)	Average latency time (ms)	Spindle start time (ms)
12	5.56	4000

Impact of block size on sequential reads		
Hypothesis: When reading a large volume of sequential data, reading the data in larger chunks requires lower processor utilization and less energy.		
Setup	Observations	Recommendations
We created a large file (around 1 GB) and read the entire file in blocks of various sizes. As a general rule of thumb for any disk I/O, we rebooted the system between runs to avoid any file system cache interference.	We measured CPU utilization and energy as we varied block size from 1 bit to 64 KB. As expected, the CPU utilization and energy required dropped as the block size increased. CPU utilization and energy usage levelled off with greater block sizes.	Use block sizes of 8 KB or greater for improved performance

Impact of native command queuing (NCQ) on random reads		
Hypothesis: Effective use of asynchronous I/O with native command queuing (NCQ) improves performance and saves energy.		
Setup	Observations	Recommendations
Store a 256 MB file in fragmented and unfragmented states. Read the files and compare the results.	When NCQ was utilized, the total time reduced by ~15% and there was a similar reduction in total energy for the task.	Applications that deal with random I/O or I/O operations with multiple files should use asynchronous I/O to take advantage of NCQ. Queue up all the read requests and use events or callbacks to determine if the read requests are complete.
Buffering during multimedia playback		
Hypothesis: For multimedia playback, reading ahead and caching media content will save energy.		
Setup	Observations	Recommendations
We compared the energy usage of reading and playing an MP3 file (4 MB) in two ways – reading in ~2 KB chunks, and reading and buffering the entire file.	Similar to the DVD playback experiment, when reading the data in small chunks the hard disk remains active and consumes more power than if we read the entire file, access it from buffer and let the hard drive go idle.	Utilize a buffering strategy in multimedia playback to minimize disk reads and save energy.
Impact of fragmentation		
Hypothesis: The performance and energy costs to read a fragmented file are greater than those of a contiguous file.		
Setup	Observations	Recommendations
Store a 256 MB file in fragmented and	As expected, the fragmented file took	Avoid by pre-allocating large sequential files

(continued overleaf)

unfragmented states. Read the files and compare the results.	longer to read – over twice as long – ~26 s fragmented and ~11 s for the contiguous file. The energy savings were proportional.	when they are created, for example SetLength in .Net* framework. Use NtFsControlFile() to aid in defragmenting files. End users can defragment their volumes periodically.
Disk I/O in multithreaded code		
Hypothesis: The performance and energy costs of multithreading can be reduced by coordinating access to shared data.		
Setup	Observations	Recommendations
For this analysis, we developed a bitmap-to-JPEG algorithm based on the IJG library that converts a large set of BMPs to JPEGs. We created a serial version of the application and several multithreaded versions: (i) two threads that split the files and work independently, competing for disk access and (ii) add a thread to coordinate the buffer read-writes and handle requests sequentially. Use queued I/O in the coordinating thread to optimize read-writes.	Thread solution 1 provided almost no performance improvement over the serial version due to I/O contention and thrashing. Solutions 2 and 3 (buffered I/O and queuing I/O) provided ~1.52–1.56 × scaling) – a significant performance gain. Solutions 2 and 3 also yielded ~30% reduction in total energy cost over the serial version.	For multiple threads competing simultaneously for disk I/O, queue the I/O calls and utilize NCQ. Reordering may help optimize the requests, improve performance and save energy. When multiple threads competing for the disk cause significant disk thrashing, consolidate all the read-write operations into a single thread to reduce read-write head thrashing and reduce frequent disk spin-ups as well.

3.2.2.2 Pre-Fetching and Caching

We briefly outline outcomes of a study to determine if pre-fetching and caching can save energy during DVD playback (for details, see Chabukswar, 2009). The study analysed the power consumption of three different DVD playback software applications (DVD App 1, 2 and 3) with the multiple out-of-box configurations available whilst taking power measurements – primarily maximum power-saving mode versus no power-saving mode. The workload used for the analysis was a standard-definition DVD movie that was included with the MobileMark 2005 (MobileMark, 2005, 2007) benchmarking tool.

Table 3.3 shows the actual measured energy usage for the three DVD playback applications. It is valuable to note from these data that the difference between the worst-case energy consumption (App 2, 10 143 mWh) and the best-case energy consumption (App 3, 6023 mWh) is over 4000 mWh and appears to be entirely due to the design choices made by the application developers. This is an energy savings of about 40%. Even a 10% energy savings on a 4-hour battery would provide 24 minutes more battery life on a standard notebook PC.

From the results of the studies performed, three guidelines emerge that can help save energy during DVD playback:

- **Buffering:** Apply buffering techniques, which can reduce DVD power consumption by 70% and overall platform power consumption by about 10%, compared to other techniques.
- **Minimize DVD drive use:** Reduce DVD spin-up, spin-downs and read accesses in order to save energy.
- **Let the OS manage the CPU frequency:** Allow the OS to set the appropriate P-state, adjusting the CPU frequency as needed. (We do not recommend changing the CPU power scheme to run the processor at the highest available frequency.)

3.2.3 Context Awareness

Humans naturally use context to understand our world, makes decisions and adapt to the environment.

Context awareness in computers means that they can sense the environment in which they are operating and software can be designed to react to changes in the environment.

Table 3.3 Energy consumed during DVD playback

Application	Mode	DVD energy (mWh)	CPU energy (mWh)	Platform energy (mWh)
DVD App 1	No save	869.84	663.92	6618.76
	Max save	263.41	762.99	6039.41
DVD App 2	No save	897.82	3329.53	10 143.56
	Max save	895.57	1064.02	7509.18
DVD App 3	No save	780.93	703.25	6202.04
	Max save	781.04	554.87	6023.57

Context awareness was first introduced by Schilit, Adams, and Want (1994, p. 89). The objective is to create applications that can respond or adapt to changes in the environment. For the physical environment, this requires sensors and the ability to generate events or state changes to which the applications can react. Examples of context-aware behaviour are as follows:

- A PC or smartphone warns you when your battery has reached a low-energy state.
- A notebook PC responds to a change from AC to DC power by automatically dimming the display.
- A tablet PC or smartphone responds to ambient light level and adjusts display brightness.
- A notebook PC quickly parks the hard drive heads when sensors detect that the device is falling – to avoid a head crash.
- A handheld device writes cached data to flash memory when the battery is getting critically low.

Embedded systems are particularly context aware because, in many cases, they are designed specifically to monitor environmental conditions from sensor data and react to them. The use of sensors is growing rapidly in smartphones and tablets and includes light sensors, gyros, accelerometers, Global Positioning System (GPS) receivers, near-field communications and others.

Context awareness makes our devices 'smarter', and the behaviour of applications can be passive or active. A passive response to a change in context would be to ask the user what action to take ('Switch to power-save mode?') or to acknowledge that the state change has occurred ('You have 10% battery left. OK?'). An active response would be to take action automatically either as a built-in feature (dim the display in a dark room) or as a user configurable option (skip the full-system virus scan when on battery). We believe software applications can take advantage of context awareness to save energy. We will look at two examples here and suggest some others for further research.

3.2.3.1 Awareness of Power Source

Does it benefit an application to know the source of power – for example, if a notebook PC is plugged into an AC power source or operating on battery – and accordingly tailor its operational modes or application behaviour? Consider the following scenarios:

- Should your virus checker start a full-system scan when you are running on battery?
- Should your BluRay movie player application provide you with the option to deliver longer playback when operating on battery, possibly sacrificing some quality?
- Are you willing to give up some special effects in games to get more game play on a single battery charge?

If you answer yes to any of these questions, then it is important for the application to be aware of whether the platform is plugged into a continuous power source (AC) or operating on battery (DC). In Windows, you can achieve this by querying a unique GUID called GUID_ACDC_POWER_SOURCE (Microsoft Corporation, 2007). Armed with this information, you can adapt the application's behaviour and possibly deliver extended battery life for the use.

The logical next step is to receive a notification when the power status changes. To get this notification, your application must register for the event. Important event notifications include the switch from AC to DC power and reaching a battery threshold. Below is some sample code to register for the AC–DC change event. More details can be found at Microsoft Corporation (2010a).

```
HPOWERNOTIFY ACDCNotificationHandle;
ACDCNotificationHandle = RegisterPowerSettingNotification(
GUID_ACDC_POWER_SOURCE,
DEVICE_NOTIFY_WINDOW_HANDLE);
```

3.2.3.2 Platform Power Policies

Microsoft Windows provides built-in power policies – 'High performance', 'Balanced' and 'Power saver'. They give the system user the option to choose between better performance and better battery life.

Application software can use power policies in the following ways:

1. *Adjust application behaviour based on the user's current power policy*. Windows provides a method to query for the current power policy. Similar to the query for the AC–DC setting, the application would query a GUID called GUID_POWERSCHEME _PERSONALITY.
2. *Change application behaviour in response to a change in power policy*. This requires that the application register for an event notification. To register for that event, your application would use a mechanism that would look similar to this:

   ```
   HPOWERNOTIFY ACDCNotificationHandle;
   ACDCNotificationHandle = RegisterPowerSettingNotification(
   GUID_ACDC_POWER_SOURCE,
   DEVICE_NOTIFY_WINDOW_HANDLE);
   ```

3. *Change the power policy to suit the application behaviour*. The application must first determine if the system will allow a policy change and then make the change if necessary. When the application is finished, it is best practice to return the power policy back to its original state. To change the power policy, you must call the Win32 application programming interface (API) *PowerSettingAccessCheck* to determine if the user has access rights to override the power settings. This API call queries for a group policy override for specific power settings.

   ```
   DWORD WINAPI PowerSettingAccessCheck (
   __in POWER_DATA_ACCESSOR AccessFlags,
   __in_opt const GUID *PowerGuid);
   ```

   The API will return the active power settings identified by the GUID, allowable values and default values for AC and DC. For more information on how to use this API, see Microsoft Corporation (2011).

3.2.3.3 Other Context-Aware Behaviours

Developers may also consider the status of other components on the platform and use that information for intelligent application behaviour and energy savings. It might be useful to know information about the status of components such as network cards, Bluetooth, Wi-Fi, universal serial bus (USB) devices and monitors. For example, should an application continue to render video if the monitor has turned off due to a timeout or if the application window is minimized?

Another set of devices to consider are local area network (LAN) cards and radios. Networking increases energy consumption not just because the LAN card uses energy for transmitting and receiving data, but also because it will remain in an active state for a long period of time on the chance that some useful network communication may occur. PCs and set-top boxes are the most notable examples of this. The Microsoft System Event Notification Service (SENS) can help alleviate this and other mobile application issues. The SENS API, distributed with the Platform Software Development Kit (SDK), provides a simple function call for checking if the network connection is alive and another that will ping a specified address for you. In addition to these functions, you can also register with the service to receive events when a connection is made or lost, to ping a destination or even as an alternative method to detect when the system changes power states (battery on, AC ON or battery low).

3.2.4 Idle Efficiency

Idle Power for mobile platforms is defined as the power consumed when the system is running in ACPI S0 state with software applications and services running but not actively executing workloads. In this state, there should be minimal background activity. Figure 3.6 shows energy measurements taken whilst a computer was running an office productivity suite. The *idle floor* is about 8 W. By examining the C-state data from this run, we

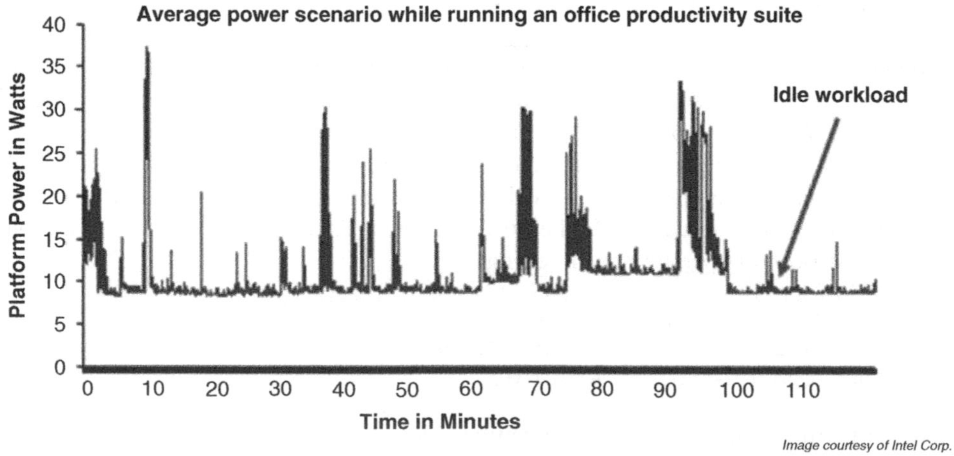

Figure 3.6 Platform power profile whilst running an office productivity suite.

determined that even with application activity, the platform was in C0 only 5–10% of the time. In other words, the processor was in an *idle* state, something lower than C0, 90–95% of the time. The challenge is to lower the idle floor by improving application *idle efficiency* which will lead to a significant increase in battery life. This also benefits average power scenarios and helps all but the most demanding (thermal design power (TDP)–like) workloads.

3.2.4.1 Deep C-State Residency

One of the key requirements for achieving idle efficiency is to keep the platform in deeper C-states for as long a duration as possible. For a platform in idle state, ideally the residency in the deepest C-state (C6/C7) should be more than 90%. Software should aim to keep the number of C-state transitions coming and going out of deep C-state as low as possible. Frequent C-state transitions from C6/C7 to C0 are not energy efficient. Activity should be coalesced whenever possible to allow for higher residencies in deep C-states. This concept was verified by measuring captured power data from the idle platform and a single-threaded application with two processes that communicate frequently with each other, each waiting for the other to complete. Each process ran for a very small duration (~50 μs). In a multicore system, when these two processes are scheduled on two different cores, the communication between these two processes generates an interprocessor interrupt (IPI). Whilst one process is waiting for the other to complete, the core with the waiting process goes into a lower power C-state. This sort of frequent C-state transition impacts power consumption in two ways:

- The energy requirements to enter and exit deep C-states are nontrivial. When the C0 (active) duration is very small, the latency to transition in and out of the C-states in comparison is appreciable and may result in net energy loss.
- The hardware policy may demote the C-state to a lower state based on heuristics. Even if the frequent C-state transition behaviour occurs for only 2–3 ms in a 15.6 ms window, hardware polices may either demote the core C-state or reopen the package-level cache, and this will impact power for the remaining ~12–13 ms of idle period.

To reduce C-state transitions in applications and services, it is recommended not to split a task between processes and threads unless parallel execution can occur. If it is necessary that a task be split between processes, then schedule the work so that the number of C-state transitions can be reduced. Also, applications and services should coalesce activity whenever possible to increase idle period residency.

3.2.4.2 OS Timer Resolution

The default system-wide timer resolution in Windows is 15.6 ms, which means that every 15.6 ms the OS receives a clock interrupt from the system timer hardware. When the clock interrupt fires, Windows performs two main actions: It updates the timer tick count if a full tick has elapsed, and it checks whether a scheduled timer object has expired. A timer tick is an abstract notion of elapsed time that Windows uses to consistently track the time of day and thread quantum times. By default, the clock interrupt and timer tick are the same, but Windows or an application can change the clock interrupt period.

Many applications call *timeBeginPeriod* with a value of 1 to increase the timer resolution to the maximum of 1 ms to support graphical animations, audio playback or video playback. This not only increases the timer resolution for the application to 1 ms, but also affects the global system timer resolution, because Windows uses at least the highest resolution (i.e. the lowest interval) that any application requests. Therefore, if only one application requests a timer resolution of 1 ms, the system timer sets the interval (also called the system timer tick) to at least 1 ms. Generally, setting the timer to a value less than 10 ms can negatively affect battery life. Modern processors and chipsets, particularly in portable platforms, use the idle time between system timer intervals to reduce system power consumption. Various processor and chipset components are placed into low-power idle states between timer intervals. However, these low-power idle states are often ineffective at lowering system power consumption when the system timer interval is less than 10 ms.

If the system timer interval is decreased to less than 10 ms – including when an application calls *timeBeginPeriod* with a resolution of 1 ms – the low-power idle states are ineffective at reducing system power consumption and system battery life suffers. System battery life might be reduced as much as 25%, depending on the hardware platform. The reason is that transitions to and from low-power states incur an energy cost. Therefore, entering and exiting low-power states without spending a minimum amount of time in the low-power states may be more costly than if the system simply remained in the high-power state.

Windows 7 comes with a command line utility called *PowerCfg* (Microsoft Corporation, 2010b). Using the */energy* option, PowerCfg can be used to determine whether an application has increased the platform timer resolution. Run the PowerCfg utility when the application is running and examine the resulting energy report to see if the application changed the platform timer resolution. PowerCfg will also show the entire call stack for the request. The report lists all of the instances of increased platform timer resolution and indicates whether the process hosting the application increased the timer resolution.

It is important that application developers understand the power impact of using high-resolution timers and set them to the lowest resolution that meets the performance requirements of the application for the specific platform. Applications and services should use the lowest timer resolution possible that meets the performance requirements of the application. If the application requires a high-resolution periodic timer, increase the timer resolution only when the application is active and then return the timer to its default state after the application exits. Software applications should minimize the use of APIs that shorten the timer period. In Windows this includes, but is not limited to, the timeBeginPeriod Multimedia Timer API and NtSetTimerResolution low-level API. Instead, applications should use the newer timer-coalescing API supported by the OS such as SetWaitableTimerEx (API) and KeSetCoalescableTimer (a device driver interface, or DDI) in Windows 7. Some other recommendations are as follows:

- If your application must use a high-resolution periodic timer, enable the periodic timer only whilst the required functionality is active. For example, if the high-resolution periodic timer is required for animation, disable the periodic timer when the animation is complete.

- If your application must use a high-resolution periodic timer, consider disabling use of the periodic timer and associated functionality when a power-saving power plan is active or when the system is running on battery power.

3.2.4.3 Background Activity

Frequent periodic background activity increases overall system power consumption. It impacts both the processor and chipset power. Long-running, infrequent events also prevent the system from idling to sleep. Background activity on the macro scale (e.g. minutes or hours) such as disk defragmentation, antivirus scans and the like are also important for power. Windows 7 has introduced a unified background process manager (UBPM) to minimize the power impact from background activities. The UBPM drives scheduling of services and scheduled tasks and is transparent to users, IT pros and existing APIs. It enables trigger-start services. For instance, many background services are configured to autostart and wait for rare events. UBPM enables the trigger-start services based on environmental changes. Some of the environmental change activities include device arrival or removal, IP address change, domain join and so on. An example a of trigger-start service is starting Bluetooth services only when the Bluetooth radio is currently attached. Some of the other Windows 7 improvements to minimize frequent idle activity are as follows:

- Elimination of transmission control protocol (TCP) distributed program call (DPC) timer on every system timer interrupt;
- Reduction in frequency of USB driver maintenance timers;
- Intelligent timer tick distribution;
- Timer coalescing.

Table 3.4 summarizes the methodologies for energy conservation presented in this section and highlights their potential benefits. Note that the energy saved and other benefits will vary significantly and depend heavily on the specific application and workloads.

3.3 Evaluating and Measuring Software Impact to Platform Power

To improve the energy efficiency of application software and to optimize power in mobile platforms, it is important to understand the impact on power consumption of the different hardware functional units. Various tools are available to provide a high-level estimate of the power consumed by a mobile platform. Whilst these tools may be sufficient to understand the high-level power consumption of a particular platform, they do not provide fine-grained details of specific components. The more accurate and invasive method to measure power is to use data acquisition (DAQ) tools where specific hardware components are instrumented and more granular power measurement can be logged. DAQ tools require an instrumented platform for actual power measurement.

3.3.1 Fluke NetDAQ® (Networked Data Acquisition Unit)

The Fluke NetDAQ is one of a class of DAQ tools that can be used to measure platform power consumption whilst running different applications on the system. A NetDAQ has

Table 3.4 Energy-saving software methodologies

Category	Technique	Description	Benefits
Computational efficiency: better application performance leads to energy savings.	Efficient algorithms	Use known algorithms that deliver the best performance and obtain the corresponding power benefit.	Race to idle. Energy benefits should be proportional to performance benefits.
	Multithreading	Parallelize the work whenever possible to take advantage of multiple cores.	Limited by Amdahl's law, but using more cores with balanced multithreading can deliver significant gains.
	Vectorization	Take advantage of SIMD for instruction-level data parallelism.	With AVX, perform eight simultaneous floating point operations instead of serially; race to idle for lower power.
Data efficiency: minimize data movement and keep data close to reduce unnecessary activity and save energy.	Manage disk I/O	Know the physical properties of disk drives and the cost of reading and writing data – use methods to minimize.	Experiment with reading and writing various record sizes to achieve optimal energy savings.
	Prefetching or caching	Reduce drive spin-up or spin-down by prefetching data during streaming workloads.	Hard drive and optical drive spin-up uses much more energy than sustained operation – prefetching data with high probability of access saves energy.
Context awareness: let the system be aware of the context and environment in which it is operating and respond accordingly. Intelligent application behaviour saves energy.	AC/DC	Know when the platform is operating on battery and when this situation changes.	When on DC, alter application behaviour to save battery life.
	Thresholds	Know when the battery reaches critical thresholds.	Alter application behaviour to save the last bit of battery power.
	Power policies	Know the current power policy; know when the power policy changes.	Choose application behaviours that are consistent with chosen power policies; provide user with choices.

Table 3.4 (*continued*)

Category	Technique	Description	Benefits
Idle efficiency: minimize unnecessary activities and processor interrupts.	C-states	Avoid splitting tasks unless parallel execution can occur; coalesce activity whenever possible.	Reducing C-state transitions keeps the processor in a low-power state longer.
	Timer resolution	Enable high-resolution timers only when the required functionality is active.	Highly granular timers cause significant, useless energy consumption at idle, and prevent CPU from entering deep C-states.
	Background activity	Use a unified background process manager to enable trigger-start services as opposed to polling.	Registering for events that trigger responses is far more efficient and effective than polling for activity.

many channels (10–100) that may be programmed individually to perform virtually any signal conditioning function the user requires. NetDAQ logger software for Windows is a configuration and data management programme for the NetDAQ Systems. The details of a NetDAQ setup are as follows:

- The target PC has a special motherboard with built-in sense resistors. For each target component (i.e. CPU), all sense resistors are wired and soldered at both ends before being connected to a module attached to the NetDAQ unit.
- The NetDAQ has modules that are attached with individual wires to the target PC and measures the current and voltage drop across the sense resistors. The NetDAQ is connected to the host PC via a cross-over network cable.
- The host PC can be any IA32 system with NetDAQ logger software installed on it. The logger collects the measured current and voltages and calculates the average power (W). The sampling interval can be changed on the basis of individual analysis.

3.3.2 Software Tools

Tools are an important asset for tuning software for performance and energy efficiency. The better your tools, the easier it will be for your developers to create powerful applications on top of any platform. The power tools discussed here help diagnose energy problems with the applications and system and provide a starting point towards creating energy-efficient apps and platforms.

3.3.2.1 Windows 7 PowerCfg

As mentioned in this chapter, *PowerCfg* is a command line tool that lets users control their system's power management settings. Users can use PowerCfg to view and modify power plans and to detect common energy efficiency problems when the system is idle. Used with the */energy* option, PowerCfg provides an HTML report or a checklist of problems based on a snapshot of the system's energy consumption over a 60 s period. Users can detect power policies, sleep states that are supported in the system, USB devices that are not suspending and applications that have increased the platform timer resolution. Using PowerCfg, typical diagnostics are generated and the following issues are reported:

- Processor utilization: overall utilization and per-process utilization;
- Power policy settings: idle timeouts, processor power management (PPM) configuration and wireless power save mode;
- Platform timer resolution requests;
- Outstanding power requests: display, sleep and away;
- Platform capabilities: sleep state availability, display dimming capability, firmware validation problems and Peripheral Component Interconnect Express (PCI Express) active state power management (ASPM) status;
- Battery capacity: battery static data and last full-charge capacity or design capacity;
- USB device selective suspend issues.

To see the available options for PowerCfg, on a Windows Vista or Windows 7 system, run the command line tool as administrator and type 'powercfg /?'. For further details on PowerCfg, refer to Microsoft Corporation (2010b).

3.3.2.2 PowerInformer

PowerInformer (Intel Corporation, 2008) is a tool developed by Intel to provide basic power-relevant statistics to a developer. Developers can use these statistics to optimize their application against battery life constraints whilst meeting performance requirements. PowerInformer features include the following (see Figure 3.7):

- Battery and power status indicators;
- Processor (physical, core and logical) detection;
- Percentage time of C1, C2 and C3 states of the system and of all logical processors;
- Average residency of C1, C2 and C3 states of the system and of all logical processors;
- Percentage time of the system and of all logical processors;
- Percentage time of the P stages of the system;
- System calls per second;
- Interrupt rate of the system;
- Disk I/O operation (access, read and write) rates;
- File I/O operation (control, read and write) rates.

3.3.2.3 Energy Checker

The Intel® Energy Checker SDK was developed to help software developers measure software energy efficiency and write energy-aware software. *Energy-aware software* should be capable of measuring and reporting dynamically its energy efficiency metrics. The SDK was designed to simplify this task, so the software vendor can focus on developing

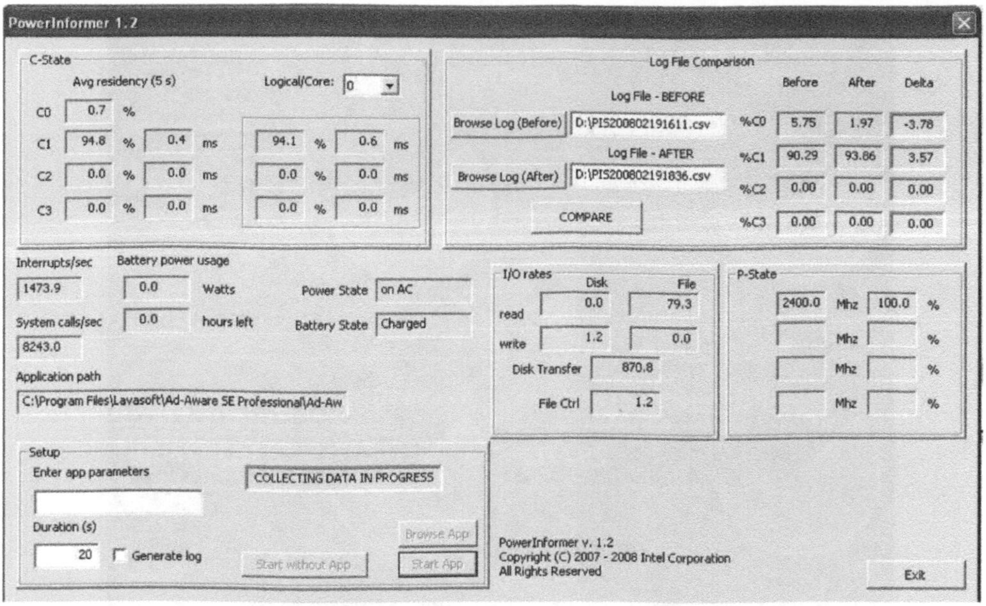

Figure 3.7 Snapshot of the PowerInformer tool.

the heuristics required to save energy. The Energy Checker API provides the functions required for exporting and importing counters from an application. A counter stores the number of times a particular event or process has occurred, much like the way an odometer records the distance a car has travelled. Other applications can read these counters and take actions based on current counter values or trends derived from reading those counters over time. The core API consists of five functions to open, reopen, read, write and close a counter. In practice, using the API exposes metrics of 'useful work' done by an application through easy software instrumentation. For example, the amount of useful work done by a payroll application is different from the amount of useful work performed by a video-serving application, a database application or a mail server application. All too often, activity is measured by how busy a server is whilst running an application rather than by how much work that application completes. The Energy Checker SDK provides a way for the software developer to determine what measures of 'useful work' are important for that application and expose those metrics through a simple API. Figure 3.8 shows a sample screenshot of the Energy Checker. More information on the SDK can be found at Intel Corporation (2010).

3.4 Summary

Energy efficiency will be crucial for the computing industry in the future both to increase battery life for mobile platforms and to reduce energy expenses for desktops, server platforms and data centres. The demand for higher performance from mobile devices and new usage models will also continue to grow. The world is moving towards green

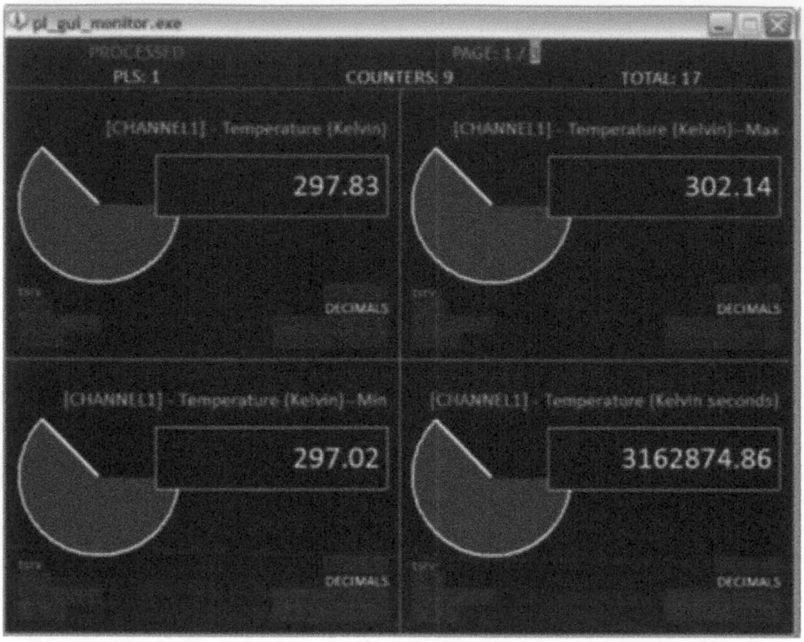

Figure 3.8 Intel energy checker monitor window with simulated data.

technologies, and consumer demand for longer battery life in mobile devices will continue to increase.

As discussed in this chapter, software behaviour can have a significant effect on platform power consumption and battery life. Modern processors and platforms have many energy-saving features, particularly for gaining performance improvements and the ability to enter low-power states when idle. But to benefit from these features, software should harness and work in harmony with these features. Software developers should do the following:

- Take advantage of performance features by emphasizing computational efficiency.
- Be frugal with data movement to improve data efficiency.
- Implement intelligent application behaviours by exploiting context awareness.
- Seriously consider the impact of software at idle to improve idle efficiency.

There are many free tools from Intel and others to help you get started. Even small improvements when amplified across millions of systems can make a dramatic difference.

Acknowledgements

The experiments and data summarized in this chapter are based on years of experimentation and research conducted by engineers of Intel Corp. We would like to acknowledge the tireless efforts and contributions of Rajshree Chabukswar, Jun De Vega, Karthik Krishnan, Manuj Sabharwal and Jamel Tayeb.

Review Questions

1. How do processor C-states save energy?
2. What are some programming methods used to achieve computational efficiency?
3. Explain how data buffering can save energy.
4. Give a few examples to illustrate how context awareness leads to 'smarter' devices.
5. How much more battery life can be obtained from a 60 W h battery if we reduce the idle floor of the system from 8 to 6 W?

Discussion Questions

1. Has the US Energy Star programme been effective? Can you envision an Energy Star rating for software applications? What properties of the software would you measure?
2. Some argue that the effort required to implement energy-efficient methods in software does not deliver sufficient return on investment. Can energy efficiency be an effective differentiator in software products?
3. As a developer, what tools would be the most useful in developing energy-efficient software? Can you think of new system features that would make it easier to get the feedback needed for better software design decisions?

References

Arnout, G. (2005) Data-efficient software and memory architectures are essential for higher performance and lower power. *Information Quarterly*, **4** (3), 53–57.

Chabukswar, R. (2009) DVD Playback Power Consumption Analysis. Intel Corporation working paper, http://software.intel.com/en-us/articles/dvd-playback-power-consumption-analysis/ (accessed April 2012).

De Vega, J. and Chabukswar, R. (2009) Data Transfer over Wireless LAN Power Consumption Analysis. Intel Corporation working paper, http://software.intel.com/en-us/articles/data-transfer-over-wireless-lan-power-consumption-analysis/?wapkw=data+transfer++wireless+power (accessed April 2012).

Intel Corporation (2008) Intel PowerInformer. Intel Corporation working paper, http://software.intel.com/en-us/articles/intel-powerinformer (accessed April 2012).

Intel Corporation (2010) Intel Energy Checker SDK, http://software.intel.com/en-us/articles/intel-energy-checker-sdk (accessed April 2012).

Intel Corporation (2011) Energy-Efficient Platforms: Considerations for Application Software and Services, http://download.intel.com/technology/pdf/322304.pdf (accessed April 2012).

Krishnan, K. and De Vega, J. (2009) Power Analysis of Disk I/O Methodologies. Intel Corporation working paper, http://software.intel.com/en-us/articles/power-analysis-of-disk-io-methodologies/ (accessed April 2012).

Maxon GmbH (2010) CINEBENCH 11.5, Run on Windows 7 and an Intel Core i7 Processor-Based Software Development Platform. CPU Energy Measurements Obtained Using a Utility to Capture CPU Counter Data. This Test Was Performed without Independent Verification by Maxon GmbH and the Maxon GmbH Makes no Representation or Warranties as to the Result of the Test. The CINEBENCH is Copyright © 2010 MAXON Computer GmbH, All Rights Reserved.

Microsoft Corporation (2007) Application Power Management Best Practices for Windows Vista. Microsoft Corporation working paper, http://www.microsoft.com/whdc/system/pnppwr/powermgmt/pm_apps.mspx (accessed April 2012).

Microsoft Corporation (2010a) Power Policy Configuration and Deployment in Windows. Microsoft Corporation working paper, http://msdn.microsoft.com/en-us/windows/hardware/gg463243.aspx (accessed April 2012).

Microsoft Corporation (2010b) Using PowerCfg to Evaluate System Energy Efficiency. Microsoft Corporation working paper, http://msdn.microsoft.com/en-us/windows/hardware/gg463250.aspx (accessed April 2012).

Microsoft Corporation (2011) Power Setting Access Check Function. Microsoft Corporation working paper, http://msdn.microsoft.com/en-us/library/aa372761(v=VS.85).aspx (accessed April 2012).
MobileMark (2005 and 2007) MobileMark, http://www.bapco.com (accessed April 2012).
Schilit, B., Adams, N. and Want, R. (1994) Context-aware computing applications. In IEEE Workshop on Mobile Computing Systems and Applications (WMCSA'94), Santa Cruz, 2003, pp. 89–101 (http://sandbox.parc.com/want/papers/parctab-wmc-dec94.pdf (accessed April 2012).

Further Reading

Capra, E., Formenti, G., Francalanci, C. and Gallazzi, S. (2010) The impact of MIS software on IT energy consumption. In European Conference of Information Systems, 2010.
Ellison, M. (2010) *Energy Efficiency for Information Technology*, Intel Press, Santa Clara, CA
Microsoft Corporation (2009) Windows Timer Coalescing. Microsoft Corporation working paper, http://msdn.microsoft.com/en-us/windows/hardware/gg463269.aspx (accessed April 2012).
Microsoft Corporation (2010a) Energy Smart Software. Microsoft Corporation working paper, http://msdn.microsoft.com/en-us/windows/hardware/gg463226.aspx (accessed April 2012).
Microsoft Corporation (2010b) Mobile Battery Life Solutions for Windows 7: A Guide for Mobile Platform Professionals. Microsoft Corporation working paper, http://msdn.microsoft.com/en-us/windows/hardware/gg487547.aspx (accessed April 2012).
Microsoft Corporation (2010c) The Science of Sleep. Microsoft Corporation working paper, http://msdn.microsoft.com/en-us/windows/hardware/gg463260.aspx (accessed April 2012).
Microsoft Corporation (2010d) Timers, Timer Resolution, and Development of Efficient Code. Microsoft Corporation working paper, http://msdn.microsoft.com/en-us/windows/hardware/gg463266.aspx (accessed April 2012).
Microsoft Corporation (2010e) ACPI/Power Management – Architecture and Driver Support, Microsoft Hardware Developer Central. Microsoft Corporation working paper, http://msdn.microsoft.com/en-us/windows/hardware/gg463220.aspx (accessed April 2012).
Steigerwald, B., Chabukswar, R., Krishnan, K. and De Vega, J. (2008) Creating Energy-Efficient Software. Intel Corporation working paper, http://software.intel.com/en-us/articles/creating-energy-efficient-software-part-1/ (accessed April 2012).
Steigerwald, R., Lucero, C., Akella, C., and Agrawal, A. (2012) Energy Aware Computing – Powerful Approached for Green System Design, Intel Press.
Stemen, P. and Miller, G. (2005) Windows Vista: Developing power-aware applications. In lide Presentation, SDC 2005, http://download.microsoft.com/download/c/d/5/cd5154e8-d825-4e14-89c8-8b0eb9dda203/pdc_2005_developingpower-awareapplications.ppt (accessed April 2012).

4

Sustainable Software Development

Felipe Albertao

Department of Environmental Computing, IBM Research – China, Beijing, China

Key Points

- Discusses how software (a virtual asset) can negatively impact the environment.
- Illustrates the importance of considering software's social and economic aspects.
- Examines current approaches to address environmental issues related to software.
- Introduces the notion of sustainable software development.
- Presents a methodology to measure the sustainability performance of software projects.
- Illustrates the application of the methodology with a real-world case study.

4.1 Introduction

In recent years, green IT has gained attention across the IT industry, especially in organizations that maintain energy-intensive resources such as data centres. Although most of the focus has been on minimizing hardware's energy consumption and improving resource utilization, very little attention is paid to the environmental impact of software. Software is commonly regarded as neutral due to its virtual nature, but its indirect impact is in fact real. The most obvious impact is the higher energy consumption caused by inefficient software, but other issues, such as increasing e-waste caused by existing computers becoming obsolete due to software demands, are greatly ignored by software professionals.

A recent study (Swann, 2010) estimates that almost 2.5 billion PCs will be rendered obsolete by 2013 as they cannot support the higher resources demanded by software upgrades or newer software. Though most of these computers are usable and in working condition, software requirements effectively make them unusable. Further, only about

Harnessing Green IT: Principles and Practices, First Edition. Edited by San Murugesan and G.R. Gangadharan.

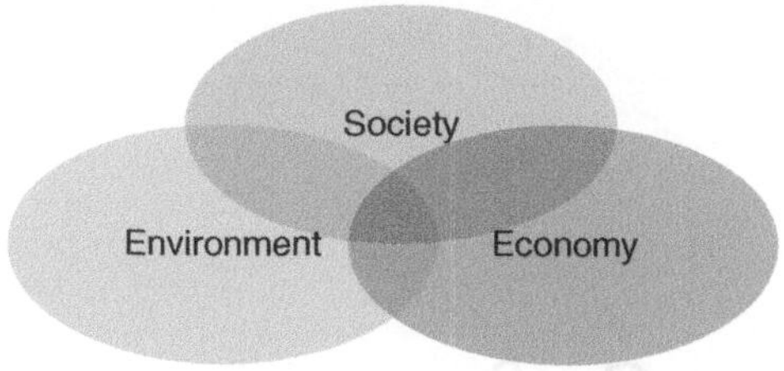

Figure 4.1 Sustainability encompasses environmental, social and economic dimensions.

20% of these discarded computers will be properly disposed of and/or recycled, whilst the rest of the e-waste, which contains highly toxic materials, will be dumped in landfills (Krikke, 2008) thus polluting soil, water and air.

Software also creates social issues besides its environment impact. For example, lack of accessibility support (i.e. support for disabled persons) effectively excludes people from the workforce. In addition, ill-designed and hard-to-use software demands more training and user support which might increase software's carbon footprint, particularly if it involves printing and distributing hardcopy of training materials and additional travel. E-waste also creates a social issue, since most of the dumped and highly toxic components are shipped illegally to developing countries, where they are handled by untrained workers without protective gears, effectively risking their lives and putting additional burden on the community.

The terms green and sustainability are often used interchangeably, but there is a subtle difference: Whilst *green* normally refers to environmental aspects, *sustainability* encompasses environmental, economic and social dimensions (Figure 4.1).

These three dimensions are integrated and interrelated:

- Economic growth without addressing its environmental impact diminishes quality of life.
- Environmental protection without considering local culture and traditions creates social injustice.
- Social disruptions like riots and war jeopardize the environment and the economy.
- A healthy economy enables a better environment and social welfare.

In advocating sustainable software, we include all three sustainability factors – environment, society and the economy – and align them to the project's business goals. It is imperative to adopt a holistic approach, considering not only the environmental aspects but also social and economic issues.

4.2 Current Practices

Unlike other engineering disciplines such as environmental and civil engineering, currently there are no well-established standards or practices to effectively manage sustainability in software projects. In the context of software, most of the effort on software sustainability focuses on the maintenance of legacy systems, and they do not address software sustainability in terms of environmental, social and economic aspects.

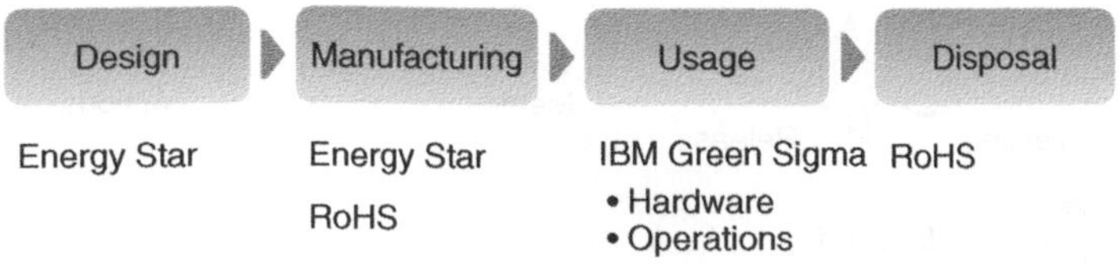

Figure 4.2 Methodologies and standards that cover the computer hardware life cycle.

In the 1990s Eckart Wintzen, founder of the dutch IT company BSO/Origin, implemented a practice called environmental accounting (van Bakel, 1996) which required each software project team to keep track of resources used during implementation (such as electricity) to assess their environmental impact. Since accurate tracking was complex, managers were then instructed to estimate resources used by the team members, such as paper used, travel and meetings. The estimated impact was then converted into cash amounts and reinvested in environmental projects. Whilst the practice was criticized for not being consistently quantifiable, it helped to raise awareness about the environmental impact in the context of software projects. In this chapter, I present a new sustainable software development methodology based on my previous research (Albertao, 2004), which was directly inspired by Wintzen's pioneering work.

As Figure 4.2 shows, there are several methodologies and standards that cover the life cycle of computer hardware (design, manufacturing, usage and disposal), where the main concerns are lower energy and water consumption in data centres, lower carbon emissions, use of less toxic materials and environmentally friendly disposal of unused hardware. For example, Energy Star and Restriction of Hazardous Substances (RoHS) are now industry standards, and IBM Green Sigma is a generic framework that applies Lean Six Sigma strategies to reduce water and energy usage, and can also be used on various business operations, including IT operations.

However, these methodologies and standards do not address environmental concerns related to software, such as system longevity (minimize e-waste), algorithmic efficiency (minimize energy consumption), project's carbon footprint (minimize carbon emissions) and support for disabled persons (address societal and economic issues, such as digital inclusion and disability inclusion).

4.3 Sustainable Software

Sustainable software is software that is developed considering its positive and negative impact on the environment, society and the economy, whilst still delivering the value for which the software is intended.

Having discussed the negative impacts associated with software, it is not realistic to simply expect companies to remove product features or ask programmers to simply take care of the problem without a systematic approach. Just like quality and security, sustainability should be integrated as an orthogonal aspect of the software development process. For instance, 'quality' is built into software or other products through a series of actions adopted across the development cycle, supported by metrics, that eventually increases the overall quality of the product. Sustainability should be integrated with a similar systematic

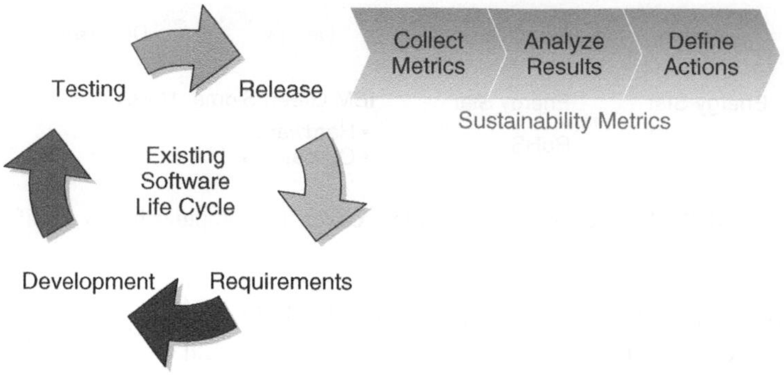

Figure 4.3 Sustainable software methodology.

approach, with incremental steps driven by trade-off decisions, supported by a pragmatic analysis of its properties, across the entire development process.

We present a process and a set of metrics that software developers and project managers can use to quantify factors that impact the environment, society and the economy. It fits any software development model without disrupting existing practices. Its main objective is to promote sustainability ideals across the organization whilst delivering business value. It also embraces the continuous improvement ethos like IBM Green Sigma and Six Sigma.

This methodology is integrated at the end of the existing software life cycle when the product is released (see Figure 4.3), and it includes three steps:

1. Metrics are collected at the end of development cycle.
2. Metrics are analysed based on their environmental, social and economic benefits.
3. Corrective or refined actions are formulated for the next development cycle and release of the product.

The goal of this approach is not to label whether a system is 'sustainable' or 'not sustainable.' Instead, it aims to measure and improve the overall *sustainability performance* across several product releases. This practice allows us to create an environment of 'pro-sustainability' across the organization, by adopting small but meaningful improvements where processes are constantly measured and evaluated.

4.4 Software Sustainability Attributes

To evaluate the sustainability performance of a given software system, we must first outline what attributes of the system we want to improve, and examine their impact and benefits. In other words, we need to define what a *sustainable software system* means in the first place.

As previously discussed, *sustainability* is an orthogonal property-like quality, and as such we will borrow a software-engineering concept called quality attributes to define sustainability. *Quality attributes* (Bass, Clements, and Kazman, 1997) (also known as nonfunctional requirements) are overall system attributes that impact the system's operation as opposed to its functions or features, and are normally used to analyse architectural trade-offs. They also provide a foundation for defining metrics and understanding their benefits.

Although there are several quality attributes (for a comprehensive list, refer to the Wikipedia article 'List of System Quality Attributes'; Wikipedia, 2010), the following attributes are most relevant to sustainability performance:

- **Development-related attributes:** These are the attributes that impact the development process, and key among them are the following:
  - **Modifiability:** The ability to make changes quickly and cost-effectively.
  - **Reusability:** The degree to which system components can be reused in other systems.
  - **Portability:** The ability of the system to run under different computing environments.
  - **Supportability:** The system's ability to be easily configured and maintained after deployment.
- **Usage-related attributes:** These are the attributes that impact the usage at runtime. They are as follows:
  - **Performance:** The time the system takes to respond to user requests.
  - **Dependability:** The ability of a system to function as expected at any given time.
  - **Usability:** Features that make a system easy to use.
  - **Accessibility:** The system's ability to allow users to access the system regardless of the user's location, or the type of computer or access device used.
- **Process-related attributes:** These are the attributes that impact project management. They are as follows:
  - **Predictability:** The ability to accurately estimate the effort and cost involved in developing software upfront.
  - **Efficiency:** The effort towards deliverables that add direct value to the customer, as opposed to the effort towards deliverables necessary to run the project.
  - **Project carbon footprint:** The net carbon emissions arising from the development of the software.

Quality attributes were originally created to minimize the cost or effort required during system development, maintenance and use, whilst maximizing the system's value. However, these attributes can also be used to analyse the (indirect) environmental and social impacts of a given system. For example, good performance improves the user's productivity (thus minimizing effort and cost), but it also indirectly minimizes e-waste because the system can be deployed on older computers.

Though many may not recognize it, these software attributes bring environmental, social as well as economic benefits.

- **Modifiability and reusability:** Less effort in introducing changes minimizes the resources used by the development team as well as the amount of waste, and hence reduces the carbon footprint.
- **Portability:** Software that can run on different environments increases flexibility and minimizes e-waste because it can run on existing hardware, for example by installing a less demanding OS like Linux to run the application. Portability also reduces the costs of adoption, and therefore the application is accessible to more users.

- **Supportability:** Less effort in configuring and operating the system minimizes the use of physical resources such as books and training required to support the system.
- **Performance:** Increased performance with even less resources minimizes e-waste by allowing the system to be deployed on older computers.
- **Dependability:** A system that functions reliably and as expected minimizes the need for additional resources because users do not have to deal with recurring unplanned tasks or emergency maintenance.
- **Usability:** By reducing the usability barrier, the system is available to a broader cross-section of users. Also, better usability of a system reduces the amount of training required, thus minimizing the use of books, travelling and other resources.
- **Accessibility:** It allows the system to be used by minorities, the elderly, people with disabilities, non-English-speaking communities and the illiterate population.
- **Predictability:** A team that develops software in a predictable manner has to deal with fewer emergencies and unplanned activities, therefore minimizing its usage resources (office resources, computer equipment, electricity, etc.).
- **Efficiency:** A more efficient software team optimizes the use of physical resources.
- **Project carbon footprint:** Decreasing the software team's carbon footprint directly reduces the amount of greenhouse gas emitted.

Table 4.1 presents a brief summary of environmental, social and economic benefits that can be derived by improving each of the software sustainability attributes.

4.5 Software Sustainability Metrics

To assess the greenness and improvements in environmental performance, we need to quantify each one of these attributes. Table 4.2 presents suitable metrics for each of the sustainability attributes. These metrics are commonly used in software engineering, and most of these measurements can be done or collected automatically (which is discussed in this chapter).

4.5.1 Modifiability and Reusability

Of all the attributes, modifiability and reusability are perhaps the most common in software projects, because they directly affect the programmer's productivity. For instance, in object-oriented systems it is a common practice (Martin, 1994) to measure and minimize the degree of dependency among classes, as highly interdependent classes are difficult and risky to change.

To find the distance from main sequence, a prime measure of modifiability, we first need calculate *instability* and *abstractness* – both are measures of reusability. Instability measures the potential impact of changes in a given package. A package is considered stable when it has no dependencies on outside classes. However, it is undesirable to have a system that is completely stable, since that would make it unchangeable. In view of this, we also calculate abstractness, which measures how much a package can withstand change through the use of abstract classes. We then calculate the *distance from main sequence*,

Table 4.1 Software sustainability attributes and their environmental, social and economic benefits

	Development-related attributes				Usage-related attributes				Process-related attributes		
	Modifiability	Reusability	Portability	Supportability	Performance	Dependability	Usability	Accessibility	Predictability	Efficiency	Project footprint
Environmental benefits											
Minimize e-waste by extending the lifetime of old hardware.			✓		✓						
Minimize e-waste through less effort in producing and maintaining the existing system.	✓	✓									
Minimize the use of physical resources.				✓			✓		✓	✓	
Minimize resource consumption.					✓	✓					✓
Social benefits											
Reduce technology adoption cost.			✓		✓						
Minimize learning barriers.				✓			✓				
Enable technology to minorities.								✓			
Economic benefits											
Minimize support costs.	✓										
Improve productivity.		✓			✓					✓	
Accelerate time to market.		✓									
Increase potential market.			✓					✓			
Minimize maintenance costs.				✓		✓	✓				
Increase customer satisfaction.							✓				
Minimize risk of budget overrun.									✓		

Table 4.2 Software sustainability attributes and their metrics

Attribute	Metric(s)
Modifiability	Distance from Main Sequence
Reusability	Instability and Abstractness
Portability	Estimated System Lifetime
Supportability	Support Rate
Performance	Relative Response Time
Dependability	Defect Density, Testing Efficiency and Testing Effectiveness
Usability	Learnability, Effectiveness, Error Rate and Satisfaction
Accessibility	Accessibility Requirements Score
Predictability	Estimation Quality Rate
Efficiency	Project Efficiency
Carbon footprint	Number of Offsite Meetings, Long-Haul Roundtrips and others (depends on the nature of the project)

which represents the balance between instability and abstractness, by measuring how far a package is from the idealized balance.

$$\text{Instability} = \text{Efferent Couplings}/(\text{Afferent Couplings} + \text{Efferent Couplings})$$

where Afferent Couplings is the number of classes outside a package that depend upon classes within the package, and Efferent Couplings is the number of classes inside a package that depend upon classes outside the package.

Instability ranges from 0 to 1, where 0 means the package is maximally stable and 1 means the package is maximally unstable.

Abstractness is the number of abstract classes in a given package divided by the number of concrete classes in a given package. It ranges from 0 to 1, where 0 means the package is completely concrete and 1 means it is completely abstract.

$$\text{Distance from Main Sequence} = \text{Abstractness} + \text{Instability} - 1$$

It ranges from 0 to 1, where 0 means the package has the ideal balance and 1 means the package requires redesign and refactoring.

These metrics help us to identify whether the package needs to be optimized in the next release.

4.5.2 Portability

An objective of sustainable software development is to minimize e-waste by limiting the implementation of software features that would render reasonably recent hardware obsolete. Since this is a subjective goal, we try to quantify it by finding the *estimated system lifetime*, which is an estimation of the year when the hardware required to run the system reached the market. The intent is to make a reasonable judgement that the new system will not force the target desktops to be unnecessarily upgraded. For more information on how to estimate this metric, refer to Section 4.6.1.

4.5.3 Supportability

Another objective is to minimize the amount of post-deployment support required by the system, which would in turn reduce the amount of resources needed. One could use metrics already gathered by the system support team, such as number of calls and average time to resolve tickets. For new systems one can use a metric devised from the usability study, called the support rate. For further information on the usability study, refer to Section 4.6.1.

Support Rate = User's Questions That Required Assistance/Number of Minutes System Was Used in a Usability Study Session.

4.5.4 Performance

A measure of performance is relative to the objective of the system. Since our goal is to improve user productivity, we use the relative response time metric captured during the usability study.

Relative Response Time = Number of Tasks with an Unacceptable Response Time/Total Number of Tasks Tested.

4.5.5 Dependability

The goal is essentially to minimize defects, which are costly from both business and environmental standpoints, because it causes more resources to be wasted. We use three common quality assurance metrics to evaluate dependability: Defects Density (the amount of defects compared to the system's size), Testing Efficiency and Testing Effectiveness. As the use of Defect Density alone could be misleading if the testing process is faulty, we also use the Testing Efficiency and Testing Effectiveness metrics.

- Defect Density = Known Defects (Found but Not Removed)/Lines of Code (LOC);
- Testing Efficiency = Defects Found/Days of Testing;
- Testing Effectiveness = Defects Found and Removed/Defects Found.

4.5.6 Usability

Quality attributes are used not only to assess quality or (in our case) sustainability, but also by usability experts. For improving software ease of use, Jakob Nielsen (n.d.), a leading usability expert, recommends the following attributes:

- **Learnability:** How easy is it for users to accomplish basic tasks the first time they encounter the design?
- **Efficiency:** Once users have learned the design, how quickly can they perform tasks?

- **Memorability:** When users return to a design after a period of not using it, how easily can they re-establish proficiency?
- **Errors:** How many errors do users make, how severe are these errors and how easily can they recover from the errors?
- **Satisfaction:** How pleasant is it to use the design?

A usability study is required to measure these attributes, which are defined as follows:

- Learnability = Minutes to Accomplish First Critical Task without Assistance/Minutes of Usability Test/Minutes System Was Used by User;
- Efficiency = Tasks Completed/Total Tasks Tested;
- Error Rate = Tasks Which Were Completed but Deviated from Normal Course of Action/Total Tasks Tested;
- Satisfaction = Score Based on Subjective User's Feedback.

Whilst a formal usability study is a complex subject and beyond the scope of this chapter, a simplified method for carrying out the study is outlined in Section 4.6.1.

4.5.7 Accessibility

Accessibility can be measured based on the following requirements, adapted from Ball State University's Web Accessibility Initiative (Ball State University, 2002):

- Support for motor-impaired users;
- Support for visually impaired users;
- Support for blind users;
- Support for users with language and cognitive disabilities;
- Support for illiterate users;
- Internationalization and localization support.

Each of these requirements is measured on a 4-point scale: 0 (non-existent), 1 (not adequate), 2 (acceptable) and 3 (adequate).

Most of these requirements are provided (or not provided) by the user interface (UI) platform used to develop the system, whilst some of them require the implementation of new measurements. Also, some of these items may not be relevant depending on the demographics of the target users: For instance, it does not make sense to provide support for illiterate users in a system that targets technical users who are professionally required to be literate.

4.5.8 Predictability

The goal is to measure how effectively the development team is able to estimate effort and cost. In traditional projects, we can obtain this metric by simply counting the number of days a project was delayed. However, in agile-based projects a project is never late, since agile methodologies have fixed time but variable scope. In such projects we count how many iterations were overestimated or underestimated based on an acceptable threshold (say, +/– 20%) by simply comparing the number of points allocated at the beginning of the iteration with the number of points actually used at the end.

- Estimation Quality Rate (for Traditional – Waterfall – Software Development Life Cycle Projects) = Planned Days/Actual Days;
- Estimation Quality Rate (for Agile Software Development Projects) = Number of Underestimated or Overestimated Iterations/Number of Total Iterations.

4.5.9 Efficiency

Project efficiency is measured by the effort towards deliverables that add direct value to the customer (e.g. coding and manuals) as opposed to project-related effort (e.g. infrastructure maintenance and project management). The efficiency can be represented in hours or points, depending whether your project is based on a waterfall or agile methodology.

4.5.10 Project's Carbon Footprint

To measure the project's carbon footprint, rather than quantifying the amount of all the resources used during a project, which may be hard to do, one can track the activities that can potentially cause a negative impact on the environment, such as the following:

- Work-from-home days;
- Long-haul round trips;
- Number of conference calls;
- Number of offsite meetings.

Metrics should be selected based on the nature of the project. For example, a project involving a globally dispersed team is likely to hold many conference calls, but that fact alone does not necessarily mean that the team's footprint is low. In addition, some metrics might be considered beneficial from an environmental standpoint but harmful to other areas of the project. For example, holding less physical meetings might have a positive environmental impact, but it can negatively impact the team's cohesiveness and motivation, which could ultimately jeopardize the project's sustainability.

Note that the goal of these metrics is not to answer questions such as 'How much CO_2 does my team emit?' (which is hard, if not impossible, to track), but instead to spark discussions like 'Why not visit clients by train instead of car?' The key is to select sensible and simple metrics, and stick with them across several product releases.

4.6 Sustainable Software Methodology

4.6.1 Collecting Metrics

Having defined the 'why' (benefits) and the 'what' (attributes and metrics), in this section we outline 'how' to obtain the metrics (see Table 4.3). Some of the metrics can be collected automatically, whilst others are likely to be already available in your project.

Table 4.3 Techniques used to collect the metrics

Attribute	Metrics	Code metrics tools	Simplified usability study	Platform analysis	Existing project statistics
Modifiability and reusability	Instability Abstractness Distance from Main Sequence	✓			
Portability	Estimated System Lifetime			✓	
Supportability	Support Rate		✓		✓
Performance	Relative Response Time		✓		
Dependability	Defect Density Testing Efficiency Testing Effectiveness	✓			✓
Usability	Learnability, Efficiency and Error Rate Satisfaction		✓		
Accessibility	Accessibility Requirements Score			✓	
Predictability	Estimation Quality Rate				✓
Efficiency	Project Efficiency				✓
Footprint	Project specific				✓

4.6.2 Code Metrics Tools

Metrics such as instability, abstractness, distance from main sequence and LOC are standard in software engineering, and most development environments have several tools to obtain such metrics automatically. The following are some code metrics tools for specific languages or development environments:

- **Java:**
  - IBM Rational Software (commercial): http://www-01.ibm.com/software/rational/
  - Eclipse Metrics (open source): http://metrics.sourceforge.net/.
- **NET:**
  - NDepend (commercial): http://www.ndepend.com/
- **C++:**
  - CppDepend (commercial): http://www.cppdepend.com/
- **Adobe Flex:**
  - FlexMetrics (open source): http://opensource.adobe.com/wiki/display/flexpmd/Flex Metrics
  - ItDepends (open source): http://code.google.com/p/it-depends/
  - How to get the LOC count: http://dougmccune.com/blog/2007/05/10/analyze-your-actionscript-code-with-this-apollo-app/
- **Multilanguage:**
  - Sonar (open source): http://www.sonarsource.org/

4.6.3 Simplified Usability Study

Measurement of support rate, relative response time and the four metrics of the usability attribute require a usability study. Usability studies can be complex, and in large projects they are normally handled by a separate team of professionals (user experience designers or usability engineers). For small to midsized projects, however, a simplified usability study method is described here which can be completed in a few hours.

One or more subjects are required for the usability test. The subject's profile will depend on the target audience of the application being tested. For instance, an outsider can be recruited if the system is intended to be used by people with no previous knowledge (e.g. a Web application). However, if previous knowledge is required to use the system, then a person who is familiar with the subject matter should be recruited (the subject should not have previous knowledge of the system being tested). Recruit someone who can be classified as a new user, so the learning ramp-up required to use the system can be measured.

Then, a list of small tasks to be performed by the subject(s) must be created. The tasks in the list must follow an order that can be performed during a single test session, and they should cover the most important use cases a user is expected to accomplish the first time the subject encounters the system. The tasks must have sufficient information to allow the subject to accomplish specific tasks without assistance: for example, a task should not request something vague like 'Navigate around the map', but instead specify 'Find river X in the map'. The tests should be designed so that the entire task can be completed within 10–15 minutes.

During the actual test, the subject should be observed and the time taken to complete each task should be measured. Help should be provided only when the subject specifically requests assistance, or when he or she is clearly stuck on a task. The results of each test should be recorded: 'The task was completed without assistance', 'The task was completed with assistance' or 'The task was completed but deviated from the expected path' (i.e. the subject accomplished the task by using a different path than was normally expected). At the end of the session, feedback about the subject's overall satisfaction about usability should be asked.

Also, the system response time of each task should be recorded: good, slow or unacceptable. There are quantifiable ways to track response time (e.g. a tool like Firebug could be used to measure page load times on Web applications), but simple subjective feedback is sufficient for the purposes of this study, based on the subject's own observation or on complaints during the test. A form like in Table 4.4 can be used to record test session data.

Finally, compile the following data that will allow you to calculate support rate, relative response time and the four usability metrics:

- Number of minutes to accomplish the first critical task without assistance;
- Total number of minutes the test session took;
- Number of tasks completed;
- Number of tasks completed but deviated from normal course of action;
- Number of tasks that required assistance;
- Total number of tasks.

Table 4.4 Usability test results

Task number	Task description	Time to complete	Task completed without assistance	Task completed with assistance	Task completed but deviated	System response time
1			❍	❍	❍	❍ Good ❍ Slow ❍ Unacceptable
2			❍	❍	❍	❍ Good ❍ Slow ❍ Unacceptable
3			❍	❍	❍	❍ Good ❍ Slow ❍ Unacceptable

Satisfaction feedback:

4.6.4 Platform Analysis

To estimate system lifetime and the Accessibility Requirement Score, identify the minimum hardware and software requirements of the platform on which the system will run or be deployed, and the platform's accessibility compliance.

To estimate the system lifetime, we first start by listing all the major underlying software components used by the system, both client and server, such as Java, Flash Player, a database and others. We then find the software and hardware requirements based on the documentation of each component, and based on information available online (on the manufacturer's Web site or Wikipedia) we gather the year the component or required hardware was released. For example, Java 6 was released somewhat recently, but the documentation mentions that it supports Internet Explorer 6 SP1, and through Wikipedia we found that IE6 SP1 was released in 2002. The assumption here is that if IE6 SP1 was released in 2002, it is likely that a computer manufactured in 2002 will run IE6 SP1. We use the same approach for hardware requirements: For example, a software component requires an 'Intel or AMD (Advanced Micro Devices) processor running at 1 GHz', and we found in a news article that the first 1 GHz Intel chips came out in 2000.

The estimated system lifetime is the most recent year that we can find for this analysis, and we normally add two more years, assuming that this is the amount of time that it takes for a product to become broadly available. The idea is that if the year found is too recent (e.g. the system lifetime is 2010) we should try to mitigate that because it likely will force users to upgrade their existing hardware. Normally we do not consider memory and hard-disk requirements because they are not constraints per se: Normally they are standard and interchangeable (they can be reused on old and new computers). Client and server requirements should be analysed separately, and the client requirements are normally the most relevant because they impact the largest number of physical computers, and servers tend to be more powerful and commonly reused across the organization.

Obtaining the accessibility information is usually fairly simple, search online for '[your UI platform name and version] Section 508'. Section 508 is part of the US Rehabilitation Act, and it became a standard for accessible products. You will search for the platform on which your UI relies: For example, if your application uses Java 6 on the server side and Adobe Flash Player 10 on the client side, then you would search for 'Flash Player 10 Section 508'.

4.6.5 Existing Project Statistics

Most software projects already track metrics like number of defects or effort in some capacity, either manually (using spreadsheets or documents) or automatically (using management tools, such as bug-tracking systems and support ticket systems). These metrics are normally public within the organization, because they are useful to all team members, and you can collect them from the following sources:

- Project management;
- Testing and quality assurance team;
- Customer support team.

It is a good practice to involve these teams during the sustainability analysis, as this would create a sense of buy-in and involvement for people across the entire organization.

4.7 Defining Actions

Based on the value of the attributes measured or estimated, one can identify the attributes that need to be improved in the next development–release cycle, and select the key goals for the next release cycle, based on the following:

- *Business value*: the degree to which the goal supports the system's objectives.
- *Effort required for implementation*: the feasibility or likelihood that the goal will be actually implemented.
- *Sustainability value*: the degree to which the goal would be to bring environmental, social and/or economic benefits.

This criteria list helps the selection of goals that can realistically be implemented. If we evaluate the goals solely by their sustainability benefits, it is unlikely that they will be implemented because there would not be organizational buy-in. A realistic goal is one that brings tangible sustainability benefits, but is also a win–win for decision makers, business managers concerned about profitability and project managers concerned about cost (effort).

Chosen goals are to be reported and evaluated by the project team during the next product release. Goals are translated into requirements that are treated by the development team as normal feature requests.

Goals must be specifically defined based on quantifiable and realistic metrics, such as 'Improve learnability level by 30%'. *Realistic* does not necessarily mean small. Although most continuous improvement actions are small but continuous steps, there are also opportunities for breakthrough improvements.

4.8 Case Study

In this section, we present the results of the sustainability performance analysis, applied to a real-world software project (Albertao *et al.*, 2010). The project started from scratch, with no previous releases, and the actual coding and testing took around three months. The back end was developed in Java, and the front end in Adobe Flex.

4.8.1 Modifiability and Reusability

Table 4.5 shows Afferent Couplings, Efferent Couplings, Instability, Abstractness and Distance metrics for the project source code for both Java (back end) and Flex (front end). The metrics indicate a high number of packages that require redesign (D close to 1). The most likely cause for such instability is the fact that packages were organized by design patterns (beans, business, servlets and I/O) rather than their actual functions. The key conclusion is that the packages should be reorganized by system functionality.

4.8.2 Portability

The project depends on the following platforms and components: Adobe Flash Player 10, Java 6 on Windows XP, IBM SPSS Statistics 18, GeoServer and PostgreSQL. By investigating its minimum hardware requirements, the team has estimated that the system can run on hardware as old as from 2003, which is an acceptable timeframe based on the

Table 4.5 Modifiability and reusability metrics for the package

Package	Afferent couplings	Efferent couplings	Instability	Abstractness	Distance
Java: map.bean	8	2	0.20	0	0.80
Java: map.io	2	3	0.60	0	0.40
Java: common	1	0	0	0	1
Java: kpi.servlet	0	1	1	0	0
Java: map.business	0	4	1	0	0
Flex: comp	2	19	0.90	0	0.10
Flex: comp.key	1	1	0.50	0	0.50
Flex: kpi	1	1	0.50	0	0.50
Flex: beans	21	1	0.04	0	0.96
Flex: maps	1	18	0.95	0	0.05
Flex: business	1	1	0.50	0	0.50
Flex: events	20	1	0.05	0	0.95

types of PCs used by the project's target users, and therefore the system is not going to require unnecessary hardware upgrades.

4.8.3 Supportability

The project is a Web-based system, not requiring installation on the user's desktop. Desktop-based systems can also use the Estimated Installation Time metric, which is the amount of time the user takes to install the product without assistance.

4.8.4 Performance

The project's usability study indicated one task with an unacceptable response time from a total of 11 tasks, or a relative response time of 0.09.

4.8.5 Dependability

- **Defect density:** Known Defects (Found but Not Removed)/LOC:

  4 known defects/2111 LOC = 0.002

- **Testing efficiency:** Defects Found/Days of Testing:

  9 defects found/16 hours of testing = 0.56

- **Testing effectiveness:** Defects Found and Removed/Defects Found:

  5 defects removed/9 total defects found = 0.55.

4.8.6 Usability

- **Learnability:** 0.43 Minutes to Accomplish First Critical Task without Assistance/8.3 Minutes System Was Used by User = 0.05.
- **Efficiency:** 5 Tasks Completed without Assistance/11 Tasks = 0.45.
- **Error rate:** 2 Tasks Which Were Completed but Deviated from Normal Course of Action/11 Tasks = 0.18.
- **Overall satisfaction about usability:** Satisfactory. User felt difficulty due to user's lack of knowledge in the subject matter (water management).

  Table 4.6 shows the results of the usability study.

4.8.7 Accessibility

Score: 0 = non-existent, 1 = not adequate, 2 = acceptable and 3 = adequate.

- **Support for motor-impaired users:** 1 = Flash Player 10 supports motor control, but the system does not provide shortcuts.

Table 4.6 Results of the usability study

Number	Task	Seconds to complete	Completed	Response time
1	Select English language	26	Yes	Good
2	Find the Xi River in the map (let user try to figure out how to find it – the idea is to find out whether the user will scroll around or click directly on the buttons)	41	Deviated	Good
3	Find the ShangSi Reservoir (let user try to figure out how to find it)	32	Deviated	Good
4	Find the Hun River in the map through the labels shown above the map (let user try to figure out how to click on the number inside the box)	75	With assistance	Good
5	Name the lakes available in the map	23	Yes	Good
6	Map zoom-in and zoom-out	7	Yes	Good
7	Access the pipe fault prediction application (under 'water supply')	85	With assistance	Good
8	Run a data audit analysis	127	With assistance	Unacceptable
9	Go back to overview	17	Yes	Good
10	See sewage-related performance metrics	32	With assistance	Good
11	Add a key performance indicator to the monitor dashboard	33	Yes	Good
		Total: 498		

- **Support for visually impaired users:** 1 = Flash Player 10 supports colour adjustments, but it does not include features for low-vision users, such as zoom-in or font sizing.
- **Support for blind users:** 2 = Flash Player 10 supports screen readers.
- **Support for users with language and cognitive disabilities:** 0 = The system uses very technical language, and no investigation was carried out to find out what professionals with such disabilities in the water management industry do to overcome such challenges.
- **Support for illiterate users:** 2 = The system has no support for illiterate users, although it is extremely unlikely that the target users (water management professionals) will be illiterate.
- **Internationalization and localization support:** 2 = The system supports English and Standard Mandarin, the most common languages spoken by the target users. The system does include a few localized features such as dates; however, additional changes are necessary such as correctly translating indicators that use the Chinese character *wan* (which means '10 000') to the English *thousand* or *million* (e.g. '78 million' instead of '7800 ten-thousand').

4.8.8 Predictability

The project team used a variation of the extreme programming methodology, based on points instead of hours worked. Firstly, the points initially estimated at the beginning of each iteration were compared with the points used at the end of each iteration. Then, the estimation quality rate metric was calculated by dividing the number of iterations where the difference was ±20% by the number of total iterations in the project. The result was zero, given that no iteration had more or less than 20% difference in points.

4.8.9 Efficiency

In the project, 38 points were used in infrastructure-related tasks, out of a total of 310 points (12.25%). Therefore the project efficiency is 88%.

4.8.10 Project's Footprint

The team has chosen two metrics that reflect resource-intensive activities, such as transportation to and from the office and long-haul trips:

- **Work-from-home days:** 2 days out of 165 total team days (33 project days × 5 team members) = 1.21%.
- **Long-haul roundtrips:** By airplane: 6; by train: 0.

4.8.11 Results and Actions

Based on the analysis above, the following assessment was made:

1. **Modifiability and reusability:** Packages organized by design instead of functionality.
2. **Portability:** No action required.
3. **Supportability:** No action required.
4. **Performance:** Low response time of the 'data audit analysis' function.
5. **Dependability:** No action required.
6. **Usability:** No action required.
7. **Accessibility:** Shortcuts not available; zoom-in or font sizing not available; Chinese *wan* was not correctly translated.
8. **Predictability:** No action required.
9. **Efficiency:** No action required.
10. **Project's Footprint:** Team members rarely work from home; no trips by train.

Based on the above analysis and expected business value, effort and sustainability value, the following specific sustainability improvement goals were defined for the next release of the software:

1. Improve the 'data audit analysis' response time by 50%.
2. Redesign the package structure and improve the distance metric on at least five packages.
3. Prioritize train trips whenever possible.

4.9 Conclusions

The goal of this methodology is to extract quantifiable and reliable metrics, so they can be consistently managed and improved. However, it is very difficult to connect the benefit implemented in the software with the actual physical benefit. That would be possible only if there is an extensive collection of case studies that would allow us to research the actual physical impact of the implemented actions. A collection of case studies would also be helpful in defining industry benchmarks for each one of the metrics.

Although substantial effort was made to make the metrics quantifiable, some of them are still based on subjective criteria. In addition, some of the metrics are still somewhat hard to gather manually. A tool to automatically gather some of these metrics would be extremely helpful to address both issues.

This methodology is intended to be a first step, and by no means does it try to cover all possible sustainability-related indicators. Our goal is to remove some of the guesswork in implementing sustainability initiatives by offering a practical starting point. Considering that the biggest barrier for adoption is the lack of awareness regarding the physical impact of software, it is recommended to start with a subset of the metrics (specifically, the ones that can be obtained automatically). The results of such a study can then be used as a venue within the organization for discussions about the impact of software production on the environment and society, in order to get the buy-in from the different stakeholders.

Review Questions

1. How can software impact the environment?
2. Distinguish between 'green' and 'sustainable'.
3. What is sustainable software?
4. What are the quality attributes of software?
5. What are the attributes relevant to assessing sustainability performance?

Discussion Questions

1. Why it is necessary to include software development and maintenance as part of an organization's green IT strategy?
2. Does your organization's green IT or software strategy consider social and economic issues in addition to environmental concerns? If not, why is it not integrated with the organization's corporate responsibility strategy (which normally considers social and economic concerns)?
3. What metrics are collected in your current project? Is there a process in place to analyse and improve these metrics?
4. How can an organization use software sustainability for competitive advantage?
5. What legal liabilities might an organization be subjected to by not addressing accessibility or social concerns in software products?

References

Albertao, F. (2004) *Sustainable Software Engineering: Master's Practicum*, Carnegie Mellon University, Pittsburgh, PA.

Albertao, F., Xiao, J., Tian, C. *et al.* (2010) Measuring the sustainability performance of software projects. In IEEE International Conference on E-Business Engineering (ICEBE).

van Bakel, R. (1996) Origin's original. *Wired Magazine* 4.11. http://www.wired.com/wired/archive/4.11/es_wintzen_pr.html (accessed April 2012).

Ball State University (2002) Web Accessibility Initiative: How People with Disabilities Use the Internet, http://www.bsu.edu/web/bsuwai/use.htm (accessed April 2012).

Bass, L., Clements, P. and Kazman, R. (1997) *Software Architecture in Practice*, SEI Series, Carnegie Mellon University, Pittsburgh, PA.

Krikke, J. (2008) Recycling e-waste: The sky is the limit. *IEEE IT Professional*, **10** (1), 50–55.

Martin, R. (1994) OO Design Quality Metrics: An Analysis of Dependencies, http://www.objectmentor.com/resources/articles/oodmetrc.pdf (accessed April 2012).

Nielsen, J. (n.d.) Usability 101: Introduction to Usability, http://www.useit.com/alertbox/20030825.html (accessed April 2012).

Swann, P. (2010) *Software Marketing and E-waste: Standards for Sustainability*, Nottingham University, http://communications.nottingham.ac.uk/News/Article/Software-bloat-to-cause-environmental-timebomb-academics-warn.html (accessed April 2012).

Wikipedia (2010) List of System Quality Attributes, http://en.wikipedia.org/wiki/List_of_system_quality_attributes (accessed April 2012).

5

Green Data Centres

Charles G. Sheridan[1], Keith A. Ellis[1], Enrique G. Castro-Leon[2] and Christopher P. Fowler[3]
[1]*Intel Labs Europe, Intel Corporation, Leixlip, Ireland*
[2]*Intel Architecture Group, Intel Corporation, Hillsboro, OR, USA*
[3]*Intel/SAP Research Colab, Queen's Island, Belfast, Ireland*

Key Points

- Outlines key sustainability challenges associated with data centres and strategies to mitigate energy consumption.
- Describes a holistic approach to IT and facilities energy management in a data centre.

5.1 Data Centres and Associated Energy Challenges

The ever increasing digitization of modern life has resulted in the increased deployment of data centre facilities. Data centres are complex ecosystems that interconnect elements of the information and communication technology (ICT), electrical and mechanical fields of engineering, and, as identified within the much cited Global e-Sustainability Initiative (GeSI) *Smart 2020* report (GeSI, 2008), they represent the fastest growing contributor to the ICT sector's overall carbon footprint.

Since initial public adoption in the early 1990s, the Web has evolved to become a global platform that touches the lives of billions across the world on a daily basis. In support of business, education, news media, social participation and scientific discovery, the Web has changed humanity's opportunity and outlook for today and the future.

The growth of the Internet has been fuelled in part by the proliferation of digital technology and humanity's natural desire to communicate. We have transformed from mere consumers of information, via old-school television, radio and print media, into

Harnessing Green IT: Principles and Practices, First Edition. Edited by San Murugesan and G.R. Gangadharan.

producers of digital content. We use, and contribute to, blogs, wikis, photo-sharing portals, social-networking sites, online auctions and much more.

Driven by the Web 2.0 revolution and a tech-savvy generation, new concepts are entering the global lexicon, such as the digital *prosumer*, the net generation, the citizen journalist, open-source collaboration and crowd sourcing. This social and digital media revolution, characterized by the rise of Google, YouTube, Facebook, Flickr, Twitter, eBay and Amazon (to name a few), has resulted in an increasing demand for data storage and processing capacity that is showing no signs of abating.

In enterprise computing too, the outsourcing of business information technology (IT) requirements via *cloud computing* is motivating further impetus, resulting in the demand for larger and more efficient data centre services. Cloud-computing service provision is now, of itself, a business model, with Web-based companies marketing virtualized capacity as a 'pay-as-you-use' commodity. Cloud computing is posited as a natural progression to our digital existence, offering storage and synchronized access to our music, videos, photos and documents, from anywhere anytime, all of which is facilitated via a globally expanding fleet of data centres.

According to data centre energy consumption trends collected by the Green Grid, the overall power consumption of data centres in the United States was projected to reach 3.5% of total US power consumption in 2011. Koomey (2007) suggests that worldwide servers consume about 120 TWh of electricity, whilst GeSI (www.gesi.org/) suggests that data centres will account for approximately 18% of the ICT sector's carbon footprint by 2020. In short, the need to provide data-processing services from data centres has never been greater. But these technological, commercial and social advances are not without cost and provision needs to be made to negate the environmental impact of such rapid ICT and hence data centre growth.

As such, the impact of data centre facilities is a key concern for both companies (in achieving sustainability targets) and governments (which are placing increased scrutiny on data centre consumption and associated carbon dioxide (CO_2) emissions). The 2007 'Report to Congress on Server and Data Center Energy Efficiency' (US Environmental Protection Agency, 2007) and the European Commission's 2008 'Code of Conduct on Data Centres Energy Efficiency' are testimony to that increased focus.

'Green' data centres seek to address these concerns and challenges by more effectively incorporating energy-efficient design together with high-efficiency power delivery, high-efficiency cooling and increased utilization of renewable-energy sources (RESs). Such facilities seek a balance that places environmental sustainability on an even keel with financial considerations. In fact green data centres are seen as a competitive advantage that positively contributes to the financial viability of the enterprise, and in this chapter we outline and discuss some of the key elements and concepts to consider.

Sections 5.2 and 5.3 introduce key data centre IT and facilities infrastructure that should be understood in terms of greening data centre operations. Subsequently, Section 5.4 outlines IT management considerations and strategy. Section 5.5 follows with an overview of key metrics in the context of energy-efficient operation. In Section 5.6 we discuss a data centre management case study before ending with conclusions and suggestions for further reading.

5.2 Data Centre IT Infrastructure

In an efficient modern green data centre there are two layers of infrastructure: the IT infrastructure and facilities infrastructure (discussed in Section 5.3). By *IT infrastructure*, we mean the server technology, networking systems and storage provided within a typical data centre.

This section discusses the following key elements of IT infrastructure of a data centre:

- Server design and server systems development in support of efficient data centre service provision and the range of service function.
- The role of networking within a data centre.
- The role of storage and the types of storage provision.
- The changing shapes of data centre IT platforms through system innovation.

5.2.1 Servers

IT servers take many forms and provide many different services and functions, but the fundamental goal is the same: They provide a service as part of a bipartite communication between a client and a server.

A server may be a software program connected locally on the same hardware machine, or remotely via networking infrastructure. Servers are generally a software or hardware system designed to carry out a dedicated function: e-mail server, Web server, print server or database server. Within a data centre the IT hardware used to host a software server may differ in design, efficiency and function. A server may be designed to host a particular operating system (OS), and within a data centre there may be capacity for different OSs. Each server *machine* will consist of the physical hardware, the OS and the software service. This mix of options feeds directly into the design choices and characteristics of a data centre and must be considered early on in the IT infrastructure development process.

A server machine designed for a data centre will have very different characteristics from a machine designed for home or office use. This is primarily due to the nature of its ultimate use, where large numbers of servers are networked via router and switch technology with gateway machines coordinating huge numbers of client requests for services. As such, a data centre server will typically be *headless*; that is, there is no monitor or mouse connected. This design is due to the *machine-to-machine* service interaction mode, typical of data centres, where human intervention is required only when something goes wrong, or a machine requires maintenance. In this case, human interaction is required for administration, setup and maintenance, and a control terminal is then provided with a monitor, keyboard and mouse interface. For large-scale data centres, a full Network Operations Centre may be present.

Onboard a data centre server, the central processing unit (CPU), onboard memory, networking interface and software are optimized for the intended purpose. For example, a database server may have a larger onboard memory capacity to enable queries to be processed in memory, reducing the seek time needed to access data stored on networked disc space.

As with a home computer, data centre servers need to be housed in a suitable form-factor to enable efficient integration into the wider data centre infrastructure.

5.2.1.1 Rack-Mounted Servers

Rack-mounted servers come in two sizes, 19 or 23 in., though the smaller of the two is the standard. Fitting a racked server into a standard-width cabinet is a fairly straightforward procedure, with the machine housing providing predrilled *ears* that align precisely with the vertical posts of the rack cabinet. For heavy equipment, or that which requires regular access to replace or maintain components of the server hardware, a rail-mounting system is also a standard feature of a rack. This allows for access behind the faceplate to be made as simply as opening a drawer in a piece of furniture.

The ease with which servers may be added and accessed makes rack-mounted servers particularly convenient for retrofitting low-density environments. The standard rack server container and mounting system standard dictates the number of physical machines that may be housed. The current standard enables 42 standard *units*, with each server consider one unit (1U).

5.2.1.2 Blade Servers

The blade system design differs from that of a rack design in some fundamental ways. Racked servers are self-contained individual machines with power and network cabling for each unit. In contrast, blades are housed within a blade system container, which is mounted in a standard cabinet. The blade system provides the power and networking for all the blades housed within the system. Onboard cooling and uninterruptible power supply (UPS) requirements may also be provided by the blade cabinet system. This design, whereby the common support infrastructure (power, networking and cooling) is separated out into a common house system, enables greater density of machine within a standard cabinet – 42 servers for a rack scales to 128 for blades, giving a far greater density or capacity using the blade system design.

Physical dimension may at first not appear relevant to green data centres. But as racks transition to blades, the capacity of the data centre in terms of hosting physical machines also increases as does the energy requirement.

5.2.1.3 Containers

The next logical step in server configuration design for data centres was the self-contained data centre module. Shipped inside a standard-sized transport container, of the type used for shipping goods overseas or via heavy-goods vehicles, container-based data centres provide an off-the-shelf solution to data centre needs. Designed to be self-contained, their energy and connectivity requirements are known upfront. The data centre customer need only hook up the required power and network cabling capacity to have a fully functioning data centre. The advent of data centres housed in shipping containers seems a perfectly logical one and is merely a scaling up of the same modular approach taken by a 42U rack-mounted system.

Modularization in design, from racks through to containers, allows for rapid scaling and easy replacement, with old or failing units swapped out with a replacement or higher specification units swapped in as demand requirements change. Modularization also allows for ease in power management as energy requirement scales as a function of computing capacity.

Before discussing newer optimizations in data centre design that maintain the benefits of modularization but do not attract the same energy demands as capacity increases, Sections 5.2.2 and 5.2.3 detail the networking and storage elements of the IT infrastructure.

5.2.2 Networking

The gateway machine of a data centre will sit at the entrance to the data centre. Its primary function is protocol translation in and out of the data centre, acting as the connection point between the data centre's internal local area network (LAN) and the wide area network (WAN) outside of the data centre – in most cases, the Internet Service Provider's network.

The millions of requests, for Web page content (hits), e-mail or database query results, need to be received by the software services hosted within the data centre. Once inside the data centre's LAN, each message must be routed to a server instantly able to satisfy the request. Depending on the scale and network complexity of a data centre, multiple routers will deployed to direct message traffic, routing messages to different sectors of the internal network. Routers use routing tables and message address standards to manage the traffic within the data centre. A router will forward a message to the next address on the path (a *hop*), or simply drop the message if it does not have a next hop for the particular message. This simple process means that routers may be configured to manage the vast quantities of messages flowing through the centre's networking cables.

Whilst a router will work at the network layer, *switches* may be deployed to manage messages across a number of different layers – although ordinarily they work at the data layer. A primary function of the switches within a data centre network is to link different network segments. Depending upon how the centre's network of servers has been configured, the system designers will deploy a number of switches to optimize and manage the message or data flow between all the network segments in the data centre. This will include servers, storage and gateway.

The *backbone* within the data centre is there to provide high-capacity connectivity between different network segments within the data centre. It will ordinarily be of a much higher bandwidth capacity than the segments connected to it, to allow for the greater capacity of traffic flow between multiple locations. The backbone will often need to handle the full two-way message capacity of the data centre.

5.2.3 Storage

Data storage is a critical element of data centre design. A number of options exist, each of which caters to the requirements of other elements in the overall IT infrastructure choices made. The key differentiator in storage type lies in the way the client machine – in our case, the data centre server – logically *sees* the storage medium. This will play a part in how the server manages the space and the access protocols available for accessing the data stored.

Network-attached storage (NAS) appears to the client machine as a network-based file server able to support the Network File System (NFS) protocol. A client machine then maps a *network drive* to a disc share that appears locally to the NAS. The NAS then manages the access to the file space via client-side requests using the NFS protocol. In order to manage the NFS access from many clients, the NAS is built in such a way as to become a server in its own right – a dedicated and optimized machine with the specific task of serving and managing network file space. Issues around speed of access may become apparent if the connecting network bandwidth or the local memory cache of the NAS is not sufficient for the expected access traffic. Careful consideration is therefore required when designing this type of storage.

As mentioned, the key difference between NAS and storage area networks (SANs) is the way the client machine views the space. In a SAN, the disc space appears as local to the client machine. This is a key point that enables the client (our data centre servers) to use disc management utility software to configure and optimize the space to best suit the needs of the server application. The same issues around connectivity bandwidth exist with a SAN configuration, as like the NAS they are positioned within the data centre's network and connected via standard network cables; however, SAN is considered a more logically efficient file server access provisioning system.

Despite the difference, we should note that the choice between NAS or SAN is not mutually exclusive. Also they are not the only choices we have. Direct access storage (DAS) is another option, where the disc storage is connected exclusively to the server machine – although this may have greater limiting factors such as ease of remote management and backup options. The key point to consider, as with all data centre design, is clear and reasoned design decisions based on the requirements and anticipated uses of the data centre as a whole. In many cases, the full range of storage options will be used to gain the optimum performance whilst driving down energy demands and cost.

5.2.4 IT Platform Innovation

Physical hardware computing is only half the story of data centre design. As with physical servers, networking and storage design, innovations in software platforms and OS virtualization have resulted in the ability to modularize systems into separate servers (as services) at the software level. This advance enables efficiencies in infrastructure provision due to the separation of concerns between hardware resources and virtualized software provision. A brief look at the evolution of IT platform infrastructures towards fully virtualized cloud-based systems is discussed throughout the rest of this section.

5.2.4.1 Server Farm (Cluster)

Cluster computing is characterized by multiple, physically discrete machines, closely linked to provide the logical interface of a single machine. Often associated with the parallelization of processing algorithms, cluster computing requires dedicated and highly specialized middleware to form the complex message-passing infrastructure required to manage the cluster's physical resources. The parallel processing capability would split and schedule individual requests across the large number of individual server machines, each configured to compute a result. The results of individual processes would then be collated together to form the final result. The savings in parallelizing the workload is the principle use and research interest for cluster computing.

5.2.4.2 Grid Computing

The increasing demands of the scientific research community gave rise to research into grid computing as a natural progression to clusters. As data sets increased in size and the demands for processing capabilities to analyse data in a timely manner also grew, a new approach was sought. The core aim of grid computing was to integrate disparate resources across organizational domains into what became termed virtual organizations. For example, a database server in one domain may be integrated with a networked cluster in another domain, to form a powerful data analytics platform. Grid computing, however, presents a few issues including security management across multiple domains, the complexity of handling the interaction state and the realities of processing vast data sets across a network. As a result the approach did not gain traction beyond academic circles. It was not until some clever thinking and the adoption of a Web services approach – common in the e-commerce domain – that a breakthrough was made in Internet-scale data analytics.

5.2.4.3 Service Orientation

Service-oriented architecture (SOA), of which Web service is one instantiation, promotes a separation of concerns between service implementation (software) and service hosting (server hardware). It is a means of providing both data and processing resources over a network that decouples the service instantiation from a machine-readable service interface. This enables system designers to deploy network services that are accessible and addressable using standard Internet protocols. The Web Service Description Language (WSDL) was used to describe interfaces with request and response messages transported using Simple Object Access Protocol (SOAP) and HTTP – a standard Internet protocol. Universal Resource Identifiers (URIs) are used to uniquely address an individual server in the same way that a Web address uniquely identifies a Web page resource. Through service orientation a system may leverage the full power of the Internet's inherently scalable message-addressing and message-routing capabilities and in turn enables scalable distributed systems to be deployed over a WAN. With increases in Internet bandwidth overcoming issues in grid computing, service orientation has proved more viable in the longer term.

5.2.4.4 Virtualization

An additional approach to compute server provision is virtualization. Rather than a single hardware machine supporting a single OS, that in turn hosts a single server application (Web server, mail server, etc.), a virtualized system enables a single hardware machine running a single OS to host multiple virtual machines, which may or may not be running the same OS. This leads to a single host machine running multiple virtual machines. Virtualization presents the opportunity to scale the service provision within a data centre, make far more efficient use of hardware resources, reduce running costs and reduce energy consumption. Hence, it proved to be a breakthrough technology in data centre IT infrastructure design, enabling a far more efficient use of resources with a much reduced impact in terms of energy consumption.

5.2.4.5 Cloud Computing

The combination of SOA and virtualization gave rise to a further innovation in computing resource provision: cloud computing. Cloud computing makes a separation of concerns between *service*, *platform* and *infrastructure*, with each of these layers being virtualized and provided as a service in itself. Networking is used to communicate between different service layers and the application services supported.

Infrastructure as a Service (IaaS) provides the fundamental virtual machine upon which a server may be built. Platform as a Service (PaaS) enables the provision of the required software platform stack upon which the final service is designed to run. Finally, Software as a Service (SaaS) enables the specific application to be packaged as a service and deployed on the virtual platform. This stack of virtualized services enables a complete large-scale server system to be built and deployed across the IT infrastructure of the data centre. The approach maximizes the use of hardware resources with each physical machine hosting a number of virtual machines. (For further information on cloud computing, refer to Chapter 16.)

5.3 Data Centre Facility Infrastructure: Implications for Energy Efficiency

Data centres range from closet-sized operations to megasized facilities, and their function at its simplest is to store, process and move information. For efficient and effective service provisioning, data centre IT infrastructure needs to be carefully designed. However, from a facilities perspective, IT infrastructure is simply a power-consuming, heat-producing ‘critical black box’ whereby the energy used for providing services is dissipated as heat by IT infrastructure – processors, memory, input–output systems and other components.

Consequently, the two main functions of the supporting infrastructure are as follows:

1. Ensure that the IT and facilities are supplied with power at all times.
2. Keep the data centre at the required temperature by removing the heat generated.

Throughout this section, we discuss the energy implications of these objectives. In focussing on the supporting infrastructure, we assume that all electrical power delivered to the IT equipment is related to ‘useful work’; of course, as alluded to in Section 5.2, this is an oversimplification with underutilized systems consuming significant power in legacy data centres.

5.3.1 Power System

In terms of power, the primary difference between a normal office or home environment and a data centre relates to the ‘criticality’ of the electrical load. Losing power in most situations is nothing more than an inconvenience, whereas losing power to critical IT services (e.g. in the case of a financial institution) can be extremely disruptive, even catastrophic. To avoid such disruption, a data centre employs an UPS together with a battery bank to ensure that smooth and uninterrupted power is supplied to the critical IT load.

Power distribution units (PDUs), which usually contain electrical transformers, are also used to smooth the alternating current (AC) power and to distribute that power to the IT equipment racks within the data centre. Within the IT equipment, AC power is subsequently converted to direct current (DC) power which is utilized by the individual IT components.

If electrical supply is lost, the UPS utilizes the batteries to provide 'ride-through' power to the critical load. The objective of providing the ride-through power is to allow time for support electrical generators (usually diesel powered) to come online until the mains power supply is restored.

Another feature of most data centre electrical power systems is the practice of having redundant paths and systems from the substation level right through to the server power supply level, thus ensuring power availability in the event of any single point failure in one of the paths. This offers another level of resilience, and in the event of a problem with one path the other will supply power to the IT infrastructure. The typical power path is illustrated in Figure 5.1.

As shown above, AC power is supplied to the main utility station and routed via switch gear to the substation supporting the data centre. Under normal operation the UPS acts as a filter smoothing the incoming AC and routing to the PDUs whilst at the same time the AC power charges the DC batteries. In an electrical outage the battery DC power is converted to AC and routed via the PDUs to the IT equipment racks until such time as the backup generators can come online to support the IT load.

Data centre electrical supply has traditionally centred on redundancy, the level of which is often described in terms of N + 1, N + 2, 2N, and so on, where N equals the required number of units required to meet the desired power capacity. Having one UPS unit supply capacity means one point of failure, and as such a combination of smaller units is typically used. For example, in a data centre requiring 800 kW one could install two 400 kW modules but if one failed 50% of capacity is lost. Installing four 200 kW units

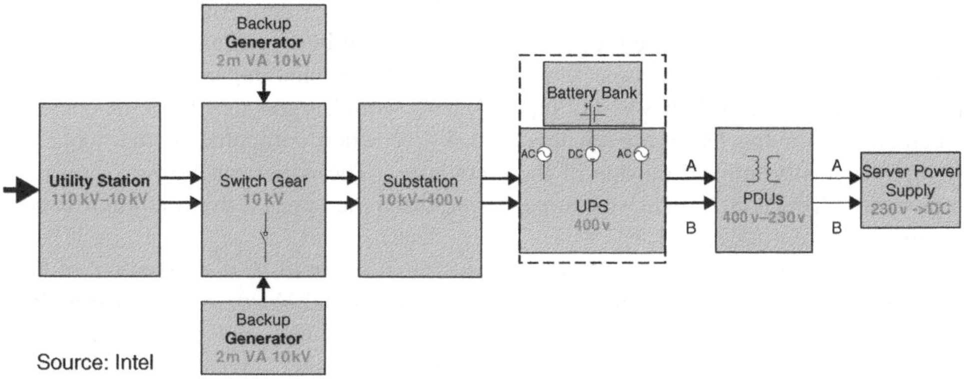

Figure 5.1 Typical dual-power path to the IT load (United Kingdom and Ireland).

would result in a more favourable 20% capacity drop should one fail. But of course a 20% drop is not tolerable when dealing with critical services. A redundant N + 1 configuration would employ five 200 kW modules, 1000 kW in total. Now if a single module were lost the required 800 kW of capacity is maintained. In this case, then, 'N' = 4 modules and the '+1' equals one additional module. N + 2 would equal 1200 kW, and in a 2N scenario an additional module would be installed for every required module: 2 × 4 modules of 200 kW each, for a total capacity of 1600 kW. The level of resilience has strong implications for energy efficiency, as does the level of load placed on the UPS. The reasoning for this is that electrical load is shared across all modules, which are less efficient at lower loading capacities.

Best practice is to utilize a reduced number of high-efficiency PDUs and a modular, high-efficiency UPS that can dynamically match capacity to IT load. It is also worth examining whether all IT loads are indeed 'critical', and moving noncritical services to mains power. In short, the challenge in any data centre is to achieve a redundancy versus energy efficiency balance that is optimal for the given business need – a task which, like IT infrastructure, is best addressed at the design phase of any facility.

5.3.1.1 AC versus DC Power

Given the inefficiency of the AC/DC/AC/DC conversion process prominent in UPS-supported data centres and the fact that IT components ultimately utilize DC power, there have been renewed calls to move data centres to a DC-based power infrastructure. The theoretical case for DC power encounters little argument as the reduced number of conversions (i.e. one), where facility supply to the data centre is AC, results in reduced conversion losses and hence greater efficiency.

Where there is contention, however, is in relation to the level of potential savings. This argument tends to centre on the misinterpretation of studies such as the 2007 LBNL lead report (Tschudi *et al.*, 2007) on 'DC Power for Improved Data Centre Efficiency (DCE)' which indicated that 'an improvement of over 28% is possible in an average data centre'. The key thing to note here is that this statement referred to 'an average data centre' (i.e. one with a legacy AC UPS system).

The study did in fact suggest DC improvement over best-in-class AC systems of 5–7%. This order of improvement is consistent with the Pratt, Kumar, and Aldridge (2007) study evaluating 400 V DC in data centres compared to existing best-in-class AC. Indeed, calls for the move to DC tend to come from the United States and Japan where the typical data centre utilizes a 480/208 V AC input. Others would argue that the efficiencies to be gained by moving DC are even less than 5–7% when compared to the 400/230 V AC input typically utilized outside of these countries. The American Power Conversion Corporation (APC, 2007, 2011) white papers on the topic suggest that the improvement is in the order of 1.25%.

Whether the percentage is 5%, 7% or even 1.25%, it is not to be dismissed out of hand as in larger data centres the savings could be quite substantial. Also, as identified by Pratt *et al.*, whilst 'delivery efficiency improvements ... alone may not justify the change by itself ... the combination of high efficiency with the other advantages ... including higher reliability, simplified implementation due to lack of phasing requirements and harmonic mitigation, and reduced components cost, makes for a compelling case in considering the adoption of facility-level . . . dc distribution'. Additionally, DC distribution is an efficient means of combining renewable energy resources (RESs) of power which are invariably DC, such as solar panels. The question remains, given these advantages why has a switch to DC not occurred en masse?

The answer is actually a historical one relating to the so-called *current wars* of the 1880s personified by the Thomas Edison versus Nikola Tesla rivalry, in which AC, posited by Tesla, became the standard due to advantages relating to long-distance distribution and safety at the consumer device level. AC's transmission advantage stems from the ease at which it can be stepped up or down using a transformer between high and low voltages. Until recently, there had been no economically viable means of doing this for DC. Why is this important? Well, the main issue when transmitting power over long distances relates to the inherent resistance of the copper wire whereby losses increase with distance. Losses are proportional to the square of current, and what that means is if voltage is doubled the level of current required to deliver the same power can be halved, thus proportionally reducing the losses. That is why power is transmitted at such high voltage: to minimize the level of current required and hence the level of losses incurred. In terms of safety at the consumer device level, AC has a typical frequency of 50 or 60 Hz which means that the voltage zeroes out 100 or 120 times a second and as such negates potential arcs. This is not the case with DC, and as such there is not the same inherent level of safety.

Of course today, high-voltage direct current (HVDC) transmission can be economically implemented, whilst safety features can be built into the appliance at the plug level. But whilst the traditional advantages of AC may no longer stack up, what we have is a historically established incumbent, whereby the capital cost to change is likely to exceed potential savings. That said, in situations where a roll-out of new infrastructure is planned, especially when taking a facilities-level view, DC can now make a viable case for implementation thus renewing the 'war of currents' debate.

5.3.2 Cooling

As stated in this chapter, from a facilities engineering perspective the IT servers and equipment are simply heat-producing 'black boxes' supported by infrastructure such as UPSs, PDUs and fan motors that themselves produce heat. The objective of cooling is to ensure that components within the IT equipment do not overheat, causing damage or degrading the performance and thus impacting service. The job at hand is, in fact, heat removal as opposed to cooling, based on the principle that heat always moves from a warm object to a cool one; however, the phrases *heat removal* and *cooling* are used interchangeably.

The most common means of cooling is by means of convection, which is the transfer of energy between an object and its environment, due to circular motion of a fluid (e.g. water) or a gas (e.g. air). Some emerging cooling solutions utilize *direct touch* – conduction – to remove heat from servers and IT equipment; however, they are not commonly used to date.

Air remains the dominant medium used to cool IT equipment at the server level, whereby the internal components of the server transfer their heat to cool air which is drawn by server fans across the devices and subsequently directed out the back of the chassis.

In the majority of data centres, server racks sit front-to-front to form cold aisles and back-to-back to form hot aisles. Typically, within these facilities one of three types of

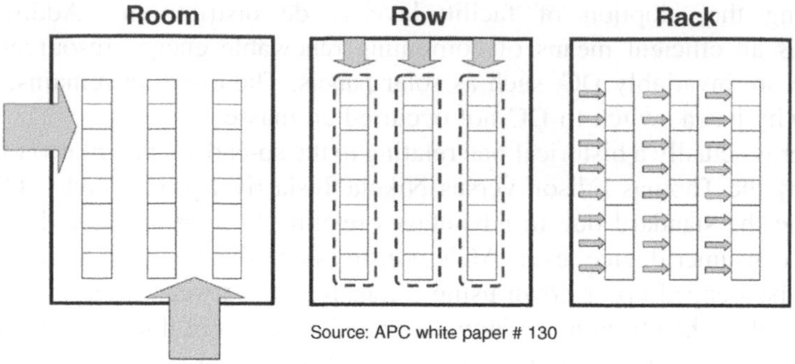

Figure 5.2 Room, row and rack level cooling.

air-based systems is utilized, all three of which employ a computer room air conditioner (CRAC) or computer room air handler (CRAH). The systems can be characterized by location and size – namely, 'room-based' large units, 'row-based' medium units or 'rack-based' small units (see Figure 5.2).

'Row-based' distribution is more efficient than 'room-based' systems, due to shortened air paths, whilst 'rack-based' systems are the most efficient given the reduced power required to move air within the confines of the rack itself. However, they are but one element of an overall cooling system.

Under usual operation, heat within the air is transferred via the CRAC or CRAH at the room, row or rack level, to a liquid medium, normally water, chilled water or glycol. This heat is subsequently transported externally and dissipated to the outside air. How efficiently this is done depends on pipe run distance, the presence or absence of a refrigeration cycle and the collective efficiency of individual components such as chillers, pumps, and so on.

Wet-side or water-side economization is one best practice employed to reduce energy consumption by minimizing reliance on costly mechanical refrigeration. In wet-side economization, the internal setup of the data centre is the same as in any typical facility, encompassing one of the three configurations discussed here. The difference occurs in the back end of the system where, for example, in a typical chilled-water system an additional condenser water loop is utilized. The return water of the chilled-water loop transfers its heat to the condenser water loop via a heat exchanger (HEX) and is ultimately dissipated to the external environment via a dry cooler or an evaporative tower.

But opportunity to feasibly utilize economization depends on the ability to operate at server inlet temperatures around 21 °C or above. This normally means that some form of cold or hot aisle containment (see Figure 5.3) needs to be deployed to prevent supply and exhaust air from mixing. The reason is that mixing requires the need to overcool supply air in order to guarantee desired inlet temperatures to servers in high rack positions. An optimal server inlet temperature allows for higher supply/return water temperatures and thus increases the useful operation of economizers.

Air-side economization, sometimes referred to as direct-free air cooling or natural cooling, represents current best practice in terms of energy-efficient heat removal and is, perhaps surprisingly, the simplest system of those employed from a mechanical perspective. In direct-free air cooling ambient outside air is drawn into the DC and across the

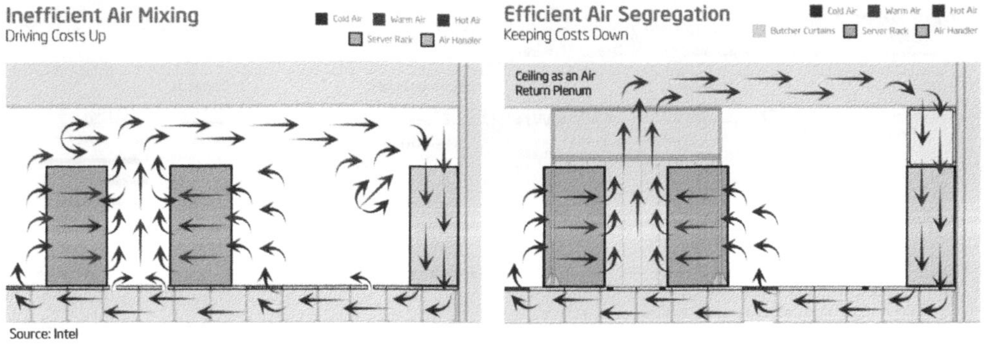

Figure 5.3 An example of air containment.

servers, with the exhaust simply directed out into the outside air. Under normal operation, fan-energy consumed in moving the air is the only cost, although refrigeration backup is usually incorporated for situations when ambient air is higher than the desired inlet temperature.

Having briefly looked at the various types of systems, it should be apparent that from an energy efficiency perspective one would ideally avoid refrigeration whilst attempting to strike an effective balance between redundancy and energy efficiency in terms of support infrastructure, specifically cooling and power systems. An important theme is to move from fixed supporting infrastructure to dynamic and best practices, and as such the use of variable frequency drives (VFDs) on pumps and fans needs to be considered along with air management and economization. As stated, the efficiency of all the individual elements that constitute the ecosystem plays a part, as does the effective management of same, and infrastructure management is a subject to which we now turn.

5.3.3 Facilities Infrastructure Management

As discussed the data centre is a complex ecosystem and in the classical management sense needs to be monitored, measured and managed effectively. Best practice is moving towards a holistic approach that spans both IT and facilities infrastructure, and as such the line between support and IT infrastructure management tools is becoming blurred. However, traditionally management has been siloed and based on fixed maximum requirement service-level-agreements (SLAs).

For effective data centre infrastructure management (DCIM), facilities' operational decision support tools and dashboards often need to integrate data from a variety of information systems such as building management systems (BMSs), facilities management systems (FMSs), security, capacity, power and even weather information systems (see the mock-up in Figure 5.4). The facilities manager needs to consider the interconnectedness of the ecosystem whilst managing to defined metrics. Data centre metrics is an important and somewhat burgeoning theme addressed specifically in Section 5.5.

With the help of DCIM tools, a data centre professional should be able to locate and visualize both static and dynamic information. This might range from viewing standard capacity information like 'What U-space, network ports and power are available?' to

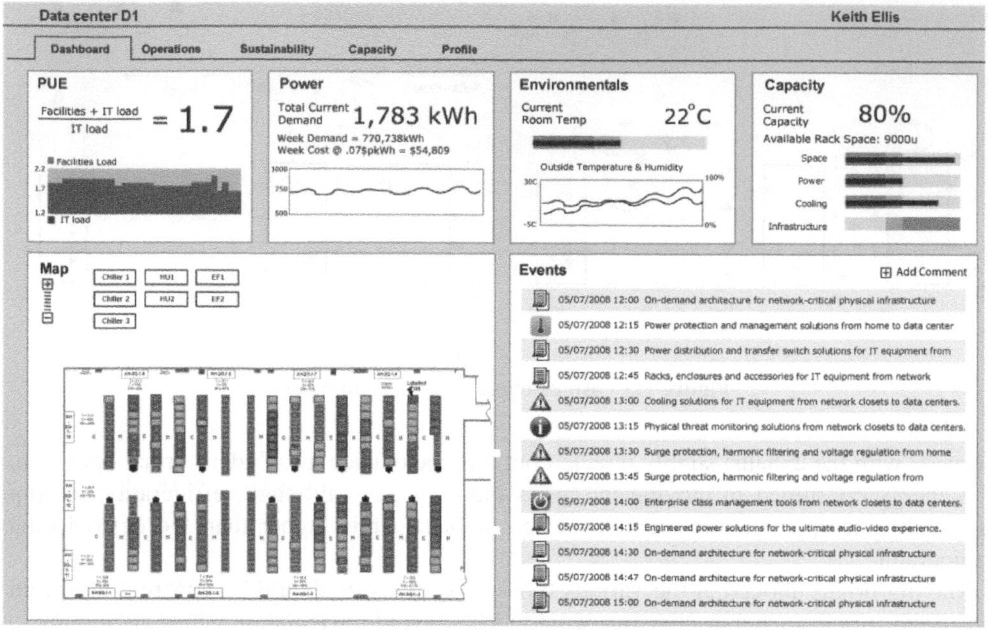

Source: Intel

Figure 5.4 A holistic data centre view using DCIM.

understanding 'What if?' scenarios like 'How will landing a new blade server affect the airflow CFM (cubic feet per minute) requirements of neighbouring servers?', 'What is the optimal landing zone for server X?' and such things. The tool should also help one to understand more traditional facilities issues like 'What is our level of chiller consumption?' and 'What level of variance exists between our different units?'

Such systems and tools require the integration of diverse information sources, and increasingly the trend is towards the integration of IT sensor information into the management of the facilities infrastructure. For example, temperature and humidity sensors within the servers themselves can be used in the logic that drives CRAC or CRAH fan speed and cooling coil position.

5.4 IT Infrastructure Management

5.4.1 Server Power

The traditional approach for data centre operators to meet SLAs has been through provisioning for peak demand, for not just daily peaks but also seasonal ones, and to top it off with a generous safety margin to allow for demand growth through the expected planning horizon of the deployed equipment. The net effect is systems that are grossly overprovisioned most of the time, with average utilization rates in the single digits. Implicit assumptions in this mode of operation are data centres with generous headroom for growth and energy costs that constitute a small fraction of the data centre's total cost of operations, which do not reflect the present-day reality. These assumptions are less likely to hold due to increasing equipment demand on the data centre infrastructure. Unfortunately, even when the situation becomes clearly unsustainable, there are perverse dynamics that tend to preserve the status quo, for instance a system of split incentives where server equipment may be under the care of an IT organization with a charter to provide the best service levels with overprovisioning as the tool of choice. Even worse, departmental boundaries may prevent sharing servers, contributing to pervasive underutilization. On the flip side, the company's energy costs may be borne by the facilities organization under a different cost centre with no say on server management policies.

5.4.1.1 Need for Server Power Management

As discussed, new applications, especially in the support of social media applications, have increased the demand for data centre services exponentially. The total energy use for powering and cooling servers in data centres has also been growing, albeit at a much smaller rate because of improved equipment and practices. Nonetheless, energy costs are getting chief information officer (CIO)–level visibility providing impetus for globally coordinated power management strategies.

In this backdrop, progress in server power and energy management technology in the past five years or so has been through improvements in CPU fabrication processes. CPU power efficiency matters from the standpoint that CPUs constitute one of the most energy-intensive components in a server. Improved CPU energy efficiency enables increased computation rates per watt expended. Another area of significant improvement has been in the area of power-proportional computing. Power-proportional computing is the ability of servers to dynamically throttle power demand in response to workload.

Server systems are most efficient when fully loaded. Based on the management practices mentioned here, servers are rarely operated to capacity – not even close. The pesky issue is a 'pay-to-play' dynamic in effect with the power-proportional computing properties of present-day servers: Even when servers are idling (i.e. delivering zero work), they are already consuming about 50% of the full load power. The situation is imposed by the state of technology, similar to that of automobiles powered with internal combustion engines consuming substantial fuel whilst idling. Electric or hybrid electric vehicles are more efficient in this respect, consuming very little fuel when the vehicle is not moving.

In principle, best outcomes take place when applications get to decide when to apply specific policies and what the trade-offs for these policies should be. If too much is applied, users are inconvenienced (i.e. the SLA is not met). Solution architects and application engineers may need to roll back the application of a power policy until trade-offs are acceptable.

In essence, this is an instance of the classic feedback mechanism. As a matter of fact, for Intel-based servers there are feedback mechanisms already in operation: Servers provisioned with Intel® Node Manager (Node Manager) technology implement a feedback loop where a server is given a consumption target. Power supplies conforming to the Power Management Bus (PMBus) have embedded sensors to measure real-time server power consumption. Firmware that runs in the management engine (ME) microcontroller embedded in the chipset can compare the actual power consumption against the consumption target and regulate the processor voltage and speed as a control mechanism until the

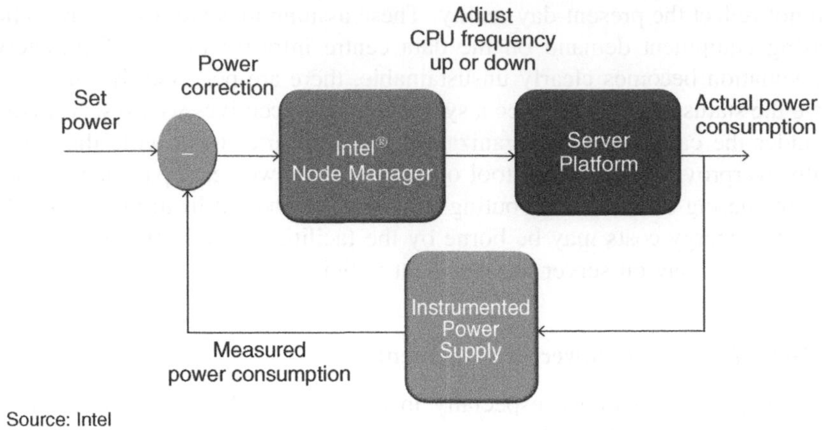

Figure 5.5 Server power management control loop.

target power consumption is attained. This mechanism is called power limiting or, more affectionately, power capping. Figure 5.5 depicts the Node Manager feedback loop. Voltage and CPU frequency are pre-set by the P-states under the Advanced Configuration and Power Interface (ACPI) standard.

In sum, this feedback control mechanism becomes really useful when it is placed under application control because it opens the opportunity to regulate the equipment profile to match workload demand whilst minimizing the inconvenience factor. Moving forward, power efficiency becomes more nuanced than having a goal of optimal efficiency only at 100% workload. Systems need to be efficient through their operating range and architected to be efficient to any target SLA. Most systems are capable of delivering beyond the SLA. To the extent that the system delivers more than what the SLA requires, the operator can reduce cost through the application of a more aggressive power policy. Conversely, the operator can't underdeliver on the SLA because that creates a liability and the possibility of customer complaints. Node Manager becomes valuable in that it allows placing power control under specific application policies.

5.4.1.2 Server Power Management in the Data Centre

Power management represents a collection of IT processes and supporting technologies geared towards optimizing data centre performance against cost and structural constraints, for instance increasing the deployable number of servers per rack when racks are subject to power or thermal limits makes power consumption more predictable and easier to plan for.

As mentioned in this chapter, server equipment represents the most energy-intensive portion in a data centre, and the server infrastructure constitutes a logical starting point for any comprehensive data centre power monitoring and control strategy. Furthermore, because of the data centre power usage effectiveness (PUE), covered in Section 5.5.1, opportunities for synergy exist between improvements in server efficiency and reduced data centre cooling requirements. For static power management, the relationship is implicit. More sophisticated dynamic schemes call for inserting data centre cooling into the control loop for additional gains.

The range of power capping attainable is a function of the server architecture. For current-generation servers, the range is in the order of 20–30% of a server's peak power consumption. The payback for the adoption of power management practices can be substantial. However, it can only happen in the context of a strategy, institutional learning and process maturity. A strategy would assume an evolution towards the deployment of increasingly sophisticated management schemes.

The first opportunities at the early stages come from the adoption of monitoring technologies. Even this level of monitoring offers low-hanging fruit opportunities, as knowing how power is allocated provides the first insight about what can be improved. Beyond the monitoring stage, a minimalist approach consists in using a power-capping capability as a guard rail to enable a tighter utilization of the available power.

The effect of these practices on application performance would be invisible to applications yet would allow data centre operators to schedule power consumption to actual power instead of less accurate estimates. These policies are applicable to traditional, nonconsolidated corporate data centres as well as newly consolidated data centres.

A more aggressive application of power capping includes the enforcement of power quotas and workload prioritization. At this point more gains become possible through further optimizations that include time-varying power caps and power policy–driven server shutdowns, whilst the highly variable nature of cloud computing brings opportunities for the application of dynamic policies not practical in traditional data centres. These more sophisticated policies are more appropriately applied to virtualized cloud data centres used to deliver cloud-computing services.

The integration of server power monitoring and control technology with sophisticated IT processes allows reduction goal setting in data centre energy consumption, not just instantaneous power reduction. Of course, it is important that this integration be interoperable across equipment providers to accommodate the diversity of equipment in the data centre.

5.4.2 Consolidation

In the remainder of the section, we present a number of usage models in a logical sequence from the simple to complex. The first three apply mostly to nonvirtualized, consolidated environments where the OS runs on bare metal. These use cases assume static capping where the level is set once and does not get changed during normal operations.

A usage model for a system is formally defined as a collection of data describing the system's usage within a stated context. The usage model data describe the interactions between the user and the system at a level that identifies the system's benefits to the user. The context for all usage models in this document is their application to virtualized cloud data centres.

The focus is on policy-based usages. A *policy* refers to a course or method for action chosen from a number of alternatives and applicable to specific conditions. Policies are preferably defined in terms meaningful to the user, not in some obscure platform-specific entities such as P-states.

For instance, *power monitoring* is to be defined in terms of server platform consumption, and the policy is to be in effect based on the time of day. A policy mechanism that provides only CPU power or is defined in terms of the processor's internal P-states would not be very useful because it requires the user to map these artefacts to units meaningful to the workload. Even if the user is willing to do this work upfront, the translation would not necessarily be consistent across implementations, leading to equally inconsistent outcomes.

Table 5.1 captures three usage models applicable to consolidated data centres. The list is not exhaustive by any measure. The usage models are ordered by increasing complexity and integration requirements as well as by the increasing number of Intel Node Manager Technology features utilized. The virtualized cloud data centre represents the most general application context.

For each scenario there are one or more use cases. The following paragraphs cover the usage scenarios in Table 5.1. Tables 5.2 and 5.3 outline one of the use cases in the right column of Table 5.1. Not all the use cases are highlighted for brevity, but all assume deployed server equipment with a power- and thermal-monitoring capability. If we go back 10–15 years, power used to be an afterthought for servers deployed in data centres. Even today, some of the old practices still persist. For this particular use case, in many facilities today the power bill still comes bundled with the facilities charge and is managed by a different group from the IT infrastructure.

Table 5.1 Consolidated data centre server power management usage models

Usage model	Benefits	Use cases
Perform real-time server power monitoring	Reduce stranded power by scheduling available data centre power to actual server power consumption	Real-time monitoring of power consumption Manage data centre hot spots Power and thermal scheduling Power trending and forecasting
Power guard rail: Impose power guard to prevent server power consuming beyond a pre-set limit	Deterministic power limit and guaranteed server power consumption ceiling	Maximize server count per rack and therefore CapEx return on investment (ROI) per available rack power when rack is under power budget with negligible per server performance impact
Static power capping: Operate servers under a permanent power-capped regime	Operate under impaired power availability conditions	Maximize per rack performance yield when rack under power budget Application power optimization Application performance compensation Business continuity: Continue the operation in the presence of power outages

Table 5.2 Manage data centre hot spots, power and thermal scheduling

Description	Shift virtual machines around in a server pool to optimize power and thermal behaviours. In a server pool operating under a power budget, optimize operating equipment to available power. Shut down selected servers in pooled applications such as front-end Web servers when called for by power limitations
Actor(s)	Data centre operators and solution architects
Event flow	Relocate workload virtual machines to optimize and rebalance power and thermal margins based on measurements Optimize the number of servers across pools whilst monitoring temperature and power consumption to check for excursions
Exceptions	Adjust the number of servers in the pool to limit power excursions
Benefits	Number of servers deployed are optimal for a given power budget across server pools

Table 5.3 Data centre power use trending and forecasting

Description	Use historical power consumption data to develop forecasting models for data centre planning
Actor(s)	Data centre operators and solution architects
Event flow	Develop statistical models, such as time series analysis autoregression and moving average (ARMA) models to map future power and energy use against available data centre power to plan for data centre remodels, expansion and migrations
Exceptions	None
Benefits	Power consumption forecast models are now based on actual power demand data

Furthermore, a large number of established data centres were not originally designed to factor in increased power densities, and are quickly reaching their load-bearing limits, both in terms of available infrastructure to power more servers and to keep the physical infrastructure from exceeding thermal limits. Yet, due to lack of visibility, data centre planners need to significantly overprovision power to provide enough of a cushion because falling short is not an option. This is not efficient use of infrastructure and capital resources. Table 5.2 briefly captures the use case for managing data centre hot spots.

Aggregation software such as Intel® Data Centre Manager can be used to keep a log of all the power readings taken in the managed system. The data establish a useful track record for the purposes of trending and forecasting in power scheduling and data centre planning.

5.4.3 *Virtualization*

The opportunities for reducing energy use using power-capping technology alone are limited. If energy reduction is to be significant, power cuts need to be deep and sustained over time. For instance, if the policy in effect is capping as a guard rail, capping seldom kicks in, if at all. Furthermore, some energy savings are possible under a permanently capped regime, but these are limited by the capping range, or by the need to remove the capping policy to optimize performance yield.

Whilst a single server has a baseline power consumption of 50% and does not allow for much algorithmic flexibility, the floor for a group of servers managed as a pool is defined by the power consumed during sleep, which is a lot less than that of an idling server.

Virtualized cloud data centres introduce additional degrees of freedom that are not available under traditional operating models where there is a hard binding between servers and the applications which they run. Cloud applications run in virtualized environments allowing the dynamic consolidation of workloads. Under these circumstances there will be a designated nucleus of highly utilized servers efficiently processing the workloads due to the high loading, thus allowing the other servers to be put into a low-energy sleep state until needed.

Policies under dynamic power management take advantage of additional degrees of freedom inherent in virtualized cloud data centres as well as the dynamic behaviours supported by advanced platform power management technologies. Power-capping levels are allowed to vary over time and become control variables by themselves. Selective equipment shutdowns enable reductions in energy consumption, not just power management. These shutdowns alter the profile and topology of the equipment, and hence we call this scheme *dynamic reconfiguration*, whilst the action of shutting down servers specifically is typically called server parking.

The trade-off for dynamic policies is additional complexity: If the capping level becomes a control variable, this means a mechanism to exert this control needs to be implemented. The applicability for the more complex cases in Section 5.6 may be narrower, requiring long-term planning and a transformation strategy. However, significant reductions in energy use, not just power use, are possible for applications amenable to this kind of treatment.

Virtualized cloud data centre environments introduce a number of operational degrees of freedom not possible in traditional data centres. Firstly, applications hosted in virtualized cloud data centres run on virtualized OSs, that is, the OS does not run on the bare metal but is mediated through a virtualization hypervisor. The practical effect is that applications are no longer bound to a physical host and can be moved around within a pool of servers to optimize the overall power and thermal performance of the pool. Secondly, the loose binding between applications and hosts allows treating a group of hosts as pooled resources, allowing optimizations as a group that were not possible with individual machines, such as powering down some equipment during low demand. Virtualized data centres make possible three more sophisticated usages as shown in Table 5.4.

5.4.3.1 Integrated Data Centre Power Management

A platform-assisted thermal management approach adds 'smarts' to cooling solutions for data centres (see the use cases outlined in Tables 5.5 and 5.6). Assume we enable

Table 5.4 Virtualized data centre power management usage models

Usage model	Benefits	Use cases
Time-varying power capping: Adjust server performance profile to workload demand	Optimize infrastructure for quality of service (QoS) to match target service-level agreement (SLA)	Match capping set points to workload Provide support for multiple service classes
Manage data centre energy consumption for time-varying workloads	Cut electricity costs	Make a dynamic reconfiguration to achieve extreme power-proportional computing
Carry out integrated data centre power	Power optimization realized across server, communications and storage	Use server sensor data to optimize cooling equipment set points

Table 5.5 Building data centre thermal maps

Description	Build a real-time spatial temperature profile using server sensors
Actor(s)	Application and solution architects
Event flow	Learning phase: Set up management application with a database containing server (x, y, z) coordinates in the data centre and to read the server inlet temperature sensors Operational phase: Perform regular scan of server inlet temperatures; record and plot
Exceptions	Management application enforces policies when hot regions are detected
Benefits	Enable real-time temperature readouts in the zone where a pool of servers is located

Table 5.6 Set CRAC temperature set points

Description	Coordinated management of ICT and data centre cooling equipment
Actor(s)	Application and solution architects; data centre operators
Event flow	Facilities management applications (i) aggregate server power consumption data and temperature inlet information across a pool of servers and (ii) adjust CRAC set points optimally
Exceptions	Distributed control and modelling algorithms is still under research
Benefits	Match server cooling demand to building cooling supply and increasing data centre efficiency

management applications to read temperature and possibly other data from instrumentation embedded in server platforms. The presence of this instrumentation effectively constitutes a vast sensor network whose potential has not been tapped to date. One possible application is to build a real-time thermal map for the server grid to complement the real-time power monitoring and control capability enabled by Intel® Node Manager.

5.5 Green Data Centre Metrics

Metrics are essential to the holistic, effective and efficient management of the data centre ecosystem, and the following section covers some of the more important metrics to consider.

5.5.1 PUE and DCiE

PUE and its reciprocal data centre infrastructure efficiency (DCiE) are metrics introduced in the February 2007 Green Grid whitepaper 'Green Grid Metrics: Describing Data Centre Power Efficiency'. In fact, in the original paper DCiE was called data centre efficiency; however, there was some confusion as to whether the metric inferred efficiency of the IT equipment, and as it does not it was changed to DCiE. This highlights a very important point in that both PUE and DCiE are metrics that give an indication as to the effective use of power by 'supporting infrastructure' only. All power directed to the IT load itself is assumed to produce 'useful work'. This, as alluded to throughout this chapter, is not an accurate assumption, but for the purpose of understanding supporting infrastructure it is irrelevant. Figure 5.6 indicates how PUE is calculated.

PUE has become the de facto metric used in data centres with respect to energy consumption. PUE is calculated by dividing total facility power (i.e. all power-consuming elements that constitute the data centre eco-system) by IT equipment power. The metric indicates how effectively or energy efficiently one is supporting the IT load. Ideally PUE would equal 1, meaning that no additional energy is consumed to support the IT load. So the lower the PUE value, the better; and conversely the higher the DCiE value, the better. For example, if total power was 200 kW and IT power was 100 kW, then PUE would be $200/100 = 2$, and for DCiE it would be $100/200 = 0.5$ or 50%. What both mean in this case is that for every 1 W supplied to the IT equipment, another 1 W is required to support it. For more information on PUE and DCiE, see the Green Grid Web site (http://www.thegreengrid.org).

Energy efficiency is but one perspective on a data centre's design and operations, resilience and security being two others. Nevertheless, the focus here is on green metrics, and in addition to PUE the Green Grid has proposed a suite of xUE metrics such as carbon usage effectiveness (CUE) and water usage effectiveness (WUE) (see Table 5.7).

Whilst these metrics are useful as recognized by the Green Grid and other organizations, the focus now needs to centre on IT load and defining 'useful work done'. As it stands, understanding the breakdown between valued services, OS overhead and idle time is an extremely arduous process and current work is shifting towards this challenge.

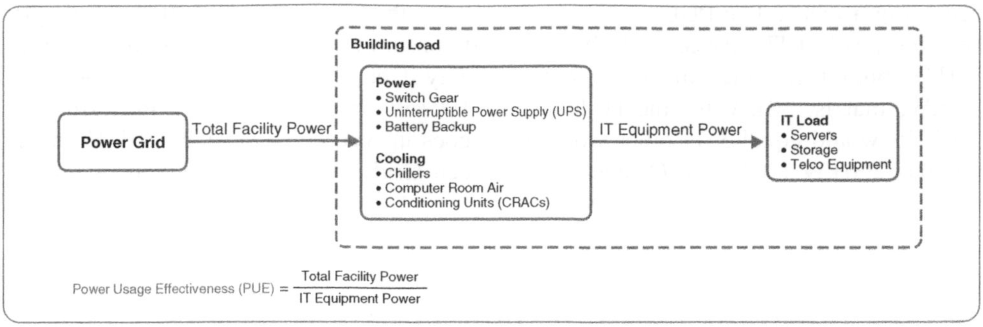

Source: Intel

Figure 5.6 Calculating PUE.

Table 5.7 The Green Grid xUE metrics

Metric acronym	Metric name	Formula or detail	Unit
PUE	Power usage effectiveness	Total data centre energy and IT equipment energy	Unit-less
CUE	Carbon usage effectiveness	CO_2 emissions caused by the total data centre energy and IT equipment energy or CEF × PUE were CEF = $kgCO_2eq/kWh$ for the grid and/or on-site generation	$kgCO_2eq/kWh$
WUE	Water usage effectiveness (site)	Annual site water usage and IT equipment energy	L/kWh
WUE_{source}	Water usage effectivencss (site + source)	(Annual source water usage + annual site water usage) / IT equipment energy	L/kWh

5.5.2 *Power versus Energy Consumption*

Whilst metrics like 'watts per square foot of work cell' (Patterson *et al.*, 2007) help us to understand power density design and infrastructure provisioning, xUE metrics help us to understand how effectively one's infrastructure and resources are used in supporting the IT equipment. However, if one is to make informed decisions regarding energy, it follows that a metric for the measurement of power and/or energy should be employed.

It might seem obvious but it is very important that data centre operators use power or energy consumption (kW and/or kW H) as their prime metrics in conjunction with metrics like PUE. If the focus is to reduce energy consumed in delivering valued IT services, then using a metric like PUE on its own may drive the wrong decision. If, for example, the same level of IT service could be delivered consuming 50 kW less than the previous 100 kW, but our facilities infrastructure was largely fixed, then our total load would equal 150 kW, that is, 50 kW for the IT load plus 100 kW for the supporting infrastructure, and PUE would equal 3, in other words PUE goes up yet we have saved 50 kW on our previous 200 kW total load. Of course, the Green Grid do not advocate a focus on any single metric and industry consensus is that a suite of metrics need to be applied in order to holistically manage the data centre.

5.6 Data Centre Management Strategies: A Case Study

The European Organization for Nuclear Research (CERN) is one of the largest and most respected scientific institutions in the world carrying out research into fundamental physics and using some of the most complex scientific instruments to study the basic constituents of matter and the universe.

5.6.1 Challenges

CERN had to improve the performance of its data centre whilst minimizing the power and energy consumption. It needs to ensure its computing platform has the highest possible throughput to process the 15 PB of data per year expected from the Large Hadron Collider (LHC) experiments and to distribute the data to be analysed worldwide. It had the capacity of 2.9 MW electrical power (not counting the power for cooling and ventilation) IT needs to ensure an optimal balance of performance and power consumption.

5.6.2 Tested Solution

The Intel® Xeon® processor 5500 series was evaluated in three flavours of varying power needs and performance levels against a series of benchmark tests.

5.6.3 Impact

- **Increased efficiency.** Tests showed that the new-generation processor delivers a 36% energy efficiency improvement over the previous generation for CERN's environment.
- **Lower power use.** By enabling the Intel Xeon processor 5500 series' simultaneous multithreading (SMT) feature, efficiency of the new platform can be boosted by up to 20%.

CERN's flagship is the LHC, a massive underground 27 km circumference particle accelerator that is used for some of the organization's groundbreaking research. CERN operates the primary computing centre (Tier 0) to store all data from the LHC experiments, to support the first event reconstruction and to distribute the data to 11 Tier 1 centres around the world, which will store a further copy of all data.

CERN openlab, a collaboration between CERN and industrial partners, supports its Worldwide LHC Computing Grid (WLCG) project by investigating various platforms to find the ideal solution for data filtering, the calibration process and data analysis, simulation and event reconstruction. The openlab team also follows technology developments closely and evaluates new promising technologies in views of enhancing the computing environment of CERN and its partners.

5.6.4 A Thorough Evaluation

When the new-generation Intel® Xeon® processor 5500 series was launched, CERN openlab was keen to assess its performance and energy-saving features. It chose to evaluate three different flavours of the processor (L5520, E5540 and X5570) with different levels of performance and cost in order to identify the most effective platform. All three types of the processor were evaluated with its SMT and Turbo modes both on and off to illustrate clearly the impact of these new features.

The evaluation units were tested based on a multiple-usage environment. First, a series of energy measurements were made using a power analyser and power-intensive benchmarks (CPUBurn[1] and LAPACK[2]) to measure electricity usage under intensive load conditions. The second stage of the testing investigated each processor model's performance credentials, using the SPEC CPU20064 benchmark suite.

It was adapted to run multithreaded on an x86 architecture using Intel's Threading Building Blocks (TBBs). Having completed these assessments, the team went on to test both the SMT and Turbo modes included in the new-generation Intel Xeon processor 5500 series. The SMT feature was found to boost the computing platform's performance by between 15% and 20%. Based on the test results, CERN openlab demonstrated that the new low-voltage Nehalem architecture (L5520) is 36% more efficient in terms of performance per watt than the best previous Intel® Xeon® processor 5400 series using a DDR2 solution.

To achieve the same performance with servers of the previous generation, 720 additional servers would be required entailing a much higher capital expenditure and energy cost over the three-year life cycle. Based on the average European electricity cost (€0.15 per kWh), we estimated the energy and cost savings: over 5.5 million kWh or €850 000 over three years (for details, see Table 5.8).

Table 5.8 Estimation of cost and energy savings

E5410-based server (200 W)	(200 W) 0.2 kW
720 systems	144 kW
Operation 24 h × 365 d	1 261 440 kWh
Plus 50% for cooling	1 892 160 kWh
Cost per year	€283 824
Total energy saving over life cycle	5 676 480 kWh
Total energy cost saving over life cycle	€851 472

[1] See CPU Burin-in: http://www.cpuburnin.com.

[2] Linear Algebra PACKage (LAPACK), a software library, contains routines for solving problems in numerical linear algebra: http://www.netlib.org/lapack/.

5.7 Conclusions

The ICT sector has a unique opportunity to enable energy efficiency improvements and carbon emission reductions in other sectors. However, if the sector is to realize its potential it must first 'walk the walk' in terms of sustainable ICT operations, products and services.

We have learnt that the pervasiveness of ICT and the ever increasing digitalization of modern life have resulted in the increased deployment of data centres, which now represent the fastest growing contributor to the overall ICT carbon footprint, and as such the 'greening' of these facilities represents a core element in the sector walking the walk.

Greening data centres require a holistic approach that measures, monitors and manages IT equipment and services together with the supporting infrastructure that maintains data centres. Energy efficiency advancement at the integrated circuit (IC) level has been mirrored by marked improvements in server, storage and network equipment efficiency, whilst innovations in software platforms and OS virtualization have resulted in the ability to modularize systems into separate servers or services at the software level, thus increasing the utilization of physical assets and with it energy efficiency.

These advancements, specifically in virtualization and service-oriented architectures, have given rise to further innovations, such as cloud computing, which makes a separation of concerns between service, platform and infrastructure. Cloud offers the potential for energy-efficient service provisioning and arguably allows for greater accessibility to data-mining and analytics capabilities which have traditionally been the bastion of large corporations.

IT technological change, of course, has implications for the growth and resource-efficient operation of data centre facilities, specifically for the supporting infrastructure that powers and cools the server, storage and network equipment. Within legacy data centres it is not atypical that for every 1 W delivered to the IT equipment, another one or more is required by the supporting infrastructure.

The correct sizing and deployment of high-efficiency UPSs and PDUs are essential to reduce both losses and inefficiencies in supplying resilient power to the critical load of the data centre. The savings to be gained by moving to DC systems is a matter of much discussion with likely gains to be in the order of 1–8%. This level of payback would perhaps not alone justify a retrofit scenario but would be significant in new-build situations.

Cooling and air movement used in cooling represent 60–80% of total support infrastructure consumption. Air is the dominate means of cooling, and best practices such as cold or hot aisle containment help to reduce energy consumption. The main energy cost associated with cooling relates to the refrigeration cycle, and best practice is to utilize some form of economization in order to reduce or eliminate its need. Where climate allows, we see a move to direct free air cooling as the most efficient means of cooling given its low electrical energy consumption and the fact that it does utilize a significant level of water.

Central to the sustainable operation of data centres is a holistic measurement, monitoring and management strategy, and DCIM-like tools assist in that regard. IT and facilities infrastructure management is crucial so as to dynamically match IT and support systems consumption and indeed to match overall consumption to valued work done. A suite of metrics are essential for measuring resource consumption and energy efficiency.

To conclude, it should be apparent that data centres are indeed complex ecosystems that require a systemic approach in ensuring effective sustainable operations, in terms of both IT and supporting infrastructure. In short, the enabling potential of ICT cannot be underestimated; the sector has a challenge and responsibility in ensuring this growth is powered by the most resource-efficient 'green' facilities possible.

Review Questions

1. What is fuelling the growth for data centre capacity?
2. Describe a high-capacity modern data centre, and compare this to a typical legacy data centre.

Discussion Questions

1. Describe the key facilities and IT components within data centres.
2. Describe the key challenges in managing data centre operations.

References

APC (2007) A Quantitative Comparison of High Efficiency AC vs. DC Power Distribution for Data Centers, White paper #127, http://www.apcmedia.com/salestools/NRAN-76TTJY_R0_EN.pdf (accessed April 2012).

APC (2011) AC vs. DC Power Distribution for Data Centers, White paper #63, http://www.apcmedia.com/salestools/SADE-5TNRLG_R6_EN.pdf (accessed April 2012).

European Commission (2008) Code of Conduct on Data Centres Energy Efficiency. http://ec.europa.eu/information_society/activities/sustainable_growth/docs/datacenter_code-conduct.pdf (accessed April 2012).

GeSI (2008) Smart 2020: Enabling the Low Carbon Economy in the Information Age, http://www.smart2020.org/_assets/files/02_Smart2020Report.pdf (accessed April 2012).

Koomey, J.G. (2007) Estimating Total Power Consumption by Servers in the U.S. and the World, http://sites.amd.com/de/Documents/svrpwrusecompletefinal.pdf (accessed April 2012).

Patterson, M.K., Costello, D.G., Grimm, P.F., *et al.* (2007) Intel White Paper 'Data Center TCO: A Comparison of High-Density and Low-Density Spaces, http://www.intel.com/technology/eep/datacenter.pdf (accessed April 2012).

Pratt, A., Kumar, P. and Aldridge, T.V. (2007) Evaluation of 400V DC Distribution in Telco and Data Centers to Improve Energy Efficiency, http://ieeexplore.ieee.org/stamp/stamp.jsp?arnumber=04448733 (accessed April 2012).

Ton, M., Fortenbery, B. and Tschudi, W. (2007) DC Power for Improved Data Center Efficiency, http://hightech.lbl.gov/documents/data_centers/dcdemofinalreportjan17-07.pdf (accessed April 2012).

US Environmental Protection Agency (2007) Report to Congress on Server and Data Center Energy Efficiency. http://www.energystar.gov/ia/partners/prod_development/downloads/EPA_Datacenter_Report_Congress_Final1.pdf (accessed April 2012).

Further Reading and Useful Web Sites

- About the Green Grid: http://www.thegreengrid.org/about-the-green-grid
- Tools: http://www.thegreengrid.org/library-and-tools.aspx
- http://www.apc.com/prod_docs/results.cfm?DocType=Trade-Off%20Tool&Query_Type=10
- http://www.intel.com/itcenter/itatintel/index.htm
- http://ivi.nuim.ie/research/dcspm.shtml
- http://www.microsoft.com/environment/greenit/

6

Green Data Storage

Pin Zhou[1] and Nagapramod Mandagere[2]
[1]Storage Systems Research, IBM Almaden Research Center, San Jose, CA, USA
[2]Storage Systems and Service Research, IBM Almaden Research Center, San Jose, CA, USA

Key Points

- Outlines energy consumption of data storage and introduces concepts of storage energy management.
- Compares power consumption characteristics of different storage solutions and media.
- Highlights different energy management techniques for hard disks.
- Describes system-level energy management schemes using RAID, power-aware data layout and hierarchical storage management (HSM).
- Examines the role of virtualization in energy management.
- Explores the energy management challenges in cloud storage.

6.1 Introduction

Data storage solutions vary widely in their complexity, configuration and size based on the nature of the data, access patterns and the importance of the data. Also, the power consumption of different data storage solutions varies widely. For instance, in high-performance computing data centres, which typically consume lots of central processing unit (CPU) resources but store less data, storage accounts for about 10% of the overall data centre energy consumption. In enterprise data centres, which typically do a mix of computation and data storage, 25% of total energy is consumed by storage systems. Although in current systems, storage power consumption seems minor when compared

Harnessing Green IT: Principles and Practices, First Edition. Edited by San Murugesan and G.R. Gangadharan.

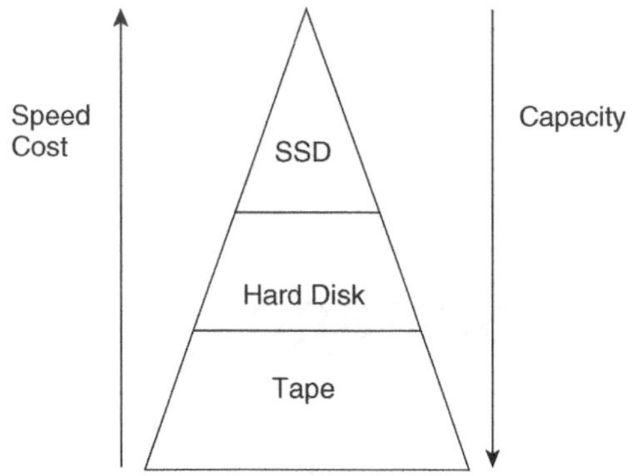

Figure 6.1 Storage media types.

to the power consumption of computing and of heating, ventilation and air conditioning (HVAC) resources, with the projected growth of data, both online and offline, storage systems are becoming more significant power consumers and contributing to greater carbon footprints. Hence there are increasing interest and need to make date storage systems greener.

Most data are typically stored in hard disk–based storage systems. However, storage solutions based on flash drives or solid-state drives (SSDs) are gaining increased traction particularly for storing frequently accessed data. Near-line or offline data are typically stored using tape-based storage systems. Figure 6.1 shows different types of storage media. The cost of storage and access speed increases from tape to SSD, whilst total storage capacity usually increases from SSD to tape. In other words, a system usually contains less faster and more expensive storage than slower and cheaper storage. Currently, massive arrays of idle disks (MAIDs) and disk virtual tape libraries (VTLs) are increasingly starting to displace tape.

Storage energy management can be classified into hard-disk energy management and system-level energy management. Among the different main storage devices – namely, hard disks, tapes and SSDs – hard disks consume more power than tapes and SSDs. Therefore, hard-disk energy management assumes greater significance in storage energy management. The main techniques for energy management of individual disks are state transitioning, caching and dynamic rotations per minute (DRPM). System-level energy management focuses on system-wide management across different or multiple components or devices. Energy management techniques for redundant array of inexpensive disks (RAID) systems, power-aware data layout such as MAID and Copan, tiered storages, virtualized storage and cloud storage fall in this category.

The chapter is organized as follows. Section 6.2 provides a background of the power characteristics of different data storage components, namely, hard drives, tapes and solid-state disks. A deep dive into energy management techniques used for one of the most prevalent media types, hard drives, is presented in Section 6.3. Specifically, we discuss state transitioning, caching and dynamic rotation control strategies. Building on these techniques, Section 6.4 discusses system-level energy management, which encompasses many of these coordinating strategies and components. We conclude the chapter with a brief summary and directions for further research in the area of storage energy management in Section 6.5.

6.2 Storage Media Power Characteristics

The operational characteristics of different devices highly influence their power consumption. In this section, firstly we describe the different operational states and their power characteristics in hard disks, followed by the characteristics of tapes and conclude by summarizing the characteristics of an emerging storage media type, SSDs.

6.2.1 *Hard Disks*

Hard disks are the most common nonvolatile storage media. A hard disk drive (HDD) contains disk platters on a rotating spindle and read-write heads floating above the platters. The read-write heads encode data magnetically. Power consumption of a hard disk in different operational (power) states can differ considerably, and energy management techniques aim to effectively exploit this feature. Power consumption of magnetic hard disks is a function of its rotational speed and the data access rate. Most power is consumed by the rotating spindle, followed by the head assembly that moves along the platters to the requested sectors or logical block addresses (LBAs) and the buffers used for queuing requests and requested data. The total power consumption (P_{total}) of a hard disk is the sum of the power consumed by the spindle motor ($P_{spindle}$), the power consumed by the head movement (P_{head}) and the power consumed by other components (P_{other}) which is relatively small, has less variation and includes the power consumed by buffers (P_{buffer}).

$$P_{total} = P_{spindle} + P_{head} + P_{other}$$

The power consumed by the spindle motor ($P_{spindle}$) is directly proportional to the square of its angular velocity (ω), that is, $P_{spindle} \propto \omega^2$. A hard disk is either rotating at its full speed or not rotating at all; therefore, $P_{spindle}$ *is power consumed at full speed* ($P_{fullspeed}$) *or zero*. The power consumed by the head movement (P_{head}) is dictated by the disk access pattern. Random access causes more head movements than sequential accesses, and thus leads to higher head power consumption.

In addition, when disks are placed in large disk array–based systems, the array controllers and enclosures consume an additional 1–2 W of power per disk.

Hard drives are in one of the following four states: active, standby, idle or sleep (Figure 6.2). These states are governed by the power states of the three main subcomponents – the spindle motor, head assembly and device electronics.

In the active state, all the three components are powered on and input–output (I/O) is serviced. The head assembly and the buffer are both on, and the spindle is rotating at its full speed. The power consumption in active mode is defined as follows: $P_{active} = P_{fullspeed} + P_{head} + P_{other}$. In this state, power consumption varies based on the degree of head movement. If read-write requests are sequential in nature, head movement is relatively minimal and hence power consumption is mainly determined by the spindle's rotational speed.

In the idle state, only the spindle motor and device electronics are on and the head typically does not consume any power in this state. The head assembly and the buffer are

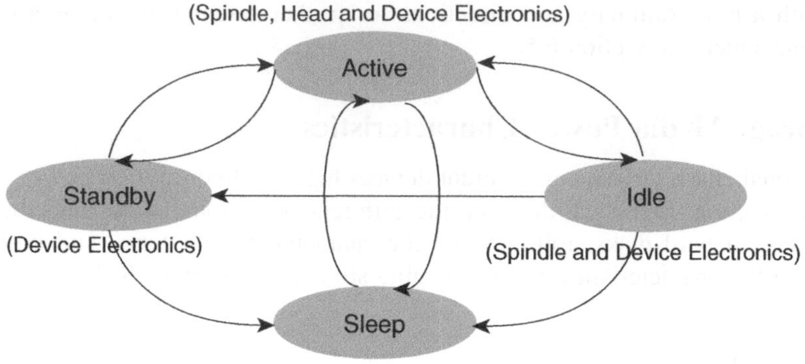

Figure 6.2 States of mechanical hard disk drives.

both on, and the spindle is rotating at full speed. However, in this state no requests are actually being serviced, and thus $P_{head} \approx 0$. Power consumed is mainly determined by the spindle's rotational speed, $P_{idle} = P_{fullspeed} + P_{other}$. Transiting between the idle and active states is instantaneous.

In the standby state, only the device electronics are on. In this state, the commands received on the interface are queued for servicing. The spindle is at rest ($P_{spindle} = 0$), but the buffers are on which facilitates queuing of new requests, and the disk is still able to respond to diagnostic queries by the controlling system. Power consumed in this state, $P_{standby} = P_{other}$, is very little compared to the active or idle state. The main disadvantage, however, is the transitioning from standby to idle or active takes a long time, typically about 8–10 seconds to get the spindle running at its specified speed.

In the sleep state, all components are off and hence any requests will result in IO timeouts or errors. Important to note here is the difference in transitioning times between different states and the power consumed for the transition. Switching from the standby to active state involves restarting the spindle motor and hence is on the order of seconds, typically about 8–10 seconds. Further, peak current during the transition is significantly higher than during steady-state usage.

State transitioning (a process of transitioning a hard disk to different operational states based on its access pattern or idle period) is a commonly used technique for storage energy management. To increase the idle periods, which are required for state transitioning to work well, disk accesses are minimized by caching.

Hard disks can be accessed by the host system via different types of bus. Based on the bus type, hard disks can be categorized into advanced technology attachment (ATA), also called integrated drive electronics (IDE), serial advanced technology attachment (SATA), small computer system interface (SCSI), serial attached SCSI (SAS) and fibre channel (FC). Each of these hard drive categories has different power characteristics as they have different hardware and operational profiles, such as their type of magnetic material used, number of platters, amount of buffering and rotational speed. For instance, SCSI, SAS and FC drives are typically targeted at enterprise computing and hence have high rotational speeds leading to higher active or idle power consumptions as compared to ATA, IDE and SATA drives.

6.2.2 Magnetic Tapes

Magnetic tape is another medium for data storage. It is made of a thin magnetic coating on a long, narrow strip of plastic. To store data on magnetic tapes, a tape drive uses a motor to wind the magnetic tape from one end to another and through tape heads to read, write and erase the data.

Magnetic tape is still a major data storage medium especially in some industries such as radio and TV broadcasting because of its very low storage-per-bit cost compared to that of hard disks. Although its areal density is lower than the density of disks, the capacity of tape is still very high (i.e. similar to disks) due to its larger amount of surface area compared to disk surface. The large capacity and cost advantage makes magnetic tapes a viable alternative, particularly for backup and archiving.

Further, the average energy consumption of tape drive is much less compared to a hard drive as it consumes power only when it reads or writes. Power consumption in the idle or retention state is zero. The cost of maintaining a tape library, which can be amortized over thousands of tape cartridges, is negligible.

6.2.3 Solid-State Drives (SSDs)

Recently, SSDs have gained increased adoption due to their better performance potential and higher power efficiency. Unlike electromechanical HDDs which contain spinning disks and movable heads, a SSD uses solid-state memory (i.e. nonvolatile memory) to store persistent data and has no moving parts. Hence, compared to HDDs, SSDs have lower access time and power consumption.

Today's SSDs use nonvolatile *not AND* (NAND) flash memory. There are two types of flash memory: multilevel cell (MLC) and single-level cell (SLC) flash memory. SLCs store a single bit in a single memory cell, whereas MLCs store multiple bits in a single cell by allowing each cell to store multiple electrical states. For example, a four-level MLC stores 2 bits in a single memory cell. Typically, MLCs are cheaper and have greater storage density, but are slower than SLCs.

SSD has rapidly increased in popularity as the primary data storage medium for mobile devices, such as phones, digital cameras and sensor devices, notebook computers and tablets. Its features include small size, low weight, low power consumption, high shock resistance and fast read performance. SSD has also started to penetrate the markets from laptops and PCs to enterprise-class server domains. Enterprise-class SSDs provide unique opportunities to boost I/O-intensive applications' performance in data centres. Compared to hard disks, SSDs are very attractive for the high-end servers of data centres due to their faster read performance, lower cooling cost and higher power savings. SSDs have the lowest power consumption rate of active devices when compared with both dynamic random-access memory (DRAM) and hard disks. For example, the power consumption for a 128 GB SSD is about 2 W, that of a 1 GB DRAM dual in-line memory module (DIMM) module is 5 W, and for a 15 000 RPM, 300 GB (7200 RPM, 750 GB) hard drive, it is around 17.5 W (12.6 W). This efficiency can mainly be attributed to the nonmechanical nature of these devices.

Data in SSD is read or written in units of pages. The read time for a page in SSD is about 20 times faster than a page read from hard disks. Unlike hard disks, there are no differences in terms of time between random reads and sequential reads. SSD is best suited for caching data between memory and hard disks since the hard disks still hold the advantage of cost and storage capacity. However, the relatively low write performance and longevity problems of SSD require new and innovative solutions to fully incorporate SSDs into the high-end servers of data centres. Unlike conventional disks, where read and write operations exhibit symmetric speed, in non-enterprise SSDs, the write operation is substantially slower than the read operation. This asymmetry arises because flash memory does not allow overwrite and write operations in a flash memory must be preceded by an erase operation to a block. Typically a block spans 64–128 pages, and live pages from a block need to be moved to new pages before the erase can be done. Furthermore, a flash memory block can be erased only a limited number of times. The slow write performance of non-enterprise SSDs and the wear-out issues are the two major concerns. Existing approaches to overcome these problems through modified flash translation layer (FTL) are effective for sequential write patterns; however, random write patterns are still very challenging.

6.3 Energy Management Techniques for Hard Disks

To reduce the energy consumption of hard disks, different techniques and methodologies are being adopted. Three commonly used energy management techniques for hard disks are state transitioning, caching and dynamic RPM.

6.3.1 State Transitioning

Given that in a hard disk, the spindle motor consumes most of the power, state-transitioning techniques try to turn off the spindle motor or keep it in standby mode during idle periods. The disk transitions to standby or off mode if there is no request to be served. If the disk idle period is not long enough, the time overhead of *spin down* and *spin up* can affect the disk response time significantly. Moreover, the power consumed by transitioning itself might exceed the power saving gained from a low-power state during the short idle period. If the disk is already idled for the threshold time, it transitions to standby mode. If it stays in standby mode for another threshold of time without requests, it can further transition to off mode. In this approach, the historical information is used to predict the future access pattern. Different variations on access prediction are based on historical information. Most on-going research and development in state transitioning revolve around idle period prediction and minimizing the performance impact of these transitions on disk responsiveness (as the transition time is usually around 8–10 seconds). Some state-transitioning techniques provide a performance guarantee (for details, see Li *et al.*, 2004).

6.3.2 Caching

In order to speed up access for both read and write requests, enterprise storage solutions typically have huge amounts of cache in conjunction with regular disks. Further, to make use of the cache to aid in disk power management, various techniques are recommended.

These cache management techniques or algorithms aim to minimize disk power usage, either by minimizing disk access or by increasing the length of idle periods.

One could in effect use huge caches to increase the idle periods of disks and in doing so can help more disks to transition to the sleep state, thereby improving energy efficiency. The cache management algorithms partition-aware least recently used (PALRU) (Zhu *et al.*, 2004) and partition-based LRU (PBLRU) (Zhu, Shankar, and Zhou, 2004) are centred on this idea. PALRU classifies all disks based on access patterns into two classes – priority (disks with fewer cold misses and longer idle times) and regular – and maintains two separate LRU queues. At the time of an eviction decision, first the regular queue elements are chosen as victims. If the regular queue is empty, the algorithm chooses elements from the priority queue. PBLRU, however, differentiates between disks by dynamically varying the number of allocated cache blocks per disk. It divides the cache into multiple partitions (one per disk) and adjusts the size of these partitions periodically based on workload characteristics. The simulation results with online transaction processing (OLTP) traces show that PALRU consumes 14–16% less energy and PBLRU consumes 11–13% less energy than traditional LRU. On the other hand, for the Cello96 trace (file system trace), PALRU saves less than 1% energy over LRU whilst PBLRU is 7.6–7.7% more energy efficient than LRU.

Since write requests in enterprise storage devices almost never get written directly to target disks (they are cached instead), another technique is to use write offloading as a mechanism to conserve disk power usage (for details, see Narayanan, Donnelly, and Rowstron, 2008). Write offloading facilitates complete spin downs of volumes periodically, thereby aiding in significant power savings. By using write offloading, about 45–60% energy savings can be achieved in write-dominated application environments.

6.3.3 Dynamic RPM

Dynamic RPM in which the rotation speed of a hard disk is varied based on workload is another technique for hard disk energy management. It assumes availability of multispeed hard disks, and power consumption increases with the speed of rotation.

In dynamic RPM, the rotational speed of the disk is altered based on the desired response time of disks and the performance requirement. A fast response time that is greater than the specified or expected threshold is a waste of performance. The idea here is to limit this wastage of performance by switching the rotational velocity of the disk to a lower value that still yields acceptable performance. Practical implementation of this approach is limited by the feasibility of developing a single disk that can change speeds in a cost-effective manner, but simulation results reveal that a dynamic RPM scheme can yield a power savings of up to 60%.

6.4 System-Level Energy Management

Storage systems' energy consumption could be managed effectively at the system level taking into consideration media type, data characteristics, data access patterns and overall system operation. Common techniques for managing energy consumption at the system level include RAID with power awareness, power-aware data layout, HSM, storage virtualization and cloud storage.

6.4.1 RAID with Power Awareness

Redundancy is a key feature of most enterprise storage solutions. Mechanisms like RAID play a key role in providing different levels of redundancy. In such systems, scheduling redundancy-related operations could be exploited for power management.

Energy-efficient redundant and inexpensive disk array (EERAID) is a RAID engine aimed at minimizing the energy consumption of RAID disks by adaptively scheduling requests to various disks that form the RAID group (Wang, Zhu, and Li, 2008). Specifically, by controlling the mapping of logical requests to a RAID stripe, the disk idle period of a subset of disks is maximized facilitating the spin down of these disks. For RAID 1, a windowed round-robin scheduler that dispatches a window of requests to one RAID disk before switching to the other RAID disks – and vice versa – can be used. For RAID 5, a transformable read scan be used. The main idea is that for a read request of a stripe that is currently on spun down disk, the stripe is reconstructed using other data blocks and parity blocks. Further, a power-aware de-stage algorithm is proposed to accommodate write requests in the design of EERAID.

Power-aware redundant array of inexpensive disks (PARAID) (Weddle *et al.*, 2007) dynamically varies the number of powered-on disks to satisfy this varying load. In addition, to tackle the problem of high penalties due to requests for data on spun down disks, PARAID maintains a skewed data layout. Specifically, free space on active and idle disks is used to store redundant copies of data that are present on spun down disks. A gear is characterized by a number of active and idle disks, and a gear upshift amounts to an increasing number of powered-on disks to cope with increased performance demand and similarly a gear downshift amounts to spinning down additional drives in response to a reduction in system load. The prototype built on a Linux software RAID driver shows a power savings of about 34% as compared to a power-unaware RAID 5.

Hibernator is a disk array design for optimizing storage power consumption (Zhu *et al.*, 2005). It assumes the availability of multispeed disks and tries to dynamically create and maintain multiple layers of disks, each at a different rotational speed. Based on performance, the number of disks in each layer and the speed of the disks themselves are adjusted. A disk speed determination algorithm and efficient mechanisms for exchange of data between various layers are used. Based on trace-driven simulations, an energy savings of about 65% for file system–based workloads can be realized (Zhu *et al.*, 2005). An emulated system with a DB2 transaction-processing engine showed an energy savings of about 29%.

6.4.2 Power-Aware Data Layout

Controlling disk access by optimizing data layouts is another way of skewing a disk access pattern (i.e. changing a disk's idle periods). The technique called popular data concentration (PDC) works by classifying the data based on file popularity and then migrating the most popular files to a subset of disks, thereby increasing the idle periods of the remaining disks (Pinheiro and Bianchini, 2004). Maximizing idle time helps in making more transitions to standby state, and hence more power can be conserved. One limitation of this approach is that access of unpopular files could potentially involve turning on or spinning up a disk, which could typically take about 8–12 seconds before actual data access can be made.

MAID is another technique that involves data migration (Colarelli and Grunwald, 2002). Unlike PDC, MAID tries to copy files based on their temporal locality. MAID uses a small subset of disks as dedicated cache disks and uses traditional methods to exploit temporal locality. The remaining disks are turned on on-demand. However, this scheme also suffers from the fact that files that have not been accessed in the recent past could potentially have a retrieval time totalling tens of seconds. Due to this high performance penalty, MAID is more suited for disk-based archival or backup solutions. Copan Systems' archival data storage systems use this technique and outperform traditional archival and backup products in terms of both performance and power consumption.

The limitation of applicability of MAID to online storage systems can be overcome by the technique called GreenStore (Mandagere, Diehl and Du, 2007) which uses application-generated hints to better manage the MAID cache. Cache misses are minimized by making use of application hints, thereby making this solution more suitable for online environments. This opportunistic scheme for application hint scheduling consumes up to 40% less energy compared to traditional non-MAID storage solutions, whereas the use of standard schemes for scheduling application hints on typical MAID systems is able to achieve energy savings of only about 25% compared to non-MAID storage.

6.4.3 Hierarchical Storage Management

HSM, also called tiered storage, is a way to manage data layout, and is widely used in industry. It is implemented in storage systems by IBM, VERITAS, Sun, EMC, Quantum, CommVault and others. In HSM, data are migrated between different storage tiers based on data access patterns. Different storage tiers have significant differences in one or more attributes – namely, price, performance, capacity, power and function. HSM monitors the access pattern of the data, predicts the future usage pattern of the data, stores the bulk of cold data on slower devices (e.g. tapes) and copies the data to faster devices (hard disks) when the data become hot. The faster devices act as the caches of slower devices. HSM is typically transparent to the user, and the user does not need to know where the data are stored and how to get the data.

One example of two-stage HSM is that frequently accessed data are stored on hard disks and rarely accessed data are stored on tapes. Data are migrated to a tape if they are not accessed for a threshold of time, and are moved back to a hard disk again upon access. The data movement is automatic without the user's intervention.

The FC disks, SATA disks and tapes can form a three-stage HSM. If the data become cold (i.e. they are not accessed for a period of time), it will first be migrated from high-speed and high-cost FC disks to lower-speed but lower-cost SATA drives, and will finally be moved from SATA disks to tapes that are even much slower and cheaper than SATA if the data are not used for a longer period of time.

Moving data from hard disks to tapes, or from FC disks to SATA disks and then to tapes, can not only reduce the storage costs but also reduce the power consumption of the storage system by storing rarely accessed data to low-power devices.

An emerging trend is the integration of SSDs into the storage hierarchy. In HSM consisting of SSDs and disks, hard disk power management techniques like state transitioning can also be integrated for power saving. Specifically, by using the SSD tier above the hard disk tier as a layer of large cache, hard disk idle periods can be extended and access to disks can be optimized. If an SSD can be used for caching the most frequently accessed files and the first portion of all the other files, the hard disks can be put into standby mode most of the time to save energy. The most frequently accessed data will be accessed from SSD. This will provide not only better energy saving but also faster access time. When a file stored on hard disk is accessed, the first portion of the data can be accessed from SSD. This will buy some time for the hard disk to spin up from standby into active mode.

6.4.4 *Storage Virtualization*

Storage virtualization is another key strategy for reducing storage power consumption. With storage virtualization, access to storage can be consolidated into fewer number of physical storage devices, which reduces storage hardware costs as well as energy costs. Moreover, those devices will have less idle periods due to workload consolidation, which greatly improves the energy efficiency of storage systems.

Storage virtualization is commonly used in data centre storage and for managing multiple network storage devices, especially in a storage area network (SAN). It creates a layer of abstraction or logical storage between the hosts and the physical storage devices, so that the management of storage systems becomes easier and more flexible by disguising storage systems' actual complexity and heterogeneous structure. Logical storage is created from the storage pools, which are the aggregation of physical storage devices. The virtualization process is transparent to the user. It presents a logical space to the user and handles the mapping between the physical devices and the logical space. The mapping information is usually stored in a mapping table as metadata. Upon an I/O request, these metadata will be retrieved to convert the logical address to the physical disk location. Figure 6.3 illustrates an example of storage virtualization.

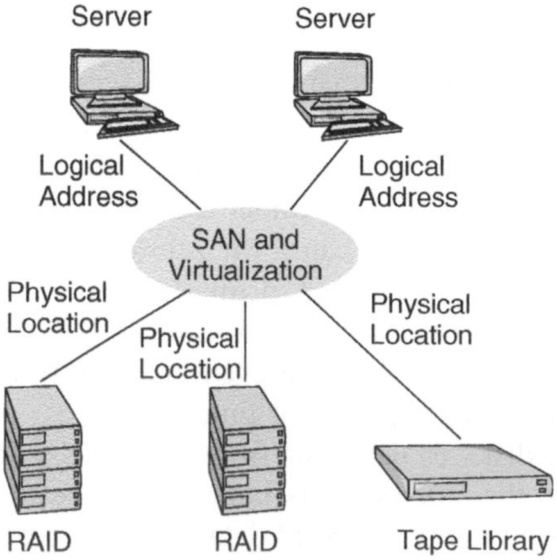

Figure 6.3 Storage virtualization.

Virtualization makes management easier by presenting to the user a single monolithic logical device from a central console, instead of multiple devices that may be heterogeneous and scattered over a network. It enables non-disruptive online data migration by hiding the actual storage location from the host. Changing the physical location of data can be done concurrently with on-going I/O requests.

Virtualization also increases storage utilization by allowing multiple hosts to share a single storage device, and by data migration. The improved utilization results in a reduction of physical storage devices, and fewer devices usually mean less power consumption. Furthermore, since more workloads go to a single device due to the improved utilization, each device becomes more energy efficient due to less and shorter idle periods.

6.4.5 Cloud Storage

As shown in Figure 6.4, *cloud storage* refers to online storage generally offered by third parties, instead of storing data to the local storage devices. Those third parties, or hosting parties, usually host multiple data servers (storages) which form the data centres. The user stores or accesses data to or from the data servers using the Internet through a Web-based interface and will pay the cloud storage provider for the storage capacity that he or she uses. In general, the fee charged by the service providers is much less than the costs of maintaining local storage for most individual users, small and medium-size companies and even enterprises.

IT and energy costs are reduced because the user does not need to buy and manage his or her own local physical storage devices, perform storage maintenance like replication and backup, prevent over-provisioning, worry about running out of storage space and so on. All of these complex and tedious tasks are offloaded to the cloud storage provider. The convenience, flexibility and ease of management provided by cloud storage, as well as the affordable costs, make cloud storage very attractive and increasingly popular.

Cloud storage relieves local IT administrators from complex storage power management tasks by offloading them to the cloud service provider. The service provider can use sophisticated techniques for minimizing power consumption by storage systems. For example, with a large data footprint, a large amount of storage devices and different workloads from different users, the service provider can lay out the data in a power-aware way or organize the data using HSM. The provider can also use storage virtualization to consolidate the workloads from different users to a single storage device to improve storage

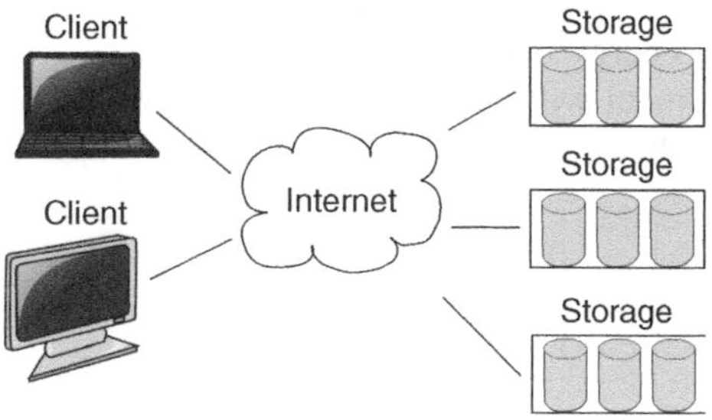

Figure 6.4 Cloud storage.

efficiency and reduce the device's idle time. The concept of cloud storage provides great opportunities for improving storage efficiency and forming greener storage compared to traditional local storage, although security and reliability are still major issues.

6.5 Summary and Research Areas

In summary, storage systems use different media types – hard disks, tapes and solid-state drives – and each medium has very different power and performance characteristics. Storage system energy management can be done at the disk level and/or at the system level. Common disk-level energy management techniques are state transitioning, caching and dynamic RPM. Techniques for system-level energy management are RAID with power awareness, power-aware data layout, HSM, storage virtualization and cloud storage.

As part of future study on energy management in storage systems, it may be worthwhile to examine how to collect and utilize semantic information or hints from higher layers of computer systems, such as applications, for better energy management. Another challenging area of study could be optimizing a whole system's energy consumption instead of only the storage system's energy consumption, as this would require a sophisticated understanding of interaction among different subsystems in terms of energy consumption.

Review Questions

1. Why is there an increasing need for green data storage?
2. What are the different power states of a hard disk?
3. Describe common energy management techniques for hard disks.
4. What are the major system-level energy management schemes? Briefly describe and compare them.

Discussion Questions

1. Discuss the use of semantic information or hints from higher layers (such as applications) for better energy management.
2. How can we guarantee performance while saving energy? For example, when using state transitioning, how can one ensure that the disk will be brought up to an active state shortly before it is accessed?
3. Describe the grouping of data based on access characteristics (such as hot data and cold data) to facilitate energy management.
4. In cloud or an environment with multiple replicas, how can we selectively shut down the power for some replicas to reduce the energy consumption without sacrificing the reliability?

References

Colarelli, D. and Grunwald, D. (2002) Massive arrays of idle disks for storage archives. Paper presented at the 2002 ACM/IEEE Conference on Supercomputing, Los Alamitos, CA, November.

Li, X., Li, Z., David, F. *et al.* (2004) Performance directed energy management for main memory and disks. Paper presented at the 11th International Conference on Architectural Support for Programming Languages and Operating Systems, Boston, MA, October.

Mandagere, N., Diehl, J. and Du, D. (2007) GreenStore: Application-aided energy-efficient storage. Paper presented at the 24th IEEE Conference on Mass Storage Systems and Technologies, Washington, DC, September.

Narayanan, D., Donnelly, A. and Rowstron, A. (2008) Write off-loading: Practical power management for enterprise storage. Paper presented at the 6th USENIX Conference on File and Storage Technologies, San Jose, CA.

Pinheiro, E. and Bianchini, R. (2004) Energy conservation techniques for disk array-based servers. Paper presented at the 18th International Conference on Supercomputing, New York, November.

Wang, J., Zhu, H. and Li, D. (2008) ERAID: Conserving energy in conventional disk-based raid system. *IEEE Transactions on Computers*, **57** (3), 359–374.

Weddle, C., Oldham, M., Qian, J. *et al.* (2007) PARAID: A gear-shifting power-aware raid. Paper presented at the 5th USENIX Conference on File and Storage Technologies, Berkeley, CA, February.

Zhu, Q., Chen, Z., Tan, L. *et al.* (2005) Hibernator: Helping disk arrays sleep through the winter. *SIGOPS-Operating Systems Review*, **39** (5), 177–190.

Zhu, Q., David, F.M., Devaraj, C.F. *et al.* (2004) Reducing energy consumption of disk storage using power-aware cache management. Paper presented at the 10th International Symposium on High Performance Computer Architecture, Washington, DC, February.

Zhu, Q., Shankar, A. and Zhou, Y. (2004) PB-LRU: A self-tuning power aware storage cache replacement algorithm for conserving disk energy. Paper presented at the 18th Annual International Conference on Supercomputing, New York, June.

7

Green Networks and Communications

Cathryn Peoples, Gerard Parr, Sally McClean and Philip Morrow
School of Computing and Information Engineering, University of Ulster, Coleraine Campus, Coleraine, UK

Key Points

- Presents the drivers and benefits of energy-efficient computer networks and communications.
- Describes energy-efficient networking solutions from the perspective of reduced carbon cost (e.g. of data centres) and improved operational sustainability (e.g. of wireless mobile devices).
- Outlines energy-efficient networking objectives of green protocols and proposed green management strategies.
- Evaluates the bit count associated with traditional network protocols.
- Presents exemplar context data required for management systems with green objectives across domains.
- Discusses, with case studies, the contrasting energy-efficient networking requirements of the United Kingdom and India.

7.1 Introduction

Roll-out of the Internet of Things and increase in the range of applications supported online have resulted in demands on network capacity which are greater than before. More than 70% of people with broadband at home in the United Kingdom describe it as essential, and a typical consumer there spends nearly half of his or her time whilst awake using telecommunications products and services (Department for Culture, 2009). This growth can be attributed to application tailoring to meet user needs, high levels of

Harnessing Green IT: Principles and Practices, First Edition. Edited by San Murugesan and G.R. Gangadharan.

quality of service (QoS) and the affordability of broadband services. Continued expansion of the telecommunications market worldwide has, however, attracted concern over future network success if services continue to be provided in the current manner. 'Success' in this respect refers to a nonnegative impact on the environment, continued market penetration through sustained affordability for end users and operators, and maintained levels of QoS. Already, however, there are indications of negative impact on the environment from increasing telecommunications use, reduced affordability through rising electricity cost, and potentially reduced levels of QoS through change in the devices on which applications are run and the nature of service provision. In terms of the environmental consequences, the IT industry in 2009 was attributed to be responsible for approximately 10% of global electric power consumption (Phippa, 2009). In 2007, the information and computer technology (ICT) sector was estimated to be responsible for 2–3% of global carbon emissions (The Climate Group, 2008).[1] Whilst negative environmental impacts alone are unlikely to be the limiting force on network roll-out in the future, there are social and government-enforced obligations to prevent further damage to the environment. Optimizing the efficiency of IT operational strategies has therefore become a priority to halt further damage to the environment and the reputation of the Internet. There is therefore a growing need for green networking and communications.

7.1.1 Green Network Communications and Management: Background

The IT industry has been criticized for its contribution to carbon emissions and failure to respond to negative impact on the climate (Phippa, 2009). Efforts have therefore been made on this front, and IT energy efficiency is now of high priority as evidenced through the publication of documents such as *Smart 2020: Enabling the Low Carbon Economy in the Information Age* (The Climate Group, 2008) and *Digital Britain* (Department for Culture, 2009). Reduction in carbon emissions will occur as a result of government regulations and schemes. For instance, in the United Kingdom the Climate Change Act 2008 (Department of Energy and Climate Change, 2008), UK Low Carbon Transition Plan (HM Government, 2009), Carbon Reduction Commitment (CRC) Energy Efficiency Scheme 2010 (Department of Energy and Climate Change, 2010) and Climate Change Levy (HM Revenue and Customs, 2011) are in force. In India,[2] similar schemes, such as the Energy Conservation Act 2001 (Ministry of Power, Government of India, 2011), are enforced by the Bureau of Energy Efficiency. Overall, the objective of these schemes is to minimize carbon emissions associated with all aspects of life. These schemes however, are not specific to the development or use of energy-efficient IT, and for the time being, the way in which network efficiency is achieved is an independent venture and not even the responsibility of telecom regulators.

---

[1] Whilst this includes operation of hardware and does not necessarily refer only to network communications (the focus of this chapter), this estimation is important to reinforce the importance of improving the operational efficiency of all elements associated with the communication process, from the client device, through the access–metro–core–metro–access network, to the destination.

[2] The background to the drive for energy-efficient networking is explored from UK and Indian perspectives given the authors' involvement with the India-UK Advanced Technology Centre of Excellence in Next Generation Networks, Systems and Services at the University of Ulster.

The International Telecommunication Union Telecommunication Standardisation Sector (ITU-T) standardizes telecommunications operation on an international basis to build a fair and competitive environment. The UK telecommunications industry is regulated by the Office of Communications (Ofcom) which oversees operation to ensure fairness to customers by promoting competition, protecting against offensive material, governing licensing procedures, researching the market and addressing complaints in accordance with the ITU-T's requirements. In working towards the achievement of green IT, it released the report *NGNs and Energy Efficiency* in 2008 which recognizes the negative contributions of next-generation networks (NGNs) on climate change and examines the efficiency of telecommunications networks and applications (International Telecommunication Union, 2008). The ITU-T has defined *Principles for the Management of Next Generation Networks* (International Telecommunication Union Telecommunication Standardisation Sector, 2006), a key objective of which is to increase networks' autonomy to optimize performance in response to real-time dynamics and trends. Whilst reduction of communication carbon cost is not defined explicitly as an ITU-T management principle, it is implied in the specification of the need to meet next-generation networking requirements by delivering services to, 'any place, any time and on any device, through any customer-chosen access mechanism', and assisting network operators and service providers to 'conduct their business efficiently' (International Telecommunication Union Telecommunication Standardisation Sector, 2006). Solutions should subsequently be energy efficient by default in the future to meet this requirement in accordance with ITU-T objectives.

The Telecom Regulatory Authority of India (TRAI) is responsible for regulating operation of telecommunications networks in India. Sustainable services are a particular requirement of Indian networks, with the increasing roll-out of wireless technology in regions which are remote and have harsh terrain. Sustainability relates to energy efficiency: The financial cost to use network services for a population with lower disposable income will be less expensive if the number of bits associated with each transmission are reduced, and operators can provide lower cost services with reduced consumption of network resources.

7.1.2 The Challenge of Next-Generation Networks

NGNs pose a challenge in the provision of energy-efficient solutions given their transportation of data with a range of QoS requirements and tolerance of lower than optimum services. Applications which may be transmitted across NGNs include:

1. those with real-time interactivity requirements and ability to accommodate slight loss (e.g. voice);
2. those with real-time interactive requirements and inability to cope with loss (e.g. online multiplayer games);
3. those without real-time requirements but which cannot cope with any loss (e.g. file transfer) and
4. those without real-time requirements and with ability to cope with slight loss (e.g. video download).

Energy-efficient communication capabilities therefore need to support these varying QoS requirements. Furthermore, NGNs use a number of carrier types to support the diverse range of applications, with traffic potentially traversing multiple technologies on the path between source and destination. A transmission between communicating end points may, for example, travel between nodes connected using wired links in the data centre or network core or across wireless links to a mobile device. QoS therefore needs to be supported in and redefined for environments with different levels of ability to support application requirements.

These characteristics of NGNs drive the way in which energy-efficient networking solutions should be provisioned – where network intelligence occurs autonomously in response to real-time dynamics, context should be collected to drive the energy efficiency process and assert appropriate actions for each network type and in response to the nature and requirements of the transmission being sent. Next-generation green-networking solutions therefore need to take into account the characteristics of client devices, networks and applications, the configurations possible for each, the level of service commonly achieved across each network portion and the ability to support application QoS requirements to optimize efficiency of operation, level of service achieved and diversity of solutions applied.

7.1.3 Benefits of Energy-Efficient Networks

Energy efficiency strategies are subsequently being developed for use in NGNs, and energy constraints and efficiency objectives of telecommunications operations influence the management strategies deployed. When power saving is applied in a notebook computer, for example, the display screen backlight dims as part of a battery conservation technique. In contrast, when power saving is applied in a wireless sensor network, an intermediary node may have functionality to 'shut down' so that only limited probe packets are distributed to determine its need to 'awaken' and become partially or fully functional. A selection of domains, illustrated in Figure 7.1, for which energy efficiency is a limiting force on operational ability (e.g. delay-tolerant networks), from which environmental concerns though the volume of emissions arise (e.g. data centres) and for which intelligent energy management (EMAN) is important (e.g. mobile devices), are considered by the authors in the provision of green-networking solutions. In the case of smart homes, for example, intelligent EMAN is becoming important due to the desire for 'always-available' services and ranges of devices which may be networked using the Internet Protocol (IP). The QoS achievable will be higher when devices are available in an on-demand fashion; as a result, users may therefore be more likely to leave devices powered on (at least in standby mode) and disable low-power options for convenience, presenting an opportunity for intelligent and autonomous management of devices to improve efficiency.[3] In a data centre, in contrast, environmental issues arise due to the volume of devices in plants which are ready to service client requests and the associated plant management costs (including lighting and air conditioning) incurred whilst maintaining a suitable operating environment. Energy-efficient networking is also important in rural farming regions (Singh, 2006); wireless

[3] Whilst existing in a standby mode results in improved operational power efficiency, the International Energy Agency (IEA) has estimated that the standby mode of operation could be resulting in 1% of world greenhouse gas emissions (Climate Neutral Network, Information and Communication Technologies, n.d.).

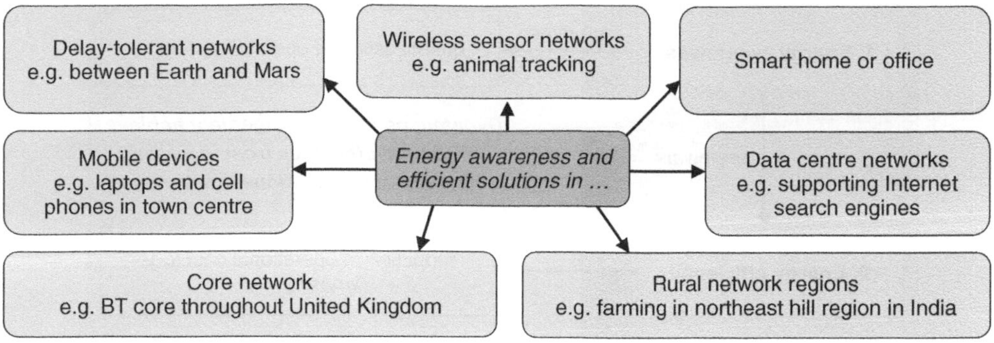

Figure 7.1 Domains with energy efficiency network requirements for improved sustainability and reduced cost.

solutions are more easily deployed and less costly to roll out in these regions. Efficient use of wireless resources helps to maximize the network's lifetime and operational ability, farmer utility received from the network and satisfaction with services provided. Drivers for improving energy efficiency within different operating environments therefore vary, whilst the priority and desire to reduce carbon emission remain constant between each.

7.1.4 Objectives of Green Networking

Across the range of domains, objectives of green network communication and management solutions include the following:

- Minimizing the carbon footprint of delivery networks;
- Improving operational sustainability in wireless networks;
- Minimizing the financial cost for operators to transmit;
- Allowing application QoS to be achieved within network resource constraints;
- Reducing load on the network and hence per transaction power consumption;
- Removing the digital divide between urban and rural areas;
- Contributing to industrial standards.

Regardless of having improved sustainability, the overall requirement of green IT across domains is to decrease the number of bits per transmission so that energy demands are curtailed, power cost lowered and carbon emissions reduced. Energy efficiency objectives from this point of view therefore involve reducing power consumption in wired networks, and in wireless networks also include maximizing operational sustainability. The contrasting requirements of efficiency in two exemplar domains, the data centre and wireless sensor network, are compared. In wireless sensor networks, node power resources are constrained: A study by Sensys Networks (2007) identified that average battery lifetime is between 23 and 35 days. Objectives in this scenario therefore prioritize sustainability to maximize the network's operational lifetime. In data centre networks, in contrast, there is a high degree of redundancy to minimize response time and maximize performance when responding to client requests. The carbon cost per square metre is, however high,

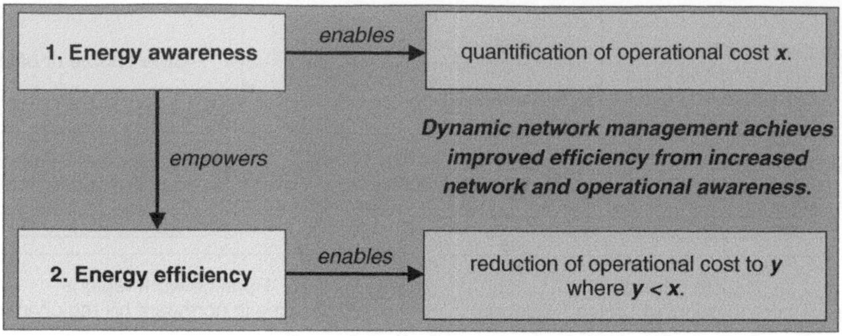

Figure 7.2 Components of next-generation green networks.

with projected server power densities of 20 000 W/m^2 (Schmidt *et al.*, 2004). Minimizing energy consumption in this environment is therefore a core objective of NGN equipment. Sustainability and cost reduction requirements are approached with equal importance in the development of green networking solutions, both being a consequence of more efficient operation. In improving the efficiency with which communications occur, cost per transmission will be reduced and sustainability improved.

7.1.5 Core Components in Green-Networking Technology

To achieve sustainable and lower cost services through green technology, networks require two core capabilities (Figure 7.2): energy awareness and energy efficiency. *Energy awareness* refers to the network's ability to quantify energy cost per packet, and identify if power constraints are becoming a limiting force on its ability to operate or if carbon emissions are increasing above a threshold. *Energy efficiency* describes the network's ability to reduce carbon contributions from those incurred prior to the application of energy efficiency and extend the network's lifetime whilst maintaining QoS.

Energy awareness empowers networks with capabilities, absent previously, for efficiency objectives. Empowering this ability enables reorganization of the way in which communication occurs, including the operations at each stack layer and management function in general. Network communication protocol standards traditionally focus on achievement of reliability for applications with stricter QoS requirements or a faster response time for those without. Mechanisms for improved efficiency should, however, be incorporated in a cross-layer approach in next-generation green networks (NGGN) such that these objectives may continue to be achieved in parallel with optimized operation.

7.2 Objectives of Green Network Protocols

In empowering the network with energy awareness and efficiency ability, it is necessary to understand protocol overhead in terms of mandatory fields in packet headers and control packets currently used to manage transmissions. The objective of this section is therefore to gain an appreciation for the way in which protocols may be optimized whilst application

QoS is maintained, and to understand mandatory content carried within protocol headers. This leads to identification of ways in which protocols may be optimized such that their degree of reliability is maintained through reducing the number of bits associated with each, the cost of which to transmit may be incurred during any transaction, and hence energy efficiency improved.

7.2.1 Energy-Optimizing Protocol Design

Network efficiency can be enhanced by the design of protocols used. Reducing the number of bits associated with a transmission and minimizing network load will optimize communication efficiency. Where fewer bits are transmitted, less processing operation will be required at nodes, fewer finite power resources consumed during transmission and less carbon emitted, along with less congestion in the network, fewer retransmissions and an overall more optimized process. From the point of view of network protocols, the number of bits involved can be reduced by[4] (i) minimizing the number of overhead packets per protocol, (ii) minimizing the number of mandatory bits per protocol, (iii) minimizing retransmission attempts and (iv) maximizing the number of successful data packets sent. These four objectives of optimization are as follows:

- **Objective 1: minimizing the number of overhead packets O per protocol:**

$$\underset{n \in N^{*(i,j;G)}}{\mathit{minimize}} \quad O \tag{7.1}$$

  where O represents the number of overhead packets associated with a transmission, pushed from each node n where $n \in N^{*(i,j;G)}$ is the set of all nodes traversed across sublinks on path (i,j) between source and destination devices in network G. 'Overhead' in this case refers to control and management packets transmitted across the network in support of the protocol design. In the case of the Ad hoc On-Demand Distance Vector (AODV) protocol (Perkins, Belding-Royer, and Das, 2003), for example, a broadcast packet is sent when a connection between nodes which wish to communicate is needed. Intermediary nodes forward the message towards the destination; when the message is received at a node with a route to the destination, it communicates this detail with the source node, which subsequently begins to use the route. In minimizing the number of overhead packets used to support protocol operation, optimization in power requirements can be achieved.

- **Objective 2: minimizing the number of mandatory M bits per protocol:**

$$\underset{n \in N^{*(i,j;G)}}{\mathit{minimize}} \quad M \tag{7.2}$$

  where M is the number of mandatory bits associated with a protocol for packets pushed from each node n using the protocol where $n \in N^{*(i,j;G)}$ is the set of all

[4] To set the context for which protocol costs are being considered: A network can be considered as a graph $G = V(E)$ composed of $V := V(G)$ nodes and $E := E(G)$ links. A path p between communicating end points is composed of one or more subpaths $(v,i)(i,j), \ldots (k,h)$ between a source v and destination h. Path $p_{i,j}$ represents all sublinks of this path, connected by intermediary nodes. The transmission will pass through zero or more intermediary nodes n whilst traversing sublinks on the end-to-end path (i,j).

nodes traversed across sublinks on path (i,j) between source and destination devices in network G. *Mandatory bits* include those transmitted alongside application data in packets encapsulated at each stack layer. (For more detail on mandatory bits applied in encapsulated packets for a selection of protocols, see Section 7.2.2.) In minimizing the number of mandatory bits associated with a protocol, fewer resources will be required to support packet transportation, leading to an overall more optimized, and subsequently efficient, communication.

In parallel with optimizing the number of bits associated with a network transaction, sufficient detail and capability should be maintained such that operational performance is achieved. Further objectives in the design of energy-efficient protocols therefore include the following:

- **Objective 3: minimizing retransmission attempts R:**

$$\underset{n \in N^{*(i,j;G)}}{\mathit{minimize}} \quad R \tag{7.3}$$

where R is the number of retransmission attempts associated with traffic pushed from each node n where $n \in N^{*(i,j;G)}$ is the set of all nodes traversed across sublinks on path (i,j) between source and destination devices in network G. 'Retransmissions' refer to data packets sent more than once through the network when reliable protocol mechanisms have been applied in the instance that application packets have been lost or received incorrectly. One or more retransmissions may be sent in response.

- **Objective 4: maximizing the number of successful data packet sends S:**

$$\underset{n \in N^{*(i,j;G)}}{\mathit{maximize}} \quad S \tag{7.4}$$

where S is the number of packets sent successfully from each node n where $n \in N^{*(i,j;G)}$ is the set of all nodes traversed across sublinks on the end-to-end path (i,j) within network G.

Objectives 1 and 2 can be influenced by protocol design. Network costs in general are calculated as a function of the traffic volume passing across links, nodes and client devices. This volume varies in relation to the number of active ports at nodes on the end-to-end path, residual node memory resources, reliability mechanisms associated with protocols carrying traffic through nodes and overhead required to enable the protocol to achieve its control and management function. Ideally, the objectives defined in Equations 7.1–7.4 will be achieved simultaneously. This requirement set presents a *constrained optimization challenge*, however, due to attempts to achieve minimization across competing parameters simultaneously. Minimizing the volume of protocol overhead (using approaches defined in Equations 7.1 and 7.2) may impact the number of successful data packet sends and subsequent number of retransmissions. It will therefore not be possible to achieve minimization and maximization of all characteristics as outlined in Equations 7.1–7.4. Due to this constrained optimization challenge, objectives defined in Equations 7.1 and 7.2 should therefore be prioritized in the design of a protocol optimized for energy purposes whilst objectives defined in Equations 7.3 and 7.4 are maintained at least above a threshold.

7.2.2 Bit Costs Associated with Network Communication Protocols

Reducing the overhead costs associated with protocols will improve their energy efficiency. Minimum costs of network protocols and typical overhead volumes associated with packets sent using each protocol are therefore explored in this section to highlight the network resources required for protocols to operate and lead to optimization of their design through identification of inefficiencies.

7.2.2.1 Internet Protocol v4 (IP) Cost

Mandatory bits included in IP packet headers according to Request for Comments (RFC) 791 (Postel, 1981a) are shown in Table 7.1. Application data are appended to this IP control information, with the volume v of data being $1 <= v <= \text{MTU}$, restricted by the Maximum Transmission Unit (MTU) of the link to which the node is attached. Additional field options may be appended to IP packets on a transmission-specific basis to supplement the information available, as shown in Table 7.2.

The overall minimum cost of IP packets is therefore the sum of those in Table 7.1, and will be incurred by all packets on the end-to-end path passed between communicating nodes. IP modules implement the Internet Control Message Protocol (ICMP) defined in RFC 792 (Postel, 1981b), and ICMP messages are sent using the IP packet header (with an IP header Protocol field value of 1). ICMP reports problems with IP packet processing and can therefore send a range of error-reporting packets. This includes a Destination Unreachable Message (packet type 3), with fields included, as shown in Table 7.3.

Other ICMP packet types include Time Exceeded Message (type 11), Parameter Problem Message (type 12), Source Quench Message (type 4), Redirect Message (type 5), Echo (type 8) or Echo Reply Message (type 0), Timestamp (type 13) or Timestamp Reply

Table 7.1 IPv4 packet header format

Field	Number of bits
Version	4
Internet header length	4
Type of service	8
ID	16
Flag	3
Fragment offset	13
Time to live	8
Protocol	8
Checksum	16
Source address	32
Destination address	32
Options	Variable (zero or more options)
Padding	Variable

Table 7.2 Optional IPv4 packet header fields

Optional IP packet field	Number of bits
End of option list	–
No operation	–
Security	16
Compartments	16
Handling restrictions	16
Transmission control code	24
Loose source and record route	Variable
Strict source and record route	Variable
Record route	Variable
Stream identifier	4
Internet timestamp	Variable

Table 7.3 ICMPv4 destination unreachable message packet header format

Field	Number of bits
Type	8
Code	8
Checksum	16
Internet header + 64 bits of original data datagram	64

Message (type 14) and Information Request (type 15) or Information Reply Message (type 16). The sizes of each of these packets are constant, with the code and type field varying as a function of the message type. Taking into account the packet header structure used by IPv4 and ICMPv4 protocols, *there is a minimum of 144 bits in an IPv4 packet before application traffic is encapsulated and 96 bits in an ICMPv4 packet*.

Whilst IPv4 continues to be the most widely used version of the IP, IPv6 (Deering and Hinden, 1998) is used to support the rapid growth in the number of Internet users. In addition, IPv6 demonstrates a greater level of efficiency in its design, with the header fields restricted to those shown in Table 7.4.

IPv6 supports flexibility in its operation through use of an Options header (which contains the following fields: Option Type (8 bits), Option Data Length (8 bits) and Option Data (variable)). Option types include those which are read on a hop-by-hop manner and those read at the destination node only (both containing the fields Next Header (8 bits), Header Extension Length (8 bits) and Options (variable)). ICMPv6 (Conta, Deering, and Gupta, 2006) also demonstrates improved efficiency. Packets are divided into error and informational messages: The number of error messages is reduced from those provisioned in ICMPv4, and include only Destination Unreachable (type 1), Packet Too Big (type 2), Time Exceeded (type 3) and Parameter Problem (type 4) packets. Fields included within the Destination Unreachable packet, for example, include those used by ICMPv4. It is therefore through reduction in the number of packets used which improves

Table 7.4 IPv6 packet header format

Field	Number of bits
Version	4
Traffic class	8
Flow label	20
Payload length	16
Next header	8
Hop limit	8
Source address	128
Destination address	128

its operational efficiency. With all header fields being mandatory, *there is therefore a minimum of 320 bits in an IPv6 packet before application traffic is encapsulated and 96 bits in an ICMPv6 packet*.

Whilst IP is the common protocol used across all Internet communication, a selection of others, with their costs explored in this section, may be applied at the other stack layers.

7.2.2.2 Routing Information Protocol (RIP) Cost

At the network layer, mandatory fields associated with packets transmitted using the Routing Information Protocol (RIP) according to RFC 2453 (Malkin, 1998) include Command (8 bits), Version (8 bits) and RIP Entry (between 1 and 25 entries). The RIP Entry is composed of the following fields: Address Family Identifier (16 bits), Route Tag (16 bits), IPv4 Address (32 bits), Subnet Mask (32 bits), Next Hop (32 bits) and Metric (32 bits). With each attribute being mandatory in all packets and the RIP Entry of variable length (with the potential of an array of information), *there is a minimum of 176 bits of overhead in RIP packets*.

7.2.2.3 AODV

The routing protocol AODV (Perkins, Belding-Royer, and Das, 2003) supports a number of packet types, which include the Route Request (RREQ), Route Reply (RREP), Route Error and Route Reply Acknowledgement. With regard to the RREQ message as an example, packet fields include Type (8 bits), Flags including Join, Repair, Gratuitous RREP, Destination Only and Unknown Sequence Number (all 1 bit), Reserved (11 bits), Hop Count (8 bits), RREQ ID (32 bits), Destination IP Address (32 bits), Destination Sequence Number (32 bits), Originator IP Address (32 bits) and Originator Sequence Number (32 bits). With all attributes being mandatory in each packet, *there is therefore 192 bits of overhead in the AODV RREQ message*.

7.2.2.4 User Datagram Protocol (UDP) Cost

At the transport layer of the stack, mandatory fields of User Datagram Protocol (UDP) packets according to RFC 768 (Postel, 1980) include the Source Address (16 bits),

Destination Address (16 bits), Length (16 bits) and Checksum (16 bits). The volume of application data appended to each packet is controlled by the MTU of the link to which the node is attached. As each attribute is included in all packets transmitted using UDP, *there is therefore 64 bits of overhead in UDP packets prior to the encapsulation of application data*.

7.2.2.5 Transmission Control Protocol (TCP) Cost

Mandatory bits associated with Transmission Control Protocol (TCP) packets according to RFC 793 (Postel, 1981c) include the Source Port (16 bits), Destination Port (16 bits), Sequence Number (32 bits), Acknowledgement Number (32 bits), Data Offset (4 bits), Reserved (6 bits), Control (6 bits), Window (16 bits), Checksum (16 bits), Urgent Pointer (16 bits) and the variably sized fields Options and Padding. As in the case of the IP and UDP protocols, the volume of application data appended to each packet is controlled by the MTU of the link to which the node is attached. With the header fields included in all packets transmitted using TCP, *there is therefore a minimum of 160 bits in TCP packet headers prior to encapsulation of application data*.

7.2.2.6 RTP

The Real-Time Protocol (RTP) packet header according to RFC 3550 (Schulzrinne *et al.*, 2003) contains the fields Version (2 bits), Padding (1 bit), Extension (1 bit), Contributing Source (CSRC) Count (4 bits), Marker (1 bit), Payload Type (7 bits), Sequence Number (16 bits), Timestamp (32 bits), Synchronization Source Identifier (32 bits) and CSRC Identifier (0–15 items, 32 bits each). With each attribute being used in all RTP packets, *there is therefore a minimum of 96 bits in RTP packets prior to the encapsulation of application data*.

7.2.3 Objectives of Green Network Protocols

Through exploring the range of header fields in a selection of commonly used protocols at different stack layers, potential opportunities to improve their efficiency have been identified. In the development of green network protocols, objectives therefore include the following:

1. Improving utilization of cross-layer detail between protocols unpacked at different stack layers;
2. Minimizing or eliminating redundancy in header detail;
3. Optimizing the protocols in their design through removal of support for older versions.

A cross-layer approach promises the greatest improvements in energy efficiency (Almi'ani, Selvakennedy and Viglas, 2008), allowing problems and/or inefficiencies at each layer to be tackled in a consistent manner. When a protocol header is adapted, cross-layer compatibility will ensure that any attributes removed are not needed at other layers. Similarly, attributes incorporated for improved energy intelligence should be utilized at a maximum number of layers for optimum efficiency.

To improve their efficiency, these objectives are applied to protocols evaluated in Section 7.2.2 as follows:

- Meeting Objective 1
  - Header detail may be better reused between stack layers in the case of the IP. The time to live (TTL) field is applied by the IP and also in the RSVP header, for example. As the network layer is traversed at each node, the attribute therefore need not be included in all headers but only in those used lower in the stack, and appended when being unpacked at the previous header layer.
- Meeting Objective 2
  - Inclusion of the *ToS* field in the IP header may be considered unnecessary at this layer. It describes the packet's precedence, acceptable delay, volume of throughput and degree of reliability required. This detail may instead be gleaned from the TTL attribute which is also included in the header by default in an approach optimized for energy efficiency. On the other hand, the TTL can be captured from the ToS field and it need not be appended to the header instead. The nature of detail retained in these fields means that only one attribute is needed, not both.
  - The need to include *source and destination addresses* in a range of packet headers used at different stack layers may also be questioned. Source and destination addresses are included, for example in MAC, IP, AODV, UDP, TCP and SNMP packet headers. Optimized UDP may, however, omit source and destination addresses from the packet header. This detail will be carried by the routing protocol and need therefore not also be replicated at the transport layer.
  - The inclusion of a *checksum* within each protocol header can also be reconsidered for improved efficiency. Determined on an application-specific basis, it may be possible to optimize the inclusion of a checksum in all protocol headers, particularly in the case where the application can cope with a small degree of error, for the objective of optimizing communication energy efficiency.
  - There may be redundancy in the header fields provisioned for IPv6. The *hop limit* field, for example, may be replaceable with the *traffic class* field only. The traffic class field can be used to indicate the acceptable delay associated with a packet stream (traffic classes remain undefined in RFC 2460), thereby removing the need to include both fields in the packet header.
  - In the case of ICMPv6, there may be an opportunity to reduce the amount of redundancy associated with the protocol: Whilst there are fewer error message types used by this protocol in relation to those used by ICMPv4, it may be possible to restrict the range of error codes. With regard to the destination unreachable message, for example, there are seven optional error codes for reasons why the destination is unreachable. Three of these may, however, not be needed, including the options 'Beyond Scope of Source Address', 'Address Unreachable' and 'Reject Route to Destination', which could instead be replaced with the single error code, 'No Route to Destination'.
- Meeting Objective 3
  - With regard to provision for support of updated versions of the protocol, this is the case with the Internet Group Management Protocol (IGMP) Version 3 defined

in RFC 3376 (Cain *et al.*, 2002) which also supports packet types associated with older versions of the protocol.

7.3 Green Network Protocols and Standards

Minimum costs associated with a selection of network protocols incurred through their encapsulation of application data with mandatory header detail were explored in Section 7.2. The management function of protocols represents overhead in the sense that all packets sent do not contain application traffic and all data in packets are not application traffic. As they are additional expenses incurred during network communications, they represent potential avenues where optimization may be achieved. This section therefore acts as a bridge between identification of protocol costs and approaches proposed by the authors to provision green-networking solutions, and it involves discussion of the state of the art in green communication protocols and operational management. Through exploration in this section, the current research gap with regard to energy-efficient networking standards can be defined.

7.3.1 Strategies to Reduce Carbon Emissions

Business for Social Responsibility (BSR, 2009) suggests strategies to reduce carbon emissions at all stages of the business life cycle in general, from product manufacture to distribution. They suggest that carbon reductions are achievable by

1. Enabling cleaner sourcing and manufacturing;
2. Lowering emissions in transit;
3. Enabling cleaner warehouse operations;
4. Reducing transit distances;
5. Removing nodes or legs;
6. Reducing total volume and/or mass shipped;
7. Consolidating movements;
8. Contributing to reductions elsewhere; and
9. Increasing recycling and reuse.

These techniques to reduce carbon emissions are not specific to telecommunications networks and consider carbon emitted during physical transportation of resources, development and production costs and onsite day-to-day operation. Whilst applied generically across businesses irrespective of their domain, we relate these to NGGN state-of-the-art strategies to demonstrate their versatility with regard to reducing carbon emissions in general, with processes involved during the communication of data having the same (albeit scaled-down) energy-associated impact.

7.3.2 Contributions from the EMAN Working Group

The EMAN Working Group is involved in the conversion of 'work in progress' Internet drafts (their primary contributions are summarized in Table 7.5) into formal RFC

Table 7.5 Contributions of 'work in progress' Internet drafts

'Work in progress' Internet draft	Contribution
MIB for energy, efficiency, throughput and carbon emission (Sasidharan, Bhat, and Shreekantaiah, 2010)	Defines MIB attributes required to calculate the carbon emission of network elements, with attributes including power consumed whilst performing packet throughput when idle, when operating with full power and to operate with half power
Definition of managed objects for energy management (Quittek *et al.*, 2010a)	Defines MIB structures required to appreciate the energy characteristics associated with network transactions, including a power state MIB, energy MIB and battery MIB
Energy monitoring MIB (Claise *et al.*, 2011)	Defines a number of non-operational and operational states in which nodes can exist to optimize energy efficiency, including standby, ready, reduced-power and full-power modes
Benchmarking power usage of networking devices (Manral, 2011)	Defines a power usage calculation for network devices, with attributes including the number of active ports and their utilization
Requirements for power monitoring (Quittek *et al.*, 2010b)	Defines requirements when calculating the energy consumption cost of network devices, which includes consideration for monitoring granularity and information required (state, state duration and power source)

documents. In general, these drafts define management information base (MIB) structures designed to empower networks with energy awareness such that efficiency may be achieved. In *MIB for Energy, Efficiency, Throughput and Carbon* (Sasidharan, Bhat, and Shreekantaiah, 2010), for example, calculation of carbon emissions includes energy consumption, operational efficiency and utilization of each device attribute. *Requirements for Power Monitoring* (Quittek *et al.*, 2010b) supplements Sasidharan, Bhat, and Shreekantaiah (2010) by defining requirements to perform energy calculations. This involves ensuring that all network components are monitored and that attributes collected include the current state and time spent in each state, total energy consumed at a device and since the last monitoring interval, and current battery charge, age, state and time when last used. The *Energy Monitoring MIB* (Claise *et al.*, 2011) collects attribute details which include power cost per packet, duration of power demand intervals and maximum demand in a window. This Internet draft also considers compliance with MIB monitoring processes, with support for both reading and writing context from and to MIBs. Modes of improved operational efficiency are also suggested in this standard, and 12 power states may be applied to nodes in response to collected context. When related to the BSR's principles, these strategies can be compared to enabling cleaner warehouse operations by improving understanding of the real-time environment and enforcing timely and appropriate actions to it.

7.3.3 Contributions from Standardization Bodies

The European Telecommunications Standards Institute (ETSI) Environmental Engineering group defines techniques to monitor and control telecommunication infrastructure in response to collected context and predefined alarm conditions. Their drafts therefore define alarms, events and measurements necessary to provide the level of management required. In European Telecommunications Standards Institute (ETSI) (2010), *AC Monitoring Diesel Back-Up System Control and Monitoring Information Model*, for example the minimum range of events which should be monitored on a backup generator are defined, with alarms being raised if an undefined stop, start failure, fuel leakage or battery charger failure occurs. In ETSI, Environmental Engineering (2009), the monitored attributes of a DC power system control are defined. Alarms are raised when conditions include testing for battery failure, battery over-temperature and low-voltage output. These drafts further highlight the range of context which must be collected on an application-specific approach and the tailoring of alarms in relation to the domain in which management is applied. When compared to the BSR's strategies, integration of alarms such as those proposed by ETSI relate to lowering emissions in transit by suspending operations when environment conditions are insufficient to support it.

IEEE 802.3, the Energy Efficient Ethernet (EEE) Study Group, is actively involved in reducing the power required to operate Ethernet technology. Primary contributions in the IEEE Standard 802.3az include a low-power state for activation during idle periods and times of low utilization (low-power idle (LPI)). This mode is applied in relation to link status and observed traffic flow. The standard also includes an alert signal which can be used to awaken those connections which have been sent to the sleep state when data arrive for transmission across an Ethernet link. When compared to the strategies proposed by the BSR, EEE relates to consolidating movements across primary links whilst suspending those across links which are not used as frequently.

7.3.4 Context Detail to Drive Energy Efficiency

The EMAN working group has proposed MIB structures specific to the challenge of improved communication efficiency; ETSI defines alarms and measurements to control operation of power systems, and the IEEE defines strategies to optimize the power required to operate Ethernet technology. In addition, independent researchers propose solutions for application in individual domains and/or in response to a specific operational challenge at a specific stack layer, as in Ye, Heidemann and Estrin (2004) and Rhee *et al.* (2005).

Taking into account developments in the field which provision information with regard to the nature of context required, the way in which it should be monitored, relevant evaluations and actions which may be applied, there is a research gap in that solutions have been provided in an ad hoc manner. In response to this, we have suggested that there are benefits to be achieved by applying domain-specific solutions to the collection and monitoring of context, evaluation and application of optimization strategies. Referring to Figure 7.1, which shows a range of domains that could benefit from improved efficiency networking solutions due to a desire to improve sustainability and/or reduce operational costs due to a currently high volume of carbon emissions, the range of context which may be required in a solution applied across domains to drive the optimization process is presented in Table 7.6. Context attributes are collected to drive intelligent decision

Table 7.6 Domain-specific context data required to achieve energy efficiency

Network domain	Context used in each domain (per node)	Context used in each domain (in the wider environment between client and destination devices)
Data centre	*At an individual server within the data centre, context includes* server utilization, packet arrival rate (packets/second), power consumption rate (Watts/second), job completion rate (seconds), operational state (per node and per port), processing delay (seconds) and page faults (faults/page)	Bandwidth availability (bits per second), temperature (°C), power consumption rate (Watts per second) and operational state of neighbours (per node and per port)
Delay-tolerant network	*At an individual spacecraft deployed in deep space, context includes* tilt of solar panel (degrees), propagation distance from neighbours (seconds), critical activities, temperature (°C), line-of-sight connectivity with neighbours (true or false), residual battery capacity (units), received signal strength (dB) and operational state (per node and per port)	Wind speed (miles per hour), location of neighbours (x, y and z co-ordinates), residual battery capacity at neighbours (units), strength of signal arriving at neighbours (dB), operational state of neighbours (per node and per port), time of day, time of year, bit error rate (packets per second) and bandwidth availability (bits per second)
Mobile device	*For a mobile phone or laptop, context includes* backlight (% brightness), residual battery capacity (units), application type of service, device type, memory capacity (bits), device-critical activities, packet-sending rate (packets per second) and location (x, y and z co-ordinates)	Time of day (hours, minutes and seconds), bandwidth availability (bits per second) and location of neighbours (x, y and z co-ordinates)
Core	*At an individual router/switch in the network core, context includes* throughput (bits per second), utilization (%), operational state (per node and per port), energy cost per packet (Watts), packet-processing delay (seconds) and packet arrival rate (packets per second)	Bandwidth availability (bits per second), retransmission count at neighbours (packets per second), residual memory capacity at neighbours (bits) and bit error rate (packets per second)

(*continued overleaf*)

Table 7.6 (*continued*)

Network domain	Context used in each domain (per node)	Context used in each domain (in the wider environment between client and destination devices)
Rural region	*At an individual networked device (client device or intermediary router), context includes* residual battery capacity (units), location (x, y and z co-ordinates), retransmission count (packets per second), packet transmission rate (packets per second), power cost per packet (Watts per packet) and packet arrival rate (packets per second)	Temperature (°C), bandwidth availability (bits per second), residual battery capacity at neighbours (units) and time of day (hours, minutes and seconds)
Smart home and office	*At an individual networked device, context includes* use of solar panel (true or false), device critical activities, operational state (per node and per port), time spent in state, energy cost per packet (Watts), time of last node sleep (hours, minutes and seconds) and sleep duration (seconds)	Bandwidth availability (bits per second), time of day (hours, minutes and seconds), location of nodes (x, y or z co-ordinates) and operational state of neighbours (per node and per port)
Wireless sensor network	*At an individual sensor, context includes* residual battery capacity (units), node location (x, y and z co-ordinates), operational state (per node and per port), propagation distance from neighbours (metres), temperature (°C), retransmission count (packets per second) and residual node memory (bits)	Temperature (°C), time of day (hours, seconds and minutes), location of neighbours (x, y and z co-ordinates), residual battery capacity at neighbours (units) and residual memory capacity at neighbours (bits)

making in terms of detail required on each individual node within the domain and also across the network within the wider environment. In exploring the problem domain in this way, optimization solutions in a range of environments which use different context and to which a range of contrasting evaluations should occur and actions can be applied are realized. Furthermore, in extension to standalone solutions identified in the literature, an integrated context-aware management solution which is cross-layer compatible across domains can also be developed (such as that proposed by the authors, the Energy-Efficient Context-Aware Broker or e-CAB; Peoples, Parr, and McClean, 2011), with a potential deployability and sustainability improvement in an approach similar to the TCP/IP and

Open Systems Interconnection (OSI) protocol stacks upon which the Internet's success to date has been built.

7.4 Conclusions

Energy-efficient networking is explored in this chapter from the perspectives of reducing the energy cost to communicate, and improving device sustainability when an operation is supported by finite-resource technology. These requirements are approached with equal priority in the development of energy-efficient network solutions, allowing improved efficiency to be achieved for both wired and wireless communications. Exploration from this perspective takes into account the range of domains in which energy-efficient networking solutions can be applied to improve performance in terms of both application QoS and user quality of experience. Energy-efficient networking solutions are explored in this chapter from the perspective of reduced carbon costs and improved operational sustainability.

Green network protocols transmit fewer bits than standard default protocols developed with reliability as opposed to energy efficiency as core operational objectives. Green networking includes the selection of least-cost paths in terms of node number queuing delay, carbon and financial cost, maximization of node and link resources and use of optimized protocols. We have described an energy-efficient design that includes optimization of the number of overhead packets which control protocol operation and the number of mandatory management bits associated with each packet sent using the protocol.

Acknowledgements

The research presented in this chapter is supported by the India-UK Advanced Technology Centre of Excellence in Next Generation Networks, Systems and Services (IU-ATC), which is funded by the UK Engineering and Physical Sciences Research Council (EPSRC) Digital Economy Programme and Government of India Department of Science and Technology (DST). Working as part of a larger cross-border collaboration, the research described in this chapter has been conducted at the University of Ulster by the UK project team involved with the Theme 6 project, 'Cross-Layer Energy Aware Network Management'. We thank Professor Ashok Jhunjhunwala in his role as Academic Lead for the IU-ATC in India, and our Theme 6 counterparts at the Indian Institute of Technology Madras.

Review Questions

1. Why do next-generation networks make the need for energy efficiency more important than in network operation previously?
2. How does the drive for reduced carbon cost and improved operational sustainability relate to the common objective of energy-efficient networking?
3. What are the two main strategies which can be applied to reduce the operational cost associated with network communications?

4. What is the constrained optimization challenge which arises in response to achieving the objectives of energy-efficient network communications?
5. Which are exemplar domains that can benefit from the application of energy-efficient networking due to either reduced carbon cost or improved operational sustainability?
6. What are the objectives of green networking and communication which can benefit user and operator needs alike?
7. What are the outstanding research issues which remain with regard to achieving green networking and communication?
8. In the protocols evaluated in Section 7.2, which has the greatest number of minimum mandatory bits included in its packet header?
9. What have been the contributions from the Working Group involved in the field of energy management?
10. Why is energy-efficient networking important in light of the increased number of renewable power plants?

Discussion Questions

1. Why have energy optimizing approaches to date primarily concentrated on switching nodes or ports on a node to exist in a sleep state as opposed to optimizing the structure and/or operation of network communication protocols within the stack as a whole?
2. Is it too big a task to begin to reorganize the network protocol stack and design of protocols operating within it for improved energy efficiency purposes given its successful operation for 40 years since the Internet was first established?
3. In what way should standards currently under review by the Energy Management Working Group be extended or supplemented to provide improved energy management functionality as opposed to simply a definition of MIB structures?
4. Energy management is important in delay-tolerant networks where the sustainability of expensive missions could be improved to maximize scientific discovery. Autonomic energy efficiency in this domain has, to date, not been a key research focus. Why?
5. Integrating energy modelling and enforcing efficiency practices are relatively limited in the network management software available to date. Why is this the case given the volume of research currently on-going in this field?

References

Almi'ani, K., Selvakennedy, S. and Viglas, A. (2008) RMC: An energy-aware cross-layer data-gathering protocol for wireless sensor networks. In Proceeding of 22nd IEEE International Conference on Advanced Information Networking and Applications, March, pp. 410–417.

Business for Social Responsibility (2009) Value Chain Approaches to a Low Carbon Economy: Business and Policy Partnerships: A Discussion Paper for the World Business Summit on Climate Change in Copenhagen, May, pp. 1–13.

Cain, B., Deering, S., Kouvelas, I. *et al.* (2002) Internet Group Management Protocol, Version 3, Network Working Group Request for Comments 3376, October.

Conta, A., Deering, S. and Gupta, M. (2006) Internet Control Message Protocol (ICMPv6) for the Internet Protocol Version 6 Specification, Internet Engineering Task Force Request for Comments 4443, March.

Claise, B., Chandramouli, M., Parello, J. and Schoening, B. (2011) Energy monitoring MIB, work in progress as an IETF Internet draft, July.

Deering, S. and Hinden, R. (1998) Internet Protocol, Version 6 (IPv6) Specification, Internet Engineering Task Force Request for Comments 2460, December.

Department for Culture (2009) Media and Sport and Department for Business, Innovation and Skills, Digital Britain Final Report, June, pp. 1–245, http://www.official-documents.gov.uk (accessed April 2012).

Department of Energy and Climate Change (2008) The Climate Change Act 2008, http://www.decc.gov.uk/en/content/cms/legislation/cc_act_08/cc_act_08.aspx (accessed April 2012).

Department of Energy and Climate Change (2010) The CRC Energy Efficiency Scheme Order 2010, http://www.legislation.gov.uk/ukdsi/2010/9780111491232/contents (accessed April 2012).

ETSI, Environmental Engineering (2009) ES 202 336-2 v1.1. *Environmental Engineering (EE): Monitoring and Control Interface for Infrastructure Equipment (Power, Cooling, and Environment Systems Used in Telecommunication Networks): Part 2: DC Power System Control and Monitoring Information Model*, March, pp. 1–26.

European Telecommunications Standards Institute (ETSI) (2010) ES 202 336-5 v1.1.1. *Environmental Engineering (EE): Monitoring and Control Interface for Infrastructure Equipment (Power, Cooling and Building Environment Systems used in Telecommunication Networks); Part 5: AC Diesel Back-Up Generator System Control and Monitoring Information Model*, January, pp. 1–18.

HM Government (2009) The UK Low Carbon Transition Plan: National Strategy for Climate and Energy, 15 July, pp. 1–220, http://centralcontent.fco.gov.uk/central-content/campaigns/act-on-copenhagen/resources/en/pdf/DECC-Low-Carbon-Transition-Plan (accessed April 2012).

HM Revenue and Customs (2011) Climate Change Levy, http://customs.hmrc.gov.uk (accessed April 2012).

International Telecommunication Union (2008) NGNs and Energy Efficiency, ITU-T Technology Watch Report #7, August, ICU, Geneva.

International Telecommunication Union Telecommunication Standardisation Sector (2006) Series M: Telecommunication Management, Including TMN and Network Maintenance; Series Y: Global Information Infrastructure, Internet Protocol Aspects and Next-Generation Networks – Principles for the Management of Next Generation Networks, pp. 1–64.

Malkin, G. (1998) RIP Version 2, Internet Engineering Task Force Request for Comments 2453, November.

Manral, V. (2011) Benchmarking Power Usage of Networking Devices, work in progress as an IETF Internet draft, January.

Ministry of Power, Government of India (2011) The Energy Conservation Act 2001, http://www.powermin.nic.in/acts_notification/energy_conservation_act/introduction.htm (accessed April 2012).

Peoples, C., Parr, G. and McClean, S. (2011) Context-aware characterisation of energy consumption in data centres. In Proceeding 3rd IFIP/IEEE International Workshop on Management of the Future Internet, May 2011, pp. 1250–1257.

Perkins, C., Belding-Royer, E. and Das, S. (2003) Ad Hoc On-Demand Distance Vector (AODV) Routing, Network Working Group Request for Comments 3561, July, pp. 1–36.

Phippa, A. (2009) Who makes IT professionals environmentally aware? European Community in Information Technology (ERCIM) News 79, Special Theme: Towards Green IT, October, p. 16.

Postel, J. (1980) User Datagram Protocol, Internet Engineering Task Force Request for Comments 768, August.

Postel, J. (1981a) Internet Protocol, Internet Engineering Task Force Request for Comments 791, September.

Postel, J. (1981b) Internet Control Message Protocol, Internet Engineering Task Force Request for Comments 792, September.

Postel, J. (1981c) Transmission Control Protocol, Internet Engineering Task Force Request for Comments 793, September.

Quittek, J., Winter, R., Dietz, T. and Dudkowski, D. (2010a) Definition of Managed Objects for Energy Management, work in progress as an IETF Internet draft, April.

Quittek, J., Winter, R., Ditz, T. *et al.* (2010b) Requirements for Power Monitoring, work in progress as an IETF Internet draft, July.

Rhee, I., Warrier, A., Aia, M. and Min, J. (2005) Z-MAC: A hybrid MAC for wireless sensor networks. In ACM SenSys, November 2005, pp. 1–12.

Sasidharan, S., Bhat, K.P. and Shreekantaiah, S. (2010) MIB for Energy, Efficiency, Throughput and Carbon Emission, work in progress as an IETF Internet draft, January.

Schmidt, R.R., Belady, C., Classen, A. *et al.* (2004) Evolution of data center environmental guidelines. *American Society of Heating, Refrigerating and Air-Conditioning Engineers (ASHRAE)*, **110** (Pt. 1), 559–566.

Schulzrinne, H., Casner, S., Frederick, R. and Jacobson, V. (2003) RTP: A Transport Protocol for Real-Time Applications, Internet Engineering Task Force Request for Comments 3550, July.

Sensys Networks (2007) Measurement of Sensys™ Wireless Sensor Battery Life, pp. 1–8, http://www.sensysnetworks.com (accessed April 2012).
Singh, S. (2006) Selected success stories on agricultural information systems. Asia-Pacific Association of Agricultural Research Institutions, AAPARI Publication 2006/1, http://www.apaari.org/wp-content/uploads/2009/05/ss_2006_01.pdf (accessed April 2012).
The Climate Group (2008) Smart 2020: Enabling the Low Carbon Economy in the Information Age, pp. 1–87.
Ye, W., Heidemann, J. and Estrin, D. (2004) Medium access control with coordinated adaptive sleeping for wireless sensor networks. *IEEE/ACM Transactions on Networking*, **12** (3), 493–506.

Further Reading and Useful Web Sites

- Bureau of Energy Efficiency: www.bee-india.nic.in
- Energy Management Working Group mailing list: eman@ietf.org
- European Telecommunications Standards Institute (ETSI) Environmental Engineering: http://www.etsi.org/WebSite/technologies/EnvironmentalAspects.aspx
- IEEE P802.3az Energy Efficient Ethernet Task Force: http://grouper.ieee.org/groups/802/3/az/public/index.html
- International Telecommunication Union Telecommunication Standardisation Sector (ITU-T): www.itu.int/ITU-T/
- The Office of Communications: www.ofcom.org.uk
- Telecom Regulatory Authority of India (TRAI): www.trai.gov.in/

8

Enterprise Green IT Strategy

Bhuvan Unhelkar
MethodScience, Sydney, Australia

Key Points

- Emphasizes the need for close alignment between business goals and strategies for carbon reduction.
- Highlights the business drivers that encourage the development and implementation of enterprise green IT strategies.
- Outlines the dimensions along which green IT strategies are implemented – economy, technology, processes and people.
- Describes the crucial steps and considerations in developing green IT strategies.
- Discusses the challenges in implementing green IT strategies and approaches that help ameliorate those challenges.
- Outlines some green IT metrics that can be used in practice.

8.1 Introduction

Green information technology (green IT) strategies are essentially business strategies that integrally incorporate carbon emission reduction and other environmental considerations in their formulation and execution. Successful green IT strategies give due consideration to an organization's objectives, industrial context and sociocultural environment. The value of this crucial alignment between business, technology and society has been anticipated and advocated by Alvin Toffler (1975) and others. Today, this alignment is reflected in the need for the holistic growth of organizations, particularly in the context of the environment (see Pearce, 1989). As a result, an organization's decision makers have to align and synchronize their business, environmental and societal interests. This alignment and the business drivers for becoming and remaining green comprise the basic premise of this chapter: the development of green IT strategies.

Harnessing Green IT: Principles and Practices, First Edition. Edited by San Murugesan and G.R. Gangadharan.

Green IT strategy is, therefore, a strategic business approach that does not separate environmental considerations from business goals. The alignment of an organization's business strategies with its environmental consciousness can be best viewed as an intersection between its business and environmental sustainability interests. As a result, effective green IT strategies need to continuously foster and demonstrate their value to business stakeholders.

Green IT strategies comprise business issues, leadership and decision making, critical thinking and business architecture, technology (including information and communications technology (ICT)) as well as soft issues such as people, their morale and their motivation. A green strategic approach includes an organization's structure, dynamics, macro-economic incentives, compliance constraints and need to align corporate social responsibility (CSR) with mainstream corporate business. Ghose (2011) has provided a very good discussion of approaches to green IT strategies that consider a holistic approach to environmental consciousness based on micro- and macro-economic factors. An in-depth discussion of these various aspects of a green IT strategy, also known as an environmentally responsible business strategy (ERBS), is presented by Unhelkar (2011).

The strategic scope of green IT is much beyond its immediate or tactical advantages (see Figure 8.1). IT is a producer of carbon emissions that impact the environment throughout a product's life cycle, including during its use. When considering IT as a producer of carbon emissions, immediate benefits can be gained by reducing its usage. The simple, preliminary approach to carbon reduction is to switch off computers and monitors when not in use and to reduce network traffic.

A more comprehensive approach, however, ensues when IT is used as a strategic enabler of carbon emissions reduction, as shown in Figure 8.1 as 'IT as Enabler' of carbon reduction. In this layer, IT systems and processes are put to use to reduce the carbon emission of not only IT systems but also the entire organization. Eventually, the 'Green Enterprise', shown in the layer of Figure 8.1 immediately surrounding 'IT as Enabler', results from green IT strategies that include the organizational infrastructure, people, policies, law, standards, metrics and all associated processes – including the supply chain and marketing irrespective of the involvement of IT in these processes. This third layer, green enterprise, is the focus of this chapter. Eventually, multiple organizations will collaborate with each other beyond their organizational boundaries to establish

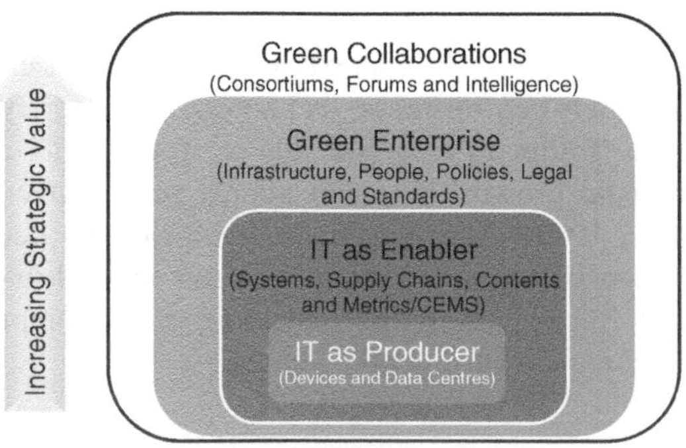

Figure 8.1 Green enterprises are over and beyond green IT.

industry- and national-level strategies – an important discussion but beyond the scope of the chapter.

The hallmark of such green business strategies is that they provide a much more robust foundation for sustainability to the organization than focussing only on IT as represented by the inner rectangle in Figure 8.1. Thus, business optimization processes such as Lean or Six Sigma, whether IT focussed or not, become important to the greening of an organization. Optimization and/or elimination of unnecessary activities within business processes drive up not only business efficiency but also carbon efficiency. Thus, green business strategies are combinations of extending and/or redefining existing business strategies as well as coming up with new strategies that have a specific environmental focus.

The type, size and location of a business all influence the way in which green IT strategies are formed and implemented. Therefore, discussion on what motivates an organization to formulate green IT strategies needs to be followed by a discussion on the dimensions along which an organization needs to transform itself. The four dimensions of economy, technology, processes and people provide the foundation for creating a roadmap, or project plan, for implementing a green IT strategy. A comprehensive green IT strategy thus has underlying philosophy, drivers and motivators for businesses to undertake these strategies, specific steps to develop such a strategy, dimensions along which the strategy can be executed and relevant metrics and measurements.

8.2 Approaching Green IT Strategies

The conceptual framework for green IT strategies discussed in this chapter is based on earlier ideas by Unhelkar and Dickens (2008) and further refined by Unhelkar (2011). In addition to the green IT strategies discussed here, a few other green IT frameworks are worth considering. To model an enterprise from an environmental perspective, Philipson (2009) has refined RMIT University's original framework for green IT (Molla, 2009) into a comprehensive green IT framework that can be used in practice. A procedural model towards sustainable information systems management (Murugesan, 2007, 2008a, 2008b; Schmidt *et al.*, 2009; Worthington, 2009) contributed to these models and frameworks for green IT, resulting in valuable input into the development of a green IT strategy.

An important consideration in developing a green IT strategy is the timeframe of its influence. For example, if the organization only views 'IT as Producer' of carbon footprint (see Figure 8.1), then simple measures like switching off monitors and computers when not in use can be brought about immediately. A more strategic approach to carbon footprint reduction will involve other measures and take a longer timeframe to achieve. Given the urgency of reducing the carbon footprint and complying with legislation, business is often faced with the need to implement tactical solutions to meet immediate needs and showcase the benefits of green IT, which may then become the incumbent or are replaced by longer term solutions (Sherringham and Unhelkar, 2011).

Effective green strategies result from an approach that cuts across all the tiers and silos of an organization. Such strategies come from individual understanding, leadership, vision, knowledge about the organization's structure and dynamics, awareness of the organization's operational nuances and people's (i.e. stakeholders') attitude toward change. The green strategic mindset acknowledges these vital initial efforts especially for the visibility they add to the initial effort, and it adopts a long-term, integral, all-encompassing effort.

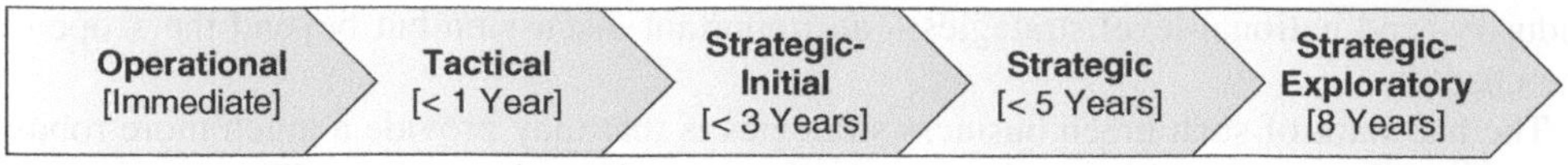

Figure 8.2 The evolving nature of green IT strategies on organizations over the next few years.

Green ICT can be used to both deliver tactical solutions for businesses to obtain some quick gains and meet legislative needs as well as enable longer term strategic solutions across a group of organizations that form a green business ecosystem.

Figure 8.2 shows the range of impact of green IT strategies on an organization (based on Unhelkar, 2011). This impact, or time-based range, of green IT strategy's influence within and across an organization ranges from operational to strategic-exploratory.

- **Operational (immediate).** Simple, immediate action taken by an organization with respect to green IT. For example, switching off the computer monitors when not in use or not printing on paper whenever possible are immediate actions, also called the low-hanging fruits. Whilst these are the most visible actions, they do not require what is considered a strategic approach. Simply inform users that they need to switch off computers when not in use, or implement an internal method to charge the users' cost centre for the use of paper. Feedback in terms of carbon usage per action, developing a consensus amongst a group of users and initial training is helpful in getting these operational green IT initiatives off the ground. Many early adopters of green IT have done precisely this.
- **Tactical (within one year).** At a tactical level, the organization needs about one year to build up its ability to reduce carbon emissions. Examples of these tactical actions include the replacement of the organization's existing computer monitors with green, flat-screen monitors, or replacing mobile gadgets and networking equipment within a year. Similarly, recycling programmes can be put together by managers for their respective departments that will encourage staff to have processes for recycling paper and reducing printing.
- **Strategic-initial (within three years).** The three-year timeframe for impact of green IT initiatives is based on strategic initiatives. These initiatives would include the senior leadership of the organization including a dedicated 'C-level' role (such as a chief sustainability officer). These green IT strategies are formulated and approved by the board, have substantial budgetary backing and are based on a holistic approach to greening that included the organization's data centres, buildings, supply chains, disposal strategies and even sales and marketing. Implementing green policies, using software and applying metrics will provide tremendous value to a green enterprise transformation – and that value will itself be maximized by keeping a 3–5-year timeframe for implementing those strategies and plans.
- **Strategic (within five years).** This green IT strategy is a further extension of the aforementioned three-year strategy but has greater depth and breadth of coverage. For example, in addition to reengineering efforts over the three-year period, this strategy would also bring about a complete attitude change in people at all levels, reorganize the business architecture and implement substantial governance mechanisms for the board. The physical infrastructure, such as buildings and data centres, will also undergo a major

revamp in this period. Strategic use of carbon data involves not only collecting and reporting data, but also identifying risks and opportunities associated with the greening and also plotting trends and patterns in terms of internal carbon savings and external carbon credits and trading. Green IT strategies thus expand into the areas of capacity planning for the organization, resourcing and skills (human resource) strategies, technology acquisitions, risk management and governances. Furthermore, the organization will be influenced by and, in turn, influence other partnering organizations through collaborative efforts. Renewable energy sources are explored and consumed – with fully automated, systems-based measurement, reporting and monetizing.
- **Strategic-exploratory (within eight years).** A green IT strategy over an eight-year time period will have to continuously explore the possibilities of carbon reduction and strive to align them with the business, which would also be changing over that time period. Therefore, such a long-term approach would require strategists to imagine the future in terms of technologies and business and incorporate it into the green IT strategy. Such explorations are important, especially for large and global organizations as well as government bodies, as they result in a think tank–based output that enables organizations to prepare for multiple, futuristic technologies. For example, such organizations will have the resources to create prototypes and measure the impacts of, say, nanotechnologies and biomimicry (technologies that mimic nature to get the best carbon results) on their carbon emissions. Coming close to a decade in future, one would expect the carbon economy to be a truly mainstream economy (with carbon trading on the stock exchange) requiring organizations to deal with carbon in all of their processes, people and technologies.

Carbon trading in future is inevitable, and the carbon factor will play a crucial role in the stock exchange of the future. Therefore, one of the most crucial considerations for an organization's decision makers is to engender a change of mindset from a tactical one to a strategic one. This is an inherently challenging situation in a market-driven economy, where all micro- and macro-economic levers are pulled by the organization to boost its share prices.

8.3 Business Drivers of Green IT Strategy

Businesses need compelling reasons to undertake and implement green IT strategies. Business drivers of green IT (Trivedi and Unhelkar, 2010; Unhelkar, 2011) can be grouped into six categories as shown in Figure 8.3: (i) costs (including energy costs and operational costs), (ii) regulatory and legal, (iii) sociocultural and political, (iv) new market opportunities, (v) enlightened self-interest and (vi) a responsible business eco-system. Green IT strategies, policies, design, implementation and practice find necessary impetus by a combination of one or more of these drivers. The influence of these drivers on green IT strategies are discussed in this section.

8.3.1 Cost Reduction

Cost reductions provide an excellent driver for an organization to come up with a comprehensive green IT strategy. As a result of a green initiative, cost reduction could be

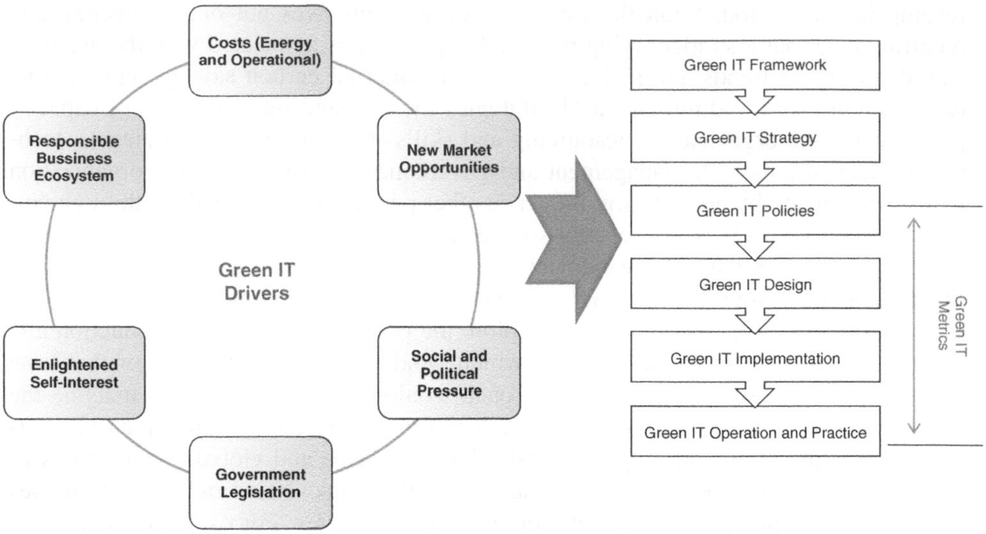

Figure 8.3 Business drivers for green IT strategies (www.methodscience.com).

derived from minimizing energy consumption (improving energy efficiency), reducing the use of raw materials and equipment, recycling equipment and waste and optimizing storage and inventory. Whilst efforts to reduce costs can provide an impetus for carbon emission reduction, organizations undertaking green transformations need to be aware of the investment that they must incur as a result of their greening effort. For example, optimizing a business process can eliminate the need for a desktop machine but, instead, there may be a need to replace that desktop with a mobile device. Virtualizing a data centre, whilst improving resource utilization and reducing cooling costs, will require some initial investment from the business for implementing virtualization. At the organizational level, costs associated with a green enterprise transformation programme need to be factored in along with the anticipated cost reduction due to the transformation.

8.3.2 Demands from Legal and Regulatory Requirements

Government rules and regulations comprise a major driver for many green enterprise transformation programmes. The relative importance given to the regulatory factor, as compared with other factors such as organization self-initiation, customer demand and pressure from society, are the highest – 70% as reported by Unhelkar (2011). Regulatory acts such as National Greenhouse and Energy Reporting (NGER) (www.climatechange.gov.au/reporting; Australian Government, 2011a) and the Carbon Pollution Reduction Scheme (CPRS) (www.climatechange.gov.au) require organizations to mandatorily report their carbon emissions if they are above a certain threshold level. Regulatory bodies also provide some basic calculators to enable greenhouse gas calculations. An example one such calculator is the NGER calculator OSCAR (Online System for Comprehensive Activity Reporting; Australian Government, 2011b). These calculators are used to determine an organization's total carbon emissions that can be used to decide whether the organization will require mandatory reporting. In addition to the basic calculators, green information systems also source external regulatory data (such as permissible emissions figures), and store, analyse and broadcast the results that enable an organization to monitor and improve its performance. These organization-specific green information systems are more sophisticated than the basic calculators provided by the regulatory bodies (Unhelkar and Philipson, 2009).

8.3.3 Sociocultural and Political Pressure

Sociocultural and political pressure become major driving forces when an organization's society recognizes the environment as of significant value and is interested in protecting it. Such acceptance of the environment's importance by the society brings pressure on the organization to change. For example, the increasing popularity of and adherence to Earth Hour (last Saturday of March in most countries), wherein almost all large edifices around the world switch off their electrical power for all non-essential things for an hour, or Earth Day (22 April in the United States and 20 March by the United Nations) have a corresponding bearing on many large businesses' sustainability strategies. This 'groundswell' of opinions also leads to corresponding shifts in political viewpoint. As a result, the organization is forced to seriously reconsider its business priorities and processes in light of the environment. Whilst the scale and nature of the benefits of such CSR for an organization can vary depending on the nature of the enterprise, and are difficult to quantify (Garito, 2011), their importance should not be discounted.

8.3.4 Enlightened Self-Interest

Self-interest comes into play when an organization, on its own accord, realizes the need to be, and the benefits of being, environmentally responsible and creates or adopts a green strategy. It may include a range of interests including the organization's desire to undertake a genuine *common* good, the need of business leadership to achieve personal satisfaction or maintain or raise employee morale or simply the decision makers' understanding that costs can be reduced and customers more satisfied with a self-interest approach that also helps the environment. The desire to achieve brand recognition based around environmental sustainability or an understanding of its impact on business continuity also forms part of this driver (Cartland, 2005). This driver can thus translate into self-motivation and has the potential to be an effective green driver for businesses. A variation of this driver, known as incentive-driven compliance (IDC), incorporates innovation and self-motivation within its environmental approach for better carbon compliance.

8.3.5 Collaborative Business Ecosystem

If a large organization that has myriad different associations with its many collaborating smaller sized organizations changes its direction and priorities, then those collaborating organizations also have to change their priorities accordingly. When such a large organization embarks on environmentally sustainability programmes in a major way encompassing its supply chain, an entire ecosystem made up of the business partners, suppliers and customers and internal users organizations, together with the industry and the corresponding business consortiums in which the organization exists, is affected. These various stakeholders and associations are invariably pushed into implementing environmentally responsible initiatives and strategies. This happens by virtue of the multiple interactions – physical and electronic – that are undertaken in the course of daily business activities. This scenario is demonstrated by HP, wherein not only are the environmental impacts monitored and managed by the organization, but also, by virtue of its own management and active involvement with the members of its supply chain, the overall carbon impact of the activities of HP's suppliers is also reduced (Velte, Velte and Elsenpeter, 2008). In addition to the impact of collaborating organizations in a business ecosystem, there are also considerations of superimposition of long-term trends upon short-term markets (Goel *et al.*, 2011). Such superimpositions bring about major business changes and restructuring in favour of ideas that are environmentally friendly.

8.3.6 New Market Opportunities

Global environmental awareness, corresponding legislations and sociocultural and political pressure on businesses have created opportunities for new markets that did exist or were not even envisaged a few years ago. For instance, these new markets can create and provide products and services that assist other organizations in achieving their green initiatives and goals. Thus, we are talking about not only 'businesses that are green' but also 'green as a business offering'. For example, carbon emissions management software (CEMS) is a new breed of software applications that are now available. The developers of these new software applications have discovered a market that did not exist before. Similarly, smart meters to measure carbon emissions, opportunities to apply new standards for the optimization of emissions and new architecture and design of low-carbon gadgets comprise markets that are likely to grow in the carbon economy.

Despite the discussion on the aforementioned drivers for businesses to undertake green initiatives, practical experience suggests that these green strategy drivers are usually interpreted by organizations in their own ways. For example, as described by Godbole (2011), within the health care sector, hospitals have significant challenges with disposal of hazardous waste, whilst insurance companies are more concerned with reducing paper use or decreasing power consumption in their data centres. Thus, in practice, these drivers will result in a combination of drivers for the business to initiate green IT – depending on what it considers as its own key environmental and business issues. In the development of a green IT strategy, not only do these drivers need independent analysis, but also they need to be studied together to see their overall impact on the organization.

8.4 Business Dimensions for Green IT Transformation

Once the drivers that provide the impetus to the business for its green initiatives are identified and documented, they lead to discussion on the areas of business that are likely to be affected by the changes. The changes resulting from green IT initiatives transform the organization and, therefore, understanding them is an integral part of a green IT strategy. An organization changes or transforms along four different lines or dimensions (Unhelkar, 2009, 2010) – economy, technical, process and people – as highlighted in Figure 8.4.

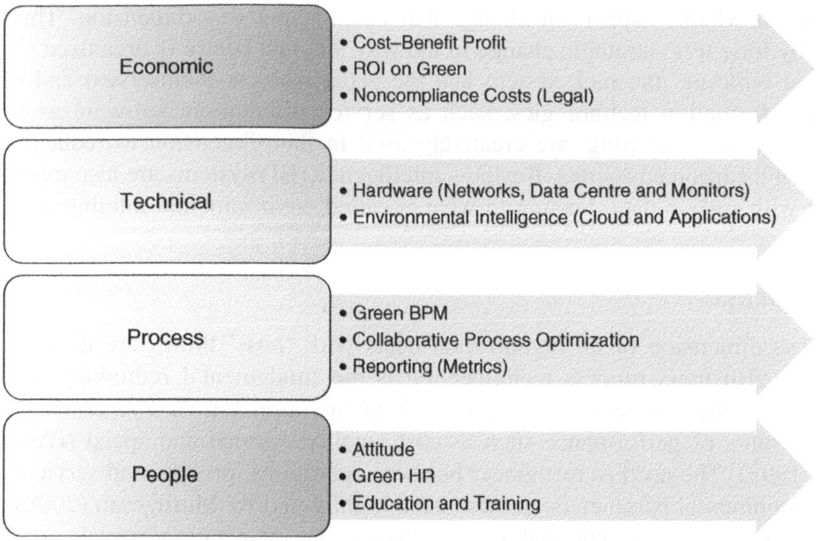

Figure 8.4 Economy, people, process and technology dimensions in a green IT strategy implementation.

These business transformation dimensions are applicable to any kind of transformation, and can be also understood as the factors that will change as an organization changes.

8.4.1 Economy

Economic considerations are one of the key factors in an organization's decision to implement environmental policies and systems. The costs associated with green transformations and the return on those costs are the first ones to appear in the minds of leaders and those in charge of the green transformation. Therefore, this is a primary dimension along which green transformation occurs in an organization. These include the cost–benefit analysis and a financial return on investment (ROI) analysis. Economic growth in the current economy is usually associated with increase in carbon emissions. This is particularly true of the developing economies, where all industries are on the rise – leading to increase in emissions across the board and not just restricted to a particular organization. For example, this economic dimension brings friction between the 'developed' and the 'developing' worlds – as was evident from the Copenhagen summit in 2009. The dichotomy between the developed world's consumption of resources and its demand for BRIC (Brazil, Russia, India and China) and other developing countries to reduce their carbon footprint towards conserving the environment for the future can lead to economic and legal quagmires.

8.4.2 Technology

In this context, by *technology* we mean an organization's hardware, network infrastructure, software and applications. This is also the more 'popular' and visible aspect of green IT. Switching off monitors, virtualizing servers and eschewing printing on physical paper are the initial, visible aspects of change that occur along this dimension. This is then followed by long-term strategic change in the way the data centre is organized (including its physical building, the rack system and the actual servers themselves) and operated. Emerging information technologies, such as service orientation, software as a service (SaaS) and cloud computing, are creatively used in this dimension to reduce an entire organization's carbon emissions. Business intelligence (BI) systems are also extended and enhanced with carbon data, leading to what is called environmental intelligence.

8.4.3 Process

The process dimension of an organization deals with 'how' things are done within an organization. Business process reengineering is the fundamental rethinking and radical redesign of business processes to achieve dramatic improvements in critical, contemporary measures of performance such as cost, quality, service and speed (Hammer and Champy, 1993). The need to reengineer business operations, process and services according to environmental parameters has also been highlighted by Murugesan (2008a). Green business process management (BPM) is wherein an organization models, studies and optimizes its processes in order to improve its green credentials. This work involves optimizing existing processes and introducing new green-aware processes that will not only reduce carbon emissions but also enhance customer experience.

The process dimension of an organization is perhaps the most visible one, and it is often used to judge the level of ecological responsibility for an organization's green ICT. This is because the process dimension has immediate and measurable effects on a business operation's carbon footprint. It also has effects on clients, vendors and business partners in the collaboration. The process' carbon footprint and compliance for green ICT operations by other business partners can serve as a good proxy for measuring the effectiveness of green ICT initiatives within the organization. Proactively maintaining devices and systems, outsourcing noncore service functions and taking precautionary actions such as installing antivirus and antispam software can all contribute to optimized support processes and reduced carbon footprint. Governance frameworks such as ITIL and CoBIT and process optimization such as Lean and Six Sigma can be used to impact an organization's business processes for carbon reduction.

8.4.4 People

The most difficult and perhaps most complex dimension of a green enterprise transformation is people. Whilst the people aspect of an organization's behaviour has been studied to great depths, in this discussion the focus is on the attitudes of individuals and the sociocultural setup in which they operate in the context of the environment. The same sociocultural driver that drives the organization towards green IT also provides challenges when the organization actually undertakes that transformation. In addition to the individual employee and the customer at the grassroots level, there is a significant challenge in addressing the people dimension in the context of business leadership for green IT transformation.

An enterprise-wide green strategy is best driven from the top of the organization in order to ensure its success. Leadership within this people aspect, such as that by senior directors and chief officers, is a deciding factor in an environmental initiative. The involvement of senior management in bringing about a change in the people dimension is vital – and it has to be done at an early stage of a green initiative, though such involvement from senior leadership requires a substantial commitment in terms of time, money and other resources. Making the key stakeholders fully aware of the importance of the green initiative for the organization and, through them, promoting the initiative to bring about fundamental changes in attitudes are keys to success.

Finally, it is worth reiterating that there is no single driver, dimension or green IT strategy that will fit all organizations. Although the discussion here has distilled the commonalities in these aspects of a strategy, still organizations need to identify, develop and implement their own specific short- and long-term green strategies. Thus, these various aspects of green IT drivers and dimensions have to be tailored to suit the industry sector, as well as the size (small or large) and type (product or service) of the organization; see the Sidebar, 'Industry Verticals and Shades of Green IT Strategies'. Thus business drivers of green IT get applied in different combinations and with varying emphasis.

Industry verticals and shades of green IT strategies	
Education	A service industry in which processes are important. Green IT can be used in collecting and promoting educational material globally. Online education mechanisms, sharing of online classrooms and tutorials can provide significant advantage in terms of reduced infrastructure and, therefore, reduced carbon.
Hospital and medicine	In addition to the processes and people relating to green IT, attention should also be paid to the fact that major IT revolutions have resulted in high-end medical equipment which, whilst saving lives, also reduce hospitals' carbon footprint. This medical equipment, together with IT systems and support, make up a substantial amount of carbon emissions.
Entertainment	Has significant infrastructure as well as operational carbon costs. For example, most high-carbon-emitting equipment such as televisions, cable TV, theatres and gaming is studded with carbon-generating gadgets. There is a need to calculate the carbon footprint by separating the procurement and installation, operation and disposal of equipment.
Finance	Information technologies and systems are heavily used in the financial world, right from providing prices for stocks through to completing trades. The entire global wealth generation and growth depend on these high-end servers and equally high-end communication equipment that have direct carbon impacts.

(*continued overleaf*)

Industry verticals and shades of green IT strategies	
Security	In a different, security-conscious new world, the security vertical is replete with electronic gadgets that produce significant carbon emission. Furthermore, with security gadgets, it is almost mandatory that they all operate for a 24/7 duration. Therefore, gadgets such as alarm systems in homes, vehicles and business premises, and the associated TV monitoring, recording and analysis, have a tremendous carbon cost in addition to the actual costs of having and operating these devices.
Telecommunications	Clearly an infrastructure type of organization, with challenges in terms of procurement and installation of large (and many times public) infrastructures. The carbon footprints of the installations are much higher than those of the operations. End-user devices and applications supporting telecom business (such as billing and operational support) also need to be studied from their procurement and operational emissions viewpoint.
Banking	Although a financial services industry, the IT infrastructure and applications used in the banking sector are staggering. Banking vertical is a very high emitter of carbon emissions and, as such, requires strategies that span both services and infrastructure aspects of green IT.
Packaging	A unique product-based industry that is involved in producing and delivering packaging materials in myriad different forms. Reusability and recycling of packaging materials as well as innovative ways of creating packaging are likely to impact environmental sustainability in a major way in this vertical. Green IT can be used as a support mechanism to facilitate optimized production of packaging.

8.5 Organizational Considerations in a Green IT Strategy

Key practical factors that need to be recognized and considered in the creation of a comprehensive green IT strategy for businesses are as follows:

- Base the green IT strategy on a firm belief that carbon footprint reduction and management are not averse to achieving business outcomes – and, in fact, could leverage business outcomes.
- Stay abreast of the holistic and subjective nature of the concept of a green enterprise that encompasses personal, individual and attitude challenges.

- Move away from the desire of organizations to focus only on gaining immediate benefits towards a more holistic approach. The attractiveness of the so-called low-hanging fruits – such as immediately switching off physical carbon-emitting hardware (e.g. monitors and data servers) – may shadow potentially holistic carbon reduction.
- Create multiple provisions to tackle the uncertainty of legislation and standards relating to carbon emissions.
- Integrate an organization's existing packages and systems with CEMS.
- Incorporate cost–benefit analysis in metrics associated with green projects, thereby focussing on payback on the environmental initiatives.
- Manage risks associated with the use of technology-based initiatives such as cloud computing, BI and knowledge management in the area of green initiatives.
- Pay due consideration to the design and construction (wherever possible) of buildings and associated infrastructures. There is opportunity for substantial reduction in the emissions of an infrastructure if attention is paid to its initial design and construction from a carbon reduction viewpoint.
- Consider data centres as specialized buildings that house data and computing servers as well as an organization's network equipment – requiring strategic attention in the early stages of their construction and installation.
- Provide education and training (attitude and culture) to the staff to change current attitudes and outline the path for change, but also consider green human resources support that encourages attitude changes.
- Consider and make provisions for technology (hardware, servers and network) upgrades that will invariably occur as the organization strategizes for a green transformation. This consideration includes reusing and recycling existing hardware as well as implementing strategies for replacing it with new, more carbon-efficient hardware.
- Consider applications and systems upgrades in two major areas – firstly, to upgrade existing applications and systems to enable the incorporation of carbon data within them and, secondly, to strategize for new CEMS that is dedicated to collecting, storing, analysing and reporting only on carbon data.
- Undertake green process reengineering and management – making use of erstwhile reengineering strategies that include identification, modelling and process optimization.
- Include green metrics and measurements that form part of identifying an organization's 'as is' state and modelling its 'to be' state.
- Ensure that legal compliance is an integral part of green IT strategies. Legal requirements can vary from local and state legislations to carbon legislations at the national level. There are also international consortiums and summits that dictate legal requirements and need to be incorporated in the ERBS.

8.6 Steps in Developing a Green IT Strategy

After giving due consideration to the wide-ranging organizational factors influencing the development of green IT strategy, this section describes the actual steps in developing a green IT strategy. The resulting strategy document may differ depending on the type, size, location and industrial vertical, and those variations will have to be factored in.

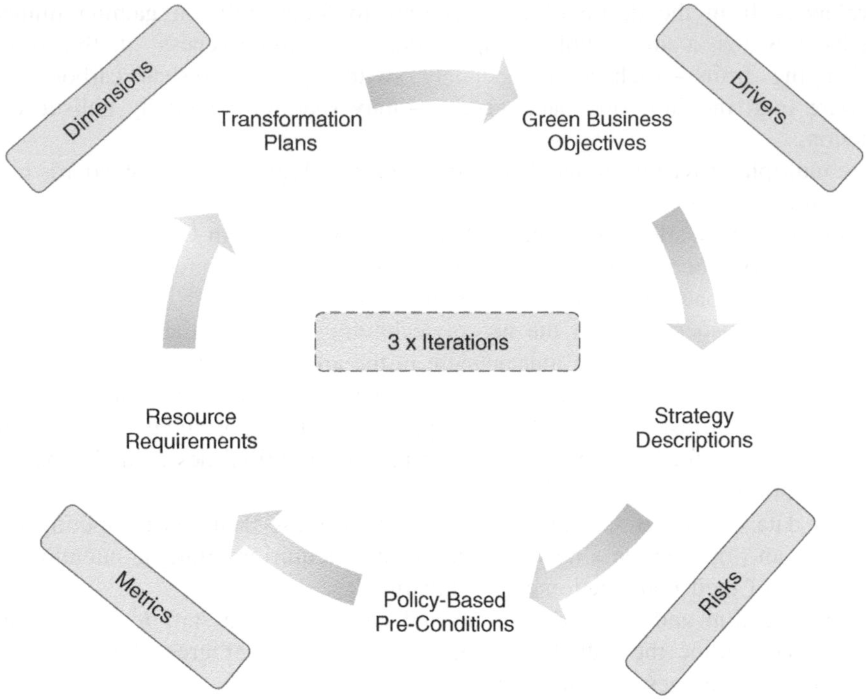

Figure 8.5 Steps in developing a green IT strategy (www.methodscience.com).

The following are the major steps that can be executed iteratively (three times) to produce a green IT strategy (see Figure 8.5).

- **Aligning green IT strategy with business objectives.** Green business objectives are the core objectives for a business undertaking green transformation. As discussed in this chapter, these objectives need to be aligned with an organization's carbon and business goals. The key drivers impacting the organization will provide an understanding of the business objective in becoming green. For example, if cost reduction is the key driver, then that will be reflected in the business objective listed in the green IT strategy – and corresponding metrics applied to it.
- **Strategy descriptions.** This section of the strategy will detail the approach the organization will take in becoming green. The green transformation dimension (economic, technical, process and people) will provide input into the strategy description. The length of time required for implementation (for example, three years) will also come into play here. Organizations can easily take 1–3 months (or more, depending on an organization's size) to develop their green IT strategy descriptions. Strategy descriptions lead to green enterprise transformation projects that influence the organization. This also requires an understanding of the current strategic plan if one exists. Strategy descriptions can be based on SMART (specific, measurable, attainable, realistic and timely) goals (The Climate Group 2008).

- **Transformation plan and timeline.** Developing a green enterprise transformation plan is the final and important step in developing a green IT strategy. A *transformation plan* is a project plan that contains tasks, roles and deliverables together with a timeline for delivery. Usually, this transformation project plan provides the roadmap for transformation. This plan is generally divided into two parts – a high-level roadmap that identifies major areas of work, deliverables and timelines, which can be followed by a detailed, task-by-task project plan that makes use of all known project and programme management techniques.
- **Iterations and risks.** Development of a green IT strategy should not be a unidirectional process. Instead, it should be developed as an iterative process going through all drivers, dimensions, risks and metrics more than once, as depicted in Figure 8.5. All influencing factors, such as the drivers, dimensions, metrics and risks, are also summarized in Figure 8.4. Typically, you may need three iterations to arrive at a final, comprehensive and actionable green IT plan. These iterations, sometimes ranging over a period of 3–6 months, may also include observing industry trends and new developments with respect to green IT. The green policies have to be revised based on these trends. These iterations also indicate an approach to implementing the policies – which should also be based on iterations. Iterative refinements of the policies are expected during practice. However, the concepts of continuous improvements in processes, people and technologies that provide impetus to a lean business initiative also apply here.

8.7 Metrics and Measurements in Green Strategies

Metrics for green IT performance of an organization can be based internal ROI goals and/or on legal reporting requirements. Whilst the ISO 14000 series of standards can provide an excellent starting point for the Key Performance Indicators (KPIs) for green IT, CEMS can be used to automate, measure and report on carbon emissions and the carbon footprint.

Following are some typical KPIs that must be embedded in an organization that is undertaking green strategies.

- **Economic outcome.** Reduce energy consumption by 10% of its current level per year for three years; increase green services (e.g. the addition of one detailed insurance service dedicated to green).
- **Technical.** Use virtualized data servers for all warehoused data; use smart meters to record, repost and control emissions.
- **Process.** Optimize supply chain management to reduce or reengineer individual processes.
- **People.** Train people for green IT at all levels. Telecommute once a week to reduce emissions.

The KPI groups described here can be further expanded in greater detail, and they will have their own nuances depending on the dimension to which they belong. For example, a KPI that is entirely focussed on carbon reduction irrespective of cost considerations may not be acceptable to an organization's economic dimension. Alternatively, a technologically advanced energy-efficient cooler might use less energy and hence have lower operational cost, but the capital expenses towards such a cooler will be part of the economic dimension. Thus, KPIs should regularly tie business efficiency with carbon reduction efficiency. Savings in carbon related to an organization's various aspects, such as production, sales and marketing, research and development and administration, need to be related to savings in costs.

8.8 Conclusions

Beginning with the basic premise that carbon reduction initiatives should not be separate from an organization's business goals, this chapter outlined the concept of green IT strategy from an immediate, tactical approach to a long-term strategic approach. The six drivers that provide the necessary impetus to an organization to undertake green business transformation and the four dimensions (economic, technical, process and people) along which such transformation can take place were discussed. Steps and process (iterations) for developing enterprise green IT strategy were presented. The future of green IT strategies is in developing and embedding them in an organization's regular business processes, monitoring the results and demonstrating the carbon savings that will provide the basis for activities such as carbon trading in the emerging carbon economy.

Review Questions

1. Discuss the drivers for businesses to implement green IT strategy. Illustrate with relevant real-world examples.
2. Explain the business dimensions for green IT transformation.
3. Discuss the organizational considerations in formulating enterprise green IT strategy.

Discussion Questions

1. What are the business drivers for green IT? Which, according to you, is the most compelling of these drivers and why?
2. What strategies would you use for green business transformation? Which of the four dimensions discussed in this chapter is the most challenging to you?
3. Describe how you would iteratively develop a comprehensive green IT strategy.
4. Create a green IT metric for each of the four dimensions of a green IT strategy.
5. Select and examine an organization's recent green IT strategy, and discuss it merits and limitations. How would you revise the strategy to address those limitation and take into consideration current developments and requirements?

References

Australian Government (2011a) Clean Energy Regulator, National Greenhouse and Energy Reporting, http://www.cleanenergyregulator.gov.au/National-Greenhouse-and-Energy-Reporting/Pages/default.aspx (accessed April 2012).

Australian Government (2011b) OSCAR v6.12.11.0: NGERS Calculator, Department of Climate Change and Energy Efficiency, https://www.oscar.gov.au/Deh.Oscar.Extension.Web/Content/NgerThresholdCalculator/Default.aspx (accessed April 2012); also see http://www.cleanenergyregulator.gov.au/National-Greenhouse-and-Energy-Reporting/Pages/default.aspx (accessed April 2012).

Cartland, S. (2005) Business continuity challenges in global supply chains. In *Global Integrated Supply Chain Systems* (ed. Y. Lan and B. Unhelkar), IDEAS Group Publishing, Hershey, PA, pp. 320–339.

Garito, M. (2011) Balancing green ICT business development with corporate social responsibility (CSR). In *Handbook of Research in Green ICT: Technical, Business and Social Perspectives* (ed. B. Unhelkar), IGI Global, Hershey, PA, pp. 607–620.

Ghose, A. (2011) Green strategic alignment: Aligning business strategies with sustainability objectives, in *Handbook of Research in Green ICT: Technical, Business and SocialPerspectives* (ed. B. Unhelkar), IGI Global, Hershey, PA, pp. 184–196

Godbole, N. (2011) In *Handbook of Research in Green ICT: Technical, Business and Social Perspectives*, IGI Global, Hershey, PA, pp. 470–479.

Goel, A., Amit Goel, A., Tiwary, A. and Schmidt, H. (2011) Approaches and initiatives to green IT strategy in business, in *Handbook of Research in Green ICT: Technical, Business and Social Perspectives* (ed. B. Unhelkar), IGI Global, Hershey, PA, pp. 169–183.

Hammer, M. and Champy, J. (1993) *Reengineering the Corporation: A Manifesto for Business Revolution*, Harper Collins, London.

Molla, A. (2009) An exploration of green IT adoption, drivers and inhibitors. In Annual Conference on Information Science and Technology Management (CISTM 2009) July 13–15.

Murugesan, S. (2007) Going green with IT: Your responsibility towards environmental sustainability. *Cutter Consortium Business-IT Strategies Executive Report*, **10** (8), 1–24.

Murugesan, S. (2008a) Harnessing green IT: Principles and practices. *IEEE IT Professional*, **10** (1), 24–33.

Murugesan, S. (ed.) (2008b) Can IT go green: Special issue. *Cutter IT Journal*, **21** (2), 3–5.

Pearce, D. (1989) *An Economic Perspective on Sustainable Development*, Environmental Economics Centre, London.

Philipson, G. (2009) Green IT and Sustainability in Australia, report by Connection Research, Australia, http://www.connectionresearch.com.au (accessed April 2012).

Schmidt, N.-H., Erek, K., Kolbe, L.M., and Zarnekow, R. (2009). Towards a procedural model for sustainable information systems management. In *42nd Hawaii International Conference on System Sciences. 2009*.

Sherringham, K. and Unhelkar, B. (2011) Strategic business trends in the context of green ICT, in *Handbook of Research in Green ICT: Technical, Business and Social Perspectives* (ed. B. Unhelkar), IGI Global, Hershey, PA, pp. 65–82.

The Climate Group (2008) SMART 2020: Enabling the Low Carbon Economy in the Information Age, http://www.smart2020.org/_assets/files/Smart2020UnitedStatesReportAddendum.pdf (accessed April 2012).

Toffler, A. (1975) *The Third Wave*, Bantam, New York.

Trivedi, B. and Unhelkar, B. (2010) Role of mobile technologies in an environmentally responsible business strategy, in *Handbook of Research in Green ICT: Technical, Business and Social Perspectives* (ed. B. Unhelkar), IGI Global, Hershey, PA, pp. 233–242.

Unhelkar B. (2009) *The Business Transformation Process*, Cutter Consortium, Arlington, MA.

Unhelkar B. (2010) *Environmentally Responsible Business Strategies for a Green Enterprise Transformation*, Cutter Consortium, Arlington, MA.

Unhelkar, B. (2011) *Green ICT Strategies and Applications*, Taylor & Francis, New York.

Unhelkar, B. and Dickens, A. (2008) Lessons in implementing “Green” business strategies with ICT. *Cutter IT Journal*, Special Issue on “Can IT Go Green?” (ed. S. Murugesan), **21** (2), 32–39.

Unhelkar, B. and Philipson, G. (2009) The development and application of a green IT maturity index. In Proceedings of the Australian Conference on Software Measurements, ACOSM2009, November.

Unhelkar, B. and Trivedi, B. (2009) Merging web services with 3G IP multimedia systems for providing solutions in managing environmental compliance by businesses. In Proceedings of the 3rd International Conference on Internet Technologies and Applications (Internet Technologies and Applications, ITA 09), Wrexham, North Wales, September 8–11.

Velte, T., Velte, A. and Elsenpeter, R. (2008) *Green IT: Reduce Your Information System's Environmental Impact While Adding to the Bottom Line*. McGraw-Hill, New York.

Worthington, T. (2009) ICT Sustainability: Assessment and Strategies for a Low Carbon Future eBook, http://www.tomw.net.au/ict_sustainability/ (accessed 20 December 2011).

9

Sustainable Information Systems and Green Metrics

Edward Curry[1] and Brian Donnellan[2]

[1]*Digital Enterprise Research Institute, National University of Ireland, Galway, Ireland*
[2]*Innovation Value Institute, National University of Ireland, Maynooth, Kildare, Ireland*

Key Points

- Introduces green and sustainable informatics and metrics as a tool to monitor and drive sustainable behaviour.
- Describes the multilevel nature of green metrics with examples at the regional, organizational, functional, product/service, and individual levels.
- Provides an overview of the metrics and standards for greenhouse gas reporting, life cycle impact analysis, energy efficiency within data centres and assessing the maturity of sustainable information and communication technology (SCIT) within organizations.
- Illustrates applications of the Natural Step Framework to develop a sustainable strategy for local government, with relevant KPIs.

9.1 Introduction

It is estimated that information and communication technology (ICT) is responsible for at least 2% of global greenhouse gas (GHG) emissions (Webb, 2008). The first wave of green Information Technology (green IT), *greening of IT,* aims to reduce 2% of global emissions from IT by reducing the footprint of ICT by actions such as improving the energy efficiency of hardware (processors and disk drives), and waste from obsolete hardware. The second wave of green IT, *greening by IT*, also called Green IT 2.0 or Sustainable IT (Murugesan and Laplante, 2011), is shifting the focus towards reducing the remaining 98% by focussing on the innovative use of IT and Information Systems (IS) in business processes to deliver positive sustainability benefits beyond the direct

Harnessing Green IT: Principles and Practices, First Edition. Edited by San Murugesan and G.R. Gangadharan.

footprint of IT, such as monitoring a firm's emissions and waste to manage them more efficiently. The potential of *IT for greening* to reduce GHG emissions has been estimated at approximately 7.8 Gt CO_2 of savings in 2020, representing a 15% emission cut in 2020 and £600 billion (US$946.5 billion) of cost savings (Webb, 2008). The use of IT for greening will play a key role in the delivery of benefits that can alleviate an estimated five times the GHG footprint of IT itself (Enkvist, Nauclér, and Rosander, 2007).

Relevant and accurate data, information, metrics and key performance indicators (KPIs) are critical to supporting sustainable practices, and the need to manage this information has led to the emergence of green information systems (GIS) as a field in itself. There is substantial potential for green IS to bring together business processes, resource planning, direct and in-direct activities and extended supply chains to effect positive changes across the entire activities of governments, organizations and individuals. Green IS is the engine driving both the strategic and operational management of sustainability. Organizations pursuing a sustainability agenda will need to consider their green IS (Watson, Boudreau, and Chen, 2010) to be as critical as their other operational IS such as finance or production.

Whilst distinction between green IS and green IT exists (Boudreau, Chen, and Huber, 2008), in this chapter we will consider the broad need for *sustainable information* to support both *green for IT* and *IT for green*. As sustainable information is needed at both the macro and micro levels, it will require a multilevel approach that provides information and metrics that can drive high-level strategic corporate and regional sustainability plans as well as low-level actions like improving the energy efficiency of an office worker.

The chapter starts with an overview of the need for multilevel sustainable information, and introduces the wider context of sustainability frameworks, principles and tools. It then examines the information requirements and methods utilized at multiple levels including regional (regional sustainability plan), organization (GHG emission reporting), business function (data centre energy efficiency), individual (commute tracking), and product and service (life cycle assessment (LCA)). It also examines how the sustainability capability of an organization can be examined to determine its effectiveness and highlight areas for further research.

9.2 Multilevel Sustainable Information

Sustainability requires information on the use, flows and destinies of energy, water and materials including waste, along with monetary information on environment-related costs, earnings and savings. This type of information is critical if we are to understand the causal relationships between the various actions that can be taken and their impact on sustainable performance. However, the problem is broad in scope and the necessary information may not be available, or may be difficult to collect. Improving sustainability performance, especially through changing the way an organization or activity operates, requires a number of practical steps which will include the need for a systematic approach for information gathering and analysis.

In order to tackle the problem, it is important to break it down into smaller, manageable pieces by adding boundaries and scopes to activities to make them more manageable. A 'boundary' or 'scope' can be drawn narrowly for a specific activity (e.g. to consider only the emissions that arise directly from that activity) or broadly (including emissions indirectly associated with the activity).

We will look at the problem of sustainability from the perspective of a multilevel information problem, where individual levels are used to provide a scope and boundary for activities (see Table 9.1).

Information can flow between levels as necessary, allowing the granularity of the problem to be set as needed. This allows the sustainable information to be tackled at high or low levels of detail. In order to avoid a myopic view of the benefits of sustainable

Table 9.1 Multilevel sustainable information

Level	Stakeholders	Information requirements	Information regarding
Regional/City	Public administration, policymakers, politicians, corporations, citizens, and regulators	Regional sustainability plans, movement and transport, biodiversity and environmental impacts, health and well being, resource management, waste disposal	Regional energy consumption Energy consumption by sector GHG emissions per capita GHG intensity of energy consumption
Organizational	Executive team, shareholders, citizens, regulators, suppliers and consumers	Corporate sustainable reports, sustainability plans, sustainable business objectives, business function performance, and so on	Total energy consumption Total electricity consumption Percentage of renewable energy sources
Functional	Function management team, organization management and employees	Function sustainability performance, functions sustainability objectives and so on	Facility electricity consumption Internal electricity consumption DC electricity consumption
Individual	Citizens and employees	Direct and indirect cost of actions of the individual, private travel, energy use, work commute and impacts of products and services consumed	Business travel Employee commuting Employee IT energy use
Product or service	Product producers and consumers	Analysis of the sustainability impacts of the product or service, manufacturing cost, usage cost, disposal cost and so on	Server electricity consumption Laptop electricity consumption

information and to understand its real impacts, we must first understand and examine the bigger picture of sustainability.

9.3 Sustainability Hierarchy Models

Sustainability is a complex and broad subject. In order to make sense of the various frameworks and tools, Hitchcock and Willard (2008) created a hierarchy of sustainability models that is illustrated in Figure 9.1.

- **Natural laws:** The laws imposed upon us by Mother Nature such as the Law of Conservation of Mass and Energy, Law of Entropy and Laws of Thermodynamics.
- **Frameworks:** High-level conceptual rules for sustainability that conform to natural laws.
- **Principles:** General and sector-specific guidelines that detail sustainable practices and actions.
- **Tools:** Methodologies, standards and strategies for implementation.

As natural laws are well described by their respective disciples, for the remainder of this section we will focus on the bottom three levels of the hierarchy, starting with frameworks for sustainability.

9.3.1 Sustainability Frameworks

In order to improve the understanding and communication of sustainability issues and to provide high-level definitions of sustainability, a number of frameworks have been proposed. Natural Capitalism, The Natural Step, Ecological Footprint and the triple bottom line (TBL) are popular frameworks and are described in this section. These frameworks are used to reach a shared mental model of sustainability, providing concrete definitions and scoping for concepts and terms (Hitchcock and Willard, 2008). The frameworks can be used to develop high-level visions and planning for sustainability activities.

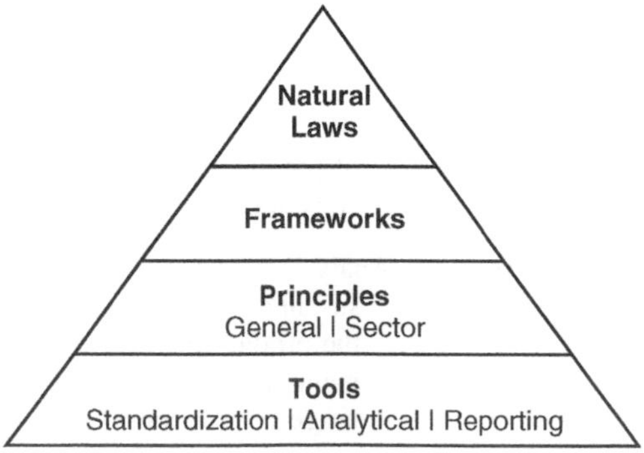

Figure 9.1 Hierarchy of sustainability models (adapted from Hitchcock and Willard, 2008).

9.3.1.1 Natural Capitalism

The concept of Natural Capitalism, an extension of the economic concept of capital to the natural environment (Hawken, Lovins, and Lovins, 1999), is to look at the environment as a system that yields a valuable flow of goods and services (e.g. fish, trees and other such things). Natural capitalism requires the following shifts in business practices: Radically increase productivity in the use of natural resources; shift to biologically inspired production models and materials; move to a 'service-and-flow' business model; and reinvest in natural capital.

9.3.1.2 The Natural Step

The objective of The Natural Step (Nattrass and Altomare, 1999) is to help reduce the potential causes of environmental problems. This framework defines four system conditions, derived from the Laws of Thermodynamics, for a sustainable society. In a sustainable society, nature's functions and diversity must not be systematically subjected to (1) increasing concentrations of substances extracted from the Earth's crust, (2) increasing concentrations of substances produced by society and (3) degradation by physical means. Furthermore, (4) resources must be used fairly and efficiently to meet the basic needs of people worldwide (Table 9.2).

9.3.1.3 Ecological Footprint

The ecological footprint (Rees, 1992; Wackernagel and Rees, 1996) is the measure of environmental impact of particular actions on the Earth's natural resources and ecosystem functionality. It compares human demand with the Earth's ecological capacity to regenerate. The assessment can be used at the individual, city or regional level to estimate how much of the Earth (or how many planet Earths) it would take to support humanity if everybody lived a given lifestyle.

Table 9.2 The natural step framework: system conditions and sustainability principles

System conditions	Sustainability principles
Concentrations of substances extracted from the Earth's crust	Eliminate our contribution to the progressive build-up of substances extracted from the Earth's crust (e.g. heavy metals and fossil fuels)
Concentrations of substances produced by society	Eliminate our contribution to the progressive build-up of chemicals and compounds produced by society (e.g. dioxins, polychlorinated biphenyls (PCBs) and dichlorodiphenyltrichloroethane (DDT))
Degradation by physical means	Eliminate our contribution to the progressive physical degradation and destruction of nature and natural processes (e.g. over-harvesting forests and paving over critical wildlife habitat)
In that society, people not subject to conditions that systemically undermine their capacity to meet their needs	Eliminate our contribution to conditions that undermine people's capacity to meet their basic human needs (e.g. unsafe working conditions and not enough pay to live on)

9.3.1.4 Triple Bottom Line (TBL)

The TBL framework (Elkington, 1998) allows an organization to focus on not only its economic bottom line, but also its environmental and social 'bottom lines'. TBL expands the scope of responsibility for an organization from shareholders and owners to also include stakeholders – anyone who is influenced, either directly or indirectly, by the actions of the organization.

Other sustainability frameworks include cradle to cradle (McDonough and Braungart, 2002), biomimicry (Benyus, 1997), social return on investment (Scholten and Olsen, 2006) and the sustainability helix.

9.3.2 Sustainability Principles

Below the high-level frameworks are a broad range of principles that provide guidance on the sustainability practices needed to achieve the objectives set out in higher level frameworks. Principles are typically created via a group or community process with the aim to produce a number of aspirational statements to provide guidance (often common sense) on sustainability.

General principles for sustainability are broad guidelines that can be applied within any domain or sector. Two well-known general principles, mentioned in this section, are the 3 Rs and Earth Charter. Sector-specific principles complement general principles with guidance to help translate what sustainability means within the context of a sector such as government, international business or higher level education.

9.3.2.1 Reduce, Reuse and Recycle (3R's)

Reduce, *Reuse* and *Recycle* are three waste management strategies that are used collectively within a waste hierarchy known as the 3 Rs. The 3 Rs classify the strategies according to the desired order of use: It is better to reduce than reuse, and better to reuse than recycle. The aim of the waste hierarchy is to extract the maximum practical benefits from products and to generate the minimum amount of waste.

9.3.2.2 Earth Charter

The Earth Charter is an international declaration on the principles needed to build a just, sustainable and peaceful global society. The Earth Charter proposes that environmental protection, human rights, equitable human development and peace are interdependent and indivisible.

9.3.3 Tools for Sustainability

At the bottom of the hierarchy are the sustainability tools that provide guidance and best practices. Sustainability tools come in many forms, from methodologies used to help determine the environmental impact of a steel water bottle, to certifying the design and construction of a building. Sustainability tools can be general purpose, such as the GHG Protocol for emissions reporting, or specific to a sector, like the Leadership in Energy and Environmental Design (LEED) for green building certification. A detailed list of sustainability tools is given in this chapter's Appendix. These tools provide sustainability information needed to make sustainable decisions and drive sustainable behaviour. Many of these tools can be classified as *IT for green* or as an opportunity for IT to 'green' processes or activities outside of IT.

9.4 Product Level Information

Understanding the impacts of a product or service requires an analysis of all potential impacts associated with a product, process or service for its entire life cycle. This is achieved using a technique known as life cycle assessment.

9.4.1 Life-Cycle Assessment

Life-cycle assessment (LCA), also known as life cycle analysis, is a technique to systematically identify resource flows and environmental impacts associated with all the stages of product and service provision. LCA provides a quantitative cradle-to-grave analysis of the products or services' global environmental costs (i.e. from raw materials through materials processing, manufacture, distribution, use, repair and maintenance and disposal or recycling). The demand for LCA data and tools has accelerated with the growing global demand to assess and reduce GHG emissions from different manufacturing and service sectors (Horne, Grant, and Verghese, 2009).

LCA can be used as a tool to study the impacts of a single product to determine the stages of its life cycle with most impact (Levi Strauss & Co., 2009). LCA can also be used as decision support when determining the environmental impact of two comparable products or services (Goleman and Norris, 2009).

9.4.2 The Four Stages of LCA

For a LCA, both ISO 14040 (ISO, 2006a) and 14044 (ISO, 2006b) standards follow four distinct phases process, which are briefly described here.

1. **Goal and scope definition:** It is important to ask the right question to ensure whether the LCA is successful. The first step in this process is the framing of the key questions for the assessment. Typical steps include defining the goal(s) of the study, determining what type of information is needed to inform decision makers, defining functional units (environmental impact, energy efficiency, life span, cost per use, etc.), defining the system boundaries and studying perspective, allocation principles, environmental impact assessment categories and level of detail.
2. **Inventory analysis:** The second phase involves data collection and modelling of the product and service system with process flow models and inventories of resource use and process emissions. The data must be related to the functional unit defined in the goal and scope definition and include all data related to environmental (e.g. CO_2) and technical (e.g. intermediate chemicals) quantities for all relevant unit processes within the study boundaries that compose the product system. Examples of inputs and outputs include materials, energy, chemicals, air emissions, water emissions, solid

waste, radiation and land use. The results of a life cycle inventory provide verified information about all inputs and outputs in the form of elementary flow to and from the environment from all the unit processes involved in the study.

3. **Impact assessment:** The third phase evaluates the contribution to selected impact assessment categories, such as 'climate change', 'energy usage' and 'resource depletion'. Impact potential of the inventory is calculated and characterized according to the categories. Results can then be normalized across categories (same unit) and weighted according to the relative importance of the category; both of these actions are voluntary according to the ISO standard.
4. **Interpretation:** The final phase involves interpretation of the results to determine the level of confidence and communicate them in a fair, complete and accurate manner. This is accomplished by identifying the data elements that contribute significantly to each impact category, evaluating the sensitivity of these significant data elements, assessing the completeness and consistency of the study and drawing conclusions and recommendations based on a clear understanding of how the LCA was conducted and the results were developed (Skone, 2000).

9.4.3 CRT Monitors versus LCD Monitors: Life Cycle Assessment

A comprehensive environmental LCA of the traditional cathode ray tube (CRT) and newer liquid crystal display (LCD) monitors was conducted through the EPA's Design for the Environment (DfE) programme. The objective of the study (Socolof, Overly, and Geibig, 2005) was to evaluate the environmental and human health life cycle impacts of functionally equivalent 17 in. CRT and 15 in. LCD monitors. The study assessed the energy consumption, resources input and pollution produced over the lifetime of the equipment. The cradle-to-grave analysis was divided into three stages: (i) cradle to gate (manufacturing), (ii) use and (iii) end of life (disposing or reusing). Each stage was assessed for the energy consumed, materials used in manufacturing and associated waste. Components manufactured in different locations, where energy sources can differ due to the way local energy is produced, such as coal versus nuclear, were taken into account.

A sample of the results from a life cycle environmental assessment is presented in Table 9.3. In summary, the LCA concluded that LCD monitors are about 10 times better for resource usage and energy use, and five times better for landfill use. However, LCDs are only 15% better for global warming because the LCD manufacturing process uses sulphur hexafluoride, a significant GHG.

9.5 Individual Level Information

In a similar manner to other levels, understanding impacts at the level of an individual requires a holistic view of activities. Primary sources of emissions for an individual will include the life cycle of products and services they purchase and use, the construction (LCA of material and construction) and operation of their residence (energy use, water use and waste disposal and recycling) and private travel (especially emissions from long-haul flights).

The ability for individuals to understand the impacts of their activities is critical. Online carbon calculators are a popular mechanism to calculate impact; however, these may

Table 9.3 Life cycle analyses of CRT and LCD monitors

	17 in. CRT	15 in. LCD
Total input material	21.6 kg	5.73 kg
Steel	5.16 kg	2.53 kg
Plastics	3 lb.	1.78 kg
Glass	0.0 kg	0.59 kg
Lead–oxide glass	9.76 kg (0.45 lb. of lead)	0.0 kg
PCBs	0.85 kg	0.37 kg
Wires	0.45 kg	0.23 kg
Aluminium	0.27 kg	0.13 kg
Energy (in manufacturing)	20.8 GJ	2.84 GJ
Power drawn	126 W	17 W
Energy (use – five years at full power)	2.2 GJ	850 MJ

have significant limitation including static calculation, a lack of personalization and limited capacity for historical analysis. However, tools are improving for individuals. For instance, home energy usage is an area that has seen the early adoption of real-time monitoring systems with the on-going development of smart meters and the Smart Grids. Studies have shown that energy conservation improves if residents receive real-time feedback on their energy usage; one study in Ontario showed the average household reduced its electricity usage by 6.5% (Mountain, 2006). Another interesting development is the utilization of smart phones as a low-cost means to determine the impacts associated with commuting.

A significant contribution to CO_2 emissions levels is the daily commute by an individual. In response to addressing this challenge, a group of Volvo employees wanted to develop an IT solution that would motivate people to reduce the emission cost of their daily commute by measuring the time, efficiency and environmental impact of their commuting. By using a small application on mobile phones, Volvo turned the device into a CO_2 pedometer to calculate the environmental impact of each commute, whilst helping them to make the right daily choices of transport modes towards efficiency and sustainability. In a 2009 pilot, Volvo employees were able to reduce their CO_2 footprint by 30% in just one month's time.

This app was transformed into a global service and launched as Commute Greener!, which is able to help companies, cities and individuals around the world understand how to commute in a greener way (Commute Greener, 2010). The system aggregates the commute data of individuals to build commute patterns that are useful for decision making at higher levels, for understanding the commute pattern within a city or for providing information for a company. This information can be used to optimize public transport, company shuttles and carpooling. Efforts such as Commute Greener and Smart Grids show how tracking information at the individual level can benefit the individual directly, and also be aggregated at a higher level of analysis to benefit a region or community.

9.6 Functional Level Information

An organization typically comprises multiple functions or operating divisions and departments including marketing, finance, operations, human resources and research and development. Sustainability issues at the functional level are related to business processes and the value chain; they involve the development and coordination of resources through which the overall organization's objectives and goals can be executed efficiently and effectively.

A close relationship exists between organization level and functional level metrics, and it is important that metrics at both levels be aligned. Typically, metrics at the functional-level will be more granular to provide specific detail on the operations of the function. Functional level metrics can then be aggregated into an organization level metric.

Monitoring energy usage for an IT function can involve metrics around building energy usage (lights and heat), staff computer energy usage and in particular energy used within data centres. In Section 9.6.1, we examine energy usage within the data centre and the role of metrics.

9.6.1 Data Centre Energy Efficiency

The power needs of data centres may range from a few kilowatts for a rack of servers in a closet, to several tens of megawatts for large facilities. Power usage in a data centre goes beyond the direct power needs of servers to include networking, cooling, lighting and facilities management. The US Environmental Protection Agency (EPA) estimates that servers and data centres are responsible for up to 1.5% of the total US electricity consumption (EPA, 2007) or roughly 0.5% of US GHG emissions for 2007. The same report also highlights that significant power consumed by data centres is not used on computation; for every 100 W supplied, only 11.2 W were used for computation. With electricity costs the dominant operating expense of a data centre, it is vital to maximize the centre's operational efficiency to reduce both the environmental and economic costs (Belday *et al.*, 2008). In this section, we focus on metrics that help to understand a data centre's energy efficiency.

9.6.2 Data Centre Power Metrics

Developed by the Green Grid, power usage effectiveness (PUE) is a measure of how efficiently a data centre uses its power. PUE measures how much power the computing equipment consumes in contrast to cooling and other overheads uses. PUE is defined as follows:

$$PUE = Total\ Facility\ Power/IT\ Equipment\ Power$$

The reciprocal of PUE is data centre infrastructure efficiency (DCiE) and is defined as follows:

$$DCiE = 1/PUE = IT\ Equipment\ Power/Total\ Facility\ Power \times 100\%$$

IT equipment power includes the load associated with all of the IT equipment, such as compute, storage and network equipment, along with supplemental equipment used to monitor or otherwise control the data centre including Keyboard Video Mouse (KVM) switches, monitors, workstations and laptops. *Total facility power* includes everything that supports the IT equipment load such as power delivery (uninterruptible power supply (UPS), generators, batteries, etc.), a cooling system (chillers, computer room air conditioning units (CRACs), direct expansion air handler (DX) units, pumps and cooling towers), compute, network, storage nodes and other loads such as data centre lighting.

9.6.3 Emerging Data Centre Metrics

When assessing the financial health of a business, one should not look at one metric in isolation. The same is true for assessing the efficiency of a data centre. Whilst PUE and DCiE have proven to be effective industry tools for measuring infrastructure energy efficiency, there is a need to measure the operational effectiveness of the data centre. To this end, a number of metrics are under development to measure dimensions including resource utilization and environmental impact. Each of these metrics provides data centre operators more visibility into where opportunities for further efficiency improvements exist.

- **Carbon usage effectiveness (CUE):** Measures data centre–specific carbon emissions, which are emerging as an extremely important factor in the design, location and operation of a data centre. CUE, combined with PUE, can assess the relative sustainability of a data centre to determine if any energy efficiency and/or sustainable energy improvements need to be made. Note: CUE does not cover the emissions associated with the data centre or the building itself. CUE is define as:

$$CUE = CO_2 \ emitted \ (\mathrm{kgCO_2\ eq})/unit\ of\ energy\ (\mathrm{kWh}))$$
$$\times\ (Total\ Data\ Centre\ Energy/IT\ Equipment\ Energy)$$

- **Energy reuse effectiveness (ERE):** Many data centres are now recovering waste energy from their operations and reusing it outside of the data centre such as heating office space or homes. Since PUE does not consider these alternate uses for waste energy, the ERE metric is used.

$$ERE = (Total\ Facility\ Power - Power\ Reuse)/IT\ Equipment\ Power$$

- **Data centre energy productivity (DCeP):** DCeP quantifies useful work compared to the energy it requires. It can be calculated for an individual IT device or a cluster of computing equipment. DCeP is a sophisticated metric where useful work and energy are compared relative to a user-defined time limit.

$$DCeP = Useful\ Work\ Produced/Total\ Data\ Centre\ Energy\ Consumed\ over\ time$$

- **Data centre computer efficiency (DCcE):** DCcE – and its underlying submetric, server compute efficiency (ScE), enables data centre operators to determine the efficiency of their compute resources, which allows them to identify areas of inefficiency. The metric can reveal unused compute resource within a data centre making it easier for data centre operators to discover unused servers (both physical and virtual) and then decommission or redeploy them.
- **Environmental consumer chargeback:** Carbon dioxide and environmental damage are gaining acceptance as viable chargeable commodities. Using environmental chargeback models (Curry et al., 2012b) data center operators can "chargeback" the environmental

impacts (i.e. CO_2 emissions), in addition to the financial costs, of their services to the consuming end-users. Environmental chargebacks can have a positive effect on environmental impacts by linking consumers to the indirect impacts of their service usage, allowing them to understand the impact of their actions.

Energy consumption metrics do not tell the full story of the impacts of data centres on the environment. In order to understand the full environmental burden of a data centre a full life cycle assessment of the data centre facilities and IT equipment is needed. These additional costs should not be under-estimated. Take, for example, Microsoft's data centre in Quincy, Washington that consumes 48 MW (enough power for 40 000 homes) of power. In addition to the concrete and steel used in the construction of the building, the data centre uses 4.8 km of chillers piping, 965 km of electrical wire, 92 900 m^2 of drywall and 1.5 metric tons of batteries for backup power. Each of these components has its own impact that must be analysed in detail. This level of analysis is discussed later in the chapter.

9.7 Organizational Level Information

Whilst specific measures may differ, sustainability is important to organizations from all sectors – from service-based organizations to manufacturing organizations, from national government to local authorities and city councils. Sustainability strategy and direction are determined at the organization level based on macro concerns; identifying the overall sustainability goals of the organization, determining the types of businesses and activities in which the organization should be involved and defining organizational responsibilities.

Organizations need to determine their goals and objectives for sustainability. Typically, organizational sustainability goals involve one or more of the following:

- Develop significant capabilities and a reputation for sustainability leadership.
- Keep pace with industry or stakeholder expectations.
- Meet minimum compliance requirements and reap readily available benefits.

Agreeing on one's desired business posture on sustainability will have a significant impact on business and thus on necessary goals and priorities. It is important to be clear about the organization's business objectives and the role of sustainability in enabling those objectives.

Performance metrics and KPIs are used to measure environmental, social and economic impacts, and to ensure the delivery of strategic (and sustainability-related) objectives. Further, they help to ensure the alignment of organizational activities and performance to sustainable strategy. Sustainability performance measures and KPIs help organizations to establish progress against sustainability goals and to ensure that they cover their environmental, social and economic impacts. A sample of widely used TBL KPIs typically found in organization level sustainability reports, also known as integrated reporting (Eccles and Krzus, 2010), is provided in Table 9.4.

9.7.1 Reporting Greenhouse Gas Emissions

The GHG Protocol is the most widely used international accounting tool for government and business leaders to understand, quantify and manage the emissions of all six major

Table 9.4 A summary of widely used KPIs in sustainability reports

Economic indicators	Environmental indicators	Social indicators
Revenues	Investments in environmental protection	Raises awareness and upholds organization's values, code of conduct and principles
Operating costs	Greenhouse gas emissions	Total workforce by employment type, contract and region
Operating margin	Spills	Hours worked
Operating profit	Water use	Employee turnover
Employee wages	Waste (hazardous and nonhazardous)	Minorities in management
Employee benefits	Employee commuting	Benefits for full-time and part-time employees
Payments to providers of capital	Environmental and polluting fines	Employee education and training expenditure
Payments to government in taxes	Total energy consumption	Percentage of employees receiving regular performance and career reviews
Research and development	Renewable energy consumption	Flexible working arrangements
Sustainable innovations	Facility energy consumption	Employee satisfaction
Customer satisfaction	Internal energy consumption	Remuneration and bonuses related to sustainable development
Product safety and quality	Data centre energy consumption	Injuries and accidents
Capital and exploration expenditure	Business travel (flights)	Child labour
Sales and marketing	Fleet fuel consumption	Community contribution
General and administration	Paper consumption	Losses of customer data
	Noncompliance with regulations and voluntary codes	
	Sites with a (certified) environmental management system	

GHGs: carbon dioxide (CO_2), methane (CH_4), nitrous oxide (N_2O), hydrofluorocarbons (HFCs), perfluorocarbons (PFCs) and sulphur hexafluoride (SF_6). Many of these gases have a 'global warming potential' that is many times greater than that of CO_2. The GHG emissions generated directly and indirectly by an organization can be classified into three 'scopes', based on the source of the emissions. The scope of emissions is illustrated in Figure 9.2. The GHG Protocol is based on five principles (relevance, completeness, consistency, transparency and accuracy) and lays out a sequence of steps that organizations should follow to account for and report their emissions of GHG. These include the following:

1. Defining the geographical boundaries within which the organization operates.
2. Setting organizational boundaries.
3. Identifying reporting entities at the corporate and facility levels.
4. Deciding emission scopes (1, 2 and/or 3) and which GHGs are to be reported.
5. As appropriate, adopting estimating protocols specific to their sector(s) of industry.
6. Establishing a base year and setting targets for future years.

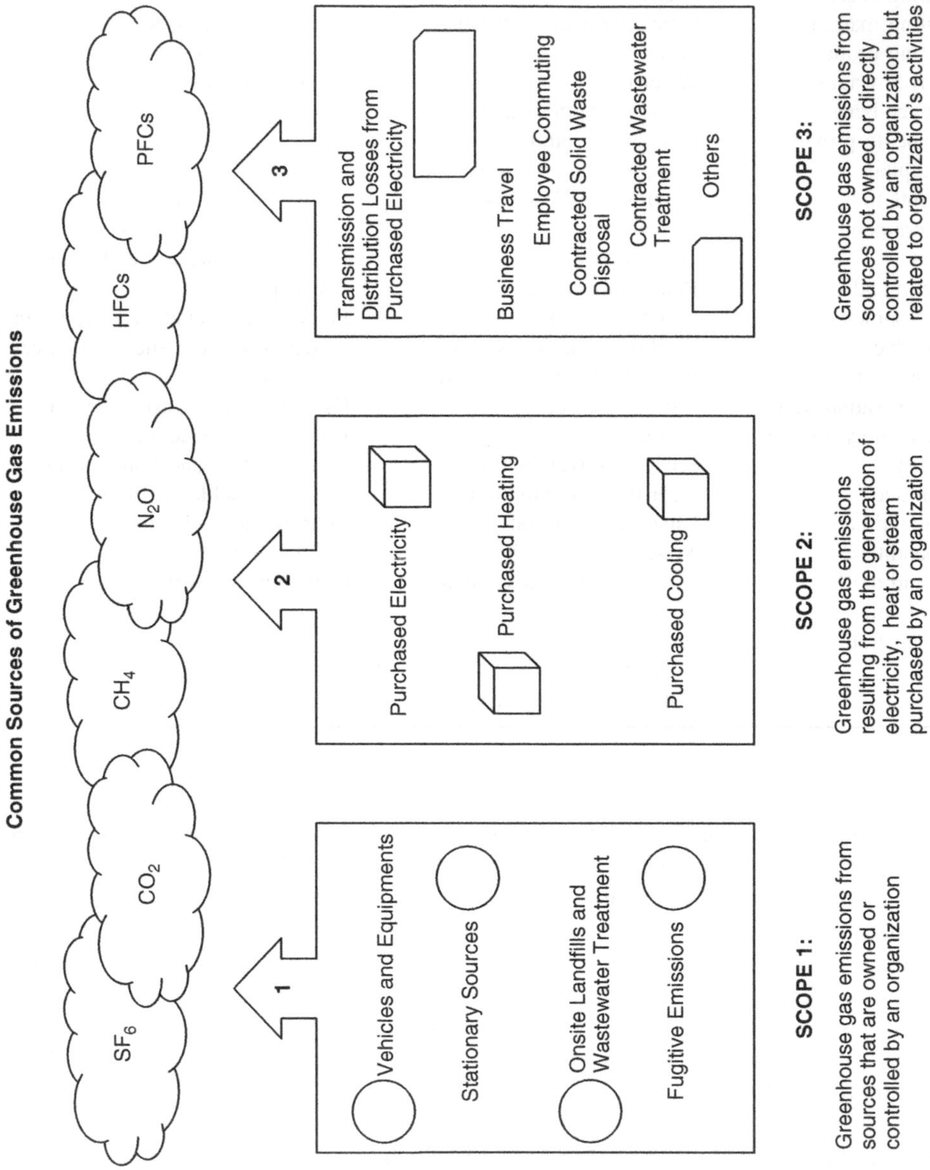

Figure 9.2 Scopes of greenhouse gas emissions.

9.8 Regional/City Level Information

It is critical that we understand the impacts that regions have on people and the environment. Understanding the relationship between economic, environmental, and social factors is essential for the authorities within a region to manage their approach to sustainability. In 2008, for the first time in human history, over half the world's population live in cities in addition, cities are responsible for generating more than 80% of global GDP yet they occupy just 2% of the world's land surface. The challenge of developing sustainable city regions is likely to become more complex as populations continue to migrate to urban centres.

Strong leadership and governance plays a key role in enhancing a regions sustainability through plans and policies that enhancing resource efficiency and embrace new technologies to improve levels of sustainability through careful management and planning. To ensure that the region is moving towards sustainability the baseline and trend information across all aspects of the region must be made using indicators to track the progress of key aspects of the region such as energy use, total employment rate or level of mental well-being, and to use this information to effect positive change. These indicators should be contextualized with a set of region statistics against which the indicators can be measured or analysed (i.e. population, population density, age dependency ratios, geographical size, national and regional gross domestic produce and gross national product, consumer price indices, life expectancy, etc.).

To contextualise a regions performance in an international context it is possaible to benchmark against peer regions, for city regions a number of benchmarks are available. The European Green City Index is a collaboration between Siemens and the Economist intelligence unit developed. The 2009 index compared 30 European Cities with one another along 30 different criteria, both qualitative and quantitative. The Index considers eight themes; CO_2 emissions, energy, buildings, transport, water, waste & land use, air and environmental governance. The Carbon Disclosure Project has a wealth of experience in monitoring the GHG emissions from companies; they are extending the project to the city scale. Carbon Disclosure Project for Cities initiative allows cities to disclose their emissions data and benchmark their performance against other cities.

9.8.1 Developing a City Sustainability Plan: A Case Study

We examine how Dublin City Council went about developing its sustainability plan.

In January 2009, Dublin City Council began preparation of its new *Dublin City Development Plan 2011–2017,* as required under Ireland's Statutory Planning Process. The Dublin City Council used the Natural Step Framework, summarized in Table 9.2, to define a generic 'golden standard' planning process to help the local authority better leverage its internal resources and refine governance systems to achieve long-lasting cultural change from within to accelerate the city's progression towards sustainability.

Dublin City Council operationalized the framework through an implementation schema (Ny *et al.*, 2006, 2008) composed of five specific levels: systems level, purpose level, strategic level, actions level and tools level. The City Council developed a governance model based on these levels as detailed in Table 9.5.

Table 9.5 Sustainability governance plan of Dublin City Council

Level	Practical application of framework
Joined-up systems	Six themes identified to build alliances
Vision	Vision of a sustainable Dublin
Strategy	Development plan policies
Actions	Implementation of development plan Development management Guiding principles Sustainable standards Objectives
Tools	Monitoring body and indicators

Source: Dublin City Council (2010).

This integrated approach is useful as it helps 'avoid the tendency in planning to focus only on a subset of issues or areas ignoring broader, connected issues leading to a need to expand the system boundaries' (Waldron *et al.*, 2008). The integrated action plan arising out of this approach is given in Table 9.6.

Examples of indicators used to support the Dublin City Council sustainability plan are provided in Table 9.7. However, as illustrated by Table 9.6, this information is spread across many initiatives and functions within the council, and with partners. Sustainable information management is a significant challenge for the council.

9.9 Measuring the Maturity of Sustainable ICT

IT organizations need to develop a sustainable information and communication technology (SICT) capability to deliver sustainability benefits both internally and across the enterprise. However, due to the new and evolving nature of the field, few guidelines and guidance on best practices are available. In order to assist organizations understand the maturity of their SICT capability, a number of tools for measuring SICT maturity have been developed including the G-readiness framework (Molla *et al.*, 2008; O'Flynn, 2010) which provides a benchmark score against SICT best practices, or the Gartner Green IT Score Card which measures corporate social responsibility (CSR) compliance. In the remainder of this section, we examine the SICT–Capability Maturity Framework (SICT-CMF) from the Innovation Value Institute (IVI). The SICT-CMF Maturity provides a comprehensive assessment to determine current maturity level and a set of practices to increase SICT capability; performing an assessment allows an organization to identify capability gaps and identified opportunities to improve SICT performance.

9.9.1 A Capability Maturity Framework for SICT

The SICT–CMF gives organizations a vital tool to manage their sustainability capability (Curry *et al.*, 2012; Donnellan, Sheridan, and Curry, 2011). The framework provides

Table 9.6 Integrated sustainability plan of the Dublin City Council

Action	Water	Waste	Transport	Biodiversity and parks	Sustainable society	Procurement	Energy
Action at work scheme		X					
Active leakage reduction	X						
Allotments strategy				X			
Bike-to-work scheme			X		X	X	
Biodiversity action plan				X			
Cycling training programme			X		X		
Region water conservation	X						
Energy action plan							X
Energy smart community							X
Framework for Sustainable Dublin (FSD)					X		
Green procurement guide						X	
Hydro power	X						X
Kilbarrack Flagship Project	X	X	X	X	X	X	X
Litter management plan		X		X			
Mary's Lane project		X	X				X
Minus 3% project							X
Mobility management			X				
Parks and landscape strategy				X			
Energy action plan							X
Sustainable drainage systems (SuDS)	X			X			
Switch off campaign							X
Water tap tips	X						
Transport eco-awareness			X				X
Water conservation policy	X						X
Water mains rehabilitation project	X						
Workplace travel plan			X		X		

Source: Dublin City Council (2010).

Table 9.7 Indicators used in the Dublin City Council's sustainability plan

Theme	Indicators	Example
Transport	Vehicle fleet fuel usage for reporting period. Broken down into fuel type (e.g. diesel, petrol or biofuel). Equivalent CO_2 emitted.	Between 8 November and 9 October, Dublin City Council used about: 3.3 million L of diesel 61 500 L of petrol 4 800 L of biofuel This is equivalent to 8105 tonnes of CO_2 per annum.
Waste recycling	Total waste from offices for reporting period. Broken down into percentage of waste recycled.	For 2009 Dublin City Council offices disposed of about 32 000 bags of waste in landfill and 40 300 bags of waste were sent for recycling. This equates to a recycling rate of 56% for waste generated in Dublin City Council offices.
Water use	Volume of water consumed in offices for reporting period.	The volume of water used in civic offices was 20 432 m^3 between 8 September and 9 August. From 9 September to 10 August, the volume used was 18 197 m^3. This is a reduction of 11%.
Biodiversity and parks (zoned land)	Amount of land zoned in the development plan for amenity and open space lands, green network, waterways protection, recycling facilities and so on	The total amount of Z9 (amenity and open-space lands and green network), Z11 (waterways protection) and Z12 (institutional land including recycling facilities, etc.) lands zoned in the Dublin city development plan in 2008 was 2882 ha.
Energy use	Total electricity and gas usage in council offices for reporting period	Total electricity and gas usage in council buildings between 1 January and 31 December 2009 was: Electrical usage: 49 533 019 kW h Gas usage: 96 919 704 kW h

Source: Dublin City Council (2010).

a comprehensive value-based model for organizing, evaluating, planning and managing SICT capabilities. Using the framework, organizations can assess the maturity of their SICT capability and systematically improve capabilities in a measurable way to meet their sustainability objectives (Curry *et al*., 2012a). The SICT–CMF offers a comprehensive value-based model for organizing, evaluating, planning and managing SICT capabilities, and it fits within the IVI's IT–CMF (Curley, 2004, 2007).

The SICT–CMF assessment methodology determines how SICT capabilities are contributing to the business organization's overall sustainability goals and objectives. This gap analysis between what the business wants and what SICT is actually achieving positions the SICT–CMF as a management tool for aligning SICT capabilities with business sustainability objectives.

The framework focusses on the execution of four key actions for increasing SICT's business value:

- Define the scope and goal of SICT.
- Understand the current SICT capability maturity level.
- Systematically develop and manage the SICT capability building blocks.
- Assess and manage SICT progress over time.

9.9.2 Defining the Scope and Goal

Firstly, the organization must define the scope of its SICT effort. As a prerequisite, the organization should identify how it views sustainability and its own aspirations. Typically, organizational goals involve one or more of the following:

- Develop significant capabilities and a reputation for environmental leadership.
- Keep pace with industry or stakeholder expectations.
- Meet minimum compliance requirements and reap readily available benefits.

Secondly, the organization must define the goals of its SICT effort. It is important to be clear on the organization's business objectives and the role of SICT in enabling those objectives. Having a transparent agreement between business and IT stakeholders can tangibly help achieve those objectives. Significant benefits can be gained even by simply understanding the relationship between business and SICT goals.

9.9.3 Capability Maturity Levels

The framework defines a five-level maturity curve for identifying and developing SICT capabilities:

1. **Initial:** SICT is ad hoc; there is little understanding of the subject and few or no related policies. Accountabilities for SICT are not defined, and SICT is not considered in the system's life cycle.
2. **Basic:** There is a limited SICT strategy with associated execution plans. It is largely reactive and lacks consistency. There is an increasing awareness of the subject, but accountability is not clearly established. Some policies might exist but are adopted inconsistently.

3. **Intermediate:** A SICT strategy exists with associated plans and priorities. The organization has developed capabilities and skills and encourages individuals to contribute to sustainability programmes. The organization includes SICT across the full system's life cycle, and it tracks targets and metrics on an individual project basis.
4. **Advanced:** Sustainability is a core component of the IT and business-planning life cycles. IT and business jointly drive programmes and progress. The organization recognizes SICT as a significant contributor to its sustainability strategy. It aligns business and SICT metrics to achieve success across the enterprise. It also designs policies to enable the achievement of best practices.
5. **Optimizing:** The organization employs SICT practices across the extended enterprise to include customers, suppliers and partners. The industry recognizes the organization as a sustainability leader and uses its SICT practices to drive industry standards. The organization recognizes SICT as a key factor in driving sustainability as a competitive differentiator.

This maturity curve serves two important purposes. Firstly, it is the basis of an assessment process that helps to determine the current maturity level. Secondly, it provides a view of the growth path by identifying the next set of capabilities an organization should develop to drive greater business value from SICT.

9.9.4 SICT Capability Building Blocks

Whilst it is useful to understand the broad path to increasing maturity, it is more important to assess an organization's specific capabilities related to SICT. The SICT framework consists of nine capability building blocks (see Table 9.8) across the following four categories:

- *Strategy and planning*, which includes the specific objectives of SICT and its alignment with the organization's overall sustainability strategy, objectives and goals
- *Process management*, which includes the sourcing, operation and disposal of ICT systems, as well as the provision of systems based on sustainability objectives and the reporting of performance
- *People and culture*, which defines a common language to improve communication throughout the enterprise and establishes activities to help embed sustainability principles across IT and the wider enterprise
- *Governance*, which develops common and consistent policies and requires accountability and compliance with relevant regulation and legislation.

The first step to systematically develop and manage the nine capabilities within this framework is to assess the organization's status in relation to each one.

The assessment begins with a survey of IT and business leaders to understand their individual assessments of the maturity and importance of these capabilities. A series of interviews with key stakeholders augments the survey to understand key business priorities and SICT drivers, successes achieved and initiatives taken or planned. In addition

Table 9.8 Capability building blocks of SICT

Category	Capability building block	Description
Strategy and planning	Alignment	Define and execute the ICT sustainability strategy to influence and align to business sustainability objectives.
	Objectives	Define and agree on sustainability objectives for ICT.
Process management	Operations and life cycle	Source (purchase), operate and dispose of ICT systems to deliver sustainability objectives.
	ICT-enabled business processes	Create provisions for ICT systems that enable improved sustainability outcomes across the extended enterprise.
	Performance and reporting	Report and demonstrate progress against ICT-specific and ICT-enabled sustainability objectives, within the ICT business and across the extended enterprise.
People and culture	Adoption	Embed sustainability principles across ICT and the extended enterprise.
	Language	Define, communicate and use common sustainability language and vocabulary across ICT and other business units, including the extended enterprise, to leverage a common understanding.
Governance	External compliance	Evangelize sustainability successes and contribute to industry best practices.
	Corporate policies	Enable and demonstrate compliance with ICT and business sustainability legislation and regulation. Require accountability for sustainability roles and decision making across ICT and the enterprise.

to helping organizations understand their current maturity level, the initial assessment provides insight into the value placed on each capability, which will undoubtedly vary according to each organization's strategy and objectives. The assessment also provides valuable insight into the similarities and differences in how key stakeholders view both the importance and maturity of individual capabilities as well as the overall vision for success.

Plotting current levels of maturity and strategic importance lets an organization quickly identify gaps in capabilities. This is the foundation for developing a meaningful action plan. Figure 9.3 shows the results of an organization's assessment of the importance of capabilities versus its own assessment of its current maturity in those capabilities.

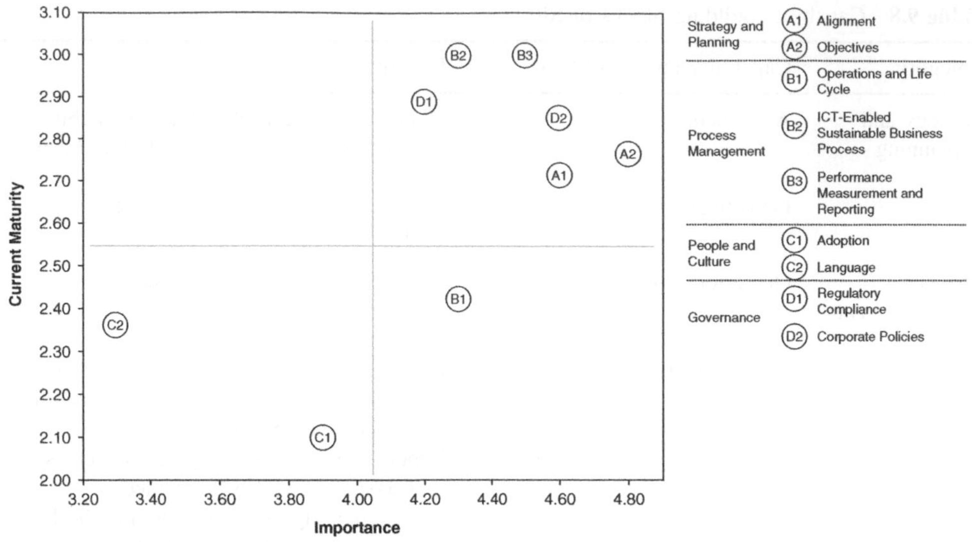

Figure 9.3 Maturity level versus importance plotted for each capability building block.

Figure 9.4 shows the consolidated survey results, resulting in an overall maturity level for each capability building block. This organization is close to level-3 maturity overall but is less mature in some individual capabilities. It views alignment and objectives under the strategy and planning category as the most important capability building blocks, but it has not achieved level-3 maturity in these areas. It also views operations and life cycle as important capabilities, but its maturity level for that building block is even lower (level 2).

9.9.5 Assessing and Managing SICT Progress

With the initial assessment complete, organizations will have a clear view of current capability and key areas for action and improvement. However, to further develop SICT capability, the organization should assess and manage SICT progress over time by using the assessment results to achieve the following goals:

- Develop a roadmap and action plan.
- Add a yearly follow-up assessment to the overall IT management process to measure over time both progress and the value delivered from adopting SICT.

Agreeing on stakeholder ownership for each priority area is critical to developing both short-term and long-term action plans for improvement. The assessment results can be used to prioritize the opportunities for quick wins – that is, those capabilities that have smaller gaps between current and desired maturity and those that are recognized as more important but might have a bigger gap to bridge.

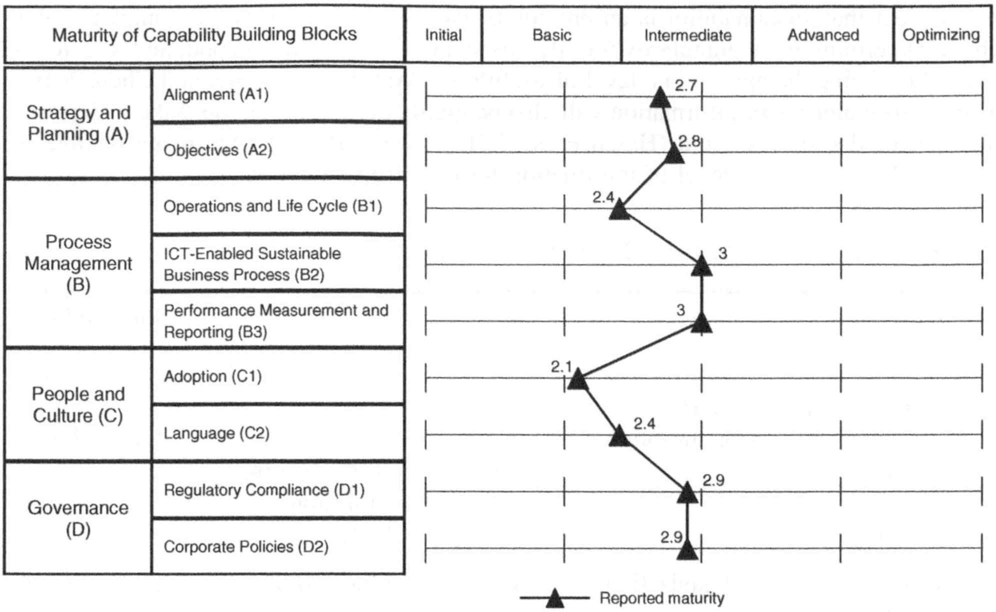

Figure 9.4 Aggregated results for the current maturity level from the assessment.

9.10 Conclusions

The next wave of green IT will tackle broad sustainability issues outside of IT. Sustainable IT has significant potential to contribute to sustainability and to enhance existing sustainability practices. Sustainability information is needed at both the macro and micro levels; it will require a multilevel approach that provides information and metrics that can drive high-level strategic corporate and regional sustainability plans, as well as low-level actions such as improving the energy efficiency of an office worker.

Many organizations think sustainability requires a significant transformational change, yet the ultimate goal is to embed sustainability into business-as-usual activities. In aiming to improve sustainability, organizations are facing both business and technical challenges that are complicated by the inherent breadth of information (Curry *et al.*, 2011), which spans the full value chain through an enterprise.

Whilst organizations are fighting a data deluge within their information systems (Cukier, 2010), there is a significant lack of data on sustainability concerns. A 2010 survey of more than 600 chief information officers and senior IT managers highlighted that few organizations are performing well at measuring the effectiveness of their sustainability efforts (O'Flynn, 2010). The paucity of sustainable information within organizations is a significant challenge and one that needs to be addressed if sustainable IT efforts are to deliver on their potential.

With the relative immaturity of practices within organizations, effective use of metrics is an emerging area (O'Flynn, 2010). The development of effective metrics is complicated by the fact that sustainability is an enterprise-wide issue that spans the complete value chain. Determining the granularity for effective data is not well understood, and research is needed to define the appropriate level of usefulness (Watson, Boudreau, and Chen, 2010). The appropriateness of information will also be highly dependent on the stakeholders and the task or decision at hand (Hasan *et al.*, 2011). Green IS will need to be flexible to provide the appropriate level of information for the given situation.

Appendix: Sustainability Tools and Standards

Standard name	Level	Description	Jurisdiction
General reporting and GHG			
GHG Protocol: accounting and reporting standard	Organization	Internationally recognized procedure for preparing verifiable emission reports (2004)	International
ISO 14064-1, 2 and 3: GHG accounting and verification	Organization or project	Modelled on the GHG Protocol; used to quantify, report and verify GHG emissions	International
The Climate Registry (TCR): General Reporting Protocol	Organization	Guidelines and calculation tools for voluntary emissions reporting programmes	North America
BSI PAS 2050: specification for the assessment of life cycle GHG emissions of goods and services	Product or service	Detailed technical specifications for the carbon footprint of goods and services (2008)	International
BSI PAS 2060: specification for the demonstration of carbon neutrality	Organization	Details quantification, reduction and offsetting of GHG emissions to achieve and demonstrate carbon neutrality (2010)	International

Standard name	Level	Description	Jurisdiction
UK Department for Environment, Food and Rural Affairs (DEFRA) Guidance: How to Measure and Report Your GHG Emissions	Organization	Procedure for organizations to measure and reduce GHG emissions (2009)	United Kingdom
GHG Protocol: Product and Supply Chain Standards	Product	–	International
ISO 14067-1 and 2	Product or service	Standard to quantify and communicate the GHG emissions of goods and services; builds on life cycle assessments (ISO 14040/44) and environmental labelling and declarations (ISO 14025)	International
Climate Disclosure Standards Board (CDSB)	Organization	Standard guidelines for corporate reporting of emissions	International
Global Reporting Initiative (GRI) Guidelines	Organization	Version G3 launched in 2006, standard guidelines for sustainability reporting	International
Life cycle costing	Product or service	A process to determine the sum of all the costs associated with an asset including acquisition, operation, maintenance and disposal costs	Standards by countries

(*continued overleaf*)

Standard name	Level	Description	Jurisdiction
Government			
Smart growth	General principles	Urban planning and transportation theory that concentrates growth in urban centres	International
New urbanism	General principles	Urban design movement that promotes walkable neighbourhoods of housing and jobs	International
Industrial ecology	General principles	The study of material and energy flows through industrial systems and their effects on the environment	International
Manufacturing			
Waste from Electrical and Electronic Equipment (WEEE) and Restriction of Hazardous Substances (RoHS)	Product	EU law in 2003, setting collection, recycling and recovery targets of electrical goods	Europe
REACH	Product	EU regulation in 2006, addressing the production and use of chemical substances and their potential impacts on human health and environment	Europe
EUP	Product	EU directive in 2005, addressing the security of its energy supply and its potential impacts on human health and environment	Europe

Standard name	Level	Description	Jurisdiction
LCA, ISO 14040	Product or service	A process to evaluate the effects that a product has on the environment throughout its entire life cycle	International
Design for environment	Product or service	US EPA Programme in 1992, working to prevent pollution and its and its risk on human health through design approaches that reduce environmental impacts of a product	United States
Cradle to cradle	Product or service	Biometric approach to the design of systems that models human industry in a way that materials are viewed as nutrients circulating in healthy and safe metabolism	International
EPEAT	Product	Global registry for greener electronics, covering the most products from the broadest range of manufacturers, ranking products as gold, silver or bronze based on a set of environmental performance criteria	International
Green seal	Product or service	Third-party, nonprofit, standards development body since 1989	United States
Hannover Principles	Buildings or objects	Copyrighted in 1992, a set of statements about designing buildings and objects with forethoughts about their environmental and sustainable impacts	International

(*continued overleaf*)

Standard name	Level	Description	Jurisdiction
Product stewardship andelectron paramagnetic resonance (EPR)	Product or service	An approach whereby everyone who is involved in the product life cycle takes the responsibility to reduce the environmental impacts, for example through moving the costs to producers and consumers instead of taxpayers	International
Precautionary principle	General principle	An approach whereby if a policy or an action is suspected to be harmful with no scientific evidence, the ones who take the action have to prove that it is not harmful	International
Building			
LEED	Building	Incepted in 1998 by USGBC, a green building certification system, providing third-party verification that a building or community was designed and built using strategies intended to improve environmental performance	North America
BREEAM	Building	Incepted in 1990 by UK BRE, a green building certification system	United Kingdom
Natural resources			
Food alliance	Organization	Started in 1993, defines and promotes sustainability certification standards in agriculture and food industry	North America

Standard name	Level	Description	Jurisdiction
Marine Stewardship Council	Organization	Founded in 1997, defines and promotes sustainability certification standards in fishery and seafood industry	International
Forest Stewardship Council and Sustainable Forestry Initiative	Organization	Defines and promotes sustainability certification standards for the responsible management of the world's forests	International
Green Globe	General principles	Based upon the Agenda 21 plan of the Rio Earth Summit of 1992; provides a set of principles for local, state, national and international action on sustainable development in travel and tourism industry	International
STEP	Organization	Comprehensive, global sustainable tourism certification programme	International

Acknowledgements

The work presented in this chapter has been funded by Science Foundation Ireland under Grant No. SFI/08/CE/I1380 (Lion-2) and by Enterprise Ireland under Grant CC/2009/0801. We would also like to thank Souleiman Hasan and Gabriel Costello for their assistance.

Review Questions

1. Explain the hierarchy of sustainability models. What is the role of sustainability frameworks, principles, and tools?
2. What are multi-level models needed?
3. What are the key metrics for data centre energy efficiency?

4. What is LCA? Explain the four stages of LCA.
5. Discuss the maturity of SICT capabilities.

Discussion Questions

1. How sustainable is your organization, education institute or personal lifestyle?
2. What activities have the largest impacts on sustainability? How could they be measured?
3. What would a life cycle assessment of your day's activities involve? Consider both direct and indirect impacts.
4. What mertics could be used to track the activity? How could an information system help you reduce your impacts?

References

Belday, C., Rawson, A., Pfleuger, J. and Cader, T. (2008) Green Grid Data Centre Power Efficiency Metrics: PUE and DCIE, Green Grid, http://www.thegreengrid.org/Global/Content/white-papers/The-Green-Grid-Data-Center-Power-Efficiency-Metrics-PUE-and-DCiE (accessed April 2012).

Benyus, J. (1997) *Biomimicry: Innovation Inspired by Nature*, William Morrow & Company, New York.

Boudreau, M., Chen, A. and Huber, M. (2008) Green IS: building sustainable business practices, in *Information Systems: A Global Text Project* (ed. R. Watson), University of Georgia, Athens, GA, http://globaltext.terry.uga.edu/ (accessed April 2012).

Commute Greener (2010) Commute Greener! TM, http://www.commutegreener.com/ (accessed April 2012).

Cukier, K. (2010) A special report on managing information: Data, data everywhere. *The Economist*, February 25.

Curley, M. (2004) *Managing Information Technology for Business Value*, Intel Press, Santa Clara, CA.

Curley, M. (2007) Introducing an IT capability maturity framework, in *Proceedings of the 9th International Conference on Enterprise Information Systems*, Springer, Berlin, pp. 21–26.

Curry, E., Hasan, S., ul Hassan, U. *et al.* (2011) An entity-centric approach to green information systems. In *Proceedings of the 19th European Conference on Information Systems (ECIS 2011)*, Helsinki, Finland.

Curry, E., Guyon, B., Sheridan, C., and Donnellan, B. (2012a) Developing an Sustainable IT Capability: Lessons From Intel's Journey. *MIS Quarterly Executive*, **11** (2), 61–74.

Curry, E., Hasan, S., White, M.,and Melvin, H. (2012b) *An Environmental Chargeback for Data Center and Cloud Computing Consumers, in First International Workshop on Energy-Efficient Data Centers (ed. J. Huusko, H. de Meer, S. Klingert, and A. Somov)*, Springer Berlin, Heidelberg.

Curry, E. and Donnellan, B. (2012) Understanding the maturity of sustainable ICT, in *Beyond Efficiency: Business Process Management for the Sustainable Enterprise* (ed. J.v. Brocke, S. Seidel and J. Recker), Springer, Berlin, pp. 203–216.

Donnellan, B., Sheridan, C. and Curry, E. (2011) A capability maturity framework for sustainable information and communication technology. *IT Professional*, **13** (1), 33–40.

Dublin City Council (2010) Dublin City Council Sustainability Report, http://www.dublincity.ie/Documents/Sustainability%20Report%5B1%5D.pdf (accessed April 2012).

Eccles, R.G. and Krzus, M. (2010) *One Report: Integrated Reporting for a Sustainable Strategy*, John Wiley & Sons, Inc., Hoboken, NJ.

Elkington, J. (1998) *Cannibals with Forks: The Triple Bottom Line of 21st Century*, New Society Publishers, Gabriola Island, BC.

Enkvist, P.A., Nauclér, T. and Rosander, J. (2007) A cost curve for greenhouse gas reduction, *McKinsey Quarterly*, **1**, 35–45.

EPA (2007) EPA energy star program report to congress on server and data centre energy efficiency, public law. *Public Law*, **109**, 431.

Goleman, D. and Norris, G. (2009) How green is my bottle? *New York Times*, April 19, http://www.nytimes.com/interactive/2009/04/19/opinion/20090419bottle.html (accessed April 2012).
Hasan, S., Curry, E., Banduk, M. and O'Riain, S. (2011) Toward situation awareness for the semantic sensor web: Complex event processing with dynamic linked data enrichment. *In 4th International Workshop on Semantic Sensor Networks 2011 (SSN11)*, Bonn, Germany, pp. 60–72.
Hawken, P., Lovins, A. and Lovins, L.H. (1999) *Natural Capitalism: Creating the Next Industrial Revolution*, Little, Brown and Co., Boston.
Hitchcock, D. and Willard, M. (2008) *The Step-by-Step Guide to Sustainability Planning*, Earth Scan Publishing, London.
Horne, R., Grant, T. and Verghese, K. (2009) *LCA: Principles, Practice and Prospects*, CSIRO Publishing, Collingwood, VIC.
ISO (2006a) 14040. *Environmental Management – Life Cycle Assessment – Principles and Framework*, International Organisation for Standardisation (ISO), Geneva.
ISO (2006b) 14044. *Environmental Management – Life Cycle Assessment – Requirements and Guidelines*, International Organisation for Standardisation (ISO), Geneva.
Levi Strauss & Co. (2009) A Product Lifecycle Approach to Sustainability, http://www.levistrauss.com/sites/default/files/librarydocument/2010/4/Product_Lifecyle_Assessment.pdf (accessed April 2012).
McDonough, W. and Braungart, M. (2002) *Cradle to Cradle: Remaking the Way We Make Things*, North Point Press, New York.
Molla, A., Cooper, V., Corbitt, B. *et al.* (2008) E-readiness to G-readiness: Developing a green information technology readiness framework, *Proceedings of the 19th Australasian Conference on Information Systems 2008*, University of Canterbury, Christchurch, NZ, pp. 669–678.
Mountain, D. (2006) *The Impact of Real Time Energy Feedback on Residential Electricity Consumption: The Hydro One Pilot*, McMaster University, Hamilton, ON.
Murugesan, S. and Laplante, P.A. (2011) IT for a greener planet. *IT Professional*, **13** (1), 16–18.
Nattrass, B. and Altomare, M. (1999) *The Natural Step for Business: Wealth, Ecology and the Evolutionary Corporation*, New Society Publishers, Gabriola Island, BC.
Ny, H., Hallstedt, S., Robèrt, K-H. *et al.* (2008) Introducing templates for sustainable product development through a case study of televisions at Matsushita Electric Group. *Journal of Industrial Ecology*, **12** (4), 600–623.
Ny, H., MacDonald, J.P., Broman, G. *et al.* (2006) Sustainability constraints as system boundaries: An approach to making life-cycle management strategic. *Journal of Industrial Ecology*, **10**, 61–77.
O'Flynn, A. (2010) Green IT: The Global Benchmark, white paper, Fujitsu, Tokyo.
Rees, W.E. (1992) Ecological footprints and appropriated carrying capacity: What urban economics leaves out. *Environment and Urbanisation*, **4** (2), 121–130.
Scholten, N. and Olsen, G. (2006) *SROI A Guide to Social Return on Investment*, Lenthe Publishers, Amstelveen, the Netherlands.
Skone, T.J. (2000) What is life cycle interpretation? *Environment Program*, **19**, 92–100, doi: 10.1002/ep.670190207
Socolof, M.L., Overly, J.G. and Geibig, J.R. (2005) Environmental life-cycle impacts of CRT and LCD desktop computer displays. *Journal of Cleaner Production*, **13** (13–14), 1281–1294.
Wackernagel, M. and Rees, W. (1996) *Ecological Footprint: Reducing Human Impact on the Earth*, New Society Publishers, Gabriola Island, BC.
Waldron, D., Robèrt, K.-H., Long, P. *et al.* (2008) *Guide to the Framework for Strategic Sustainable Development, Strategic Leadership Towards Sustainability*. Blekinge Institute of Technology, Karlskrona, Sweden.
Watson, R.T., Boudreau, M-C. and Chen, A.J. (2010) Information systems and environmentally sustainable development: Energy informatics and new directions for the IS community. *MIS Quarterly*, **34** (1), 23–38.
Webb, M. (2008) *Smart 2020: Enabling the Low Carbon Economy in the Information Age*, The Climate Group, London.

Further Reading and Useful Web Sites

(All sites accessed April 2012.)

General

- Global Footprint Network: http://www.footprintnetwork.org/en/index.php/GFN/

Reporting

- GHG Protocol: http://www.ghgprotocol.org/
- EPA Climate Leaders: http://www.epa.gov/climateleaders/
- Global Reporting Initiative: http://www.globalreporting.org
- Carbon Disclosure Project: http://www.cdproject.net
- The UN Conference on Trade and Development (UNCTAD) *Manual for the Preparers and Users of Eco-Efficiency Indicators*: http://www.unctad.org/en/docs/iteipc20037_en.pdf
- UK Department for Environment Food and Rural Affairs – *Environmental Key Performance Indicators: Reporting Guidelines for UK Business*: http://www.defra.gov.uk/publications/2011/03/25/environmental-kpi-guidelines-pb11321
- UNCTAD guidance on corporate responsibility indicators in annual reports: http://www.unctad.org/en/docs/iteteb20076_en.pdf

IT and Data Centre Energy Efficiency

- The Green Grid: http://www.thegreengrid.org/
- The Uptime Institute: http://www.uptimeinstitute.org/
- Climate Savers Computing: http://www.climatesaverscomputing.org/
- EU Code of Conduct for Data Centres: http://re.jrc.ec.europa.eu/energyefficiency/html/standby_initiative_data_centers.htm
- Energy Star: http://www.energystar.gov/
- Chapter 5 of this book, 'Green Data Centres'

Product and Service Life Cycle Assessment

- The Sustainability Consortium: http://www.sustainabilityconsortium.org/
- Walmart Sustainability Index: http://walmartstores.com/Sustainability/9292.aspx
- Jeffrey Ball, 'Green Goal of "Carbon Neutrality" Hits Limit', *Wall Street Journal*, December 30, 2008: http://online.wsj.com/article/SB123059880241541259.html
- Levi Strauss & Co. – Life Cycle of a Jean: http://www.levistrauss.com/sustainability/product/life-cycle-jean
- EPA Desktop Computer Displays a Life Cycle Assessment: http://www.epa.gov/dfe/pubs/comp-dic/lca/

Tools and Carbon Calculators

Reporting

- GHG Calculation Tools: http://www.ghgprotocol.org/calculation-tools
- SAP Sustainability Report: http://www.sapsustainabilityreport.com/
- eXtensible Business Reporting Language (XBRL): http://www.xbrl.org

Product and Service Life Cycle Assessment

- Earthster: http://www.earthster.org/
- OpenLCA: http://www.openlca.org/

10

Enterprise Green IT Readiness

Alemayehu Molla and Vanessa Cooper
School of Business IT and Logistics, RMIT University, Melbourne, Australia

Key Points

- Presents a green IT readiness, or *G-readiness*, framework, to display the input, transformational and output capabilities in greening IT.
- Defines the nomological structure of the framework and offers a series of propositions linking the G-readiness dimensions.
- Offers mechanisms to explain the organizational capability in sustainable management of the IT infrastructure and in the IT department's role to promote enterprise-wide sustainability.

10.1 Introduction

The pairing of information technology (IT) and the environment is now referred as green IT. The emerging notion of green IT raises questions such as how green IT is, and how IT can enable a business's green strategy. In the context of 'green' and 'IT', a few perspectives have emerged. To refer to the preservation of environment, whilst many use the terms green (Murugesan, 2008; Molla, 2008), some use the terms sustainability (Elliot, 2007; Elliot and Binney, 2008; Maruster, Faber, and Peters, 2008) and eco-sustainability (Chen *et al.*, 2008; York *et al.*, 2009). Likewise, although the terms IT, information systems (IS) and information and communications technologies (ICTs) are used interchangeably (Capra and Merlo, 2009; Elliot, 2007; Elliot and Binney, 2008), sometimes these terms are used to refer to different things (Chen *et al.*, 2008; York *et al.*, 2009). To get a better understanding of green IT and green IT management frameworks, it is therefore important to examine the use of the terms green and IT in green IT.

The concept of IT is complex. There is a difference between the *technical IT infrastructure* and the *IT human and managerial capability* (Broadbent and Weil, 1997; Byrd and

---

Harnessing Green IT: Principles and Practices, First Edition. Edited by San Murugesan and G.R. Gangadharan.

Turner, 2000; Ravichandran and Lertwongsatien, 2005). The IT technical infrastructure is commonly defined as a pyramid of four layers: the physical infrastructure (e.g. cooling, ventilating and power delivery), IT network and communications technologies (e.g. physical servers and network devices), shared services (e.g. enterprise-wide databases and electronic data interchange (EDI)) and business applications that utilize the shared infrastructure (e.g. sales analysis and purchasing) (Broadbent and Weil, 1997). The IT *human capability* pertains to 'the experiences, competencies, commitments, values and norms of the IT personnel delivering the IT products and services' (Byrd and Turner, 2000). The *managerial capability* comprises the management of all IT activities, including strategic foresight concerning changes in the business, IT and wider environment (Ravichandran and Lertwongsatien, 2005). Human, technological and relationship resources influence the functional capabilities of IT departments which in turn impacts the capability of IT to support an organization's core competencies. Figure 10.1 presents a pictorial representation of IT infrastructure and capability.

The greening of the IT infrastructure implies that eco-sustainability consideration has to be incorporated within the IT technical and human infrastructure and IT managerial capability dimensions of the IT infrastructure. This leads to questions such as the following:

- How do enterprises succeed in greening their IT?
- What capabilities do IT departments need to develop in applying environmental sustainability criteria to manage IT?

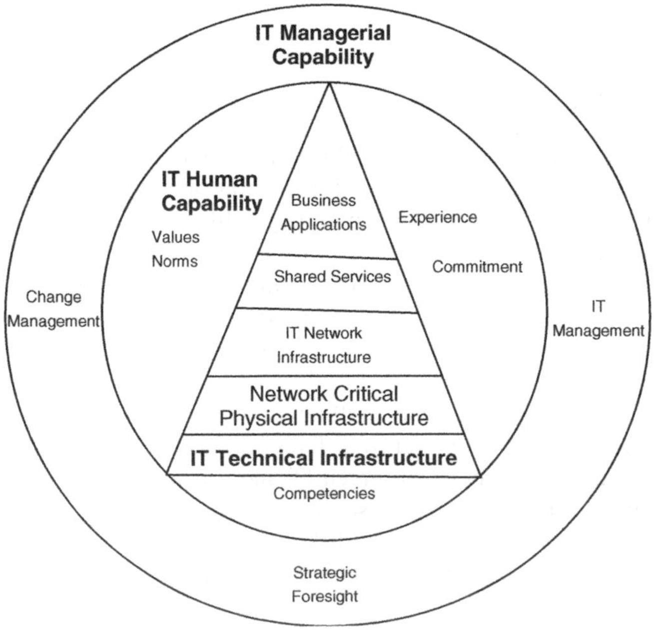

Figure 10.1 The IT infrastructure and capability perspective.

To answer these questions, a number of green IT models and strategies have been proposed in both practitioner and academic publications. From practitioners' perspective, green IT adoption can take place either through green-led or market-led mechanisms (Info-Tech, 2007). *Green-led adoption* occurs when green believers and green communities promote green IT, whereas *market-led adoption* occurs when green IT is led by market forces and innovative enterprises. To tackle both IT and enterprise-wide environmental sustainability responsibility, chief information officers (CIOs) can adopt a systematic and continuous approach of investigating the opportunities and threats associated with greening IT, developing strategies and business operations for IT, deciding the role of IT in providing tools and insights and leading change to respond to the opportunities and threats.

Like practitioners, researchers have suggested several green IT strategies and procedures. Murugesan (2008) recommends three approaches – the *tactical incremental*, *strategic* and *deep green* approaches. Whilst the tactical incremental approach comprises preserving existing IT infrastructure and policies and incorporating simple measures (such as energy consumption reduction) to achieve moderate green goals, the strategic approach involves conducting an environmentally oriented audit of a company's IT infrastructure use and developing a comprehensive green plan and initiatives to address broader green goals. The deep green approach expands the measures of the strategic approach to fundamentally redesign the IT infrastructure in a way that neutralizes greenhouse gas emissions. Likewise, Schmidt *et al.*, (2009) describe a procedural model for sustainable management of IT. The procedure covers assessment, identification of measures, prioritization, implementation, monitoring and evaluation.

Whilst these works have contributed towards a clearer understanding of the procedures and approaches that organizations can follow to green their IT, we need a conceptually coherent and comprehensive framework to nurture the capabilities that IT departments have to develop to implement procedures and strategies, green their IT and benefit from the potential interrelationships among these capabilities. In addition, IT managers need to follow a systematic assessment to evaluate their green IT progress. In this chapter, we present a green IT readiness (G-readiness) framework that helps to foster green IT adoption in enterprises.

10.2 Background: Readiness and Capability

Although the term readiness has been used to explain organizational change, IS business process reengineering (BPR) and innovation implementations, it has also become very popular in the e-commerce and e-government areas. Several researchers and practitioners have used the *readiness* or *e-readiness* concept in studies and global reports (Lai *et al.*, 2006; Mia and Dutta, 2007). At a global scale, the World Economic Forum publishes its annual report on the 'network readiness' of countries (Mia and Dutta, 2007). There are two main notions to the use of the 'readiness' concept: (i) readiness as a precursor condition (or set of conditions) for the implementation of change, IS or digitization (e.g. e-business or e-government) innovations (Guha *et al.*, 1997; Raymond, Bergeron, and Rivard, 1998; Todd, 1999) and (ii) readiness as an indicator of the agility of a business and a capability that needs constant building, rebuilding and upgrading (hence maturity) (Clark and Cavanaugh, 1997; Mia and Dutta, 2007). In this chapter, we follow the notion of readiness as a capability.

Organizational capability can be explained using the resource-based view theory (Barney, 1996; Rivard, Raymond, and Verreault, 2006). The resource-based view of the firm considers firms to be heterogeneous bundles of resources whose characteristics can predict organizational success (Barney, 1996; Bharadwaj, 2000). An organization's capability differentiates it from its competitors and can affect organizational performance. Capabilities could be tangible or intangible firm-specific processes and assets that represent firms' ability at coordinating and deploying resources (Amit and Schoemaker, 1993; Bhatt and Grover, 2005). It can also include functional skills and cultural perceptions to manage change and innovation. Capabilities emerge over time through complex interactions among tangible and intangible resources (Bharadwaj, 2000; Ravichandran and Lertwongsatien, 2005). Overall, though, capabilities could be input, transformational and output based (Lado, Boyd, and Wright, 1992). *Input capabilities* refer to firms' physical, capital and human resources. In particular, human resource capabilities include the training, experience, judgement and insights of managers and workers. *Transformational capabilities* transform inputs into outputs, and include innovation to generate new processes, products and services as well as organizational culture, learning and adaptation. *Output capabilities* refer to firms' tangible products and services and intangible output.

Extending these views to green IT, capabilities represent the tangible and intangible assets, resources and processes by which firms deploy eco-sustainability considerations in building and managing their IT infrastructure. Thus, a firm's capability to green its IT can be understood by looking at the permeation of eco-sustainability in a company's IT and IT department's input (IT human resources), transformation (the routines and processes that IT management follow to deliver its services) and output (the IT products, systems and practices that are delivered to support the wider organization). These dimensions are related to the concept of the IT infrastructure discussed in Section 10.2.

An analysis of existing green IT practitioner publications illustrates the importance of using the input, transformational and output capabilities in green IT. As a basic input capability, greening IT requires changing the mindset of IT personnel and IT management (Accenture, 2008; Capra and Merlo, 2009; Gartner, 2008; Mines, 2008). In terms of transformational capability, policy, governance and measurement are central (CFO, 2009; Elliot, 2007; Elliot and Binney, 2008). In terms of output capability, there are a number of technologies that are considered to be green and there is an increasing push for green data centres (Accenture, 2008). Thus, green IT covers not only technical considerations but softer practices as well.

10.3 Development of the G-Readiness Framework

G-readiness refers to the maturity of environmental considerations, whether they're part of a coherent set of IT management policies, they have been adopted into IT human and managerial operational practices or they have been built into concrete IS. It demonstrates the comparative levels of green IT development among enterprises and serves as a benchmark for understanding IT's contribution to support an enterprise's environmental sustainability strategy.

G-readiness consists of five components: *attitude*, *policy*, *practice*, *technology* and *governance*. The attitude dimension of G-readiness is an element of the IT human

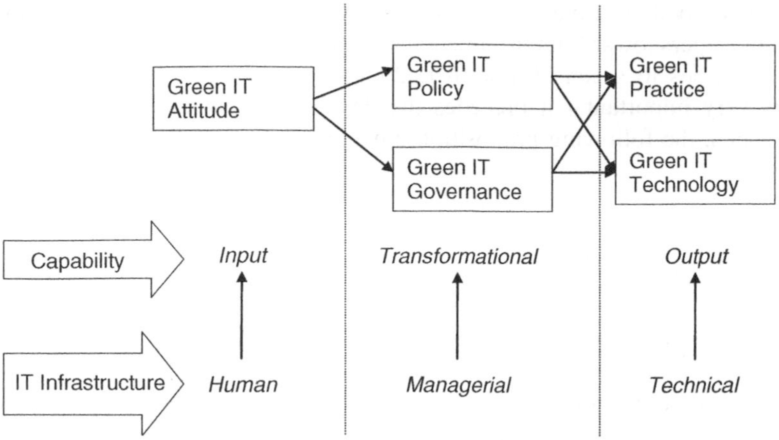

Figure 10.2 The nomological structure of G-readiness.

infrastructure and represents the green IT input capability. The policy and governance components are elements of IT managerial capability and represent its transformational capability. The technology and practice components are elements of the IT technical infrastructure and represent its output capability.

> G-readiness is an organization's capability as demonstrated through the combination of green IT attitude, policy, practice, technology and governance in applying environmental criteria to its IT technical infrastructure as well as within its IT human infrastructure and management across the key areas of IT sourcing, operations and disposal to reduce IT business process and supply chain related emissions, waste and water use.

Figure 10.2 presents a descriptive nomological structure of G-readiness.

10.3.1 Green IT Attitude

An *attitude* represents an enduring positive or negative feeling about some object or issue (Eagly and Chaiken, 1993). Attitudes are learned dispositions and are often the result of experiences. In the context of climate change, two major attitudes are prevalent. Most submit that the climate is changing at an alarming rate and that human (including business) activities are the main causes of the change (IPCC, 2007; Stern, 2008). On the other hand, some are sceptical about the causes and impacts of climate change (Royal Society, 2007). This group maintains that the climate is always changing and its impact is not as severe as most believe. Correspondingly, organizations are likely to adopt very different attitudes at the corporate level in dealing with eco-sustainability, and these differing attitudes will impact their expectations of green IT (CFO, 2009; Hart, 1997; Info-Tech, 2008). *Green IT attitude* is defined as an organization's IT human infrastructure's sentiment towards climate change, and refers to the extent to which IT people are aware and concerned about the impact (both positive and negative) of IT on eco-sustainability. The attitude of IT people and managers towards environmental sustainability and the role of IT is a key factor in initiating actions to green IT (Gartner, 2008). Having a favourable attitude towards green IT is very important – it precedes the development of green IT transformational capability. Thus, the following proposition emerges:

Proposition 1: Firms with IT people and managers who believe that environmental issues are important are more likely to have a relatively well-developed green IT policy, and a relatively matured green IT governance mechanism.

10.3.2 Green IT Policy

Organizations should develop their green IT policy aligned with its overall environmental policy and initiatives. *Green IT policy* encompasses the frameworks the organization puts in place to apply environmental criteria in IT-related activities. It defines the extent to which green issues are encapsulated in an organization's procedures guiding the sourcing, use and disposal of the IT technical infrastructure, the activities of the IT human infrastructure and the use of IT in the wider enterprise (Gartner, 2008; Olson, 2008). The maturity of green IT policy reflects whether environmental considerations are systematically permeating the IT activity value chain and are repeatable, or are disorganized and based on uncoordinated efforts. Policy captures an organization's intent to green IT. However, not all policies are expected to be smoothly implemented, nor are all practices expected to be policy led. Thus we arrive at the following propositions:

Proposition 2: Firms with a relatively well-developed green IT policy are more likely to have greener technical IT infrastructure.

Proposition 3: Green IT practices are more likely to flourish in firms that have a relatively well-developed green IT policy.

10.3.3 Green IT Governance

Green IT governance is the operating model that defines the administration of green IT initiatives and is closely related to the policy construct. Roles, responsibilities, accountability and control for green IT initiatives need to be clearly established. Businesses should decide whether the responsibility for green IT initiatives should be delegated to the CIO or the environmental sustainability manager (CFO, 2009; Gartner, 2008). For example, in ANZ Bank and Deloitte, IT leads green IT initiatives, whilst in some other institutions, IT's role is restricted to providing either tools or insights (Gartner, 2008). Deloitte's green IT operating model is based on a three-step process of planning sustainability measures, implementing and tracking the measures and addressing green organizational change (Deloitte, 2010). Green IT governance also includes allocating budget and other resources to green IT initiatives and defining metrics for assessing the impacts of green IT initiatives. Indeed, governance capabilities will require standard administrative processes for developing green IT initiatives to be put in place. This leads to the following two propositions:

Proposition 4: Green IT practices are more likely to flourish in firms with a relatively well-developed green IT governance mechanism.

Proposition 5: Firms with relatively well-developed green IT governance are more likely to have a high level of green IT technical infrastructure.

10.3.4 Green IT Practice

Green IT practice pertains to the actual application and realization of eco-sustainability considerations in IT infrastructure sourcing, operation and disposal. Organizations are likely to vary in the practice of analysing the green track record of IT hardware, software and services providers (CFO, 2009). They are also likely to vary in their practice in operating the IT and network-critical physical infrastructure in data centres and beyond data centres throughout the organization in an eco-friendly manner (Accenture, 2008; CFO, 2009; Velte, Velte, and Elsenpeter, 2008). For example, some are enforcing the Advanced Configuration and Power Interface (ACPI) to slow down processors. In 2005, IBM USA's telework programme involved over 20 000 employees, saving more than 5 million gallons of fuel and avoiding more than 50 000 tons of CO_2 emissions. A number of companies either recycle their IT hardware at the end of its life or dispose of it in an environmentally friendly way (CFO, 2009; Mitchell, 2008). For instance, Deloitte's green IT practices involve 'replacing traditional computers with thin laptops (Samson, 2008), for new data centres, and introducing application centralization and platform standardization'. Green IT practices would contribute positively to greening the IT technical infrastructure.

Proposition 6: Firms that apply eco-considerations in IT infrastructure decisions are more likely to have a green IT technical infrastructure.

10.3.5 Green IT Technology

The *technological* dimension refers to technologies and IS for (i) reducing the energy consumption of powering and cooling corporate IT assets (such as data centres), (ii) optimizing the energy efficiency of the IT technical infrastructure, (iii) reducing IT-induced greenhouse gas emissions, (iv) supplanting carbon-emitting business practices and (v) analysing a business's total environmental footprint (Accenture, 2008; Caldelli and Parmigiani, 2004; Chen *et al.*, 2008; Elliot and Binney, 2008; Info-Tech, 2007). For example, SAP's Recycling Administration Application can help organizations to meet regulatory reporting and documentation requirements, manage recycling declaration and payment processes more efficiently and reduce the risk and cost of environmental reporting. The SAP Environmental Compliance application is designed to help 'organizations ensure compliance with environmental laws and policies and reduce associated costs, efforts and risks on (the) plant and corporate level. It streamlines all environmental processes by seamless integration with operations control data, production control systems, and components from SAP software for environment, health and safety, enterprise asset management, materials management, the SAP Manufacturing Integration and Intelligence (SAP MII) application, business intelligence and knowledge management'.

10.4 Measuring an Organization's G-Readiness

To illustrate the utility of G-readiness in practice, in this section we present a brief case study of a green IT consultancy firm that works with client organizations to determine their current 'G-readiness' capability, with a view to assisting them in improving this. Data were collected via semistructured interviews with the firm's two principals and by document analysis, including green IT consultancy reports developed by the firm and information published via the company Web site.

10.4.1 G-Readiness Consultancy Services

Connection Research (2010; http://www.connectionresearch.com.au/), Australia is a market research firm specializing in sustainability issues and, in particular, sustainability issues for IT. The firm has two principals, two employees and approximately six part-time consultants. The firm's key customers include trade associations, government agencies and medium-large organizations. Connection Research provides market data to clients collected via direct methods such as surveys and through comparing such data with data from the Australian Bureau of Statistics.

Assessing the G-readiness of organizations is one of Connection Research's key areas of business. The firm uses the G-readiness framework described in this chapter, albeit adopting alternative terminology in places and an alternative graphical representation. For example, attitude, policy, behaviour (practice), technology and metrics (governance) form central constructs. Connection Research also identifies four 'pillars' of green IT within its consultancy services, namely, life cycle, end-user computing, enterprise and data centres and the role of ICT as an enabler. Each of these pillars is also included in the G-readiness framework described in this chapter, for example *life cycle* encompasses procurement, recycling and reuse and disposal issues.

To develop its framework, Connection Research initially administered a survey based on the framework to 500 organizations around the world and asked them to rate themselves on a 1–5-point scale. Since the survey was first administered, it has been repeated by Connection Research in Australia, England, India and the United States. The framework and survey instrument are publically available to encourage as much use as possible and, thus, build an increasingly comprehensive database.

The firm then uses the results of the survey as a means to benchmark its clients against other organizations. Essentially an organization completes the survey and compares itself across each dimension (described further in Section 10.4.2) to other organizations across different industry sectors and also different countries.

Based on the client firm's initial result in the survey, Connection Research provides additional services to client organizations. There are two versions of these services. The first is a 'Green IT Report Card' of approximately four pages, which provides a breakdown of the client's performance across the five dimensions and pillars of green IT compared to other organizations in its industry and at the national total. The report card includes a brief reflection on the client's performance across each area and offers broad suggestions of how performance could be improved.

The second set of services is the 'Readiness Index'. This product involves a more comprehensive consultancy process where more individualized services are offered to the client company. These services are offered in greater detail and generally via face-to-face methods. The product provides customized advice to the client about its objectives for green IT and explains how this relates to each of the five dimensions of green IT. This consultancy service can focus on calculating the index across all five dimensions, or it can focus on one dimension. Typically the service results in a report, prepared for the individual client, reflecting on their performance in terms of industry and national averages.

Connection Research also provides green IT training services to client organizations based on the G-readiness framework, Report Card and Readiness Index.

The next section provides a brief summary of how the G-readiness index is derived.

10.4.2 Calculating the G-Readiness Index via a Survey Instrument

As foreshadowed in Section 10.4.1, a simple application of G-readiness is its use by practitioners to measure the current green IT capabilities of an organization and to identify areas that need improvement. Such an assessment is inherently subjective. If it is done by a group of managers for a single organization, it first requires developing a shared understanding of G-readiness items.

An initial instrument to measure G-readiness is reported in Molla, Cooper, and Pittayachawan (2009). In this study, measurement items for the five G-readiness constructs – attitude, policy, governance, practice and technology – were generated via a literature review. These items formed an initial instrument to survey CIOs of large organizations in Australia, New Zealand and the United States to test the validity and reliability of the developed model and instrument. Ultimately, 10 factors (subcomponents) and 32 items were confirmed using confirmatory factor analysis (CFA), the LISREL 8.8 programme and convergent validity, discriminant validity and factorial validity tests (for further information, see Molla, Cooper, and Pittayachawan, 2009).

The resulting instrument can be implemented as a tally sheet with which managers (either individually or as a group) can evaluate their performance across the 32 items on a scale from 1 (*low*) to 7 (*high*). The item scores can be averaged to produce the average scores of 10 subcomponents. On the basis of a 7-point scale, the maximum value of a subcomponent is 7. The subcomponent score can then be averaged to produce a score for the five basic components of G-readiness. Aggregating the five components will yield a G-readiness score out of a maximum of 35. In this study, there were 143 respondents and their G-readiness score was calculated at 19.3, which can be interpreted as average (Figure 10.3). Individual firms could therefore use the instrument to calculate their score and compare their result to the average results of the 143 firms that participated in the survey.

10.5 Conclusions

Businesses are under increasing pressure from customers, competitors, regulators and community groups to implement sustainable business practices. Balancing economic and environmental performance is therefore a key strategic issue for businesses. G-readiness is a critical organizational capability to make our environment ecologically sustainable.

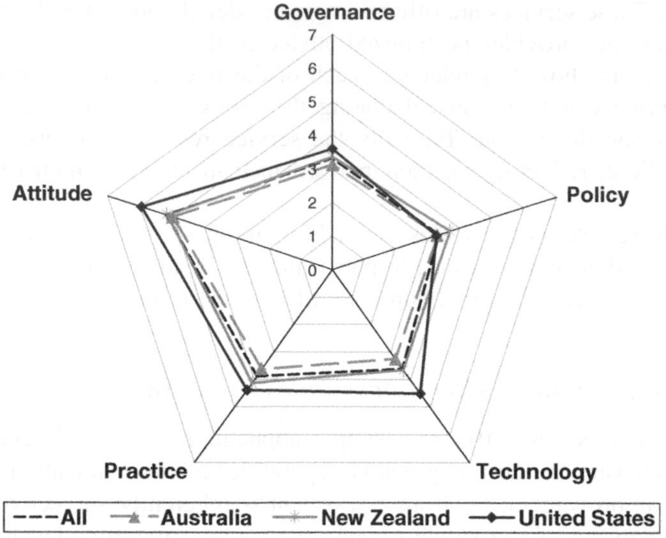

Figure 10.3 G-readiness results for Australia, New Zealand and the United States (Molla, Cooper, and Pittayachawan, 2009).

In this chapter, we presented a theoretically grounded definition and model of G-readiness as a capability. The G-readiness model will allow IT managers to approach green IT from not only the IT technical infrastructure but also the human and managerial perspectives. In addition, the model, rather than viewing green IT from one domain of the IT activity chain, is based on a life cycle approach covering IT sourcing, operation and disposal.

Illustrated with a brief case study, this chapter has demonstrated the use of G-readiness in practice. The case study highlighted how the metrics provided by the G-readiness framework can be turned into a series of indices, which then allow organizations to be compared to each other and to themselves over time.

Future refinement and evaluation of the proposed model will be useful to advance knowledge on green IT. Firstly, research that develops a measurement instrument to operationalize G-readiness would be extremely valuable. This contributes to the cumulative tradition of green IT research, which is inseparable from measurement. Secondly, additional empirical validation of the proposed model by testing the hypothesized relationship among the different G-readiness factors, and by exploring the relationship between the G-readiness factors and other antecedent and/or consequent variables of interest, can be another opportunity for research. An enrichment of the proposed model such as adding a construct or a relation or alternative ways of organizing the net constitutes offers another avenue for research.

Review Questions

1. Discuss different strategies and approaches for green IT and their managerial implications.

2. Describe the strengths and weaknesses of the G-readiness framework.
3. For your study, identify an organization. Using the framework suggested in this chapter, analyse it to assess its G-readiness, and compare your findings with the examples discussed in this chapter or presented elsewhere.

Discussion Questions

1. Discuss the importance of environmental sustainability in IT management.
2. What are the differences and similarities of green IT and IT for green? Is it possible to assess an organization's capability to use IT for green by the same framework and indicators as green IT?
3. What must business and other organizations that are considering greening their IT do to gain better value from their green IT initiatives?

References

Accenture (2008) Data Centre Energy Forecast Final Report, www.accenture.com (accessed April 2012).

Amit, R. and Schoemaker, P. (1993) Strategic assets and organizational rent. *Strategic Management Journal*, **14**, 33–46.

Barney, J. (1996) Looking inside for competitive advantage. *Academy of Management Executive*, **9** (4), 49–61.

Bharadwaj, A. (2000) A resource-perspective on information technology capability and firm performance: An empirical investigation. *MIS Quarterly*, **24** (1), 169–196.

Bhatt, G.D. and Grover, V. (2005) Types of information technology capabilities and their role in competitive advantage: An empirical study. *Journal of Management Information Systems*, **22** (2), 253–273.

Broadbent, M. and Weil, P. (1997) Management by maxim: How business and IT managers can create IT infrastructures. *Sloan Management Review*, **38** (3), 77–92.

Byrd, T.A. and Turner, D.E. (2000) Measuring the flexibility of information technology infrastructure: Exploratory analysis of a construct. *Journal of Management Information Systems*, **17** (1), 167–208.

Caldelli, A. and Parmigiani, M. (2004) Management information system – a tool for corporate sustainability. *Journal of Business Ethics*, **55** (2), 159–171.

Capra, E. and Merlo, F. (2009) Green IT: Everything starts from the software. European Conference of Information Systems, http://www.ecis2009.it/papers/ecis2009-0014.pdf (accessed April 2012).

CFO (2009) The Next Wave of Green IT: IT's Role in the Future of Enterprise Sustainability, www.CFO.com (accessed April 2012).

Chen, A.J.W., Boudreau, M.C. and Watson, R.T. (2008) Information systems and ecological sustainability. *Journal of Systems and Information Technology*, **10** (3), 186–201.

Clark, C.E. and Cavanaugh, N.C. (1997) Building change-readiness capabilities in the IS organization: Insights from the Bell Atlantic experience. *MIS Quarterly*, **21** (4), 425–456.

Connection Research (2010) Green IT in Australia, http://www.connectionresearch.com.au/ (accessed April 2012).

Deloitte (2010) Green IT the Fast-Track to Enterprise Sustainability, http://www.deloitte.com/assets/Dcom-Belgium/Local%20Assets/Documents/EN/Services/be-cio-green-it-260110.pdf (accessed April 2012).

Eagly, A. and Chaiken, S. (1993) *The Psychology of Attitudes*, Harcourt Brace Jovanovich, Fort Worth, TX.

Elliot, S. (2007) Environmental sustainable ICT: A critical topic for IS research? In Pacific Asia Conference Information Systems 2007, Auckland, New Zealand, AIS, 4–7 July (ed. F. Tan and J. Thong).

Elliot, S. and Binney, D. (2008) Environmentally sustainable ICT: Developing corporate capabilities and an industry relevant IS research agenda. Pacific Asia Conference Information Systems, Suzhou, China, July 4–7, 2008.

Gartner (2008) Going Green: The CIO's Role in Enterprisewide Environmental Sustainability, Gartner EXP Premier, May.

Guha, S., Varun, G., Kettinger, W.J. and Teng, J.T.C. (1997) Business process change and organizational performance: Exploring an antecedent model. *Journal of Management Information Systems*, **14** (1), 119–154.

Hart, S.L. (1997) Beyond greening: Strategies for a sustainable world. *Harvard Business Review*, **85** (3), 58–68.

Info-Tech (2007) 11 Green Initiatives Your Peers Are Cultivating, Info~Tech Research Group, July 30, pp. 1–14.

Info-Tech (2008) North America Underperforms in Green IT Attitudes and Actions, Info~Tech Research Group, January, pp. 1–15.

IPCC (2007) Summary for Policymakers, Climate Change 2007: Climate Change Impacts, Adaptation and Vulnerability, http://www.ipcc.ch/pdf/assessment-report/ar4/wg2/ar4-wg2-spm.pdf (accessed April 2012).

Lado, A.A., Boyd, N.G. and Wright, P. (1992) A competency-based model of sustainable competitive advantage: Toward a conceptual integration. *Journal of Management*, **18**, 77–91.

Lai, F., Dahui, L., Wang, J. and Hutchinson, J. (2006) An empirical investigation of the effects of e-readiness factors on e-business adoption in China's international trading industry. *International Journal of Electronic Business*, **4** (3–4), 320–339.

Maruster, L.F., Faber, N.R. and Peters, K. (2008) Sustainable information systems: A knowledge perspective. *Journal of Systems and Information Technology*, **10** (3), 218–231.

Mia, I. and Dutta, S. (2007) The Global Information Technology Report 2006/2007, World Economic Forum, Geneva.

Mines, C. (2008) The Dawn of Green IT Services, Forrester Research, http://cebit.portel.de/uploads/media/Green-IT_Forrester_Mines_02-2008.pdf (accessed April 2012).

Mitchell, R.L. (2008) Green by Default, *ComputerWorld*, http://www.computerworld.com/pdfs/LFG_green_IT_2008.pdf (accessed April 2012).

Molla, A. (2008) GITAM: A model for the acceptance of green IT. In 19th Australasian Conference on Information Systems, Christchurch, New Zealand, December 3–5, 2008.

Molla, A., Cooper, V.A. and Pittayachawan, S. (2009) IT and eco-sustainability: Developing and validating a green IT readiness model. In International Conference of Information Systems, Phoenix, AZ, December 15–18.

Murugesan, S. (2008) Harnessing green IT: Principles and practices. *IT Professional*, **10** (1), 24–33.

Olson, E.G. (2008) Creating an enterprise-level 'green strategy'. *The Journal of Business Strategy*, **29** (2), 22–30.

Ravichandran, T. and Lertwongsatien, C. (2005) Effect of information systems resources and capabilities on firm performance: A resource-based perspective. *Journal of Management Information Systems*, **21** (4), 237–276.

Raymond, L., Bergeron, F. and Rivard, S. (1998) Determinants of business process reengineering success in small and large enterprises: An empirical study in the Canadian context. *Journal of Small Business Management*, **36** (1), 72–86.

Rivard, S., Raymond, L. and Verreault, D. (2006) Resource-based view and competitive strategy: An integrated model of the contribution of information technology to firm performance. *The Journal of Strategic Information Systems*, **15** (1), 29–50.

Royal Society (2007) Climate Change Controversies: A Simple Guide, http://royalsociety.org/policy/publications/2007/climate-change-controversies/ (accessed April 2012).

Samson, T. (2008) The ROI of Green IT, http://www.infoworld.com/d/green-it/roi-green-it-797 (accessed April 2012).

Schmidt, N., Erek, K., Kolbe, L. and Zarnekov, R. (2009) Towards procedural model for sustainable information systems management. In Proceedings of the 42nd Hawaii International Conference on Systems Sciences.

Stern, N. (2008) The economics of climate change. *American Economic Review*, **98** (2), 1–37.

Todd, A. (1999) Managing radical change. *Long Range Planning*, **32** (2), 237–244.

Velte, T.J., Velte, A.T. and Elsenpeter, R. (2008) *Green IT: Reduce Your Information System's Environmental Impact While Adding to the Bottom Line*, McGraw-Hill, New York.

York, P.T., Watson, R.T., Boudreau, M.C. and Chen, A. (2009) Green IS: Using information systems to encourage green behaviour. Paper presented at the 2009 Academy of Management Annual Meeting, Chicago, August 7–11, 2009.

11

Sustainable IT Services: Creating a Framework for Service Innovation

Robert R. Harmon[1] and Haluk Demirkan[2]
[1]*School of Business Administration, Portland State University, Portland, OR, USA*
[2]*W.P. Carey School of Business, Arizona State University, Tempe, AZ, USA*

Key Points

- Reviews the current state of the development of sustainable IT services.
- Discusses the factors driving the development of green and sustainable IT.
- Examines the sustainability dimensions of IT: service, temporal, cost, organizational, economic, environmental and societal sustainability.
- Discusses the corporate sustainability, social responsibility and IT.
- Summarizes the service-dominant logic with business, customer and societal values.
- Discusses the steps to integrate sustainable IT with business strategy.
- Explores the best practices from major IT to non-IT companies.
- Recommends a set of guidelines for sustainable IT services development.

11.1 Introduction

Over the past two decades the terms green computing and green IT have come into common usage to define strategies, processes and practices focussed on reducing the environmental impacts of information technology. From its inception with the US Environmental Protection Agency's (EPA) 1991 Green Lights programme for energy-efficient lighting and the 1992 Energy Star programme for computers and monitors, green IT

Harnessing Green IT: Principles and Practices, First Edition. Edited by San Murugesan and G.R. Gangadharan.

has evolved significantly. One of the objectives of green IT is to reduce IT's energy consumption and thus the cost of computing. More recently, the linkage of energy use with carbon generation and elevated concerns about IT's impact on the environment and potential contribution to climate change has enabled reducing energy use to be positioned as 'green' (Harmon and Auseklis, 2009).

The increasing energy costs of data centres comprise a primary driver behind the current manifestation of the green IT movement. Enterprise-scale data centres can easily account for half of a technology company's energy bill and corresponding carbon footprint (Forrest *et al.*, 2008; McKeefry, 2008). The rapid uptake of cloud-based computing models and rising energy costs has exacerbated this trend with the costs for data centre computing and cooling expected to rise as organizations become more data intensive (Goodin, 2006; Hamm, 2008). Since cost reduction has a direct impact on business value, green IT at its core will likely remain focussed on cost reduction for the foreseeable future. In addition to energy costs, other drivers for the continued development of green IT are (i) the continuing rapid growth of the Internet use, (ii) increasing data centre power density, (iii) increasing cooling requirements, (iv) restrictions on energy supply and access, (v) the growing awareness of the environmental impact of computing and (vi) regulatory compliance (Harmon and Auseklis, 2009).

The relationship between energy use, carbon footprints and associated costs as the primary drivers of the first wave of green IT is direct and simple: Energy cost reduction also reduces the organization's environmental footprint. Green IT issues impact energy efficiency, IT budgets, legal compliance and risk reduction, datacentre design, server virtualization, supply chain optimization, product design, manufacturing, e-waste, air pollution, water pollution, hazardous materials, recycling and reuse (Harmon and Auseklis, 2009). To gain from customer or brand equity, businesses should make their green initiatives and credentials visible to customers and other stakeholders, and recent research suggests that firms should be developing products and services that can be positioned on their environmental and social responsibility credentials (Esty and Winston, 2009; Harmon and Auskelis, 2009; Murugesan, 2008, 2010; Nidumolu *et al.*, 2009; Pohle and Hittner, 2008; Senge *et al.*, 2008).

The second wave of green IT is service based and will enable firms to embrace the development of sustainability solutions as a business strategy. Sustainable IT services (SITS) move beyond the first-wave green IT issues to focus on the long-term importance of an organization's IT unit to the firm, its customers and society at large. This will be accomplished by aligning IT with corporate environmental and social responsibility strategy. The IT unit will become a key enabler of corporate sustainability (CS) strategy through the development and implementation of an innovation platform for new IT service-based business models (Harmon *et al.*, 2010). SITS is service innovation that redefines markets, transforms the competitive landscape and forces companies to change the way they think about opportunities and value creation. SITS-based solutions have the potential to revolutionize business models by turning environmental and social responsibility problems into business opportunities for the firm, its customers and society at large.

As green IT and SITS are complementary and sequential concepts on the same developmental roadmap, it is useful to conceptualize them as domains within the larger sustainable IT construct. Sustainable IT is the overarching concept that encompasses green IT as its first wave and SITS as its second wave. The sustainable IT construct extends from its initial focus on energy use and legal compliance through its higher order developments in terms of new processes and new business models that derive from a SITS innovation platform.

11.2 Factors Driving the Development of Sustainable IT

The development of sustainable IT, and its green IT and SITS domains, is the direct result of several market forces and enabling factors. Table 11.1 summarizes the forces that are driving the development of sustainable IT. For green IT, the primary drivers are energy efficiency and legal compliance. Concurrently, political and social forces are focussing on the environmental costs associated with IT, especially the potential impact on climate change. Although it is likely that a cap-and-tax or carbon-trading regime will not be fully implemented in the United States, the EPA, some state and local governments, nongovernmental organizations (NGOs) and consumer groups are continuing to pressure companies in terms of their environmental strategies, especially their carbon footprints (Parenti, 2010).

The development of SITS recognizes the migration from product-oriented green IT to service development as IT organizations transition from internally focussed cost and compliance issues to externally focussed sustainability-driven innovation (Demirkan *et al.*, 2008). SITS brings the IT organization into alignment with the corporation's CS strategy. SITS involves the integration of software, hardware, telecommunications networks, data, maintenance, technical support, customer service and consulting that is necessary to design, deploy, operate and maintain SITS (Harmon *et al.*, 2010). Increasingly, SITS will evolve to cloud-based solutions. This is already happening as firms such as IBM, HP and Oracle are launching SITS-based services that were initially developed for internal use (Harmon and Demirkan, 2011). SITS is a force for disruptive change for IT organizations. It will require IT managers to shift their priorities from internal efficiencies to customer- and societal-focussed value creation (Deloitte Touche Tohmatsu, 2009).

11.2.1 The Sustainability Dimensions of IT

IT performance requirements are precise and unforgiving. The technology must be capable to meet demand, availability and capacity management requirements. IT systems must work as expected and need to be ready all the time. IT has to be cost effective, deliver customer and business value and generate positive return on investment (ROI). Sustainable IT must enable business to meet these requirements or it will not be pursued. Sustainable IT is 'everything you need to keep IT going indefinitely' (Clifford, 2009).

Table 11.2 presents the dimensions and top-level requirements for sustainable IT. The first set of requirements – *organizational sustainability dimensions* – focusses on enabling the creation of business value. The emphasis is on the viability of IT products, services and the IT organization itself. *Service sustainability* emphasizes the development of effective and reliable processes for the creation and delivery of IT services. *Temporal sustainability* means that the IT organization must be run as a business that innovates to justify its existence over time. *Cost sustainability* in the short run contributes to business value

Table 11.1 Driving forces for sustainable IT: green IT and SITS dimensions

Green IT	Sustainable IT services (SITS)
Lower energy costs = increased business value from IT	Trend towards IT service innovation as the leading source of value and competitive advantage
Compliance with green IT standards and government regulations for energy use, materials and processes	Need to transform IT operations to reflect service orientation, sustainability requirements and business strategy alignment
Declining IT budgets	Need to align IT strategy with corporate sustainability (CS) strategies
Rapid growth of the Internet	Need to address IT's total economic, environmental and social impact
Rapid growth of IT, especially data centres	CS environmental and social responsibility reporting such as triple bottom line (TBL) reporting
Rapid increase in energy costs	New market opportunities driven by sustainability requirements
Increasing energy use by data centres and IT operations	Corporate branding and positioning strategies
Concerns about energy availability and access limitations	Trend towards cloud-based IT services
Increasing data centre power density	Smart technology initiatives
Increasing data centre cooling requirements	Increased customer value and societal value from IT services
Low server utilization rates	
Restrictions on energy access and availability	
Drive for IT energy efficiency (reduced costs)	
Concerns about IT's impact on the environment (carbon footprint)	
Stakeholder activism: government, NGOs, consumers and community groups	

through efficient operations (Dubie, 2009; Nagata and Shoji, 2005). *Organizational sustainability* ensures that the IT organization has the requisite leadership, personnel, skills and resources to address changing operational demands (Clifford, 2009).

The second group of sustainability dimensions – triple-bottom-line sustainability dimensions – deals with how IT organizations do business and serve as catalysts for economic, environmental and social change. Whilst the triple bottom line is a core feature of sustainability reporting, much debate still swirls around its conceptualization, efficacy, implementation costs and desirability (Global Reporting Initiative, 2006; Norman and MacDonald, 2004; Pava, 2007; Robins, 2006). *Economic sustainability* deals with the necessity that the IT organization meets revenue and profit goals to remain in business. As such, it depends on successful organizational sustainability. It also relies on the environmental and societal effectiveness of the firm. There is an expectation, over time, that economic sustainability will be enhanced by the organization's ability to meet environmental and social responsibility goals (Savitz and Weber, 2006).

In an ecological context, IT services must be able deliver customer and business value with minimal long-term impact on the Earth's resources. The goal for *environmental sustainability* is for IT services to meet the needs of the present generation without compromising the ability of future generations to meet their needs (Savitz and Weber, 2006;

Table 11.2 Sustainability dimensions of information technology

Organizational sustainability dimensions
Service sustainability: All systems are ready all the time for effective delivery of IT services. Managing performance, keeping services running smoothly, security, systems recovery and keeping versions current are considerations.
Temporal sustainability: This involves understanding the role of IT, its customers, business conditions and the value to be created to ensure business viability.
Cost sustainability: Ensure IT efficiency through controlling acquisition, operating costs, life cycle costs and replacement costs. For example, green IT focusses on low power consumption and high levels of resource utilization to lower costs.
Organizational sustainability: Effective leadership, employees, skills and resources are the keys to a strong organization that can meet requirements and manage change.
Triple-bottom-line sustainability dimensions
Economic sustainability: The IT organization must support the firm's revenue and profit goals. Over time, it is expected that ecological and social responsibility requirements will present service innovation opportunities that enhance economic performance.
Environmental sustainability: In an ecological context, IT services must be able deliver customer and business value by meeting the needs of present customers without compromising opportunities for future generations.
Societal sustainability: This dimension includes meeting legal requirements, ethical standards and societal norms and taking responsibility for the societal impacts of IT products and services on employees, consumers, communities and other stakeholders. This includes not only mitigation of negative outcomes but also avoidance whenever possible.

Wellsandt and Snyder, 2009). Finally, IT will need to take on increasing responsibilities in the *societal sustainability* arena. This dimension is less well defined in terms of IT's current operations, and IT managers may not yet have much visibility of social responsibility issues. It includes adherence to the law, ethical standards, societal norms and embracing responsibility for the societal impacts of IT products and services on employees, consumers, communities and other stakeholders. In some instances, the business purpose of social responsibility actions may not be apparent or directly remunerative, but are pursued for the good of society without attribution. The challenge for IT managers is to devise a proactive strategy to include societal interests in corporate decision making (Senge *et al.*, 2008).

The seven IT sustainability dimensions described here can apply to both green IT and SITS, but they do not apply evenly. Green IT is characterized more by economic (especially cost) and environmental sustainability dimensions. SITS will be more characterized by the service delivery, environmental and social responsibility dimensions. Although the temporal, organizational, cost and economic dimensions are important, triple bottom line (TBL) practitioners believe these dimensions will be satisfied if the organization is successful in meeting its environmental and social responsibility performance goals (Savitz and Weber, 2006).

11.2.2 Corporate Sustainability, Social Responsibility and IT

CS and corporate social responsibility (CSR) are very similar constructs with areas of overlap and points of difference (for details, see Montiel, 2008). Both have similar conceptualizations of the *economic* (business performance and profits), *environmental* (ecological and regulatory compliance) and *social responsibility* (social, ethical and philanthropic) dimensions of sustainability (Bansal, 2005). CS researchers are more environmental purists and take a systems view where the economy and society are part of a greater ecological system. They focus on the 'intrinsic value' of the environment for its own sake independent of the potential benefit for humans or business. CS practitioners are more likely to proscribe an activity or go to great lengths to correct a business practice if it is perceived to have adverse environmental impacts. The emphasis on 'climate change' is a good example of the CS orientation.

CSR researchers view the underlying dimensions individually and look at the environment as a source of benefits for society, or 'use value'. Environmental and social impacts should be minimized, mitigated, avoided or resolved favourably, but not necessarily proscribed. Both approaches embrace stakeholder interests and encourage collaboration. To be recognized as socially responsible, firms must address all of these issues in the course of their businesses and, hence, CS and CSR are converging and essentially equivalent (Montiel, 2008). We will, therefore, use this broadly integrated CS concept as the underlying discipline for the discussion of sustainable IT and conceptualization of SITS.

The primary goals and initiatives that characterize the green IT and SITS dimensions of sustainable IT are summarized in Table 11.3. Many IT professionals tend to define green IT from narrow economic and ecological perspectives. Mostly they ignore the broader CS social responsibility dimensions or engage to some degree with stakeholders as necessary. The terms green IT and green computing, by evoking this narrow perspective, obscure the true potential of information technology to become the innovation engine for sustainability-focussed services.

To improve IT's alignment with overall CS efforts, the emphasis needs to be on service innovation, especially for solutions that address ecological, ethical-social and philanthropic dimensions of sustainability as a means for achieving economic success. This second wave of sustainable IT reflects a shift in customer requirements from the tangible cost benefits of IT as a product (high performance at reduced costs) to the more intangible benefits of sustainable IT as a service for implementing socially responsible business models such as creating services to support the economical provision of sustainable water management in less developed countries (Demirkan and St. Louis, 2008; Senge, 2008).

IT organizations have been able to develop innovative green IT solutions. The problems are well defined and the benefits, especially in terms of cost reduction, are tangible and achievable in a relatively short time period. IT organizations have a high degree of familiarity with the technology and its applications, implementation and operation which are internal to the organization. For the broader CS-focussed IT services, the IT organization is, however, likely to be poorly prepared to understand the full range of social responsibility issues, much less design services to address them. The existing communications gap between the IT organization and its customers, both internal and external, and the questionable alignment between IT and business strategy will be challenged to new levels as IT managers try to ordain the complexities of CS.

Table 11.3 Corporate sustainability perspectives of the green IT and sustainable IT services (SITS) dimensions of sustainable IT

	Economic (performance and profits)	Environment (ecological)	Environment (legal compliance and standards)	Social responsibility (ethical-philanthropic)
Green IT	Cost savings and business value Energy cost reduction Outsourcing operations Headcount reduction Travel cost reduction Telecommuting Risk management (impact on employees, shareholders and other stakeholders)	Green IT practices and processes Power and workload management Renewable energy Thermal load management Virtualization Grid computing Server and client refresh Data centre and IT infrastructure Product design Green and clean technology Modularity Low-carbon materials Dematerialization Recycling Reuse and remanufacturing E-waste Decommissioning and disposal Green data centres Life cycle management Supply chain optimization Teleconferencing Cloud computing	Meets regulations and standards Waste Electrical and Electronic Equipment (WEEE) directive Restriction of Hazardous Substances (RoHS) directive Registration, Evaluation, Authorization and Restriction of Chemical Substances (REACH) Eco-design of Energy-Using Products (EuP) Electronic Product Environmental Assessment Tool (EPEAT) Energy Star EPA carbon regulation 2011 ISO 14000 environmental management Leadership in Energy and Environmental Design (LEED) certification Green IT Infrastructure Library (Green ITIL) UN Intergovernmental Panel on Climate Change (IPCC) Risk management (impact of noncompliance)	Stakeholder engagement The green grid Climate savers computing initiative The uptime institute Open cirrus partnership Voluntary codes Nongovernmental organizations (NGOs) Risk management (impact of not being engaged)

(continued overleaf)

Table 11.3 *(continued)*

	Economic (performance and profits)	Environment (ecological)	Environment (legal compliance and standards)	Social responsibility (ethical-philanthropic)
Sustainable IT services (SITS)	Innovation leadership Sustainable IT services innovation platform (start with environment and extend to social responsibility) Create customer and societal value through innovative solutions Competitive advantage Triple-bottom-line (TBL) reporting Integrated sustainable IT reporting Risk management (long-term profitable business)	Environmental leadership through SITS innovation Sustainable IT is a key driver and enabler of corporate sustainability strategy Sustainability-as-a-service applications (SITS) with applications for smart energy-efficient operations, renewable energy, green supply chain, green manufacturing and sustainable water (to name a few)	Regulations and standards leadership Be widely known as the environmentally responsible industry leader Drive new environmental standards before they are imposed Cost–benefit analysis includes ecological and societal value Risk management (manage the regulatory and standards processes)	Social responsibility leadership through SITS innovation CS leadership through SITS leadership Sustainable organizational culture Customer value requirements and expectations Societal value expectations Strategic philanthropy Stakeholder management Social justice initiatives Public relations Brand equity Social tracking and monitoring Risk management (stakeholder management)

Service innovation is the future of corporations, and information technology will provide the infrastructure for its development and delivery. SITS will need to become a core competence of sustainable (i.e. viable over the long term) IT organizations.

11.3 Sustainable IT Services (SITS)

With the on-going shift in the IT industry from product-oriented to service-oriented business models such as cloud-based IT services, the underlying technology for developing SITS is at hand. IT organizations need to develop the business case for its implementation (Demirkan and Goul, 2008). We define SITS from a total societal value perspective as the aggregate value available to society from the systematic integration and alignment of the individual IT service components for the purpose of creating superior societal value. These components include software, hardware, telecommunications networks, data, maintenance, technical support and consulting that are necessary to design, deploy, operate and maintain innovative sustainable IT solutions (Harmon *et al.*, 2009). In broader terms, SITS strategies seek to optimize the societal bottom line of the firm, its customers and other stakeholders to meet the TBL economic, environmental and social responsibility criteria for defining organizational success. A primary goal for SITS is to enable the firm to monetize the fulfilment of its CS responsibilities by developing innovative IT service solutions.

Developing sustainable IT capability is becoming essential for business success. By developing the services dimension, sustainable IT becomes a force for meeting organizational needs. SITS are about aligning IT with CS strategy to achieve market-leading business value, customer value and societal value for relevant stakeholders. The broader based environmental and social responsibility (legal-compliance and ethical-philanthropic) requirements are driving the development of SITS. It will manifest from a comprehensive review of potential opportunities throughout the value chain and corporate ecosystem. Government, NGOs and market forces are making sustainability reporting a mandatory requirement for corporations. Companies are responding and need help from the IT organization which will be required to support a corporate-level approach to sustainability. With IT at the core of most business processes and a core competence for business competitiveness, IT organizations will need to transform themselves to become key players in the development of CS strategy.

11.3.1 Developing a Service-Dominant Logic

Vargo and Lusch (2004a), in their seminal work on the topic, advocated for a service-centred view of business that has the following requirements:

1. Identify or develop service-oriented core competencies, knowledge and skills that represent potential competitive advantage.
2. Identify potential customers (or other stakeholders) that can benefit from the competencies.
3. Engage in collaborative relationships that involve customers (and stakeholders) in developing customized, competitively compelling value propositions to meet specific needs.
4. Monitor service outcomes to improve customer collaboration and firm performance.

To implement such a service-centred approach, it is important for IT managers to understand the conceptual differences between products and services, the types of value created by each and how they are delivered. It involves understanding the distinction between the goods-dominant (G-D) logic paradigm and the service-dominant (S-D) logic paradigm. G-D logic views 'services' from a product perspective as 'add-ons' or intangible products that may be offered on an after-sale basis (Vargo and Lusch, 2009, 2008a). In this view, services are designed and conceptualized as outputs, essentially intangible products, that 'add value' that is created and then delivered to the consumer for compensation. It is an 'arms-length' transaction. Therefore, G-D logic is based on a value-in-exchange conceptualization.

Conversely, S-D logic envisions services to be product independent, although goods can play a role in service provisioning (Vargo and Lusch, 2004a). The value proposition is service centred. Service value is always co-created with customers. It is based on the value-in-use concept. Co-creation involves the process of proposing value, the acceptance of the proposal and the realization of the proposal by two service systems (Spohrer *et al.*, 2008). These systems engage each other to apply and integrate resources in order to co-create value and realize the service experience. Since the customer is actively engaged with the 'provider' in the co-creation of value, the outcome of the service experience should, by definition, be more customer oriented and satisfying.

The distinctions between G-D logic and S-D logic are useful for assessing the evolving nature of sustainable IT from a product orientation to a service orientation. The first wave of sustainable IT with its focus on green computing is an artefact of G-D logic that focusses on the product dimensions of business value to reduce costs (energy in this case) and increase benefit (lower carbon footprint) without directly engaging customers or other service systems on a co-creation of value basis. Green IT by nature is a traditional design-build-sell approach that creates value-in-exchange. SITS, in contrast, must engage both internal and external customers and other members of its business ecosystem to be successful. Its foundation is collaboration that facilitates the co-creation of value propositions on a value-in-use basis. In short, for sustainable IT to be viable in the long term, it must become a true service that can create sustainable customer value.

11.3.2 Business Value, Customer Value and Societal Value

IT operations have a demonstrable impact on the bottom line of the corporation. Business value is defined as the overall value that results from IT products and services that is realized by the corporation (Sward, 2006). To optimize business value, IT spending must be aligned with corporate business strategy. Increased revenues or lower costs that can improve ROI are evidence that business value is being created. Successful investments in innovative IT solutions, such as green IT, are primary drivers of business value (Baldwin and Curley, 2007; Sward, 2006). Although business value ultimately depends on creating value for the customer, business value objectives are primarily about generating returns for the corporation. Therefore, business value tends to focus on short-term, cost-based solutions that are relatively quick and easily quantifiable. Green IT fits well in this paradigm with metrics that include energy cost reductions, headcount reduction, productivity increases, uptime, risk avoidance and cost avoidance. This internal focus can

Table 11.4 Green IT and SITS value dimensions

Value dimension	Green IT	Sustainable IT services (SITS)
Business value	Cost reduction is primary driver Internal IT focus Goods-dominant (G-D) logic Products and ancillary services Co-produced Value-in-exchange Low engagement or collaboration Short term	Not a primary driver in the short term Business value results if customer value and societal value are successfully created
Customer value	Secondary driver of adoption Customer focus is not strong Goods-dominant (G-D) logic Products and ancillary services Co-produced Value-in-exchange Low engagement or collaboration Short-term time horizon	Primary driver of adoption Service-dominant (S-D) logic IT services provisioned by products and infrastructure Co-created with customers Value-in-use High engagement and collaboration Short-term to long-term time horizon
Societal value	Minimal consideration of societal value Green IT can have a beneficial impact on societal value, but it is not the primary strategic focus	Primary driver of adoption Service-dominant (S-D) logic IT services provisioned by products or infrastructure Co-created with stakeholders Value-in-use High engagement and collaboration Long-term time horizon

Adapted from Harmon *et al.* (2010).

overlook the long-term best interests of the customer, society, the business and ultimately the IT organization as well.

Green IT with its focus on products and systems is G-D logic in nature and focussed on the creation of business value (see Table 11.4). Products and systems may be co-produced with customer input (co-production is the standard new product development process), and then delivered to customers. This hand-off characterizes value-in-exchange. Customer requirements are recognized but value is not co-created. The short-term focus on costs and the lack of sustained engagement and collaboration with customers and other stakeholders do not assure that customer or societal value is created. The primary focus on creating business value, which is the orientation of most IT organizations, is not amenable to the development of a SITS orientation.

Customer value may be defined as the overall benefit derived from a product or service, as the customer perceives it, at the price the customer is willing to pay (Harmon *et al.*, 2009; Sheth *et al.*, 1991). A customer value orientation becomes the foundation for IT organizations to engage the customer both individually and collectively (as markets) as the focus of their business. From a G-D logic perspective, customer engagement might mean conducting market research to determine customer requirements for new products and services, developing and delivering the new products and then seeking customer satisfaction feedback (Harmon *et al.*, 2010). This is product co-production and value-in-exchange, an implementation of G-D logic. Alternatively, the SITS concept requires a continuous engagement between two service systems (provider and customer) to co-create value to meet economic, ecological and societal requirements. This situation describes the S-D logic co-creation of value-in-use for an IT service (Vargo and Akaka, 2009). However, in markets characterized by technological innovation customer value can change rapidly, whether or not that value is co-created. Some customers may be willing to look at their long-term needs in a societal context, but for most IT customers cost and performance are the primary value drivers (Deloitte Touche Tomahtsu, 2009).

The definition of societal value is characterized by subjective interpretations of value. If the organization is dealing with renewable energy systems, water and wastewater systems, pollution, recycling and other tangible issues, it is likely that well-defined parameters and strategies can be developed. If the issues are world hunger, social justice, environmental justice, income inequality or neglected social services, the opportunity for highly subjective interpretations of value is greatly increased. However, pressures for business organizations to build social responsibility into their business models will continue to increase (Savitz and Weber, 2006). Societal value may be defined as achieving commercial success in a manner that honours ethical values and respects people, communities and the natural environment (Porter and Kramer, 2006).

Managers often perceive environmental and social responsibility goals to be in conflict with business goals. Government regulations, NGOs and consumer activists may pressure or mandate companies to take actions that increase costs or proscribe business practices are currently profitable and difficult to change. Social responsibility requirements are seldom aligned with the corporation's business strategy. Therefore, from a corporate perspective and certainly from an IT manager perspective, efforts to improve societal value are difficult to define and not associated with current or anticipated business practices.

Most green IT efforts have been G-D logic approaches that mitigate risk, lower cost or try to enhance corporate reputations without really engaging stakeholders. They are internally focussed and, to the extent that solutions are made available to external customers, they comprise value-in-exchange, generally without consideration of value co-creation. What is needed is a market-focussed S-D logic approach that genuinely engages stakeholders on a sustainability-as-a-service basis to co-create value-in-use that not only enhances society and delights customers, but brings business success as well.

11.3.3 SITS as Service Science

Service science's purpose is to develop a discipline that supports the application of scientific rigour to the practice of services and the development of innovative business models (Vargo and Lusch, 2008b). This is particularly important for IT services since the transition of IT organizations from product orientation to service orientation has just begun. Historically, most technology-related research has been focussed on product development and manufacturing innovation. The producer was separated by space and time from the consumer as products were produced away from the market. Product standardization supported the goals of efficiency and profit maximization. Conversely, service involves the interaction of producers, consumers and value network partners to co-create value through the collaboration of service systems (Vargo and Lusch, 2004a). This is exactly the transition that is taking place as sustainable IT moves from product-centric green IT to service-centric SITS.

IT managers are key players in this transition. They need to think of service (a process) that can be manifested in two ways: (i) IT products and infrastructure as provisioning agents for the development and delivery of high-value services and (ii) pure play services. If one conceives of value being created in terms of a flow of services delivered from a common platform (such as cloud-based services) rather than one-off sales of tangible products with add-on minor services, then it is possible to conceive of a scalable service system. This is a complementary relationship with IT services representing recurring revenue opportunities with high profit potential that leverage the IT system platform. As hardware becomes commoditized and software can be hosted anywhere, pure play services can be developed. This is happening with smart phone wireless applications and with third-party-hosted software.

As the IT organization moves from value-in-exchange product models to value-in-use service models, the importance of intangible value becomes apparent. Intangible value necessitates an understanding of the knowledge, emotions and experience factors that are associated with the design and delivery of services. Service is knowledge intensive, and the co-creation of value is predicated on a two-way exchange of knowledge. In addition, these collaborations with customers have high emotional valence that sets expectations for the service experience. Knowledge and emotions are then recalibrated as the customer assesses the value received from the service experience. These customer interactions influence customer value perceptions which, in turn, influence satisfaction, loyalty and the firm's brand reputation. The challenge then is to convert these important intangibles into negotiable forms of value (Steiner and Harmon, 2009).

Although both products and services can exhibit tangible and intangible properties, they differ in how these properties become actionable. *Operand* resources, often associated with products, are typically tangible and require some activity to be performed on them to become useful. Alternatively, *operant* resources have dynamic intangible properties that can be readily used to produce a desired result. Services are characterized by high knowledge content, the ability to create and engage emotions and the facility to co-create solution-based experiences, all of which are highly operant in nature. The ability to create these operant intangible resources is a primary core competency of successful service organizations and the source of their competitive advantage (Vargo and Lusch, 2004a).

The distinction between operand (product) and operant (service) resources can impact the manner in which value is created and perceived by managers and customers (Lusch and Vargo, 2008). From a G-D logic perspective, value is considered to be a property of the product that was added during its transformation from raw materials. When this product is sold, the value is transferred to the buyer (value-in-exchange). To increase value, it must be 'added' to the product; it is a product cost. Therefore to increase value, costs must be increased. For service, value exists if and only if it is perceived by the customer. In S-D logic, a service is defined as 'the application of competencies (skills and knowledge) for the benefit of another party' (Vargo and Lusch, 2008b). Therefore, 'service' (singular) is always exchanged for service. 'Services' (plural) are intangible units of output that may be provisioned by products or provided directly (pure service).

Service is a common denominator process for social and economic exchange (Vargo and Akaka, 2009). In S-D logic, a firm can offer a value proposition to a customer only to meet a specific need. If that proposition is accepted, then the value will be co-created with the customer for the proposition to be realized. The value is not inherent in the service definition itself. It is determined by the customer's perception of the results of the service outcomes or experience. It is the embodiment of the notion of value-in-use and critical to the development of SITS (Vargo and Lusch, 2004a).

11.4 SITS Strategic Framework

Although the need for the development of strategies for the development and delivery of SITS has been apparent for many years, there is no extant body of literature on strategies or best practices. But SITS strategy is nascent and being pursued on a fragmented, incremental, 'greener IT' basis (Daoud, 2008; Deloitte Touche Tohmatsu, 2009).

As the imperative to develop a SITS orientation becomes more apparent (as it has for companies such as IBM and HP), IT managers will need to consider the full CS impact of their product and service designs in addition to the traditional focus on costs and business value generation. The primary driver of sustainable IT, both green IT and SITS, is CS, especially as it applies to a firm's impact on the economy, environment and society at large (Savitz and Weber, 2006; Zarella, 2008). Therefore, IT managers will need to work across the functional areas of the organization to ensure an integrated organization-wide SITS strategy that aligns with overall CS strategy.

SITS development and deployment will likely to be slower than that of green IT. It will take time for firms to understand a market that is early in its formation. CS requirements and outcomes are harder to measure in terms of the customer and societal value generated. Due to the front-end costs and lack of visibility about returns, it may be difficult for small companies to offer SITS solutions, although there will eventually be start-ups or spin-offs with SITS business models. At present, it is the larger IT companies in which SITS is starting to get traction. They are packaging applications developed for internal use (mostly green IT solutions) and marketing them to their customers (HP, 2008; IBM, 2008; Pohle and Hittner, 2008; Watson *et al.*, 2009; Wellsandt and Snyder, 2009). The cost-driven, first-wave green IT initiatives will continue to be foundational to SITS. Energy costs will continue to rise and IT will become more pervasive, especially in rapidly growing areas such as Asia, ensuring that greener IT will always be needed. However, it is the market-focussed SITS-oriented business models that offer the most innovation potential. Value migrates from commoditized product-based business models to high-value service models that are better able meet customer value requirements (Slywotzky, 1996).

11.4.1 The SITS Value Curve

There is a paucity of SITS-oriented applications that address CS goals, but we can begin to see the logic of how SITS will develop by its early implementations (Harmon and Demirkan, 2011; Olson, 2008). Firms are changing their policies and practices to lower costs and minimize their environmental impact, but such efforts are not usually integrated with CS. Projects have focussed on customer safety, legal and regulation compliance, product design, sustainable processes, stakeholder engagement, strategic social

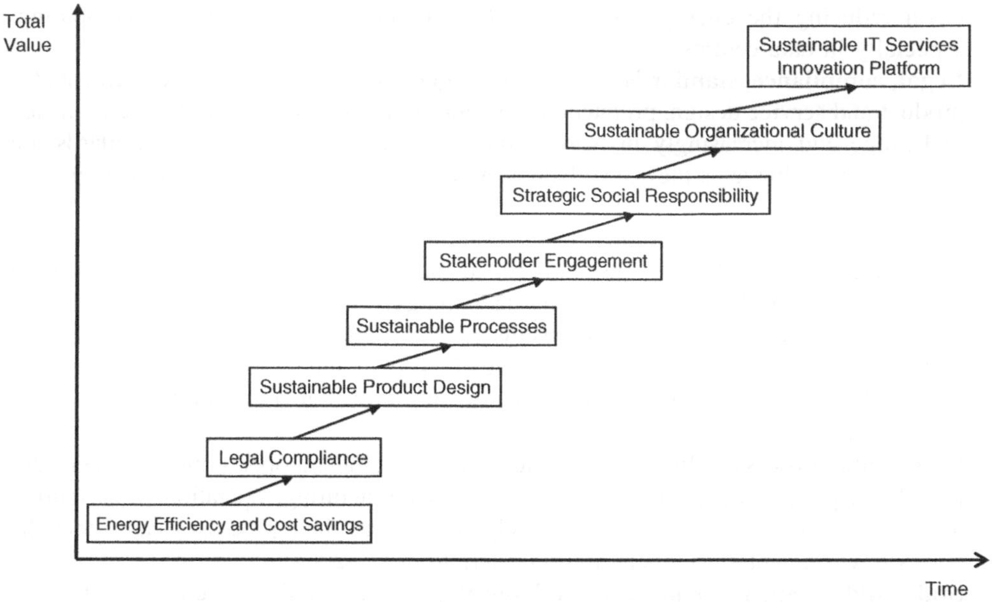

Figure 11.1 The SITS value curve.

responsibility, sustainable organizational culture and efforts to protect the brand. What is needed is a value roadmap with sequential steps that results in an integrated approach to developm an innovation platform for sustainable IT.

One approach is for companies to view their current activities against a CS value curve to obtain a perspective on what the next steps should be. The SITS Value Curve (Figure 11.1), adapted from IBM Business Value Institute's CSR Value Curve, depicts a path from cost–risk mitigation efforts to the development of an integrated core strategy (Pohle and Hittner, 2008). It conceptualizes the value migration path that starts with energy efficiency, cost savings and compliance activities and migrates through subsequent steps to the strategic apex of the sustainable IT innovation platform. When organizations have successfully met the goals of each step at the lower levels of the curve, they can continue their journey upward towards more strategic activities and higher levels of value creation in a sequential fashion. Our conceptualization recognizes green IT initiatives as a starting point along a value migration path that culminates with a SITS-driven sustainable IT innovation platform that supports overall CS efforts.

The following strategy development milestones depict the firm's (and IT organization's) maturation from focussing on costs and compliance at the low end to embracing the organizational change necessary to create a high-value SITS-based growth platform for the implementation of CS innovation. The major milestones along the curve are as follows:

1. **Energy efficiency and cost savings:** The starting point for SITS value creation is efficiency. The initial step along the curve recognizes the linkage between energy use by IT products and operations and overall carbon dioxide generations. The emphasis

is on reducing the energy costs and carbon footprints associated with computing, especially in data centres.

2. **Legal, compliance, standards and risk management:** CS-associated requirements for product and service design, production, operations and distribution are well established in Europe and increasingly in North America. These regulations and standards are spreading worldwide as they are adopted by national governments, manufacturers and marketers (see Table 11.3 for a representative listing of regulations and standards).
3. **Sustainable product design:** This value milestone includes clean technology, both 'clean tech' (new technology to address environmental problems) and 'green tech' ('end-of-pipe' remediation technology.) Clean tech includes renewable energy, transportation, water and wastewater, air pollution, materials, smart manufacturing, agriculture, recycling and waste. It also includes design for environment (DfE), design for recycling (DfR), e-waste minimization and cloud-based service applications (mostly green IT).
4. **Sustainable processes:** Includes IT systems, energy-efficient operations, the green supply chain, product development, engineering, manufacturing, operations, distribution and marketing. All of these functions rely on IT, and their processes can affect the firm's environmental and social impact (Barreto *et al.*, 2007).
5. **Stakeholder engagement and collaboration:** Stakeholders include customers, employees, business partners, investors, community members, industry associations, NGOs and the government with a report card on how the company is doing with its sustainability commitments. The goal is to build partners in sustainability to enable the co-creation of higher value services with superior brand power (IBM, 2008). Industry associations include the Green Grid, the Climate Savers and the Uptime Institute.
6. **Strategic social responsibility:** This milestone addresses the need to align corporate philanthropy and social responsibility initiatives with business goals. Drucker (1984) posited the notion that social responsibility can present the firm with strategic business opportunities. He called this 'taming the dragon'. Public relations and word of mouth should make stakeholders aware of the company's social commitment (Pohl and Hittner, 2008).
7. **Sustainable organizational culture:** Creating a common culture based on sustainability empowers employees to become more aware of issues, opportunities and the actions required for achieving a desired result (Olson, 2008). It involves setting clear goals and objectives and developing a code of conduct to guide business activity (Pohle and Hittner, 2008).
8. **SITS Innovation Platform:** SITS integrates the value innovation potential of all the sustainable IT dimensions into a platform for market growth. SITS creates growth by identifying new market opportunities, collaborating to co-create value and creating innovative solutions to drive business performance. Emerging applications are cloud-based SaaS with both wired and mobile Internet implementations.

As the recent study by Lubin and Esty (2010) on the quality and IT movements of the 1980s and 1990s reveals, business megatrends tend to share a common development pattern. Lubin and Esty identified four distinct stages that pioneering companies navigate as they migrate from efficiency-based strategies to disruptive innovation. The first stage is characterized by cost savings, the second stage by product and process reengineering, the

Table 11.5 Sustainable IT strategy migration

Stage	Megatrend strategy dimensions	Sustainable IT strategy migration	Sustainable IT wave
1	Reduce costs, waste and risk	Energy efficiency, cost savings Legal compliance, standards setting and risk management	First wave: green IT
2	Reengineer and redesign products and business functions	Sustainable product design Sustainable IT processes	
3	Transform the core business and integrate new ideas	Stakeholder engagement and collaboration–value co-creation Strategic social responsibility – ‘taming the dragon’ Sustainable organizational culture	Second wave: sustainable IT services
4	Develop new business models for disruptive innovation and differentiation	Sustainable IT services (SITS) innovation platform external market focussed and service oriented	

Adapted from Harmon and Demirkan (2011).

third stage by the transformation of the core business and the fourth stage by the creation of new business models that enable differentiation.

Table 11.5 integrates the milestones from the SITS value curve with the megatrends stages. The milestones fit well with the megatrends stages. Stages 1 and 2 are characterized by first-wave green IT milestones of energy efficiency and cost savings, legal compliance, sustainable product design and the development of sustainable IT processes. Stages 3 and 4 migrate sustainable IT to SITS development through the reengineering of processes, products and business functions. Stage 3 milestones are stakeholder engagement, strategic social responsibility and sustainable organization culture which serve to transform the organization through the inculcation of efficacious new ideas. The culmination of the value curve migration process is the creation of the SITS innovation platform. These applications will typically include cloud-based software as a service (SaaS) applications, both wired and wireless, that enable customers to address sustainability requirements. We will address these applications in the “SITS Leadership and Best Practices” section of this chapter.

11.4.2 Integrating Sustainable IT and Business Strategy

To be effective, CS initiatives need to be aligned and integrated with business strategy. However, a key problem for managers desiring to develop effective sustainable IT programmes is the disconnect between these two strategies (Porter and Kramer, 2006). A more business strategy–oriented approach to CS is needed. Green IT initiatives that are uncoordinated and lack an integrated approach may not have much business impact. Businesses must integrate a sustainability perspective into their strategic framework used to identify new markets, develop new technologies, understand competition and establish partnerships and alliances. To integrate sustainability initiatives into IT and business strategy, the following steps, adapted from Porter and Kramer, are recommended:

1. **Identify points of intersection:** The first step is to identify where sustainability issues intersect with the IT organization in the normal course of business. These are called inside-out linkages, where IT strategy impacts the environment. This could include everything from data centre design, IT operations, air and water pollution emissions, water use and the use of IT applications to protect the environment. Outside-in linkages indicate where and how external sustainability requirements impact the IT organization in terms opportunities, constraints and risks. Understanding the dynamics at the points of intersection can provide insights about future opportunities and the creation of competitive advantage.
2. **Understand the competitive context:** *Competitive context* refers to the dynamics of the industry and its key players. It refers to the quantity and quality of business resources, the rules that govern competition, competitors' capabilities, the size and sophistication of demand, the firm's value chain members' availability and capability and the key stakeholders' characteristics and capabilities. The IT organization needs to understand the relationships, how and where sustainability issues will impact them and the potential for developing partnerships and alliances.
3. **Choose sustainability issues to address:** IT managers must choose high-impact sustainability issues that intersect with its key business initiatives. Ideally the choice will align with CS initiatives to create shared value that provides a meaningful benefit for the environment while providing value for the business. To ensure that the IT organization can meet its business goals, sustainability issues that are in the firm's strategic interest should be given priority. *General social responsibility issues* might be important to society, but are not affected by or affect the IT organization. *Value chain sustainability issues* that directly impact the IT organization might present a business opportunity. *Competitive context sustainability issues* that can significantly affect the competitiveness of the IT organization and the firm should be given the highest priority (Porter and van der Linde, 1995). A method for evaluating and prioritizing sustainability issues needs to be developed.
4. **Create a sustainability agenda:** The IT organization should engage the firm's stakeholders to identify sustainability opportunities. Porter and Kramer advise managers to choose between responsive sustainability and strategic sustainability for agenda development. *Responsive sustainability* appeals to good citizenship by responding to stakeholder demands. However, responsive sustainability often deals with generic issues of little strategic value. It does not impact the competitive context. *Strategic sustainability* raises the bar to focus on issues that directly impact the competitive context and transform value chain activities to enhance sustainability whilst supporting business strategy. However, some stakeholders may not appreciate the firm acting in its own best interests.

5. **Create a sustainability dimension for all value propositions:** To address sustainability strategy, the IT organization will need to ensure that sustainability principles are at the heart of its value proposition. IBM has been successful in organizing its sustainability efforts around the concept of a 'smarter planet'. This positioning provides a unifying theme for the value proposition (IBM, 2008).

11.5 Sustainable IT Roadmap

A strategic-planning roadmap (Phaal *et al.*, 2004) for sustainable IT is outlined in Table 11.6. It presents roadmap elements for both the first-wave green IT and the second-wave SITS in the following categories: time horizon, market segments, products and services, technology, compliance and reporting, organization and value goals (Harmon, Daim, and Raffo, 2010). The roadmap assessment will provide a snapshot of the current state and the future development path for sustainable IT.

11.5.1 Time Horizon

First-wave green IT strategy has reached a mature stage. The time horizon for the roadmap elements is the present and near term (2–3 years in the future). SITS, however, is still in its formative stage and the developmental elements presented in Table 11.5 represent initiatives over an intermediate term of the next five to seven years.

11.5.2 Market Segments

The current target market for sustainable IT is the 'cost-centric' green IT market (Deloitte Touche Tohmatsu, 2009; Harmon and Auseklis, 2009). Two subsegments exist, one focussed on energy efficiency in data centres and other on the energy efficiency of IT operations. The primary supplier is the IT organization that serves internal business customers (Harmon and Auseklis, 2009). For the SITS-oriented CS segment, there are two subsegments: 'eco-proactive' and 'social proactive'. IT firms are beginning to target the eco-proactives with service-based ecological applications that were initially developed for internal users (HP, 2008; IBM, 2008). By extension we believe that a social responsibility–motivated socially proactive segment will evolve over the intermediate term. We expect that a cost-centric green IT segment will eventually be absorbed by the eco-proactive segment as more SITS-based applications address what had been green IT issues.

11.5.3 Products, Services and Technologies

We will discuss the product and service dimensions jointly since many of the solutions in the green IT and SITS markets are still in the early stages of technological development and deployment and have not been systematically configured or integrated in terms of fully featured products and services in many cases. Key technologies for greening a data centre are as follows:

Table 11.6 Sustainable IT strategic-planning roadmap elements

Roadmap category	First wave: green IT	Second wave: SITS
Time horizon	Present Near term	Near term Intermediate term
Market segments	Cost-centric segments (reduce energy costs and environmental footprint) Data centres IT operations	Corporate sustainability segments (sustainable IT innovation leadership) Eco-proactive Social-proactive
Products and services	Green IT products and systems Green data centre and energy-efficient products Green IT operations and eco- and cost-efficient products	IT-enabled corporate sustainability services Sustainable IT services (SITS) Social-sustainable SITS Eco-sustainable SITS
Technologies	Leverage technology for IT efficiency Virtualization, server design, power and workload management, infrastructure, cloud computing, green buildings, green tech, green tech, e-waste, DfE, DfR, and so on	Leverage technology for competitive advantage SITS applications SaaS Mobile cloud Remote sensing Smart systems
Compliance, regulations, standards and reporting	Green IT regulations and standards WEEE, EuP, RoHS, REACH, EPEAT, Energy Star, EPA, LEED, ISO 14000, Green ITIL and so on	Environmental and social reporting Triple bottom line, CS and CSR reports, NGO reporting, environmental-social reporting and integrated sustainable IT reporting
Organizational changes	Traditional IT organization with green elements IT organization with green IT functions IT organization with sustainable IT office	Sustainable IT organization Sustainable IT aligns with CS or CSR Integrated sustainable IT culture
Value goals	Business value is primary focus Customer value is secondary	Customer value and societal value focus Business value is achieved as a result

- **Virtualization:** Data centre virtualization enables increased server utilization by pooling applications on fewer servers whilst using less power, physical space and labour. Multiple operating systems can run concurrently on a host server which can be segmented into several 'virtual machines' each with a separate operating system and application.

Fewer servers mean lower energy costs for computing and cooling, less headcount and improved manageability (Ou, 2006; Ryder, 2008).

- **Server design:** Energy-efficient servers use multiple core, dynamic frequency and voltage-scaling technologies to increase peak level performance whilst reducing energy use (Barroso and Holze, 2007; Wellsandt and Snyder, 2009).
- **Power and workload management:** Power and workload management software adjusts the processor power states to match workload requirements (Wilbanks, 2008).
- **Data centre infrastructure:** Infrastructure includes chillers, power supplies, storage devices, switches, pumps, fans and network equipment. Energy efficiency is improved by retrofitting old data centres or building new ones.
- **Green data centre buildings:** Intel's newest data centre in Haifa, Israel has received a Leadership in Energy and Environmental Design (LEED) Gold rating for Intel from the US Green Building Council (Miller, 2009). A Fannie Mae data centre was the first facility to achieve this rating in 2005. LEED standards cover energy efficiency, water conservation, recycled materials, low-emission paints and carpeting and sustainable landscaping.
- **Cloud computing:** A hosted computing model where massively scalable IT platforms and applications are provided as a 'service' (Rhoton, 2009). Developers can create and deploy high-performance services that the user can access through a browser from any location (Greer, 2009).

The sustainable IT innovation platform integrates SITS applications (SaaS) with green IT solutions and will eventually target social issues. Major SITS applications include electric power supply management (conventional and renewable), water and wastewater management, traffic and public transportation management, Smart Grid management, intelligent levee management and data-based modelling of environmental systems. Other applications include 'clean tech' and 'green tech', the mobile cloud, remote sensing and smart systems solutions (Deloitte Touche Tohmatsu, 2009; Greer, 2009; Siegele, 2010).

11.5.4 Compliance, Regulations, Standards and Reporting

Sustainability directives and regulations are focussed primarily on first-wave green IT products. CS and CSR reporting requirements will affect both green IT and SITS with the latter encompassing social reporting as well.

11.5.4.1 Green IT Regulations and Standards

Major global green IT regulations and standards are as follows:

- The European directive on Waste and Electrical and Electronic Equipment (WEEE) mandates free return of obsolete equipment to sellers to reduce electronic waste. DfE is a primary strategy to address WEEE requirements (Hanselman and Pegah, 2007).
- The European directive on the Restriction of Hazardous Substances (RoHS) is associated with WEEE and restricts lead, mercury, cadmium and other substances used to manufacture electronics (Hanselman and Pegah, 2007).

- Restriction, Evaluation and Authorization of Chemicals (REACH) regulates chemical production and use for health and environmental purposes (Schneiderman, 2009).
- Eco-Design of Energy Using Products (EuP) regulates products' life cycle energy efficiency (Schneiderman, 2009).
- The Electronic Product Environmental Assessment Tool (EPEAT), an international product registry, rates IT products on environmental criteria.
- The Energy Star 5.0 standard regulates energy efficiency for desktops, workstations and notebooks (Shah, 2009).
- The EPA's carbon dioxide regulations took effect 2 January 2011. The initial industry targets are power plants and oil refineries which will increase the costs of electrical and transportation energy (Chipman, 2010).
- ISO 14000 is a standard for environmental management systems (EMS). It provides a template for setting requirements, guidelines and implementation roadmaps for setting up an EMS (Esty and Winston, 2009).
- The green Information Technology Infrastructure Library (ITIL) v3 provides various mechanisms for helping IT managers to consider the full life cycle costs of every IT service – from design and development to support and retirement – in terms of their actual business value (Kalm and Waschke, 2009).

11.5.5 SITS Standards and Reporting

Due to the early stage of SITS development, there are no established standards or reporting requirements. Evidence of the effectiveness of SITS is not pervasive. However, standards will evolve as government regulators, companies, industry associations, NGOs, customers and other stakeholders gain experience with the capabilities and limitations of SITS applications. The results of SITS applications (both green IT and social oriented) will be included in triple bottom line reporting, annual reports, CS and CSR reports, NGO report cards and corporate marketing materials.

11.5.6 Organizational Changes

IT organizations will become more responsive to market forces and as a result more oriented towards pursuing opportunities in sustainable IT. Most IT organizations have already embraced green IT. These efforts are central to IT operations. Leading companies are establishing sustainable IT offices or departments with similar functions (Wellsandt and Synder, 2009). The next step is to align the IT organization with CS strategy. To accomplish this, IT organizations will have to transform from an inward-looking support function to a market- and society-oriented strategic function. This will involve a major change in organizational culture, leadership and employee qualifications from a support group that is highly technical to a strategic services group that embraces innovation for the betterment of society.

11.5.7 Value Goals

We include the value goals dimension to emphasize value motivations of green IT and SITS strategies. Both green IT and SITS initiatives need to create business value or they would not be considered. However, there has been a major departure in the manner of how business value is achieved. For green IT, business value is the primary motivation. Achieving favourable ROI through cost efficiencies is the goal. The process is controlled by the IT organization and does not rely on co-creation with a customer. For SITS strategy, business results are based on co-creating value to satisfy customer value expectations and subsequently address customers' societal needs. If these goals are met, competitive advantage can be achieved, strong brands can be developed and the sales and profitability can result in increased business value. Customer value and societal value are the primary motivations for SITS which, if achieved satisfactorily, can result in the creation of business value.

11.6 SITS Leadership and Best Practices

As the SITS concept takes shape and gets deployed, it is useful to envision it as a smart system for societal information technology (Siegele, 2010). Smart systems are based on pervasive connectivity, remote sensors and business intelligence (BI) processes. It is this convergence of the digital and physical worlds with inexpensive monitoring tools that will foster the development and deployment of SITS applications. Smart systems are enabling innovative new services and business models, and a dominant trend is to apply smart systems technology to sustainability solutions.

Several companies' approaches to SITS development from a smart systems or *system-of-systems* perspective are outlined throughout the rest of this section.

11.6.1 IBM

Developing smart systems that enable cities to become more sustainable is a huge opportunity for IT firms. IBM's Smarter Planet initiative brings together the best thinking of business, government and society to create smart system solutions for sustainable development, societal progress and economic growth. To better manage the urban environment, IBM adopts a system-of-systems approach. This initiative's focus is to make energy, transportation, cities, business systems and organizations more intelligent and sustainable. IBM is developing smart system sustainable IT solutions to manage data centres, Smart Grids, smart cities, renewable energy, water systems, green buildings, health care, intelligent communities, railroad operations, supply chains and highway systems for energy conservation, climate protection, safety and healthy living. IBM has also undertaken initiatives for clean tech product designs, packaging, recycling and product end-of-life management. The key elements of the smart system are the infrastructure, equipment, sensors and software that make up the network, data collection and analytical capability as well as the software that delivers the service. In the short run, the biggest impact on sustainability is to make old infrastructure run better, but the learning that takes place will inform the development of future cities. IBM has leveraged its early leadership in IT services to become the leader in the development and delivery of SITS-based solutions (IBM, 2008).

11.6.2 Cisco Systems, Inc.

Cisco has launched a Smart+Connected Communities initiative to transform physical communities to connected communities for the purpose of achieving the CS goals of economic, social and environmental sustainability (Cisco, 2010). The Cisco approach is to use intelligent networking capabilities to integrate services, community assets, information and people into a single pervasive solution: services delivered anytime and anywhere. Echoing John Gage's assertion that the 'network is the computer', Cisco promotes the network as the platform for the development and delivery of services that transform physical communities to connected communities. The network will constitute the foundation for the city of the future by enabling services for buildings, transportation, utilities, security, entertainment, education and health care to name a few applications. Everything is connected, intelligent and green. One hoped-for outcome is that citizens and businesses will have unprecedented levels of collaboration, productivity and economic growth without compromising the environment (Cisco, 2010).

With the network as the delivery platform, Cisco envisions eight service experiences.

1. The Home Experience enables consumers to access and manage services from their homes, or wherever they choose. Dimensions of the Home Experience include small business and entrepreneurship opportunities, entertainment, fitness, energy and water consumption, health care and online education.
2. The Office Experience offers energy, security, telecommunications, mobile and IT systems management services as well as other applications associated with office operations and building management.
3. The Wellness Experience uses the Cisco Medicinal Grade Network to simplify communications between doctors and patients. This includes electronic clinical records, images and virtual doctor visits using Cisco's video collaboration technology. The idea is to provide a care-at-a-distance experience that creates a live face-to-face experience with greater convenience, better access and faster point-of-care deployment.
4. The Learning Experience enables online learning with integrated video technology.
5. The Shopping Experience combines shopping, entertainment and social dimensions to enhance onsite mall shopping. It involves reserved parking, real-time personalized sales incentives at specific stores or mall-wide, car or home delivery of purchases and reserved babysitting.
6. The Travel Experience helps communities manage road traffic flows using mobile command centres. Solutions involve rerouting, real-time transit information and parking reservations. The goal is to integrate all modes of transportation and travel accommodations with businesses and individuals over a mobile-enabled network.
7. The Fan Experience enables sports fans to connect with their favourite teams through interactive and personalized services. Fans can buy or upgrade tickets, view customized video feeds, order food, purchase merchandise and interact with other fans at the event by using their mobile phone.
8. The Government Experience facilitates engagement between citizens and government. The network enables access to information and fast links to government services, both face-to-face and online.

Cisco's first Smart+Connected Community is Songdo City near Seoul, Korea. The project is a showcase for green technology as well as a test bed for the Cisco smart 'experiences' (Siegele, 2010).

11.6.3 Siemens AG

Siemens has an 'IT for sustainability' SITS-oriented service line for data centre efficiency, energy management, building, industrial automation, Smart Grids, smart meters, electromobility (electric care software engineering) and cloud computing. It is one of only a few companies to offer fully featured SITS models that integrate IT processes and software services (Siemens, 2009).

11.6.4 HP

HP has identified four topics on which it focusses its CS efforts: energy, health care, education and supply chains. Global citizenship is one of HP's seven corporate objectives. It engages with customers, NGOs, governments, regulators and other stakeholders to share views, discuss best practices, develop standards and influence policy decisions. It efforts span the full range of CS dimensions: economic, environment, compliance, ethics, philanthropy and social responsibility. HP uses sustainable design principles for its products, works with suppliers to reduce environmental footprints, practices green IT energy strategies for energy use in data centres and business operations and follows product life cycle management (reuse, recycling, end of life and e-waste). The company launched the Global Workplace Initiative to reduce its physical footprint, use resources more efficiently and reduce HP's climate impact. It markets SITS solutions for materials management, facilities management, energy efficiency, water and wastewater management, video collaboration, employee travel and commuting management, manufacturing, supply chain, logistics and distribution, warehouse management, imaging and printing and sustainable building design (HP, 2009).

11.6.5 Intel Corporation

Intel has been a leader in green IT initiatives for over a decade. It has effective programmes for energy and water use efficiency, emissions, hazardous materials, energy-efficient products, recycling and electronic waste. The company also takes an active role in ensuring labour, safety and environmental responsibility for its supply chain members. Social responsibility programmes are targeted at education quality, the digital divide and workforce diversity. The company has embraced cloud computing and software as service applications. As this process matures Intel, which is placing increased emphasis on software and service development, should be in a position to offer SITS solutions to its customers and supply chain members (Intel, 2009; Wellsandt and Snyder, 2009).

11.6.6 Microsoft Corporation

Microsoft has developed numerous products and solutions to address green IT issues with SITS-oriented applications for energy-efficient computing, environmental management, green data centres, environmental dashboards and BI solutions for sustainability initiatives. The OneLab initiative consolidated several of the company's development labs to save energy and increase operational efficiency. Microsoft also offers solutions for unified communications, travel management, fleet management, supply chain and transportation (Microsoft, 2010).

11.6.7 Oracle

Oracle has developed environmental sustainability management software solutions for manufacturers and commercial facilities. Their Sustainability Sensor Data Management solutions help organizations monitor energy use, greenhouse gas (GHG) emissions and other environmental factors. The system uses smart meters, building management systems and data analysis to deliver comprehensive visibility of real-time environmental performance (Oracle, 2010).

11.6.8 Google

Google has a sustainability programme that is green IT oriented. They have developed initiatives for carbon neutrality, green data centres, green workplaces and renewable energy. SITS-like applications are few. Of note is the Google Earth Engine, a database of images that supports the development of systems to monitor, report and verify changes in the environment such as deforestation, floods, droughts, glaciers and other factors associated with climate change. Google PowerMeter provides consumers with access to detailed information about their home energy use throughout the day in association with utilities such as San Diego Gas & Electric. Google also has invested in geothermal, hydro, wind and solar energy and plug-in vehicles.

11.6.9 Apple

Apple has internal green IT programmes for energy efficiency, limiting GHG emissions, material efficiency, restricted substances, recycling and supplier responsibility across its supply chain. No SITS-oriented initiatives are mentioned on its Web site (Apple, 2010).

11.6.10 Samsung

Samsung has a well-developed green IT approach to sustainability. It has an Eco-Innovation programme for energy efficiency, water use, pollution and hazardous substance control, green operations, product design, recycling, waste management and health and safety. Social responsibility initiatives involve low-income families and youth, local community projects, and partnerships with NGOs and governments for social development projects. Samsung does not have identifiable SITS initiatives (Samsung, 2009).

11.6.11 Pachube

Pachube.com, a London start-up, bills itself as helping users connect to build the Internet of Things. It has developed a SITS-oriented service that enables users to share sensor data that they use to build smart services. One user uploaded temperature readings from his office and used Pachube's system to control his cooling fan. Users share data and apps. Users who want to use Pachube's system to build proprietary mobile and Web applications are charged a fee (Pachube, 2011; Siegele, 2010).

11.6.12 SeeClickFix

SeeClickFix.com is an app for iPhone, Android and Blackberry smartphones that allows citizen users to report things that need a solution to neighbourhood groups, news outlets, government agencies and NGOs. It uses smart phones and their users in a remote-sensing 'crowdsourcing' model to get things done. This smart system application could be readily adaptable as a platform for SITS-oriented environmental or social responsibility data collection. It could speed up the identification of problems and development of CS solutions (SeeClickFix, 2010; Siegele, 2010).

11.7 Conclusions

Companies are moving beyond internally focussed green IT initiatives to the development of SITS. This chapter has introduced and reviewed the current state of the development of SITS. The following set of recommendations for SITS development is intended to guide the IT manager in the transition to an IT organization that is fully aligned on CS goals.

1. Focus your sustainability efforts where you can make the most impact and be innovative in developing SITS that support your business model.
2. Get senior management committed to developing and supporting SITS as a major strategic initiative.
3. Align sustainability goals with CS strategy. Set sustainable IT goals that fit the business and enable growth and profitability opportunities for the company.
4. Link sustainability to your technology and the core competencies of your company and IT organization. Do what you do best and let SITS leverage your capabilities.
5. Develop SITS for internal use first. Once you have perfected the service, market it to your customers, suppliers and new markets.
6. Develop SITS as a smart system. Smart systems incorporate functions of sensing, actuation and control. They are capable of identifying, describing and analysing a situation and taking decisive action based on the available data in a predictive or adaptive manner, thereby performing smart actions. SITS at its core is based on BI principles.
7. Collaborate and otherwise engage with your stakeholders to develop SITS solutions. Build a sustainable organizational culture. SITS should benefit the company, but do not forget to be a good corporate citizen.
8. Define metrics and monitor the outcomes from SITS initiatives. Adapt the strategy and implementation to improve stakeholder collaboration and service performance.

11.8 Summary

Organizations are under increasing pressure to adopt sustainable business practices as the societal costs of IT have become more apparent. Initial efforts to address the environmental impact of IT have focussed on minimizing energy costs and the ecological footprints of IT products and operations. However, this green IT orientation does not address the potential for IT to become a key enabler of overall CS strategy. As IT departments embrace a more strategic role, future success will be determined by the ability to meet market requirements, governmental regulations and societal expectations. To address this opportunity, IT managers will need to move beyond narrow operational requirements and harness IT's ability to develop innovative new services that will define the future of CS and social responsibility efforts. SITS, applications that provide innovative solutions for corporate ecological and societal issues, represent an excellent opportunity for IT organizations to become indispensable players in developing essential new markets. This chapter reviews the current state of the development of SITS, describes the factors driving the development of green and sustainable IT, then demonstrates the sustainability dimensions of IT including service, temporal, cost, organizational, economic, environmental and societal sustainability. The service-dominant logic with business, customer and societal values is also discussed. This chapter also reviews the newest practices from companies like IBM, Cisco Systems, Siemens, HP, Intel, Microsoft, Oracle, Google, Apple, Samsung, Pachube and SeeClickFix and provides a set of guidelines for SITS development.

Review Questions

1. Outline the current state of development of sustainable IT services.
2. What are the driving factors for the development of green and sustainable IT?
3. How are corporate sustainability, social responsibility and IT related to each other?
4. How should companies move from a goods-dominant logic to a service-dominant logic by utilizing business, customer and societal values?
5. How can an organization integrate sustainable IT with its business strategy?
6. What is a sustainable IT services innovation platform? What capabilities should it have?
7. On what will the major SITS-oriented applications be focussed in five years?
8. How can companies implement sustainable IT services development practices?

Discussion Questions

1. Discuss the primary sustainability dimensions of IT.
2. How are organizations implementing sustainable IT services practices? Discuss with real-world examples.

References

Apple (2010) Apple and the Environment, http://www.apple.com/environment/reports/ (accessed April 2012).
Baldwin, E. and Curley, M. (2007) *Managing IT Innovation for Business Value*, Intel Press, Santa Clara, CA.
Bansal, P. (2005) Evolving sustainability: A longitudinal study of corporate sustainable development. *Strategic Management Journal*, **26** (3), 197–218.

Barreto, L., Anderson, H., Anglin, A. and Tomovic, C. (2007) Product Lifecycle Management in Support of Green Manufacturing: Assessing the Challenges of Global Climate Change. In Proceedings of the International Conference on Comprehensive Product Realization 2007 (ICCPR2007), June 18–20, Beijing.

Barroso, L.A. and Holze, U. (2007) The case for energy-proportional computing. *IEEE Computer*, **40**, 33–37.

Chen, A.J.W., Boudreau, M.-C. and Watson, R.T. (2008) Information systems and ecological sustainability. *Journal of Systems and Information Technology*, **10** (3), 186–201.

Chipman, K. (2010) EPA-Texas Feud Escalates over New Carbon Regulations. *Bloomberg Businessweek*, December 28, http://climate.aib.org.uk/article/68129/EPA-Texas-Feud-Escalates-Over-New-Carbon-Regulations (accessed April 2012).

Cisco (2010) *Smart+Connected Communities: Changing a City, a Country, the World*, Cisco Systems, Inc., http://www.cisco.com/web/strategy/smart_connected_communities/overview.html (accessed April 2012).

Clifford, A. (2009) Sustainable IT. it.toolbox.com: Project Management Community, http://it.toolbox.com/blogs/minimalit/sustainable-it-30157 (accessed April 2012).

Daoud, D. (2008) Beyond Power: IT's Roadmap to Sustainable Computing, IDC white paper, http://m.softchoice.com/files/pdf/about/sustain-enable/Beyond_Power.pdf (accessed April 2012).

Deloitte Touche Tohmatsu (2009) *The Next Wave of Green IT*, CFO Research Services, CFO Publishing Corp., Boston.

Demirkan, H. and Goul, M. (2008) Process and services fusion impact assessment: SSME findings from industry collaboration and the need for competency centers, in *Service Science, Management and Engineering: Education for the 21st Century* (ed. B. Hefley and W. Murphy), Springer, New York, pp. 257–262.

Demirkan, H., Kauffman, R.J., Vayghan, J. *et al.* (2008) Service-oriented technology and management: Perspectives on research and practice for the coming decade. *Electronic Commerce Research and Applications*, **7** (4), 356–376.

Demirkan, H. and St. Louis, R. (2008) Computing IT's Give-and-Take Role in Sustainability, Knowledge@W. P. Carey, April 23, http://knowwpcarey.com/article.cfm?aid=470 (accessed April 2012)..

Drucker, P. (1984) The new meaning of corporate social responsibility. *California Management Review*, **26** (2), 53–62.

Dubie, D. (2009) How to Cut IT Costs with Less Pain. http://www.networkworld.com/news/2009/012609-companies-cutting-costs.html (accessed April 2012).

Esty, D.C. and Winston, A.S. (2009) *Green to Gold*, John Wiley & Sons, Inc., New York.

Forrest, W., Kaplan, J.M. and Kindler, N. (2008) Data Centers: How to Cut Carbon Emissions and Costs. *McKinsey Quarterly*, (14), http://www.mckinseyquarterly.com/Data_centers_How_to_cut_carbon_emissions_and_costs_2255 (accessed April 2012).

Global Reporting Initiative (2006) Sustainability Reporting Guidelines, G3 Framework, https://www.globalreporting.org/resourcelibrary/G3-Sustainability-Reporting-Guidelines.pdf (accessed April 2012).

Goodin, D. (2006) IT Confronts the Datacenter Power Crisis, *InfoWorld*, http://www.infoworld.com/t/platforms/it-confronts-datacenter-power-crisis-220 (accessed April 2012).

Greer, M. (2009) *Software as a Service Inflection Point: Using Cloud Computing to Achieve Business Agility*, IUniverse, Inc., New York.

Hamm, S. (2008) It's Too Darn Hot, Businessweek.com, March 20, http://www.businessweek.com/magazine/content/08_13/b4077060400752.htm (accessed April 2012).

Hanselman, S.E. and Pegah, M. (2007) The wild wild waste: E-waste. In SIGUCCS '07 Conference on User Services, October 7–10, pp. 157–162.

Harmon, R.R. and Auseklis, N. (2009) Sustainable IT services: Assessing the impact of green computing practices. In PICMET 2009 Conference Proceedings, PICMET/IEEE, July, pp. 1707–1717.

Harmon, R.R., Daim, T. and Raffo, D. (2010) Roadmapping the future of sustainable IT. In Technology Management for Global Growth, PICMET/IEEE, Phuket, Thailand, July, pp. 361–370.

Harmon, R.R. and Demirkan, H. (2011) The next wave of sustainable IT. *IT Professional*, **14**, 19–25.

Harmon, R.R., Demirkan, H., Auseklis, N. and Reinoso, M. (2010) From green computing to sustainable IT: Developing a sustainable service orientation. In Proceedings of the 43rd Hawaii International Conference on System Sciences (HICSS-43), January.

Harmon, R.R., Demirkan, H., Hefley, B. and Auseklis, N. (2009) Pricing strategies for information technology services: A value-based approach. In Proceedings of the 42nd Hawaii International Conference on System Sciences (HICSS-42), January.

HP (2008) Global Citizenship Customer Report, Hewlett-Packard Company, http://www.hp.com/hpinfo/globalcitizenship/08gcreport/pdf/fy08_gcr.pdf (accessed April 2012).
HP (2009) HP Global Citizenship Report, Hewlett-Packard Company, http://www.hp.com/hpinfo/globalcitizenship/09gcreport/pdf/fy09_fullreport.pdf (accessed April 2012).
IBM (2008) 2007–2008 Corporate Responsibility Report, http://www.ibm.com/ibm/environment/annual/IBM_CorpResp_2007.pdf (accessed April 2012).
Intel (2009) Corporate Responsibility Report, Intel Corporation, http://www.intel.com/content/www/us/en/corporate-responsibility/corporate-responsibility-2009-report.html (accessed April 2012).
Kalm, D. and M., Waschke (2009) The New Color of ITIL: Green, MainframeZone.com, http://www.mainframezone.com/article/the-new-color-of-itil-green (accessed April 2012).
Lubin, D.A. and Esty, D.C. (2010) The sustainability imperative: Lessons for leaders from previous game-changing megatrends. *Harvard Business Review*, May, 42–50.
Lusch, R.F. and Vargo, S.L. (2008) The service-dominant mindset, in *Service Science, Management and Engineering: Education for the 21st Century* (ed. B. Hefley and W. Murphy), Springer, Berlin, pp. 89–96.
McKeefry, H.L. (2008) A high-energy problem. eWeek, March, http://www.eweek-digital.com/eweek/20080324?pg=53#pg53 (accessed April 2012).
Microsoft (2010) Innovating to Improve the Planet, http://www.microsoft.com/environment/product_solutions.aspx (accessed April 2012).
Miller, R. (2009) LEED for Datacenters Draft Released, DatacenterKnowledge.com, February 3, http://www.datacenterknowledge.com (accessed April 2012).
Montiel, I. (2008) Corporate social responsibility and corporate sustainability: Separate parts, common futures. *Organization and Environment*, **21** (3), 245–269.
Murugesan, S. (2008) Harnessing green IT: Principles and practices. *IT Professional*, **10** (1), 24–33.
Murugesan, S. (2010) Making IT green. *IT Professional*, **12**, 4–5.
Nagata, S. and Shoji O. (2005) Green process aiming at reduction of environmental burden. *Fujitsu Science and Technology Journal*, **41** (2), 251–258.
Nidumolu, R., Prahalad, C.K. and Rangaswami, M.R. (2009) Why sustainability is now the key driver of innovation. *Harvard Business Review*, September, 57–64.
Norman, W. and MacDonald, C. (2004) Getting to the bottom of the triple bottom line. *Business Ethics Quarterly*, **14** (2), 243–262.
Olson, E.G. (2008) Creating an enterprise-level green strategy. *Journal of Business Strategy*, **29** (2), 22–30.
Oracle (2010) Accelerate Sustainability Initiatives through Oracle's Sustainability Sensor Data Management for Public Sector, Oracle white paper, http://www.oracle.com/us/products/applications/green/sustainability-ssdm-323527.pdf (accessed April 2012).
Ou, G. (2006) Introduction to Server Virtualization, Techrepublic.com, http://www.techrepublic.com/article/introduction-to-server-virtualization/6074941 (accessed April 2012).
Pachube (2011) You Can Help Build an Open Air Quality Sensor Network, Pachube blog, December 7, http://blog.pachube.com/2011/12/you-can-help-build-open-air-quality.html (accessed April 2012).
Parenti, C. (2010) Green strategy now, *The Nation*, December 2, http://www.thenation.com/article/156812/green-strategy-now (accessed April 2012).
Pava, M. (2007) A response to 'Getting to the bottom of the Triple Bottom Line'. *Business Ethics Quarterly*, **17** (10), 105–110.
Phaal, R., Farrukh, C.J.P. and Probert, D.R. (2004) Technology roadmapping – a planning framework for evolution and revolution. *Technology Forecasting and Social Change*, **71**, 5–26.
Pohle, G. and Hittner, J. (2008) Attaining Sustainable Growth Through Corporate Social Responsibility, IBM Institute for Business Value, white paper, http://www.ibm.com (accessed April 2012).
Porter, M.E. and Kramer, M.R. (2006) Strategy and society: The link between competitive advantage and corporate social responsibility. *Harvard Business Review*, December, 78–92.
Porter, M.E. and van der Linde, C. (1995) Toward a new conception of environment-competitiveness relationship. *Journal of Economic Perspectives*, **9** (4), 97–118.
Rhoton, J. (2009) *Cloud Computing Explained*, Recursive Press.
Robins, F. (2006) The challenge of TBL: A responsibility to whom?. *Business and Society Review*, **111** (1), 1–14.

Ryder, C. (2008) Improving Energy Efficiency through Application of Infrastructure Virtualization: Introducing IBM Websphere Virtual Enterprise, The Sageza Group, white paper, 13 pp.

Samsung (2009) Sustainability Report: Harmony with People, Society, and Environment, http://www.samsung.com/us/aboutsamsung/citizenship/download/2009_Our_Sustainability_Report.pdf (accessed April 2012).

Savitz, A. and Weber, K. (2006) *The Triple Bottom Line: How Today's Best-Run Companies are Achieving Economic, Social and Environmental Success – and How You Can Too*, Jossey-Bass Publishers, San Francisco.

Schneiderman, R. (2009) Regulatory compliance means going the extra mile. *Electronic Design*, January 29, http://www.electronicdesign.com (accessed April 2012).

SeeClickFix (2010) The Battle for Control of Smart Cities, SeeClickFix blog, December 16, http://seeclickfix.blogspot.com/2010/12/battle-for-control-of-smart-cities.html (accessed April 2012)..

Senge, P., Smith, B., Kruschwitz, N. *et al.* (2008) *The Necessary Revolution: How Individuals and Organizations Are Working to Create a Sustainable World*, Doubleday, New York.

Shah, A. (2009) Energy Star 5.0 boosts energy efficiency for PCs. *ComputerWorldUK*, July 1, http://www.computerworlduk.com/news/it-business/15491/energy-star-50-boosts-energy-efficiency-for-pcs/?print (accessed April 2012).

Sheth, J.N., Newman, B.I. and Gross, B.L. (1991) *Consumption Values and Market Choices: Theory and Applications*, Southwestern Publishing Company, Cincinnati, OH.

Siegele, L. (2010) It's a Smart World: A Special Report on Smart Systems. *The Economist*, November 6, 1–18.

Siemens (2009) IT for Sustainability Relies on the Intelligent Use of Resources, Siemens Portfolio of Sustainable Development, http://cn.siemens.com/cms/cn/English/it-solutions/Documents/IT_for_Sustainability_e_RY.pdf (accessed April 2012).

Slywotzky, A.J. (1996) *Value Migration: How to Think Several Moves Ahead of the Competition*, Harvard Business School Press, Boston.

Spohrer, J., Vargo, S.L., Caswell, N. and Maglio, P. (2008) The service system is the basic abstraction of service science. In Proceedings of the 41st Hawaii International Conference on System Sciences (HICSS-41), January.

Steiner, F. and Harmon, R.R. (2009) The impact of intangible value on the design and marketing of new products and services: An exploratory approach. PICMET 2009 Conference Proceedings, PICMET/IEEE, July, pp. 2066–2079.

Sward, D. (2006) *Measuring the Business Value of Information Technology*, Intel Press, Santa Clara, CA.

Vargo, S.L. and Akaka, M.A. (2009) Service-dominant logic as a foundation for service science: Clarifications. *Service Science*, **1** (1), 32–41.

Vargo, S.L. and Lusch, R.F. (2004a) Evolving to a new dominant logic for marketing. *Journal of Marketing*, **68** (1), 1–17.

Vargo, S.L. and Lusch, R.F. (2004b) The four service marketing myths: Remnants of a goods-based, manufacturing model. *Journal of Services Research*, **6** (4), 324–335.

Vargo, S.L. and Lusch, R.F. (2008a) Service-dominant logic: Continuing the evolution. *Journal of the Academy of Marketing Science*, **36** (1), 1–10.

Vargo, S.L. and Lusch, R.F. (2008b) A Service logic for service science, in *Service Science, Management and Engineering: Education for the 21st Century* (ed. B. Hefley and W. Murphy), Springer, Berlin, pp. 83–88.

Watson, B.J., Sharma, R.K., Charles, S.K. *et al.* (2009) Creating a sustainable IT ecosystem: Enabling next-generation urban infrastructures. In 2009 ISSST IEEE International Symposium on Sustainable Systems and Technology, May, pp. 1–6.

Wellsandt, S. and Snyder, S. (2009) Building a Long-Term Strategy for IT Sustainability. Intel Information Technology, white paper, 12 pp. http://communities.intel.com/community/openportit/it (accessed April 2012).

Wilbanks, L. (2008) Green: My favorite color. *IT Professional*, **10**, 63–64.

Zarella, E. (2008) Sustainable IT: The Case for Strategic Leadership, KPMG IT Advisory, white paper, http://kpmgcarbonadvisory.com (accessed April 2012).

Useful Web Sites

- The Green Grid (www.thegreengrid.org) is a nonprofit organization that develops standards to measure data centre efficiency.
- The Climate Savers Computing Initiative's member companies commit to purchasing energy-efficient desktops and servers, and to broadly deploying power management strategies (www.climatesaverscomputing.org).
- The Uptime Institute (www.uptimeinstitute.org) provides educational and consulting services for maximizing data centre uptime availability and sustainable IT standards. The Institute promotes learning through conferences, site tours, benchmarking, best practices and abnormal incident collection and analysis for its 100 large enterprise members. It also certifies data centre tier levels and site resiliency.
- www.cleantech.org is a virtual research institute at the centre of clean tech.
- The Electronic Product Environmental Assessment Tool (EPEAT) is an international product registry that rates IT products on environmental criteria (www.epeat.net).
- The Energy Star 5.0 2009 standard (www.energystar.gov) regulates energy efficiency for desktops, workstations and notebooks.

12

Green Enterprises and the Role of IT

Joseph Sarkis
Graduate School of Management, Clark University, Worcester, MA, USA

Key Points

- Provides an overview of various green initiatives within and between organizations.
- Presents a comprehensive overview of various green enterprise activities and functions and their role with IT.
- Discusses the roles of IT and IS in greening enterprises.

12.1 Introduction

Enterprises are becoming greener, and IT plays major roles in greening an enterprise. In this chapter we provide an overview of various green initiatives within and between organizations. Based on the value chain perspective and focussing on various organizational functions, we provide an overview of the organization and greening activities. We then outline inter-organizational aspects of greening which include purchasing and logistics relationships amongst organizations. The general greening strategies, practices (routines), policy and process characteristics across the internal and external value chains set the stage for evaluating and integrating IT considerations. Whether for the greening of physical and usage aspects of actual capital equipment or the application of IT tools and software for greening purposes, various green value chain dimensions, in-bound logistics, purchasing, production, distribution and outbound logistics, design and marketing, inter-organizational relationships and reverse logistics (closing the loop) are addressed in this chapter. We identify some practices which organizations can complete with various

Harnessing Green IT: Principles and Practices, First Edition. Edited by San Murugesan and G.R. Gangadharan.

greening policies such as environmental management systems (EMS), green procurement, design for the environment, life cycle analysis, green marketing and green logistics and transportation, which are all evaluated here.

For planning and controlling each of the value chain functions of organization, IT can effectively be used. For example, IT could be harnessed for life cycle assessment (LCA), environmental management system, environmental performance measurement systems and design for environment and even green supplier and customer management. In terms of capital equipment and the tangible physical product, green IT means that purchasing greener technologies, using IT in service settings, manufacturing these systems (if it is an IT company) or managing the end of life of IT equipment all have implications for greening the enterprise.

E-commerce business practices, which are heavily dependent on IT, have significant inter-organizational implications. For instance, replacing physical goods such as printed books with information goods, also called dematerialization, can eliminate significant waste and reduce the carbon footprint associated with physical product manufacturing, delivery and management. Reductions in inventory, warehousing, return of products and obsolescence can all be improved with effective information technology and information systems (IT and IS) that can be used for design, planning and implementing value chain activities.

The roles of IT and IS in greening the enterprise will be detailed, and a summary of various potential and actual practices will help organizations evaluate the costs and benefits of green IT practices from the perspective of the overall enterprise and inter-enterprise relationships.

12.2 Organizational and Enterprise Greening

Organizations have been experiencing various pressures from a variety of stakeholders that require them to address their environmental impacts and contribute to environmental sustainability by greening their enterprise. Several drivers for greening enterprises go beyond simply meeting compliance requirements. There are at least four business value dimensions for enterprise greening: cost reduction, revenue generation, resiliency or business continuity and legitimacy ('the right to do business'). The greening of IS and IT comprises critical aspects of these efforts for gaining business value. *Green IS* refers to improving the flow and management of information, whilst *green IT refers* more to the hardware and other infrastructure that can be better managed and designed from an environmental perspective. Both these dimensions are important and interrelated. The business value argument is necessary to help organizations more effectively manage the resources they target towards these efforts. The bottom-line and competitive dimensions of the organization are influenced by green IT and IS.

Elimination or reduction of waste reduces the cost. Consumption of excessive resources such as energy and paper essentially means there is inefficiency and increased costs. The most common example is less energy usage, but IS practices such as the paperless office are also examples. In 2009 the US House of Representatives saved US taxpayers $2000 a day in energy costs due to more efficient IT equipment usage. In the United Kingdom it has been reported that the Department for Work and Pensions will save 200 million sheets of paper per year by reducing the number of printers and switching to default duplex printing; the Home Office will save £2.4 million (US$3.9 million) per year by eliminating unused IT equipment and improving the efficiency of remaining machines and the Crown Prosecution Service will save £2.35 million by replacing its 9500 computers and 2500 printers every five years instead of every three years.

Organizations may realize extra revenue through green IT and IS practices. By-products and former waste products may find alternative uses instead of non-value-adding disposal to landfills. IT products and materials that are returned may be recycled, remanufactured and resold, potentially as 'green' products. Thus, what may have been viewed as a cost centre for organizations (a net cost is incurred by a particular product or departmental activity) may become a revenue generator or profit centre. Another method to potentially generate revenue is in regions of the world where the cap-and-trade systems for greenhouse gases may exist. The parlaying of credits by reducing greenhouse gas emissions may become unexpected revenue streams, as carbon credits may be sold (Sarkis and Tamarkin, 2005).

Business continuity has many dimensions but means having the resources to remain in business and deliver products or services to customers, making sure your organization and partners are resilient. If organizations are unsustainable, they may use up their resources, materials may not be as easily available and/or their costs can dramatically increase. By managing supply chains in a sustainable way, such as by making sure that hazardous materials are not in IT products, it is more likely that long-term continuity will occur.

To operate effectively and with little stakeholder conflict, organizations need to develop their 'right to do business'. This value-adding dimension is related to furthering the reputation and legitimacy of organizations that have green IT and IS practices in place. Industries or companies that are viewed as socially irresponsible will have greater barriers and thus difficulty when attempting to complete their business activities in various regions, or difficulties when seeking to expand their organizational capacity in current locations. Extending the life of IT products by donating to charity can also improve an organization's image and reputation (Shah and Sarkis, 2003). Table 12.1 provides a summary of these business value dimensions that can help organizations manage their green IT and IS practices. Appropriate justification and management of these systems can be not only environmentally beneficial but also economically and competitively valuable.

12.2.1 The Green Enterprise: A Value Chain Perspective

Figure 12.1 describes activities and operations within an organization's value chain. Within this systemic perspective of the organization, activities begin with procurement and inbound logistics functions that introduce materials and services into the organizational system. These materials are transported from various vendors. The policies for selection of vendors, including transportation and delivery services, are a central issue for purchasing agents. Thus, the selection of material, services and suppliers may become critical for the purchasing function to help guarantee the environmental performance of their supply chain and materials. Relationships with suppliers including environmentally oriented selection, development and supplier management are needed for effectively greening the procurement function. These materials are then stored or the services are utilized, and may be managed under the auspices of the purchasing function.

Table 12.1 Business value dimensions

Cost reduction	Revenue generation	Resiliency	Legitimacy and image
Decrease the cost of production by retrieving returned and recycled material from IT equipment. Reuse collected material in production which drives down production cost.	Lengthen the life of an IT product by reselling and reusing older systems to locations that cannot afford newer systems.	An organization may lose its license to operate or become less profitable if the IT products it manufactures are not taken back but left to enter other markets.	Having IS systems that are green will help to improve organizational and product image.
Reduce energy usage.	Develop new information systems that allow for managing of an enterprises environmental processes and practices.	The lack of information related to environmental performance may cause business shutdown.	

An important strategic activity for an enterprise is the design of products and processes. Each of the major functions will be profoundly influenced by the design of the product and the process. This influence should be managed with the cross-functional inclusion of various functions and suppliers in the design of processes and products. Designs should now address new ecological themes as life cycle analysis and design for the environment concepts.

The production (transformation) function in a typical manufacturing organization is composed of assembly and fabrication (service organizations would focus on transformation in different ways such as information transformation and locational transformation). Within this function, environmental issues such as closed-loop manufacturing, total quality environmental management, de-manufacturing and source reduction make some form of value-adding contribution, even though some of them also influence other functional areas. The role of EMS, such as ISO 14000–accredited systems, will be critical aspects of managing production function activities and aspects within organizations.

Outbound logistics includes such activities as transportation determination, packaging, location analysis, warehousing and inventory management (for finished goods and spare parts). In these areas, the environmental implications from transportation mode selection and the amount and type of packaging are critical environmental dimensions of organizations. Activities such as using recyclable containers and green fleets and efficiently designing and managing warehousing and inventory play roles in managing an enterprise's

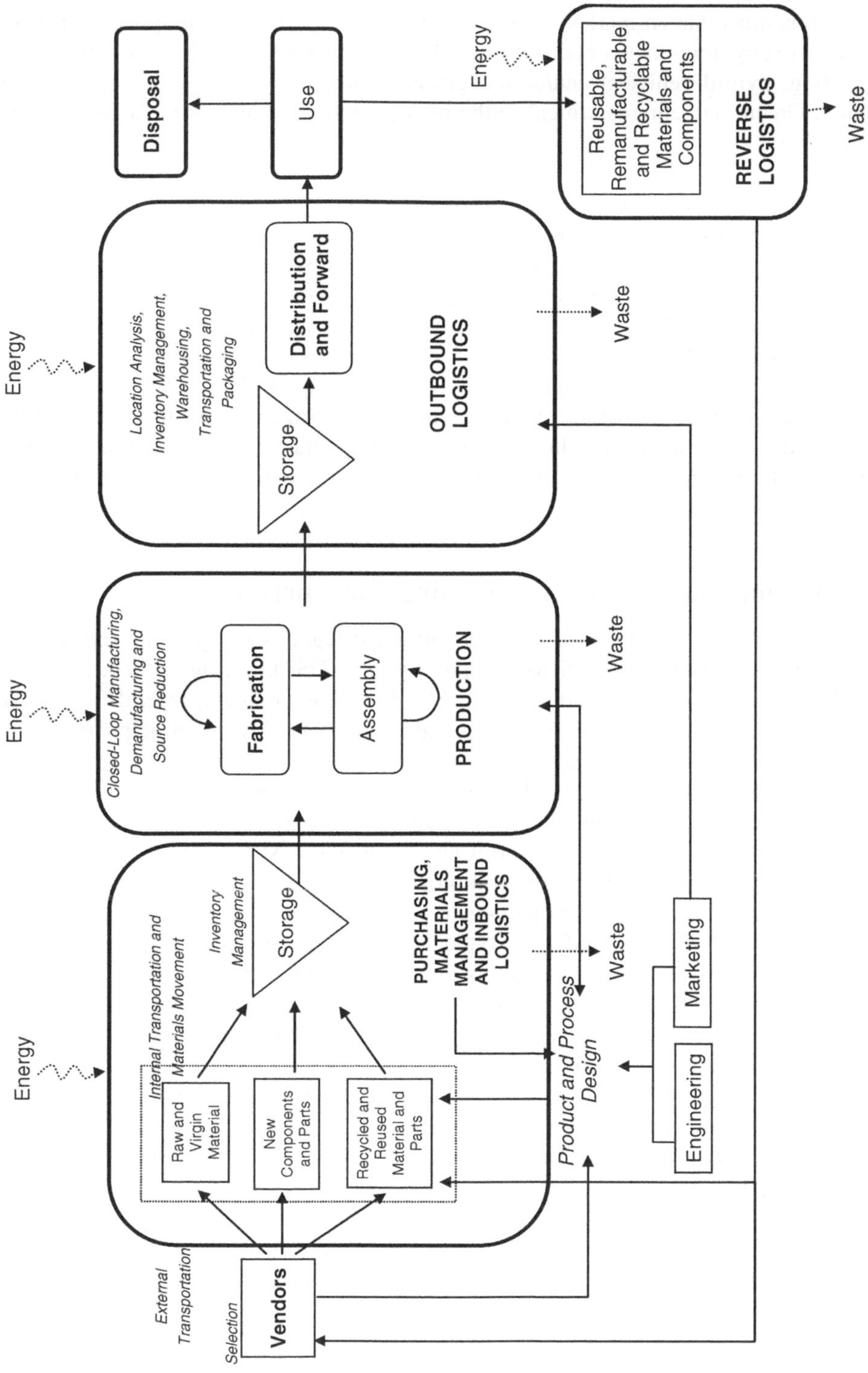

Figure 12.1 Materials, product and information flow: forward and reverse logistics. *Source*: Adapted from Sarkis, 2001.

ecological footprint. Marketing's role is important for activities within this stage of organizational functions. Green marketing has proven to be an effective component of green enterprise strategy for many organizations. Green marketing may focus on the green products (e.g. hybrid vehicles) and/or the greening of processes (e.g. reducing carbon footprints). Green marketing is critical to the management of an enterprise's green image and reputation.

The 'use' external activity is the actual consumption of the product, a situation where product stewardship plays a large role. At this stage, field servicing may occur, but from an environmental perspective the product or materials may be disposed or returned to the supply chain through the reverse logistics channel. This step of the process is known as closing the loop and the closed-loop supply chain. Within this reverse channel, the product may have reusable, recyclable or remanufacturable characteristics. The reverse logistics function may feed directly back to an organization's internal supply chain or to an external vendor, starting the cycle again. As each of these supply chain activities consumes energy and generates some waste, reductions in energy usage and waste generation are issues that need to be addressed throughout the supply chain. IS and the movement of information rather than the movement of materials (information substitution) can greatly enhance this reduction.

12.3 Information Systems in Greening Enterprises

Organizational IS can be separated into four major categories of systems: the transaction processing system (TPS), decision support system (DSS), management information system (MIS) and executive support system (ESS). In addition to these, recently a new category of IS, environmental management information system (EMIS) that helps to manage environmental aspects is emerging.

TPS are focussed at the operational level of an organization and deal with real-time and very short-term information requirements. MIS and DSS are typically focussed at the middle management (tactical-planning) level of an organization. MIS's role is to summarize and aggregate in reporting and communication systems the company's operational information. Typically this information is aggregated to intermediate time scales ranging from weekly to yearly information. DSSs are typically analytical tools that help middle-level managers make relatively routine decisions and use information from various levels of the organization. ESSs focus on the needs and requirements of upper management and aid their focus on strategic management of the organization. Information is typically aggregated from the lower level systems and summarized in longer term perspectives ranging into years and focussing on nonroutine-type decisions (Laudon and Laudon, 2010).

Table 12.2, using this IS categorization, summarizes the various roles of the levels and system types for a few enterprise functions as examples. The categorizations include examples of the type of environmental information and data, tools or reporting required for each function and at the various levels. Many of these items show the prevalence and pervasiveness of IS throughout the whole organization and their implications for greening an enterprise. These various functions and green IS management aspects are discussed further in this chapter.

Table 12.2 Summary of various information system categories and environmental activities by organizational function

Managerial decision level	Operational level	Management level		Strategic level
Functional area	Transaction processing systems (TPS)	Management information systems (MIS)	Decision support systems (DSS)	Executive support systems (ESS)
Engineering and design	New product requirements, and environmental liability	Economic justification models for designs, and design for environment (DFE) decision tools	LCA inventory data	Environmental product and process performance
Procurement	Updating inventory of environmentally sensitive material	Reports concerning environmental performance of suppliers	Supplier selection decision models with environmental factors	Due diligence merger information, and superfund liability information
Manufacturing and production	E-mail reminders of permit thresholds	Daily and weekly levels of hazardous wastes generated from processes for Toxics Release Inventory (TRI) reporting	Disassembly production planning tools	Global, yearly emissions changes, and environmental technology information
Sales and marketing	Daily sales of environmentally sensitive materials	Information on different green promotion successes	Forecasting tools for green product requirements	Green consumer data
Logistics	Amount of packaging returns for day and scheduling of reclaimed materials	Reports on daily and weekly fuel usage	Simulation tools for transportation and energy planning and network design	Long-term data and plans for transportation fleet
Finance	Daily transactions of greenhouse gas emissions permits	Financial environmental budget reports	Capital budgeting DSS tools integrating environmental factors	Shareholder value percentage for socially responsible funds

(*continued overleaf*)

Table 12.2 (*continued*)

Managerial decision level	Operational level	Management level		Strategic level
Accounting	Daily recording information on environmental accounting data	Internal and external environmental audit information	Environmental balanced scorecard system	Social and environmental report structure and standards
Human resources	Updating material safety data sheets (MSDSs)	Environmental training records	Personnel selection for environmental programmes	Environmental and safety requirements in union negotiations

12.3.1 Environmental Management Information Systems

EMISs include hardware, software, people, procedures and tasks that manage environmental information and support environmental and other managers in managing environmental issues within and between organizations. We will focus on software and systems that are used to manage an organization's environmental and greening activities. The usage of such systems also extends to intra-enterprise activities. We begin this section with an overview of the software and database dimensions of EMIS.

12.3.2 Software and Databases

Environmental software programmes cover everything from auditing and managing emissions to analysing energy and minimizing waste. Traditional environmental software as part of IS has focussed on internal practices. More recent aspects of software systems include the utilization of LCA which goes beyond organizational boundaries. Design for environment databases also plays a role and helps integrate supplier and vendor data and processes. A summary of the major software and database systems are shown in Table 12.3.

An integrated enterprise resource planning (ERP) system, as shown in Figure 12.2, can cover many of the environmental management IS software types, database types and organizational functions.

12.3.3 ERP EMISs

Many ERP systems offer a multitude of data with environmental relevance, but they mainly focus on substance classification, hazardous material and disposal criteria. Much of these data could not be used for monitoring and controlling material, energy and water consumption or material or energy flows. The integration of ERP systems with more advanced environmental IS tools helps to address this limitation (Eun *et al.*, 2009).

Table 12.3 Software and database aspects of an environmental management information system (EMIS)

Type	Description
Mass flow and process flow software	Software enabling the construction of full mass flow input and output at different company levels. Helps the user develop a process or mass flow diagram that depicts the sequence of operations for all products. Narrow focus on environmental data.
Life cycle software	Link environmental interaction to environmental impact, and assess these aspects for the whole product life cycle. Assist managers in assessing the environmental impacts of each stage of the life cycle of a product, from raw material extraction through transport, design, development, sale and return.
Environmental risk and impact assessment software	Identifies and assesses risks and impacts associated with activities at the site level. Focusses on specific events and calculates vulnerability, probability, frequency and potential consequences. Assesses direct and indirect impacts of an activity.
Environmental cost assessment software	For use in identifying and assessing costs associated with various environmental activities including clean-up, remediation and process changes due to environmental considerations, related to environmental risk and impact assessment software.
Application, modelling and simulation software	Enables the user to construct models of processes and sites. Helps managers visualize impacts, and how they interact or react in different scenarios. Geographic information systems are usually elements of this software.
Regulatory software	Focusses on government environmental, health and safety regulations, workplace assessments, health and safety project management, illness records and injury statistics. Text of environment-related laws and regulations with guidance and comments also exists.
Waste management software	Manages data for hazardous and solid waste – from profiling and manifesting to calculating, monitoring and tracking at thc operational level
Permit management and MSDS software	Provides management, processing, tracking and reporting support for permit, submission and monitoring compliance status. Also provides immediate information on materials in production chain. May be related to life cycle and other information software. Databases containing knowledge of chemical substance characteristics, international standards for hazard labelling and so on.
Environmental management system software	These packages contain tools for facilitating the implementation of an environmental management system. Some also contain the documentation for ISO 14001 and the European Union's EMAS. Used for implementation of environmental management standards – for example, ISO 14001 or EMAS. Tracking, managing documents, scheduling and monitoring tasks for each element and aspect of these standards may be included.
Integrated and modular software	A system that combines a number of the modular software types mentioned in this table. The larger IT framework could be Web based. Enterprise resource planning systems may contain these modules.

Adapted from Rikhardsson (1998), Moore (2002) and Makarova (2008).

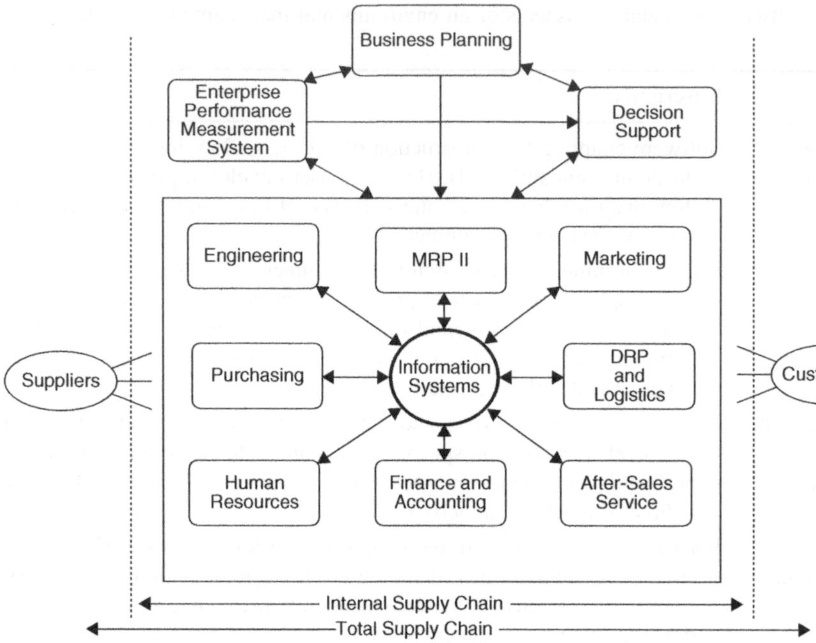

Figure 12.2 Typical ERP system with modules and relationships.

EMIS have typically been designed as stand-alone, isolated, software tools such as waste administration packages. Integration and adequate co-operation of environmental and ERP functionality require an emphasis in their common base: the physical flow model. Environmental harm directly connected to production is related to physical flows entering and leaving the production process.

Enterprises are obliged to deal with data on energy and raw materials consumption, on discharge and on emissions. From a costing point of view, physical flows are also important, even if they were not accounted for traditionally, because they are imposed gradually to specific costs like taxes, tariffs and levies. The essential units for most EMISs are physical ones: mass units (kg) and energy units (MJ), each measured over a definite unit of time. The time unit depends on the availability of data, and on the scope (instrumental, operational, tactical and strategic) that is considered. Also, other operational units are often required, like volume, surface, number of items and so on, with appropriate conversions between units also easily accessible. Of course, the relationship between physical data and environmental data is usually dependent on industry, and appropriate accounting of materials and their environmental implications is needed.

Another unique aspect of environmental information and the IS design is the need to consider multiple stakeholders: supply chain partners (i.e. suppliers and customers), regulatory authorities, consumer organizations, unions, insurance companies and the community. EMIS waste and emissions data would require similar controls and accuracy, as do product and material data in standard ERP systems.

Standard information that would be available from ERP systems for LCA includes material and product information, process and work flow information, supply chain information and information about waste (Eun *et al.*, 2009).

12.3.3.1 Materials and Products Information

Material and product data are available through a bill of material (BOM). Although BOMs and supporting inventory control systems provide some insight into the composition of materials flows, this usually is not sufficient from an environmental point of view. This product and material information is on technical aspects, quality, product specifications and so on. Environmentally relevant data, however, only partially overlap the BOM and material requirements planning (MRP) data. BOM material and product composition can be represented on different levels and in different ways. These levels may include (Lambert and Jansen, 2000) elements, compounds, materials and parts or component assemblies (e.g. bolts or motors).

A BOM usually includes no weight of components or only incomplete information on weight. In addition, components are reported and not materials or substances as needed for a LCA inventory. Supporting processing materials (solvents and lubricants) are also not included in these BOMs. An example is a printed circuit board listed as a component; this would include data on the supplier, type number, dimensions and functionality which can be obtained from a BOM. Yet, physical properties like mass, the presence of hazardous materials and components and the coarse composition may be missing.

Given regulatory policy such as the 'Restrictions on Hazardous Substances' (ROHS), manufacturers are required to know the prohibited substances in their products. BOM represents a single product or assembly, or a group of products, which can aid recognition of any RoHS-restricted substances in the final product. A component's testing report is a crucial document in determining where RoHS-restricted substances exist within its manufacture.

Clearly, this type of information would be necessary in an environmentally integrated ERP system. Integrating a BOM with a material safety data sheet (MSDS) is one way of furthering both environmental and product information.

12.3.3.2 Process and Work Flow Information

Process flow charts are part of ERP systems, especially in ISO 9000–certified organizations. This information may be used to describe the material and energy flows in an LCA. Work orders may contain a relatively complete data set about materials, components, required resources and the job task order. Using this information, process flow charts can be generated to track production related data for resource and energy use.

12.3.3.3 Supply Chain Information

Primarily, transportation and logistics-type information could be useful for environmental management reasons. Supplier information can be used to calculate the transportation effort to the company. In addition, the kind of delivery is registered in the conditions of the supplier. Transportation methods within a company can be obtained from the work order. The distribution methods from a company can be obtained from the sales and distribution functionality of an ERP system.

12.3.3.4 Information about Waste

This information includes types and quantity of waste, and the product that generated the waste.

Logistics and procurement-scheduling modules may also provide valuable information from an environmental perspective. Transportation planning will identify weights, modes of transport, distances and other information that can be used to evaluate the carbon footprint of the organization's logistics function.

12.3.4 ERP Challenges and Deficiencies with Respect to EMIS

Integrating ERP with EMIS systems raises a number of managerial and technological challenges and issues. A number of issues are related to the difficulty of integrating the two systems:

- No one ERP system exists that meets the needs of companies with diverse and multi-dimensional EMIS requirements, even within the same industry.
- Data are usually at highly aggregated levels.
- There is only partial registration of the BOM's components: registration of components and their weights but not materials or substances.
- There is no integration of energy use, water use or emissions into water, air or land.
- The entire life cycle is not included, and recycling and reuse are not considered.
- There is no capability to generate reports for EMS or LCA, for example inventory analysis.
- Units are in batch- or lot-sized operational control–type units.

12.3.5 Integrating Environmental and LCA Information with ERP

As mentioned, some ERP systems have environmental, health and safety (EH&S) modules included in them. For example, the SAP R/3 system has an integrated EH&S module and provides operational solutions for hazardous substance management, product safety, dangerous good management and waste management. Yet, the characteristics and linkages necessary for a full corporate analysis linking them to various functional and supply chain decisions have not been advanced.

There have been some structural systems models that show a more extensive linkage between EMIS, LCA and ERP. The functionality of an ERP system should include various managerial and functional decision levels. Using the managerial decision-making hierarchy to link these two has been recommended. Others (de la Pena, Gomez, and Rautenstrauch, 2004) have advocated that ERP systems need integration of mass and energy flow models for effective integration. This integration is necessary since, as we shall see in this chapter, business process models are required for systems analysis and design approaches for implementing enterprise-wide IS.

A consortium of German industry and schools has been investigating the development of standards called Publicly Available Specification (PAS) 1025 for the standardization of an exchange format between ERP and EMIS systems. This exchange is eventually meant to be a two-way integration since ERP data are useful for EMIS and EMIS data can be used for ERP such as in cost-accounting modules (Wohlgemuth, Niebuhr, and Lang, 2004).

12.3.6 Electronic Environmental and Sustainability Reporting

Environmental communication and environmental and sustainability corporate reporting are tools to communicate a company's (environmental) performance, demonstrate its management systems and present its responsibility, among other items. As environmental data are continuously dynamic and growing, the corporate report may eventually have to be a living document. Internally, processes need to be in place to gather the information and put it into an appropriate format to be reported. Thus, the use of business process management and workflow management has been recommended to develop these systems. Workflow processes have been standardized by the Workflow Management Coalition (http://www.wfmc.org/).

Within the electronic commerce field, the most common language used for communication and reporting standardization is Extensible Markup Language (XML). In fact, many EMS are currently under design to arrive at the corporate report. XML-based documents have a precisely defined structure. XML can be seen as a large family of technologies and languages that permits structuring document contents, formatting documents and transforming documents into other documents or other functions. XML documents have a strict structure, yet they offer the flexibility needed for the presentation of various kinds of information required in the reporting process. XML-based reports are also a suitable tool for Internet and cross-media reporting. A history and development of Internet-based enterprise environmental reporting can be found in Isenmann, Bey, and Welter (2007).

12.4 Greening the Enterprise: IT Usage and Hardware

A driving force in greening IT from a manufacturing perspective is the adoption of environmentally friendly materials, procedures and practices in the design, manufacture and delivery of IT systems.

The environmental implications of hardware production are quite extensive. Electronic products require significant 'clean' requirements. Higher purity requirements mean a greater need for energy and materials. For example, a 2 g memory chip may require 1.3 kg (1300 g) of material resource input, whilst an average desktop personal computer and cathode ray tube (CRT) monitor requires 10 times its weight in water, fossil fuels and chemicals as material and resource inputs (Kuehr and Williams, 2004). Large quantities of energy, materials and chemicals are consumed during the production phase, not all of which will be contained in the final products. Modern electronics and computing equipment consists of over 1000 materials, including lead and cadmium in computer circuit boards, lead oxide and barium in the monitor's CRTs and mercury in switches and flat screens (Babbitt, Williams, and Kahhat, 2011; Basel Action Network, 2002; Zhou *et al.*, 2011). Thus, the management of hardware and its usage is critical to organizational greening.

In this section we examine green IT standards that enterprises seeking to purchase, develop and manufacture green IT hardware could adopt.

12.4.1 Environmental Information Technology Standards

Green IT standards have emerged recently. One of the major efforts towards greening IT product is the Electronic Product Environmental Assessment Tool (EPEAT) that helps identify greener computers and other electronic equipment. It is a powerful tool for enhancing an enterprise's sustainability performance.

EPEAT is a three-tiered, point-based system. There are 23 required criteria to meet the lowest level of EPEAT certification, which is EPEAT Bronze. These criteria cover the entire life cycle of a product, from a reduction of the toxic materials used in production, to the energy it uses whilst in operation, and the recyclability of its materials at the end of life. Products that meet all 23 criteria receive Bronze certification, and those that meet an additional 14 or 21 optional criteria receive Silver or Gold certification, respectively. Table 12.4 summarizes the categories for the 23 EPEAT-required criteria. A total of 28 additional, optional criteria exist.

Other standards such as Energy Star and IEEE Standard 802.3az-2010 influence design. For instance, consider Ethernet network systems; as much as 90% of the time, an Ethernet connection is idle but still drawing power. A new standard, IEEE Standard 802.3az-2010, requires a dual-power state for Ethernet connections, high power and lower power, that can cut down the energy used during those idle times.

These standards provide valuable guidelines for manufacturers' eco-design (design for the environment) and for meeting and achieving green IT goals.

12.4.2 Green Management of Data Centres

Internally for enterprises, there are many activities that can help green the usage of IT. One of the most critical energy users within an enterprise with around-the-clock usage is the data centre. File servers and centralized data storage devices are predominant. The management of these centres is critical to the overall greening of IT whether the enterprise is service or manufacturing oriented. A number of strategies and practices have been recommended to make data centres greener, especially from an energy-saving perspective (Info-Tech Research Group, 2007). For detailed coverage of greening data centres, refer to Chapter 5.

12.5 Inter-organizational Enterprise Activities and Green Issues

A number of inter-organizational enterprise (extended enterprise) activities can be made greener by leveraging IS and technologies. Among them are three activities that are gaining growing interest: electronic commerce and purchasing, reverse logistics and demanufacturing operations as well as eco-industrial parks (Sarkis, 2006). These activities

Table 12.4 EPEAT required (mandatory) criteria for IT equipment

- Reduction and elimination of environmentally sensitive materials
  - Compliance with provisions of European RoHS directive upon its effective date
  - Reporting on amount of mercury used in light sources (mg)
  - Elimination of intentionally added short-chain chlorinated paraffin (SCCP) flame retardants and plasticizers in certain applications
- Materials selection
  - Declaration of postconsumer recycled plastic content (%)
  - Declaration of renewable or bio-based plastic materials content (%)
  - Declaration of product weight (lbs.)
- Design for end of life
  - Identification of materials with special handling needs
  - Elimination of paints or coatings that are not compatible with recycling or reuse
  - Easy disassembly of external enclosure
  - Marking of plastic components
  - Identification and removal of components containing hazardous materials
  - Minimum 65% reusable or recyclable
- Product longevity or life cycle extension
  - Availability of additional three-year warranty or service agreement
  - Upgradable with common tools
- Energy conservation
  - Energy Star®
- End-of-life management
  - Provision of product take-back service
  - Provision of rechargeable battery take-back service
- Corporate performance
  - Demonstration of corporate environmental policy consistent with ISO 14001
  - Self-certified environmental management system for design and manufacturing organizations
  - Corporate report consistent with the EPA's Performance Track or the Global Reporting Initiative (GRI)
- Packaging
  - Reduction or elimination of intentionally added toxics in packaging
  - Separable packing materials
  - Declaration of recycled content in packaging

Source: http://www.epeat.net/Criteria.aspx

also reveal a variety of issues that can be encountered across enterprise boundaries. In this section, we examine these activities and the issues that we might face in greening them.

12.5.1 Electronic Commerce and Greening the Extended Enterprise

Electronic commerce (e-commerce) is the process of buying and selling goods and services electronically through computerized or mobile communication systems using various technologies such as the Internet, the World Wide Web and electronic data interchanges. E-commerce can occur between business and consumers (B2Cs), businesses and other businesses (B2Bs) and consumers and consumers (C2C). There are environmental implications and issues for all these types of transactions, and greening implications occur from all these areas. The impact can be from both an information-sharing perspective and a usage or process perspective.

The Internet and World Wide Web have helped reduce information asymmetry. Information asymmetry is when one party has more information for a transaction than another party. Environmental information, whether it was for reactive purposes (e.g. compliance) or proactive purposes (e.g. locating recyclable materials), was not easily available to all parties. Now people and organizations can quickly locate and act upon environmental information from various organizations. The reduction in information asymmetry necessitates organizations becoming more environmentally sound, especially from a social legitimacy perspective and information-based policy instruments. The role of e-commerce as a conduit of environmental information is best exemplified by the preparation and delivery of environmental reports. One of the more interesting areas of environmental reporting is how to provide a mechanism and structure for organizations to complete environmental reporting.

By implementing e-commerce, firms are likely to better manage their inventories through better information sharing and, for example, *postponement* which means the delay of product differentiation. All this contributes to less waste and obsolete products which are fundamental factors for green, ecologically friendly practices (Sarkis, Meade, and Talluri, 2004). E-commerce makes it possible for companies to directly do B2C business, reducing the need for retail shops or other intermediary services along the supply chain. Consumers can quickly gather price and product information through the Internet and base their buying decision on these attributes. Also the convenience of home shopping is one major reason behind the popularity of e-commerce and its potential environmental benefit. That is, consumers and companies can have products delivered from centralized locations versus driving to and from individual outlets. Less or no packaging is required for information products that can be delivered online. However, there may be some drawbacks such as fragmentation of the fulfilment services as small orders have to be delivered to a large number of dispersed customers, which cannot be regarded as effective in terms of time use and emissions (Edwards, McKinnon, and Cullinane, 2010). Some experts believe that e-commerce, rather than making the supply chain more effective, may increase transport distances resulting in increased pollution.

12.5.2 Demanufacturing and Reverse Logistics

To help extend the life of IT products or materials, a system that will allow for the management of IT hardware is needed. Managing and incorporating a reverse-logistics channel is necessary in this circumstance (Meade, Sarkis, and Presley, 2007). This necessity may be not only voluntary (e.g. competitive advantage) but also due to regulatory requirements such as the Waste Electrical and Electronic Equipment (WEEE) regulations in Europe, Japan and China. Thus, managing this 'closing' of the loop across enterprises for product and materials stewardship is important. Figure 12.3 provides a summary design of a - loop system. There are multiple loops that can be considered including immediate reuse back

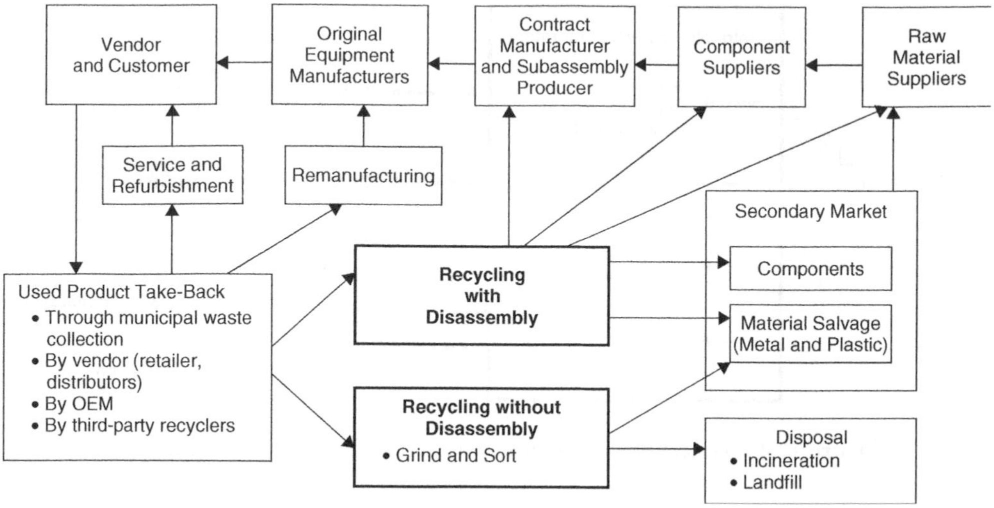

Figure 12.3 A closed-loop system for IT products and materials. *Source*: Sarkis and Park, 2008.

to the consumer market, remanufacturing of equipment around a core (e.g. motherboard), disassembly and recycling with removal and reuse of various parts or recycling without disassembly through destruction of the original equipment and material. Markets exist for each of these dimensions, and the value of each would need to be determined. Much of the value is driven by pricing for products and materials on the market.

The operations in the materials recovery portion of the physical plant typically involve the acquisition of products and materials. Two in-bound flows of material exist. The first flow of material goes directly to the disassembly portion of the facility. The second flow of material goes to a sorting section to determine the category of material. The material may be (i) stored as is in the warehouse facility or (ii) tested. Testing functions like a 'triage unit' which determines whether a product is working (reused, as is), needs some simple 'remanufacturing' or needs to be disassembled for recovery of reusable components or recyclable material. Depending on the material inflow, some material will require little processing, whilst others will require a significant amount of processing. Figure 12.4 summarizes the various input sources and types of outputs of this facility. Computer and electronics components form the overwhelming material that is processed within an asset materials recovery operation (AMRO), although office furniture and other office-based products and materials also arrive for processing. Typically, intact parts are removed, tested and stocked as spares. Precious metals, (gold, platinum and silver) are extracted and resold. Plastic, glass and other materials are recycled. In some cases, with efficient operations, less than one-tenth of 1% of the material ends up in landfills.

12.5.3 Eco-Industrial Parks and Information Systems

Eco-industrial parks are formed by either physically or virtually locating organizations whose by-products may be utilized by other organizations within the park (Geng *et al.*,

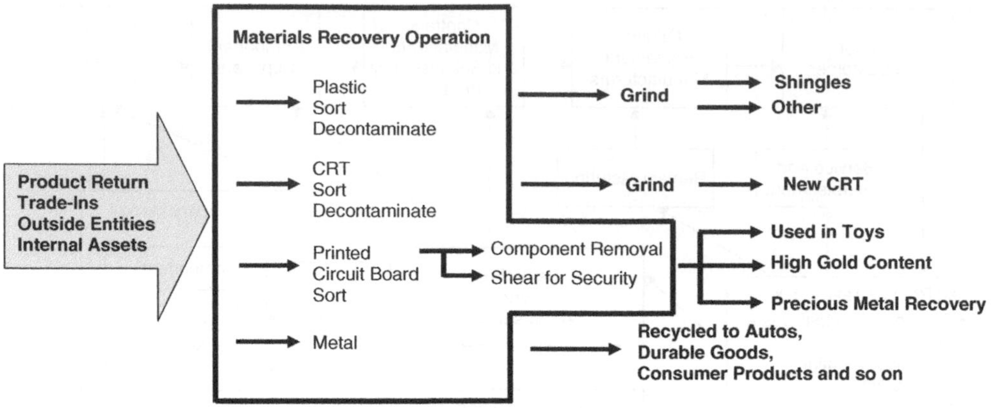

Figure 12.4 Typical flows and operations of a demanufacturing facility.

2012). That is, one organization's waste (by-product) may be another organization's raw material. Environmental information plays important roles in the planning, design, construction, management and retrofit of eco-industrial parks, in industrial symbiosis and in by-product exchange network synthesis. One of the key approaches to improve environmental performance and production management efficiency is to integrate members' environmental information into a park management system.

Software and development systems for eco-industrial parks have been developed since the mid-1990s. A recent survey (Grant *et al.*, 2010) of 17 of these systems shows that their major purposes (functionalities) are (i) opportunity identification, (ii) opportunity assessment, (iii) barrier removal, (iv) commercialization and adaptive management and (v) documentation, review and publication. It was found that many of the tools were for specific situations or regions. Their development was based on the requirements of the developer and not necessarily for broader application.

Eco-industrial parks are a core dimension of China's Circular Economy policy. Much of this policy is heavily reliant on the 'informatization' of China's industry and government agencies. An informatization strategy focusses on promoting informatization in concert with industrial policy encouraging informatization in enterprises. Informatization provides a potentially powerful foundation for eco-industrial development (Fang, Cote, and Qin, 2007). For example, environmental IS at the municipal level is being led by local Chinese environmental protection bureaus. Inter-organizational environmental IS is also recommended for establishment within industrial parks and zones to provide integrated and reliable data. Such data would include eco-industrial park member surveys, detailed information about inputs and outputs of materials, environmental monitoring and other data. Life cycle analysis and material flow analysis tools and information will help eco-industrial parks guide eco-industrial development. 'Symbiotic synergies' such as the exchange of by-products among organizations within eco-industrial parks would be aided (Fang, Cote, and Qin, 2007).

Eco-industrial parks within a larger community (city or province) working together in a broader system may have eco-symbiotic relationships at many levels, similar to an organism that has subsystems working together in a mutually beneficial manner (e.g. the circulatory and respiratory systems in humans). Open-source and distributed systems that can communicate at many levels are needed to enable this situation (Zhijun and Nailing, 2007). The Internet, e-commerce and other relationships amongst different organizations that share knowledge, expertise and data will be needed. This type of system is probably the least developed of the organizational innovations that cross organizational boundaries. Adaptive and dynamic IS that can evaluate and link these organizations at multiple levels, such as geographic IS and mobile information technologies, can prove useful in managing this organizational innovation (Sarkis and Zhu, 2008).

Systems that can manage waste exchanges that occur across and between organizations, a virtual eco-industrial symbiosis, will be needed. An example of such a Web exchange–type tool appears in China's construction industry and is called Webfill (Chen, Li, and Wong, 2003). Webfill is an e-commerce platform to encourage the exchange of residual materials and construction waste for reuse and recycle among different construction sites and material regeneration manufacturers.

12.6 Enablers and Making the Case for IT and the Green Enterprise

Greening an enterprise by harnessing IT or through business process reengineering investment requires thoughtful evaluation and justification by management. Some solutions, such as the policy of favouring the purchase of greener equipment, is easy to implement. Some may require significant investment and justification such as greening full data centres with the latest technologies. In each of these situations, chief information officers (CIOs) must work with a greening and sustainability team to aid in the integrative process.

There are four major categories of enablers for green IT (Seidel *et al.*, 2010): strategy definition, organizational support, motivation and traceability.

- **Strategy definition:** A clear target definition for *sustainability* is required. Supporting corporate strategic measures need to focus beyond economic metrics, towards inclusion of values associated with economic and greening responsibilities. Thus, introducing business case measures for environmental issues can show substantive top management support.
- **Organizational support:** The main organizational enablers for the successful adoption of any sustainable practices are top management support. With regard to top management support, having the commitment from two chief executives – CEO and COO – ensures strategic commitment and support for making organizational change. Bottom-up support may be equally important.
- **Motivation:** According to self-determination theory, both extrinsic and intrinsic motivational factors play a role in adopting new business programmes. Intrinsic motivation is more effective for greening. Intrinsic motivation is an important personal characteristic to achieve bottom-up support. Extrinsic motivation will require more formal procedures and rewards.
- **Traceability:** This is in the sense of transparency and measurement, also important enablers for greening IT. IT also plays an important process role since measurement systems are heavily reliant on software and IS.

As outlined earlier, organizations can gain business value from greening activities. The development of a business case highlighting major business value items is necessary for effective adoption of the practices. A range of tools are available for business case and performance evaluation. Many of these tools have strategic and operational characteristics in addition to incorporating tangible and intangible factors. However, further studies are desired on these tools' issues and nuances and how they may need to be adjusted for greening IT (see Presley, Meade, and Sarkis, (2007), for an overview).

12.7 Conclusions

Greening any enterprise could be accomplished more effectively by appropriate design, implementation, adoption and overall management of IT and IS. This chapter presented a brief overview of various green enterprise activities and functions and their role with IT. There are both internal and extended enterprise implications and concerns that were identified throughout the chapter. Not only is greening the enterprise associated with the usage aspect of IT, such as energy savings, but also IT and IS support of green processes and the actual hardware characteristics are all part of the greening dimensions. There are numerous business value dimensions that an organization can pursue to help justify green IT, but there are also costs and disadvantages associated with green IT efforts. Careful consideration of these various elements needs to be integrated into any managerial evaluation.

Managers must realize the complexity of these issues, and interdisciplinary teams for greening and managing green IT are needed. In some cases, inter-organizational and stakeholder agents will be necessary for the appropriate introduction of systems, technology and processes. This chapter's outline of the various issues can provide some initial insight. Numerous other topics and concerns also exist at multiple levels of analysis including the regional, supply chain, enterprise, departmental and individual levels. The field certainly has room to grow and develop from both a practice and research perspective.

Review Questions

1. Identify and discuss the four major ways in which organizations can gain value by greening an enterprise.
2. What are the major elements of the value chain, and how does 'closing the loop' relate to the value chain?
3. What are the major categories of information systems within an organization? Provide examples of greening enterprise activities at each level.
4. How do enterprise resource planning systems integrate with greening enterprise activities? What are the challenges in integrating them?
5. How can green inter-organizational activities be supported with IT and IS activities?

Discussion Questions

1. What will motivate industry to adopt IT greening practices? Is helping the environment for the environment's sake a motivational goal?
2. Can organizations green their IT activities without external pressure or demand?

3. Are there any activities that you, as an employee or citizen, can do to aid and support the greening of enterprise IT?
4. What barriers exist to greening organizations from an IT perspective?
5. How do you get organizations and agents outside the purview of your organization to adopt green IT practices?
6. Outline your views, pros and cons, on greening an entire enterprise.

References

Babbitt, C.W., Williams, E. and Kahhat, R. (2011) Institutional disposition and management of end-of-life electronics. *Environmental Science and Technology*, **45** (12), 5366–5372.

Basel Action Network (BAN) (2002) Silicon Valley Toxics Coalition Export Harm: The High-Tech Trashing of Asia, BAN, Seattle, WA.

Chen, Z., Li, H. and Wong, C.T.C. (2003) Webfill before landfill: An ecommerce model for waste exchange in Hong Kong. *Journal of Construction Innovation*, **3** (1), 27–43.

Edwards, J.B., McKinnon, A.C. and Cullinane, S.L. (2010) Comparative analysis of the carbon footprints of conventional and online retailing: A "last mile" perspective. *International Journal of Physical Distribution and Logistics Management*, **40** (1/2), 103–123.

Eun, J.H., Son, J.H., Moon, J.M. and Chung, J.S. (2009) Integration of life cycle assessment in the environmental information system. *The International Journal of Life Cycle Assessment*, **14** (4), 364–373.

Fang, Y., Cote, R.P. and Qin, R. (2007) Industrial sustainability in China: Practice and prospects for eco-industrial development. *Journal of Environmental Management*, **83** (3), 315–328.

Geng, Y., Fu, J., Sarkis, J. and Xue, B. (2012) Towards a national circular economy indicator system in China: An evaluation and critical analysis. *Journal of Cleaner Production*, **23** (1), 216–224.

Grant, G.B., Seager, T.P., Massard, G. and Nies, L. (2010) Information and communication technology for industrial symbiosis. *Journal of Industrial Ecology*, **14** (5), 740–753.

Info-Tech Research Group (2007) Top 10 Energy-Saving Tips for a Greener Data Center, http://www.infotech.com/ (accessed April 2012).

Isenmann, R., Bey, C. and Welter, M. (2007) Online reporting for sustainability issues. *Business Strategy and the Environment*, **16** (7), 487–501.

Kuehr, R. and Williams, E. (2004) *Computers and the Environment: Understanding and Managing Their Impacts*, Kluwer Academic Publishers, Dordrecht.

Lambert A.J.D., Jansen, M.H. and Splinter, M.A.M. (2000) Environmental information systems based on enterprise resource planning. *Integrated Manufacturing Systems*, **11** (2), 105–112

Laudon, K. and Laudon, J. (2010) *Management Information Systems*, Prentice Hall, Upper Saddle River, NJ.

Makarova, Y. (2008) Greening business information systems: a case of Volvo information technology. Master's thesis, IIIEE, Lund University, Sweden.

Meade, L., Sarkis, J. and Presley, A. (2007) The theory and practice of reverse logistics. *International Journal of Logistics Systems and Management*, **3** (1), 56–84.

Moore, M.A. (2002) A strategic, systems approach to understanding environmental management information systems. *Environmental Quality Management*, **11** (4), 65–73.

de la Pena, G.B., Gomez, J.M. and Rautenstrauch, C. (2004) Integrated material flow management and business information systems. In 18th International Conference on Informatics for Environmental Protection, CERN, Geneva, Switzerland.

Presley, A., Meade, L. and Sarkis, J. (2007) A strategic sustainability justification methodology for organisational decisions: A reverse logistics illustration. *International Journal of Production Research*, **45** (18–19), 4595–4620.

Rikhardsson, P.M. (1998) Information systems for corporate environmental management accounting and performance measurement. *Greener Management International*, **21**, 51–70.

Sarkis, J. (2006) *Greening the Supply Chain*, Springer, London.

Sarkis, J., Meade, L. and Talluri, S. (2004) E-logistics and the natural environment. *Supply Chain Management: An International Journal*, **9** (4), 303–312.

Sarkis, J. and Park, J. (2008) Understanding the linkages between IT, global supply chains, and the environment. *Cutter IT Journal*, **21** (2), 13–18.

Sarkis, J. and Tamarkin, M. (2005) Real options analysis for 'green trading': The case of greenhouse gases. *Engineering Economist*, **50**, 273–294.

Sarkis, J. and Zhu, H. (2008) Information technology and systems in China's circular economy: Implications for sustainability. *Journal of Systems and Information Technology*, **10** (3), 202–217.

Seidel, S., Recker, J.C., Pimmer, C. and vom Brocke, J. (2010) Enablers and barriers to the organizational adoption of sustainable business practices. In Proceeding of the 16th Americas Conference on Information Systems: Sustainable IT Collaboration around the Globe, Lima, Peru, August 12–15, 2010.

Shah, S. and Sarkis, J. (2003) PC disposition decisions: A banking industry case study. *Environmental Quality Management*, **13**, 67–84.

Wohlgemuth, V., Niebuhr, C. and Lang, C. (2004) Exchanging environmental relevant data between ERP systems and industrial environmental management information systems using PAS 1025. In 18th International Conference on Informatics for Environmental Protection, CERN, Geneva, Switzerland.

Zhijun, F. and Nailing, Y. (2007) Putting a circular economy into practice in China. *Sustainability Science*, **2** (1), 95–101.

Zhou, X., Nixon, H., Ogunseitan, O. *et al.* (2011) Transition to lead-free products in the US electronics industry: A model of environmental, technical, and economic preferences. *Environmental Modeling and Assessment*, **16** (1), 107–118.

13

Environmentally Aware Business Process Improvement in the Enterprise Context

Konstantin Hoesch-Klohe and Aditya Ghose
Decision Systems Laboratory, School of Computer Science and Software Engineering, University of Wollongong, New South Wales, Australia

Key Points

- Explains the functions and goals of business process management (BPM) and green BPM in particular.
- Demonstrates how to identify a process or activity's environmental impact.
- Discusses process improvement in the enterprise context.
- Compares trade-off analysis with impact and change propagation analysis.

13.1 Introduction

There is a global consensus on the need to reduce our collective carbon footprint. Whilst much research attention has focussed on developing alternative energy sources, automotive technologies or waste disposal techniques, we often ignore the fact that the ability to optimize (existing) operations to reduce a mission's impact is fundamental to this exercise. Business process management (BPM) technology, with its focus on understanding, modelling and improving business processes, is a key starting point. Process modelling technology has applications beyond what we would traditionally describe as business processes – we can also model and improve manufacturing and other 'physical' processes. We will use the term Green BPM to describe a novel class of technologies that leverage and extend existing BPM technology to enable process design, execution and

Harnessing Green IT: Principles and Practices, First Edition. Edited by San Murugesan and G.R. Gangadharan.

monitoring in a manner informed by the environmental performance of process designs and instances (Ghose *et al.*, 2009).

The ability of BPM technology to redesign and optimize operations in a sustainable manner has been identified by several researchers. For example, Ghose *et al.* (2009) proposed a first research agenda on green BPM, highlighting the need to assess and improve processes at the design, instance and process ecosystem level (considering multiple related business process). Likewise, Nowak, Leymann, and Mietzner (2010) emphasized the need for business process re-engineering (BPR) methods particularly in the information and communication technologies (ICT) context. Cleven, Wortmann, and Winter (2010) conducted an empirical investigation on the use of process performance management (PPM) (concerned with the measurement and improvement of business process performance) for establishing and maintain sustainable processes. Houy *et al.* (2010) looked at potentials and challenges of process improvement and redesign as part of the BPM life cycle.

Though much has been written on the applicability of BPM to contribute to the environmental sustainability challenge, few frameworks or practical means currently exist which support the process analyst in a green BPM exercise. This chapter provides an overview of a green BPM framework and offers some practical guidelines on green BPM. Being able to assess the environmental performance of an activity or a process is central for any analysis exercise – in the words of Lord Kelvin, 'If you cannot measure it, you cannot improve it'. So, firstly, we outline a set of methods for identifying the environmental impact of a business activity or a process. Next, we summarize the concepts behind a decision support tool for environmentally aware business process design and improvement, which is currently developed as part of the Abnoba framework (Hoesch-Klohe and Ghose, 2010a, 2010b, 2010c). Finally, we outline how a change and optimization analysis can be performed within the enterprise ecosystem, beyond traditional process optimization and redesign. We exemplify this by providing example cases.

13.2 Identifying the Environmental Impact of an Activity or Process

To be able to reason about and improve the environmental performance of a business process, we need information on various activities involved in the business process and the environmental impact of each activity. In the following, we sketch four methods that can help an analyst in this task: educated guess by an expert, derivation from a resource model, activity-based costing (ABC) and carbon dioxide accumulation. These methods are intended to support the discrimination and ranking of different process design realizations, but they are not means for carbon accounting. For ease of explanation, we will use the measure *carbon dioxide emission* (CO_2 emission) for the on-going elaboration of this section, but note that other measures like waste generation or water and air pollution, can be equally handled.

13.2.1 Educated Guess by an Expert

In this method, an expert (e.g. an external consultant or the process owner) assesses each business activity. The assessment is based upon the knowledge of the expert. This method cannot provide detailed CO_2 emission figures and we therefore recommend to abstract away from quantitative figures to an qualitative scale, such as the *traffic light scale*, where 'red' denotes a 'high' CO_2 emission impact, whilst 'green' denotes a moderate impact. This method allows the process owner to get a quick overview of the tentative performance of each business activity.

13.2.2 Derivation from a Resource Model

In this bottom-up method, the CO_2 emission value for an activity is determined by capturing the resources that an activity requires to be executed, the way the activity uses the resources and the intensity of the activity. Resources and activities are linked via a usage–cost relationship which reflects a CO_2 emission value for the intensity and way in which a resource is used. For example, an activity 'Print document X' might use a printer resource with an intensity of 15 pages, which results in 200 g CO_2. Whilst we omit a detailed elaboration here, further information can be found in Hoesch-Klohe and Ghose (2010b).

The accuracy of deriving the CO_2 emission is dependent on the number of resources modelled. Whilst the method allows identifying detailed carbon emission figures for each activity, it can be cumbersome due to the potentially high complexity of creating and managing the resource models.

13.2.3 Carbon-Dioxide Accumulation

This method assumes that activities (atomic activities or sub-processes) are associated with emission figures and is used to aggregate these values to the processes level. It complements bottom up approaches like 'derivation from a resource model'. We start by identifying all alternative paths through the business process. This is either done manually or via tool support (e.g. Hinge, Ghose 2009). For each path we accumulate the emission values of its participating activities. In case a single CO_2 value is required for the process, we can average the values associated with each path. However, this might be erroneous due to the fact that some rarely executed paths might skew the mean emission value. To avoid this issue, we recommend to weight each path with respect to its execution probability (such information can be taken from run-time data like execution logs) – if available. More information on emission accumulation can be found in Hoesch-Klohe and Ghose (2010b).

13.2.4 Activity-Based Costing

ABC (Kaplan and Anderson, 2004) is a top-down method to trace costs to cost objects. Whilst in most of the times cost is associated with money, we can also think of carbon emission or waste as cost. The ABC method is applicable if the total cost of an organization is available. This, for example, is the case for electricity consumption where the total consumption is known due to the electricity bill or electricity meter. The electricity consumption can then be traced (using appropriate drivers) to the business capabilities. Electricity can then be converted into a CO_2 emission equivalent, using either numbers provided by the electricity provider or an average value provided by the respective government. More information on using ABC for the environmental assessment of activities or business processes can be found in Emblemsvag and Bras (2001) and Recker, Rosemann, and Gohar (2010).

13.3 A Decision Support Tool for Environmentally Aware Business Process Improvement

In an environmentally aware business process improvement exercise, the objective is to find process design alternatives (redesigns) that have a lower environmental impact than the current as-is design. This is a challenging exercise for a human analyst since the range of possible process redesign decisions is large. Further, there is higher likelihood of an erroneous design decision, which might result in nonrealization of organizational goals. Therefore, decision support system assisting the analyst in a process optimization exercise is required. Whilst existing work (e.g. Netjes, Reijers, and Aalst, 2009) on automated process improvement focusses on paralleling activities note that this does not necessarily have a positive impact on a process' environmental impact.

In the Abnoba framework (Hoesch-Klohe and Ghose, 2010a, 2010b, 2010c), we provide a semi-automated system that uses a library of best practice process fragments (snippets) for business process improvement. Essentially, the system replaces fragments of an as-is process design with more environmentally friendly fragments drawn from the library. At the same time, the system ensures that (i) the desired functionality of the process is still realized and (ii) the process design can be provisioned by the resource context of the enterprise.

13.3.1 Some Preliminaries

The system requires all activities of a business process design to be annotated with their *immediate effects*, resource requirements and environmental impact figures. An *immediate effect* is a context-independent specification of functionality, denoting the outcome of executing the respective activity. This allows us to leverage the ProcessSEER (Hinge, Ghose, and Koliadis, 2009) tool for semantic effect accumulation, which enables us to point at any point in the process design and get feedback on what is achieved if the process design would have been executed up to this point. This is needed to ensure that a given process redesign continues to have the desired functional outcome. A *resource requirement* states that an activity requires a resource. An activity can be provisioned by the resource context if all resource requirements are met. The number of valid business process redesigns is therefore constrained by the underlying enterprise resource context, and we might have to drop a process redesign candidate because we are not in possession of the required resources.

13.3.2 The Business Process Improvement System

Process improvement is performed in five steps. An overview of these steps is given in Figure 13.1 (adapted from Hoesch-Klohe and Ghose, 2010a).

1. **Given an as-is process design:** It is disassembled into all its process fragments. A process fragment is a (sub-) process with a single entry and a single exit point. For example, each activity (Figure 13.2a), sequence of activities (Figure 13.2b) or activities between a gateway split and merge (Figure 13.2c) are process fragments.

   Splitting a process design into its process fragments allows us to isolate functionality in the hope that it can be replaced by a fragment from the library with similar functionality and a lower environmental impact.

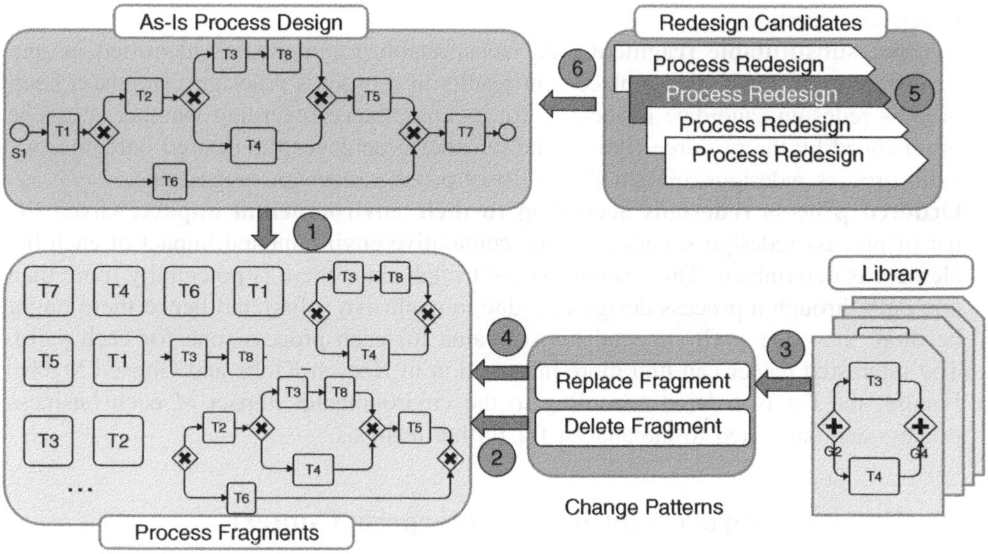

Figure 13.1 An overview of the business process improvement system.

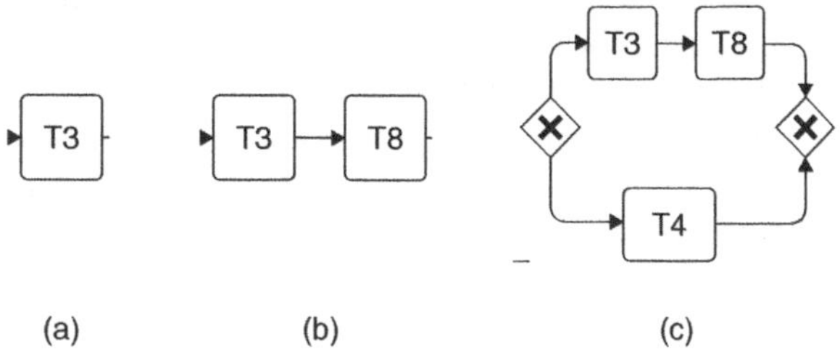

Figure 13.2 Examples of process fragments.

2. **All obsolete fragments are removed from the as-is design:** Process designs evolve over time and hence might include fragments which are not needed anymore to satisfy goals correlated with the business process. We identify obsolete fragments by checking for whether each identified process fragment can be deleted, such that the resulting process design continues to satisfy the correlated goals (desired functionality) and is compliant.
3. **A capability library is used to search for substitutable fragments:** The capability library constitutes a set of (semantic and provisioning constraint annotated) process fragments that the enterprise can provide, as well as fragments from external 'best practice' process designs. Conceptually, the library could also include services (which can be seen as complex activities), derived from a service broker. For each fragment of the as-is process design, we search for a substitutable fragment in the capability library such that this fragment includes the semantic effect of the as-is design fragment under consideration.
4. **Replace substitutable fragments:** All substitutable fragments, as identified in step 3, are replaced. Each such replacement results in a process redesign candidate. Each process redesign candidate is checked for its compliance regarding whether it can be provisioned by the resource context and whether it achieves the desired outcome. All valid process redesigns are added to a list of process redesign suggestions.
5. **Ordered process redesigns according to their environmental impact:** Given the list of process redesign suggestions, the cumulative environmental impact of each list element is determined. This exercise is not trivial, since there is potentially more than one path through a process design (i.e. due to exclusive splits) and hence there might be more than one environmental impact value for each process (one for each path). The interested reader can find more information in Hoesch-Klohe and Ghose (2010b). Finally, the list is ordered according to the environmental impact of each business process and suggested to the analyst for further analysis.

13.4 Process Improvement in the Enterprise Context

In Section 13.3, we elaborated on a system for business process improvement, which ensures that each suggested process redesign meets goal and resource requirements. By doing so, we ensure that the process redesign is 'fitting' into the enterprise environment in which it is executed. Hence, the enterprise context in which the process redesign is executed acts as a set of constraints for which we seek to find a solution. This approach is appropriate, if we are satisfied with our enterprise context and do not wish to make further changes besides redesigning the business process under consideration. However, we might be willing to accept further changes to our enterprise environment (e.g. give up some constraints) if further optimization potentials can be activated.

We are, therefore, interested in exploring the a process redesign's impact on the enterprise environment and how the enterprise context can be optimally adapted to the original change. We refer to this type of analysis as *impact and change propagation analysis*. Since there can be more than one solution (resolving all constraint violations), we are interested in identifying the one which has the most preferred properties, such as the solution which results in an overall lower environmental impact, and/or the solution which contains as little change as possible to the original enterprise context, allowing an organization to protect its existing investments in infrastructure and resources. We refer to the assessment of each candidate solution as a *trade-off analysis*.

To be able to perform this kind of analysis, the enterprise context has to be captured. In this section we refer to the enterprise context as an *enterprise ecosystem*, hinting at its vulnerability to change and need for a balanced state, to which we refer as equilibrium.

13.4.1 The Enterprise Ecosystem

An enterprise ecosystem can be captured by a set of enterprise entities and a set of relationships or dependencies that can be established between these entities. Here we restrict our analysis to the entities and relationships provided by the i* modelling notation (Yu and Mylopoulos, 1994). The i* notation allows one to model the intentional actors within and across organizational boundaries, their goals, behaviours as well as interdependencies. Note that these entities are also part of existing enterprise architecture frameworks like Zachman (1999), TOGAF (The Open Group, 2009a) or ArchiMate (The Open Group, 2009b).

We consider the following enterprise entities:

- **Actor:** An actor (e.g. a department, unit or role) is an entity that performs actions to realize its goals (intentions).
- **Behaviour:** Behaviour describes the actions performed by an actor.
- **Goal:** A goal describes what an actor seeks to achieve and is the justification for performing its behaviour. Functional goals are of Boolean nature: either the goal is achieved, or it is not achieved.
- **Key performance indicator (KPIs):** A KPI describes the nonfunctional preference of an actor with respect to a certain measure (e.g. CO_2 emission). KPIs allow us to discriminate between alternative designs or realizations.
- **Resource:** A resource is a relevant (physical or nonphysical) entity that is required to provision an activity.

Given these enterprise entities, a variety of *relationships and dependencies* can be established between them. We consider the following relationships in our analysis:

- **Actor dependencies (between actors):** A actor–dependency relation denotes that one actor depends upon another actor.
  - **Resource dependency:** An actor depends upon another actor to have access to a resource.
  - **Activity dependency:** An actor depends upon another actor to perform a certain action.
  - **Goal dependency:** An actor depends upon another actor to bring about a condition in the world (the actor is free to choose how to bring about the condition).
- **Realization relation (between business processes and goals):** A realization relation between a goal and a business process denotes that the process provides the means to achieve the goal. The relationship holds if the effects of executing the business process entail the goal achievement conditions.

- **Provisioning relation (between resources and an activity):** A provisioning relation between an activity and a resource denotes that the activity requires the resources to be executed. A business process can be provisioned by a given resource context, if all resource requirements for its subtask are satisfied.
- **Refinement relation (between goals and between activities):** A refinement relation between two entities denotes that one is a more detailed description of the other. This allows for specification of entities at multiple levels of abstraction, ranging from the generic to the detailed.

13.4.2 Enterprise Ecosystem Equilibrium

An *enterprise ecosystem equilibrium* describes a desired state of the enterprise ecosystem in which:

1. all goals are realized by a set of business process or are further refined by other goals;
2. all business processes are justified – they either realize a goal or a dependency relationships to another actor;
3. all activities can be provisioned – all their resource requirements are satisfied; and
4. all dependency relationships between any two actors can be satisfied.

This first rule ensures that each goal, which is not further refined, can be realized by a business process. Since goals on the operational level are refinements of strategic goals, failing to ensure realization can lead to not achieving organizational strategies. The second rule ensures that superfluous business processes, adding no value to the enterprise, do not exist. The third rule ensures that all behaviour can be provisioned by the existing resource context – the enterprise is in possession of the required resources. This last rule ensures that all dependencies between internal actors (e.g. departments) as well as external actors (e.g. customers) are satisfied.

We refer to an enterprise ecosystem that is not in the state of equilibrium (any of the rules is not satisfied) as a perturbed enterprise ecosystem. It is obvious that an enterprise that operates with a perturbed enterprise ecosystem is misaligned and threatens its competitive advantage.

13.5 Impact and Change Propagation Analysis

The objectives of impact and change propagation analysis are to (i) identify the consequences of a business process change to the enterprise ecosystem equilibrium and (ii) re-establish a state of equilibrium given a perturbed enterprise ecosystem.

13.5.1 Identifying the Consequences of a Business Process Change

A given change in a business process can introduce the following ecosystem perturbation:

1. **Resource perturbation:** The business process redesign candidate cannot be provisioned by the resource context, because a resource in the enterprise ecosystem does

not exist which fits the resource requirements. For example, a new 'order supply' process requires a material management (MM) system resource, which does not exist in the ecosystem.
2. **Goal perturbation:** The business process redesign candidate does not realize the fulfilment conditions of the goal(s) associated with the original as-is design. For example, one of the fulfilment conditions of a goal to 'ensure supply' might be to 'receive and store order confirmation'. A process redesign that does not have the effect of receiving and storing the order information does not satisfy the fulfilment condition, and consequently it does not realize the goal.
3. **Activity–dependency perturbation:** The dependency relation between two actors cannot be satisfied if the depender (the actor upon which another actor depends) cannot provide the dependum (the resource, activity or goal) upon which the depending actor depends. A previously satisfied actor dependency might become unsatisfied if the depender makes changes to his goal, processes or resources. For the case of a process redesign candidate, the redesign candidate might result in nonsatisfaction of an activity dependency to an actor who depends on the original as-is process design to realize her goals.

Note that for this discussion we only consider perturbation scenarios that result from changing (redesigning) a given business process. Other scenarios can be considered as well. For example, an enterprise might seek to change its strategies and explore the consequences of such an action to the operational actor-level goals, business processes and inter-actor dependencies.

13.5.2 Re-Establishing a State of Equilibrium

Given a perturbed enterprise ecosystem, caused due to a process change, the following scenarios emerge for resolving a resource, goal or activity–dependency perturbation.

13.5.2.1 Resolving Resource Perturbation

Given an enterprise ecosystem perturbation, due to a business process that cannot be provisioned by the resource context, we identify the following options to handle this scenario:

1. **Acquire the resource:** In this scenario the enterprise buys the required resources and integrates them into their enterprise ecosystem. However, caution has to be given to the monetary and environmental price of the resource, such that acquiring the resource does not eliminate the results of the business process improvement exercise.
2. **Replace existing resource:** In this scenario the acquired resource replaces an existing resource in the enterprise ecosystem. However, this might impact other business processes, which were provisioned by the replaced resource, resulting in a new resource perturbation. Hence, it must be ensured that these process designs can be provisioned by either resolving the new resource perturbation or redesigning the impacted process designs (which again might cause perturbation).
3. **Acquire access to the resource:** In this scenario the enterprise acquires access to the resource via another actor, which was not in the scope of the enterprise ecosystem

before (e.g. via an external actor). This results in a resource dependency with the new actor, which has to be captured in the ecosystem.

4. **Outsource business functionality:** In this scenario, business functionality (a business process, service or activity) is outsourced to another actor, which either desires the resource or has access to it. This results in an activity dependency to that actor.
5. **Reject process redesign candidate:** In this scenario neither of the previous scenarios is acceptable to the enterprise and hence the business process redesign is rejected.

13.5.2.2 Resolving Goal Perturbation

Given an enterprise ecosystem perturbation, due to a business process that cannot realize the correlated goal(s), we identify the following options to handle this scenario:

1. **Give up fulfilment conditions:** In this scenario the fulfilment conditions that cannot be satisfied by the process redesign are given up. For example, the enterprise might realize that the fulfilment conditions are too onerous and that the goal could also be realized by achieving a less restrictive set of fulfilment conditions.
2. **Give up goals:** In this scenario the goal, which cannot be realized by the process redesign, is given up. However, this might result in the parent goal (and subsequent parent goals) not being satisfied anymore,[1] which might impact existing inter-actor goal dependencies. The consequences of this must be explored as well.
3. **Reject process redesign candidates:** In this scenario neither of the previous scenarios is acceptable to the enterprise and hence the business process redesign is rejected.

13.5.2.3 Resolving (Activity-) Dependency Perturbation

Given an enterprise ecosystem perturbation, due to an (activity) dependency not being satisfied anymore, we identify the following options to handle this scenario:

- **Depending actor accepts nonsatisfiability:**[2] The actor which depends upon the business functionality accepts the nonsatisfiability of the activity dependency, gives up the activity dependency and assesses the impact (see the list item 'goal perturbation' in Section 13.5.1 and see Section 13.5.2.2).
- **Outsource business functionality:** In this scenario the depending actor gives up the activity dependency and establishes a new activity dependency with a new (external) actor providing the business functionality.
- **Actor creates business functionality:** In this case the depending actor gives up the activity dependency and establishes the required business functionality within her boundaries. However, this might result in a resource perturbation, which needs to be resolved (see Section 13.5.2.1).

[1] This might result in the need to change the parent goals or in some cases even the enterprise strategies, which again might result in a further perturbation, due to new child goals and the need to realize them via business functionality, which again needs to be provisioned, and so on. As mentioned in this discussion, we only focus on the change due to a business process redesign.

[2] In this scenario we assume that the depending actor is part of the enterprise.

- **Reject process redesign candidate:** In this scenario neither of the previous scenarios is acceptable to the enterprise and hence the business process redesign is rejected.

Given the different scenarios on resolving a perturbed enterprise ecosystem as well as the possible combination of these scenarios, multiple restored enterprise ecosystem equilibriums are possible. In the following trade-off analysis, we provide means to juxtapose these different equilibrium candidates.

13.6 Trade-Off Analysis

A given process change might require us to choose between different consequent changes (if we do not handle the enterprise context as a fixed constraint) to maintain an enterprise ecosystem equilibrium. However, some of these consequent changes might undo the improvements gained from the process redesign, whilst others might activate further improvements. We hence need means to identify the most desired equilibrium candidate. This is determined in a trade-off analysis. We identify two ways to discriminate among distinct ecosystem equilibriums: (i) the cost to bring about a change and (ii) the environmental performance of operating with respect to an ecosystem equilibrium candidate.

13.6.1 Cost to Bring about the Change

When new resources are acquired, process designs changed, new goals derived and new dependencies established, monetary *costs* arise. For example, costs might arise for implementing a process redesign or acquiring a required resource. To avoid high costs we need means to assess the setup costs of each ecosystem candidate. A challenge often faced is the lack of detailed cost figure during an early phase. Assessing the 'distance' of change of an equilibrium candidate compared to the original equilibrium can help us to overcome this issue. We assume that a high-distance point needs higher implementation costs, compared to a candidate with a small distance. The distance of a candidate to the as-is equilibrium is determined by *counting the number of enterprise entities affected* (i.e. which have to be changed).

For example, consider two actors A and B, as well as an activity dependency of actor A for a business functionality provided by actor B and the intention of actor B to redesign this business functionality. Due to the intended change, actor A cannot realize all her goals anymore – there exists a perturbation of the ecosystem. As previously identified, there are multiple options to handle this scenario. We seek to juxtapose the options. The options could be (besides B giving up his intensions to change the business functionality): (i) 'Actor A creates a new business functionality' and (ii) 'Actor A outsources business functionality to another actor C'. For the first option we assume that two resources have to be acquired to satisfy the resource requirements of the newly created business functionality. One resource is directly acquired by buying it, whilst the second is acquired via a resource dependency to another actor. Assuming that there are further consequences, this makes the number of changes required for option (i) four: giving up activity dependency to actor B, creating new business functionality, buying a resource and establishing new resource dependency. For case (ii), actor A established a new activity dependency with another external actor C, which makes the number of changes for option (ii) two: giving up activity dependency to actor B, and establishing new activity dependency with actor (iii). Hence option (ii) would be preferred over option (i).

In the former case we assumed an *equal weighting* for all types of enterprise entities. However, a *different weighting* can be considered as well. For example, one could argue that establishing an activity dependency to an external actor generally involves doubling the amount of monetary costs, compared to other changes. Assuming that there are no further weightings given case (i) and case (ii) of our former example would have an equal change distance of four to the original equilibrium.

13.6.2 Environmental Operating Costs

Operating cost, in our setting, denotes the expected environmental costs for operating an enterprise according to a given enterprise ecosystem. In the following we outline two methods for discriminating between any two ecosystems – one where concrete figures for each activity are known (e.g. from the carbon wiki), and the other where only tentative figures are available (e.g. from an expert's educated guess).

Given *concrete figures* for each activity in the ecosystem, we can discriminate between two ecosystems by determining their expected total environmental impact. For each ecosystem candidate, we create a set of all (distinct) activities. We consider activities from activity–dependency relationships with external actors not part of the set, since they are performed by another company. Each activity of the set is weighted by the number of (expected) executions over a fixed period of time – this information could be taken from past experience, for example from process logs. If no such information is available, an equal weighting could be applied. Consequently, the environmental performance of an ecosystem is determined by multiplying the weighting of each activity with its environmental impact and taking the sum over all activities of the set. At the end, the enterprise ecosystem candidates are ordered according to their environmental performance.

Given (qualitative) *tentative figures* (e.g. a scale of 'red, yellow and green') for each activity of an ecosystem, we can either (i) choose the value of the least performing activity of an ecosystem as representative value for the respective ecosystem or (ii) choose the value of the best performing activity. In the former we apply a pessimistic view whilst in the later we commit to an optimistic view. This method allows a quick assessment of any two ecosystems, but the results might be skewed due to a single high- or low-achieving activity.

13.7 An Example

In the following example, let us consider the human resources (HR) department of an organization, focussing on the actors, goals, behaviour and resources that deal with job applications.

13.7.1 As-Is Scenario

As internal actors of the enterprise ecosystem, we consider the HR department as well as an IT department. The applicant is captured as an external actor.

For the HR department, we consider the *goal* (besides others) of ‘maintain staff recruitment’, which might be a refinement of a more general goal to ‘maintain staffing’. The goal ‘maintain staff recruitment’ is refined into the goals ‘job offer available’ and ‘job application handled’. The goal ‘job offer available’ requires that jobs are created and made accessible to potential applicants. The goal ‘job application handled’ requires that incoming applications are assessed and in all cases the applicant is informed about the application’s status. Note that goals should be refined to a level of abstraction, where they can be correlated with the business behaviour.

The goals given here can be correlated with the following set of process designs (being a subset of the set of all HR processes): ‘create and announce job offer’, as well as ‘assess job application and inform applicant’. In the former process, the HR department creates a job description and sends it to the IT department to manually update the job description on the organization’s Web site. The IT department is reluctant to give members of HR access to the Web site, due to security issues. The announcement of the job offer via the IT department is perceived as a bottleneck. This is due to the IT department performing irregular batch updates (once every couple of days), which lead to unnecessary long waiting times between job creation and application assessment. Moreover, already-occupied job positions are still listed, due to the HR department not having access to the current listing of job applications on the Web site and the IT department performing only sporadic updates. The out-of-date listings on the Web site result in applications on old job offers, which in turn have to be handled by the HR department. In the later process of ‘assess job application and inform applicant’, the strength as well as correctness of the job application are assessed and based on that a decision is made. In either case, the applicant is informed about the outcome.

An analysis of the effects of each process design and the goal descriptions reveals that the business process ‘create and announce job offer’ realizes the goal ‘job offer available’, whole the business processes ‘assess job application and inform applicant’ realizes the goal ‘job application handled’. Note that these business processes themselves have subprocesses, but we omit details for simplicity. Furthermore, the goals, behaviour and resources of the applicant (being an external actor) can only be assumed (from the perspective of the HR departments) and are hence not given explicitly.

The following *dependencies* can be established between the actors. The applicant depends (via goal dependencies) upon the HR department to realize the goal ‘job offer available’ as well as ‘job application handled’. The HR department depends (resource dependency) upon the applicant to submit an application to be able to ‘assess the job application’. Furthermore, the HR department depends upon the IT department to announce the job offer.

Note that other internal and external actors’ departments (e.g. finance) and their interrelationships should be considered as well, but are omitted for brevity.

13.7.2 Improvement Scenarios

Given the as-is situation, a business process improvement exercise is initiated. The following process redesigns and consequent ecosystem equilibrium candidates have been identified.

1. The process 'assess job application and inform applicant' is redesigned, such that the applicant is not informed about the status of his application, if the application is on an expired job offer. As a consequence the overhead from applications on old job offers is decreased. However, the given change results in a perturbation of the enterprise ecosystem, since the goal 'job application handled' states that *in all cases* the applicant has to be informed about the status of his application. This is not given by the redesign and hence it does not realize the given goal. A state of equilibrium can be re-established by changing the goal accordingly, for example by removing or loosening the goal requirements – we assume no further perturbation from doing so.
2. The subprocess 'announce job offer' being part of the process 'create and announce job offer' is executed by the HR department. As a consequence the HR department does not rely on the IT department to make changes to the job offer listing. However, the given change results in a perturbation of the ecosystem, since the HR department does not have access to the job listing on the Web site. An equilibrium can be restored by establishing a resource dependency from the HR department to the IT department, denoting that the HR department has access to or relies on the job listing on the Web site. We do not assume further impacts the ecosystem.
3. The manually managed Web site for listing the job offers is replaced by a content management system, where the HR department has permission to create and delete job offers. Furthermore, job offers can be correlated with a lifespan, such that they are automatically deactivated from the active listings after the lifespan is exceeded. As a consequence, the overhead from applications on old job offers is reduced and the update cycle improved. However, this requires establishing a new resource within the boundary of the IT departments (we assume the IT department will manage and own the system) and establishing a resource dependency from the HR department to the content management system resource.
4. The subprocess 'announce job offer' is outsourced to a service provider offering superior listing of job offers as well as a convincing database of job seekers. As a consequence the organization expects up-to-date listings as well as more competitive job applications, due to more job seekers being reachable. However, this change has to be reflected in the enterprise ecosystem by establishing a new task dependency to the service provider.

13.7.3 Assessing Scenarios

Given the identified enterprise ecosystem equilibrium candidates, the organization seeks to identify the most preferred candidate. As discriminator between the candidates, the organization chose to minimize monetary setup costs as well as minimize carbon dioxide emission performance.

The enterprise entities affected in the first scenario are the business process 'assess job application and inform applicant' as well as the goal 'job application handled'. We hence count two affected entities. For the second scenario the business process 'create and announce job offer' and the established resource dependency (job listing on the Web site) to the IT departments are affected. We count two affected entities.

In the third scenario a new resource (content management system) is acquired, a dependency relation from the HR department to the IT department established, and the subprocess 'announce job offer' changed accordingly. We count three affected entities. The enterprise entities affected in the third scenario are 'create and announce job offer' and the established task dependency (announce job offer) to the service provider. We count two affected entities. The distance of scenarios 1, 2 and 4 to the original ecosystem is two, and there are three affected entities for scenario 3. However, the organization decides to double-weight the creation of the content management system resource in scenario 3 as well as the task decency to the service provider. This is done to reflect higher expected setup costs.

As a result, the equilibrium candidates resulting from scenarios 1 and 2 are more preferred, with respect to setup costs (each having a distance of two to the original ecosystem), to the candidates resulting from scenarios 3 and 4 (having a distance of four and three, respectively).

In terms of CO_2 emission, the organization applies the expert method (and a scale of 'green', 'orange' and 'red', where 'red' denotes the least preferred) to assess the CO_2 performance of each candidate *relative to the original design*. The CO_2 performance of the equilibrium candidate resulting from scenario 1 is assessed as 'green' compared to the original ecosystem, since the applicant does not need to be informed in all cases. The candidates resulting from scenarios 2 and 3 are assessed as 'orange' compared to the original ecosystem, since their CO_2 performance is expected be very similar to the original. The candidate resulting from scenario 4 is assessed as 'green', since the service provider has a high reputation for offering environmentally friendly services. Note that if we would be in the game of carbon accounting, the organization not need include the outsourced service into its calculations. However, since we seek to support environmentally friendly design decisions (across organizational borders), the outsourced service is part of our analysis as well. Given the assessed CO_2 performance, the equilibrium candidates from scenarios 1 and 4 (each assessed as 'green') are preferred over the candidates resulting from scenarios 2 and 3 (each assessed as 'orange').

Given an equal weighting over setup cost and CO_2 emission, scenario 1 is identified as the most preferred enterprise ecosystem equilibrium candidate. Table 13.1 provides the setup costs and CO_2 emission performance for all candidates.

Recall that performance indicators are used to discriminate between multiple options and equilibrium candidates. Consequently, the preference relation over the candidates changes depending on the performance indicators chosen. For example, the organization could have chosen 'maximize information flow to stakeholders' as another indicator, which would have a bad impact on the candidate resulting from scenario 1, most likely resulting in a distinct preference ordering.

Table 13.1 Summary of setup costs and CO_2 performance

Scenario	Setup costs (distance)	CO_2 emission performance
1	2	Green
2	2	Orange
3	4	Orange
4	3	Green

13.8 Conclusions

In this chapter we addressed the environmentally aware design and optimization of business processes as part of a BPM exercise. Firstly, we outlined a set of methods to identify the environmental performance of a business process as a basis for process improvement. In this context, it would be interesting to investigate how the different methods can be conjointly applied, such that for each situation the most appropriate method can be chosen. Secondly, we summarized the conceptual underpinnings of a decision support system for environmentally aware business process optimization. The system focusses on design time aspects of process improvement, and it would be interesting to see how it can be extended to also take into account runtime aspects of a business process. Finally, we outlined how the process improvement analysis can be extended to an enterprise optimization analysis. We currently investigate how this analysis can be supported by decision support machinery.

Review Questions

1. How will you identify the environmental impact of a business process?

Discussion Questions

1. Give an example of how you could use a trade-off analysis to make a process greener.
2. Explain the Abnoba framework.

References

Cleven, A., Wortmann, F. and Winter, P. (2010) Process performance management as a basic concept for sustainable business process management-empirical investigation and research agenda. In Proceedings of the 1st International Workshop on Business Process Management and Sustainability.

Emblemsvag, J. and Bras, B. (2001) *Activity-Based Cost and Environmental Management*, Kluwer Academic Publishers, Dordrecht.

Ghose, A., Hoesch-Klohe, K., Hinsche, L. and Le, L.S. (2009) Green business process management: A research agenda. *Australian Journal of Information Systems*, **16** (2), 103–117.

Hinge, K., Ghose, A. and Koliadis, G. (2009) Process seer: A tool for semantic effect annotation of business process models, in *Proceedings of the 13th IEEE International EDOC Conference (EDOC-2009)* (ed. IEEE Computer Society), IEEE Computer Society Press, Piscataway, NJ, pp. 54–64.

Hoesch-Klohe, K. and Ghose, A. (2010a) Business process improvement in Abnoba, in *ICSOC 2010 International Workshops PAASC, WESOA, SEE, and SC-LOG*, LNCS, Springer, Berlin, pp. 193–202.

Hoesch-Klohe, K. and Ghose, A. (2010b) Towards green business process management. In Proceedings of the 7th International Conference on Services Computing (Industry and Application Track).

Hoesch-Klohe, K. and Ghose, A. (2010c) Carbon-aware business process design in Abnoba. In Proceedings of the 8th International Conference on Service Oriented Computing.

Houy, C., Reiter, M., Fettke, P. and Loos, P. (2010) Towards green BPM-sustainability and resource efficiency through business process management. In Proceedings of the 1st International Workshop on Business Process Management and Sustainability.

Kaplan, R.S. and Anderson, S.R. (2004) Time-driven activity-based costing. *Harvard Business Review*, November, 1.

Netjes, M., Reijers, H.A. and Aalst, W.M.P. (2009) On the formal generation of process redesigns, in *Business Process Management Workshops*, Springer, Berlin, pp. 224–235.

Nowak, M., Leymann, F. and Mietzner, R. (2010) Towards green business process reengineering, in *ICSOC 2010 International Workshops PAASC, WESOA, SEE, and SC-LOG*, LNCS, Springer,Berlin, 187–192.

Recker, J., Rosemann, M. and Gohar, E.R. (2010) Measuring the carbon footprint of business processes. In Proceedings of the 1st International Workshop on Business Process Management and Sustainability.

The Open Group (2009a) Togaf Version 9, http://www.togaf.info (accessed April 2012).

The Open Group (2009b) Archimate 1.0 Specification, http://www.opengroup.org/archimate/doc/ts_archimate/ (accessed April 2012).

Yu, E. and Mylopoulos, J. (1994) From "ER" to "AR" – modelling strategic actor relationships for business process reengineering. In Entity – Relationship Approach – ER'94 Business Modelling and Re-Engineering, pp. 548–565.

Zachman, J.A. (1999) A framework for information systems architecture. *IBM Systems Journal*, **38** (2/3), 454–470.

14

Managing Green IT

Linda R. Wilbanks
Naval Criminal Investigative Service (NCIS), Quantico, VA, USA

Key Points

- Introduces the concept of how to manage IT with a focus on environmental sustainability.
- Presents a comprehensive programme life cycle for managing green IT, starting with strategic thinking and planning.
- Describes the components necessary for successfully managing green IT.
- Illustrates how to demonstrate a strong return on investment on green IT implementation and techniques of a successful metrics programme.
- Discusses information assurance (IA) and risk management as part of the process of implementation of green IT.

14.1 Introduction

Green computing is the study and practice of using computing resources efficiently with minimal impact to the environment. It also focuses on reducing the use of hazardous materials, maximizing energy efficiency during the product's lifetime and supporting recyclability or biodegradability of defunct products and factory waste. A senior executive of an enterprise, such as a CIO, a CTO or an IT manager, can foster green innovations and take an active role in leading the development and implementation of enterprise-wide green initiatives. IT can play a central role in all green initiatives. Investing in green technology and practices has the potential to save money, make the company more efficient and competitive and accelerate the ability of the company to grow, besides saving the planet.

Several case studies and evidences confirm that IT managers utilizing green IT initiatives can make a difference to their companies' bottom line and the environment without

Harnessing Green IT: Principles and Practices, First Edition. Edited by San Murugesan and G.R. Gangadharan.

a large cost outlay. For instance, according to a US Environmental Protection Agency (EPA) estimate, the resulting annual savings from enterprise power management software for desktop computers is $25–75 per computer. Even simple steps such as these can make a huge difference when leveraged across the vast number of computers in organizations. This is a simple realistic example of return on investment of a power management software upgrade or installation.

Managing IT with a focus on environmental sustainability is a wise strategic decision. Even with minor alterations to their existing practices, IT managers and users can make a difference. This chapter focuses on practical approaches for successfully managing the implementation and utilization of green IT, presenting techniques and guidelines that will help a manager implement green IT initiatives successfully. This chapter begins with strategic planning, leadership skills and demonstrated valued added by green initiatives. It then moves onto design, illustrating the use of enterprise architecture (EA) and the incorporation of information assurance (IA). Concluding with the development phase, the process for creating an effective metrics programme will be discussed along with incorporating a risk management program, all leading to the management of successful implementation of green IT initiatives.

14.2 Strategizing Green Initiatives

Successfully formulating, implementing and managing green initiatives calls for strategic thinking, strategic planning and strategic implementation.

14.2.1 Strategic Thinking

As with everything else, you need a strategy to green your IT or enterprise. Simply starting to write a strategic plan assumes the end product, rather than clearly defining what the end product should be. Many managers, especially those with previous experience in a technical field, tend to dive right into the plan without strategically thinking where the plan should lead; they assume that strategic planning is the same as strategic thinking. Formulating and implementing green IT initiatives require strategic thinking, prior to designing the strategic approach and assuming the end state. Strategic thinking is the action taken prior to strategic planning, prior to the development of those requirements. It lets managers develop the comprehensive green vision they want to attain. Strategic planning is a formal process of defining the requirements for delivering a green IT programme – identifying what and how to get from current systems and equipment to future green ones.

Strategic thinking is a distinctive activity whose purpose is to discover novel, imaginative green strategies that offer value. This approach encourages managers to visualize potential future scenarios for the company comprehensively harnessing green IT principles and practices. It is proactive rather than reactive in nature. The focus is always on a greener future state in relation to where the company is today. This is the way to add environmental value to organizations through the selection of high payoff targets, by responding to future new environmental realities and an accelerated rate of change towards green IT.

Strategic thinking is not necessarily an innate skill, nor is it pure serendipity. It is a mental process – arising from personal and managerial experience – that must be enhanced as part of professional development. The intent in using strategic thinking is to enhance the organization's position and purpose towards green initiatives, specifically in the area of IT. Initially, the IT manager must clearly understand the fundamental business goals that are driving the move to green initiatives within the organization and then think about what it means to be green. The goal is to formulate effective strategies consistent with a business and competitive strategy; the means are the examination and validation (and possibly elimination) of policy issues through a long-term perspective. The IT manager must focus on finding and developing unique opportunities to create value by enabling provocative and creative dialogue about and with green IT initiatives.

Following strategic thinking, managers can strategically plan and develop the requirements and processes needed to attain the comprehensive vision of the program utilizing green IT components and systems.

14.2.2 Strategic Planning

Strategic planning is an organization's process of defining its strategy or direction, and making decisions on allocating its resources to pursue this strategy, including its capital and people. This is the process for determining where an organization wants to be in the short term and in the long term (3–5 years or more). Without a clear plan of the direction in which the company wants to move, green initiatives are likely to remain isolated from the rest of the business' initiatives and processes and will not form part of the company's overarching strategy (Wikipedia, n.d.).

Strategic planning starts with a prior mission statement and a vision and leads to the formulation of goals and objectives. The mission statement tells you the fundamental purpose of the organization; it defines the customer and critical processes, and informs you of the desired level of performance. A vision statement outlines what the organization wants to be or how it wants the world in which it operates to be; it concentrates on the future as a source of inspiration and provides clear decision-making criteria.

If a company is comprehensively moving towards a green environment, it should be identified in the vision statement. Even if only the IT aspect is going green, identifying that vision here identifies that at the highest company level, green is critical, which greatly strengthens the IT department's position to accomplish its green objectives.

Every IT department should have its own strategic plan that supports that of the company. In this mission statement and vision, the move towards green IT should be prominent. This plan should be approved by your upper management for full comprehensive support and then circulated throughout the management team and to all employees of the IT department. This informs everyone of the direction in which IT is moving (i.e. towards green), and encourages them to be a part of the change, thus getting the critical buy-in needed for success.

A company's management at the highest level must support the move towards green IT. Success is based on a blend of technology and business acumen. The CEO and the CIO must work together to authoritatively mandate the acceptance of changes and must persist until all adapt and accept the changes.

14.2.3 Strategic Implementation

IT should be recognized as a strategic resource, one that can make a difference and actively support the company. Peers and partners cannot always see the best ways to leverage IT as a strategic resource, so the IT manager must make it part of his or her job to ensure that IT is seen in this light, as these actions will also increase IT visibility. This increased visibility then allows the IT manager to demonstrate how green IT can have a positive value impact for the company.

As shown in Figure 14.1, you change the process by understanding the processes and procedures currently in use and the habits of the IT community of users and customers. Some valuable processes can actually hinder some green initiatives. For example, turning off computers and power strips and the end of the day prevents patches from being automatically pushed. This should not be an impediment to the greening action; IT needs to change the process of pushing patches by looking for other options, such as asking the user what time they would like the patches to be pushed or pushing them prior to the computer shutting down. New habits need to be developed that produce both real and perceived value, which means a new set of rules for IT management also. To build a green environment you must modify or abolish many old and familiar ways of doing business. There is no silver bullet or single vendor solution for IT to magically become green.

14.2.4 Enterprise Architecture Planning

Following strategic planning, the next step is to develop the architecture that is needed to support the green initiatives to maximize their impact and support their implementation.

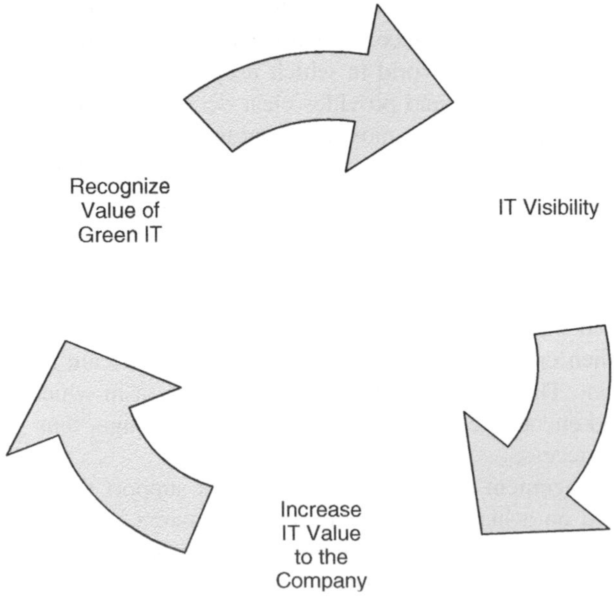

Figure 14.1 Increasing the value of green IT.

EA is a methodology for developing a series of architectural frameworks – current, intermediate and target – often known as as-is, to-be and the mitigation plan. These frameworks detail all relevant structures within the organization, including business, application, technology and data. They are a rigorous taxonomy and ontology that clearly identify what processes a business performs and give detailed information about how those processes are executed. The result is a set of artifacts that describe, in varying degrees of detail, exactly what and how a business operates and what resources are required to run the components with maximum efficiency and profits.

Moving towards a comprehensive green IT environment can be compared to remodelling a house. Firstly, the objectives and strategies of the company must be known and incorporated into the strategic planning for the new green environment. What should the new green house achieve? For example, lower energy costs reduce the carbon footprint. Most IT managers do not have the luxury of starting from scratch, throwing out all the old equipment, networks and systems and buying all-new ones, so a plan is needed.

Enterprise architecture planning (EAP) is the process of defining architectures for the use of information in support of the business and the plan for implementing those architectures. The business mission is the primary driver, followed by the data required to satisfy the mission, then the applications are built using those data, finally followed by the technology to implement these applications.

This hierarchy of activity is represented in Figure 14.2, in which the layers are implemented in order from top to bottom. EAP takes a data-centric approach to provide data quality, access to data, adaptability to changing requirements, data interoperability and sharing and cost containment. The alternative, more traditional view is that applications should be defined before data needs are determined or provided for, but puts a stronger focus on the data needed for the mission. Both can be implemented successfully.

Regardless of which model you choose, there are four layers critical to successful EAP:

- **Layer 1 – getting started:** This planning initiation layer leads to producing an EAP work plan and stresses the necessity of high-level management commitment to support and resource the subsequent steps in the process. Planning initiation includes decisions on which methodology to use, who should be involved, what other support is required and what toolset will be used.
- **Layer 2 – the vision of where we are today:** This layer provides a baseline for defining the eventual architecture and the long-range migration plan. It consists of business

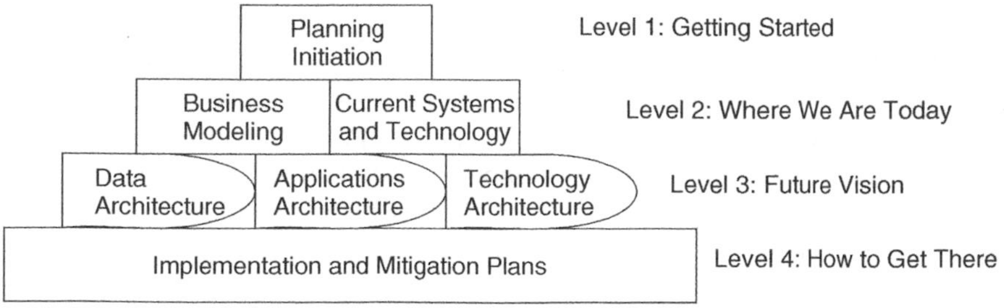

Figure 14.2 Enterprise architecture planning levels.

process modelling, which is a compilation of a knowledge base about the business functions and the information used in conducting and supporting the various business processes. It also consists of current systems and technology, a definition of current application systems and supporting technology platforms.
- **Layer 3 – the vision of where we want to be:** This layer delineates the data architecture defining the major kinds of data needed, applications architecture defining the major kinds of applications needed to manage that data and technology architecture defining the technology platforms needed to support the applications.
- **Layer 4 – how we plan to get there:** The implementation and migration plans define the sequence for implementing applications, a schedule for implementation, a cost–benefit analysis and a clear path for migration.

A successful move to a comprehensive green IT environment will start with and continually utilize EA to ensure that a strong compatible structure is built.

14.3 Implementation of Green IT

Initiating green IT management involves four key components:

1. Adopt a bottom-up or top-down approach. If you are part of the company's management team, initiate discussions on what you would like to do. If reception is poor or minimal, start with engaging with the users and getting their suggestion and initiatives that quickly demonstrate the value of green initiatives.
2. Understand the complexities and interdependencies of how products, architectures and operating procedures impact green initiatives.
3. Understand the trade-offs, the architecture and what will be required.
4. Use point solutions associated with comprehensive plans and sound architectures.

Computers and the IT infrastructure consume significant amounts of electricity and contribute to greenhouse gas emissions. IT hardware poses severe environmental problems during production and in its disposal. These are just some of the major environmental issues that an IT manager must take into consideration when initiating the change to green IT. One must consider how to make the IT infrastructure, products, services, operation, applications and practices environmentally sound while creating a sustainable environment.

While developing green initiatives, consider what employees can do personally. Simple actions such as turning off power strips are easily done by the employees both at work and at home. By educating employees and encouraging these actions, the company benefits as do the employees through the reduction in energy costs. Company-wide, for example, automatic screen savers can be enabled in computers. Procurement policies can require buying energy-efficient, environmentally computers and other hardware meeting specified Electronic Product Environmental Assessment Tool (EPEAT) and Energy Star ratings.

Most people's personal or professional agenda takes precedence over corporate aspirations. People often resist change if they are not convinced of the need for change or the potential benefits the change might bring in. Whilst the IT manager should have already demonstrated the value of green IT to the company management, he or she should also educate and convince employees by providing them with relevant information and demonstrating the value of the proposed initiatives. In order to be successful, users must be active participants. Educate employees on how to save energy, and get them involved. Seek employee's feedback, address their concerns and encourage them to participate.

Involving and engaging employees in green initiatives will strengthen the move to green and, if managed correctly, will create a wave effect. Telling people there will be an impact from utilizing a screen saver is not the same as showing them said effect and having them personally connect to it. This action will then encourage them to accept (or at least try) the next green item, and whether it is cloud computing or a new computer, the wave of acceptance and successful greening has started.

14.3.1 Return on Investment

It is the responsibility of the IT manager to identify and deliver value, and then communicate to management what value has been added. How that value is determined is the responsibility of the technical staff – ensuring that there is a tangible or intangible value is your responsibility. If you can demonstrate the value, especially initially, you create success for your team and for your goal. This success can then be built on as you move to the next phase, because you will start with the confidence of your management team.

Effective IT leaders not only manage well, but also help business counterparts play their roles in making good decisions that produce operational and financial improvements in business performance. For example, more energy-efficient desktops reduce energy consumption. The reduction in the use of energy reduces the costs of running the building, supporting that manager. But the IT manager can assist the facilities manager even further through the investigations and selection of computerized systems that manage the building's energy consumption, such as load-sharing software or software that manages the temperature, lowering the temperature when possible and raising it when necessary. By working together, the IT manager and the facilities manager can move the building towards green and reduce costs successfully.

Green IT does not have to be an all-or-nothing movement; it can be incremental, as funding supports the changes. It is the job of the IT manager to manage continuous IT improvements: As these improvements are scheduled and planned, look for green solutions. Thorough understanding of the dynamics of continuous and discontinuous change helps the CIO accomplish the task of moving the company towards green.

Clients usually have no insight into the factors that affect their IT costs, and no understanding of how to decrease their IT costs while supporting green IT. It is the IT manager's job to show value in terms they understand. Often this will require breaking down the factors. For example, in upgrading a data center to a green environment, an IT manager will need to break down the costs, such as cooling and energy consumption. An IT manager must make these factors known regarding how they fit into the objectives that he or she are trying to achieve, and why those objectives are important to the company.

For example, assume that an IT manager is upgrading a data center, doing one server rack at a time. Although this may not be viewed as an incremental project, the manager still can show value at each stage in terms of green IT. As the equipment is purchased, place emphasis on the value added by the new equipment (e.g. it is made of X% recyclable material, as opposed to the Y% in the old boxes). This comparison is necessary to make sure that upper management understands the value of the change. Just telling them what percentage is recyclable does not mean anything to a non-IT manager, and sometimes not even to an IT manager. In order to impress them with the percentage change, and hence get credit for the first step towards green, both numbers are necessary.

At the next step, the first installation, which is always the hardest and often where unexpected problems are found, should address problems as quickly as possible so as not to mar the success of the project. After the first installation, an IT manager should give the team credit for installing the equipment on time, and any downtime hopefully can be minimized. If the installation took longer than expected or had unanticipated problems, then the manager should acknowledge them also.

After the first component is installed, announce it, making sure to discuss the decrease in the amount of energy used for the amount of cooling needed. At the end of the project, again announce how the new green IT equipment has made a difference to the environment and energy consumption.

It often is helpful to publicize improvements and outcomes. For example, if you are replacing servers with more energy-efficient, less heat-producing servers, one way to visibly demonstrate value is to take the upper management or your boss on a brief tour of the facility prior to the replacement. Have them feel the heat being emitted and see the push of cooling needed. After the changes, arrange another tour, again showing how little heat is emitted. Measure the temperature before and after the replacement, and record your improvements.

In showing the value added of green IT, you need to find ways to describe *value added*, besides running IT at lower costs. Demonstrate how IT can not only assist in green movements, but also help the business become more successful. Transform that IT into more than a cost of doing business, more than just a commodity, such as electricity. Focus on contributions to business performance and outcomes, not just the performance of the machines. This process is demonstrated in Figure 14.3.

14.3.2 Metrics

For the manager implementing a green IT programme, the challenge is to show that an improvement has been achieved and that moving to green has made a difference. Metric programmes are initiated to demonstrate the improvements or benefits.

In order to demonstrate the difference, the first step in developing a metrics programme is to identify the program's goals or objectives. For example, a goal may be to reduce energy costs. Next define the attributes that are to be measured; an example of these may be heating or cooling costs, or energy consumed by desktop computers or servers.

Continue forward by clarifying and quantifying the goals by specifying questions and identifying metrics and data that are needed. For example, how much energy is consumed by the current desktops, what is the energy usage of a green desktop, what is the current energy usage in the data center now and how does it change as new green servers are implemented? The final and very critical step is to close the loop – provide management with answers to their questions based on the metric analysis. The key to continued success of a metrics program is immediate, visible benefits. It must do the job it was designed to do and supply management with usable information to solve their current problem in a timely fashion.

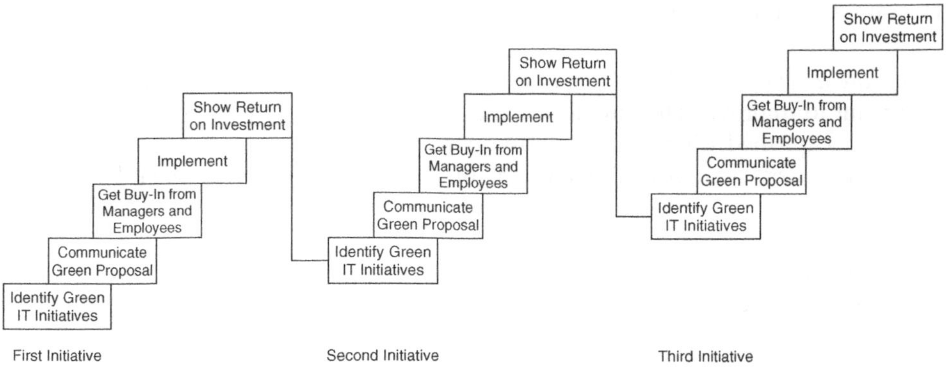

Figure 14.3 Progressive implementation of green initiatives.

Metric programs are based on raw data and measurements collected from multiple sources. Successful metrics programs should initially focus on what data should be collected and the data collection format. There is an overwhelming amount of data available that can be very expensive to collect and may not provide any answers.

Data collection can be expensive if not carefully monitored – the temptation is high to collect all possible data and then decide how to use it later. This type of process generally leads to failure because the quantity of data now overshadows its quality. Thus, extraneous data should be discarded.

Data collection should be an intricate part of the work structure, automated whenever possible. Automation increases the accuracy and decreases interruptions. Automated input is also preferable; research indicates that electronic forms tend to be completed faster and more accurately than paper forms. Existing systems and data should be used whenever possible. Also, metric programs can successfully evaluate processes, but the temptation to use the resulting metrics to evaluate the people performing the processes must be resisted.

It is difficult, if not impossible, to place a dollar amount on the benefits of a metrics program because, as in the case of risk management, you are trying to measure something that did not happen. The benefits derived are also applicable not only to the current project but also to future projects. The sooner benefits are seen by management and developers, the faster metrics programs progress. Metric programs should be designed to show visible benefits as soon as possible, as this is the key to continued support (Rosenberg, 1996).

14.3.3 The Goal–Question–Metric (GQM) Paradigm

Managers often have difficulty in determining where and how to start a metrics program. The goal–question–metric (GQM) paradigm is a simple mechanism that provides a framework for developing a metrics program by formalizing the characterization, planning, construction, analysis, learning and feedback tasks. The paradigm does not provide specific goals but rather a framework for stating goals and refining them into questions to provide a specification for the data needed to help answer goals; it provides a relatively simple technique to initiate a metrics program.

The GQM paradigm consists of three steps:

1. *Generate a set of goals based upon the needs of the organization*. Determine what it is you want to improve. This provides a framework for determining whether or not you have accomplished what you set out to do.
2. *Derive a set of questions*. The purpose of these questions is to quantify the goals as completely as possible. This requires the interpretation of fuzzy terms within the context of the development environment.
3. *Develop a set of metrics which provide the information needed to answer the questions*. In this step, the actual data needed to answer the questions are identified and associated with each of the questions. As data items are identified, it must be understood how valid the data item will be with respect to accuracy and how well it captures the specific question (Rosenberg, 1996).

14.4 Information Assurance

IA is defined in the US government's *National Information Assurance Glossary* as,

> Measures that protect and defend information and information systems by ensuring their availability, integrity, authentication, confidentiality, and non-repudiation. These measures include providing for restoration of information systems by incorporating protection, detection, and reaction capabilities. (Wikipedia, n.d.).

IA is the practice of managing risks related to the use, processing, storage and transmission of information or data and the systems and processes used for those purposes. Whilst focussed dominantly on non-information in digital form, the full range of IA encompasses not only digital but also analogue or physical forms.

The IA process typically begins with the enumeration and classification of the information assets to be protected. Next the IA practitioner will develop a risk assessment that will lead to a risk management plan that involves mitigating, eliminating, accepting or transferring the risks and considers prevention, detection and response. IA must be considered and built in to ensure that the new green IT components do not have a negative impact on the security of the network. Recycling IT components is a great way to improve the IT footprint, but we need to move with caution when managing a classified environment. Most classified equipment is deemed unacceptable for recycling. Make sure the group doing the recycling does not get carried away and recycle components that should not be recycled for security reasons. Use your strong IA plan to help determine what is appropriate for recycling.

14.4.1 Risk Management

Risk management helps avoid disasters, rework and overkill; it also stimulates win–win situations. The objectives are to identify, address and eliminate risk items before they become threats to the success of implementing green initiatives. Risks have two

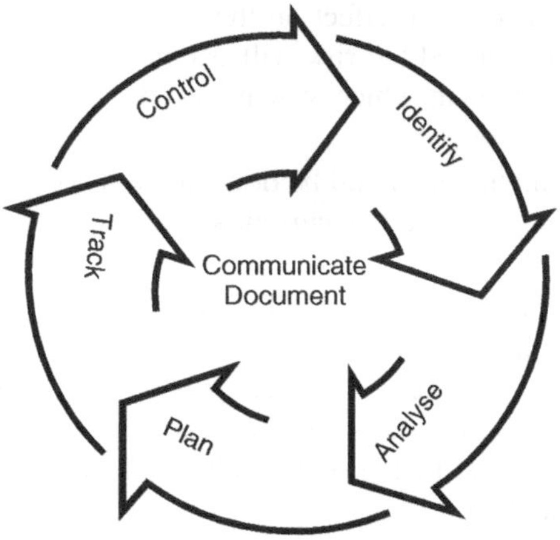

Figure 14.4 Continuous risk management: principle functions.

characteristics: (i) *uncertainty*: An event may or may not happen and (ii) *loss*: An event may have unwanted consequences or losses.

Thus, risk involves the likelihood that an undesirable event will occur, and the severity of the consequences of should that event occur. Risk management aims to do the following:

- Identify potential problems and deal with them when it is easier and cheaper to do so before they are problems and before a crisis exists.
- Focus on the project's objective and consciously look for things that may affect quality throughout the production process.
- Allow the early identification of potential problems (the proactive approach) and provide input into management decisions regarding resource allocation.
- Involve personnel at all levels of the project as needed.
- Increase the chances of project success.

The paradigm shown in Figure 14.4 illustrates the set of continuous risk management functions throughout the life cycle of a project. Risks are usually tracked in parallel whilst new risks are identified and analysed, and the mitigation plan for one risk may yield another risk. Implementing green IT initiatives is a continual process, as new opportunities arise to increase the green environment. New initiatives may present new risks which must be managed in order to ensure project success.

Risk assessment involves the following six steps:

1. **Identify:** Consider risks before they become problems and incorporate this information into the project management process.
2. **Analyse:** Examine the risks in detail to determine the extent of the risks, how they relate to each other and which ones are the most important. Analysing risks comprises three basic activities: evaluating the attributes of the risks (impact, probability and timeframe), classifying the risks and prioritizing or ranking the risks.

   (a) **Impact:** The loss or negative effect on the project should the risk occur
   (b) **Probability:** The likelihood the risk will occur
   (c) **Timeframe:** The period in which you must take action in order to mitigate the risk.
3. **Plan:** Decide what, if anything, should be done about a risk or set of related risks, and develop mitigation strategies based on current knowledge of project risks. The purpose of this plan is to
   (a) Make sure the risk's consequences and sources are known;
   (b) Develop effective plans;
   (c) Plan efficiently (only as much as needed or will be of benefit);
   (d) Produce, over time, the correct set of actions that minimize risk impacts of (cost and schedule) while maximizing opportunity and value; and
   (e) Plan important risks first.
4. **Track:** Track the process by which risk status data are acquired, compiled and reported. The purpose of tracking is to collect accurate, timely and relevant risk information and to present it in a clear and easily understood manner to the appropriate people or group. Tracking is done by those responsible for monitoring 'watched' or 'mitigated' risks. Tracking status information becomes critical to performing the next function in the continuous risk management paradigm, control.
5. **Control:** Make informed, timely and effective decisions regarding risks and their mitigation plans. This process takes in tracking status information and decides exactly what to do based on the reported data. Controlling risks involves analysing the status reports, deciding how to proceed and then implementing those decisions.
6. **Communicate and document:** Ensure *all* personnel understand the risks of mitigating to green. Communication and documentation are essential to the success of all other functions within the paradigm and are critical for managing risks.

Continuous risk management is critical for success because it involves identifying areas of concern before they become problems that can potentially have a negative impact on implementation and success (Rosenberg, 1999).

14.5 Communication and Social Media

Communication to stakeholders and stakeholder participation are keys to the success of green initiatives. Among other channels, social media can be used for communicating among stakeholders green initiatives, their progress and their benefits as well as to get their feedback and to engage and involve them. Judiciously using these technologies allows you to present your authoritative stance on the advantages of implementing green IT initiatives.

Start by establishing the IT department as the social authority expert in the field of green IT and that the benefits that can be derived with minimal disruption to the workforce. By becoming the social authority, you become the influencer and have the opportunity to pull other employees outside the IT department into the push towards green IT.

One of the foundational concepts of social media, however, is that you cannot completely control your message through social media but you begin to participate in the conversation with the objective of becoming a relevant influence in it. Be careful in your conversations, as the participation must be cleverly executed; people are resistant to direct or overt 'marketing'. Credibility is important: Always back up your statements with clear facts, but do not overwhelm conversation participants. Build trust slowly but continually. The most effective marketing approaches revolve around honestly convincing people of genuine intention, knowledge and expertise in green IT through providing valuable and accurate information on an on-going basis with a marketing angle overtly associated. If this approach is successfully executed, the message itself will begin to develop naturally, the IT organization will be viewed as the authority and users will naturally begin to gravitate to them for additional information.

No project can be successful without comprehensive communication to all levels within the company. Everyone must support the move to green IT, but in order to support it, they must know about it and understand the value.

14.6 Case Study

As an IT manager of an organization, you are invited to develop a green IT programme to reduce overall IT energy consumption by 15% during the next year.

The first step is to come up with clear, realistic expectations; many strategic plans are written fairly generically and can be implemented in different ways. Focus your strategy in the right direction and channel the expectation into the area where you have the highest probability of success. Start strategic thinking and planning.

The next step is to find if any budget was allocated to this new initiative. Assuming no additional funding, you need to look at where your budget for the current year has been allocated. If upgrades of desktops and servers are in the current budget, moving to energy-efficient desktops and servers may be a way to meet the objective. Energy-efficient servers would reduce the amount of energy consumed for cooling.

Then identify potential risks, and outline the measures to minimize the impact of risks.

Metrics must be utilized to clearly demonstrate you have met the company's objectives for green IT. Start with the current utility costs, and estimate these for the data centre; use Energy Star ratings to find out how much energy is used by the current desktops. When purchasing the new IT hardware, specify Energy Star ratings and/or EPEAT-grade products and estimate the savings.

Finally, communicate the plan to your management and seek its approval and support. Widely publicize your plan and the expected benefits to the employee-users and engage them in your greening efforts. Follow this up by discussing what green IT initiatives you propose to implement over the next 3–5 years that will make a major difference, and as part of your proposal include resource requirements and return on investment estimates.

In your near-term green IT proposal, include the following:

- An explanation of the project, written without technical jargon.
- A realistic cost estimate; include cost of personnel, hardware, software and others. Have a high-level estimate as well as a very detailed estimate (in the backup data) that demonstrates that your cost estimate is comprehensive.
- A timeline for completion; be realistic, as you will be held to these deadlines.
- Return on investment: how will the company benefit by the green IT project?

- Metrics that will be used to show the project is on course, at a very high level.
- Identify potential risks, if any, and demonstrate how the risks will be mitigated.
- Specify your proposed role and that of others involved in this initiative.

In writing a green IT proposal, include options, starting with quick wins that are not expensive through the optimal solutions.

14.7 Summary

Green IT management starts at the conception phase of any programme with the strategic design – how to fit this program into the strategic vision of the company. Leadership skills are important when these strategic plans are implemented, and in green management they are critical. An aspect of IT design that must be utilized after strategic planning is Enterprise Architecture. One important management component when implementing green IT initiatives is the demonstration of value added; approaches and examples are given to assess managers' problems and funding new green IT issues. Any changes to the IT architecture, networks and systems always require a good manager to ensure that all Information Assurance requirements are met; IA cannot effectively be added at the end, but must be built in to be effective. Comprehensive communication with all stakeholders is required for the success of green IT initiatives, and social media can be effectively used for communication and for engaging users towards green initiatives.

Review Questions

1. What is the difference between strategic thinking and strategic planning?
2. How do you, as the IT manager, get your senior manager to recognize the value of green IT initiatives?
3. How would you estimate return on investment on a green IT initiative?
4. Identify potential risks in the implementation of a green IT technical project or programme.

Discussion Questions

1. Which is more important, strategic thinking, strategic planning or enterprise architecture? Do you need all three, or will any two of the three suffice?
2. What are some of the highest risks when implementing green IT project and how would you mitigate them?
3. Why bother to include users and customers in the discussions on green IT projects?

References

Rosenberg, L.R. (1996) Developing a successful metrics program. In Software Technology Conference, Salt Lake City, Utah, April 1996.
Rosenberg, L.R. (1999) Continuous risk management: A NASA program initiative. In Software Technology Conference, Salt Lake City, Utah, May 1999.
Wikipedia (n.d.) Enterprise Architecture, http://en.wikipedia.org/wiki/Enterprise_architecture (accessed April 2012).

15

Regulating Green IT: Laws, Standards and Protocols

Tom Butler
University College Cork, Cork, Ireland

Key Points

- Delineates the global regulations governing green IT.
- Discusses the scope of emerging regulations and public policy on the direct and enabling effects of green IT.
- Explores the complex web of regulatory, business and other forces acting on all organizations to adopt green IT strategies.
- Considers the future of green IT in the context of the growth in regulatory and other pressures.
- Challenges the conventional wisdom on self-regulation on environmental issues.

15.1 Introduction

Organizations in the electrical, electronics and information and communication technology (ICT) sectors are confronted with a plethora of diverse regulations and other influences whose purpose is to make their products environmentally friendly. Likewise, business organizations are increasingly subject to regulatory, social and other pressures to deploy green IT and implement green IT–based applications.

The term *green IT* refers to information technologies that have minimum *direct effects* on the environment in that they (i) consume low amounts of electrical energy in operation and standby modes, (ii) contribute minimally to greenhouse gas (GHG) emissions when in use (e.g. using desktop and/or server virtualization), (iii) are designed for the environment and are therefore in compliance with regulations on hazardous and restricted substances

Harnessing Green IT: Principles and Practices, First Edition. Edited by San Murugesan and G.R. Gangadharan.

and (iv) can be easily disposed of, reused or recycled (cf. GeSI, 2008; Murugesan, 2008; OECD, 2009a, 2009b).

Green IT–based software applications also have *enabling effects* in that they help reduce GHG emissions associated with social and organizational processes, products and services (cf. GeSI, 2008; Watson, Boudreau, and Chen, 2010). Depending on the context in which they are used, green IT–based applications typically perform one or more of the following functions:

1. Monitor and report on GHG emissions.
2. Control and report on waste, toxic and hazardous materials use.
3. Manage energy-consuming facilities such as offices, manufacturing facilities and other buildings, including data centres.
4. Enable design for environment (DfE).
5. Help redesign business processes to make them energy efficient.
6. Enable energy-efficient logistics and transport throughout the supply chain.
7. Enable dematerialization of travel and other physical carbon-intensive artefacts.
8. Integrate with existing IT-based platforms to make them and/or the business processes they support energy efficient (cf. Boudreau, Watson, and Chen, 2008; Butler and McGovern, 2009; GeSI, 2008).

These points are echoed in several key practitioner studies which refer to the direct and enabling effects of green IT (cf. GeSI, 2008). As climate change is considered to be the greatest threat to the environment in the twenty-first century (OECD, 2009a, 2009b), the major focus of regulators and those who influence the law makers (e.g. Greenpeace, the World Wildlife Fund (WWF), etc.) is on GHG emissions reductions.

This chapter will illustrate that the advances made in making IT green were driven by increased global regulation in the area of toxic substances, e-waste, energy efficiency and GHG emissions reduction. However, there are several other influences of a nonregulatory nature, such as standards (e.g. Electronic Product Environmental Assessment Tool (EPEAT), Energy Star, Flower Label, ISO 14001, etc.) and protocols (Greenhouse Gas Protocol). Whilst effectively optional, various standards have become, in effect, obligatory for organizations due to customer or public demands, the emergence of environmentally sustainable public and private sector procurement policies and increased market competition based on leveraging environmental credentials. The influence exerted by social movements and nongovernment organizations is also shaping organizational strategies on environmental sustainability, whilst also influencing government regulatory measures (Reid and Toffel, 2009). Collectively such influences have helped promote technological innovation to ensure that the direct effects of green IT are realized. The realization of the enabling effects of green IT applications, which are required to reach 2020 targets, will require a similar concentration of forces.

This chapter presents an overview of the combination of regulatory, nonregulatory, and other influences being brought to bear on business and IT organizations so that they might leverage the direct and enabling effects of green IT. The following section charts the global regulatory environment as it relates to the manufacture and use of green IT. The third section delineates nonregulatory initiatives by governments, standards bodies and social movements. The final section discusses the findings and offers several conclusions.

15.2 The Regulatory Environment and IT Manufacturers

As seen from Figure 15.1, electrical, electronics and IT manufacturers face a significant challenge in maintaining compliance with global regulations on environmental issues. However, manufacturers are not passive consumers of environmental legislation; they actively lobby regulators, both individually and collectively, to shape current and future environmental laws that govern their processes and products. In a global context, the European Union (EU) has arguably led the way in regulating these and other industry sectors with onerous environmental laws based on the Restriction of Hazardous Substances (RoHS) Directive, the Waste Electrical and Electronic Equipment (WEEE) Directive, the Registration, Evaluation and Authorisation of Chemicals (REACh) Regulation, the Eco-Design for Energy Using Products (EuP) Directive and its amended Battery Directive (2006/66/EC), which regulates the manufacture and disposal of batteries in the European Union.

These laws have enormous implications for all electrical, electronics and IT manufacturers (Butler, 2010; Butler and McGovern, 2009). For instance, RoHS, REACh and the Battery Directive impact the design and manufacture of IT, whilst EuP focusses on the power consumed during use; WEEE addresses the take-back, recycling and disposal of each artefact. These laws have been emulated from China to California, and from Canada to Australia. It must be noted that industry associations (Institute of Electrical and Electronics Engineers (IEEE), etc.) and dominant corporations (e.g. Dell, IBM, HP and Siemens) were typically consulted when such laws were being drafted; alternatively, individual corporations and their trade associations lobbied to have the draft laws on RoHS, WEEE, REACh and EuP changed and various exemptions obtained. The figure

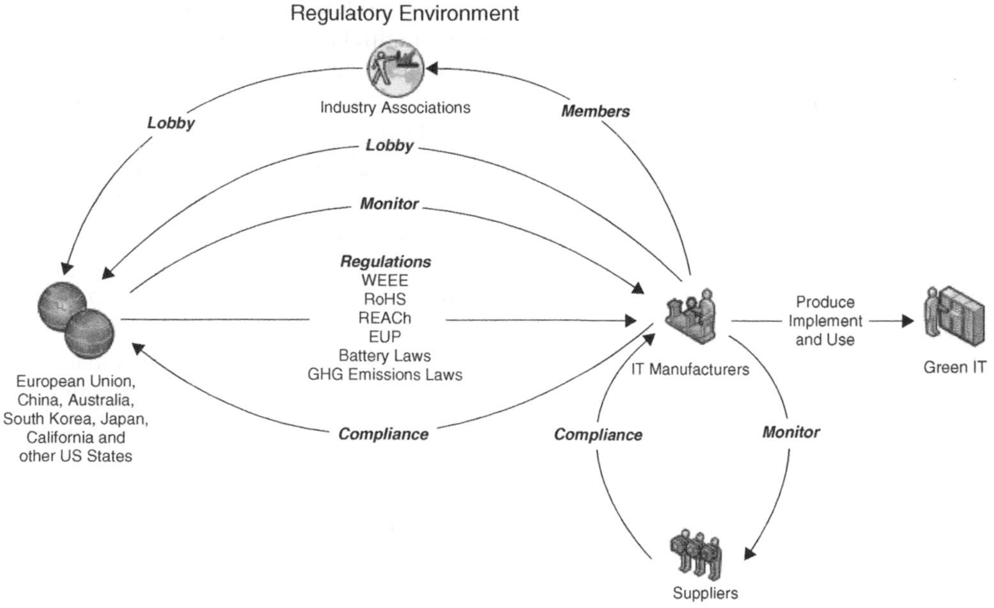

Figure 15.1 The global regulatory environment for the electrical, electronic and IT sectors.

also illustrates that suppliers, which often do not trade directly into regulated markets, also need to be in compliance, with the responsibility to monitor them placed on original equipment manufacturers (OEMs) and those at the end of the supply chain who actually place products on the market.

15.2.1 RoHS

The RoHS Directive was instituted by the European Union in February 2003 and came into force on 1 July 2006. Subsequently, each EU member state transposed the directive into, what were often idiosyncratic, national laws. The RoHS Directive restricts the use of hazardous materials in products that cause environmental pollution during the disposal and recycling of electrical, electronic and IT equipment. The substances currently targeted by RoHS are mercury, lead, cadmium, hexavalent chromium, polybrominated biphenyls (PBBs) and named polybrominated diphenyl ethers (PBDEs). PBBs and PBDEs are types of brominated flame retardants (BFRs) used in plastics found in IT equipment and cables. The list of hazardous substances is to be increased in the near future: These include nickel plating, polyvinyl chloride (PVC), gallium arsenide, antimony trioxide, liquid crystals, cobalt and 42 BFRs. Eliminating these substances will pose a significant challenge for manufacturers.

Several general exemptions were made in the original RoHS Directive to cover medical devices and monitoring and control instruments; EU member states publish a list of specific exemptions currently in force.[1] Table 15.1 illustrates the IT equipment currently covered under RoHS. Significantly, computer servers and IT networking equipment were exempted until 2010, due to potential problems with the use of lead-free solder. Indeed, such were the focus and consequences of restrictions on the use of lead in solder (the glue that holds all electronic circuits together) that it was colloquially known as the lead directive. The fun for manufacturers began, however, with initial interpretations of the directive and its institution into laws in member states. The following excerpt from the directive provides a useful point of departure for this discussion: 'A maximum concentration value of 0.1% by weight in homogeneous materials for lead, mercury, hexavalent chromium, polybrominated biphenyls (PBB) and polybrominated diphenyl ethers (PBDE) and of 0.01% weight in homogeneous materials for cadmium shall be tolerated. Homogeneous material means a unit that cannot be mechanically disjointed in single materials'.

A practical example will illustrate the challenge facing IT manufacturers. A typical laptop has over 200 discrete parts sourced, ultimately, from hundreds of suppliers in a global supply chain. When it is disposed of and/or recycled, the different parts or subcomponents may be mechanically separated out. Hence, EU RoHS stipulates that none of the individual parts may exceed the limits set for restricted substances. Cadmium is used as a stabilizer or colouring agent in plastics; however, exposure to the chemical can harm human kidney function. Companies could be forgiven for thinking that if cadmium levels in a laptop were lower than the 0.01% threshold, then the device is compliant. However, if the cadmium levels in any of the individual cables or in individual elements of the plastic case was 0.02%, for example, then the entire device would be noncompliant and would need to be withdrawn from the market. An example of the consequences

[1] See http://www.bis.gov.uk/nmo/enforcement/rohs-home/rohs-exemptions (accessed April 2012).

Table 15.1 IT equipment covered under RoHS

Equipment categories
Mainframes
Minicomputers
Servers (exempt from lead-free solder until 1 January 2010)
Routers, switches, and so on
Printers
Personal computers (including the CPU and all peripheral devices)
Laptop computers
Notebook computers
Notepad computers
Copying equipment
Electrical and electronic typewriters
Pocket and desk calculators
User terminals and systems
Facsimile machines
Telex
Telephones – all types
Video conferencing and so on
All other products and equipment for the collection, storage, processing, presentation or communication of information by electronic means

comes from Sony's experience with its PlayStation. Although unrelated to the RoHS legislation, approximately 1.3 million PlayStation 1 game consoles were impounded in the Netherlands in the run-up to Christmas 2001 because they contained noncompliant levels of cadmium in the cable sheathing. The withdrawal of the games console cost Sony in terms of both reputation and loss of revenue.

The real problem for IT manufacturers is that they are so heavily dependent on upstream suppliers (Tier 1 to n). This makes it extremely difficult for an individual IT manufacturer to properly assess whether particular components sourced from upstream suppliers are compliant with regulations or corporate standards and codes of conduct. Indeed, the vice president of one division of a leading Fortune 100 ICT company admitted to the author that of the 5000 suppliers feeding into his division, he trusted only one in terms of being RoHS compliant.

15.2.2 REACh

The introduction of the REACh Regulation in June 2007 complicated matters significantly for IT manufacturers, as it requires organizations to declare the possible dangers associated with chemical combinations in their products both in use and on disposal. REACh also places disclosure requirements to the extent that customers and organizations like Greenpeace have access to information on regulated substances in use. Failure by EU-based IT manufacturers, or importers or EU-based agents of non-EU suppliers, to register with the European Chemicals Agency (EChA) substances of very high concern (SVHC) contained in IT equipment in volumes of over 1 tonne per annum or in concentrations above 0.1%, will result in exclusion of the equipment from the European Union. SVHCs are carcinogenic, mutagenic, toxic for reproduction or persistent bioaccumulatives. In 2008, REACh listed 15 SVHCs. In January 2010, the list grew to 29, and in 2012 it is likely to reach 135 (something which will particularly impact IT manufacturers). IT equipment is considered as a finished product under REACh: As such, the reporting obligation relates to SVHCs that may be emitted during normal use. Nonetheless, as many components are imported in significant volumes into the European Union, the implications of REACh are significant and extend beyond this regulatory domain, as downstream manufacturers and business customers and consumers are demanding proof of compliance.

15.2.3 WEEE

The WEEE Directive, which was instituted in February 2003, establishes collection, take-back and recycling targets and related obligations for IT equipment and broader categories of electrical and electronic devices. The responsibility for the take-back, disposal, recycling and reuse of WEEE is placed on manufacturers. This seemingly innocuous piece of legislation has caused headaches for IT manufacturers, not only in taking responsibility for their products' end of life, but also in gathering accurate information for reporting purposes. With EU WEEE, the producer is responsible – physically and financially – for their products, whether the end users are individual consumers or corporate clients. Take, for example the transposition into law of WEEE in Sweden. In order to bring order to what could have been a chaotic process, the Swedish government created a compliance and take-back system for IT products. Swedish local governments were made responsible for collecting WEEE and transporting it to a collection centre. However, equipment producers provide the collection centres for take-back. Producers trading into Sweden must finance the take-back of all products placed on the market after August 2005 and for historical products if a replacement is bought. In addition, the cost of equipment take-back is allocated according to the current market share of equipment producers. The problem for global IT manufacturers is that each member state implements different types of WEEE systems. Thus, IT manufacturers placing products in all of the European Union's 27 member states need to comply with WEEE on a state-by-state basis and participate in what are heterogeneous WEEE-based systems. This poses a high level of complexity for manufacturers.

In sum, the implementation of WEEE and RoHS Directives resulted in sophisticated, highly differentiated, legal instruments in EU member states. The REACh regulation adds to this regulatory complexity, despite the fact that it is uniform in its application in EU member states. To further complicate matters, this body of legislation is not easy to comprehend and then apply to a firm's R&D, operations, products and logistics processes. It is clear that the task of maintaining compliance with, for example, RoHS will become even more burdensome as the European Union moves to include new substances on top of the original six covered under EU RoHS.

Environmental laws in other jurisdictions are no less stringent. The US Environmental Protection Agency (EPA) has a significant body of legislation covering hazardous substances across the whole range of manufacturing sectors. Significantly, individual US states such as California and New Jersey are following the European Union's lead in introducing exacting WEEE- and RoHS-like laws. Korea, Australia and Canada, have introduced legislation similar to the RoHS and WEEE directives, whilst in China, a directive known as the China RoHS, or the Methods for the Control of Pollution by Electronic Information Products Directive, came into force in March 2007. Japan has the most stringent and comprehensive set of environmental laws outside of the European Union.

It is clear that the need to address compliance legislation in different geographical locations adds complexity for global IT manufacturing organizations; however, determining the applicable regulation for a given geographical area can be complicated by the problem of understanding which products are covered, or are exempt, by sets of seemingly conflicting regulations. Understanding which products are covered by or exempt from sets of complex and apparently conflicting regulations is clearly an intimidating, information-intensive task (Butler, 2010; Butler and McGovern, 2009). One way or another, the issues created by EU legislation for manufacturing firms are significant in that the requirements in each section of the various transposed laws in 27 member states will have to be enumerated, and understood, if they are to be properly addressed. This, however, only scratches the surface of the regulatory mountain facing IT manufacturers and business organizations using IT.

15.2.4 Legislating for GHG Emissions and Energy Use of IT Equipment

The EC EuP Directive 2005 32/EC focuses on energy efficiency in electrical, electronic and IT products. This law sets challenging targets for energy savings of up to 9% in the majority of electrical, electronic and IT products from 2008 to 2016. When this directive was transposed into law in EU member states, it required IT manufacturers (among others) to make voluntary compliance declarations on the energy used in the design, packaging, delivery and recycling of products across supply chains, in addition to the energy consumed during use. The directive extends voluntary Energy Star–like standards in EU member states such as Blue Angel in Germany and Nordic Swan in Scandinavia. Another example of EuP-like legislation comes from Canada, whose Action on Standby Power Development is a standard covering standby limits for consumer electronics products. This regulation aims to reduce the power consumption of electronic devices including IT, by setting minimum performance standards for new products, and making existing standards even more stringent. Essentially, it implements the 1-W Initiative, which aims to bring standby power to 1 W per device. The new standby power limits are equivalent to those in the State of California's energy legislation.

15.3 Nonregulatory Government Initiatives

Governments across the world have reshaped the IT manufacturing industry through environmental laws. The United States, the European Union (particularly Germany) and Japan have also initiated and supported several industry standards (discussed in this chapter) and adopted wider nonregulatory initiatives. Take, for example, research by the OECD (2009a) that reports on 50 government programmes and 42 industry initiatives aimed at achieving energy savings and GHG emissions reductions through the direct and enabling effects of green IT. Table 15.2 provides an abridged elaboration of the most notable of the government-sponsored initiatives.

Table 15.2 Government-sponsored green IT initiatives

Regulation or policy-making body	Law, regulation or policy standard
European Union	The Eco-Label (Flower Label) standard mandates that an environmental impact analysis be conducted on products or services throughout their life cycle. The analysis should include life cycle stages such as the extraction of raw materials, production, distribution and disposal or recycling.
Germany	German Sustainability in the Information and Communication Technologies initiative. The Blaue Engel (Blue Angel) eco-label covers more than 3600 products, including papers, oil burners, wall paints and IT equipment.
United Kingdom	Greening of Government ICT Strategy: The British government developed a Green ICT Scorecard with evaluated constituent departments, agencies and so on, using 32 key indicators, including 18 ICT-related metrics. Areas covered include green policy, governance of policies, energy efficiency, waste management, supplier management, procurement, buildings and energy management and behaviours.
Denmark	Action Plan for Green IT. This has two major strands the first of which aims to (i) foster reductions in the environmental impact of IT use in private sector organizations by promoting green IT to businesses, (ii) adopt the same approach to promote energy-efficient IT to children and teenagers, (iii) provide green IT guidelines for the public sector and (4) create a knowledge base for energy consumption and GHG emissions calculations. The focus of the second strand is to (i) foster R&D on green IT, pervasive computing and e-government; (ii) the transfer of green IT knowledge and technologies and (iii) green IT knowledge sharing using international conferences on green IT hosted in Denmark.
Finland	The government's central procurement is invested in a limited company called Hansel Ltd. This organization works with the Finnish Environment Institute to develop and apply rigorous environmental criteria for public-tendering procedures including IT.
Japan	Green IT Promotion Council: The council consists of members from academia, industry (nationally and internationally) and government or the public sector. The green IT initiative aims to (i) generate R&D on energy-efficient IT, (ii) promote awareness of the environmental impacts of IT and (iii) institute education initiatives aimed at management of the environment and green IT.

Whilst one thinks of government in terms of regulation, it must also be remembered that they institute nonregulatory initiatives; indeed Section 15.4 describes their input into generating industry standards. Likewise, it must be remembered that governments are also large users of IT products and services. In the United Kingdom, for example, government accounts for approximately 35% of the IT market, with expenditures of up to £17 billion annually. The same can be said of other leading OECD countries where e-government is now the norm, rather than the exception. Thus, government organizations are heavy users of IT: Accordingly, they are conscious of the fact that they could contribute to IT-related environmental problems, if they did not take action on the use of toxic chemicals, hazardous substances, e-waste and IT-related GHG emissions. Hence many adopt rigorous environment-focussed procurement policies and other measures. Governments also recognize that IT-based applications are key enablers of GHG reductions and offsets (OECD, 2009a, 2009b). Hence, they institute programmes such as those described in Table 15.2.

As government departments and organizations are not exempt from mandatory reporting of GHG emissions in countries such as the United Kingdom, public policy of a nonregulatory nature will increasingly impact IT manufacturers and service providers alike. Take, for example, that the UK public sector is governed by the Carbon Reduction Commitment (CRC) Energy Efficiency law from 2010. In line with this new law, and in keeping with other environmental obligations described here, the UK public sector has also adopted stringent policies on green IT procurement and outsourcing – thereby placing pressures on suppliers not covered by the CRC law. The US public sector is also preparing itself for mandatory GHG emissions reporting in the near future. It is also significant that whilst the US government did not regulate on the EPEAT standard, in 2007 it passed an executive order to all US federal bodies to purchase only EPEAT-certified IT (Ryan, 2008).

15.4 Industry Associations and Standards Bodies

There are numerous industry associations associated with the IT and related industry sectors. These include umbrella groups such as the sector-specific Electronic Industries Alliance (EIA), the Consumer Electronics Association (CEA), the Storage Networking Industry Association (SNIA), the Green IT Promotion Council (Japan) and the Information Technology Industry Council (ITI). These organizations promote green IT among industry members, whilst also lobbying to limit the scope and impact of regulations. In addition, such associations are typically represented on, or influence the deliberations of, standards bodies. Some of these bodies are also associated with sector-based environmental movements such as the Climate Savers Computing Initiative and the Global e-Sustainability Initiative (GeSI).

The GeSI is encouraging sustainable development in the IT and telecommunications sectors. Its *SMART 2020 Report* (GeSI, 2008) is, perhaps, one of the most influential documents on green IT. GeSI advocates programmes to reuse and recycle IT equipment, in addition to the promotion of green IT applications that enable smart buildings and smart transportation systems. The Climate Savers Computing Initiative promotes the use of green IT and its direct effects in lowering GHG emissions. Climate Savers Computing members commit to deploying energy-efficient personal computers and servers (i.e. Energy Star/EPEAT compliant) and to apply available power management features to reduce emissions. Significantly, the WWF plays a key role in both of these industry movements.

One function of industry standards is to disseminate best practices across organizations in a particular sector. Others such as ISO 14000 series span several sectors. The International Standards Organization (ISO) and IEEE, and nongovernment organisations (NGOs) like the Green Electronics Council, are among the most influential of such bodies.

Table 15.3 illustrates several key standards governing both process and product where green IT is concerned.

The ISO 14000 standards series addresses several aspects of environmental management: Specifically, ISO 14001 and ISO 14004 provide for the requirements and guidelines for environmental management systems (EMSs). The ISO14060 series covers both process- and product-related GHG emissions. However, the most widespread industry standard comes from the EPA Energy Star initiative, which concentrates on the energy consumption of products in use. Almost all major manufacturers now produce Energy Star–compliant products. However, in 2006, the Green Electronics Council, which includes the EPA, the US Department of Energy and other industry standards bodies, went beyond this standard by introducing EPEAT. This extensive standard has pushed the envelope on green IT standards (see Table 15.3).

15.5 Green Building Standards

As identified by the GeSI's *Smart 2020* report, the enabling effects of green IT could make a significant contribution in environment-oriented, green IT–enabled building design and management. There are two rival standards in use globally: the US Leadership in Energy and Environmental Design (LEED) Standard, which is a green building rating system developed by the US Green Building Council; and the United Kingdom's BREEAM (BRE Environmental Assessment Method), which is argued to be the leading and most widely used standard globally, due to the existence of UK and international versions. Both LEED and BREEAM standards implement best practice in sustainable design. Major US corporations are implementing LEED in the construction of offices and manufacturing facilities and new data centres. Indeed, the Lawrence Berkeley National Labs (LBNL) drew on LEED to arrive at its 'Environmental Performance Criteria (EPC) Guide for Data Centers'.[2] The BREEAM standard was extended to cover data centres in collaboration with the largest data centre provider globally, Digital Realty Trust.

15.6 Green Data Centres

One industry association whose influence is significant in establishing standards for data centre operation is The Green Grid. This industry association promotes user-centric models and metrics, energy efficiency standards, processes and efficient technologies for use in data centres. The Green Grid's influence on IT professionals is evident in the widespread use of the Power Usage Effectiveness (PUE) and Data Centre Efficiency (DCE) metrics for benchmarking energy efficiency. The EU also publishes and promotes the EU Code of Conduct on Data Centres, viz., the 'Code of Conduct is a voluntary commitment of individual companies, which own or operate data centers (including colo), with the aim of reducing energy consumption through the adoption of best practices in a defined timescale'.[3]

Best practices for data centre design and operation are also researched and published by the LBNL in the US. Green Grid Guidelines and the EU Code of Conduct are currently

[2] See http://hightech.lbl.gov/dc-epc.html (accessed April 2012).

[3] See http://www.ecoinfo.cnrs.fr/IMG/pdf/DC_CoC_Oct2011-CNRS.pdf (accessed April 2012).

Table 15.3 Green IT: process and product standards

Regulatory or standards bodies	Policy or standard
International Standards Organisation (ISO)	ISO 14000 series: Family of standards on environmental management systems (EMSs) ISO 14001: Specification ISO 14004: General guidelines on principles, systems and supporting techniques ISO 14015: Environmental assessment of sites and organizations (EASO) ISO 14020: Environmental labels and declarations ISO 14031: Environmental performance evaluation ISO 14040: Life cycle assessment. Principles and framework ISO 14041: Life cycle assessment. Goal and scope definition and inventory analysis ISO 14042: Life cycle management. Life cycle impact assessment ISO 14043: Life cycle assessment. Life cycle interpretation ISO 14048: Environmental management. Life cycle assessment. Data documentation format ISO 14050: Vocabulary ISO 14064: GHG accounting and verification (indeed, the ISO1406x series are particularly relevant to GHG emissions)
US Department of Energy, Green Electronics Council: Members include the US Environmental Protection Agency (EPA) and several industry standards bodies	Electronic Product Environmental Assessment Tool (EPEAT). EPEAT is based on the Institute of Electrical and Electronics Engineers (IEEE) 1680 Standard, Section 15.4 of which governs environmental performance criteria for desktop PCs, notebooks and PC monitors. The new standard is concerned with: The reduction or elimination of environmentally sensitive materials; Materials selection; Design for end of life; Product longevity and life cycle extension; Energy conservation (Section 15.4.5 covers adherence to the Energy Star standard); End-of-life management (take-back and recycling); Corporate performance (in terms of corporate social responsibility (CSR)) and Packaging (toxics and labelling).
US Environmental Protection Agency	Energy Star. It covers computer equipment, heating and cooling systems, office equipment and home electronics. Energy Star 4.0 focusses on workstations, desktop PCs and notebooks. It encompasses standby, other soft-off modes, the on or idle mode it requires and 80-plus power supply units. Energy Star 5.0 builds on this to include computer displays, digital picture frames and large video displays. Energy Star has been widely adopted.

(continued overleaf)

Table 15.3 (*continued*)

Regulatory or standards bodies	Policy or standard
US Green Building Council	Leadership in Energy and Environmental Design (LEED) Standard. Increase energy efficiency and lower GHG emissions of buildings, including data centres (with LBNL).
BRE Environmental Assessment Method (UK and Global)	BREEAM Standards. Increase energy efficiency and lower GHG emissions of buildings, including data centres (with Digital Realty Trust).

being applied by practitioners: PUE benchmarking aside, EU companies and the public sector favour the latter and US organizations the former. In 2005 the Telecommunications Industry Association (TIA) instituted the TIA-942 Telecommunications Infrastructure Standards for Data Centres, which was the first to specifically address technical aspects of data centre IT infrastructure and layout. Table 15.4 illustrates current initiatives in this area.

15.7 Social Movements and Greenpeace

Environmental concerns voiced by citizens and consumers gave rise to various social movements (den Hond and de Bakker, 2007), the most visible of which is, perhaps, the NGO Greenpeace. NGOs have been driving organizations towards environmental sustainability. Social movements such as Friends of Earth, Greenpeace and the WWF regularly target companies that are not environmentally responsible (den Hond and de Bakker, 2007; Reid and Toffel, 2009). Social movements such as the WWF and Greenpeace also have direct and indirect effects on individual organizations. The WWF is, as indicated, participating in the Global e-Sustainability Initiative and the Climate Savers Computing Initiative. In contrast to other NGOs, Greenpeace directly monitors the processes and products of leading IT corporations. It also acts in more overt ways by lobbying to change government laws and policies; hence, its activities deserve special mention as it has in many ways a greater influence over major players in the IT industry than government regulators.

In the November 2011 *Guide to Greener Electronics*,[4] Greenpeace provides a comparative analysis of 15 (down from 18 in previous years) of the IT industry's leading corporations including, for example, Apple, Hewlett Packard, Dell, Acer, Lenovo, Sony Ericsson, Motorola and Nokia. Greenpeace focusses on these ICT providers simply because their product ranges include consumer-based goods, from mobile phones to laptops. Three categories of ranking criteria are employed by Greenpeace to evaluate IT and consumer electronics manufacturers: toxic chemicals, e-waste and energy. An elaborate scorecard was developed from this to score each organization's performance on a scale of 0–10. In its November 2011 report, no organization achieves the holy grail of being the first to 'go

[4] See http://www.greenpeace.org/international/en/campaigns/climate-change/cool-it/Guide-to-Greener-Electronics (accessed April 2012).

Table 15.4 Green data centres initiatives

Regulation or policy-making body	Law, regulation or policy standard
European Union	EU Code of Conduct on Data Centres: code of best practice for the design and operation of data centres to reduce energy consumption and GHG emissions.
US Department of Energy	Industrial Technologies Programme, which focusses specifically on the energy consumption of data centres. Through its Save Energy Now/Data Centre Energy Efficiency Programme it (i) will offer free energy assessments performed by a department energy expert; (ii) is developing partnerships with data centres, national supply chain and trade associations, state and local agencies and others, aimed at knowledge sharing; (iii) is providing IT-based applications to analyse energy use in data centres and (iv) will publish case studies of best practice and other informational assets on energy efficiency. Other activities by the DoE focussed on data centres include (i) establishing data centre energy metrics; (ii) developing green IT applications and guidelines whose objectives are to continue to leverage on-going data centre energy efficiencies; (iii) providing support for third-party certification of data centre energy efficiency and (iv) promoting energy efficiency achievements by data centre by publishing the saving made.
Lawrence Berkeley National Laboratory	Research on all aspects of data centre design and operations. Leadership in energy and environmental design (LEED) criteria for data centres.
The Green Grid (US) (Department of Energy)	Establishes and diffuses user-centric models, metrics for data centres, whilst also promoting the adoption of energy efficiency standards, processes and efficient technologies for use therein. The Green Grid's influence on data centre practice is manifested in the widespread use of the power usage effectiveness (PUE) and data centre efficiency (DCE) metrics for benchmarking energy efficiency against past performance and against other data centres.
Telecommunications Industry Association (TIA)	TIA-942 Telecommunications Infrastructure Standards for Data Centres

green'. Indeed only HP is in the 'green zone' of the dashboard, although Sony Ericsson and Nokia were previously in this zone – most of the organizations score below 5/10.[5]

The first category in the scorecard covers toxic chemicals and seeks to 'stimulate substitution of hazardous chemicals in electronic products and their production processes'

[5] See http://www.greenpeace.org/international/Global/international/publications/climate/2011/Cool%20IT/greener-guide-nov-2011/guide-to-greener-electronics-nov-2011.pdf (accessed April 2012).

(Hojsik, Harrel, and Kruszewska, 2008, p. 330). The five criteria in this category are (i) the application of the precautionary principle; (ii) chemicals management; (iii) establishing a timeline for the elimination of PVCs and BFR; (iv) establishing a timeline for the phase-out of substances including all phthalates, beryllium (including alloys and compounds) and antimony and related compounds and (v) evaluating PVC-free and BFR-free models presently on the market.

In applying the second category, 'Greenpeace expects companies to take financial responsibility for dealing with the e-waste generated by their products when discarded by consumers, to take back discarded products in all countries with sales of their products and to reuse or recycle them responsibility' (Hojsik, Harrel, and Kruszewska, 2008, p. 330). The five criteria in this category cover (i) individual producer responsibility, (ii) voluntary take-back, (iii) provision of take-back or recycling information to individual customers, (iv) disclosures on amounts recycled and (v) use of recycled plastic content in products and packaging.

GHG Protocol

GHG Protocol classifies carbon emissions into three categories: Scope 1, Scope 2 and Scope 3.

- **Scope 1:** GHG emissions are generated by all sources of combustion, processing as well as the unintended leakage of gases from equipment and plant, all of which operate under the direct control of organizations.
- **Scope 2:** GHG emissions relate to electricity consumption and the energy content of steam, heating plant and cooling water.
- **Scope 3:** GHG emissions are embodied in the life cycle of products and corporate supply chains.

Greenpeace employs four criteria to evaluate electronics manufacturers in relation to GHG emissions and a fifth in relation to adopting and adhering to energy efficiency standards. These cover (i) global GHG emissions reduction support, (ii) carbon footprint disclosure, (iii) own GHG emissions reduction commitment, (iv) amounts of renewable energy used and (v) energy efficiency of new models (companies score double on this criterion). As with the other two categories, four of the criteria covering GHG emissions involve disclosure – whether of support for institutional policies or emissions using the GHG Protocol Corporate Standard:

1. The first criterion examines the political commitment of the organization, that is, 'clear support for global mandatory cuts of at least 50% by 2050 (from 1990 levels) and cuts from industrialized countries of at least 30% as a group by 2020' (Hojsik, Harrel, and Kruszewska, 2008, p. 332).
2. The second criterion examines the level of disclosure of GHG emissions. It seeks to have companies calculate and report (i) emissions from their Scope 1 (direct) and Scope 2 (indirect) operations and (ii) two stages of their supply chain (Scope 3). In

relation to this, companies should have their disclosed calculations certified according to ISO 14064, which is an emerging standard on GHG accounting and verification.
3. The third criterion is targeted at reducing GHG emissions from their own operations, and corporate disclosure forms the benchmark for this. The recommended benchmark baseline can be emissions in 2006, 2007 or 2008. Full points are awarded if companies fulfil these obligations and commit to absolute GHG reductions of 20% by 2012.
4. The fourth criterion evaluates the use of renewable energy in comparison to the total electrical energy consumed by the company. The final energy criterion evaluates the adoption of energy efficiency standards in current and future products. Greenpeace issues quarterly updates on all 18 organizations in its *Greener Electronics* reports.

Criterion 3 on GHG emissions should concern all organizations, not just large IT manufacturers, as it is not unreasonable to expect tougher regulation in this area when emissions reduction targets are not being met and the effects of climate change become more evident. Indeed, many organizations are now publishing detailed reports on GHG emissions in their corporate social and environmental reports. The problem for regulators and other societal stakeholders is accounting and verification. Apple Inc.[6] for example, discloses that 'Greenhouse gas emissions are calculated in accordance with guidelines and requirements as specified by ISO 14040 and ISO 14044'. The latter standards perform a life cycle analysis of GHG emissions, including Scope 3 emissions. In a comparison between a life cycle assessment (LCA; ISO 14040) versus GHG Protocol (ISO 14064) standards, Arthur Braunschweig[7] indicates that LCA provides for more comprehensive reports, hence Apple appears to be one of the few IT manufacturers accounting for Scope 3 emissions. Disclosure of GHG emissions is optional for many organizations. And whilst the United Kingdom is leading the way with its CRC law, over 2500 companies report their emissions to the Carbon Disclosure Project (CDP), which represents over 300 institutional investors that are concerned about climate change and the need to reduce corporate GHG emissions.

Another non-sector-specific global initiative of growing significance that IT professionals need to be aware of is the Greenhouse Gas Protocol Initiative, which is a collaboration between the World Resources Institute and the World Business Council for Sustainable Development. This NGO provides the foundation or reference point for GHG standards and programmes globally – from the ISO to The Climate Registry – in addition to structuring the GHG inventory and reporting activities of individual organizations through the GHG Protocol Corporate Standard. The latter is in widespread use in sustainability reports as is the protocol's approach to GHG accounting. Significantly, the GHG Protocol Initiative provides sector-specific toolsets for the IT industry among others.

15.8 Conclusions

Social concern about the environment has increased in its intensity and scope since the 1960s. Environmental regulation on all aspects of public and occupation health and safety resulted in better work environments and relatively cleaner environments. This occurred

[6] See http://images.apple.com/environment/reports/docs/Apple_Facilities_Report_2009.pdf (accessed April 2012).
[7] See http://www.lcaforum.ch/portals/0/df34/DF34_01_Braunschweig.pdf (accessed April 2012).

chiefly in developed Western democracies. In contrast, socialist countries saw little concern for the human environment, where the true scale and cost of toxic and nuclear pollution are now becoming evident. In the first decade of the twenty-first century, the electrical, electronics and IT manufacturing sector began to produce more environmentally friendly and energy-efficient products simply because they were obliged to do so by regulators; however, social movements and investors also had a significant effect (cf. Butler, 2010).

Instituting new laws is only one part of the equation – regulations are often ignored or circumvented. Returning to the financial crisis of 2008, for example, the financial regulations that did exist in the 2000s were often disregarded or circumvented in innovative ways (cf. Campbell, 2007). Thus, there is ample evidence to suggest that corporations cannot be trusted to self-regulate in addressing economic externalities. 'Greenwashing' products and brands has become commonplace as companies increasingly use a product's 'greenness' as a basis for competition.

Watson *et al.* (2010) indicate the need for regulation in the area of energy efficiency and GHG emissions reductions. These points are echoed elsewhere by Butler and Daly (2009). We have seen that because of the nature of global commerce, the introduction of stringent legislation in one trading block, such as the European Union, could compel all those who trade into it to comply (e.g. note the global response to RoHS, WEEE and the Battery Directive). If organizations placing products and services onto the EU market are made to account for Scope 1, 2 and 3 emissions, then unless they wish to be eliminated from this market, they must comply. Scope 3 emissions apply to the supply chain, wherever it is. The problem with regulating supply chains, however, is indicated by Egels-Zanden (2007), who report in a study of Swedish toy manufacturers that the majority of Chinese suppliers were not in compliance with the standards and codes of conduct set down by their Swedish customers. Egels-Zanden (2007, p. 45) argues that monitoring did not work well because 'Chinese suppliers successfully deceive toy retailers monitoring organizations by decoupling the formal monitored part of their organization from the actual operational part of their organization'. Field (2008) illustrates similar problems across several industries including the IT sector and cites the problems faced by manufacturers such as HP.

Energy-related cost reductions aside, organizations would not have made much progress in this regard had not the law compelled them to do so and made them accountable for noncompliance. Accordingly, the IT sector is leading the way in terms of practicing environmental sustainability, not only in the manufacture of green IT, but also in its application and use to leverage the direct and enabling effects of green IT to lower GHG emissions (cf. GeSI, 2008; OECD, 2009a, 2009b). This is a sea change in management thinking about the environment and corporate environmental responsibility, and one which augers well for the future, perhaps, if the temptation of 'greenwashing' is avoided (Butler, O'Flynn, and McGarry, 2010).

Review Questions

1. Distinguish between the direct effects of green IT and the enabling effects of green IT–based applications.
2. What levels of GHG emissions are associated with the use of IT, past, present and future?

3. What is the difference between RoHS, REACh and WEEE?
4. What is the most effective emissions reductions legislation currently in operation and why?
5. What are the consequences of noncompliance?
6. What is greenwashing? Do you think companies engage in it?
7. Do managers of IT units or businesses really care about climate change, and take measures to address the environmental impacts caused by their operations?
8. How effectively are Energy Star ratings and EPEAT rankings informing consumer purchases?
9. What do you think would happen if more IT manufacturers were included in the Greenpeace Greener Electronics study?
10. Will the emphasis on green IT come to anything besides cost savings, if any, for corporations?

Discussion Questions

1. Do you believe what you read in corporate sustainability reports? Why or why not?
2. Do we need to quantify the GHG footprint of Facebook, Google, Second Life and other social-networking sites?
3. What do you think is your contribution to IT's footprint? What measures would you take to reduce your IT carbon footprint?
4. Would you like to see corporations regulated on their use of green IT?

References

Boudreau, M.C., Watson, R.T. and Chen, A. (2008) From green IT to green IS, in *The Organizational Benefits of Green IT* (ed. B. Biros, M.C. Boudreau, T. Butler *et al.*), Cutter Information LLC, Arlington, MA, pp. 79–91.

Butler, T. (2010) Compliance with institutional imperatives on environmental sustainability: Building theory on the role of green IS. *Journal of Strategic Information Systems*, doi: 10.1016/j.jsis.2010.09.006

Butler, T. and Daly, M. (2009) Environmental responsibility and green IT: An institutional perspective. 17th European Conference on Information Systems, Verona, Italy, 2009.

Butler, T. and McGovern, D. (2009) A conceptual model and IS framework for the design and adoption of environmental compliance management systems. *Information Systems Frontiers*, doi: 10.1007/s10796-009-9197-5

Butler, T., O'Flynn, A. and McGarry, J. (2010) On institutional rationality and decision making in adopting green ICT strategies. In DSS 2010, IFIP WG 8.3 Working Conference, Lisbon, Portugal.

Campbell, J.L. (2007) Why would corporations behave in socially responsible ways? An institutional theory of corporate social responsibility. *Academy of Management Review*, **32** (3), 946–967.

Den Hond, F. and de Bakker, F.G.A. (2007) Ideologically motivated activism: How activist groups influence corporate social change activities. *Academy of Management Review*, **32** (3), 901–924.

Egels-Zanden, N. (2007) Suppliers' compliance with MNCs' codes of conduct: Behind the scenes at Chinese toy suppliers. *Journal of Business Ethics*, **75** (1), 45–62.

Field, A. (2008) What is your green strategy? *Treasury and Risk*, October, 40–44.

GeSI (2008) SMART 2020: Enabling the Low Carbon Economy in the Information Age, Global e-Sustainability Initiative, http://www.gesi.org/ReportsPublications/Smart2020/tabid/192/Default.aspx (accessed April 2012).

Hojsik, M., Harrel, C. and Kruszewska, I. (2008) Greenpeace's benchmarking of electronics manufacturer's on their corporate policies on chemicals, energy and producer responsibility for end-of-life products, in *Proceedings of the Electronics Goes Green Conference 2008+* (ed. H. Reichl, N.F. Nissen, J. Muller and O. Deubzer), Fraunhofer IRB Verlag, Stuttgart, pp. 329–334.

Murugesan, S. (2008) Can IT go green? *Cutter IT Journal*, **21** (2), 3–5.

OECD (2009a) Measuring the Relationship between ICT and the Environment, Working Party on the Information Economy, http://www.oecd.org/dataoecd/32/50/43539507.pdf (accessed April 2012).

OECD (2009b) Towards Green ICT Strategies: Assessing Policies and Programmes on ICT and the Environment, http://www.oecd.org/dataoecd/3/7/44001912.pdf (accessed April 2012).

Reid, E.M. and Toffel, M.W. (2009) Responding to public and private politics: Corporate disclosure of climate change policies. *Strategic Management Journal*, **30**, 1157–1178.

Ryan, E.J. (2008) Moving IT from a green plan to sustainable operations, in *The Organizational Benefits of Green IT* (ed. B. Biros, M.C. Boudreau, T. Butler *et al.*), Cutter Information LLC, Arlington, MA, pp. 92–108.

Watson, R.T., Boudreau, M-C. and Chen, A.J. (2010) Information systems and environmentally sustainable development: Energy informatics and new directions for the IS community. *MIS Quarterly*, **34** (1), 23–28.

Further Reading

Cabinet Office (2009) *Greening Government ICT: One Year On – A Progress Report on the Government's Greening Government ICT Strategy*, HM Government, London.

Carbon Disclosure Project (2010) Carbon Disclosure Project 2010 Global 500 Report, https://www.cdproject.net/CDPResults/CDP-2010-G500.pdf (accessed April 2012).

Ceres (2010) 21st Century Corporation: The Ceres Roadmap to Sustainability, http://www.ceres.org/Page.aspx?pid=592 (accessed April 2012).

16

Green Cloud Computing and Environmental Sustainability

Saurabh Kumar Garg and Rajkumar Buyya
Cloud Computing and Distributed Systems (CLOUDS) Laboratory, Department of Computing and Information Systems, University of Melbourne, Melbourne, Australia

Key Points

- Introduces the concept of sustainability of the new emerging cloud-computing paradigm.
- Describes different components and aspects of cloud computing.
- Discusses current research and development on making cloud computing green.
- Illustrates various levels at which energy is consumed in a cloud-computing model.
- Examines the issues and challenges in making the use of cloud computing sustainable.
- Outlines future research directions emphasizing holistic efforts needed to make clouds a viable and sustainable computing alternative.

16.1 Introduction

With the growth of high-speed networks over recent decades, there is an alarming rise in network usage composed of thousands of concurrent e-commerce transactions and millions of Web queries a day. This ever-increasing demand is handled through large-scale data centres, which consolidate hundreds and thousands of servers with other infrastructure such as cooling, storage and network systems. Many Internet companies such as Google, Amazon, eBay, Facebook, Twitter and Yahoo are operating such huge data centres around the world.

The commercialization of data centres led to cloud computing (Buyya, Yeo, and Venugopal, 2008), where computing is delivered as a service, like a utility, on a pay-as-you-go basis. Traditionally, business organizations used to invest huge amounts of capital

Harnessing Green IT: Principles and Practices, First Edition. Edited by San Murugesan and G.R. Gangadharan.

and time in acquiring and maintaining computational resources. The emergence of cloud computing is rapidly transforming this *ownership-based approach* to a *subscription-based approach* by providing access to scalable infrastructure and services on demand. Users can store, access, share and process any amount of information in the cloud. So, small or medium-sized enterprises or organizations do not have to worry about purchasing, configuring, administering and maintaining their own computing infrastructure; instead, they can draw on the computational resources offered by the cloud. They can focus on leveraging their core competencies by exploiting a number of cloud-computing benefits such as on-demand computing resources, and faster software development capabilities at lower cost. Moreover, cloud computing also offers an enormous amount of computing power to organizations which need to process tremendous amounts of data.

Therefore, many companies view clouds as not only a useful on-demand service but also a potential market opportunity. According to an International Data Corporation (IDC) report (Gleeson, 2009), global IT cloud services spending is estimated to increase from $16 billion in 2008 to $42 billion in 2012, representing a compound annual growth rate (CAGR) of 27%. Attracted by high-growth prospects, Web-based companies such as Amazon, eBay and Salesforce.com, hardware vendors such as HP, IBM and Cisco, and software firms such as EMC/VMware, Oracle/Sun and Microsoft, as well as telecom providers and others, are all investing huge amounts of capital in establishing or enlarging their cloud data centres.

Clouds are essentially virtualized data centres and applications offered as services on a subscription basis as shown in Figure 16.1. They require high energy for their operation (Bianchini and Rajamony, 2004). For instance, a typical data centre with 1000 racks needs about 10 MW of power to operate (Rivoire *et al.*, 2007), which results in higher operational costs. Thus, for a data centre, the energy cost is a significant component of its operating and upfront costs. In addition, in April 2007, Gartner estimated that the information and communication technologies (ICT) industry generates about 2% of the total global carbon dioxide (CO_2) emissions, which is equal to emissions by the aviation industry (Rivoire *et al.*, 2007). Thus, energy consumption and carbon emission by cloud infrastructures have become key environmental concerns.

Some studies show that cloud computing can actually make traditional data centres more energy efficient by using technologies such as resource virtualization and workload consolidation. The traditional data centres running Web applications are often provisioned to handle sporadic peak loads, which can result in low resource utilization and wastage of energy. A cloud data centre, on the other hand, can reduce the energy consumed through server consolidation, whereby different workloads can share the same physical host using virtualization and unused servers can be switched off. According to Accenture (Accenture Microsoft Report, 2010), small businesses saw the most dramatic reduction in emissions – up to 90% whilst using cloud resources. Large corporations can save at least 30–60% in carbon emissions using cloud applications, and midsized businesses can save 60–90%.

Contrary to the opinion given here, some studies, for example Greenpeace (Greenpeace International, 2010), observe that the cloud phenomenon may aggravate the problem of carbon emissions and global warming. The reason given is that the collective demand for computing resources is expected to further increase dramatically in the next few years because of rapid growth in the use of cloud services by businesses and individuals.

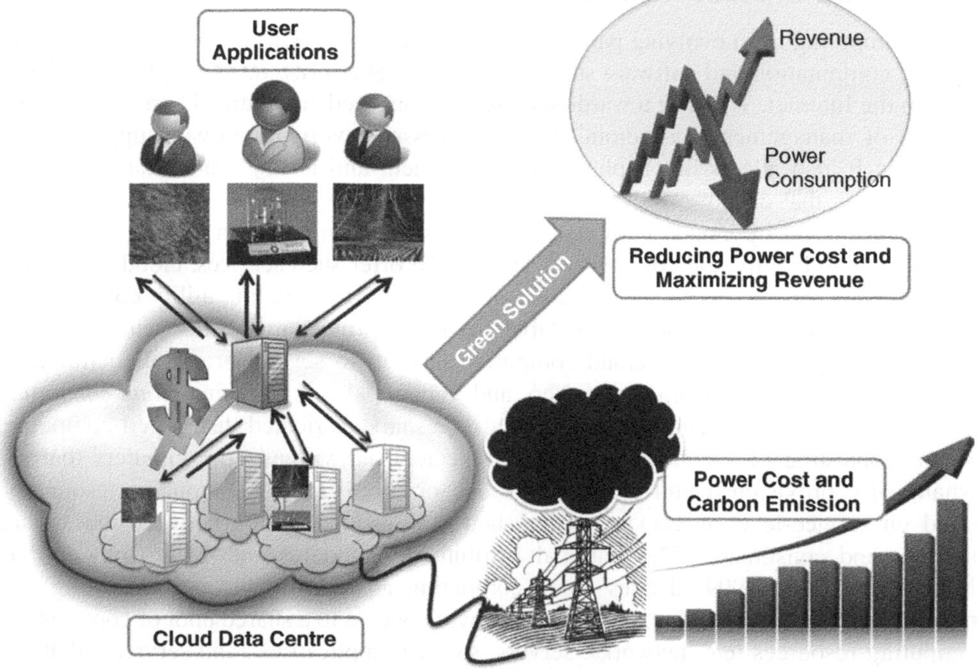

Figure 16.1 Cloud and environmental sustainability.

Table 16.1 Comparison of significant cloud data centres (Greenpeace International, 2010)

Cloud data centres	Location	Estimated power usage effectiveness	Percentage of dirty energy generation	Percentage of renewable electricity used
Google	Lenoir	1.21	50.5% coal, 38.7% nuclear	3.8
Apple	Apple, NC	–	50.5% coal, 38.7% nuclear	3.8
Microsoft	Chicago, IL	1.22	72.8% coal, 22.3% nuclear	1.1
Yahoo	La Vista, NE	1.16	73.1% coal, 14.6% nuclear	7

Even the most efficiently built data centre with the highest utilization rates will only mitigate, rather than eliminate, harmful CO_2 emissions. The reason given is that cloud providers are more interested in electricity cost reduction than in carbon emissions. The data collected by the study are presented in Table 16.1. Clearly, none of the cloud data centres in the table can be called green.

In this chapter, we explore the environmental sustainability of cloud computing by providing various technologies and mechanisms that support this goal. We also propose and recommend a green cloud framework for reducing an organization's carbon footprint in a wholesome manner without sacrificing the quality of service (QoS) (performance, responsiveness and availability) offered by the multiple cloud providers.

16.2 What is Cloud Computing?

Cloud computing is an evolving paradigm which enables the delivery of IT needs such as storage, computation and software such as office and enterprise resource planning (ERP) through the Internet. The shift towards such service-oriented computing is driven primarily by ease of management and administration processes involving software upgrades and bug fixes. It also allows fast application development and testing, particularly by small IT companies that cannot afford large investments on infrastructure. The most important advantage offered by clouds is in economies of scale; that is, when thousands of users share the same facility, the cost per user lessens. To offer such services, cloud computing encompasses many technologies and concepts such as virtualization, utility computing, a pay-as-you-go business model and scalable automatic provisioning on demand.

The growing popularity of cloud computing has led to several proposals defining its characteristics. For example, Buyya, Yeo, and Venugopal (2008) define *cloud computing* in terms of its utility to end users: 'A Cloud is a market-oriented distributed computing system consisting of a collection of interconnected and virtualized computers that are dynamically provisioned and presented as one or more unified computing resource(s) based on service-level agreements established through negotiation between the service provider and consumers'. The National Institute of Standards and Technology (NIST) (Mell and Grance, 2009) defines cloud computing as follows: 'Cloud computing is a model for enabling convenient, on-demand network access to a shared pool of configurable computing resources (e.g. networks, servers, storage, applications, and services) that can be rapidly provisioned and released with minimal management effort or service provider interaction. This Cloud model promotes availability and is composed of five essential characteristics, three service models, and four deployment models.'

Key characteristics of clouds are on-demand self-service, broad network access, resource pooling, rapid elasticity and measured service. The available service models are classified as software as a service (SaaS), platform as a service (PaaS) and infrastructure as a service (IaaS). The deployment models are categorized into public, private, community and hybrid clouds.

16.2.1 Cloud Computing Characteristics

The key characteristics exhibited by clouds are shown in Figure 16.2 and discussed here:

- **Virtualized:** Resources (i.e. compute, storage and network capacity) in clouds are virtualized, and this is achieved at various levels including virtual machine (VM) and platform levels.
- **Service oriented:** Cloud is implemented using a service-oriented architecture model where all the capabilities or components are available over the network as a service. Whether it is software, a platform or infrastructure, everything is offered as a service.
- **Elastic:** Resources (i.e. compute, storage and network capacity) required for cloud applications can be dynamically provisioned and varied, that is, increased or decreased at runtime depending on user QoS requirements.
- **Dynamic and distributed:** Although cloud resources are virtualized, they are often distributed to enable the delivery of high-performance and/or reliable cloud services.

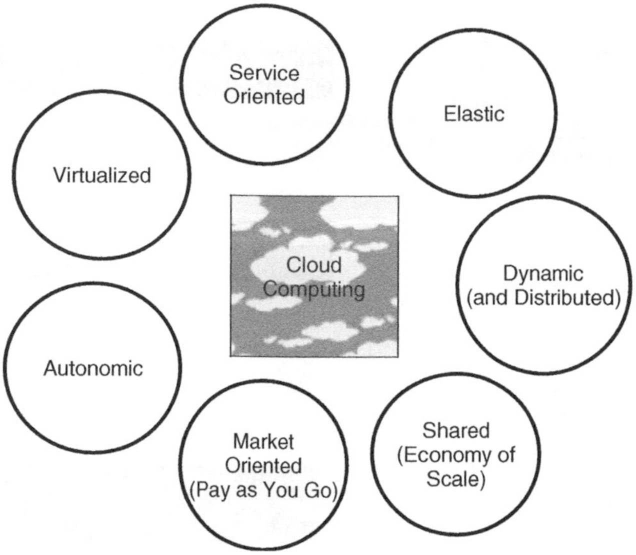

Figure 16.2 Characteristics of cloud computing.

These resources are flexible and can be adapted according to customer requirements such as software, network configuration and so on.

- **Shared (economy of scale):** Clouds are shared infrastructure where resources serve multiple customers with dynamic allocation according to their application's demand. This sharing model is also termed the multi-tenant model. In general, customers neither have any direct control over physical resources nor they are aware of the resource location and with whom resources are being shared.
- **Market oriented (pay as you go):** In cloud computing, customers pay for services on a pay-per-use (or pay-as-you-go) basis. The pricing model can vary depending on the QoS expectation of application. This characteristic addresses the utility dimension of cloud computing. That means that cloud services are offered as 'metered' services where providers have an accounting model for measuring the use of the services, which helps in the development of different pricing plans and models (Allenotor and Thulasiram, 2008). The accounting model helps in the control and optimization of resource usage.
- **Autonomic:** To provide highly reliable services, clouds exhibit autonomic behaviour by managing themselves in case of failures or performance degradation.

16.2.2 Components of Cloud Computing

Cloud computing is mainly composed of three layers which cover the entire computing stack of a system. Each of these layers offers a different set of services to end users, as described in Figure 16.3.

At the lowest layer, cloud offerings are named infrastructure as a service which consists of VMs or physical machines, storage and clusters. Cloud infrastructures can also be heterogeneous, integrating clusters, PCs and workstations. Moreover, the system

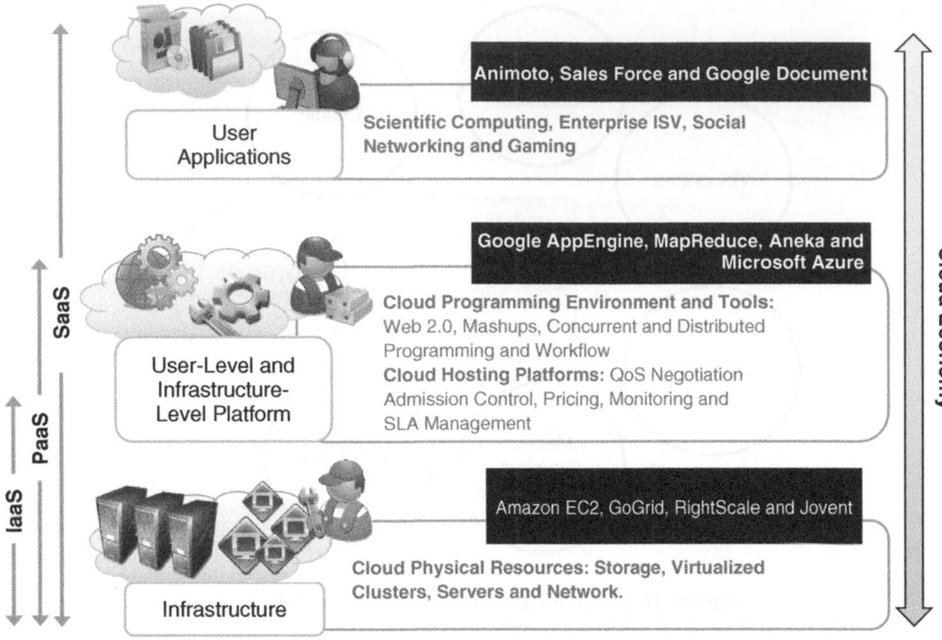

Figure 16.3 Cloud-computing architecture.

infrastructure can also include database management systems and other storage services. The infrastructure in general is managed by an upper management layer that guarantees runtime environment customization, application isolation, accounting and QoS. The virtualization tools, such as hypervisors, also sit in this layer to manage the resource pool and to partition physical infrastructure in the form of customized VMs. Depending on end user needs, the virtualized infrastructure is pre-configured with a storage and programming environment, which saves time for users who do not need to build their system from scratch.

Even though IaaS gives access to physical resources with some software configuration, for developing and testing new applications users require a variety of tools that assist them in application development. These services constitute another layer called platform as a service, offering cloud users a development platform on which to build their applications. Google AppEngine (Google AppEngine, 2010), Aneka (Vecchiola, Chu, and Buyya, 2009) and Microsoft Azure (Microsoft Azure, 2011) are some of the most prominent examples of PaaS clouds. In general, PaaS also includes the lower layer (IaaS) that is bundled with the offered service, although pure PaaS offers only the user-level middleware, which allows the development and deployment of applications on any cloud infrastructure (Charrington, 2010). The major advantage of PaaS is the cost savings in development, deployment and management cycle of new applications. PaaS providers reduce risk in terms of the upgrade costs of underlying platforms and allow cloud users to concentrate on application development.

On the topmost layer of cloud-computing architecture, the cloud services (Figure 16.3) are referred to as software as a service which is a software delivery model providing on-demand access to applications. The most common examples of such a service are customer relationship management (CRM) and ERP applications that are commonly used in almost all enterprises of any size. In general, SaaS providers also constitute other layers of cloud computing and, thus, maintain the customer data and configure the applications according to customer need. This scenario results in considerable reduction in upfront cost of purchasing new software and infrastructure. Customers do not have to maintain any infrastructure or install anything within their premises. They just require high-speed networks to get instant access to their applications. Multi-tenancy is another core feature of SaaS compared to traditional packaged software, allowing providers to outsource the effort of managing large hardware infrastructure, maintaining and upgrading applications and optimizing resources by sharing the costs among the large user base. Therefore, the SaaS model is particularly appealing for companies who get access to software configured according to their specific needs and shared between multiple users. On the customer side, the only costs incurred are the monthly software usage fee.

16.2.3 Cloud Computing Deployment Models

From the discussions here, we can say that cloud computing is a paradigm of offering on-demand services to end users. Clouds are deployed on physical infrastructure where cloud middleware is implemented for delivering services to customers. Such an infrastructure and middleware differ in their services, administrative domain and access to users. Therefore, the cloud deployments are classified mainly into three types: public cloud, private cloud and hybrid cloud (Figure 16.4).

16.2.3.1 Public Clouds

The public cloud is the most common deployment model where services are made available to anyone through the Internet. To support thousands of public domain users, data centres built by public cloud providers are quite large comprising thousands of servers with high-speed networks. Examples of popular public clouds are Amazon Web Services (AWS), Google AppEngine and Microsoft Azure. Public clouds are particularly attractive to customers with small enterprises or infrequent infrastructure usage, since these clouds provide a very good option to handle peak loads on the local infrastructure and for effective capacity planning. The fundamental characteristic of public clouds is its multi-tenancy, which is essentially achieved using sophisticated virtualization at various levels of the software stack. Being public clouds, QoS and security are the main issues that need to be ensured in their management.

16.2.3.2 Private Clouds

Private clouds are deployed within the premise of an organization to provide IT services to its internal users. Private cloud services offer greater control over the infrastructure, improving security and service resilience because its access is restricted to one or a few organizations. Such private deployment poses an inherent limitation to end user applications, that is, inability to scale elastically on demand as can be done using pubic cloud services.

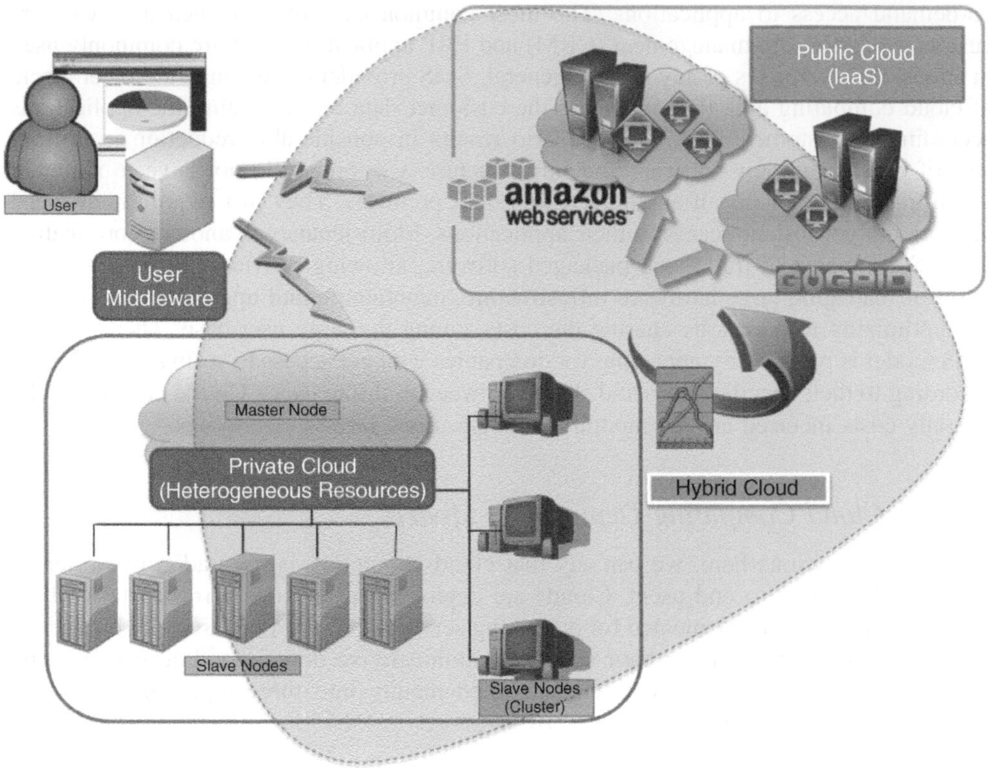

Figure 16.4 Deployment models for clouds.

16.2.3.3 Hybrid Clouds

Hybrid clouds are a deployment with the benefits of both public and private clouds. In this model, organizations deploy noncritical information and processing to the public cloud, whilst keeping critical services and data in their control. Therefore, organizations can utilize their (existing) in-house IT infrastructure for maintaining sensitive information within the premises, and can auto-scale their resources using public clouds for handling occasional peak loads. These resources or services are temporarily leased in peak load times and then released. The hybrid cloud, in general, applies to services related to IT infrastructure rather than software services.

16.3 Cloud Computing and Energy Usage Model: A Typical Example

In this section, through a typical cloud usage scenario we will analyse various elements of clouds and their energy efficiency. Figure 16.5 shows an end user accessing cloud services such as SaaS, PaaS or IaaS over the Internet. User data pass from his or her own device through an Internet Service Provider's router, which in turn connects to a gateway router within a cloud data centre. Within data centres, data go through a local area network and

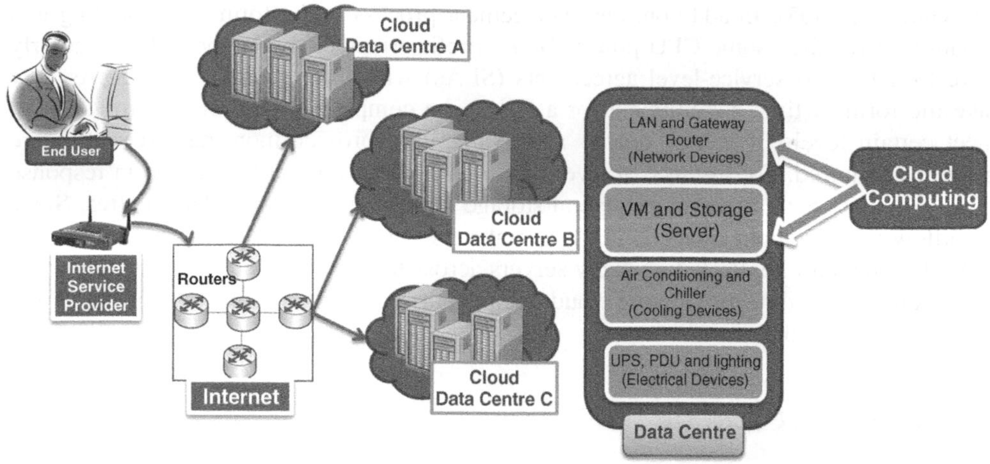

Figure 16.5 Cloud usage model.

are processed on VMs, hosting cloud services, which may access storage servers. Each of these computing and network devices that are directly accessed to serve cloud users contributes to energy consumption. In addition, within a cloud data centre, there are many other devices, such as cooling and electrical devices, that consume power. These devices do not directly help in providing cloud service, but are the major contributors to a cloud data centre's power consumption, as discussed in this chapter.

16.3.1 User and Cloud Software Applications

The first factor that contributes to energy consumption is the way software applications are designed and implemented. Cloud computing can be used for running applications owned by individual users or offered by the cloud provider using SaaS. In both cases, the energy consumption depends on the application itself. If application is long running with high CPU and memory requirements, then its execution will result in high energy consumption. Thus, energy consumption will be directly proportional to the application's profile. The allocation of resources based on the maximum level of CPU and memory usage will result in much higher energy consumption than is actually required. The energy inefficiency in executing an application emanates from inaccurate design and implementation. Application inefficiencies, such as suboptimal algorithms and inefficient usage of shared resources, lead to higher CPU usage and, therefore, higher energy consumption. However, factors such as energy efficiency are not considered during application design in most application domains other than, for example, embedded devices such as mobile phones.

16.3.2 Cloud Software Stack for the SaaS, PaaS and IaaS Levels

The cloud software stack leads to an extra overhead in executing end user applications. For instance, it is well known that a physical server has higher performance efficiency than a VM, and IaaS providers generally offer VM access to their end users (Cherkasova and Gardner, 2005). In addition, the management process in the form of accounting and monitoring requires some CPU power. Being profit oriented, service providers regularly have to adhere to service-level agreements (SLAs) with their clients. These SLAs may take the form of time commitment for a task to be completed. Thus cloud providers, to meet certain levels of service quality and availability, provide more resources than are generally required. For instance, to avoid failure, fast recovery and reduction in response time, providers have to maintain several storage replicas across many data centres. Since workflow in Web applications requires several sites to give better response time to its end user, their data are replicated on many servers across the world. Therefore, it is important to explore the relationships among cloud components and the trade-offs between QoS and energy consumption.

16.3.3 Network Devices

The network system is another area of concern which consumes a non-negligible fraction of the total power consumption. The ICT energy consumption estimates (Sarokin, 2007) just for Vodafone Group radio access network was nearly 3 TW h in 2006. In cloud computing, since resources are accessed through the Internet, both applications and data are needed to be transferred to the compute node (Baliga *et al.*, 2010). Therefore, it requires much more data communication bandwidth between a user's PC to the cloud resources than it requires application execution requirements. In some cases, if data are really large, then it may turn out to be cheaper and more carbon emission efficient to send the data by mail than to transfer through the Internet.

In cloud computing, the user data travel through many devices before they reach a data centre. In general, the user computer is connected to the Ethernet switch of his or her Internet service provider (ISP) where traffic is aggregated. The Broadband Network Gateway (BNG) network performs traffic management and authentication functions on the packets received by Ethernet switches. These BNG routers connect to other Internet routers through the provider's edge routers. The core network is further composed of many large routers. Each of these devices consumes power according to its traffic volume. According to the study conducted by Tucker (Baliga *et al.*, 2010), the public cloud is estimated to consume about 2.7 J/b in transmission and switching in comparison to 0.46 J/b for a private cloud. They found out that power consumption in transport represents a significant proportion of the total power consumption for cloud storage services at medium- and high-usage rates. Even typical network usage can result in 3–4 times more energy consumption in public cloud storage than in one's own storage infrastructure. Therefore, with the growth of cloud-computing usage, it is expected that the energy efficiency of switches and routers will play a very significant role since they need to provide a capacity of hundreds of terabits of bandwidth.

In the network infrastructure, energy consumption depends especially on the power efficiency and awareness of wired networks (Chabarek *et al.*, 2008), namely, the network equipment or system design, topology design and network protocol design. Most of the energy in network devices is wasted because they are designed to handle worst-case scenarios. Therefore, the energy consumption of these devices remains almost the same during both peak time and idle state. Many improvements are required to get high energy efficiency in these devices. For example, during low-use periods, Ethernet links can be turned off and packets can be routed around them. Further energy savings are possible at the hardware level of the routers through appropriate selection and optimization of the layout of various internal router components (i.e. buffers, links, etc.).

16.3.4 Data Centres

The cloud data centres are quite different from traditional hosting facilities. A cloud data centre could comprise many hundreds or thousands of networked computers with their corresponding storage and networking subsystems, power distribution and conditioning equipment and cooling infrastructures. Due to the large number of equipment, data centres can consume massive energy consumption and emit large amounts of carbon. Table 16.2 lists equipment typically used in data centres with their contribution to energy consumption. It can be clearly observed that servers and storage systems are not the only infrastructure that consumes energy in the data centre. In reality, cooling equipment consumes an equivalent amount of energy as the IT systems themselves. Ranganathan (2010) suggests that for every dollar spent on electricity costs in large-scale data centres, another dollar is spent on cooling.

Further energy consumption occurs due to lighting, loss in the power distribution and other electrical equipment such as UPSs. In other words, the majority of power usage within a data centre is used for other purposes than actual IT services. Thus, to achieve the maximum efficiency in power consumption and CO_2 emissions, each of these devices needs to be designed and used efficiently whilst ensuring that its carbon footprint is reduced.

16.4 Features of Clouds Enabling Green Computing

Even though there is a great concern in the community that cloud computing can result in higher energy usage by the data centres, cloud computing has a green lining. There are several technologies and concepts employed by cloud providers to achieve better utilization and efficiency than traditional computing. Therefore, comparatively lower carbon emission is expected in cloud computing due to highly energy-efficient infrastructure and reduction in the IT infrastructure itself by multi-tenancy. The key driver technology for energy-efficient clouds is 'virtualization', which allows significant improvement in the energy efficiency of cloud providers by leveraging the economies of scale associated with a large number of organizations sharing the same infrastructure. Virtualization is the process of presenting a logical grouping or subset of computing resources so that they can

Table 16.2 Percentage of energy consumption by each data centre device

Data centre subsystem	Percentage of energy used
Cooling device (chiller, computer room air conditioning (CRAC))	42
IT equipment	30
Electrical equipments (UPSs, power distribution units (PDUs), lighting)	28

be accessed in ways that give benefits over the original configuration (Smith and Nair, 2003). By consolidation of underutilized servers in the form of multiple VMs sharing the same physical server at higher utilization, companies can gain high savings in the form of space, management and energy.

According to an Accenture report (Accenture Microsoft Report, 2010), four key factors have enabled cloud computing to create lower energy usage and carbon emissions for ICT.

1. **Dynamic provisioning:** In traditional settings, data centres and private infrastructure used to be maintained to fulfil worst-case demand. Thus, IT companies end up deploying far more infrastructure than is needed. There are various reasons for such over-provisioning: (i) it is very difficult to predict the demand at a given time, which is particularly true for Web applications, and (ii) to guarantee service availability and to maintain certain levels of service quality to end users. One example of a Web service facing these problems is a Web site for the Australian Open Tennis Championship (IBM, 2008). The Australian Open Web site each year receives a significant spike in traffic during the tournament period. To handle such peak load during a short annual period, running hundreds of servers throughout the year is not really energy efficient. Such scenarios can be readily managed by cloud infrastructure. Thus, data centres always maintain the active servers according to current demand, which results in lower energy consumption than the conservative approach of over-provisioning.
2. **Multi-tenancy:** Using the multi-tenancy approach, cloud-computing infrastructure reduces overall energy usage and associated carbon emissions. The SaaS providers serve multiple companies on the same infrastructure and software. This approach is obviously more energy efficient than multiple copies of software installed on different infrastructure. Furthermore, businesses have highly variable demand patterns in general, and hence multi-tenancy on the same server allows the flattening of the overall peak demand which can minimize the need for extra infrastructure. The smaller fluctuation in demand results in better prediction and greater energy savings.
3. **Server utilization:** In general, on-premise infrastructure runs with very low utilization; sometimes it goes down as much as 5–10% of average utilization. Using virtualization technologies, multiple applications can be hosted and executed on the same server in isolation, thus leading to utilization levels up to 70%. Thus, it dramatically reduces the number of active servers. Even though high utilization of servers results in more power consumption, servers running at higher utilization can process greater workload with similar power usage.
4. **Data centre efficiency:** By using the most energy-efficient technologies, cloud providers can significantly improve the power usage effectiveness (PUE) of their data centres. Today's state-of-the-art data centre designs for large cloud service providers can achieve PUE levels as low as 1.1–1.2, which is about 40% more power efficiency than that of the traditional data centres. The server design in the form of modular containers, water- or air-based cooling or advanced power management through power supply optimization are all approaches that have significantly improved PUE in data centres. In addition, cloud computing allows services to be moved between multiple data centre which are running with better PUE values. This is achieved by using high-speed networks, virtualized services and measurement as well as monitoring and accounting of the data centre.

Due to these cloud features, organizations can reduce carbon emissions by at least 30% per user by moving their applications to the cloud. These savings are driven by the high efficiency of large-scale cloud data centres.

16.5 Towards Energy Efficiency of Cloud Computing

16.5.1 Applications

The SaaS model has changed the way applications and software are distributed and used. More and more companies are switching to SaaS clouds to minimize their IT cost. Thus, it has become very important to address energy efficiency at the application level itself. However, this layer has received very little attraction since many applications are already in use and most of the new applications are mostly upgraded versions of, or developed using, previously implemented tools. Some of the efforts in this direction are for Message Passing Interface (MPI) applications (Freeh *et al.*, 2005), which are designed to run directly on physical machines. Thus, their performance on VM is still undefined.

Various power-efficient techniques (Großschädl *et al.*, 2005; Saxe, 2008) for software designs are proposed in the literature, but these are mostly for embedded devices. In the development of commercial and enterprise applications which are designed for the PC environment, generally energy efficiency is neglected. Mayo and Ranganathan (2005) presented in their study that even simple tasks such as listening to music can consume significantly different amounts of energy on a variety of heterogeneous devices. As these tasks have the same purpose on each device, the results show that the implementation of the task and the system upon which it is performed can have a dramatic impact on efficiency. Therefore, to achieve energy efficiency at the application level, SaaS providers should pay attention in deploying software on the right kind of infrastructure which can execute the software most efficiently. This necessitates the research and analysis of a trade-off between performance and energy consumption due to the execution of software on multiple platforms and hardware. In addition, the energy consumption at the compiler level and code level should be considered by software developers in the design of their future application implementations using various energy-efficient techniques proposed in the literature.

16.5.2 Cloud Software Stack: Virtualization and Provisioning

In the cloud stack, most works in the literature address the challenges at the IaaS provider level where research focus is on scheduling and resource management to reduce the amount of active resources executing the workload of user applications. VM consolidation, VM migration, scheduling, demand projection, heat management, temperature-aware allocation and load balancing are used as basic techniques for minimizing power consumption. As discussed in this chapter, virtualization plays an important role in these techniques due to its many features such as consolidation, live migration and performance isolation. Consolidation helps in managing the trade-off between performance, resource utilization and energy consumption (Srikantaiah, Kansal, and Zhao, 2008). Similarly, VM migration (Beloglazov *et al.*, 2011) allows flexible and dynamic resource management whilst facilitating fault management and lower maintenance cost. Additionally, the advancement in virtualization technology has led to significant reduction in VM overhead which improves further the cloud infrastructure's energy efficiency.

Abdelsalam *et al.* (2009) proposed a power-efficient technique to improve the management of cloud-computing environments. They formulated the management problem in the form of an optimization model aiming at minimization of the total energy consumption of the cloud, taking SLAs into account. The current issue of underutilization and overprovisioning of servers was highlighted by Ranganathan *et al.* (2006). They present a peak power budget management solution to avoid excessive overprovisioning considering dynamic voltage scaling (DVS) and memory and disk scaling. There are several other research works which focus on minimizing overprovisioning by using virtualized server consolidation (Chase *et al.*, 2001). A majority of these works use monitoring and estimation of resource utilization by applications based on the arrival rate of requests. However, due to multiple levels of abstractions, it is really hard to maintain deployment data of each VM within a cloud data centre. Thus, various indirect load estimation techniques are used for consolidation.

Although these consolidation methods can overall reduce the number of resources used to serve user applications, the migration and relocation of VMs for matching application demand can impact user's QoS service requirements. Since cloud providers need to satisfy a certain level of service, some work focussed on minimizing energy consumption whilst reducing the number of SLA violations. One of the first works that dealt with the performance and energy trade-off was by Chase *et al.* (2001) who introduced Muse, an economy-based system of resource allocation. They proposed a bidding system to deliver the required performance level and switching off unused servers. Kephart *et al.* (2007) addressed the coordination of multiple autonomic managers for power and performance trade-offs using a utility function approach in a nonvirtualized environment. Song *et al.* (2007) proposed an adaptive and dynamic scheme for efficient sharing of a server by adjusting resources (i.e. CPU and memory) between VMs. At the operating system level, Nathuji and Schwan (2007) proposed a power management system called VirtualPower that integrates power management and virtualization technologies. VirtualPower allows the isolated and independent operation of VM to reduce energy consumption. The soft states are intercepted by Xen hypervisor and are mapped to changes in the underlying hardware such as CPU frequency scaling according to virtual power management rules.

In addition, there are works on improving the energy efficiency of storage systems. Kaushik *et al.* (2010) presented an energy-conserving self-adaptive commodity green cloud storage called Lightning. The Lightning file system divides the storage servers into cold and hot logical zones using data classification. These servers are then switched to inactive states for energy saving. Verma *et al.* (2010) proposed an optimization for storage virtualization called sample-replicate-consolidate mapping (SRCMAP) which enables the energy proportionality for dynamic input – output (I/O) workloads by consolidating the cumulative workload on a subset of physical volumes proportional to the I/O workload intensity. Gurumurthi, Stan, and Sankar (2009) proposed intra-disk parallelism on high capacity drives to improve disk bandwidth without increasing power consumption. Soror *et al.* (2008) addressed the problem of optimizing the performance of database management systems by controlling the configurations of the VMs in which they run.

Since power is dissipated in cloud data centres due to heat generated by the servers, dynamic scheduling of VMs and applications which takes into account the thermal states or heat dissipation in a data centre is proposed by several researchers. Consideration of the thermal factor into scheduling also improves the reliability of the underlying infrastructure, and the following techniques and principles can be used:

- A mathematical model for maximizing the cooling efficiency of a data centre (Bash and Forman, 2007).
- Emulation tools for investigating the thermal implications of power management (Heath *et al.*, 2006).
- Software prediction infrastructure called C-Oracle that makes online predictions for data centre thermal management based on load redistribution and DVS (Ramos and Bianchini, 2008).
- Automatic reconfiguration of thermal load management system taking into account thermal behaviour for improving cooling efficiency and power consumption; another proposition comprising thermal management solutions focussing on scheduling workloads with consideration of temperature-aware workload placement (Moore, Chase, and Ranganathan, 2006).
- Workload placement policy for a data centre that allocates resources in the areas which are easier to cool, resulting in cooling power savings (Bash and Forman, 2007).
- A framework which coordinates and unifies five individual power management solutions (consisting of hardware–software (HW–SW) mechanisms) (Raghavendra *et al.*, 2008).

16.5.3 Data Centre Level: Cooling, Hardware, Network and Storage

The rising energy costs, drive cost reduction and desire to get more out of existing investments are making today's cloud providers to adopt best practices to make data centre operations green. To build energy-efficient data centres, several best practices have been proposed to improve the efficiency of each device from electrical systems to the processor level (Moore, Chase, and Ranganathan, 2006; Ranganathan, 2010; Woods, 2010).

The first level is constructive a smart data centre and choosing its location. There are two major factors to consider: One is energy supply and the other is equipment energy efficiency. Hence, the data centres are being constructed in such a way that electricity can be generated using renewable sources such as sun and wind. Currently the data centre location is decided based on their geographical features; climate, fibre-optic connectivity and access to a plentiful supply of affordable energy. Since the main concern of cloud providers is business, an energy source is also seen mostly in terms of cost, not carbon emissions.

Another area of concern within a data centre is its cooling system which contributes to almost one-third of the total energy consumption. Some research studies (Moore, Chase, and Ranganathan, 2006; Ranganathan, 2010) have shown that uneven temperature within data centres can also lead to significant declines in IT system reliability. In data centre cooling, two types of approaches are used: air- and water-based cooling systems. In both approaches, it is necessary that they directly cool the hot equipment rather than the entire room area. Thus newer energy-efficient cooling systems are proposed based on liquid cooling, nano-fluid-cooling systems and in-server, in-rack and in-row cooling by companies such as SprayCool. Other than that, the outside temperature or climate can have a direct impact on the energy requirements of cooling systems. Some systems have been constructed where external cool air is used to remove heat from the data centre (Woods, 2010).

Another level at which data centre's power efficiency is addressed is on the deployment of new power-efficient servers and processors. Low-energy processors can reduce the power usage of IT systems to a great degree. Many new energy-efficient server models are currently available from vendors such as AMD, Intel and others; each of them offers good performance and watt system. These server architectures enable slowing down CPU clock speeds (clock gating) or powering off parts of the chips (power gating) if they are idle. Further enhancement in energy saving and increasing computing per watt can be achieved by using multi-core processors. For instance, Sun's multicore chips, each a 32-thread Niagara chip, UltraSPARC 1, consumes about 60 W, whilst the two Niagara chips have 64 threads and run at about 80 W. However, the exploitation of such power efficiency of multi-core systems requires software which can run on a multi-CPU environment. Here, virtualization technologies play an important role. Similarly, the consolidation of storage systems helps to further reduce the energy requirements of IT systems. For example, storage area networks (SANs) allow building an efficient storage network that consolidates all storage. The use of energy-efficient disks such as tiered storage (solid state, serial advanced technology attachment (SATA) or serial-attached SCSI [Small Computer System Interface] (SAS)) allows for better energy efficiency.

The power supply unit (PSU) is another infrastructure which needs to be designed in an energy-efficient manner. Their task is to feed the server resources with power by converting a high-voltage alternating current (AC) from the power grid to a low-voltage direct current (DC) which most electric circuits (e.g. computers) require. These circuits inside PSUs inevitably lose some energy in the form of heat, which is dissipated by additional fans inside the PSU. The energy efficiency of a PSU mainly depends on its load, number of circuits and other conditions (e.g. temperature). Hence, a PSU which is labelled to be 80% efficient is not necessarily that efficient for all power loads. For example, low power loads tend to be the most energy-inefficient ones. Thus, a PSU can be just 60% efficient at 20% of power load. Some studies have found that PSUs are among the most inefficient components in today's data centres as many servers are still shipped with low-quality power supplies operating at 60–70% efficiency. One possible solution is to replace all PSUs with Energy Star–certified ones. This certificate is given to PSUs which guarantee a minimum 80% efficiency at any power load.

16.5.4 Monitoring and Metering

It is essential to construct power models that allow the system to know the energy consumed by a particular device, and how it can be reduced. To measure the unified efficiency of a data centre and improve its performance per watt, the Green Grid has proposed two specific metrics known as power usage effectiveness and data centre infrastructure efficiency (DciE) (Rawson, Pfleuger, and Cader, 2008).

- PUE = Total Facility Power/IT Equipment Power.
- DciE = 1/PUE = IT Equipment Power/Total Facility Power × 100%.

For measuring and modelling the power usage of storage systems, researchers from IBM (Allalouf *et al.*, 2009) have proposed a scalable, enterprise storage modelling framework called STAMP (Stanford Transactional Applications for Multi-Processing). It sidesteps the need for detailed traces by using interval performance statistics and a power table for each disk model. STAMP takes into account controller caching and algorithms, including protection schemes, and adjusts the workload accordingly. Research from the Lawrence Berkley National Labs (Greenberg *et al.*, 2008) shows that 22 data centres measured in 2008 have PUE values in the range of 1.3–3.0. PUE of data centres can be useful in measuring the power efficiency of data centres and thus provide a motivation to improve its efficiency. To measure the power consumed by a server (e.g. PowerEdge R610), the Intelligent Platform Management Interface (IPMI) (Giri, 2010) is proposed. This framework provides a uniform way to access the power-monitoring sensors available on recent servers. Further, intelligent power distribution units (PDUs), traditional power meters (e.g. Watts Up Pro power meter) and Advanced Configuration and Power Interface (ACPI) – enabled power supplies can be used to measure the power consumption of the whole server.

16.5.5 Network Infrastructure

As discussed in this chapter, at the network level, energy efficiency is achieved either at the node level (i.e. network interface card) or at the infrastructure level (i.e. switches and routers). Energy efficiency issues in networking are usually referred to as green networking, which relates to embedding energy awareness in the design, the devices and the protocols of networks. There are four classes of solutions: resource consolidation, selective connectedness, virtualization, and proportional computing.

Resource consolidation helps in regrouping underutilized devices to reduce global consumption. Similar to consolidation, the selective connectedness of devices (Allalouf *et al.*, 2009; Allman *et al.*, 2007) consists of distributed mechanisms which allow the single pieces of equipment to go idle for some time, as transparently as possible from the rest of the networked devices. The difference between resource consolidation and selective connectedness is that the consolidation applies to resources that are shared within the network infrastructure whilst selective connectedness allows turning off unused resources at the edge of the network.

Virtualization, as discussed in this chapter, allows more than one service to operate on the same piece of hardware, thus improving the hardware utilization. Proportional computing (Allman *et al.*, 2007) can be applied to a system as a whole, to network protocols as well as to individual devices and components. Dynamic voltage scaling and adaptive link rate are typical examples of proportional computing. Dynamic voltage scaling (Allman *et al.*, 2007) reduces the energy state of the CPU as a function of a system load, whilst adaptive link rate applies a similar concept to network interfaces, reducing their capacity, and thus their consumption, as a function of the link load. The survey by Bianzino *et al.* (201) gives more details about the work in green networking.

16.6 Green Cloud Architecture

Though researchers and developers have made various components of the cloud efficient in terms of power and performance, still they lack a holistic approach to addressing the environmental impacts of cloud computing. For instance, most efforts for the sustainability of cloud computing have missed the network's contribution. Some works just focus on the redistribution of workload to support energy-efficient cooling without considering the effect of virtualization. In addition, cloud providers, being profit oriented, are looking for solutions which can reduce power consumption and, thus, carbon emission without hurting their market. To address some of this issue, we present a green cloud framework, which takes into account these provider goals whilst curbing the energy consumption of clouds. The high-level view of green cloud architecture is given in Figure 16.6. The goal of this architecture is to make the cloud green from both the user and provider perspectives.

In the green cloud architecture, users submit their cloud service requests through a new middleware Green Broker that manages the selection of the greenest cloud provider to serve the user's request. A user service request can be of three types: software, platform

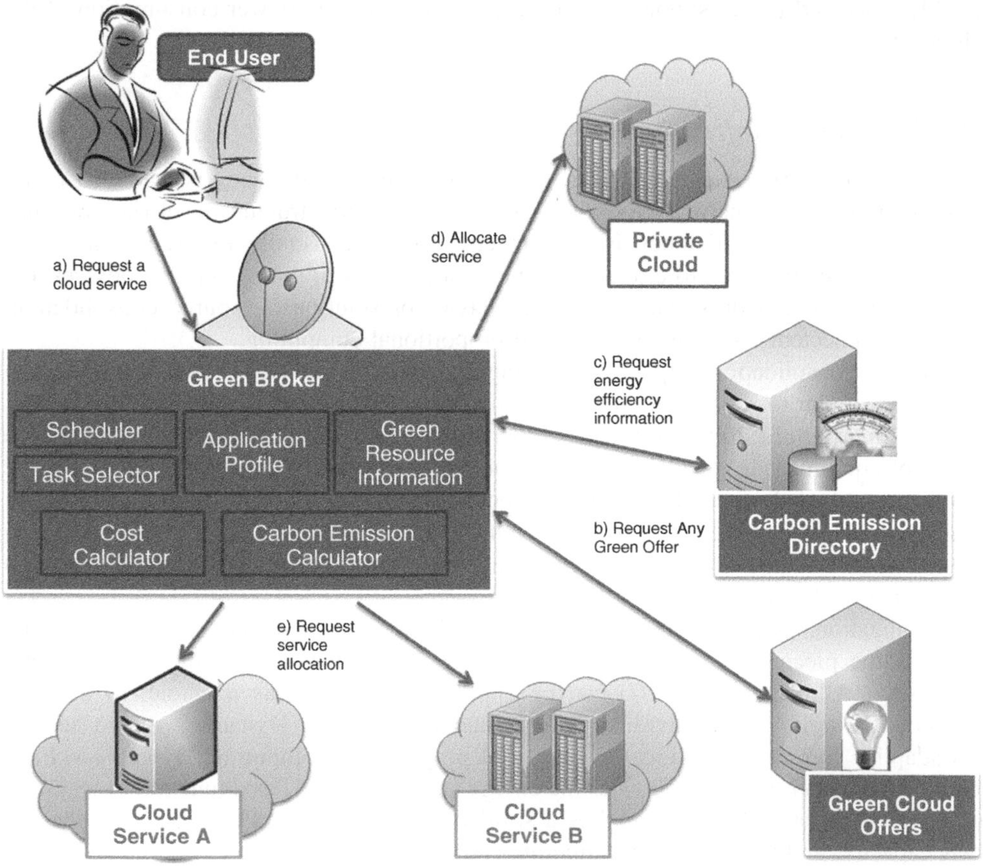

Figure 16.6 Green cloud architecture.

or infrastructure. The cloud providers can register their services in the form of 'green offers' to a public directory which is accessed by Green Broker. The green offers consist of green services, pricing and time when it should be accessed for least carbon emission. Green Broker gets the current status of energy parameters for using various cloud services from the Carbon Emission Directory. The Carbon Emission Directory maintains all the data related to cloud service energy efficiency. These data may include the PUE and cooling efficiency of the cloud data centre which is providing the service, network cost and carbon emission rate of electricity. Green Broker calculates the carbon emission of all the cloud providers who are offering the requested cloud service. Then, it selects the set of services that will result in the least carbon emissions and buy these services on behalf of users.

The green cloud framework is designed such that it keeps track of the overall energy usage of serving a user request. It relies on two main components, the Carbon Emission Directory and green cloud offers, which keep track of the energy efficiency of each cloud provider and also give incentive to cloud providers to make their service 'green'. From the user side, Green Broker plays a crucial role in monitoring and selecting the cloud services based on the user QoS requirements, and ensuring minimum carbon emissions (MCEs) for serving a user. In general, a user can use cloud to access any of these three types of services (SaaS, PaaS and IaaS), and therefore the process of serving them should also be energy efficient. In other words, from the cloud provider side, each cloud layer needs to be 'green' conscious.

- **SaaS level:** Since SaaS providers mainly offer software installed on their own data centres or resources from IaaS providers, the SaaS providers need to model and measure the energy efficiency of their software design, implementation and deployment.
  For serving users, the SaaS provider chooses the data centres which are not only energy efficient but also near to users. The minimum number of replicas of users' confidential data should be maintained using energy-efficient storage.
- **PaaS level:** PaaS providers offer in general the platform services for application development. The platform facilitates the development of applications which ensure system-wide energy efficiency. This can be done by including various energy-profiling tools such as JouleSort (Rivoire *et al.*, 2007), a software energy efficiency benchmark that measures the energy required to perform an external sort. In addition, platforms can be designed to have various code-level optimizations which can cooperate with underlying compliers in the energy-efficient execution of applications. Other than application development, cloud platforms also allow the deployment of user applications on the hybrid cloud. In this case, to achieve maximum energy efficiency, the platforms profile the application and decide which portion of the application or data should be processed in-house and in the cloud.
- **IaaS level:** Providers in this layer play the most crucial role in the success of the whole green architecture since the IaaS level not only offers independent infrastructure services but also supports other services offered by clouds. They use the latest technologies for IT and cooling systems to have the most energy-efficient infrastructure. By using virtualization and consolidation, energy consumption is further reduced by switching off unutilized servers. Various energy meters and sensors are installed to calculate the current energy efficiency of each IaaS provider and its sites. This information

is advertised regularly by cloud providers in the Carbon Emission Directory. Various green-scheduling and resource-provisioning policies will ensure minimum energy usage. In addition, the cloud provider designs various green offers and pricing schemes for providing incentives to users to use their services during off-peak or maximum energy efficiency hours.

16.7 Case Study: IaaS Provider

In this section, using a case study, we illustrate the working of the proposed green architecture and highlight the importance of considering the unifying picture to reduce energy and carbon emissions by cloud infrastructure.

The case study focusses on IaaS service providers. Our experimental platform consists of multiple cloud providers who offer computational resources to execute users' high-performance computing (HPC) applications. A user request consists of an application, its estimated length in time and the number of resources required. These applications are submitted to Green Broker who acts as an interface to the cloud infrastructure and schedules applications on behalf of users as shown in Figure 16.6. Green Broker interprets and analyses the service requirements of a submitted application and decides where to execute it. As discussed, Green Broker's main objective is to schedule applications such that CO_2 emissions are reduced and profit is increased, whilst the QoS requirements of the applications are met. As cloud data centres are located in different geographical regions, they have different CO_2 emission rates and energy costs depending on their regional constraints. Each data centre is responsible for updating this information in the Carbon Emission Directory to facilitate energy-efficient scheduling. The list of energy-related parameters is given in Table 16.3.

In order to validate our framework and to prove that it achieves better efficiency in terms of carbon emission, we have studied five policies (green and profit oriented) employed for scheduling by Green Broker.

1. **Greedy minimum carbon emission (GMCE):** In this policy, user applications are assigned to cloud providers in a greedy manner based on their carbon emission.
2. **Minimum carbon emission–minimum carbon emission (MCE-MCE):** This is a double greedy policy where applications are assigned to the cloud providers with MCE due to their data centre location and carbon emission due to application execution.

Table 16.3 Carbon emission–related parameters of a data centre

Parameter	Notation
Carbon emission rate (kg/kW h)	$r_i^{Co_2}$
Average COP	COP_i
Electricity price (\$/kWh)	p_i^e
Data transfer price (\$/GB) for upload or download	p_i^{DT}
CPU power	$p_i = \beta_i + \alpha_i f^3$
CPU frequency range	$[f_i^{\min}, f_i^{\max}]$
Time slots (start time, end time and number of CPUs)	(t_s, t_e, n)

3. **Greedy maximum profit (GMP):** In this policy, user applications are assigned in a greedy manner to a provider who executes the application fastest and gets maximum profit.
4. **Maximum profit–maximum profit (MP-MP):** This is a double greedy policy considering profit made by cloud providers with whom the application finishes by its deadline.
5. **Minimizing carbon emission and maximizing profit (MCE-MP):** In this policy, the broker tries to schedule the applications to those providers who provide minimization of total carbon emission and maximization of profit.

GMCE, MCE-MCE and MCE-MP are 'green' policies whilst MP-MP and GMP are profit-oriented policies. A more extensive account on modelling energy efficiency in a cloud data centre, experimental data and results is available in Garg *et al.* (2011).

Figure 16.7 shows the course of experiments conducted with varying users' urgency for executing their application and job arrival rate. The metrics of total carbon emission

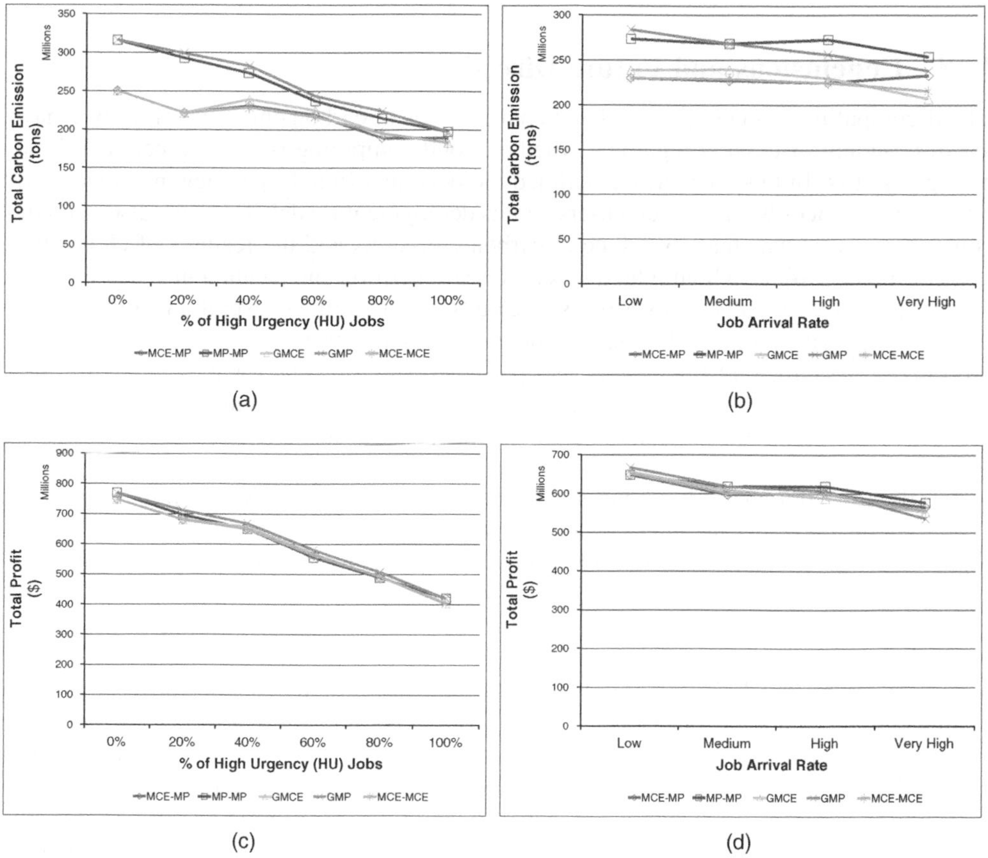

Figure 16.7 Carbon emission and profit of provider using green cloud framework. (a) Request a Cloud Service, (d) Allocate Service, (c) Request Energy Efficiency Information, (b) Request Any Green Offer and (e) Request Service Allocation.

and total profit are used since the resource provider needs to know the collective loss in carbon emission and gain in profit across all data centres. From these results, three main inferences can be made.

- Green policies reduce carbon emission by almost 20% in comparison to profit-based policies. This observation emphasizes the inclusion of overall carbon efficiency for all the cloud providers in scheduling decisions.
- With the increase in users' urgency to execute applications, the gain in carbon emission reduces almost linearly. This clearly shows how important the role of the user is in making cloud computing in general 'green'.
- Green policies also have minimal effects on the providers' profit. This clearly shows that by using energy-efficient solutions such as a Green Cloud Framework, both cloud providers and users can benefit.

These results confirm the validity of the Green Cloud Computing Framework presented in this chapter.

16.8 Conclusions and Future Directions

Cloud-computing business potential and contributions to carbon emissions from ICT have led to on-going discussion regarding whether cloud computing is really green, and if so, how green it is. In this chapter, we outlined the benefits offered by reviewing cloud computing, the services it offers to end users and its deployment model. Then, we discussed the components of clouds that contribute to carbon emissions and the features of clouds that make it 'green'. We also highlighted several research efforts and technologies that increase the energy efficiency of various aspects of clouds, and identified several unexplored areas that can help in maximizing the energy efficiency of clouds from a holistic perspective. We proposed a Green Cloud Framework and presented some results for its validation. Even though our Green Cloud framework embeds various features to make cloud computing greener, many technological solutions are still required to make it a reality:

- Efforts are required in designing software at various levels (OS, compiler, algorithm and application) that facilitates system-wide energy efficiency.
- To enable the green cloud data centres, cloud providers need to understand and measure existing data centre power and cooling designs, the power consumption of servers and their cooling requirements and equipment resource utilization to achieve maximum efficiency.
- For designing the holistic solutions in the scheduling and resource provisioning of applications within the data centre, all the factors such as cooling, network, memory and CPU should be considered. For instance, consolidating VMs, even though an effective technique to minimize the overall power usage of data centres, also raises issues related to the necessary redundancy and placement geo-diversity required to fulfil SLAs with users. It is obvious that the last thing a cloud provider will want to lose is its reputation due to bad service or violation of promised service requirements.
- Last but not least, both providers and customers are responsible to ensure that emerging technologies do not created irreversible changes which can threaten the health of human

society. The way in which end users interact with the application also has a very real cost and impact.

In conclusion, by simply improving the efficiency of equipment, cloud computing cannot claim to be green. What is important is to make its usage more carbon efficient from both user and provider perspectives. Cloud providers need to reduce the electricity demand of clouds and take major steps in using renewable energy sources rather than just look for cost minimization.

Acknowledgements

We thank Professor Thulasiram Ruppa, Dr Rodrigo Calheiros and Professor Rod Tucker for their comments on improving this chapter.

Review Questions

1. What it meant by cloud computing?
2. Why is cloud computing considered to be green?
3. What are the ways in which data centres can be made power efficient?
4. Is energy efficiency of cloud computing the same as efficiency in terms of carbon emission?
5. What is the role of each component in the Green Cloud Framework?
6. What features of cloud computing enable it to increase efficiency?

Discussion Questions

1. What are the features that make cloud computing different from other distributed system paradigms such as grid computing?
2. Will efforts to make various cloud-computing components energy efficient really reduce carbon emissions? Discuss both the positive and negative sides.
3. What responsibility do we carry at the individual level to minimize carbon emissions of ICT?

References

Abdelsalam, H., Maly, K., Mukkamala, R. *et al.* (2009) Towards energy efficient change management in a cloud computing environment. In Proceedings of 3rd International Conference on Autonomous Infrastructure, Management and Security, the Netherlands.

Accenture Microsoft Report (2010) Cloud Computing and Sustainability: The Environmental Benefits of Moving to the Cloud, http://www.accenture.com/SiteCollectionDocuments/PDF/Accenture_Sustainability_Cloud_Computing_TheEnvironmentalBenefitsofMovingtotheCloud.pdf (accessed April 2012).

Allalouf, M., Arbitman, Y., Factor, M. *et al.* (2009) Storage modelling for power estimation. In Proceedings of 2009 Israeli Experimental Systems Conference (SYSTOR '09), Israel.

Allenotor, D. and Thulasiram, R.K. (2008) Grid resources pricing: A novel financial option based quality of service-profit quasi-static equilibrium model. In Proceedings of the 8th ACM/IEEE International Conference on Grid Computing, Tsukuba.

Allman, M., Christensen, K., Nordman, B. and Paxson, V. (2007) Enabling an energy-efficient future internet through selectively connected end systems. In Proceedings of the Sixth ACM Workshop on Hot Topics in Networks (HotNets-VI), Atlanta, Georgia.

Baliga, J., Ayre, R., Hinton, K. and Tucker, R.S. (2010) Green cloud computing: balancing energy in processing, storage and transport. *Proceedings of the IEEE*, **99** (1), 149–167.

Bash, C. and Forman, G. (2007) Cool job allocation: Measuring the power savings of placing jobs at cooling-efficient locations in the datacenter. In Proceeding of 2007 Annual Technical Conference on USENIX, Santa Clara, CA.

Beloglazov, A., Buyya, R., Lee, Y.C. and Zomaya, A. (2011) A taxonomy and survey of energy-efficient data centers and cloud computing systems, in *Advances in Computers* (ed. M. Zelkowitz), Elsevier, Amsterdam, 47–111.

Bianchini, R. and Rajamony, R. (2004) Power and energy management for server systems. *Computer*, **37** (11), 68–74.

Bianzino, P., Chaudet, C., Rossi, D. and Rougier, J. (2010) A survey of green networking research. *IEEE Communications Surveys and Tutorials*, http://arxiv.org/pdf/1010.3880.pdf (accessed April 2012).

Buyya, R., Yeo, C.S. and Venugopal, S. (2008) Market-oriented cloud computing: Vision, hype, and reality for delivering it services as computing utilities. In Proceedings of the 10th IEEE International Conference on High Performance Computing and Communications, Los Alamitos, CA.

Chabarek, J., Sommers, J., Barford, P. *et al.* (2008) Power awareness in network design and routing. In Proceedings of 27th IEEE INFOCOM, Pheonix, AZ.

Charrington, S. (2010) Characteristics of Platform as a Service, Cloud Pulse blog, http://cloudpul.se/posts/the-essential-characteristics-of-paas (accessed April 2012).

Chase, J.S., Anderson, D.C., Thakar, P.N. *et al.* (2001) Managing energy and server resources in hosting centers. In Proceedings of 18th ACM Symposium on Operating Systems Principles (SOSP '01), Banff.

Cherkasova, L. and Gardner, R. (2005) Measuring CPU overhead for I/O processing in the Xen virtual machine monitor. In Proceeding of the 2005 Annual Technical Conference on USENIX, Anaheim, CA.

Freeh, V.W., Pan, F., Kappiah, N. *et al.* (2005) Exploring the energy-time trade-off in MPI programs on a power-scalable cluster. In Proceedings of the 19th IEEE International Parallel and Distributed Processing Symposium, CA.

Garg, S.K., Yeo, C.S., Anandasivam, A. and Buyya, R. (2011) Environment-conscious scheduling of HPC applications on distributed cloud-oriented datacenters. *Journal of Parallel and Distributed computing (JPDC)*, **71** (6), 732–749.

Giri, R.A. (2010) Increasing Datacenter Efficiency with Server Power Measurements. http://download.intel.com/it/pdf/Server_Power_Measurement_final.pdf (accessed April 2012).

Gleeson, E. (2009) Computing Industry Set for a Shocking Change, http://www.moneyweek.com/investment-advice/computing-industry-set-for-a-shocking-change-43226.aspx (accessed April 2012).

Google App Engine (2010) http://code.google.com/appengine/ (accessed April 2012).

Greenberg, S., Mills, E., Tschudi, B. *et al.* (2008) Best practices for data centers: Lessons learned from benchmarking 22 data centers. In ACEEE Summer Study on Energy Efficiency in Buildings, http://evanmills.lbl.gov/pubs/pdf/aceee-datacenters.pdf (accessed April 2012) .

Greenpeace International (2010) Make IT Green, http://www.greenpeace.org/international/en/publications/reports/make-it-green-cloud-computing/ (accessed April 2012).

Großschädl, J., Avanzi, R.M., Savas E. and Tillich S. (2005) Energy-efficient software implementation of long integer modular arithmetic. In Proceedings of 7th Workshop on Cryptographic Hardware and Embedded Systems, Edinburg.

Gurumurthi, S., Stan, M.R. and Sankar, S. (2009) Using intra-disk parallelism to build energy-efficient storage systems. In IEEE Micro Special Issue on Top Picks from the Computer Architecture Conferences of 2008.

Heath, T., Centeno, A.P., George, P. *et al.* (2006) Mercury and Freon: Temperature emulation and management for server systems. In Proceedings of Twelfth International Conference on Architectural Support for Programming Languages and Operating Systems, San Jose, CA.

IBM (2008) Take the Tennis to 1.9 Billion Viewers Worldwide? Done, http://www-935.ibm.com/services/au/cio/pdf/tic14027auen.pdf (accessed April 2012) .

Kaushik, R.T., Cherkasova, L., Campbell, R. and Nahrstedt, K. (2010) Lightning: Self-adaptive, energy-conserving, multi-zoned, commodity green cloud storage system. In Proceedings of the 19th ACM International Symposium on High Performance Distributed computing (HPDC '10), ACM, New York.

Kephart, J.O., Chan, H., Das, R. *et al.* (2007) Coordinating multiple autonomic managers to achieve specified power-performance tradeoffs. In Proceedings of 4th International Conference on Autonomic Computing, Florida.

Mayo, R.N. and Ranganathan P. (2005) Energy consumption in mobile devices: Why future systems need requirements-aware energy scale-down. Proceedings of 3rd International Workshop on Power-Aware Computer Systems, San Diego, CA.

Mell, P. and Grance, T. (2009) *The NIST Definition of Cloud Computing*, National Institute of Standards and Technology, Gaithersburg, MD.

Microsoft Azure (2011) http://www.microsoft.com/windowsazure/ (accessed April 2012).

Moore, J.D., Chase, J.S. and Ranganathan, P. (2006) Weatherman: Automated, online and predictive thermal mapping and management for datacenters. In Proceedings of the 3rd International Conference on Autonomic Computing, Dublin.

Nathuji, R. and Schwan, K. (2007) VirtualPower: Coordinated power management in virtualized enterprise systems. In Proceedings of 21st ACM SIGOPS Symposium on Operating Systems Principles, Stevenson, WA.

Raghavendra, R., Ranganathan, P., Talwar, V. *et al.* (2008) No "power" struggles: Coordinated multi-level power management for the datacenter. *SIGOPS Operating System Review*, **42** (2), 48–59.

Ramos, L. and Bianchini, R. (2008) C-oracle: Predictive thermal management for data centers. In Proceedings of 14th International Symposium on High–Performance Computer Architecture, Salt Lake City, UT.

Ranganathan, P. (2010) Recipe for efficiency: Principles of power-aware computing. *Communication ACM*, **53** (4), 60–67.

Ranganathan, P., Leech, P., Irwin, D. and Chase, J. (2006) Ensemble level power management for dense blade servers. *SIGARCH Computer Architecture News*, **34** (2), 66–77.

Rawson, A., Pfleuger, J. and Cader, T. (2008) Green Grid Data Center Power Efficiency Metrics, Consortium Green Grid, http://www.thegreengrid.org/Global/Content/white-papers/The-Green-Grid-Data-Center-Power-Efficiency-Metrics-PUE-and-DCiE (accessed April 2012).

Rivoire, S., Shah, M.A., Ranganathan, P. and Kozyrakis, C. (2007) Joulesort: A balanced energy-efficiency benchmark. In Proceedings of the 2007 ACM SIGMOD International Conference on Management of Data, NY.

Sarokin, D. (2007) Question: Energy Use of Internet, http://uclue.com/?xq=724 (accessed April 2012).

Saxe, E. (2008) Power efficient software. *Communication of the ACM*, **53** (2), 44–48.

Smith, J. and Nair, R. (2003) *Virtual Machines: Versatile Platforms for Systems and Processes*, Morgan Kaufmann, Los Altos, CA.

Song, Y., Sun, Y., Wang, H. and Song, X. (2007) An adaptive resource flowing scheme amongst VMs in a VM-based utility computing. In Proceedings of IEEE International Conference on Computer and Information Technology, Fukushima.

Soror, A.A., Minhas, U.F., Aboulnaga, A. *et al.* (2008) Automatic virtual machine configuration for database workloads. In Proceedings of ACM SIGMOD International Conference on Management of data, Vancouver.

Srikantaiah, S., Kansal, A. and Zhao, F. (2008) Energy aware consolidation for cloud computing. In Proceedings of HotPower '08 Workshop on Power Aware computing and Systems, San Diego, CA.

Vecchiola, C., Chu, X. and Buyya, R. (2009) Aneka: A software platform for. NET-based cloud computing, in *High Performance and Large Scale Computing, Advances in Parallel Computing* (ed. W. Gentzsch, L. Grandinetti and G. Joubert), IOS Press, Amsterdam, 267–297.

Verma, A., Koller, R., Useche, L. and Rangaswami, R. (2010) SRCMap: energy proportional storage using dynamic consolidation. In Proceedings of the 8th USENIX Conference on File and Storage Technologies (FAST'10), San Jose, California, 2010.

Woods, A. (2010) Cooling the data center. *Communications of the ACM*, **53** (4), 36–42.

17

Harnessing Semantic Web Technologies for the Environmental Sustainability of Production Systems

Chris Davis, Igor Nikolic and Gerard Dijkema
Energy & Industry Section, Faculty of Technology, Policy and Management, Delft University of Technology, Delft, The Netherlands

Key Points

- Describes our modern society as a highly networked global system, connected by mass, energy, money and information flows.
- Examines some of the tools for the collection, sharing and curation of the information that facilitates research and decision making.
- Describes an ecosystem of tools, based around Sematic MediaWiki, that enable (linked) information on networks to be stored, used and updated with minimal cost, allowing for far greater efficiency of data use.

17.1 Introduction

The modern world is dependent on complex networks of many forms (Barabasi, 2003) – a web of production chains that convert raw resources into the products and services required for society to function. These products and services include food, shelter, clothing, consumer products, flood protection through dikes, education, financial services, transportation systems, waste management and continuous and reliable electrical power supply and clean water.

Harnessing Green IT: Principles and Practices, First Edition. Edited by San Murugesan and G.R. Gangadharan.

As concerns about environmental sustainability mount, there is greater interest in understanding the *metabolic* pathways underlying these products and services as well as their material and energy use, socio-economic characteristics and environmental effects. A better understanding of this will enable us to reduce our carbon footprint, develop alternative energy sources, increase agricultural productivity with minimal impact on the environment and secure the sustained availability of metals through material recovery and recycling.

Though some companies control a significant part of particular supply chains at a national, continental or global level, the networks that form the fabric of modern society are *not* controlled or managed by a single company or government organization, but by a large number of individuals and organizations, all pursuing their own goals.

The knowledge about *what* these networks are and *how* they operate is vast and interlinked, and hence they are not the subject of a single scientific, engineering or management discipline. Further, such collective information is not contained in a single management information system. As a result, it is very difficult and tedious to trace the paths that products took on their journey from extraction of raw materials to their ultimate disposal. This complicates efforts to elucidate the energy use, land use and negative external effects associated with these paths and makes life-cycle analysis (LCA) extremely complex and difficult (Guinee, 2002). This creates an enormous challenge in our efforts to evolve towards a sustainable society, where finding a new balance between ecology, economy and equity requires us to dramatically innovate, change and transform these networks.

Information technology (IT) has enabled and helped us to shape production systems, and has had a significant impact on business administration, industrial manufacturing and management. Science, research and development, strategy and policy can be supported by powerful models and simulations. IT can aid a business in a variety of ways which helps in improving its operational efficiency and strategic advantage. Philip and Booth (2001) have identified several of these areas:

- **Survival:** Making internal operations more efficient, by automating tasks such as accounting and manufacturing.
- **Sources and resources:** Aiding in the acquisition of resources from suppliers, making the processing of these resources more efficient and helping with marketing of products and services.
- **Strategy:** Using the full potential of these resources for gaining competitive advantage.
- **Service value analysis (SVA):** Finding new business models and ways of doing things.
- **Cyberspace:** Facilitating the creation of virtual organizations by more efficiently linking employees with suppliers and customers.
- **Sustainability:** Harnessing IT aids in the management and enabling of the areas identified here.

These functions are, however, focussed on the use, role and added value of IT in single organizations.

Figure 17.1 positions a number of well-known IT systems and applications in an Ansoff matrix, where the horizontal axis indicates the degree to which a particular type of IT system is used by either a single organization or multiple organizations, while the vertical axis runs from support for a single or few activities (bottom) to multiple activities (top). In the lower-left quadrant we find the IT systems in use by business and

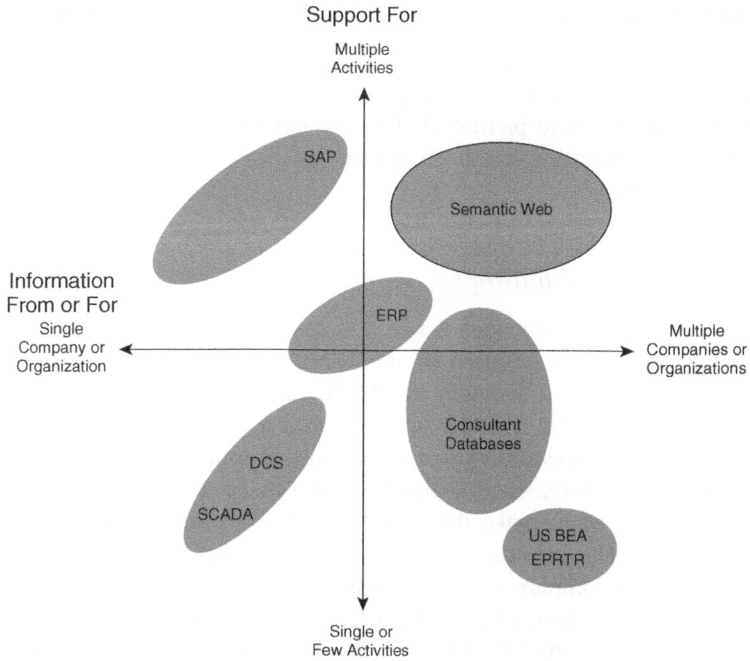

Figure 17.1 Overview of IT use and availability.

government organizations alike, such as computerized control systems (e.g. a supervisory control and data acquisition system (SCADA) or distributed control system (DCS)); design, engineering and manufacturing (computer-aided design or manufacturing (CAD or CAM, respectively); computer-aided engineering (CAE); computer-integrated manufacturing (CIM)) and enterprise resource planning (ERP) systems. The most extensive system for entire-business process management such as SAP integrates many of the functionalities of other IT systems to allow the management of every activity in a company – from ordering parts, to assembly, to billing the customer and paying employees' salary. It supports multiple activities for a single organization. In the lower-right quadrant are the databases maintained by statistics offices, such as the US Bureau of Economic Analysis (BEA), the European Pollutant Release and Transfer Registry (EPRTR) and many proprietary knowledge and databases maintained by consulting companies such as SRI-international and ChemSystems that often focus on a single sector.

The upper-right quadrant in Figure 17.1 focusses on the support of multiple activities by multiple companies – the complex network that forms the fabric of society. In this chapter, we examine the tools and technologies that populate this quadrant and help us manage these networks, our finite resources, and transform the way we cater for our needs. Thus we explore greening society through the use of IT. First, we examine the challenges we face in greening our society and the major implications for (novel) IT systems explored. Next, to address the challenges, we present a semantic software infrastructure. Then we illustrate this with examples of what is possible with semantic technologies. We conclude with a discussion and reflection on these, and an outlook on what may emerge.

17.2 Information Management for Environmental Sustainability

Approaching issues of environmental sustainability is difficult for a number of reasons. Firstly, the systems we deal with are often dynamic, complex and difficult to conceptualize. Secondly, gaining an accurate picture of these systems often requires large amounts of data, and not enough attention has been devoted to developing information systems to help manage these data.

17.2.1 Invisible Coordination

To illustrate the enormous challenges we face in evolving towards a sustainable society, consider what the economist Leonard (Read, 1956) has stated: *No single person really knows how to make a pencil*. Even in the 1950s, the components of a humble mass-produced pencil were sourced globally and involved a multitude of complex skill sets, ranging from chemistry to metallurgy to a knowledge of multimodal logistics. This is still only a small part of the story, since in order to even make a pencil, one must first make the things that are needed to make the pencil, and those things in turn also need other things to make them. The creation of what may seem like a simple artefact is in fact enabled only through a complex network composed of multiple levels of dependencies.

So, while people may not be contributing their know-how specifically with the goal of keeping humanity well supplied with pencils, this outcome emerges through coordination mechanisms embedded within economic markets. As the purchasing decisions of billions of people accumulate, propagating information signals ripple throughout the economic network. At each node in the network, these signals are interpreted by a variety of people who act on this information, whose actions in turn propagate and influence the actions of others.

Existing coordination mechanisms work quite well at creating and directing the signals that mobilize raw resources through their journey into complex products, where actors at various stages in the chain do not have to be aware of each other in order to function. However, this is also part of the problem, and these mechanisms are not very good at dealing with negative externalities, or unintended consequences where the parties responsible for an impact (e.g. pollution or resource depletion) are not the same ones that bear the costs. In other words, when cause and effect are at different ends of the chain, it can be difficult to address these problems.

17.2.2 Sustainability and Networks

While Read takes a first step in illuminating the complexity of economic networks, this is still only a small part of the whole picture. The issue is not just that these networks are connected in complex ways, but also that these networks may generate negative externalities. We need to get better at understanding *both* where these happen and *why* they happen.

Addressing sustainability issues means first identifying what these networks look like, and then understanding the types of interventions that can be made to either stop or reduce the impact of the problems. There is already a major body of work done by many research communities on understanding material and energy flows in networks (Suh, 2004). While this has provided an important foundation, it is acknowledged that this is not enough, and that we need to understand these networks as complex systems which are composed of the interactions between both social and technical networks (Dijkema and Basson, 2009).

For example, there have been persistent questions about whether more energy is needed to produce ethanol than is contained in it as an energy carrier (Farrell *et al.*, 2006). This requires looking at the energy inputs of the entire technical network from production on the farm, to transportation, to fuel production and finally delivery to the customer. While this gives a picture of what is happening, actually dealing with this issue involves understand social and economic issues such as the role of the corn industry in the United States. As another example, in considering whether the use of palm oil as a fuel source can reduce CO_2 emissions, one has to consider if the palm oil plantation was created from the conversion of peatland, since this act of land conversion results in an enormous release of greenhouse gases (Danielsen *et al.*, 2009), which may obliterate the desired benefits. Solving this is about not just understanding technologies, but also understanding the socioeconomic pressures and incentives that may drive people towards either beneficial or destructive outcomes. We need to be able to both traverse these networks by following their relevant links, and understand the context in which different elements of these networks operate. Solutions that work in one area may not work in others due to various reasons, such as existing policy and legislation, along with the details of people's backgrounds and personal experiences.

17.2.3 Need for Information Management Techniques

While we see that we face an issue of the nature of the problems we're dealing with, there is another important issue of *how we organize ourselves to solve those problems*. The way in which these networks are currently researched is usually inadequate and fundamentally limiting. This is not a complaint about the quality of individual researchers' work, but rather is an acknowledgement of the fact that while people are documenting global networks composed of interconnected processes, they do not publish their data in a form that natively enables interconnection.

In response to these problems, there has been a push towards opening up data sources, particularly by leveraging the Web as a publishing platform. This is an important first step and is not without its difficulties due to the different licences and a multitude of formats associated with the data, along with a lack of awareness that some digital formats are more useful than others.

However, simply having open data is not enough. While this is a very positive development since it greatly increases the rate at which we can find information, the true difficulty lies in connecting these data describing networks and performing quality checks over them. For example, it is not unusual to find different names for the same products. Additionally, processes may be described in a very generic way (based on the stoichiometry of chemical reactions) or to a high level of detail based on the specific configurations of actual factories. Furthermore, mass balances may not be enforced, and data may be missing.

Since we are dealing with distributed networks of processes operated by diverse entities, connecting and curating these data will require a distributed collaborative process. In other words, we need to take peer review of these data to the next level, which can be greatly leveraged by recent advances in IT which can both facilitate social processes and automate the process of data maintenance. Furthermore, we need to set aside the *mythology of data quality* and recognize that even the most official and respected sources of data still have problems.

Online collaborative projects such as Wikipedia hint at a way forward, although this is not enough, and tools are needed that can also deal with structured data that can describe networks. Additionally, we need to begin using tools that enable a more favourable economics of information gathering, and this can be challenging due to the need to incorporate large amounts of information of a diverse nature.

Many Web sites have successfully leveraged the idea of the architecture of participation (O'Reilly, 2004) – they evolve and become better as a natural by-product of user interaction. For instance, this is quite evident with a project such as Wikipedia. For further information on the mechanisms that have enabled Wikipedia to be successful, see Nikolic and Davis (2012).

From the discussion in this section, we see that there are many challenges involved in dealing with issues of sustainability. In Section 17.3, we will describe a particular combination of technologies that we believe can be used to address these issues.

17.3 Ecosystem of Software Tools

We present an example of a semantic wiki platform to deal with process chain data. This platform allows for both unstructured and structured data to co-exist on the same pages so that users can contribute plain text to a page in order to help give context, while other types of data such as inputs, outputs and measurements can be annotated in such a way that this information can be retrieved using a formal query language, just as with a database. This enables the wiki to present a user-friendly view over a database and to natively support network data. A page describing a process contains links to pages for the products that constitute its inputs and outputs. Because these inputs and outputs are annotated as being structured data, we can run queries to automatically extract the connections that can be made between different processes with common inputs and outputs.

The particular software ecosystem, described in this section, offers stability and has a large developer community behind it. For example, MediaWiki software is the wiki engine running Wikipedia, and is commonly used by many other wikis as well. Another factor is that the software mentioned here is all open source, meaning that people needing particular functionality do not need to wait for the core team of developers to find time for improvements. As a result, there are over 1700 extensions to MediaWiki. If the core software does not contain a feature you need, then it is likely that someone has written an extension that may address your needs.

17.3.1 MediaWiki

The foundation of the wiki architecture is the MediaWiki platform, which provides the basic wiki functionality. This platform allows people to easily collaboratively edit pages and create links between them. This can be seen as enabling a type of document management, where people can edit the text describing things, and also conduct online discussions about issues relevant for the project. For a full overview, consult the MediaWiki documentation; however, several useful features are highlighted in the rest of this section.

17.3.1.1 Page History

Edits to any page are automatically logged with the date and user name recorded. All previous revisions of the page are saved, meaning that one can revert the text to an earlier version if necessary. Additionally, different versions can be compared in order to highlight changes that have been made between them. This greatly aids collaborative work since you can easily pinpoint what has happened to a page since your last edit to it. These data about edits can also be used to keep track of user contributions.

17.3.1.2 List of Recent Changes

The wiki contains a 'Special:RecentChanges' page that lists all of the latest edits to the wiki for the past several days. Instead of following all of the recent changes, by using the 'watchlists' feature users can specify the set of pages that they would like to monitor changes on. This allows for a community of people with different interests to monitor different sections of the wiki. Furthermore, the list of updates for these pages can be viewed directly on the wiki, or sent to the user via e-mail alerts.

17.3.1.3 Categories

These are tags applied to pages that are used to categorize the content of them, and multiple categories can be added to a single page. Whenever a category is added to a page, the corresponding page for that category is automatically updated to include the newly tagged page. These can be used for a variety of purposes such as highlight work to be done via 'Category:Needs Verification' or 'Category:Plastics Manufacturing' for describing different types of the same technology.

17.3.1.4 Templates

This is a special type of wiki page whose content can be embedded within many other wiki pages. This is particularly useful if there is a series of instructions or messages that you wish to duplicate across many pages. Whenever you want to update this text, you simply update the template and the changes will automatically appear on all the pages that contain the template. This is a useful tool to separate data from the structure used to present it. As will be discussed in Section 17.3.2 on Semantic MediaWiki, templates also help with entering in structured data that can then be queried.

17.3.1.5 Extensions

A benefit of the large community using MediaWiki is that a significant amount of software has been written to extend the wiki's core functionality. This means that if a desired feature is missing from the wiki software, then it is not unusual to find that someone has already created an extension to implement it.

17.3.1.6 Administrative Pages

For its management, MediaWiki offers several features for monitoring and managing the content of the wiki. It allows you to manage images, find all users, list user contributions and check statistics.

While the MediaWiki software is widely used, it has some limitations. For instance, the information contained on the wiki can be navigated only one page at a time (see Figure 17.2). While the information contained in MediaWiki is readable by humans, it cannot be automatically extracted and processed by computers, since information is presented in an unstructured format. Semantic MediaWiki, however, is aimed at overcoming this limitation. For processing by computers, information needs to be presented in a structured format.

17.3.2 Semantic MediaWiki

The Semantic MediaWiki extension runs on top of the MediaWiki software, and allows for structured data to be embedded on wiki pages. It uses standards defined for the Semantic Web. In brief, the *Semantic Web* is a set of standards and technologies that allow for much easier machine processing over data distributed over the Web, which may as it develops have profound implications for how we deal with information. This allows us to have a hybrid approach to data collection, where both structured and unstructured data are contained on the same pages.

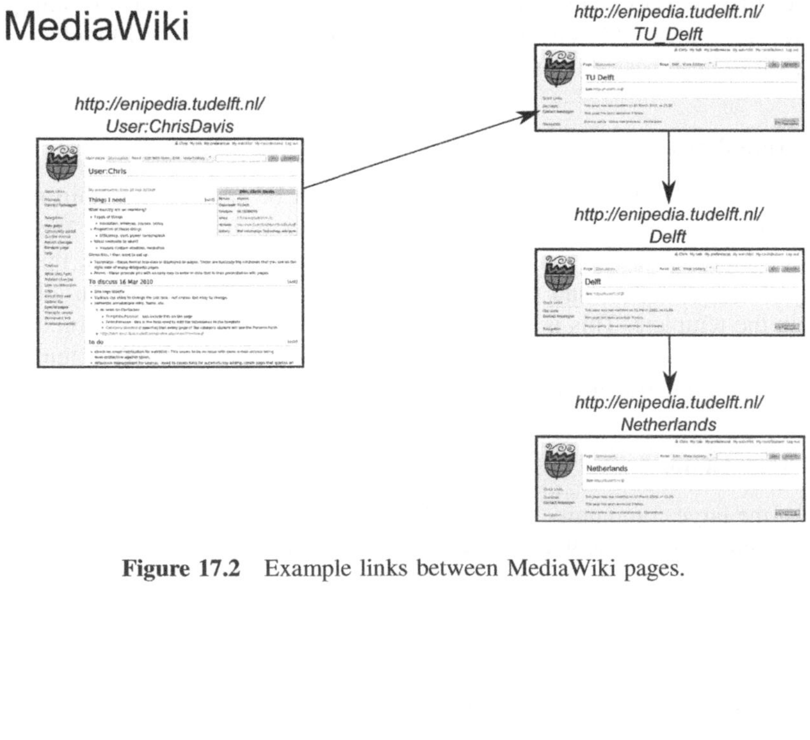

Figure 17.2 Example links between MediaWiki pages.

As shown in Figure 17.2, with a normal wiki, you can add links only between pages, and there is no meaning associated with that link. For example, you can see that my user page on the wiki contains various notes, and is also linked to a page about TU Delft, which links to a page on Delft, which in turn links to a page about the Netherlands. By reading through the connected pages, you will understand that I work for TU Delft, that TU Delft is located in the city of Delft and that Delft is a city in the Netherlands. The issue here is that the relationships between these different concepts is not machine readable, and can be processed only at the speed at which people can read. If users desire to get a listing of all the pages describing something located in Delft, they would have to search through all the pages on the site. By using Semantic MediaWiki, one can create 'typed links' by specifying a predicate (i.e. a property) associated with that link. For example, the link from the 'User:Chris' page to 'TU Delft' has the predicate of 'Employed by', which indicates the relationship between the concepts of 'User:Chris' and 'TU Delft', as shown in Figure 17.3. With this structured information, we are creating triples, or statements in the form of *subject*, *predicate* and *object*, as shown in Table 17.1. These can be understood as being simple sentences like 'Apple has colour red' and 'Red is type of colour'. With the Semantic MediaWiki software, the subject is always the name of a page. The object can be a link to another page, or a literal, which is a value that is a type of string, number or Boolean.

In practice, this system has yielded some promising results. For example, a Semantic Wiki was used as a platform for a class of MSc students tasked with evaluating eco-industrial parks (Wouters and Feldmar, 2010). These industrial parks are billed as being more sustainable than regular industrial parks, due to activities such as the reuse of waste heat and waste materials as inputs to other industrial processes. The problem is that any park can claim to be 'eco-industrial', and there had yet to be a systematic evaluation of

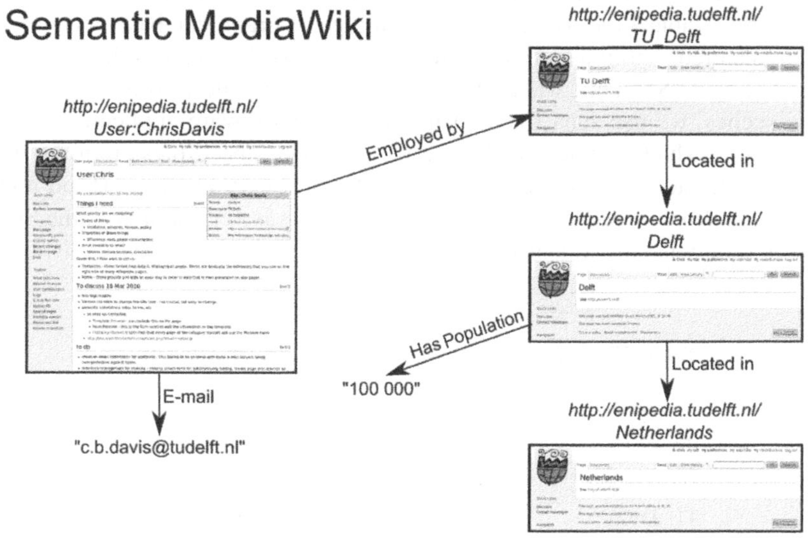

Figure 17.3 Example of semantic links between Semantic MediaWiki pages.

these claims. The wiki was an enabling factor as the students were able to document over 200 parks and 100 of the literature references describing them. The semantic nature of the wiki was used for tasks such as dynamically generating maps showing all the parks that had passed the student-defined criteria, and also highlighting the parks that still needed to be evaluated. In two months, the wiki had become the largest resource of its kind on the web, and has since been visited by researchers from over 56 countries. The visualization of these parks on a map led researchers to quickly comment on mistakes in the data. The semantic nature of the wiki enabled efficient quality control than what is practically possible if one had to read through all the pages. Further, the fact that data were live on the Web enabled us to take advantage of situations where we were in a room full of experts and were able to fix problems in real time.

The Semantic MediaWiki software is being used in projects, such as OpenEI.org, a wiki about energy topics run by the US National Renewable Energy Laboratory and the US Department of Energy (2009). Further it is also being used in other domains including, health (Boulos, 2009) and biology (Waldrop, 2008). What these projects have in common is that they all need to aggregate and manage decentralized information.

17.3.3 SparqlExtension

With the current version of Semantic MediaWiki, it is not possible to query the data contained in the wiki from external software, and to find information on the wiki, you have to use the wiki software itself. This is in contrast to typical software applications where one could use a database driver to connect to and retrieve information from the database. To fix this issue, as an extension to Semantic MediaWiki, the SparqlExtension (Chmieliauskas and Davis, 2010) developed at TU Delft is used.

This software synchronizes the structured semantic data in the wiki with a triplestore, which is a special type of database for storing triples of the 'subject–predicate–object' form as shown in Table 17.1. The triplestore is a type of graph database, meaning that the information is stored within a web of interconnected facts. Figure 17.4 illustrates how the data structured using Semantic MediaWiki in Figure 17.3 would look as a graph database. Behind the scenes, we use Jena for the triplestore, and software applications are able to access via Joseki, which provides a Web service allowing the triplestore to be queried.

The SparqlExtension allows one to use the SPARQL query language (Prud'hommeaux and Seaborne, 2008) to retrieve structured wiki data. This is very similar to the SQL query language for traditional relational databases, although it is developed explicitly to deal

Table 17.1 Example of triples in the form of *subject*, *predicate* and *object*

Subject	Predicate	Object
User:Chris	Employed by	TU Delft
TU Delft	Located in	Delft
Delft	Has population	100 000
Delft	Located in	Netherlands

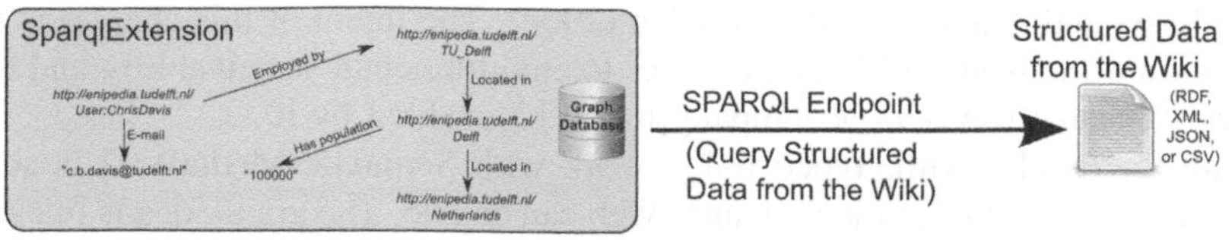

Figure 17.4 Illustration of SparqlExtension.

with graph databases. SPARQL is more powerful than the inline queries natively allowed in Semantic MediaWiki and enables one to extract complicated relationships from the data. For instance, it is possible to create SPARQL queries to search the 1200 pages describing renewable energy generation facilities on the http://OpenEI.org semantic wiki, and use this to visualize trends in the growth of renewable energy production for several different fuel sources (Davis, 2010). One of the advantages of using SPARQL is that it allows you to be as generic or as specific as you need. For example, can query 'select * where { ? x ? y ? z }' which is equivalent to asking 'find me a "something" "has something" "something else"', which will return everything in the database.

The SparqlExtension also includes a number of visualization techniques such as Google Chart Tools and Graphviz (Ellson *et al.*, 2002). The data returned from queries are reformatted and fed to the visualization module, and the resulting visualizations can be embedded directly into wiki pages.

The triplestore can be accessed through what is called a SPARQL Endpoint, which is a Web service accessible via a URL to which query strings are passed, along with other parameters that specify the format that the data should be received back in, such as RDF, XML, JSON or CSV.

While the examples described in this section involve a centralized approach, a key strength of using a semantic wiki is that the data are not locked into the site. Through the use of open standards, others can access, query and download the data for their use in common data formats such as RDF, XML, JSON and CSV. Thus the information is portable and can be reused in different applications with different tools.

Just as this extension allows easier access to information in the wiki by external programmes, it can also query remote sources (i.e. other SPARQL endpoints, running the same protocols and standards) through federated queries (Harris and Seaborne, 2010; Seaborne, 2007). This information can also be redisplayed on the wiki in output formats and visualization forms. This facilitates sharing and integrating data from different sources or applications facilitating collaboration. This is a significant feature as it allows data to be used from, or for, multiple activities of several companies and organizations. While, a 'traditional' wiki is often a solution for a single company or organization, the ecosystem of software tools that we describe here does indeed cover the aspects shown in the top-right quadrant of the matrix. We will elaborate on this here and illustrate how this is just one piece of a much larger system.

17.3.4 Semantic Web

Both Semantic MediaWiki and the SPARQLExtension use technologies developed for the Semantic Web, the intricacies of which have been described in detail by Allemang and

Hendler (2008) and Antoniou and Harmelen (2008). The intent of this chapter is to show an application of Semantic Web technologies to environmental sustainability and illustrate a social process that can both accompany it and be enabled by it.

The way that triples with 'typed links' work with Semantic MediaWiki is actually a miniature realization of what the Semantic Web can enable. The grand idea is to eventually enable this with the entire Web. Just as someone can currently create a blog post and link to a *BBC News* article without the BBC having to be concerned about this, with the Semantic Web users can create their own data sets (or collection of facts) and interlink them with other data sets without other parties having to worry about issues of ownership. This is not about creating one giant perfect database of everything, but it is about making it easier for machines to usefully navigate the intended meaning of information on the Web. For example, this collection of technologies can make it easier for consumers to compare the products offered by different companies (Hepp, 2008). This type of comparison is greatly enabled by using standard ways of describing things.

People using the Semantic Web for research may still have to deal with conflicting or erroneous facts, but the Semantic Web would make it easier to find and fix these problems. In our work, we have often encountered what we call the 'mythology of data quality', where people assume that data sets from governments and large organizations are by default very accurate. We have used Semantic Web technologies such as SPARQL to quickly search through complex relationships defined in these data sets and can with little effort usually locate certain types of common problems.

17.3.4.1 DBpedia

An easy-to-understand example of a Semantic Web application is DBpedia, which is a version of Wikipedia where structured data embedded on wiki pages has been converted into a semantic format. DBpedia extracts information about categories on pages, along with information from their infoboxes. For example, the page on the Netherlands indicates that it falls within the categories of 'Dutch-speaking countries' and 'Members of the North Atlantic Treaty Organization', among more than 10 other categories. The infobox for the Netherlands contains structured information, such as the capital, national anthem and official language. What is interesting about this approach is that DBpedia does not just list facts about the Netherlands, but also contains facts about the facts concerning the Netherlands. What DBpedia provides is a massive web of machine-readable facts. This provides opportunities for information retrieval and synthesis beyond the capabilities of traditional search engines.

The development of the DBpedia project is proceeding in several interesting directions that aim to improve its quality. One of the problems of DBpedia involves mapping between properties contained in Wikipedia infoboxes and those properties defined in the DBpedia ontology. For example, infoboxes might use different property names to describe the same types of things, and it is useful to try to use the same property name to describe these. These mappings cover an enormous number of infoboxes, meaning that it is difficult for a small team of people to maintain these. To fix this, DBpedia has created a mappings wiki (DBpedia, 2011) that anyone can contribute to, which allows people to specify how specific fields in the infoboxes should be mapped to the DBpedia ontology. These mappings are then fed to the extraction framework, which controls how it maps infobox properties to properties in the DBpedia ontology. The extraction framework (Bizer *et al.*, 2009) is responsible for reading the contents of wiki pages and extracting structured data from the infoboxes and other features such as categories and redirect links.

Another problem is that the extraction framework cannot always properly extract information. Since this software can freely be downloaded, more technical users can extend the extraction framework to better deal with difficult-to-parse information that may not be in a consistent format.

Some information on the DBpedia could be out of date. At present, the data in DBpedia are revised every few months from a database dump of Wikipedia, so there is a lag between when new information is entered into Wikipedia, and when it shows up in DBpedia. Measures such as dynamic mirroring of Wikipedia to DBpedia (Hellmann *et al.*, 2009) address this limitation.

A special feature of the ecosystem of tools described here, compared to some other combinations, is that it supports both a social dialogue regarding information collection and curation, while also allowing for rather sophisticated techniques to be applied to the data. The ability of these tools to work with the Semantic Web presents potential for further advancement.

17.4 Examples of Managing Data

In this section, we describe how this software can be used in combination with a social process to document the flows of products from their extraction as raw resources to consumption to final disposal. We employ three different types of pages. Firstly, we use pages that are used to describe different commodities or types of flows. For example, this means that there will be pages that represent the concepts of 'Polystyrene', 'Carbon dioxide' and 'Electricity'. Secondly, we use pages that describe processes that convert some set of inputs to some set of outputs. These are linked to the commodity or flow pages. Thirdly, we also create pages that can give automatically updated overviews and summaries of the state of the data that have been collected.

A key concept that supports the management of data is the use of page URLs as unique identifiers for objects. For example, there is a single page for 'Carbon dioxide', meaning that whenever a process has carbon dioxide as an output, we can link to that specific page, so we unambiguously know that these processes all have the same type of output. This helps to avoid any confusion instead of having to distinguish between pages describing 'Carbon Dioxide', 'CO_2' or 'Carbonic oxide'. The same idea is used for identifying processes. There may be a single page describing a process at a very general level based on its mass balance, while other pages may describe particular implementations of that process within actual factories.

17.4.1 Pages for Commodities

The page for a commodity acts as a hub for information about it. This contains information about alternative names, general properties and links to outside resources, some of which are retrieved by the wiki software to aid the process of data management.

While having a single page representing the concept of a particular commodity is valuable, it is still not enough. One issue is that many commodities may have different names. To get around this issue, we include on each page a link to that commodity's corresponding Wikipedia page. Including a link to Wikipedia is clearly valuable since it gives people more information. At the same time, it provides the software with more information that it can use for maintenance. By using the URL for the Wikipedia page, we can then find the corresponding DBpedia page, which can then be queried to get the alternative names. We can then for every commodity page, assign this list of alternative names and then set up a query where all the other pages that use one of these alternative names is identified, in other words, showing us the duplicate pages on the wiki. Given this information, we can then clean up the wiki by merging pages. This would be done by creating redirect links from the 'unofficial names' to the 'official name' of the page.

The way that we use DBpedia is still very limited, and we have yet to fully explore its implications. For instance, the Wikipedia pages for commodities have a wealth of information such as Chemical Abstracts Service (CAS) numbers and chemical properties such as melting and boiling points. Additionally, the categories used on the Wikipedia pages can be useful for classification. For example, the page on chlorine mentions that it is in the categories of 'Halogens', 'Hazardous air pollutants' and 'Occupational safety and health', meaning that one could easily retrieve all the other chemicals that are in these categories as well.

Another step we have taken is in linking commodities to journal articles that talk about them. The idea is that there are large numbers of studies that have structured data about processes, but these data are not in an easily obtainable format, and are often available only as a table in a PDF document. To fix this, some data entry by hand is necessary, but people need to first know where to look.

To help with this linking, several requirements need to be in place. First, we need to know what we are looking for. Users could simply use the list of commodities that they have entered by hand on the wiki, although this is likely to be limited. To jump-start this process, we have gone to Wikipedia, found the page for the template used to specify the CAS number for chemicals and then found the link to the page listing all the wiki pages using this template. Doing this gives us a list of over 6000 wiki pages, which gives a rough estimate of chemicals that will likely be mentioned in literature. By combining this with information from DBpedia about alternative names, we suddenly have several tens of thousands of search terms. The next step is that we need the actual journal articles in PDF format. These files can then be converted into plain text, and a script can be run to find the number of times each of the search terms is found in each article. Another script is then set up to take this information and write it back to the wiki pages, where links are provided to the original journal article on the publisher's site. Doing this provides functionality that is not currently available, where computer searching using crowd-sourced information from Wikipedia helps people to more effectively locate the information they need despite multiple ways of describing the same commodities.

17.4.2 Pages for Processes

The next type of pages comprises those that document processes which convert a set of inputs into a set of outputs. To facilitate the documentation process, we use the Semantic Forms Extension (Koren, 2011a) which allows one to create standard forms where people can easily enter in structured data. Figure 17.5 shows an example of this for a page

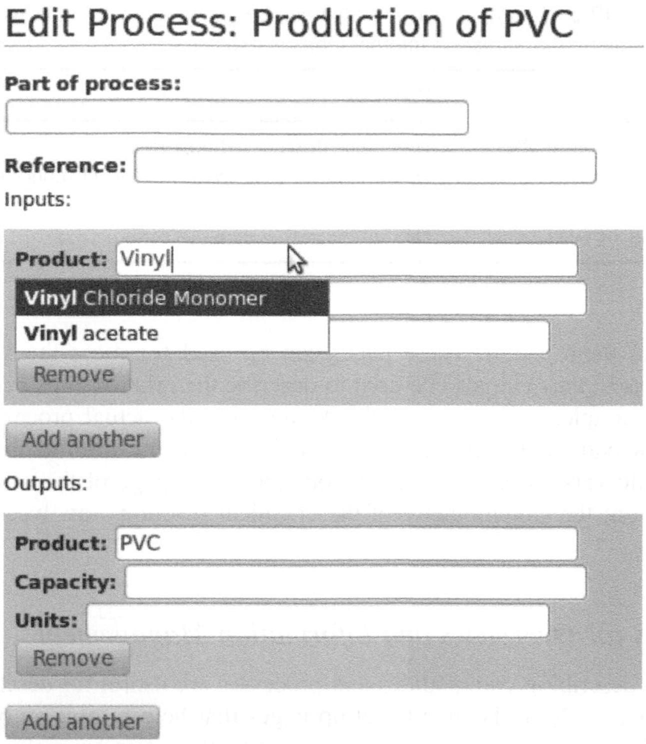

Figure 17.5 Example of editing process data with semantic forms. Automatic suggestions are based on pages for existing commodities.

describing a generic process for the production of polyvinyl chloride (PVC). We have set up the form so that for every type of input and output, we can specify the product involved, the amount (capacity) and the units that are associated with that amount. When one starts typing in 'Vinyl', several options are automatically suggested. These suggestions are dynamically generated from the list of pages on the wiki describing commodities. This ability is quite important for aligning the terms in use, so that one does not use slightly different terms or spellings for the same commodity.

With this example, we also use the Semantic Internal Objects (Koren, 2011b) in conjunction with Semantic Forms. The issue is that Semantic MediaWiki allows for the embedding of triples on a single wiki page, where the subject of the triples is the URL of the page. The problem here is that we are embedding triples which describe hierarchical data, and therefore need to be represented by different subjects. In other words, when we describe processes, we are essentially describing recipes for making things. When we describe the input and output flows of the process, we need to know more than just what the flows are; we need to have additional information, such as how much of the flows to use. As shown in Table 17.2, to do this, we use Semantic Internal Objects to create new subjects such as 'input flow #1' and so on to attach this information to.

One of the advantages of using a semantic wiki as an information-storing medium is that it allows for a flexible data structure, where one can add additional properties over

Table 17.2 Example of triples that can be encoded on a single wiki page using the Semantic Internal Objects extension

Subject	Predicate	Object
Production of PVC	Has input flow	Input flow #1
Input flow #1	Has product	Vinyl chloride monomer
Input flow #1	Has amount	1000
Input flow #1	Has units	Kilograms

time as they find them useful. These pages can be used for more than just describing individual processes; they can also be used to describe the relationships between different processes. For example, one could use this to describe the actual process configuration existing within a particular factory, while specifying that the information on that page 'is a more specific version of' information contained on a page of the same process, but derived solely from the stoichiometry of the chemical reactions involved describing the unit process.

17.4.3 Pages for Overviews and Information Management

While the pages describing commodities and processes are useful for describing concepts of things, it is also useful to be able to set up pages that help to give an overview of the data and also allow us to identify areas needing attention. For example, since we have already semantically described processes and the commodities that flow between them, it is now possible to extract a network that shows all the permutations for how different processes can connect to each other. Below is an example of the SPARQL query that is used to query the semantic structures contained in the wiki pages.

```
select ?process_1_label ?process_1
       ?product_label ?product
       ?process_2_label ?process_2 where {
   #find a flow that is an output of some process
     ?process_1_output prop:Is_output_of ?process_1 .
   #this flow is of some product
     ?process_1_output prop:Product ?product .
   #get the label of this process
     ?process_1 rdfs:label ?process_1_label .
   #get the label of the product
     ?product rdfs:label ?product_label .
   #find a flow that is an input of some process
     ?process_2_input prop:Is_input_of ?process_2 .
   #get the label of this process
     ?process_2 rdfs:label ?process_2_label .
   #this flow is of the same product as the one found above
     ?process_2_input prop:Product ?product .
}
```

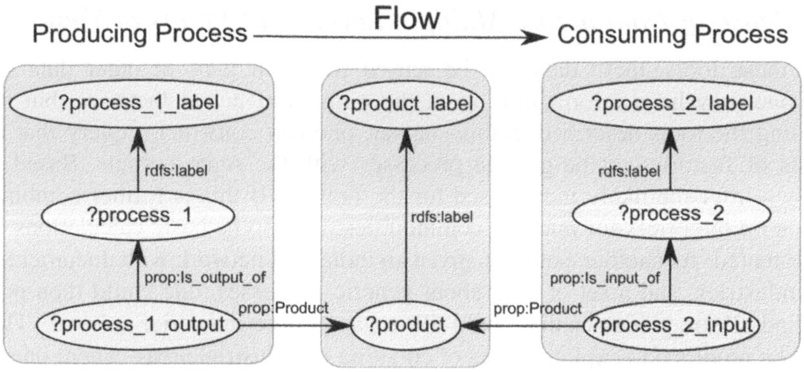

Figure 17.6 Visualization of a query used to find all the situations where the output of one process is also the input of another process.

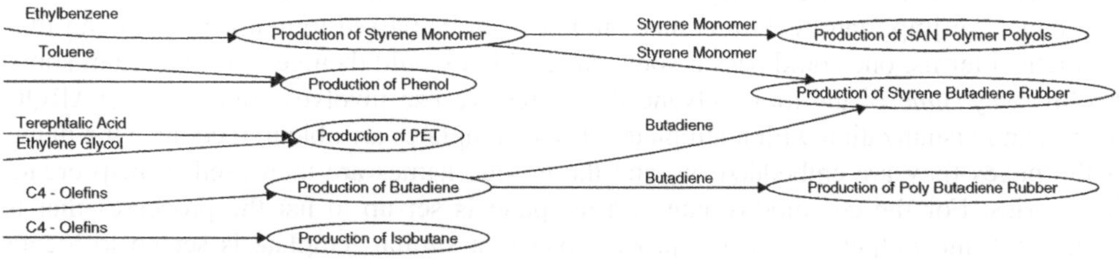

Figure 17.7 Portion of an automatically generated production network diagram. Visualized using the Graphviz library (Ellson *et al.*, 2002).

As illustrated in Figure 17.6, this query finds all the products that are an output of one process, and also the input of another process. The SPARQLExtension is used to query these data, and also visualize them in a network diagram, a subset of which is shown in Figure 17.7.

It should be noted that when SPARQL processes queries, it returns all possible permutations of results that match the desired pattern. Process networks can reveal new pathways through the network, based on compatible flows between different processes. For people looking at issues of sustainability, this may be helpful for exploring opportunities for increasing recycling or reuse of waste flows. As an example, if users were to define a process as having an output of waste heat at 200°C, they could then perform a query searching for all processes able to use waste heat of that temperature or lower as an input. Since with SPARQL, users can be as general or as specific as necessary, they could also modify the query shown here to look only at flows tagged as waste flows.

Queries can also be used to identify the boundaries of the data, such as highlighting products that are used as an input for a process, but for which its own manufacturing process is not defined. Based on this information, users are guided in the process of expanding the knowledge base, by being able to fill in information that they are aware of.

17.4.4 *Reuse of Data across Multiple Levels and Points of View*

By using these tools, these data can be reused to fill in gaps in other data sets. For example, one may have information about the outputs of actual factories, but not their inputs. Using the tools described in this chapter, one can construct a query that matches the outputs of factories to the generic processes with the same outputs. Based on this, one can then infer the likely inputs used for the factory. If this is further combined with information on the prices for relevant commodities, then some basic calculations of profit can be automated. As another example, given an industrial network with documented flows between industries, and a set of data about generic processes, one could then perform a query to find all the processes that could fill in gaps in the industrial network. The query could also be modified to explore issues of co-siting in industrial areas, where one seeks to identify utilities that may be shared, or identify industries with complementary activities.

Besides filling in gaps, the tools can navigate the data from different points of view, by using templates combined with queries. The MediaWiki software supports the use of templates, which can be thought of as wiki pages whose content is embedded on other pages. The contents of these templates can be the same as those contained on any normal wiki page. An important feature is that variables can be passed to template, meaning that in practical terms, one could pass it some data, which would then get reformatted in some 'useful' way. One of the more advanced features we use involves embedding SPARQL queries and visualization within templates. These templates are able to recognize the name of the pages they are embedded on, and these page names are then used to help create the queries. For the commodity pages, a template is set up to list the processes that it is an input and output of. For the process pages, a similar template is set up to locate the upstream and downstream processes that it can connect to based on reasoning about common inputs and output flows.

The use of a semantic wiki can to an extent facilitate the self-organization of data. Data entered in by users become part of a web of facts whose management is enabled through tools that query this web and guide the user in identifying knowledge gaps and exploring possible connections.

17.5 Challenges and Guiding Principles

In the following we discuss challenges arising from the domain-specific issues of the data and highlight helpful general principles that are applicable independent of the domain being studied.

17.5.1 *Challenges*

The Semantic Web–based tools discussed here offer a powerful system for collaborative gathering and curating of network data. While they are quite powerful and useful, several challenges remain, stemming from the nature of the networked data we are attempting to collect and curate. The key challenges are (i) conversion of data into formats used by current tools, (ii) the issue of different physical scales and levels of abstraction and (iii) the issue of the economics of data collection.

The issue of converting the data contained within the system into the different data formats used by current tools that analyse production chains is relatively easy to address. We have argued that the ecosystem of software tools described here is not a 'captive user interface' (Gancarz, 2003), and the challenge we face is not in getting data out of the system, but in getting the data into other systems, especially software tools that are designed with little thought of interoperability. We need to be able to remap the data into compatible formats. If these other tools use data formats in XML, then it is possible to use powerful tools such as XSLT (Clark, 1999), which is a translation language that allows remapping of XML documents into other formats. If XML is not used by these tools, then one would have to write custom converters. Within the field of LCA, this is already happening, and there has been significant work on creating a converter to specifically address this problem (Ciroth, 2007).

The second issue is related to the fact that economic and environmental information about processing networks involves many different physical and temporal scales. Furthermore, environmental analysis of production systems always involves a subjective choice of system boundaries. Levels of abstraction may also play a role.

Furthermore, there are issues related to the economics of data collection, specifically with regard to return on investment, in terms of the amount of benefit that people can receive given the amount of effort they put in. One should not get carried away and try to document all the properties of everything, which is clearly not feasible, since it is difficult to have a large enough community of people interested in both documenting and maintaining the data. One needs to be aware that *people need data and data need people*. It is hoped that by leveraging multiple communities with overlapping data needs, duplication of effort can be reduced, while increasing the benefits that people receive.

17.5.2 Guiding Principles

To help deal with these challenges, we have identified five guiding principles (Davis, Nikolic, and Dijkema, 2010). These are a mix of recommendations that deal with both social and technical aspects.

17.5.2.1 Connecting Both Producers and Consumers of Data

While it is important that people who need data are able to access it from those who gather it, the inability to connect this demand with supply may be either unintentional or deliberate. A key issue is that once someone compiles information, there is a question of if and how that information will be published. People gathering data may simply do so for their work, and then have it lie dormant on their hard drive where no one else can access it. They may also add it to an organizational database or knowledge management system, where a larger group of people may benefit. Alternatively, they may publish it in articles or on the Web to make it available to the rest of the world. What happens to this information is related to people's motivations, their technical skills and their concerns about how holding on to the information may lead to a strategic advantage. This last reason has led to a tension where the speed at which IT can rapidly and cheaply spread information around the world is only countered by those who can gain a competitive advantage by drastically slowing it (Brand, 1988; Clarke, 2000). While the situation with data is not the same in every domain, the trend commonly observed is that data are becoming so ubiquitous that we are seeing a shift in value away from merely possessing information, to that of having the skills to extract the relevant insights from it (Economist, 2010).

17.5.2.2 Facilitating Community Discussions and Discovery

Beyond just connecting the supply and demand of data, we also need to more effectively harness the energy of the communities working with the data. Combined with the previous guideline, this is a recognition of our statement that *people need data and data need people*. Once people have the data they need, the data need to benefit from the multitude of people exploring them. People will always find problems and have suggestions for how to improve data. This energy needs to be channelled instead of merely allowed to disperse.

17.5.2.3 Using Machine-Readable Open Formats

While sophisticated computer techniques exist for analysing data, the data need to first be in a format usable by computers. One must also realize that not all digital formats are equally useful. For example, while PDF works well for human-readable reports, it can be extremely difficult for computer programs to extract information from these files in a consistent and accurate way, even for structured items such as tables.

17.5.2.4 Using Open Standards, Open Source and Open Data

One should try to facilitate community creativity by reducing barriers where possible, while being aware that closed-source solutions will likely constrain what users can do with the information. Allow users of your data to surprise you with their creativity, and do not erect walls unless you absolutely have to.

17.5.2.5 Utilizing Shared Vocabularies

As much as possible, it is desirable to use consistent ways of describing things, since this greatly facilitates the act of searching through large amounts of data. A clear example would be to standardize a single way of describing geographic coordinates. However, it is also recognized that for certain types of information, it may be very difficult for different groups to agree on a shared vocabulary due to the complex nature of the knowledge being modelled.

17.6 Conclusions

We have explored emerging IT systems that we believe to be novel and capable of aiding the challenge of greening society. The various elements of this semantic software infrastructure have been detailed, with regard to both their technical elements and the features that support a social process. A series of examples were given to show the possibilities of this technology, based on our work in energy infrastructures and industrial networks. Through these examples, we illustrated how the process of documenting production networks is facilitated through this technology, through techniques such as using queries to highlight areas in need of attention, and also allowing the user to have multiple views over the data. From there we elucidated several challenges that will be faced in going forward, and gave guiding principles that hold promise in ameliorating the situation.

Semantic Web–based tools will help us leverage each other's work more effectively in building a much larger network of accessible knowledge. The challenge lies in scaling this up to a critical mass, and it is useful to keep in mind Metcalfe's Law (Gilder, 1993), which states that the value of a network increases exponentially with the number of users on it. This principle is being leveraged in order to jump-start the Semantic Web (Hendler and Golbeck, 2008), as evidenced through initiatives such as the Linking Open Data community project (Cyganiak, 2010; Heath, 2009).

Review Questions

1. Explain the architecture of Semantic MediaWiki.
2. What is the Semantic Web? Explain with an example.
3. How can software be used in combination with a social process to document the flows of products from their extraction?

Discussion Questions

1. How can people be incentivized to contribute when helping to build a collective database may not be part of their job description? How can issues of ownership and credit be dealt with?
2. How can we deal with the tension between centralizing and decentralizing data management?
3. The tools described here allow for documenting flows in a network. However, the information that is available may be of different qualities and levels of specificity. How do we allow these to co-exist without causing problems?
4. What are other applications that may be applied to sustainability? What are the relevant communities that may be engaged?

References

Allemang, D. and Hendler, J.A. (2008) *Semantic Web for the Working Ontologist: Modeling in RDF, RDFS and OWL*, Morgan Kaufmann, Waltham, MA.

Antoniou, G. and Harmelen, F.V. (2008) *A Semantic Web Primer*, 2nd edn, Cooperative Information Systems, MIT Press, Cambridge, MA.

Barabasi, A. (2003) *Linked: How Everything Is Connected to Everything Else and What It Means*, Plume, New York.

Bizer, C., Lehmann, J., Kobilarov, G. *et al.* (2009) DBpedia: A crystallization point for the web of data. *Journal of Web Semantics*, **7** (3), 154–165.

Boulos, M.N. (2009) Semantic wikis: A comprehensible introduction with examples from the health sciences. *Journal of Emerging Technologies in Web Intelligence*, **1** (1), 94.

Brand, S. (1988) *The Media Lab: Inventing the Future at MIT*, Penguin Books, New York.

Chmieliauskas, A. and Davis, C. (2010) Extension:SparqlExtension-MediaWiki, http://www.mediawiki.org/wiki/Extension:SparqlExtension (accessed April 2012).

Ciroth, A. (2007) ICT for environment in life cycle applications openLCA: A new open source software for life cycle assessment. *International Journal of Life Cycle Assessment*, **12** (4), 209–210.

Clark, J. (1999) XSL Transformations (XSLT) Version 1.0, http://www.w3.org/TR/xslt (accessed April 2012).

Clarke, R. (2000) Information Wants to Be Free, http://www.rogerclarke.com/II/IWtbF.html (accessed April 2012).

Cyganiak, R. (2010) About the Linking Open Data Dataset Cloud, http://richard.cyganiak.de/2007/10/lod/ (accessed April 2012).

Danielsen, F., Beukema, H., Burgess, N.D. *et al.* (2009) Biofuel plantations on forested lands: Double jeopardy for biodiversity and climate. *Conservation Biology*, **23** (2), 348–358.

Davis, C. (2010) Data Mining OpenEI.org, the US Department of Energy's Semantic Wiki, http://chrisdavis.weblog.tudelft.nl/2010/06/12/data-mining-the-us-department-of-energy (accessed April 2012).

Davis, C., Nikolic, I. and Dijkema, G.P.J. (2010) Industrial ecology 2.0. *Journal of Industrial Ecology*, **14**, 707–726.

DBpedia (2011) DBpedia Mappings, http://mappings.dbpedia.org/index.php/Main_Page (accessed April 2012).

Dijkema, G.P.J. and Basson, L. (2009) Complexity and industrial ecology. *Journal of Industrial Ecology*, **13** (2), 157–164.

Economist (2010) A Special Report on Managing Information: Data, Data Everywhere. *The Economist*, February 25, http://www.economist.com/node/15557443 (accessed April 2012).

Ellson, J., Gansner, E., Koutsofios, L. *et al.* (2002) Graphviz: Open source graph drawing tools, in *Graph Drawing*, Springer, Berlin, pp. 594–597.

Farrell, A.E., Plevin, R.J., Turner, B.T. *et al.* (2006) Ethanol can contribute to energy and environmental goals. *Science*, **311** (5760), 506.

Gancarz, M. (2003) *Linux and the Unix Philosophy*, Digital Press, Clifton, NJ.

Gilder, G. (1993) Telecosm: Metcalfe's law and legacy. *Forbes ASAP*, **152**, 158–166.

Guinee, J.B. (2002) *Handbook on Life Cycle Assessment: Operational Guide to the ISO Standards*, Kluwer Academic Publishers, Dordrecht.

Harris, S. and Seaborne, A. (2010) SPARQL 1.1 Query Language, W3C Working Draft, http://www.w3.org/TR/sparql11-query/ (accessed April 2012).

Heath, T. (2009) Linked Data – Connect Distributed Data across the Web, http://linkeddata.org/ (accessed April 2012).

Hellmann, S., Stadler, C., Lehmann, J. and Auer, S. (2009) DBPedia live extraction, in *On the Move to Meaningful Internet Systems: OTM 2009*, Springer, Berlin, pp. 1209–1223.

Hendler, J. and Golbeck, J. (2008) Metcalfe's law, Web 2.0, and the Semantic Web. *Web Semantics: Science, Services and Agents on the World Wide Web*, **6** (1), 14–20.

Hepp, M. (2008) GoodRelations: An ontology for describing products and services offers on the Web, in Knowledge Engineering: Practice and Patterns, Springer, Berlin, pp. 329–346.

Koren, Y. (2011a) Extension:Semantic Forms-MediaWiki, http://www.mediawiki.org/wiki/Extension:Semantic_Forms (accessed April 2012).

Koren, Y. (2011b) Extension:Semantic Internal Objects-MediaWiki, http://www.mediawiki.org/wiki/Extension:Semantic_Internal_Objects (accessed April 2012).

Nikolic, I. and Davis, C. (2012) Self organization in wikis, in *Inverse Infrastructures: New Phenomena in Emerging Infrastructures*, Edward Elgar Publishing, Cheltenham, UK, in press.

O'Reilly, T. (2004) The Architecture of Participation. O'Reilly Media, Sebastopol, CA.

Philip, G. and Booth, M.E. (2001) A new six 'S' framework on the relationship between the role of information systems (IS) and competencies in 'S' management. *Journal of Business Research*, **51** (3), 233–247.

Prud'hommeaux, E. and Seaborne, A. (2008) SPARQL Query Language for RDF, W3C Recommendation, http://www.w3.org/TR/rdf-sparql-query (accessed April 2012).

Read, L. (1956) *I, Pencil: My Family Tree as Told to Leonard E. Read*, Foundation for Economic Education, Irvington, NY.

Seaborne, A. (2007) Basic Federated SPARQL Query, http://seaborne.blogspot.com/2007/07/basic-federated-sparql-query.html (accessed April 2012).

Suh, S. (2004) Materials and energy flows in industry and ecosystem networks. PhD thesis, Leiden University.

US Department of Energy (2009) DOE Launches New Website to Bring Energy Technology Information to the Public, http://www.nrel.gov/news/press/2009/769.html (accessed April 2012).

Waldrop, M. (2008) Big data: Wikiomics. *Nature*, **455** (7209), 5–22.
Wouters, S. and Feldmar, N. (2010) Eco-Industrial Wiki-Platform: Increasing Efficiency in Research Through Collaboration, Egmond aan Zee, Netherlands.

Further Reading and Useful Web Sites

Below is a list of web sites that cover many similar efforts as those described in this chapter. These typically differ in the type of data and the interactions that are allowed between producers and consumers of data. Additionally, links are provided to several of the tools that we use.

- http://www.ted.com/talks/tim_berners_lee_on_the_next_web.html: The creator of the Web, Tim Berners-Lee, discusses the potential of the Semantic Web.
- http://www.sourcemap.org/: Sourcemap is an effort to crowdsource information about the supply chains for products, and their resulting CO_2 emissions.
- http://dbpedia.org/About: DBPedia is a project that republishes structured information contained on Wikipedia in a form that is accessible using Semantic Web technologies.
- http://www.chemspider.com/: Chemspider acts as a hub that links together information about chemical substances from sources spread across the Web.
- http://goodguide.com: GoodGuide is a consumer guide that aggregates sustainability information about products with regard to health and environmental effects, along with issues of corporate social responsibility.
- http://lca-data.org: The UNEP/SETAC Database Registry is an effort to create a hub for both producers and consumers of LCA data. It has a similar intent to, although it currently lacks some of the functionality of, what is described in this chapter.
- http://data-gov.tw.rpi.edu/wiki: A project by Rensselaer Polytechnic Institute to convert US government data into a form accessible using Semantic Web technologies.
- http://OpenEI.org: The Open Energy Info site is run by the US National Renewable Energy Laboratory and US Department of Energy. It uses the same software as described in this chapter, and covers a myriad of energy-related topics.
- http://mediawiki.org/: This is the wiki software used for the examples discussed in this chapter.
- http://semantic-mediawiki.org/: An extension to MediaWiki that enables the embedding of structured information on wiki pages.
- http://www.mediawiki.org/wiki/Extension:SparqlExtension: An extension to Semantic MediaWiki that allows for more sophisticated queries (using SPARQL) and allows for outside applications to query data contained on the wiki.

18

Green IT: An Outlook

San Murugesan[1] and G.R. Gangadharan[2]
[1]BRITE Professional Services and University of Western Sydney, Australia
[2]Institute for Development and Research in Banking Technology, Hyderabad, India

Key Points

- Highlights key sustainability and Green IT trends.
- Outlines what is Green Engineering and examines its principles.
- Identifies key technology enablers and their applications in sustainability projects.
- Presents examples of greening by IT: sustainability applications of RFID, Smart Grids, smart buildings and homes, green supply chain management and logistics, and green enterprise.
- Examines whether Green IT is a mega trend.
- Outlines a seven-step approach to developing and implementing Green IT strategy.
- Presents Green IT research and development directions.

18.1 Introduction

Motivated by high energy costs and the need to think more ecologically, more companies, educational institutions and individuals are adopting sustainable computing strategies, and the implementation of environmentally sustainable practices that leverage IT is gaining traction and growing in significance. IT departments and CIOs are not only making their enterprise IT greener but also driving enterprise-wide sustainability projects that improve their business' profitability, competitiveness and innovation. In the coming years, IT professionals will find green computing concepts becoming a bigger part of their work.

The chapters in this book have described various aspects of green IT focussing on hardware, software, storage, network and cloud computing as well as on standards, strategies and a green maturity framework. This concluding chapter looks at green IT trends, developments and prospects and identifies directions for further research and development.

Harnessing Green IT: Principles and Practices, First Edition. Edited by San Murugesan and G.R. Gangadharan.

18.2 Awareness to Implementation

There is growing acknowledgement of the risks of not taking action now to address our environmental problems. As a result, environmental sustainability initiatives are gaining strength and momentum. The IT sector and IT professionals and users have responsibility to help create a more sustainable environment. According to Fujitsu's *ICT Sustainability: The Global Benchmark 2011* report (Fujitsu, 2011), 'ICT is a large consumer of energy, and is globally responsible for 3% of greenhouse gas (GHG) emissions. At current rates of growth in information and computer technology (ICT) usage, this is forecast to grow to 6% by 2020. More importantly, ICT is responsible for 5–10% of the typical economy's total electricity consumption. In some organizations that rely heavily on ICT, such as banks, government and in many other administrative industries, ICT can account for up to 75% of all energy consumption'.

Whether driven by the quest to cut the increasing costs associated with energy use and waste disposal, regulatory mandates or genuine concern for the planet, a growing number of businesses are going green. As green IT is both a necessity and an opportunity, businesses and IT professionals have moved from asking 'Can IT go green?' to 'How can IT go green?'. Greening our IT products, applications, services and practices is both an economic and environmental imperative, as well as our social responsibility. Innovations in developing and adopting environmentally sustainable IT will be a key to success now and in the future. Green IT is no passing fad.

In the coming years, corporate, individual and government attention to environmental and sustainability issues is bound to intensify and IT professionals will find green computing concepts becoming an integral part of their work. Green IT principles and practices will be ingrained in several IT activities, processes and practices.

18.2.1 Green IT Trends

Companies and individuals expect IT to play significant roles in minimizing business' and individuals' environmental footprint. The following are some of the highlights of key sustainability and green IT trends:

- **Measuring and reporting footprints:** The number of businesses that measure and report their carbon emissions (carbon footprint), as part of their annual or corporate social responsibility report, continues to increase. To be transparent, businesses must themselves know how much carbon emission equivalent they generate, how much energy they consume and other factors contributing to their environmental footprint. Businesses have begun to pay more attention to the environmental friendliness of their supply chain and business partners. Many big companies have taken steps to measure their carbon footprints and small businesses increasingly are beginning to adopt this practice. Governments in a number of countries are mandating large businesses to report and reduce their energy consumption and carbon footprint.
- **Demand for green transparency:** Consumers have begun to pay attention to the green credential of products or the services they buy and use. They want to know where products are sourced, what they are made of and what their carbon footprint is. Businesses are responding to this demand by giving them more information about the environmental aspects of their products or services.

- **Customer engagement:** Savvy green businesses are not just widely publicizing their own environmental good deeds and gaining green credits, but also engaging customers and other stakeholders in sourcing their ideas and opinions and more actively in their green initiatives. For example, eBay launched a Green Team programme (www.ebaygreenteam.com) to tap into the wisdom of crowds. The programme's mission is to 'inspire the world to buy, sell and think green every day'. Over 300 000 sellers – individuals who sell goods on eBay's platform – had signed up to share ideas and views aimed at making eBay a greener sales partner. Another example is the 'GE ecomagination Challenge' (http://challenge.ecomagination.com/ideas) which seeks ideas for development and adoption of the Smart Grid and 'powering your home'.
- **Green hardware and devices:** Manufacturers are also rolling out more green computers and green electronic devices and systems. For instance, several green IT products – PCs, notebook computers, monitors, printers and others – that meet the Electronic Product Environmental Assessment Tool (EPEAT) environmental labels of Gold, Silver and Bronze are now available. Even small companies and individuals are turning to recycling and learning how to dispose of equipment in eco-friendlier ways.
- **Telecommuting:** With the use of Voice Over Internet Protocol (VOIP) services, telecommuting is becoming more popular among businesses. Companies are able to offer their employees the option of telecommuting – an attractive option in an age of high fuel prices, traffic jams and long commutes.
- **Green data centres:** Data centres that host a variety of Web applications, popular e-commerce sites and social networks are becoming greener with significant improvement in energy efficiency and use of greener, cleaner power sources for their operation.
- **Green awareness and responsibility:** Among businesses and individuals, environmental awareness and responsibility are increasing. For instance, the use of power management features and products has increased and customers who are willing pay more for green IT products are growing.

18.2.2 Green Engineering

A new discipline called green engineering is taking shape now and receiving interest. Green engineering instills environmentally conscious attitudes, values and principles, combined with science, technology and engineering practice, all directed towards improving local and global environmental quality (Virginia Tech, 2012). It promotes the adoption of environmentally friendly principles and practices early in the design and development phase of a process or product. It focusses on the design of materials, processes, systems and devices with the objective of minimizing overall environmental impact (including energy utilization and waste generation and management) throughout the entire life cycle of a product or process – from initial extraction of raw materials used in manufacture to ultimate disposal at the end of the useful life of a product (Virginia Tech, 2012).

Green engineering uses the following nine principles as guidance in the design or redesign of products and processes satisfying the constraints imposed by business, government and society such as cost, safety, performance and environmental impact (adapted from US Environmental Protection Agency, 2012):

1. Engineer processes and products holistically, carry out systems analysis and integrate environmental impact assessment tools.
2. Conserve and improve natural ecosystems whilst protecting human health and well-being.
3. Use life cycle thinking and considerations in all stages of activities.
4. Ensure that all material and energy inputs and outputs are inherently environmentally safe.
5. Minimize the depletion of natural resources.
6. Strive to prevent waste.
7. Develop and implement solutions and be cognizant of local geography, aspirations and cultures.
8. Create solutions beyond current or dominant technologies; improve, innovate and invent (technologies) to achieve sustainability.
9. Actively engage communities and stakeholders in the development of products and processes and in the entire product life cycle.

18.3 Greening by IT

Businesses can leverage IT in a number of their sustainability initiatives that make their products and services greener. Greening by IT is a key, promising trend, and is pushed by a number of drivers including cost reduction, environmental regulations and carbon tax, environmental and social responsibility, customer demands for greener products and services and societal pressure.

Greening by IT is supported by a number of enablers including technological advances not only in IT but also in other areas, green mindset and ecological thinking, the availability of new tools and systems for monitoring and control and government incentives. For instance, as highlighted in Table 18.1, a number of enabling technologies extend the scope and sophistication of sustainability projects.

The remainder of this section outlines a few examples of greening by IT: use of radio frequency identification (RFID), Smart Grids, smart buildings and homes, green supply chain management and green business (enterprise-wide environmental sustainability).

18.3.1 Using RFID for Environmental Sustainability

RFID enables improved data gathering and cross-company data integration facilitating better tracking and management of goods and services and resulting in better resource utilization and improved efficiency, among other benefits. RFID uses a noncontact, radio communication system to transfer data from a tag attached to an object, for the purposes of automatic identification and tracking. RFID tags can also hold information about the object.

RFID enables gathering information on the materials that enterprises use, their manufacturing operations, their supply chain and so forth, in order to engineer, or reengineer, products and processes to reduce costs and the impact their products have on the environment. For example, Walmart created a programme that increased the efficiency of its truck fleet by 38%. In addition to adopting new fuel-efficient technologies, Walmart believes that RFID technologies can enable more efficient replenishment and, therefore, fewer trips for trucks between distribution centres and stores (Roberti, 2009).

Table 18.1 Technology enablers and their applications

Technology	Application in sustainability projects
RFID (radio frequency identification), sensors and wireless sensor networks	Collection of real-time information from several different sources for monitoring, control and management
Internet of Things (IoT)	Access to and control of different devices, gadgets and objects through the Internet; facilitates information consolidation and coordination
Web mashups	Data and information aggregation
Decision support systems; intelligent software agents	Smart decisions
Location and context-aware systems	Context-aware control and management
Web 2.0 and social media	Creating awareness, motivating people and sharing insights and experiences
Cloud computing	Complex computation and analysis can be carried in the clouds facilitating the implementation of low-cost yet sophisticated sustainability measures that are computationally intensive and involve data sharing.

RFID is widely being used in supply chain management, transportation and logistics, asset management, health care and other areas. It is also helping to build a greener environment, by reducing vehicle emissions, protecting indigenous fauna, facilitating transport container reuse, conserving energy use in buildings, improving waste disposal, encouraging recycling and protecting the sea floor (IDTechEx, 2009). RFID's use in several green projects reveals its potential not only to enhance environmental sustainability but also to reduce costs and generate revenue by creating new commercial opportunities (Bose and Yan, 2011). RFID's contribution to green objectives also include accurately tracking a perishable item to prevent its spoilage and saving energy in operations from growing and harvesting to packaging and refrigeration.

Limitations of RFID such as the relatively high cost of tags, readers and other support systems, technical deficiencies and cross-company data integration issues remain as barriers to its widespread adoption in supply chain activities (Dukovska-Popovska *et al.*, 2010). It is, however, expected that current major limitations of RFID will be overcome in the coming years.

18.3.2 Smart Grids

Electrical power grids have now become vital for our existence, growth and development, and our total electrical power consumption continues to increase significantly – worldwide electric power consumption is expected to triple by 2050. Most of the existing power grids are over 50 years old and suffer from several problems. Their average energy efficiency is poor (about 33%), wasting energy and polluting the environment. They are also unreliable, incompatible to integrate with renewable energy sources and vulnerable to cyber-attack. Smart Grids intend to modernize the power grids by using IT and other technologies to reduce the transmission and distribution loss. It will balance the electricity supply and demand and improve the grid reliability by effectively monitoring and controlling the grid. It will also assist in optimizing resource use, and hence in enhancing environmental sustainability.

A Smart Grid is a digitally enabled power grid that gathers, distributes and acts on information about the supply and demand and the behaviour of all participants (suppliers and consumers) in order to improve the efficiency, reliability, economics and sustainability of electricity services (Wikipedia, 2012). A Smart Grid overlays an electric grid system with sensors, controls and wireless digital communication devices. Deployment of Smart Grids calls for customers to install special smart meters at their premises (some customers are, however, not willing to pay for new equipment). Much of the Smart Grid, including devices at the customers' premises, are computer controlled and interactive. A modern Smart Grid has the following features:

1. Runs more efficiently.
2. Provides higher quality power and minimizes power outages.
3. Accommodates all types of power sources and generation as well as storage options.
4. Motivates consumers to actively participate in operations of the grid.
5. Resists cyber-attacks and computer viruses.
6. Is capable of self-healing.

Smart Grids offer several operational, economic and environmental benefits such as improved efficiency, cost-effectiveness, less pollution, lower bills and fewer outages. In addition, smart grids also offer following key benefits:

- **Better integration with other energy sources:** As we seek to implement energy conservation measures and get energy from renewable resources such as solar and wind power, a Smart Grid would help make it easier to integrate photovoltaic, wind and other intermittent power sources.
- **Less power outages:** A Smart Grid uses real-time data to detect and isolate faults and to reconfigure the distribution network to minimize power outages to customers. It can anticipate equipment failures and reroute electric power autonomously to provide customers power without interruption.
- **Resilient:** A Smart Grid is more resilient and better able to handle peak power demand as wells as severe weather conditions.
- **Smarter consumption:** A Smart Grid helps consumers to change their behaviour around variable power price or billing rates. Customers could save money by shutting off appliances and using less power at times when electricity is most expensive.

IT plays key roles in enabling Smart Grids through optimization, estimation and better monitoring and control. Cloud-based Smart Grid services have begun to emerge.

18.3.3 Smart Buildings and Homes

A smart home (or building) is an intelligent home (or building) that maximizes its energy efficiency and performance by integrating various building subsystems including communications, entertainment, security, convenience and information systems. With the advent of newer technologies and advanced products, intelligent buildings are fast becoming a reality.

Buildings can be considered as energy-intensive systems throughout their whole life cycle including the design, realization (construction) and support (maintenance and renovation) phases (European Commission, 2009).

According to a World Business Council for Sustainable Development estimate (WBSCD, 2008), buildings consume ~40% of the world's energy, and almost all building complexes, manufacturing plants, retail stores, hospitals and hotels waste energy. Buildings represent a complex interdependent system comprising tenants, buildings and building equipment. Energy consumption profiles and concerns differ across locations, structures, seasons and occupancy levels. For instance, buildings account for about 40% of energy demand, and the worldwide energy consumption for buildings will grow by 45% from 2002 to 2025 (The Climate Group, 2008).

Energy efficiency in buildings could be achieved by adopting best environmentally friendly design and engineering approaches, sustainable procurement processes and conformance to building codes and regulations for energy efficiency. The renovation of existing buildings for greater energy efficiency constitutes sustainable modernization.

IT could be harnessed to improve building energy efficiency and reduce total energy consumption. For instance, energy efficiency in future smart buildings can be gained through smart building management systems and energy control management systems supported by wired and wireless sensors, multimodal interactive interfaces and multimodal context-aware systems (European Commission, 2009).

Many building professionals are unaware of the significance of energy efficiency in buildings and tend to underestimate the contribution of buildings' energy to sustainability. Greater awareness and education are needed to motivate builders and residents to use IT-enabled smart systems to reduce energy consumption and energy bills.

18.3.4 Green Supply Chain and Logistics

A supply chain is a set of organizations directly linked by one or more of the upstream and downstream flows of products, services, finances and information from a source to a customer (Mentzer *et al.*, 2001). According to the Council of Supply Chain Management Professionals (CSCMP), *supply chain management* encompasses the planning and management of all activities involved in sourcing, procurement, conversion and logistics management. It includes the crucial components of coordination and collaboration with suppliers, intermediaries, third-party service providers and customers. Supply chain management integrates supply and demand management within and across companies. Due to increasing concerns about environmental issues, organizations are required to effectively coordinate and manage their supply chain management with minimal impact on the environment.

Green supply chain management integrates environmental considerations into supply chain management including product design, material sourcing and selection, manufacturing processes, delivery of the final product to the consumers as well as end-of-life management of the product after its useful life (Srivastava, 2007; Wang and Gupta, 2011). Driven by increasing customer awareness, regulatory concerns and the need to reduce the cost and environmental impact of transportation, organizations are adopting green supply chain management practices. For instance, Dell became carbon neutral in 2008 by improving its supply chain and logistics.[1] Texas Instruments achieved 20% annual savings by reducing its transit packaging budget for its semiconductor business through source reduction, recycling and use of reusable packaging systems.[2]

Integrating environmental considerations into supply chain management has become an increasingly important issue for industry, government and academic researchers. Supply chain managers are being required to respond to new legislation, standards and regulations; changing customer demands; and demand for improved efficiency, cost effectiveness and return on investment, all whilst simultaneously being 'green'.

To green their supply chain, organization can adopt one or more of the following measures (Cognizant White Paper, 2008):

- Use IT and other technology solutions to facilitate green supply chain management with a focus on end-to-end supply chain analysis and network design.
- Pay attention to reducing inventory and identifying optimal distribution solutions adopting better information management for inventory and ordering of goods.
- Perform life cycle analysis for choosing products or solutions to minimize environmental impact.
- Adopt industry standard frameworks like SCOR version 9 to identify potential areas for green initiatives in the supply chain.
- Align green initiatives with the strategic objectives of the company.
- Follow green supply chain management best practices in implementing green initiatives.

In addition to the supply chain, sustainability initiatives could be implemented in other areas of enterprise activities, making an enterprise a 'green enterprise' as highlighted in Section 18.3.5.

18.3.5 Enterprise-Wide Environmental Sustainability

A *sustainable enterprise* or *green enterprise* is a business that has no or minimal negative impact on the environment. A business can be designated as a green business if it meets the following four criteria (Cooney, 2009):

1. It incorporates principles of sustainability into each of its business decisions.
2. It supplies environmentally friendly products or services that replace the demand for nongreen products and/or services.
3. It is greener than its traditional competitors.
4. It has made an enduring commitment to environmental principles in its business operations.

[1] http://money.cnn.com/2008/08/05/technology/dell_neutral.fortune/ (accessed April 2012).

[2] http://www.supplychainquarterly.com/topics/Global/scq200801texas/ (accessed April 2012).

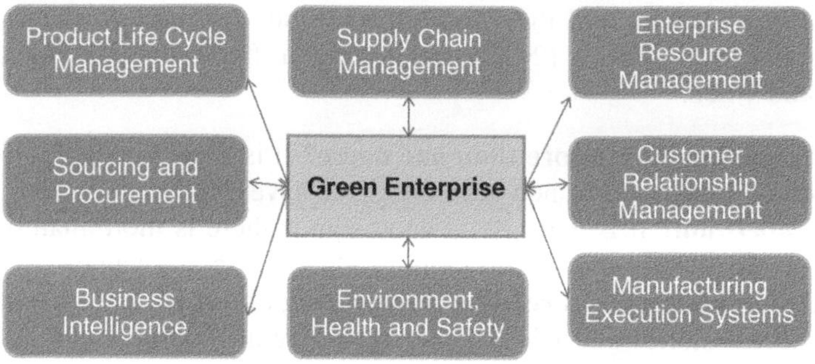

Figure 18.1 Making an enterprise greener.

A sustainable enterprise requires each of its functional units and activities (see Figure 18.1) to be green. The general guidelines for making an enterprise's functional units green are as follows:

- **Supply chain management:** Adopt techniques and plans to minimize inventory and wasted freight; adopt networked design using a carbon footprint.
- **Enterprise resource management:** Enable paperless transactions, and adopt techniques for workforce and parts optimization as well as intelligent device management.
- **Customer relationship management:** Adopt electronic means to maintain contact with customers.
- **Manufacturing execution systems:** Make proper plans for production scheduling, adopt co-product or by-product design and implement strategies for better yield management.
- **Environment, health and safety:** Monitor the environmental impact and carbon footprint, and comply with environmental, health and safety standards.
- **Business intelligence:** Include reporting systems for energy reporting and carbon footprinting.
- **Sourcing and procurement:** Select vendors by their sustainability rating.
- **Product life cycle management:** Design products that consume less energy; implement effective systems for product end-of-life management.

Thus sustainability initiatives are taking many directions, and IT can and should play a major role in all these initiatives – greening *by* IT.

18.4 Green IT: A Megatrend?

Environmental sustainability – green movement – is a 'megatrend', a transformative change in the competitive landscape like the rise of the quality movement in the 1970s and IT in the 1980s and 1990s (Lubin and Esty, 2010). The same is true for green IT.

Business executives, IT professionals and even individuals of all age groups come across many new IT developments, innovations, products and services. The challenge they face is weighing whether to pursue a technology or pass for now, and whether a technology is ripe to adopt and the value of doing so. Answers to the following five questions, adapted from Brokaw (2012), can help them find whether it is good to adopt a technology and when:

1. **Does the technology have more than one name?** It is not a good sign if the industry cannot agree on a name for a new technology or have general consensus.
2. **Is there competition?** It is generally a good sign if there is more than one provider.
3. **What does it do?** There should be clarity on its purpose and value.
4. **What kind of stories are you reading and hearing about it?** Ensure that it has clear, verifiable success stories attached. Horror stories are also helpful as they show a sign of the difficulties encountered.
5. **Has anyone made a commitment?** Explore who other users are, and what their experiences have been. If people are already adopting it, you can too.

On applying this test, one would find that green IT is ripe for widespread adoption, and has become a megatrend benefiting not only its adopters but also the entire society and the planet – now and in the future. For further information on how to make sense of IT innovation waves, see Burton Swanson (2012).

According to a MIT Sloan Management study (Kiron *et al.*, 2012), sustainability is near its tipping point, and is on the majority of companies' management agendas. Sustainability is becoming a profitable opportunity for many organizations, and at companies such as Campbell Soup, it is now a standard component of managers' performance evaluations. GreenBiz Group (2012) highlights the environmental impacts of the emerging green economy and documents what progress companies were making. It measured 20 aspects of environmental performance, from carbon emissions to paper use and recycling. According to the report, companies continue to dedicate time, money and staff to setting and meeting ambitious environmental goals.

18.4.1 Outsourcing and Environmental Attributes

Given the on-going push towards environmental sustainability, sourcers – particularly government agencies – will soon, if they are not already, start demanding a minimum level of green credentials from IT vendors in their outsourcing deals (Murugesan, 2010). This is already happening in the IT hardware arena; government agencies in their call for tenders specify particular levels of environmental attributes that the hardware has to confirm – for example an EPEAT Gold, Silver or Bronze rating. Similar demands for green credentials from vendors on IT outsourcing deals are not far away. Recognizing this, some of the major outsourcing vendors such as TCS, Infosys and Wipro in India have already implemented green measures and are showcasing their credentials. Other vendors will be required to follow suit, at least for competitive advantage; if they do not, they may have to face the consequences of not being green. Organizations need to get into the habit of measuring, reporting and improving their green credentials. The competitiveness – and perhaps even survival – of organizations may depend on their environmental credentials.

Outsourcing proposals and agreements will require the use of acceptable carbon measures that will allow comparison, justification and optimization of an organization's green credentials (Murugesan, 2010). Given the growing need for, and the importance of, green metrics and environmental certification, developments and the establishment of new green metrics that encompass end users, data centres, life cycles and overall facilities and the functions of an organization are bound to emerge.

18.4.2 Green Audit

To address accusations of 'greenwashing' – the practice of organizations exaggerating their green credentials and environmental sustainability attributes, and making claims that are untrue – a new kind of corporate audit is emerging: the green audit. Green audits assess a company's environmental credentials and its green claims for its products and services to determine whether the company's activities, practices and supply chain and/or product line can be promoted as *truly* environmentally sustainable.

18.5 A Seven-Step Approach to Creating Green IT Strategy

Although there are many common elements in making enterprises greener, there is no single green strategy that fits all enterprises. Enterprises must develop and implement their own near-term and long-term green strategies, considering their current IT infrastructure, its utilization as well as current practices and future business requirements. The following seven-step approach will help enterprises to develop and implement an enterprise green strategy (Murugesan, 2011):

1. Engage with key stakeholders like employees, senior executives and business partners, and create awareness of environmental issues and their impact on the enterprise and the environment. Also, explain to them the business value and the necessity of greening the enterprise's IT.
2. Conduct energy audits, analyse IT utilization and review IT equipment purchases and disposal policies and practices. Assess IT's environmental and cost impacts, and identify areas to be 'greened'.
3. Set SMART (i.e. specific, measurable, achievable, realistic and time-bound) green goals. To reduce your carbon footprint, formulate specific, measurable, attainable, realistic and timely internal targets along with timelines. Develop concrete criteria for measuring progress towards the goals.
4. Develop and implement a green IT policy that (i) aims to achieve high utilization of your IT systems whilst reducing energy use and (ii) helps to minimize environmental impacts of various business activities and practices.
5. Encourage, motivate and energize the workforce to follow the green path and to come up with and implement their own ideas. In addition, also encourage clients, suppliers and outsourcers to adopt green practices.
6. Monitor the progress regularly; watch industry trends and new developments. Revise the green policy as required.
7. Publicize environmental policy, actions and achievements and thereby get credits and accolades from customers, peers, industry groups, environmental advocates, government agencies and society at large. Outline tangible and intangible benefits realized as a result of adopting your green strategy.

For a generic green IT roadmap that an organization can follow and for a case study on how organizations have benefited by implementing a number of these green IT initiatives, refer to the report by the Australian Information Industry Association (AIIA, 2011). The report also highlights why green IT is important from an industry capability perspective and the economic, environmental and social benefits of green IT.

18.5.1 Balancing the Costs and Benefits of Going Green

Green initiatives may incur additional costs in terms of green software and tools that help reduce total energy consumption; green hardware meeting EPEAT gold, silver or bronze environmental ratings; creating awareness among employees and other stakeholders and reengineering business processes to reduce their carbon footprint by minimizing waste and improving efficiency. But we should start treating them as investment costs as the return on these investments over a longer term would be higher and significant.

In doing a cost–benefit analysis of a green initiative and in trying to balance costs and benefits, we should look at the total cost of ownership of IT which includes not only the initial capital expenses but also the costs of operation and of environmentally friendly disposal. We should consider both tangible and intangible benefits. Several green IT initiatives, in both private and public enterprises, demonstrate that green initiatives are helping customers save significant costs in terms of energy consumption (see AIIA, 2011). Reduction in energy consumption is a significant benefit as we encounter increasing energy costs and severe electric energy shortages in many regions.

However, green IT projects that cannot prove their worth would not succeed. Green IT projects that are poorly defined and cannot outline their benefits – both tangible and intangible – are less likely to get management's attention, support and approval. As a result the initiatives could be abandoned to save money. But now is the time to go green because new technologies offer both short-term and long-term benefits in terms of cost, environment and business. Overall, green initiatives generally turn out to be cost-saving measures rather than unnecessary expenses. Even if those initiatives do not result in cost savings, one has to consider the business impact of not going green, in terms of missed opportunities, lowered competitiveness, poor public perception and brand image and eventual environmental costs.

So, an organization needs to address sustainability issues comprehensively with a holistic perspective and long-term focus. Enterprises should start their green movement by first picking the low-hanging fruits such as placing computers in sleep or power-saving mode or switching them off when not in use by using power management tools, using thin clients where feasible, videoconferencing, printer management, using recycled paper and printer cartridges, reusing computers and so on. Enterprises should then move on to more challenging projects, like consolidating servers, making data centres green, taking measures to reduce network power consumption and helping the business in reducing its carbon footprint in other functions or activities, and then move into deeper approaches like generating and using its own renewal energy, making its operation carbon neutral.

18.6 Research and Development Directions

The field of green IT is young; yet, within a short span of time, it got the attention and interest of the IT industry, businesses, government and society. There have been major developments in recent years in terms of improving the energy efficiency of computers, virtualization, data centre design and operation and power-aware software. Several organizations and agencies have come forward to develop standards and metrics and help assist in harnessing IT to address environmental issues and create a sustainable environment. There are, however, several areas – for example technology, adoption, assessment, standards and regulation – that demand further research and development.

In the context of greening an enterprise, several questions deserve further study. For example: What should comprise an enterprise green IT strategy and policies, and how can we effectively implement them? What are the applicable regulatory requirements, and how can we comply with them? What are the *real* challenges and barriers to adopting green IT, and how can we address them satisfactorily? Further studies on the following topics are desired:

- Critical success factors in green IT adoption and how to embrace them
- Cultural influences on adopting green IT and environmentally sustainable practices
- Models and approaches for carbon footprint estimation and measurement
- Reliable tools for carbon footprint estimation
- Business green strategies and their implementation
- Best enterprise green IT practices
- The green IT maturity matrix
- Green audits.

In the technology area, further studies in the following areas are desired:

- Energy-efficient computing architecture
- Green application and system software
- Green network and communication protocols and systems
- Green storage
- E-waste disposal and recycling
- Carbon management tools.

18.7 Prospects

Green IT is a hot topic today and will remain a top priority for years to come, as environmentally sustainable IT is an economic as well as environmental imperative. It also represents a dramatic change in priorities for the IT industry. To this point, the industry has focussed on IT equipment processing power and associated equipment spending – it has not been concerned with issues such as power usage, cooling and data centre space. Going forward, however, the IT industry will need to deal with all of the infrastructure requirements and the environmental impact of IT and its use. The challenges of green IT are immense, but recent developments indicate that the IT industry has the will and conviction to tackle our environmental issues head on.

Companies can benefit by regarding these challenges as strategic opportunities. The IT sector and IT users must develop a positive attitude towards addressing environmental concerns and adopt forward-looking, green-friendly policies and practices. By successfully greening your IT systems, you can outcompete your peers, harness new opportunities and help create a sustainable environment that benefits current and future generations. You can, and should, jump on the green IT bandwagon and do your best to sustain the planet by making IT and its use greener.

We hope this book motivates you to harness the power of IT to create a sustainable environment for the benefit of current and future generations. We welcome your feedback on this book, your thoughts on green IT and your experiences in greening IT at greenITbook@gmail.com.

Review Questions

1. What are the drivers and enablers of green IT?
2. What are the significant current green IT trends? Describe with examples.
3. What does green engineering mean to you?
4. Briefly outline the role of RFIDs in improving enterprise environmental sustainability. Give examples.
5. What is meant by green supply chain management, and what are the roles of IT in it?
6. What is a smart home? How does it help in protecting our environment?
7. What is a Smart Grid and what are its features? How does it help in improving environmental sustainability?
8. Outline how an enterprise (of your choice) can implement enterprise-wide sustainability initiatives and become a green enterprise.
9. Describe an approach to create a green IT strategy.

Discussion Questions

1. Green IT – is it a passing fade? Discuss.
2. Is green IT a burden, an opportunity or both? Discuss.
3. Green initiatives may incur additional costs. Describe the costs and benefits of 'going green'.
4. Is green IT a megatrend? Discuss.
5. Develop a green IT strategy for (i) a major retail store, (ii) an educational institution (college or university) or (iii) a bank.

References

AIIA (2011) The GreenIT eBook Version 2, Australian Information Industry Association, http://www.aiia.com.au/?page=GreenITBook (accessed April 2012).

Bose, I. and Yan, S. (2011) The green potential of RFID projects: A case-based analysis. *IEEE IT Professional*, **13** (1), 41–47.

Brokaw, L. (2012) Five questions to separate "the next big thing" from the lemon. *MIT Sloan Management Review*, January 13, http://sloanreview.mit.edu/improvisations/2012/01/13/five-questions-to-separate-the-next-big-thing-from-the-lemon/ (log-in required; accessed April 2012).

Burton Swanson, E. (2012) The manager's guide to IT innovation waves. *MIT Sloan Management Review*, **53** (2), 75–83, http://sloanreview.mit.edu/the-magazine/2012-winter/53210/the-managers-guide-to-it-innovation-waves/ (log-in required; accessed April 2012).

The Climate Group (2008) SMART 2020: Enabling the Low Carbon Economy in the Information Age, http://www.theclimategroup.org/_assets/files/Smart2020Report.pdf (accessed April 2012).

Cognizant (2008) Creating a Green Supply Chain, white paper, http://www.cognizant.com/InsightsWhitepapers/Creating_a_Green%20Supply_Chain_WP.pdf (accessed April 2012).

Cooney, S. (2009) *Build a Green Small Business: Profitable Ways to Become an Ecopreneur*, McGraw-Hill, New York.

Dukovska-Popovska, I., Lim, M.K., Steger-Jensen, K. and Hvolby, H.H. (2010) RFID technology to support environmentally sustainable supply chain management. In Proceedings of the IEEE International Conference on RFID-Technology and Applications, 2010.

European Commission (2009) ICT for a Low Carbon Economy: Smart Buildings, technical report, July, http://ec.europa.eu/information_society/activities/sustainable_growth/docs/sb_publications/smartbuildings-ld.pdf (accessed April 2012).

Fujitsu (2011) ICT Sustainability: The Global Benchmark, Fujitsu Australia, https://www-s.fujitsu.com/global/solutions/sustainability/Fujitsu-ICT-Sustainability-TheGlobalBenchmark2011-Report.html (accessed April 2012).

GreenBiz Group (2012) State of Green Business Report 2012, http://www.greenbiz.com/state-green-business-2012/get-report (accessed April 2012).

IDTechEx (2009) How Green Is RFID? http://www.idtechex.com/research/articles/how_green_is_rfid_00001382.asp (accessed April 2012).

Kiron, D., Kruschwitz, N., Haanaes, K.and StrengVelken, I. (2012) Sustainability nears a tipping point. *MIT Sloan Management Review*, **53** (2), 69–74, http://sloanreview.mit.edu/the-magazine/2012-winter/53213/sustainability-nears-a-tipping-point/ (log-in required; accessed April 2012).

Lubin, D.A. and Esty, D.C. (2010) The sustainability imperative. *Harvard Business Review*, May, http://hbr.org/2010/05/the-sustainability-imperative/ar/1 (accessed April 2012).

Mentzer, J.T., DeWitt, W., Keebler, J.S. *et al.* (2001) Defining supply chain management. *Journal of Business Logistics*, **22** (2), 1–25.

Murugesan, S. (2010) IT outsourcing: Will the vendor's green credentials be a deciding factor? *Cutter Sourcing Email Advisor*, http://www.cutter.com/sourcing/fulltext/advisor/2010/src100602.html (log-in required; accessed April 2012).

Murugesan, S. (2011) Strategies for greening enterprise IT: Creating business value and contributing to environmental sustainability, in *Handbook of Research on Green ICT: Technology, Business and Social Perspectives* (ed. B. Unhelkar), Information Science Reference, Hershey, PA, pp. 51–64.

Roberti, M. (2009) RFID and the environment. *RFID Journal*, August 17, http://www.rfidjournal.com/article/view/5117 (accessed April 2012).

Srivastava, S.K. (2007) Green supply-chain management: A state-of-the-art literature review. *International Journal of Management Reviews*, **9** (1), 53–80.

US Environmental Protection Agency (2012) What Is Greening Engineering? http://www.epa.gov/oppt/greenengineering/pubs/whats_ge.html (accessed April 2012).

Virginia Tech (2012) Green Engineering Definition, http://www.eng.vt.edu/green/definition (accessed April 2012).

Wang, H.F. and Gupta, S.M. (2011) *Green Supply Chain Management: Product Life Cycle Approach*, McGraw-Hill, New York.

World Business Council for Sustainable Development (2008) Energy Efficiency in Buildings: Business Realities and Opportunities, http://www.eukn.org/E_library/Urban_Environment/Environmental_Sustainability/Environmental_Sustainability/Energy_Efficiency_in_Buildings_business_realities_and_opportunities (accessed April 2012).

Glossary

biodegradation The process of chemical dissolution of materials by bacteria or other biological means.

cap-and-trade system A market-based approach for regulating and reducing the amount of pollution emitted into the atmosphere. It allows corporations or governments to trade emissions allowances under an overall cap, or limit, on those emissions.

carbon dioxide (CO_2) A gas emitted naturally through the carbon cycle and through human activities like the burning of fossil fuels. CO_2 is the primary greenhouse gas which contributes to global warming and climate change.

carbon dioxide equivalent A quantity that represents the amount of CO_2 that would have the same global warming potential, when measured over a specified timescale, for a given mixture and amount of greenhouse gas.

Carbon Emissions Management Software (CEMS) A category of software that helps organizations manage and report their CO_2 and other greenhouse gas (GHG) emissions.

carbon emissions trading or carbon trading A form of emissions trading that targets carbon dioxide emission (calculated in tonnes of CO_2 equivalent). It is a market-based approach to minimize pollution by providing economic incentives for achieving reductions in CO_2 emission. A central authority sets a limit or cap on the amount CO_2 emission that a firm can emit, and the limit or cap is allocated, or sold to firms, in the form of permits which represent the right to emit a specific amount of CO_2 equivalent. The firm is required to hold permits (or carbon credits) equivalent to its emissions. If its emission exceeds its total permits, the firm must buy permits from those who require fewer permits – those who have lower emissions than their cap. The transfer of permits is called *trade*.

carbon footprint A measure of an organization's or entity's impact on the environment in terms of the amount of greenhouse gases produced, measured in units of CO_2 equivalent.

carbon offset A credit that an individual or organization could purchase to negate its (or another entity's) carbon footprint, thereby achieving carbon neutrality.

carbon tax Shorthand for *carbon dioxide tax*, this is an environmental tax levied on the carbon content of fuels – effectively a tax on the carbon dioxide emissions from

Harnessing Green IT: Principles and Practices, First Edition. Edited by San Murugesan and G.R. Gangadharan.

burning fossil fuels. It is a potentially cost-effective means of reducing greenhouse gas emissions. A number of countries have implemented carbon taxes or energy taxes related to carbon content. A tax on carbon emissions is not the only way to 'put a price on carbon' and thereby provides incentives to reduce the use of high-carbon fuels. A carbon cap-and-trade system and carbon emissions trading are alternative approaches. *See* 'cap-and-trade system' and 'carbon emissions trading'.

Carbon Usage Effectiveness (CUE) The ratio of total carbon dioxide emissions caused by the total data centre energy to the IT equipment energy. This metric complements a series of metrics such as power usage effectiveness (PUE). The unit of the CUE metric is kilograms of CO_2 equivalent (kgCO_2 equiv.) per kilowatt hour (kWh). *See* 'power usage effectiveness (PUE)'.

chlorofluorocarbons Organic compounds containing carbon, chlorine and fluorine that cause damage to the ozone layer.

climate change Changes in temperature and weather patterns due to certain human activity like burning fossil fuels. The changes include global average air and ocean temperature, widespread melting of snow and ice and rising global sea levels.

Climate Savers Computing Initiative (CSCI) The CSCI is driven by a nonprofit group of eco-conscious consumers, businesses and conservation organizations. Its goal is to promote the development, deployment and adoption of smart technologies that can both improve a computer's power delivery efficiency and reduce the energy it consumes when in an inactive state. As participants of this initiative, computer and component manufacturers commit to producing products that meet specified power efficiency targets, and corporate participants commit to purchasing power-efficient computing products. http://www.climatesaverscomputing.org.

cloud computing A new computing or IT paradigm in which computing resources – computing capacity, storage and applications – are delivered and consumed as a service accessed over a network. It is easily scalable and highly flexible, and users pay for the services they use.

corporate social responsibility (CSR) A form of corporate self-regulation about how companies manage their business processes to produce an overall positive impact on society. Its goal is for a company to embrace responsibility for its actions and encourage a positive impact through its activities on the environment, consumers, employees, communities, stakeholders and all other members of the public sphere. Integrated into its business model, a business' CSR policy functions as a built-in, self-regulating mechanism whereby a business monitors and ensures its active compliance with the spirit of the law, ethical standards and international norms.

data centre infrastructure efficiency (DCiE) A metric used to determine the energy efficiency of a data centre. It is the ratio of information technology equipment power to total facility power, and is expressed as a percentage.

demanufacturing The process of dismantling electronic equipment for scrap metals reclamation and component recovery.

dematerialization In the context of green IT, *dematerialization* refers to the transformation of physical goods to information goods – represented in digital form. Adopting electronic billing (e-billing) instead of paper-based billing, offering music and videos for online download rather than on CDs and DVDs, using e-books and electronic documents rather than printed books and documents and videoconferencing rather holding face-to-face meetings that may involve travel are some examples. E-commerce can reduce the need for transportation, if combined with a sustainable logistic system. In all these instances, by dematerialization, the emissions associated with these activities can be reduced.

e-waste Electronic waste, e-waste, e-scrap or waste electrical and electronic equipment (WEEE) comprises discarded electrical or electronic devices. It is one of the fastest growing segments of our waste stream.

Earth Hour A global event organized by the World Wide Fund for Nature annually on the last Saturday of March, asking people to turn off their non-essential lights and other electrical appliances for one hour to raise awareness towards the need to take action on climate change.

eco-management Activities, processes and strategies to lessen the harmful impact of human activity on the environment whilst meeting the socioeconomic, political and cultural needs of current and future generations. It also promotes the conservation and ethical use of natural resources.

Eco-Management and Audit Scheme (EMAS) A voluntary environmental management tool for companies and organizations to evaluate, report and improve their environmental performance. It also helps companies to communicate their environmental achievements to stakeholders and society in general. It was developed and is being promoted by the European Commission. http://ec.europa.eu/environment/emas/index_en.htm.

emissions trading A market-based approach to control pollution by providing economic incentives for achieving reductions in pollutant emissions. *See* 'carbon emission trading'.

Energy Star A global labelling program that segregates computers, monitors, printers and servers as well as many other electrical and electronic goods based on their energy efficiency. Energy Star specifications differ for each item. Energy Star rating 5.0 for computers became effective in 2009. A key impact of the Energy Star ratings was manufacturers introducing the sleep mode and other measures in computers and other electronic equipment to attain a higher rating. Sleep mode places the consumer's electronic equipment on standby when no user activity takes place during the pre-set time. http://www.energystar.gov.

environmental sustainability The design and provision of products and services that incorporate and promote waste minimization and the efficient and effective use and reuse of resources. Its aim is to protect the environment for the benefit of current and future generations. It is all about meeting needs and seeking a balance between people, the environment and the economy. According to the United Nations, sustainable development meets the needs of the present without compromising the ability of future generations to meet their own needs.

Electronic Products Environmental Assessment Tool (EPEAT) A popular, easy-to-use assessment tool to help organizations and individuals compare computer desktops, laptops and monitors based on their environmental attributes. EPEAT-registered products are classified as bronze, silver or gold (www.epeat.net), and they have reduced levels of cadmium, lead and mercury to better protect human health. They are more energy efficient and easier to upgrade and recycle. EPEAT is based on the IEEE 1680 Standard for Environmental Assessment of Personal Computer products. It aims to increase the efficiency and life of products, and minimize energy consumption and maintenance activities throughout the life of the product.

global warming The rising average temperature of the Earth's atmosphere and oceans and its projected continuation. In the last 100 years, the Earth's average surface temperature increased by about 0.8°C (1.4°F) with about two-thirds of the increase occurring over just the last three decades. Most global warming is caused by increasing concentrations of greenhouse gases produced by human activities such as deforestation and burning fossil fuels.

green building A resource-efficient building that uses less water, optimizes energy efficiency, conserves natural resources, generates less waste and provides healthier spaces for occupants, as compared to a conventional building. A green building reduces its carbon footprint throughout a building's life cycle design, construction, operation, maintenance, renovation and demolition.

green calculator A tool that determines the environmental impact (carbon footprint) and energy consumption and cost of a product, system, process or service.

green computing *See* 'green IT'.

green data centre A data centre in which IT systems, air-conditioning systems, electrical and mechanical systems and the buildings that house the data centre are designed and operated for maximum energy efficiency, low carbon footprint and minimum environmental impacts.

green economy An economy that results in improved human well-being and social equity, whilst significantly reducing environmental risks and ecological scarcities. It is a low-carbon, resource-efficient and socially inclusive economy. In a green economy, growth is driven by initiatives that reduce carbon emissions and pollution, enhance energy and resource efficiency and prevent the loss of biodiversity and ecosystem services.

Green Grid, the A nonprofit, open industry consortium committed to improving the resource efficiency of data centres and business computing ecosystems.

green information system (GIS) An information system that helps an organization to reduce transportation costs, support team work and meetings, track environmental information and monitor emissions and waste products to manage them more effectively.

green IT An umbrella term referring to environmentally sound information technologies and systems, applications and practices. It is the study and practice of designing, manufacturing and using computers, servers, monitors, printers, storage devices and networking and communications systems efficiently and effectively with zero or minimal impact on the environment. It is also about using IT to support, assist and leverage other environmental initiatives and to help create green awareness. Green IT encompasses hardware, software, tools, strategies and practices that help improve and foster environmental sustainability.

Green IT 1.0 and Green IT 2.0 Green IT 1.0, or the greening *of* IT, focusses making IT greener by reengineering IT products and processes to improve IT's energy efficiency, and minimize their carbon footprint and its environmental impact. Green IT 2.0, or greening *by* IT, is about empowering a range of other green initiatives harnessing IT. It encompasses activities like coordinating, reengineering and optimizing the supply chain, manufacturing activities and organizational workflows to minimize the environmental impact.

green IT audit An audit of an organization to assess the total environmental impact of its activities or of a particular product or process.

green manufacturing A method for manufacturing that minimizes waste and pollution, and uses less materials and energy. It is often achieved through better product and process design.

green networking The practice of selecting energy-efficient networking technologies and products, and minimizing resource use.

green PC A personal computer that is designed to be environmentally friendly and has a reduced carbon footprint throughout its life cycle. It is energy efficient, contains less hazardous materials and is easy to upgrade and recycle.

green power Electricity generated from renewable energy sources such as solar, wind, biomass, geothermal and hydroelectric.

green software Environmentally friendly software that helps improve the environment by consuming less energy to run or by assisting other things going green. It is also features characteristics that make its code or modules reusable.

green supply chain management (GSCM) A management philosophy and practice that embeds environmental considerations into supply chain management focussing on product design, material sourcing and selection, manufacturing processes, delivery of the final product to the consumers as well as end-of-life management of the product.

green washing The practice of organizations exaggerating their green credentials and environmental sustainability attributes, making claims that are untrue. It is an unjustified appropriation of environmental virtue. Green washing is an amalgam of the terms green and whitewash.

greenhouse gas (GHG) A wide range of different gases that can absorb thermal infrared radiation (heat) which is emitted from the earth, and then re-emit it. The most significant GHGs are CO_2, methane, nitrous oxide and CFC gases.

Greenhouse Gas Protocol (GHG Protocol) The most widely used international accounting tool for government and business leaders to understand, quantify and manage greenhouse gas emissions. *Direct GHG emissions* are emissions from sources that are owned or controlled by the reporting entity, and *indirect GHG emissions* result from the reporting entity's activities but occur at sources owned or controlled by another entity. The GHG Protocol categorizes these direct and indirect emissions into three broad scopes: Scope 1: All direct GHG emissions. Scope 2: Indirect GHG emissions from the consumption of purchased electricity, heat or steam. Scope 3: Other indirect emissions, such as the extraction and production of purchased materials and fuels, transport-related activities in vehicles not owned or controlled by the reporting entity, electricity-related activities not covered in Scope 2, outsourced activities, waste disposal and so on. http://www.ghgprotocol.org.

ISO 14001 standard The ISO 14000 standards family addresses various aspects of environmental management. ISO 14001 deals with the requirements of an environmental management system (EMS), and ISO 14004 offers general guidelines for EMSs. The other ISO 14000 standards and guidelines address specific environmental aspects such as labelling, performance evaluation, life cycle analysis, communication and auditing.

Koomey's law According to Koomey's law, the energy efficiency of computers doubles every year and a half. This conclusion, which is backed up by six decades of data, mirrors Moore's law, the observation from Intel founder Gordon Moore that computer processing power doubles about every 18 months. The power–consumption trend assumes greater relevance than Moore's law as battery-powered devices such as phones, tablets and sensors proliferate, and the environmental impacts of computers and these devices have to be minimized.

Kyoto protocol An international agreement on global warming and emissions mandating the reduction of carbon emissions, set at the UN Framework Convention on Climate Change held in Kyoto, Japan in 1997. The Protocol made computer manufacturers undertake energy audits to calculate the electricity used by their devices over their life cycle and determine the quantum of carbon dioxide emissions to take remedial action.

Leadership in Energy and Environmental Design (LEED) LEED consists of a suite of rating systems for the design, construction and operation of high-performance green buildings, homes and neighbourhoods. Developed by the US Green Building Council, LEED is intended to provide building owners and operators a concise framework for identifying and implementing practical and measurable green building design, construction, operations and maintenance solutions. *See* 'green building'. http://www.usgbc.org.

life cycle assessment (LCA) The study of all inputs and outputs of materials and energy to determine the environmental impact attributable to a product's or service's functioning over its whole life cycle.

power usage effectiveness (PUE) A metric used to determine the energy efficiency of a data centre. PUE is the ratio of the amount of total power consumed by a data centre to the power used to run the computer infrastructure within it. PUE measures how much overhead energy is required to house and cool computers inside a building relative to the amount of energy that the computers consume themselves.

recycling A series of processes – collection, separation and processing – for recovering and reusing products and raw materials, in lieu of disposing them as waste in landfills.

renewable energy The energy generated from natural and renewable (i.e. naturally replenished) resources such as sunlight, wind, rain, tides and geothermal heat. It has a smaller carbon footprint compared to energy generated by burning fossil fuel such as coal and oil. Climate change concerns, coupled with high oil prices, and government support and incentives are driving the generation and user demand for renewal energy. It is also known as *green energy* or *clean energy*.

Restriction on the Use of Certain Hazardous Substances (RoHS) The European Union's RoHS directive restricts the use of lead, mercury, cadmium, hexavalent chromium, polybrominated biphenyls and polybrominated diphenyl ether in the manufacture of electronic and electrical equipment. Implementation of the RoHS is through the Waste Electrical and Electronic Equipment (WEEE) Directive which set targets for collecting, recycling and recovering electrical goods, aimed at reducing toxic e-waste.

reuse, refurbish and recycle The philosophy that unwanted computers, monitors and other hardware should not be thrown away as rubbish, as they will then end up in landfills and cause serious environmental problems. Instead, we should refurbish, reuse or recycle (i.e. dispose of) them in environmentally sound ways. This is also known as the three 'Rs' of greening unwanted hardware.

reverse logistics All operations related to the reuse of products and materials from their point of consumption to their point of origin for the purpose of recapturing value or proper disposal.

Smart Grid Today's electric power grids are vast and energy inefficient, require excessive power generation capacity to cope with unexpected surges in energy use and allow only one-way energy flow – from provider to customer. A Smart Grid is a digitally enabled power grid that uses software and hardware tools that gather, distribute and act on information about supply and demand to enable generators to route power more efficiently, reducing the need for excess capacity. It can be integrated with renewable energy sources. The deployment of Smart Grids calls for customers installing special smart meters at their premises.

smart home or smart building A smart home (or building) is an intelligent home (or building) that maximizes its energy efficiency and performance by integrating various building subsystems including communications, entertainment, security, convenience and information systems. With the advent of newer technologies and advanced products, intelligent buildings are fast becoming a reality.

sustainability Improving the quality of human life whilst living within the carrying capacity of supporting eco-systems. In 1987, the UN World Commission on Environment and Development (the Brundtland Commission) defined *sustainable development* as that which 'meets the needs of the present without compromising the ability of future generations to meet their own needs'. Sustainability has three interdependent dimensions relating to the environment, economics and society. *See* 'environmental sustainability'.

three Rs of green IT *See* 'reuse, refurbish and recycle'.

virtualization A process of creating a virtual (rather than actual) version of something, such as a hardware platform, operating system, a storage device or network resources, with the aim to centralize administrative tasks whilst improving scalability and overall hardware resource utilization.

Index

Harnessing Green IT: Principles and Practices, First Edition. Edited by San Murugesan and G.R. Gangadharan.

Printed and bound by CPI Group (UK) Ltd, Croydon, CR0 4YY

27/10/2024

14580149-0005